HANDBOOK OF
Counselling Psychology

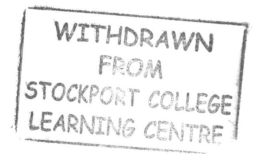

HANDBOOK OF
Counselling Psychology

edited by
Ray Woolfe and Windy Dryden

SAGE Publications
London • Thousand Oaks • New Delhi

SAGE Publications Ltd
6 Bonhill Street
London EC2A 4PU

SAGE Publications Inc
2455 Teller Road
Thousand Oaks, California 91320

SAGE Publications India Pvt Ltd
32, M-Block Market
Greater Kailash – I
New Delhi 110 048

British Library Cataloguing in Publication data

A catalogue record for this book is available
from the British Library

ISBN 0 8039 8991–1
ISBN 0 8039 8992–X (pbk)

Library of Congress catalog record available

Designed by Malcolm Harvey Young
Typeset by Mayhem Typesetting,
Rhayader, Powys
Printed in Great Britain by
The Cromwell Press, Trowbridge, Wiltshire

Contents

Contents

Contents

Acknowledgements

The editors would like to acknowledge the efforts of all those people who have contributed to the development of counselling psychology in the United Kingdom over the past fifteen years. Some of them have written for this book, but there are many others, too numerous to name, without whom counselling psychology could not have flourished in the way that it has.

The completion of such a large project as this book in a relatively short space of time owes much to the support and encouragement received from our editor at Sage, Susan Worsey.

Finally, please note that when case studies are referred to, all identifiable material has been changed and pseudonyms used to safeguard client anonymity.

Preface

The rapid development of counselling psychology in Britain over the past ten years has not been accompanied by an equivalent output of literature devoted to the needs of counselling psychologists. This book attempts to remedy that to some extent by providing a comprehensive coverage of the state of counselling psychology in contemporary Britain – its methodology, theories and practices. The book is intended to be of value both to trainee counselling psychologists and to experienced practitioners.

The key factor which distinguishes counselling psychology from counselling is the explicit recognition it affords to its base in psychological research. Each author, therefore, was asked to pay particular attention to the research evidence in her or his area of expertise and the implications of this for practice. As regards the latter, authors were invited to consider the problems and issues faced by counselling psychologists working in the field, including some of the issues associated with gender, race, disability, social class and sexual orientation.

The book is divided into six parts. The first part 'Setting the Scene', consists of a single chapter and offers an account of the development of counselling psychology in Britain with some pointers as to future directions. The question of the boundary between counselling psychology and cognate disciplines is discussed. Emphasis is placed upon the philosophy of counselling psychology.

Part 2 focuses upon the methodology of counselling psychology. It contains a double-length chapter on quantitative research and its development over time. This is accompanied by a chapter describing qualitative research methods. Counselling by its nature is not readily amenable to much traditional psychological experimental methodology and the development of counselling psychology goes hand in hand with the recent interest in and development of qualitative methodologies. The final chapter in this part examines the important question of how counselling psychologists can systematically evaluate their own practice. The three chapters together provide a detailed account of the methodology underlying the research done by counselling psychologists.

The third part highlights practice and consists of a series of eight chapters on individual paradigms. In order to encourage a standardization of approach, each writer was instructed to address their paradigm with relation to a specific series of key questions and issues:

- The underlying theory of personality and motivation.
- The process of assessment.
- The meaning of change and how it is brought about.
- The psychological theory of learning that is being employed.
- The nature of the relationship between counselling psychologist and individual client.
- Family, group and organizational applications.
- Research evidence about effectiveness.

Life cycle and developmental issues are of central concern to counselling psychologists and this theme is taken up in detail in the fourth part of the book. There are chapters, therefore, on each stage of the life course detailing the psychological issues involved and the kind of interventions made by counselling psychologists. Overall, this part links together theory and practice and this focus is maintained in the next part.

The fifth part highlights some of the major themes and contexts with which counselling psychologists are engaged. Topics covered include health and illness, the family and couples, groups, career development work, the workplace, enhancing learning skills and stress management. Together, this series of chapters provides information about the key sectors in which counselling psychologists operate: health, education and work.

The final part is concerned with the important subject of professional and ethical issues and includes chapters on ethical issues and on training and continued professional development. The two concluding chapters attempt to locate counselling psychology within a social and contextual framework. The penultimate chapter offers a view of counselling psychology as observed through a sociological lens while the final chapter engages in the challenging task of trying to look at possible future directions for counselling psychology as we move towards the next millennium.

Overall, the book offers a detailed portrait of the history, philosophy, theory, methodology and practice of counselling psychology in Britain. It is almost certainly the first such comprehensive account of its kind. The contributors include many leading counselling psychologists and our hope is that it will provide a basic foundation on which future developments can be built.

Ray Woolfe
Windy Dryden

Part One

Setting the Scene

1

The Nature of Counselling Psychology

Ray Woolfe

A brief institutional history of counselling psychology in the United Kingdom

In a classical critique of psychiatry, Szasz writes that 'the question, What is mental illness? is shown to be inextricably tied to the question, What do psychiatrists do?' (Szasz, 1962). In a similar vein, it is difficult to answer the question, What is counselling psychology, as understood in a British context?, without exploring its institutional development within the British Psychological Society.

In 1982 the Society agreed to establish a Counselling Psychology Section and at the end of that first year it had 225 members (British Psychological Society, 1993). In that year too, appeared what was the first and prior to this volume the only comprehensive British textbook on counselling psychology (Nelson-Jones, 1982).

In 1989, the Section became a Special Group (a kind of half-way house between a scientific interest group and full professional status) within the Society and by the end of 1992 had 1,208 members. These numbers were, by the Society's standards, substantial, as they made the Special Group the third largest of the Society's then 20 divisional, sectional and special group sub-systems. Only the Division of Clinical Psychology and the Occupational Psychology Section had more members. In 1992, the Society established a Diploma in Counselling Psychology in order to provide a route to chartered status for those psychologists whose professional development and expertise lay in the area of counselling psychology. Finally, full professional status was achieved in 1994 when a Division of Counselling Psychology was established and psychologists who possessed the diploma or a Statement of Equivalence to it became entitled to use the nomenclature 'Chartered Counselling Psychologist'. At the time of writing, approximately 200 persons are now able to describe themselves in this way (British Psychological Society, 1996).

Alongside the Diploma, the Society established a scheme for recognizing courses as providing part or whole exemption from the Diploma. Thus, it could be said that in the space of 12 years a new profession had been established. Although this development has been rapid, it lags far behind the development of the discipline in the USA. The American Psychological Association had set up a Division of Counselling Psychology as long ago as 1947 (see Whiteley, 1974 for a history of counselling psychology in the USA). The early thrust there had come from the vocational guidance movement and more latterly work involved with ex-service personnel in the Veterans Association.

The British developments were accompanied by the appearance of a number of journals in the field. On its inception in 1982, the Section established a journal entitled *Counselling Psychology Section Newsletter* and in 1986 this became the *Counselling Psychology Section Review*. Finally in 1989 it metamorphosed into the *Counselling Psychology Review*. In a parallel development, another but independent British journal appeared in 1988 entitled *Counselling Psychology Quarterly*.

The above account describes the development of counselling psychology in terms of what the British Psychological Society does. It is, therefore, essentially an institutionally focused history. However, it is necessary to move beyond this in order to understand what counselling psychology represents in terms of its knowledge base; its professional practices; and last but not least its philosophical orientation and value system. It is in this third domain that is to be found the key to the identity of counselling psychology.

Factors underlying the growth of counselling psychology

Counselling psychology can be defined as the application of psychological knowledge to the practice of counselling. This raises the question of why it has taken psychology so long to acknowledge counselling as other than a field of only marginal interest? In other words, what has prompted the growth of the discipline over the past decade?

It is possible to perceive the energy behind the rise of counselling psychology in Britain as deriving from six major sources, which prompted the description of counselling psychology as 'an idea whose time has come' (Woolfe, 1990). These variables are described in detail below. Inevitably there is some overlap, particularly among the first three, though this does not detract from the importance of each factor. In considering them, it should be noted that while the rise of counselling psychology as a separate discipline may be one manifestation of their influence, they have also had effects in other contexts, not least in fields such as clinical psychology and human resource development.

It should also be acknowledged that the boundaries between

counselling psychology and other psychological enterprises such as clinical and occupational are not watertight. Attempts to delineate boundaries according to work settings or practice methods reveal only that there is a great deal of overlap. The forces that influence counselling psychology are also operating in other branches of psychology. In understanding the nature of counselling psychology, therefore, it is necessary to focus on value systems rather than settings or practices. This emphasis becomes apparent when we consider the six factors in more detail. They are as follows:

- An increasing awareness among many psychologists, not just among counselling psychologists, of the importance of the helping relationship as a significant variable in working with people.
- A growing acceptance of the humanistic value system underlying counselling psychology reflected in reactions against the medical model of professional–client relationships.
- A move towards focusing the work of helpers on facilitating well-being rather than on responding to sickness and pathology.
- A developing awareness of the need for a more articulated 'scientific' basis for counselling.
- A recognition of the value of counselling psychology as a framework for human resource development within organizations.
- An appreciation that at a time of high unemployment, counselling offers an appropriate form of employment for psychology graduates.

The helping relationship

There is an increasing awareness among a large variety of helping professionals – nurses, doctors, social workers and psychologists of all kinds – that helping people involves more than the application of specific treatment regimes in a standardized fashion. Increasingly helping is being perceived as a transactional encounter between people in which the quality of the relationship is of crucial importance.

While each profession has its own special techniques, there is widespread agreement that these are most effective when embedded in a relationship which is characterized by the manifestation on the part of the helper of the core person-centred qualities of empathy, acceptance and congruence. These gained widespread recognition through the work of Rogers (1951), though it is interesting to note that something very similar had been enunciated around the same period in an influential book for social workers on the casework relationship (Biestek, 1957).

The construct 'empathy' represents a particularly well-established domain and Barkham (1988) has charted its continuing influence on psychologists over three decades. Its importance is not difficult to identify. Common sense dictates that the most purist of behaviourist practitioners, for example, must first get to know his or her client in order to discover what it is that will act as a reinforcer before a treatment regime can be applied. The acknowledgement of this fact has led to the incorporation of interpersonal skills training into the curriculum of a number of under-graduate courses in psychology. Shillito-Clarke (1987) has described such a programme.

To acknowledge the importance of interpersonal skills, however, contains within it what to traditional psychology, based around the positivist/empiricist paradigm, is the uncomfortable implication that the self of the helper also has to be acknowledged as an active ingredient in the helping process. This makes it imperative for counselling psychologists to set a lead in continuing to work on an ongoing basis at increasing the level of understanding of their own psychological processes. For this reason, personal development work and the experience of being a client feature prominently as a component of counselling psychology training as laid out in the Diploma in Counselling Psychology syllabus, which provides a yardstick for courses seeking to offer training in counselling psychology. The centrality accorded to the requirement to have undergone a minimum of 40 hours' personal psychological coun-selling is one of the critical boundary characteristics which, at the present time, distinguishes counselling psychology from other formal bodies of psychological practice.

A humanistic value base

Counselling psychology emphasizes respect for persons and the fact that each individual is separate and unique. These qualities are not of course unique to counselling psychology. What counselling psychology does, however, is to elevate these beliefs to the heart of practice. This point and the discussion which follows from it is of particular importance if one accepts what Barkham (1990a) refers to as the 'equivalence paradox'. This is the finding from comparative outcome studies that results are broadly equivalent despite technical diversity in method. He suggests that the difference between clinical and counselling psychology draws upon its own equivalence paradox: 'while the philosophies, rationales and imple-mentations of each discipline may differ, the effects in terms of skills, impact and service delivery are broadly equivalent'.

There has in recent years been a move away from what is often referred to as a medical model of professional practice in which the helper is seen as a symbolically (and sometimes actually) white-coated pro-fessional who treats the client. The former is seen as being knowledgeable and emotionally uninvolved. Emotional neutrality is seen as a pre-condition for treatment. The professional is perceived as possessing assessment and diagnostic skills based upon standardized measuring and testing procedures. In contrast the client is seen as lacking in knowledge and their emotional involvement in their own condition is perceived as a barrier to treatment. What emerges from this model is a transaction which is characterized by bipolarity. One party is seen as powerful and active; doing something to another party who is essentially a passive object. The recovery of the client is seen as dependent upon a willingness to succumb to the will of the professional.

It was the reaction of psychologists like Maslow and Rogers to this model which shaped the philosophy and ethos of counselling psychology. Although counselling psychologists employ a wide range of methods – behavioural, cognitive-behavioural, person-centred and psychodynamic – what holds this eclecticism together is a rejection of the medical model and a belief in an interactive alternative. This stresses the subjective experience and world of the client and the importance for the helper in working as a collaborator with the client in seeking to understand the client's inner reality and construal of life experiences. The notion of doing something to the client so as to cure sickness is replaced by the idea of being with the client in a manner that will facilitate the latter's personal growth and potential. In other words, the sharing of the client's inner reality helps to cement the relationship between client and helper. It is the need to understand the dynamics of this inner reality that underlies the demand for the counselling psychologist to have considerable personal experience of being in therapy in the client role.

The centrality of the humanistic value base to the practice of counselling psychology is emphasized by Duffy (1990), an American counselling psychologist, in a paper based on a distinguished visitor's address to the first annual conference of the then Special Group in Counselling Psychology. He addresses the classical 64,000 dollar question of what do counselling psychologists do that others such as clinical psychologists do not do? He suggests that the question leads into a cul-de-sac and that it is necessary to re-frame it from what counselling psychologists *do* that makes them different to one of what counselling psychologists *are* that makes them different. It is the Rogerian shift from an emphasis on doing to an emphasis on being; not so much what one does but how one does it.

Duffy develops this argument by suggesting that the way in which counselling psychologists think about what they do is important. This leads into the issue of intentionality; why do counselling psychologists do what they do? According to Duffy, 'the "why" often influences, informs and inspires the "what"'. For example, standardized psychological tests can be used as the basis for constructing a dialogue with the respondent. In the sense that counselling psychology is characterized by a way of thinking, it can be said to constitute a culture or world-view, what in German is referred to as a *Weltanschauung*, an outlook on the world.

Focus on well-being rather than sickness

Traditionally helpers have been seen as dealing with illness and sick people. Clinical psychology for example evolved in medical settings and much of the work of clinical psychologists involves the assessment and treatment of persons with significant degrees of psychological disturbance. Words such as 'clinical' and 'patient' are evocative of an illness and treatment orientation which has characterized much psychological practice.

There is a danger at this point, however, of setting up a model of a straw person which can then be conveniently knocked down. Clinical psychologists are increasingly demonstrating a concern with prevention rather than cure, as exemplified in the growth of many community-based mental health services. Primary Health Care centres staffed on a multi-disciplinary basis are increasingly replacing separate GP or psychology services. Nevertheless, there remains a difference of emphasis between clinical and counselling psychology deriving from their respective origins, histories and philosophical orientations.

Counselling psychology arose from a concern with the fulfilment of potential rather than the curing of sickness. Developmental concepts such as 'becoming what one is capable of becoming' (Rogers) and 'self-actualization' (Maslow) reflect something of the spirit behind the origins of counselling psychology which is a long way removed from the notion of curing of illness. The emphasis is on development of potential; on prevention rather than cure and on well-being rather than pathology. Alongside this is the adoption of a more holistic view of the client. This involves examining emotional and mental health in the context of an individual's location in the life cycle as well as their lifestyle and relationships.

Much of the work of counselling psychologists is, therefore, concerned with enhancing the psychological functioning, effectiveness and well-being of individuals who are not necessarily ill or in need of treatment but who have encountered problems or issues which may well be temporary but which are generating unhappiness and perhaps less than desired levels of functioning. The interventions of many counselling psychologists are likely to be time-limited, problem-focused and con-cerned with fostering the development of coping strategies. Life-span developmental issues provide the framework in which much of the work of counselling psychologists is rooted.

Duffy (1990) takes the argument a stage further in placing great emphasis on what he refers to as the 'development orientation' of counselling psychology. This involves a change of the helper's typical mind-set in which crises and problems are perceived not as evidence of pathology but as normative human experiences which pose a challenge, in the Eriksonian sense, of developmental adaptation. Experiences such as grieving, illness and separation are essentially developmental in character. Instead of a central concern with a symptom profile, he advises counselling psychologists to adopt a more dynamic view of what a disorder means developmentally in terms of the point at which the individual has reached in life and how she or he is likely to move in terms of working through the process in question. The focus is on the development of self.

In adopting a developmental approach to mental health, counselling psychology is concerned with psychoeducational programmes in a variety of life skills.

A scientific basis for counselling

Counselling psychology can be seen as reaction to the somewhat mechanistic view of human beings inherent in more traditional psychological paradigms based upon a conventional model of the nature of science and the technique of scientific investigation. This theme is developed further by the author of this chapter (and his collaborator) in the chapter in Part Six of this book which offers a sociological perspective on counselling psychology. An alternative more phenomenological view of the nature of science and of the generation of knowledge is put forward. The need for an alternative view is fostered by the fact that conventional experimental research methodologies appear to have been singularly unsuccessful in answering critical questions about which methods work with which clients in which circumstances.

It would be unfortunate, however, if counselling psychology came to be seen as anti-science, nor is this the case. Indeed its development as a discipline derives in part from the failure by counsellors to evaluate their practice, which remains as much of an art as a science. Counselling psychology can be seen as an attempt to fill this vacuum. Counselling psychologists with their training in research, assessment and evaluation have the skills to help chart the territory of evaluating process on the one hand and the link between input and output on the other. The model of the scientist-practitioner, about which more will be said later, is widely perceived as central to the emerging discipline.

Counselling psychology, therefore, can be seen as located in a pivotal position between narrow scientism on the one hand and a failure to take sufficient account of any scientific method on the other. However, in many ways it is easier to say what counselling psychology is a reaction against and what it is not, rather than to identify where it falls on the continuum outlined. This is the subject of some debate.

An interesting position has been enunciated by van Duerzen-Smith (1990) who argues that the philosophical underpinnings of counselling psychology lie in 'the immense gap left open by a psychology too devoted to narrow scientific principles to pay proper attention to what it means to be human'. She contends that psychology has lost its ability to function as an art. If the objective of the counselling psychologist is to help people to lead lives which are more fulfilled, one enters inevitably into the realms of morals and ideology, subjects which are the domain of philosophy rather than science. She suggests that the methods and insights of philosophy such as those of systematic thinking and dialogue, argument, logical analysis and dialectical processing are more important than the search for objective facts which characterizes experimental psychology.

The other side of the coin, however, has been put by Williams (1991) in a direct reply to van Duerzen-Smith. He argues that without objective criteria of competence, there is no professional basis for counselling psychology and that phenomenological approaches do not, by themselves, provide an appropriate theoretical foundation for counselling psychology.

The role of counselling psychology as a framework for human resource development within organizations

Counselling is a concept that is becoming increasingly familiar to managers across a wide variety of organizations. This manifests itself at a number of levels. At its most basic it involves a recognition of the importance of good communication and interpersonal skills in the management of people and that training in basic counselling skills helps managers to assimilate these competencies. Orlans (1989) points out how management development programmes are beginning to reflect the perceived importance of active listening and related basic counselling skills. Recent developments such as the widespread introduction of appraisal schemes has given an additional boost to this process.

At a deeper level, however, there has been a growing awareness that the principles of counselling can be of value in creating and managing organizational structures which combine efficiency with a person-centred and facilitative climate. Reddy (1987) has drawn attention to the growth of interest in counselling in work settings. This has led to the direct employment of paid counsellors or, alternatively, to providing access for staff to external counsellors employed on a consultancy basis. He also notes the spread from the USA to Britain of Employee Assistance Programmes which adopt a more broadly based approach to the overall physical and mental welfare of staff.

While counsellors have the skills to work on a one-to-one therapeutic basis, their training does not equip them to act as organizational consultants. Counselling psychologists in contrast possess the added value of being able to carry out an organizational analysis and to provide feedback about how organizational structures and systems affect the behaviour, motivation and general level of satisfaction and commitment of individuals. In this way, counselling psychologists can play an important preventive and developmental role in facilitating organizational well-being and efficiency.

Change has now become almost a way of life for many organizations within both the public and private sectors and this imposes great stress upon staff. Given a climate in which feelings can be expressed, counselling psychologists can support staff by providing them with an opportunity to talk about their work in an open fashion (see Proctor and Ditton, 1989). Lane (1990) emphasizes the importance of psychological knowledge as a basis for such organizational and consultancy work. He warns of the danger of offering 'off the shelf' packages to organizational clients and the importance of ensuring that interventions in organizations are firmly based in the scientific basis of the discipline of psychology.

While counsellors have expertise in dealing with individual clients and occupational psychologists are trained to understand organizational dynamics, counselling psychology combines these two sets of skills in a unique fashion. Cooper (1986) identified this phenomenon as long ago as 1986 when he indicated that more and more organizations in the UK are beginning to see the value of stress counselling and health promotion among their employees. Yet there was, as he put it, an irony in that there were so few psychologists available with the wide range of skills necessary to help companies to develop appropriate programmes. His prescription for filling this gap was 'a cross-bred between a clinical and occupational psychologist. An individual who has the professional counselling skills, as well as the experience and understanding (academic) of organisational behaviour'. Cooper attached the label 'clinical occupational psychologist' to this hybrid, but perhaps what he was alluding to, ahead of his time, was the emerging role of the counselling psychologist.

Counselling as a field of employment for psychologists

Legge (1987), in his formal address to the BPS as its incoming president, referred to a need for the Society to stake out new areas for psychology graduates 'if occupational colonization is one of its aims'. He identifies counselling as one such field and refers to the prestige enjoyed by counselling in the USA. Counselling is presented as an opportunity because it remains an activity in which anybody can put up a name-plate describing themselves as a counsellor or psychotherapist. There is no copyright on these terms.

Some things have moved on since 1987. The British Association for Counselling has schemes for the accreditation of counsellors, supervisors and trainers. The United Kingdom Register for Counsellors is about to come into existence and the United Kingdom Council for Psycho-therapy has been set up with its own register. Nevertheless the field remains relatively open and counselling remains still largely unregulated and what sociologists would call a 'quasi-profession'. In this vacuum, counselling psychologists with their special blend of training and skills have a significant role to play. This is more than just a rhetorical political statement. Counselling would not exist without psychology. Its knowledge base is rooted in psychology and most of its key figures were and are psychologists, often distinguished psychologists. Rogers and Maslow were both past presidents of the American Psychological Association. Without psychologists there would be little if any research carried out. Contemporary developments in counselling practice such as cognitive-behavioural methodology are rooted in advances in psychological knowledge.

In the final resort, therefore, counselling lends itself to psychologists as a field of activity by virtue of its very nature as an applied activity which would not and could not exist without the discipline of psychology. Psychology provides its theoretical and methodological foundations. There would be no counselling without psychology. The term 'colonization' seems, therefore, in the case of counselling to be highly inappropriate. How is it possible to colonize something to which one gave birth in the first place? The really interesting question is why it has taken psychology so long to acknowledge counselling as its own off-spring?

As a final comment in this section on economic factors underlying the growth of counselling psychology one might also refer to the acknowledged shortage of clinical psychologists (see Mowbray, 1989). If the supply of psychologists is insufficient to satisfy the demand for remedial workers (traditionally the domain of clinical psychology as practised within the National Health Service), it is unlikely to meet the newer and additional demand for developmental and preventive psychology services. Clinical and counselling psychologists are best regarded not as competitors but as applied psychologists, coming from different traditions, and yet with a great deal in common. If, in the end, there emerges a new category of general Health or Human Services Psychologists, it will contain elements of both these traditions.

The scientist-practitioner model

The issue of the link between science and practice is a crucial one for counselling psychology. The model of the scientist-practitioner has been widely espoused by clinical psychology as well as by counselling psychology in the USA. The model is based around the notion that an integral aspect of the role of the professional, in this case the counselling psychologist, is the need to engage on an ongoing basis in the process of researching their work. While counsellors may engage in a process of supervised reflection (the reflective practitioner), there is an expectation that counselling psychologists will engage in a more structured examination of their work with the aim of generating knowledge for debate through publication.

The topic forms the theme of one edition of *The Counseling Psychologist*, the journal of the Division of Counseling Psychology of the American Psychological Association (Division 17). Papers by Kagan et al. (1988), Meara et al. (1988) and Gelso et al. (1988) are particularly relevant and in the words of Gelso et al., while 'many counseling psychologists might prefer that the question of "clinical relevance" go away, it is clear that the issue has persisted and will continue to do so'. How then can research and practice be brought together?

Traditionally in Britain there has existed a split between science as represented by academic staff working in universities and practice as represented by field workers. To busy practitioners, particularly those in private practice, which appears to be an increasingly important source of employment for counselling psychologists, there is little or no financial incentive to engage in research. Indeed the opposite is the case. While seeing clients brings in income, writing research reports is unlikely to generate any financial return and more than that it represents income lost. However, this does not negate the importance of research. The BPS working party which established the Diploma in Counselling Psychology states that 'of central relevance . . . are empirical investigations of the processes and outcomes of counselling'. This viewpoint is echoed in the American context by Kagan et al. (1988) who identify two research-related components inherent in the future orientation of counselling psychology and in doing so articulate the model of the scientist-practitioner. These are:

1   'The value of programmatic research for both forming and informing the profession, for discerning effective intervention strategies, and for

investigating client and therapist variables as influences on counseling psychology processes and outcomes'.

2 'The essential role of research in providing a base for practice and the need for counseling psychologists to use scientific methods to evaluate their practice critically'.

The authors argue that these are necessary conditions if counselling psychology is to develop as a discipline, and this view is reinforced by Meara et al. (1988), who suggest that 'the scientist-practitioner model is an integrated approach to knowledge that recognizes the interdependence of theory, research and practice'. In Britain the importance of a 'scientist-professional' approach has been strongly endorsed by Barkham (1990a), who argues that it is 'central to the emerging discipline . . . the empirical and research basis of counselling psychology . . . is of crucial importance to the credibility of counselling psychology'.

Despite this overwhelming support for the scientist-practitioner model, the reality on the ground is somewhat different. Even in the USA where counselling psychology is well established, many practitioners seem to have rejected the task of doing research (see Watkins, 1985) and there is evidence that practitioners are largely ignorant of concerns expressed in the literature and seem to have no time other than to engage in clinical practice (see Goodyear, 1984, for example). Heppner and Anderson (1985) found that few counselling psychologists publish research findings.

The issue of methodology

The failure to do research does not necessarily imply lack of commitment to this objective and may have more to do with lack of know-how. Research methods training at undergraduate level remains heavily quantitative. Qualitative methods are still regarded as suspect and treated with reserve. At the same time, it is only too clear that counselling is not readily amenable to the old-style experimental techniques in which practitioners have largely been trained. When these two facts are set alongside each other, it is hardly surprising if many practitioners choose to eschew research.

Fortunately there has been a reaction to this state of affairs. Gelso et al. (1988) talk about the need to experiment less and describe more. 'We need to observe and empirically describe, more than we have, the intervention process.' They refer to the period 1978–88 as one of 'methodological ferment' out of which has emerged the kind of research methodology described by John McLeod in this book. There is now a significant and growing literature on qualitative research methods and this is reflected in the importance attached to this approach in the curricula of courses that are being developed in counselling psychology. The philosophical underpinning behind this new paradigm is described in chapter 27 of this book, which looks at counselling psychology from a sociological perspective.

There is of course a danger that, in advocating new approaches, the baby may be thrown out with the bathwater. An understanding of the experimental method remains important. The way forward lies not in rejecting rigour or abandoning empirical investigations but in the direction of what Gelso et al. describe as 'methodological diversity' and what Barkham (1990a) refers to as 'methodological pluralism'. Such methodological pluralism is congruent with the theoretical diversity of counselling psychologists. While data on British counselling psychologists is virtually non-existent, there is no reason to believe that the finding of the 1985 survey of Division 17 members of APA would not be replicated here. In this study, 40 per cent stated 'eclectic' as their primary theoretical orientation (Watkins et al., 1986).

The way forward

In a recent article in *The Counseling Psychologist*, Watkins (1994) identifies ten broad-based themes that seem to characterize counselling psychology in the USA. Many of these themes have already been addressed in this chapter, but it is valuable to present them as a complete set. They offer some guidelines about the issues facing counselling psychology in Britain as well as in the USA now and for the remainder of this century. In doing so, they also tell us a great deal about the nature of counselling psychology and remind us that in Britain the discipline is still very much in its infancy. The themes are as follows (they fall into five categories).

- **Research and training**
  (a) There is a growing sophistication in the formulation of research questions, in the use of statistical procedures and in knowledge of research design.
  (b) There is an increasing recognition of the need for methodological diversity.
  (c) There is an increase in commitment to making the scientific-practitioner model work.
- **Special populations**
  (d) By means of model building and continued research, there has been an increase in understanding of 'ethnic and non-ethnic minorities'.

- **Assessment, counselling, and counselling training and supervision**
  - (e) Assessment has become more refined and more integrated into othe work of the counselling psychologist.
  - (f) Great inroads have been made in understanding the 'inner workings of the counseling experience'.
  - (g) Through model building, great advances have been made in understanding counsellor training and supervision.
- **Vocational**
  - (h) The vocational arm of counselling psychology has continued to flourish and to form a key part of the identity of counselling psychology.
- **The Division of Counseling Psychology**
  - (i) The Division has become increasingly sensitive to the needs of minorities and new professionals.
  - (j) The Division has come to have a more recognized voice within the parent American Psychological Association.

In relating these themes to the UK the following brief points can be made.

Research and training

(a) While there is a considerable and increasing interest in research in Britain (see chapters 2, 3 and 4 of this book), little has been published based upon quantitative approaches (see Barkham, 1990b). The work of Shapiro and Barkham at the Applied Psychology Unit of the University of Sheffield is a notable exception. As for qualitative approaches, despite a great deal of effort, there is still a sense of coming to terms with the newer methodologies. Although Reason and Rowan's book on new paradigm research appeared as long ago as 1981, the return on the investment is still limited. The position remains very much as outlined by Barkham (1990a): one of exhortation that counselling psychology 'in establishing its role and contributing towards psychology as a knowledge base . . . must adopt a strenuous research programme encompassing both traditional and innovative methodologies'. There is still a great deal to do in achieving this ambition.

(b) Although the emphasis in Britain in recent years has been on newer research paradigms, there would be widespread agreement with the philosophy of methodological diversity.

(c) The scientist–practitioner model likewise represents an aspiration rather than a reality, although once again as the previous discussion illustrates, there would be widespread approval of the objective.

Special populations

(d) Counselling psychology has yet to make an impact in this field. The fact that there is no chapter in this book on counselling psychology in a cross-cultural context is in itself indicative of the distance that has yet to be travelled.

Assessment, counselling, and counselling training and supervision

(e) There is at the present time little literature on the role of assessment in the therapeutic process.

(f) A great deal of effort has gone into the theme of understanding the workings of counselling and this is likely to continue. Barkham (1990a) sees counselling research as having gone through three 'generations'. In the first phase, there was an emphasis on demonstrating that therapy was effective. The second phase was characterized by a search for specificity; that is to say what methods work with whom and under what conditions. In the third phase, the emphasis is on how interventions work. Barkham sees current research as having arrived at a blend of the second and third phases.

(g) There are indications that model building has been generating creative ideas in the field of supervision (see for example Hawkins and Shohet, 1989), though probably less productive in the field of training (see chapter 26 of this book).

Vocational

(h) The field of vocational guidance has been vastly influential in the development of counselling psychology in the USA, particularly in its earlier days. However Watkins suggests that while it remains important, counselling psychology students are becoming less interested in vocational than therapy-type activities. The only known research on the work of counselling psychologists in the UK was carried out in the early days of the BPS Counselling Psychology Section and as such is very dated. Based on a cohort of only 205 members and with a 65 per cent response rate, Murgatroyd found that lecturers accounted for 43 per cent of the total. Private practice was not listed as a separate category (Murgatroyd, 1983).

Personal knowledge suggests that while lecturing continues to provide a large number of counselling psychologists with an income, an increasing proportion, particularly of those entering the field, gravitate towards self-employment. Fields such as Primary Health Care and consultancy and training in the work setting have offered work opportunities on a part-time or occasional basis.

The Division of Counselling Psychology

(i) The Division of Counselling Psychology breaks new ground among BPS divisions in allowing into its membership 'Ordinary' as well as 'Accredited' Members. This allows scope for those who aspire to become Chartered Counselling Psychologists to have some say in the running of the division. The position over minority groups within the division is that very little has so far been done to acknowledge their special interests.

(j) The division is increasingly active in the general affairs of BPS and is well represented on its committees.

Conclusion

Many would argue that, increasingly, different psychological specialisms have more in common than separate them. This has led to the view that it might be sensible to dissolve the various specialisms into one general-purpose health or human services psychologist. At the present stage of its development, it would seem unwise for counselling psychology to lose its special identity, which as this chapter has sought to demonstrate is based not upon a territorial domain but upon a philosophy and a system of values. However, it is not inconceivable that a time may come when such integration might become a serious possibility. Were this to happen, what can be said with confidence is that counselling psychology will have a great deal to offer the psychological enterprise as a whole.

References

Barkham, M. (1988) 'Empathy in counselling and psychotherapy: present status and future directions', *Counselling Psychology Quarterly*, 6(1): 24–8.

Barkham, M. (1990a) 'Counselling psychology: in search of an identity', *The Psychologist: Bulletin of the British Psychological Society*, 12: 536–9.

Barkham, M. (1990b) 'Research in individual therapy' in W. Dryden (ed.), *Individual Therapy: a Handbook*. Milton Keynes: Open University Press.

Biestek, F.P. (1957) *The Casework Relationship*. Chicago: Loyola University Press. (First published in the UK in 1961 by George Allen and Unwin.)

British Psychological Society (1993) *Annual Report*. Leicester: BPS, p. 128.

British Psychological Society (1996) Private lists made available to the author as Registrar of the Board of Examiners, Diploma in Counselling Psychology.

Cooper, C.L. (1986) 'Job distress: recent research and the emerging role of the clinical occupational psychologist', *Bulletin of the British Psychological Society*, 39: 325–31.

Duerzen-Smith, E. van (1990) 'Philosophical underpinnings of counselling psychology', *Counselling Psychology Review*, 5(2): 8–12.

Duffy, M. (1990) 'Counselling psychology USA, patterns of continuity and change', *Counselling Psychology Review*, 5(3): 9–18.

Gelso, C.J. et al. (1988) 'Research in counseling psychology: prospects and recommendations', *The Counseling Psychologist*, 16(3): 385–406.

Goodyear, R.K. (1984) 'On our journal's evolution: historical developments, transitions and future directions', *Journal of Counseling and Development*, 63: 3–9.

Hawkins, P. and Shohet, R. (1989) *Supervision in the Helping Professions*. Milton Keynes: Open University Press.

Heppner, P.P. and Anderson, W.P. (1985) 'On the perceived non-utility of research in counseling', *Journal of Counseling and Development*, 63: 545–7.

Kagan, N. et al. (1988) 'Professional practice of counseling psychology in various settings', *The Counseling Psychologist*, 16(3): 347–65.

Lane, D.A. (1990) 'Counselling psychology in organisations', *The Psychologist: Bulletin of the British Psychological Society*, 12: 540–4.

Legge, D. (1987) 'Modelling a seamless robe', *Bulletin of the British Psychological Society*, 35: 241–9.

Meara, N.M. et al. (1988) 'Training and accreditation in counseling psychology', *The Counseling Psychologist*, 16(3): 366–84.

Mowbray, D. (1989) The Manpower Advisory Service Report on Clinical Psychology Services. Leicester: BPS.

Murgatroyd, S. (1983) 'Counselling psychology in Britain', *Counselling Psychology Section Newsletter*, 1: 4–12.

Nelson-Jones, R. (1982) *The Theory and Practice of Counselling Psychology*. Eastbourne: Holt, Rinehart and Winston.

Orlans, V. (1989) 'Counselling in the workplace: a review and thoughts for the future', *Employee Counselling Today*, 1(1): 3–6.

Proctor, B. and Ditton, A. (1989) 'How counsellors can add value to organisations', *Employee Counselling Today*, 1(2): 3–6.

Reason, P. and Rowan, J. (eds) (1981) *Human Inquiry: a Source Book of New Paradigm Research*. Chichester: Wiley.

Reddy, M. (1987) *The Manager's Guide to Counselling at Work*. Leicester: British Psychological Society.

Rogers, C.R. (1951) *Client-Centred Therapy: Its Current Practice, Implications, and Theory*. Boston: Houghton Mifflin.

Shillito-Clarke, C. (1987) 'Experiential interpersonal skills in the psychology curriculum: an ounce of practice is worth a pound of theory', *Review of the Counselling Psychology Section*, 2(1): 6–10.

Szasz, T. (1962) *The Myth of Mental Illness*. London: Secker and Warburg.

Watkins, C.E. Jr (1985) 'Counselling psychology, clinical psychology, and human services psychology: where the twain shall meet', *American Psychologist*, 40: 1054–6.

Watkins, C.E. Jr, Lopez, F.G., Campbell, V.L. and Himmell, C.D. (1986)

'Contemporary counseling psychology: results of a national survey', *The Counseling Psychologist*, 33: 301–9.

Watkins, C.E. Jr (1994) 'On hope, promise, and possibility in counseling psychology or some simple, but meaningful observations about our speciality', *The Counseling Psychologist*, 22(2): 315–34.

Whiteley, J.H. (1974) *Counselling Psychology: a Historical Perspective*. Schenectady, NY: Character Research Press.

Williams, D.I. (1991) 'The philosophical underpinnings of counselling psychology: a reply to Van-Duerzen-Smith', *Counseling Psychology Review*, 6(3): 8–10.

Woolfe, R. (1990) 'Counselling Psychology in Britain: an idea whose time has come', *The Psychologist: Bulletin of the British Psychological Society*, 12: 531–5.

Part Two

Methodology

2

Quantitative Research on Psychotherapeutic Interventions: Methodological Issues and Substantive Findings across Three Research Generations

Michael Barkham

The aim of this chapter is twofold. First, to set out various aspects of research methodology employed in quantitative research in counselling psychology and cognate disciplines (for example, psychotherapy). And secondly, to provide a summary of substantive findings derived from the application of quantitative methodologies across three overlapping generations of research from the 1950s to the present. Although the meaning of the term 'quantitative' research may appear obvious, it is useful to operationalize its use in this chapter. McLeod (1993) has drawn various distinctions between quantitative and qualitative approaches to research in counselling. In brief, quantitative research comprises the measurement and analysis of variables using tests, rating scales, and questionnaires which are, in turn, interpreted via statistical analyses of the data. Theoretically, quantitative research requires the researcher to be value-free, although as indicated below, this may be problematic. This view of quantitative research incorporates group contrast, correlational, naturalistic and single-case studies. The inclusion of the latter is important in light of recent criticisms directed at the field of counselling psychology: 'Counseling psychology, a field that reveres the individual . . ., virtually eschews single-case designs, a research methodology that is explicitly intended for studying the individual' (Galassi and Gersh, 1993: 525).

Within counselling psychology, the superordinate research approach should be methodological pluralism, incorporating both qualitative and quantitative methodologies. The critical point for the researcher is to select the approach which is most appropriate to the question being asked. For instance, if a practitioner wishes to know which of two counselling orientations is more effective, then this might best be addressed using a group contrast design. However, as long as, for example, audio tapes are made of the counselling sessions, then this does not preclude subsequent

---

This chapter is dedicated to the memory of Robert and Lillian Brooks.

analyses of the tapes using qualitative methods such as task analysis or discourse analysis. However, McLeod (1994) has argued that mainstream research may have been slow to adopt this pluralistic position, with the two approaches being used to 'complement' each other rather than being integrated into a study of human beings.

General caveats in research

Whether the approach is quantitative or qualitative, it is worth stating several central premises upon which any evaluation of research in counselling psychology should be based. First, all research in counselling psychology and psychotherapy is flawed: the very nature of the exercise does not enable the researcher to achieve a 'perfect' study. Research is the art of reaching a compromise without sacrificing the integrity of any particular study. This invariably involves balancing the demands of four forms of validity: internal, external, construct and statistical validity. Briefly, internal validity concerns the researcher's attempts to control the influence of competing variables which might affect the results of the study. Laboratory studies can achieve a high degree of internal validity whereas studies of counselling in naturalistic settings are more difficult. External validity concerns the researcher's attempts to ensure that the results of the study have meaning in the 'external' world. Here, naturalistic counselling achieves high external validity in contrast to laboratory studies. Construct validity involves ensuring that the phenomenon under investigation is what it purports to be. In other words, ensuring that what is being sampled or measured is the actual construct under investigation. Statistical conclusion validity requires certain elements to be present, including adequate sample size, heterogeneity of participants, etc. A range of 'threats' to each of these four types of validity can occur and these are well summarized by Shapiro (1989). Secondly, there is no such thing as a 'definitive' study. Some studies will be more conclusive than others depending upon a range of factors, but any study will always leave some questions for further investigation. Thirdly, replication is a central tenet of science. Accordingly, in looking at findings arising from counselling psychology we need to determine the extent to which they have been replicated. The centrality of this tenet gives rise to this chapter focusing on 'substantive' findings – that is, those findings which have been replicated. However, in order to capture possible intriguing and novel findings, this chapter will also include findings which are sufficiently interesting to require replication. Fourthly, there needs to be a recognition that researchers have biases, stated or unstated. This may appear contrary to the notion of quantitative research which many people perceive as 'objective'. However, researchers investigate processes which interest them and such particular interests may well lead them to make research decisions which other researchers with different perspectives would not make. In addition, decisions made during the analysis and interpretation of the data may all be influenced in subtle ways by the biases of the researchers. Accepting this view, it is logical that the content of this chapter reflects my own orientation towards research.

Structure of the chapter

In terms of adopting a strategy for presenting methodological issues and substantive findings, the chapter will progress by presenting research as comprising three successive but overlapping generations beginning with Eysenck's (1952) critique of psychotherapy. These three generations, which are detailed more fully later in the chapter, can be summarized as follows. Generation I spans the period 1950s to 1970s and addresses the outcome question 'Is psychotherapy effective?' and the process question 'Are there objective methods for evaluating process?' Generation II spans the period 1960s to 1980s and utilizes scientific rigour to address the outcome question 'Which psychotherapy is more effective?' and the process question 'What components are related to outcome?' Generation III spans the period 1970s to the present and addresses the outcome question 'How can we make treatments more cost-effective?' and the process question 'How does change occur?' Within each of these three generations, the literature is considered via a series of specific questions (such as, What intervention is most effective?) using four subheadings: (a) context (Why is this question salient?); (b) methodological issues (pertinent issues in designing research aimed to address this question); (c) substantive research findings (findings which are robust or intriguing); and (d) comment (overall judgement and impact). In this way, it is hoped to cover a range of issues combining fundamental components of good research as well as salient findings.

What this chapter does not aim to do is to provide a comprehensive coverage of all aspects of research in counselling psychology. To do so would require a considerably larger text than space allows here. However, there are two major books which present research findings: Bergin and Garfield's (1994a) *Handbook of Psychotherapy and Behavior Change* (4th edition), and Brown and Lent's (1992) *Handbook of Counseling Psychology*. There are also important books which are grounded in research methodology: Aveline and Shapiro's (1995) *Research Foundations for Psychotherapy Practice*, Watkins and Schneider's (1991) *Research in Counseling*, and Parry and Watts's (in press) *Behavioural and Mental Health Research: a Handbook of*

Skills and Methods (2nd edition). In terms of methodology, there are two excellent and very readable texts which are highly recommended: Barker, Pistrang and Elliott's (1994) *Research Methods in Clinical and Counselling Psychology*, and McLeod's (1994) *Doing Counselling Research*. From time to time, there are also special sections in quality journals which address methodological issues (for example, *Journal of Counseling Psychology*: special sections on 'Quantitative foundations of counseling psychology', 1987, and 'Qualitative research in counseling process and outcome', 1994). More broadly, there are many scientific journals which report on studies carried out in the area of counselling psychology and cognate disciplines. The key American research journals include *The Counseling Psychologist, Journal of Counseling Psychology, Journal of Consulting and Clinical Psychology, Psychotherapy*, and *Psychotherapy Research*. Key British research journals include *British Journal of Guidance and Counselling, Clinical Psychology and Psychotherapy*, and *Counselling Psychology Quarterly*.

Generation I: 1950s to 1970s
Outcome effectiveness and measuring the facilitative conditions

Prior to 1952, the field of counselling psychology and psychotherapy research was developing fast from the impact of the Second World War. In the United States there was early process work into therapist techniques using verbal response mode systems. For example, Porter (1943) worked in the area of counsellor and client behaviours and Snyder (1945) worked in a similar domain finding evidence supporting the theory that client insights follow therapists' acceptance of client attitudes and feelings. Rogers's (1942) first major publication, *Counseling and Psychotherapy*, appeared, followed later by *Client-Centered Therapy* (Rogers, 1951), which set a clear research agenda, initiating a generation of process research developing objective methods of measuring events of recorded therapy sessions. In his book he moved away from specific therapist techniques towards the theory that therapists should possess an attitude enabling the client to address their particular psychological situation. This publication provided the basis for his subsequent theory on the necessary and sufficient conditions of therapy. However, this early thrust of process work was cut across by the publication of Eysenck's (1952) critique of the effectiveness of psychotherapy which resulted in a generation of research focusing on the issue of effectiveness. As such, the overarching theme of this generation is one of 'justification' for the enterprise of psychological interventions.

Is counselling effective and, if so, how effective is it?

Context

Eysenck (1952) claimed that approximately two-thirds of all neurotics who received non-behavioural psychotherapy improved substantially within two years and that an equal proportion of neurotics who had not received treatment also improved within the same time period. This spawned a generation of research studies focusing both on the reanalyses of the data used by Eysenck and on new studies. These new studies incorporated a range of methodological components including 'control' groups and various statistical concepts, which resulted in the development of a procedure called meta-analysis. These three methodological issues, control groups, statistics and meta-analysis, are considered in the following section.

Methodological issues

Control groups   The first issue concerns the use of control groups. There are three basic designs used in psychotherapy research to address the question of effectiveness. The most basic element is a design comprising a before and after counselling comparison (often termed a pre–post comparison). In the design, all clients enter the study, complete some outcome measure pre-counselling, and then complete the same measure again post-counselling. It would be hoped that the overall mean score for the group of clients on the measure showed an improvement. However, it might be that clients improved due to events which occurred outside the counselling setting, or it may be that some would have improved in the course of time alone. Such concerns led to designs which 'controlled' for such influences. The nature of the control condition can vary. At its most simple level, it involves using a parallel group of people, matched on major demographic and psychological variables, who are offered no counselling. To achieve this, clients are randomized to one of the two conditions so as to ensure that there are no systematic differences between the two groups at this stage. They complete similar measures at equivalent times with the only difference being the treatment they receive. The post-treatment comparisons should be a reasonable test of the superiority or not of a psychological intervention over no intervention.

Ideally this would be true, but there are a number of problems with this assumption. First, if a client is told that they will be assigned to either a group receiving counselling or a group not receiving counselling, then finding that they are in the no-treatment group is likely to have a considerable effect on them (disappointment for example). Hence, far from being assured that it is a 'no-treatment' group, it is more likely to be experienced as a group who have been 'rejected' for treatment. Further, some clients in this position may act on their own accord and begin to discuss concerns with friends; that is, seek out natural support systems. The underlying point here is that a 'no-treatment' group is not as simple to implement as it sounds and, more importantly, there are inadequacies in terms of what it is actually controlling which undermine the scientific yield of the design.

A refinement of the 'no-treatment' control group arose with the 'wait-list' control group in which clients in the experiential group received treatment while a comparison group of clients were placed on a waiting list and only after the experimental group had completed treatment would the control group then receive some form of intervention. Importantly, the subsequent treatment offered to the 'wait-list' group does not have to be similar to the experimental treatment. What is important from the design perspective is that they receive something, as the purpose of the comparison group is to control for the elapsed time of treatment in the experimental group rather than a direct comparison of the subsequent intervention. This means that the subsequent treatment they are offered may be less than optimal. Obviously, this condition has some merit over the no-treatment condition but care needs to be taken in how long clients will be on a wait-list. This raises some ethical questions and it might be considered that the wait-list group should receive a condition deemed to be as effective as the experimental condition. This is a balance of ethical and scientific concerns. However, the researcher can deliver the treatment to the wait-list control group in the same form as to the original group. In this situation, the design becomes a switching replication wherein not only does the initial treatment group have a control group, but the situation is exactly reversed (that is, replicated) for the other group. Hence, there is an inbuilt replication within the study.

A third design involves a 'placebo group'. This design aims to provide the non-experimental group with a control condition for what has been generally termed 'non-specific' or 'common' factors. In other words, the placebo group is receiving the general factors associated with receiving a treatment but not the technically specific ones. Unfortunately, the problems with placebo treatments are considerable and can be considered to fall into two groups. First, all the criticisms levelled at no-treatment and wait-list controls equally apply to placebo conditions. For example, no matter what the form of the placebo treatment, it is bound to be perceived by the recipients as something 'less' than the experimental treatment. Secondly, there are issues specific to placebo conditions regarding determining what it is that is being 'controlled'. Strictly speaking, the only placebo conditions which are valid are those which employ a 'component control condition' in which the placebo is designed specifically to exclude the component of the experimental condition which is of particular interest. They are, accordingly, extremely difficult to implement and account for a minority of placebo studies. In terms of the variety of control groups, it is worth considering the overall function of any control group. Historically, a great many studies of particular interventions required a control group in order to address the primary question of whether this particular intervention was better than no intervention. As scientific knowledge is built up, the position of control groups in general needs to be questioned. If, for example, the vast majority of studies (which are deemed to pass some threshold of design adequacy) show that providing clients with a psychological intervention is consistently better than offering them no intervention, then the role of a control group whose purpose is to test for the effects of elapsed time or spontaneous remission becomes increasingly dubious both on scientific and ethical grounds. The use of a control group should be specific to an issue to which either the scientific literature cannot provide an answer or which is sufficiently ambiguous to warrant the use of a control group.

Statistical concepts Turning to the second methodological issue (i.e., statistical concepts), quantitative research has relied heavily upon the concept of statistical significance, which allows the researcher to be confident about attributing an association to something other than chance. However, Rosenthal and Rosnow (1991) have pointed out that the likelihood of obtaining a significant result is a function of both the sample size used and the size of the effect under investigation. Let us consider, first, sample size and second, effect size.

In brief, any difference between two variables can be shown to be statistically significant given sufficient power (that is, numbers of subjects). For example, this can often be seen in research using very large samples where correlations of less than 0.20 are reported as statistically significant (although such a correlation would account for only 4 per cent of the variance). The power required to detect a difference is a function of the size of effect expected and whether the test is one- or two-tailed. The norm for requisite power is usually held to be of the order of 0.80 (that is, a 4 in 5 chance of detecting a difference if one is present). Differences may well be obtained with considerably less power, which may well attest to the robustness of the finding. But findings of no difference when power is low or sub-optimal always means that the most parsimonious explanation for the null finding is low power: that is, that there was insufficient power in the design to detect the difference (which may actually have existed). While discussing the phenomenon of statistical power, it is also worth noting that increasing the number of clients in the study is not the only way of ensuring adequate power. In any design, the researcher is attempting to heighten the focus of the contrast being made, or, in other words, reduce the error variance. Hence, by ensuring that clients are homogeneous according to the variable of interest, ensuring that the form of counselling provided is delivered systematically, etc., all these will help reduce the amount of error in the study and increase the likelihood of it detecting a difference (if one is there).

The concept of an effect size (ES) introduces a metric for determining a measure of the magnitude of the relationship between independent and dependent variables, namely stating how effective a given treatment is. This is usually indexed by the following formula: $ES = (M_t - M_c)/\text{pooled SD}$ where M_t is the mean score on a given measure of the treated group, M_c is the mean score of the control group and pooled SD is the standard deviation of the treated and control groups combined. Accordingly, an ES of 1.0 indicates that the treated group is 1 standard deviation unit better than the control group at post-treatment. By referring to a table of the central distribution, we can determine that this improvement equates with 84 per cent. Hence, 84 per cent of the treated group are better than the average non-treated client. Cohen (1977) has provided guidelines for interpreting ES differences where 0.20 is small, 0.50 is medium and 0.80 is large. In comparing a treatment with a no-treatment group, we would expect a large difference (ES of 0.80 or more). Effect sizes usually relate to comparisons between treated and untreated groups. As such, they are detecting quite large effects (that is, differences between treatment and no treatment). Accordingly, the number of clients required in each group to detect a difference need not be very large. ES differences can equally apply to comparisons between two active treatment groups, in which case they would be expected to be smaller (as both interventions are active).

Meta-analysis We now turn to the third methodological issue, meta-analysis, which incorporates many of the statistical issues described in this section. When reviewing the outcome literature, reviewers would be presented with outcomes from a range of studies which invariably might be contradictory. For example, some studies might support the effectiveness of a specific intervention while others might not. In addition, some results might derive from better-designed studies than others, leading to the question of whether they should receive more weight. Hence, reviewing the cumulative literature has become increasingly difficult. One important procedure which has dominated the psychotherapeutic literature since 1977 has been 'meta-analysis'. In this procedure, individual studies themselves become the data with the aim of deriving a summary of the findings from all studies and taking into account specific features of the studies themselves. Hence, a meta-analytic study of psychological interventions for family therapy might collect all empirical studies investigating this area and delineate the dimensions on which these studies should be evaluated. The distinctive features of meta-analysis compared to other review strategies are the quantitative representation of key research findings in the studies reviewed and the statistical analysis of the distribution of findings across studies and the relationship to study features. Thus, rather than reduce data to either 'for' or 'against' (that is to say, all-or-nothing categories), meta-analysis examines both the direction and the magnitude of the effects and arrives at an overall conclusion. Further, selection of the literature is done in a determined way which can be written down and replicated by another researcher. Hence, it is far more systematic than simply scanning a range of journals. Although there are a wealth of methodological issues involved, the technique arrived at a time which enabled researchers to use individual studies in service of marshalling a more comprehensive answer about the effectiveness of psychological interventions.

Substantive findings

Prior to considering the wealth of data arising from this generation, it is appropriate to consider first the various reanalyses of the data upon which Eysenck (1952) based his critique of psychotherapy. Bergin and Lambert (1978) made a number of observations about the way Eysenck had analysed his data. For example, they noted that the most stringent improvement percentage was used for psychotherapy while the most generous was used for calculating spontaneous remission rates. Also, differing rates could be deduced depending on the criterion used. In general, their view was that conclusions drawn from the studies used by Eysenck were suspect due to their inherent limitations (not surprising given their date). In looking at more recent data, Bergin and Lambert (1978) found the rate for spontaneous remission to be 43 per cent rather than 67 per cent. Importantly, these authors also noted the finding from outcome studies that substantial change generally occurs within the initial eight to ten sessions, considerably quicker than the two-year time frame of spontaneous remission. The response of researchers to Eysenck's critique was to incorporate a control group into the research design and one exemplar design of Generation I is the study by Sloane, Staples, Cristol, Yorkston and Whipple (1975). They contrasted psychodynamic versus behavioural treatments, each with an average 14-session duration of treatment, with a wait-list control group. The total sample size used for the analysis was 90 clients with 30 clients randomly assigned to each of the three treatment conditions. The setting was a university psychiatric outpatient centre in which 54 per cent of the clients were students. The design used three experienced therapists in each of the two psychotherapy treatment conditions. The results using interview-based measures showed improvement in all three conditions but with the two active treatments being broadly similar and both superior to the wait-list condition. These gains were maintained at various follow-up intervals.

The findings from the Sloane et al. (1975) study are generally representative and were 'confirmed' several years later by the publication of the original meta-analytic study carried out by Smith and Glass (1977) and elaborated upon in their book *The Benefits of Psychotherapy* (Smith et al., 1980). The book provides a considered way through the claims and counter-claims of various researchers. They also provide a useful summary of the major reviews of this period (1961–75) prior to the use of meta-analysis. Stated as percentages of the number of studies reviewed, Eysenck (1961, 1966) found 0 per cent of studies supporting the efficacy of psychotherapy and Rachman (1971) found 4 per cent. By contrast, Bergin (1971) found 37 per cent, Meltzoff and Kornreich (1970) 80 per cent, and Luborsky, Singer and Luborsky (1975) 78 per cent. In terms of the methods used by the reviewers as to studies they either included or excluded in their reviews due to design flaws, Eysenck (1961, 1966) and Rachman (1971) excluded between 13 per cent and 74 per cent of studies while Bergin (1971) and Meltzoff and Kornreich (1970) excluded no studies. Given that many of the same studies were being sampled by the reviewers, Smith et al. (1980) noted how these findings 'illustrate the different results that arise from different methods for studying the same topic by means of a research review' (p. 23).

This 'variability' in summarizing research findings provided an excellent rationale for using meta-analytic techniques. Smith and Glass (1977) collated 475 controlled studies (that is to say, treatment versus no-treatment) across 18 differing therapy types (including placebo treatment and undifferentiated counselling). The average effect size (ES) across all studies was 0.85, indicative of a large effect for psychotherapy over no psychotherapy, indicating that the average treated person was better off than 80 per cent of non-treated people. The effects ranged from small ESs (0.14 for reality therapy) to large ESs (2.38 for cognitive therapies other than RET). The authors found little evidence for negative effects, with only 9 per cent of the measures being negative (that is, control groups were better than treated groups). In terms of overall effectiveness, the subsequent refinements of meta-analytic procedures and greater specificity, as well as the inclusion of more recent and more accomplished studies, have not delivered substantially different results, with the ESs remaining relatively stable.

In subsequent years, beyond the time frame of Generation I, many further studies have been included in meta-analytic reviews addressing the issue of 'effectiveness'. Lambert and Bergin state: 'There is now little doubt that psychological treatments are, overall and in general, beneficial, although it remains equally true that not everyone benefits to a satisfactory degree' (1994: 144). The most concise summary of findings derives from meta-analytic studies. In the area of depression, the number of studies (n) included in the meta-analysis and the effect sizes (ES) for three major meta-analytic reports are as follows: Nietzel, Russell, Hemmings and Gretter (1987), $n = 28$, ES = 0.71; Robinson, Berman and Neimeyer (1990), $n = 29$, ES = 0.84; and Steinbrueck, Maxwell and Howard (1983), $n = 56$, ES = 1.22.

In terms of more diverse presenting problems, Lambert and Bergin (1994) provide a summary table of 30 meta-analytic reviews covering a range of presenting problems and psychological interventions. Five studies (including that of Smith and Glass) are defined as 'mixed' and result in a large average ES of 0.90. The range of other studies is so diverse as not to warrant categorizing. However, they show the smallest and largest ESs (excluding control conditions) to range from 0.00 (schizophrenia; Quality Assurance Project, 1984) to 1.30 (stuttering; Andrews et al., 1980). Using only those studies ($n = 25$) which report ESs, the median ES was 0.76, which is approaching a large ES. In terms of comparisons, an ES of 0.67 is obtained from nine months of instruction in reading, while the ESs for antidepressants range from 0.40 to 0.81. Thus, as Lambert and Bergin (1994) argue, there appears to be evidence that psychological interventions are as effective, if not more effective, as medication. Apparently contrary to these substantial effects, it has been claimed that counselling/psychotherapy only accounts for 10 per cent of the outcome variance. This might appear small. However, it needs to be realized that 10 per cent variance arises from a correlation of 0.32 between counselling/psychotherapy and outcome. This is appreciably greater than other established correlations in the field: for example, correlations of 0.03 for the effect of aspirin on heart attacks, and 0.07 for service in Vietnam and alcohol consumption.

An additional question which has been raised is whether counselling is more effective than a placebo? In response, a critical point, well summarized by Lambert and Bergin, is worthy of reiteration: 'In interpreting this [placebo] research, it is important to keep in mind that failure to find incremental effects (effects beyond those attributable to common factors) for a specific therapy does not mean that psychotherapy is ineffective. Rather it means that no effect has been demonstrated beyond the effects of the common factors' (1994: 149). Lambert and Bergin (1994) provide a useful summary table of 15 meta-analytic studies whereby three two-way comparisons are made: psychotherapy vs no-treatment, placebo vs no-treatment, and psychotherapy vs placebo. The first of these comparisons produces a mean/median ES of 0.82 (i.e., very similar to that stated in the previous section). The placebo vs no-treatment comparison produces a mean/median ES of 0.42, while the placebo vs psychotherapy comparison produces a mean/median ES of 0.48.

By way of comment on the use of placebo controls, Lambert and Bergin (1994) summarize: 'we have concluded that the typical placebo controls used in outcome studies are so conceptually and procedurally flawed that they have essentially failed in their purpose of helping to isolate the active therapeutic ingredients. It is time to discontinue placebo controls and design studies with more meaningful comparison groups' (1994: 152).

Comment

In terms of outcome, Generation I research clearly established the effectiveness of psychotherapy and also provided the basis for investigating components of what might make therapy effective. With regard to the former, it might be assumed that this issue has now passed. However, two observations are worth noting. First, while the amount of research carried out has been phenomenal, Eysenck still maintains the validity of his argument (for example, 1992). Secondly, with recent changes in the service provisions for psychotherapy and counselling services within the NHS in the UK, it has again become a major issue as various stakeholders in the provision of services have begun to require outcome criteria. Hence, it is a generation of work which has come, to some extent, full circle as the demand to justify the impact of counselling and psychotherapy meets with market forces. Hence, while Generation I research may have put increasing weight on ensuring internal validity, the question of external validity has now come to prominence.

Can the therapy process (facilitative conditions) be measured?

Context

The influence of Rogers was profound in Generation I's development of objective procedures for measuring events of recorded therapy sessions. His influence has been noted as deriving from his 'respect for the scientific method and dedication to the objective study of the efficacy of his methods' (Hill and Corbett, 1993: 5). While there was a great surge of activity in pursuit of establishing the effectiveness of psychotherapy, it was largely Rogers and his students who pursued research on the process of therapy. While the earlier process work had focused on verbal response modes as indicators of therapist techniques, process measures turned to the evaluation of Rogers's facilitative conditions.

However, there is an intriguing tension between the findings of the research presented above and the assumptions underlying the research on process during Generation I. In the first edition of the *Handbook of Psychotherapy and Behavior Change*, Truax and Mitchell (1971) reviewed research on therapists' interpersonal skills. The premise for their review of particular therapists' skills was based on one particular view of the general effectiveness of psychotherapy and counselling: 'After a careful review of the relevant research literature dealing with the effects of counseling and psychotherapy, Truax and Carkhuff (1967) concluded that unfortunately Eysenck was essentially correct in saying that the *average* counseling and psychotherapy, as it is currently practised, does not result in average client improvement greater than that observed in persons who receive no special counseling or psychotherapy treatment' (1967: 301). Hence, much of the subsequent process research was premised on the assumption that specific skills training on specific therapists' variables would enhance the effectiveness of therapy.

Methodological issues

Examples of observationally based measures developed by students and colleagues of Rogers included the Experiencing Scale (Klein et al., 1970), the Client Vocal Quality Classification Scale (Butler et al., 1962) and the Accurate Empathy Scale (AES; Truax, 1961). Self-report measures which were developed included the Barrett-Lennard Relationship Inventory (BLRI; Barrett-Lennard, 1962). The last two measures (that is, the AES and BLRI) can be seen as representative of the work in this research generation and each provided a major tool for investigating the therapeutic relationship and its components which began in Generation I and spanned Generation II research (see below).

A standard approach adopted in Generation I research was to select particular 'sections' of a session either randomly or systematically. The latter approach might have involved selecting three 5-minute segments (for example, minutes 15–19, 30–34 and 45–49). This would appear 'representative' of the session. However, most studies carried out in the 1960s employed random time samples from therapy sessions when investigating Rogerian conditions. This approach reflects Generation I research because it bears the hallmark of the uniformity myth (Kiesler, 1966) which supposes that there is little fluctuation across clients, therapists and (in relation to this issue) sessions. The strategy of using random time samples assumed that it did not matter what particular segment was selected: one segment was as good as another in terms of accessing a particular therapeutic process. Such an approach appeared to be 'approved' by Rogers (see Rogers et al., 1967) who argued that small samples (for example, three samples of 2–5 minutes in length) from any given interview were sufficient to provide a basis for investigating, for example, the construct of empathy.

During this period, considerable research efforts were spent on establishing the empirical basis for associating the facilitative conditions with outcome. However, many questions arose concerning the research methodologies used which served to undermine the validity of the findings themselves.

Substantive findings

Examples of research in this early phase include the work of Rogers and Dymond (1954), who found evidence supporting the view that good outcome was associated with improvements in self-perceptions. Other research drew on the work of Whitehorn and Betz (e.g., 1954) who found, via a retrospective study of psychiatrists, that those who were successful in working with schizophrenic patients were warm and communicated with their patients in a personal manner. Similar findings arose from the various reports of the classic study of the therapeutic conditions with a group of schizophrenic patients carried out at the University of Wisconsin (e.g., Rogers et al., 1967). This study arose following publication of Rogers's (1957) paper on the necessary and sufficient conditions for change. The Wisconsin project was a major empirical investigation undertaken with schizophrenic clients and the results were later published (Rogers et al., 1967). At the same time, Truax and Carkhuff (1967) published a text which included Truax's own version of some of the Wisconsin data. There were other compendiums of research which combined 'positive' results with the development of work on the facilitative conditions (for example, Carkhuff and Berenson, 1967) as well as a major review in the first edition of the *Handbook of Psychotherapy and Behavior Change* (Truax and Mitchell, 1971). This later text marks a recognition of the fallacy of assuming uniformity. In discussing the domain of therapist variables and their role in understanding the process of psychotherapy, Truax and Mitchell (1971) stated: 'it quickly became apparent to us that we were assuming that such variables are unitary when, in fact, they are not'. They went on: 'just as therapists are not unitary, neither are specific therapist variables'. They concluded: 'Therefore, in our opinion, most if not all the research dealing with therapist characteristics needs to be re-done' (1971: 300).

Comment

One result of the research work of Generation I was to show how the 'complex personal phenomena of psychotherapy could be brought out of the private consulting room into the purview of scientific study without disrupting these phenomena beyond recognition' (Orlinsky and Russell, 1994). Hence, there was a view that any aspect of the psychotherapeutic process could be measured. In terms of process findings, the tone was decidedly optimistic and some questions have been asked about the manner in which some of the research was carried out. Garfield and Bergin (1994), in the fourth edition of the *Handbook of Psychotherapy and Behavior Change*, recount the issues surrounding the mysterious disappearance of the initial data organized by Truax in the Wisconsin project. The final publication was based on an entirely new set of ratings. Garfield and Bergin state that 'Since 1967, scholars have appeared to treat with caution any of the published reports by Truax (but not his co-authors) concerning the Wisconsin Schizophrenia Project data' (1994: 11–12).

Generation II: 1960s to 1980s
Specificity in outcome and process research

Research characterizing Generation II began in large part as a search for greater specificity in response to what became known as the 'uniformity myth'. This myth reflected the held view that clients were thought to respond similarly to particular interventions. In other words, little attention was paid to differences across clients, therapists, therapies, or across the course of therapy itself. In response to this situation, the archetypal question of this generation became encapsulated in Paul's litany: 'What treatment, by whom, is most effective for this individual with that specific problem, and under which set of circumstances?' (1967: 111). Clearly this was an important and logical step in research as it sought to address the issue of what was the most effective treatment.

In terms of process, Rogers's theory and research work paid scant attention to differences among clients. The question of whether psychotherapy is effective was seen as simplistic (Krumboltz, 1966) while process and outcome were increasingly viewed as differing across clients, therapists and therapies (Kiesler, 1966). Generation II research gained ground in the 1960s and was dominant through the 1980s. Indeed, there is still a considerable output from this generation given that some of the major outcome studies were designed and implemented in the early 1980s and hence the publications are appearing in the 1990s. In both outcome and process research, the key theme in Generation II research was 'specificity'.

Is one kind of counselling more effective than another?

Context

Once the general theme of determining the overall effectiveness of psychotherapy was instigated, Paul's matrix of specifying the various components led researchers to focus most on the differing types of interventions. In addition, the 1960s saw the rapid development of behaviour therapy within the domain of clinical psychology and fed the logical question as to whether these newer therapies (or other brands of therapy) were more effective than, for example, the verbal (for example, dynamically oriented) therapies. The research carried out in response to this question raised a number of methodological issues relating to design, measures, analyses of outcome data and statistical concerns. Each of these will be addressed in the following section.

Methodological issues

Design The design usually employed to address the above question is known as a 'comparative outcome' trial. In this situation, the main focus of interest is in comparing two (or more) active treatments. The advantages of the comparative outcome designs include their ability to ensure that any demand characteristics of the two or more conditions are broadly similar. Also, they are the best means for ensuring that the placebo effects are controlled inasmuch as they are present for both conditions. Hence, the main difference between the two or more treatments should be restricted to technical differences between the conditions. However, while this is a persuasive argument and has been the rationale for a series of studies, it needs to be noted that other proponents of the quantitative approach firmly hold to the view that a control condition should be administered (e.g., Kazdin, 1994).

The studies in this generation should be relatively sophisticated, benefiting from the lessons learned in Generation I. To provide a sense of the complexities involved, the outline design from one major comparative outcome study is presented here (the results from this study appear in the following section). The largest study to date is the National Institute of Mental Health Treatment of Depression Collaborative Research Program (NIMH TDCRP; Elkin, 1994; Elkin et al., 1989). The design comprised three research sites in which 250 clients were randomly assigned to the four treatment conditions. The four treatment conditions comprised the two psychotherapies which were of major interest – namely, cognitive-behavioural therapy (CBT) and interpersonal psychotherapy (IPT). In order to provide a standard reference condition, the third condition comprised imipramine plus clinical management (IMI-CM). Finally, a placebo condition (PLA-CM) was used primarily as a control for the drug condition and also as an imperfect control for the two psychotherapies. Among the features of the design, separate therapists were used in the two differing psychotherapies. This is termed 'nested' in which the therapists administer only one particular treatment rather than delivering all treatments. The particular treatments were documented in training manuals and the delivery of the treatments was investigated to check on therapists' adherence to the treatment protocols. This is an example of the research requiring a level of control and monitoring over the delivery of the therapy which would not normally take place in more naturalistic settings. It is also a procedure which may rest uncomfortably with the philosophy of counselling psychology.

Because both psychotherapies are active (that is to say they would both be expected to have a positive impact on psychological functioning), the effect size is likely to be appreciably smaller than for a treatment vs no-treatment design (for example, between small and medium). Logically, then, the sample size required to detect any difference will be larger. Ironically, therefore, it can be seen that in terms of resources required, it is much more difficult to carry out a contrast of two or more active treatments than it is to carry out a study using a control group (such as a wait-list control in which clients receive some subsequent treatment).

Measures It is incumbent upon users to be informed about aspects concerning the psychometric properties of measures they use and to report this basic information when using it. Basic requirements include data pertaining to validity and reliability. In terms of perspectives, outcome can be evaluated from three sources: the client, the counsellor and a third party. In contrast to many other helping professions, counselling psychology should aspire to obtain clients' perspectives on the change they have experienced. In addition, measures are based on one of two central assumptions; nomothetic or idiographic. Nomothetic measures comprise items that are invariant and that have been standardized on large samples and invariably are accompanied by norms. Idiographic measures are derived from the client's unique frame of reference and are specific to the client, a perspective which is congruent with the central role of the individual within counselling psychology.

Substantive findings

Bergin and Garfield summarize Generation II studies as follows: 'We have to face the fact that in a majority of studies, different approaches to the same symptoms (depression for example) show little difference in efficacy' (1994b: 822). This is the view summarized by Stiles, Shapiro and Elliott (1986) in their question 'Are all psychotherapies equivalent?' They posited three ways in which to understand the supposed equivalence of outcomes. The first was methodological in that equivalence could be achieved through lack of stringency in research methodology. The second argument concerned the possibility that differing therapies may be broadly equivalent due to the overriding effects of common factors. The third argument revolved around the implementation of new research strategies to detect differences.

The NIMH TDCRP implicitly addressed the first of these through implementation of one of the most stringent research designs. Findings showed that clients in the IMI-CM condition were most improved, clients in the PLA-CM condition least improved, and clients in the two psychotherapy conditions in between but generally closer to the IMI-CM condition. However, differences were not large. Indeed, there were no differences between the two psychotherapies or between either of them and the IMI-CM. Differences between the psychotherapies and the placebo condition showed only one instance of a trend towards lower scores for clients in the IPT condition as compared with PLA-CM and no significant or trend difference for CBT. Findings from a UK study comparing cognitive-behavioural (CB) with psychodynamic interpersonal (PI) therapy in two durations (8 sessions and 16 sessions) showed only a small advantage to CB over PI on the Beck Depression Inventory (Beck et al., 1961) but not on any other measures (Shapiro et al., 1994). Hence, the CB advantage was restricted to a single measure. However, there was a significant severity by duration interaction which showed that clients with high severity depression did significantly better in 16 than in 8 sessions. Findings at one-year follow-up showed that clients in the 8-PI condition did less well than clients in the other three conditions (Shapiro et al., 1995).

These findings have confirmed the view that technically different therapies result in broadly similar outcomes, a conclusion referred to as the 'equivalence paradox' (Stiles et al., 1986). It is not disputed that there is often a reported advantage to one particular method of therapy (invariably cognitive behavioural), but what is important is that the *size* of this advantage is relatively small. How such a small advantage translates into clinical status or psychological health is unclear.

Comment

In some ways, it is difficult to be conclusive about this generation of research. Some might argue that little has been gained from it, seeing the failure to identify specific differential effects as a poor outcome for a generation's work. At one level, this disappointment is understandable, especially given the huge financial cost of some of the studies. There is also the view that the full yield from the work of this generation has not been realized as it is a legitimate argument that what is still required is further specificity. What is clear is that such specificity is unlikely to be derived from further large-scale studies of the kind described above. However, the importance of the finding of broad equivalence of outcomes despite technical diversity should not be lost. Neither should it be forgotten that while 'active' treatments have consistently out-performed 'placebo' treatments, the difference between the two conditions has often been arithmetical rather than statistically significant.

Do the facilitative conditions lead to better outcomes?

Context

Process research built its base on the 'recorded' session and, in Generation II, was dominated by the work carried out to investigate the 'facilitative' conditions (i.e., empathy, warmth and genuineness). This was a logical step deriving from a theoretical basis and employing observational and self-report measures.

Methodology

A profound difficulty associated with the process research in Generation I was the lack of replication of specific findings. This arose out of the growing search for specificity contrasting with the uniformity myth. Process research applied its newly found objectivism through the use of seemingly rigorous and appropriate research designs. While the proto-typical research study in Generation I employed a random technique for sampling time periods, Generation II research moved towards employing the 'session'. This move arose from the debate as to whether therapist skills were stable across time. This point had been raised by Karl and Abeles (1969) who found that when tape recordings were sampled during any of the five 10-minute portions, there were significant differences across the segments on a sample of therapist measures. Similarly, Gurman (1973) had been critical of the single-segment sampling strategy. He sampled high and low facilitative therapists during the initial 4-minute segments in each of the five consecutive 10-minute segments and found that regardless of their absolute ratings, all therapists' relative levels of facilitativeness varied both within and across sessions. Hence, the facilitative conditions appeared not to be as consistent as Rogerian theory would have predicted. Such a position led to, for example, Gurman's (1973, 1977) 'empathic specificity hypothesis'. This hypothesis suggested that a therapist's overall facilitativeness is less predictive of treatment outcome than their level of functioning around particular issues which are more critical to the client.

Substantive findings

The core period for Generation II process research was the 1970s and there is a noticeable difference between Truax and Mitchell's (1971) review from the *Handbook* reported above and the Mitchell, Bozarth and Krauft (1977) chapter published in *Effective Psychotherapy: a Handbook of Research*. The authors of the latter text acknowledged that the former had focused too much on gross outcome and not sufficiently on the potential correlates between, for example, empathy and outcome. Hence, they stated, that 'demographic and process studies were ignored which might have answered the question: 'Which therapists, under what conditions, with which clients in what kinds of specific predicaments, need to reach what levels of these interpersonal skills to effect what kinds of client changes?', (1977: 482).

In contrast to the 1971 review which implied that the facilitative conditions were both necessary and sufficient, and that they were relatively invariant, Mitchell et al. stated that 'the mass of data neither supports nor rejects the overriding influence of such variables as empathy' (1977: 483). They went on: 'their [the facilitative conditions] potency and generalizability are not as great as once thought' (p. 483). Hence, while the authors reported some studies which supported the positive role of the facilitative conditions to varying degrees, the majority of studies they reported showed little or no direct relationship between the facilitative conditions and outcome (e.g., Sloane et al., 1975).

Comment

While process research focused largely on the facilitative conditions, which in itself became the basis for subsequent research on the thera-peutic alliance, it was, as Orlinsky and Russell (1994) observe, 'peculiarly flawed' to the extent that it virtually ceased by the late 1970s. The 'conceptual critique' specifically in relation to the facilitative conditions, combined with the increasing search for psychologically appropriate methods for investigating aspects of the therapeutic process, led to the demise of research in this area. In historical terms, the absence of a research centre linked to Rogers assisted the demise. More generally, there was probably a move away from investigating 'common' factors towards determining the more specific components of individual orientations.

Generation III: 1970s to 1990s
Cost-effectiveness and change pathways

The research included in this third generation spans the period from the 1970s through to the 1990s and incorporates what appears to be two quite diverse interests: cost-effectiveness and change mechanisms. However, these two areas can be seen to be natural developments arising from the previous two generations of research. Cost-effectiveness has become a central concern, partly driven by research interest alone but also by the interest of a variety of stakeholders. As such, it is a natural extension of the outcome research carried out in Generation I. The focus on change mechanisms reflects an extension to the issue of 'specificity' which was a feature of Generation II process research, although it might equally be construed as a reaction to it. It is an extension in terms of it retaining specificity as a hallmark but a reaction in terms of refocusing research onto the process of change.

Is 'integrative' therapy just one more brand name?

Context

The context for considering integration arises partly as a corollary to the above findings on the broad equivalence of outcomes from differing therapies. It also arises from counsellors' aspirations not to be constrained by a single theoretical orientation. Also, a perception that counsellors have multiple skills feeds the notion that the skills from a range of therapies can be utilized in response to a client's presenting problems. Certainly, recent surveys of therapists' orientations show the majority of therapists to describe themselves as 'eclectic'. It is worth noting in passing that the term 'integration' is now used considerably more than the term 'eclectic'. For example, the revised edition of the *Handbook of Eclectic Psychotherapy* (Norcross, 1986) has been entitled *Handbook of Psychotherapy Integration* (Norcross and Goldfried, 1992). Similarly, the *Journal of Integrative and Eclectic Psychotherapy* has become the *Journal of Psychotherapy Integration*. In addition, there has been a roundtable entitled 'Research directions for psychotherapy integration' (Norcross, 1993) published in the latter journal.

Methodological issues

The methodological issues in evaluating integrative therapies reflect those discussed previously as the design issues involved effectively treat 'integrative' therapy as just one more type of therapy. Perhaps, most importantly, the central problem is conceptual inasmuch as whether an integrative therapy is actually integrative or whether it is simply another brand of therapy. For example, combinations of therapies should not be viewed as integrative. What differentiates a combined therapy from an integrative therapy is the presence of an overarching integrative theory which binds the various therapeutic approaches in terms of some higher-order theory or model.

Substantive findings

Brockman, Poynton, Ryle and Watson (1987) compared cognitive-analytic therapy (CAT: Ryle, 1990) with short-term psychodynamic therapy. Specific advantages were found for CAT. However, these were found on CAT-specific measures. Comparisons of global measures showed no significant advantage to either condition. Shapiro, Barkham, Reynolds, Hardy and Stiles (1992) combined prescriptive (i.e. cognitive-behavioural) and exploratory (i.e. psychodynamic interpersonal) therapies by administering them within a session but alternating within certain constraints across the course of therapy in response to a match between client requirements and a particular overarching integrative model. The outcome for this single case was successful but requires replication. Overall, there is a dearth of direct evidence for the equivalence in efficacy, let alone superiority, of integrative therapies. Much of the argument in support of their use derives indirectly from the equivalence of outcomes. In addition, it is not clear that skills and expertise gained in one particular method of delivery transfer to a more integrated method without additional training.

Comment

The current interest in and articles emanating from this domain is considerable, but it has not been shown that integrative therapies are 'superior' to single-brand therapies. It is likely that integrative therapies are more palatable to practitioners but this is a clinical preference. Following a major workshop which focused on the research required to move this area forward, little empirical work has been carried out (Wolfe and Goldfried, 1988). Indeed, considerably more work needs to be carried out in order to provide hard data on the comparative effectiveness of integrative therapies.

Is long-term counselling more effective than short-term counselling?

Context

The 'debate' between long- and short-term counselling has gained a central focus recently, and in particular among those stakeholders who have an interest in providing a cost-effective service. While the previous question focused on the method of the intervention, this question focuses on the duration of the intervention.

Methodological issues

In determining how much of a given intervention should be delivered to a person let us first consider issues relating to open-ended vs time-limited interventions. There is, implicit in this comparison, the view that open-ended interventions will be of longer duration than time-limited interventions. However, this is not necessarily true. The vast majority of research studies investigating time-limited therapies employ durations of 12, 16 or 20 sessions. In many instances, any of these might actually be longer than an open-ended intervention, particularly if the average duration is held to be in the region of between 5 and 7 sessions. Hence, if a time-limited intervention was compared with an open-ended condition, it is likely that clients in the time-limited condition would receive more therapy than those in the open-ended condition.

As with the previous questions, power (that is to say the size of the study) is an issue. In the same way that large effects will be expected to arise from more contrasting conditions, so larger effects would be expected to occur from contrasting briefer with longer duration interventions. Of course, the main problem relates to controlling for elapsed time. Any comparison must carry out assessments at similar points in time.

In terms of what has become known as the 'dose–effect' literature, an important point is to ensure that any client has a sufficient dose in order to be able to evaluate its effectiveness. This point is akin to that in psychopharmacology in which the effectiveness of any given medication can only be determined once it has been established that a sufficient dose has been taken. In other words, it needs to be established that if no effect is obtained, that this is not attributable to the fact that not enough was given to have an effect. This notion of 'dose' may appear overly medical and contrary to the philosophy of counselling psychology. However, it is an attempt to model the match between client need and service resources.

45

Substantive findings

The major finding relating to the dose—effect literature derives from a study carried out by Howard, Kopta, Krause and Orlinsky (1986) which combined 15 outcome studies over 30 years. These authors found that the percentage of clients showing measurable improvement following specified numbers of sessions was as follows: 24 per cent after a single session, 30 per cent after two sessions, 41 per cent after 4 sessions, 53 per cent after 8 sessions, 62 per cent after 13 sessions, 74 per cent after 26 sessions, 83 per cent after 52 sessions and 90 per cent after 104 sessions. This relationship between the number of sessions received by clients and the percentage of clients showing measurable improvement was best represented by a negatively accelerating curve. This means that while the curve 'accelerates' (the percentage of clients improving gets higher as a result of more sessions), it does so 'negatively' in that the greatest improvement occurs early in therapy and then there are diminishing returns thereafter such that smaller and smaller gains are made later on in therapy in response to the provision of more sessions. However, it is worth noting that almost half of the studies (seven) had a median of 15 or more sessions, considerably more that the often-quoted averages (Taube et al., 1984). Further, the data set did not comprise cognitive-behavioural, cognitive or behaviour therapy orientations. The findings from Howard et al.'s (1986) work are interesting in how they have been used by people espousing differing view points. Howard et al. (1986) obtained two dose—effect curves: one based on therapist ratings and one on client ratings. Defence of longer-term therapy has utilized the former curve. In contrast, data from the client ratings suggests greater improvements to be derived from the initial 8 to 10 sessions. Research on brief therapies has been summarized by Koss and Shiang (1994).

Comment

Findings indicate that for many clients the greater impact of counselling or therapy occurs during the initial time frame with subsequent gains requiring more time. However, for many clients, especially those who have been severely damaged, effective therapeutic work may not be possible until considerable work has been carried out in establishing, for example, the therapeutic alliance. What this means is that there are clients for whom briefer therapies are appropriate and clients for whom longer therapies are appropriate. The issue is to determine what is best for each client. It is not necessarily true that more therapy is always the preferred option. Given limited resources, it is important to ensure that longer-term interventions are appropriately used and that they are evaluated in order to provide supporting evidence for their use.

Are the improvements realized by clients meaningful?

Context

A recent trend has been to determine the clinical significance of a particular effect. This trend has arisen within the field of clinical psychology (Jacobson and Truax, 1991) but it should also be applicable to the field of counselling psychology. However, there are important caveats to be stated and these will be addressed before providing an example of clinical significance. Chapter 4 addresses this issue in greater detail.

Methodological

There are a number of caveats regarding clinical significance. First, there will be many who will argue against counselling psychology adopting a procedure termed 'clinical' significance. Although pedantic, there is a legitimate point: the same argument could be made by occupational psychologists. Hence, there may well be a place for the term 'psychological significance' as that is what we are interested in (as opposed to statistical significance). Secondly, there needs to be a better means of appreciating the differing sizes of 'psychological' significance (in the same way as there are differing ranges of effect size). Importantly, counselling psychology addresses a range of issues, from those in which one would expect to obtain large effects to those where effects might well be extremely small. The latter might apply in those cases where interventions are made within what is a normal population with the aim of improving psychological well-being. In cases of 'life enhancement', the effects will be small unless the measures used to tap the process are extremely sensitive to the phenomenon being measured.

Substantive findings

Given that this is a procedural matter, findings relating to these procedures are more of technical interest: it is their application which is interesting. Several studies have used these procedures or variants of them. For example, Barkham and Shapiro (1990) used it in a pilot study ($n = 12$) of brief counselling for job-related distress and found that, depending on the outcome measure used, between five and eight clients met criteria for reliable and clinically significant change after only two sessions. Being able to state how many clients have reached a defined level of improvement makes results more tangible.

Comment

The trend towards being able to say that a person now belongs to a normal population is a powerful one in terms of showing the effects of an intervention. While some counselling psychologists may find the notions of 'membership' of a population at odds with the discipline, it is important to appreciate that one strength of this approach is that is places an emphasis on the individual in the context of the group or population at large. This is in contrast to inferential statistics in which the primary question being asked relates to the mean (average) of a group. However, parallel to the argument that methodological pluralism should be the aspiration, it would seem logical to embrace the same degree of pluralism in terms of analysing data. That is, researchers should consider the various ways of analysing and presenting data to ensure that the results are not biased towards one particular model or procedure of analysis.

What are the effective change pathways?

Context

Building on the developmental stages arising from Generations I and II in which process work moved from the use of random segments (1960s) to whole sessions (1970s), Generation III process research continued by beginning a rapprochement between research and clinical practice. Many features help define one generation from another but there are at least three 'shifts' in process research which help define Generation III research. One was the publication of Bordin's (1979) classic article on the working alliance which became a central focus for research into common factors in place of the facilitative conditions. A second was the publication of Hill, Carter and O'Farrell's (1983) single-case study in *Journal of Counseling Psychology*. The third was the use of new methodologies utilizing, for example, the 'events' paradigm' (e.g., Barkham and Shapiro, 1986) and 'task analysis' (e.g., Rice and Greenberg, 1984).

Research methodology

Process research is time-consuming as the data derives from what happens within sessions. The approach therefore requires the researcher to tap either some component of the session itself or to acquire some measure of the phenomenon under investigation after the session. The former strategy is greatly assisted by taking tape recordings of sessions. However, a great deal of research which focuses on in-session activities has derived from sessions selected from the course of therapy without regard to any sampling strategy. The two main options are selecting all sessions or using some theoretical rationale which is applied to determine which session (or part of a session) is to be sampled. The first strategy assumes that the researcher is interested in the course of a phenomenon across time. This is obviously a time-consuming approach but one which is central to understanding the process of change. For example, while there might be evidence that the therapeutic alliance is associated with outcome, researchers and practitioners may be most interested in how the therapeutic alliance is established and how it changes over time. The second strategy necessitates some rationale for selecting a particular session. (This strategy can obviously be used in addition to the first but not vice versa.) Staying with the therapeutic alliance as an example, the researcher may ask the client to identify a session in which he or she feels that the therapist did something to enhance the client's feeling of having a good therapeutic alliance. The client might write something at the end of the session indicating what it was. Such 'events' could then be collected for a number of clients and the data analysed in a quantitative manner. The researcher could also combine these two approaches if, for example, they have a theory that the resolution of a ruptured alliance leads to a good outcome. Here, the researcher would want to select a session in which there was evidence of a rupture and then analyse the session, and subsequent sessions, as deemed necessary.

Research investigating what counselling psychologists say in sessions has employed a variety of procedures which invariably require coding taxonomies. One level of interest has refocused on verbal response modes (VRMs) of which there are many taxonomies. In an attempt to determine common ground, a comparison of six systems was carried out (Elliott et al., 1987). A degree of commonality was found among the various systems with 'question', 'information', 'advisement', 'interpretation', 'reflection' and 'self-disclosure' common to all six systems and 'reassurance' and 'confrontation' common to four of the systems. Whatever the system used, the data (usually a transcript of the counselling session) must first be divided into meaningful units. Here, important issues underlie what a unit is. Indeed, there are a whole range of units from the 'sentence' to 'an event'. Of critical importance is that the units are reliably identified prior to using the rating system. As with all coding systems, a range of requirements is necessary. Units need to be operationally defined; independent coders trained with reported reliability statistics; multiple coders used (usually three) in which the tasks are completed independently and consideration given to the need to randomize the order if necessary. A very useful and accessible account of the many problems encountered in carrying out process research is given in Hill (1991) and Lambert and Hill (1994) – the latter covers both process and outcome.

Two particular problems have been identified regarding the validity of process research: the violation of assumptions of statistical tests; and 'fishing and error rate' problems. The first problem relates to the issue of independence (or non-independence) of data. For example, if VRM codings are obtained from a client, these codings are not independent of each other. This problem also obtains to research more generally. For example, if four counsellors each see ten clients, the pairing of those ten clients with the same counsellor do not make the dyads independent of each other. Hence, the degrees of freedom may more appropriately be taken from the number of counsellors rather than the number of clients. The second problem relates to error rate and is especially salient in process research. For example, Wampold and Poulin (1992) highlight this problem, citing a study by Hill and colleagues (Hill et al., 1988) which contained more than 300 statistical tests. We might expect 15 of these (five in every 100) to occur by chance alone, hence leading to a number of findings which could be described as 'false positives'. Corrections need to be made when so many statistical tests are carried out. A further issue in process research involves attributing causality. Process research invariably lacks the degree of experimental manipulation seen in outcome studies and researchers need to be careful with respect to cause-and-effect relationships.

Substantive findings

The review of process and outcome in psychotherapy by Orlinsky, Grawe and Parks (1994) summarized a wealth of material relating to possible effective pathways. They identified stability of treatment arrangements and counsellor adherence to a treatment model as showing promise. They identified 'patient suitability' and 'therapist skills' as particularly robust with over two-thirds of studies in each of these areas reporting significant findings. In terms of therapeutic operations, the authors summarized three areas: problem presentation; expert understanding; and therapist intervention. With regard to problem presentation, the cognitive and behavioural processes within the client's problem presentation are related to outcome. Findings on 'expert understanding' target client problems and client affective responses during sessions. In terms of therapist interventions, there appears to be substantial evidence supporting experiential confrontation as well as interpretations. In addition, paradoxical intention appears to show a consistent relationship with outcome. In terms of the therapeutic bond, this showed strong associations with outcome, especially when assessed from the client's perspective.

The use of VRMs in various research studies has shown that therapists use responses which are consistent with their theoretical orientation (Elliott et al., 1987). Relating VRMs to immediate outcomes (that is to say, in-session), a range of studies identified 'interpretation' (or responses closely allied to it) as being 'effective'. For example, O'Farrell, Hill and Patton (1986) found interpretation to be related to a decrease in client problem description and an increase in experiencing and insight, while Barkham and Shapiro (1986) found 'exploration' (a response between interpretation and reflection) to be associated with client and helper experiences of perceived empathy. However, the role of therapist 'intentions' is just as important. Horvath, Marx and Kamann (1990) found clients' ability to identify the intention of the counsellor depended, in addition to other factors, upon the stage of therapy with understanding increasing from initial to mid-therapy and then decreasing. Factors accounting for this may involve the intentions becoming more complex or tacit as therapy develops. The complex relationship between these factors (for example, response modes and intentions) is summarized by Sexton and Whiston (1994): 'Based on a variety of complex factors (experience, training, client behavior), counselors develop intentions or goals that guide their choices of intentions or response modes. After each counselor response, the client reacts (decodes, interprets and experiences) and responds. In response, the counselor develops an adjusted intention and subsequent response mode. Over time these patterns become stabilized in client and counselor expectations' (1994: 21).

However, it has been found that response modes account for very little of the outcome variance, even for immediate outcome. Hill reports that 'therapist intentions and client experiencing in the turn preceding the therapist intervention each contributed more to the variance than did response modes' (1990: 289). She sites her intensive analyses of eight single cases (Hill, 1989) in which she found that 'client personality, therapist orientation and personality, and adequate therapeutic relationship, and events external to therapy all influenced whether or not clients incorporated changes begun in therapy' (1990: 289).

Research into the effectiveness of interpretations has been summarized by Orlinsky et al. (1994). These authors cited a total of 38 findings from 16 studies, of which 24 findings were positively related to overall outcome, 11 showed no association, and three showed negative associations. Hence, while two-thirds of the findings showed a positive association between interpretations and outcome, inspection of their data (Orlinsky et al., 1994: 303) in which 11 studies yielded sufficient information for the reviewers to determine effect sizes, showed the average size of this effect to be small (ES = 0.21). Garfield (1990), albeit basing his views on a previous review (Orlinsky and Howard, 1986), when only half of the reported findings supported the link with a positive outcome, was also somewhat sceptical. Research into the accuracy of therapist interpretations has been carried out by Crits-Christoph, Cooper and Luborsky (1988) who found that accuracy of interpretation was the best predictor of outcome. However, rather surprisingly, it was not related to improvements in the therapeutic alliance. However, Garfield (1990) has offered some criticisms of this particular research: for example, the mean ratings of 'accuracy' ranged from 1.49 to 1.81 on a 4-point scale with anchor points of '1' ('no congruence') and '4' ('high congruence').

The 'events' paradigm has yielded findings which bridge the use of quantitative and qualitative approaches. In terms of the most and least helpful events in therapy, clients have reported the most helpful impacts to be problem solution, awareness and reassurance (Llewelyn et al., 1988). The least helpful was reported to be 'unwanted thoughts'. This latter finding, while not surprising, raises the point that clients and therapists have differential perspectives, with the clients experiencing 'unwanted thoughts' as negative while therapists may well see it as a necessary stage for the client to progress through towards improved psychological health.

Comment

This area of research has combined much of the more 'technical' and quantitative research efforts. However, difficulties undoubtedly occur when evaluating specific techniques and many researchers within this domain have contrasting views. For example, Garfield has stated that there is 'no truly strong support for the accuracy of interpretation as a process variable of importance . . . the interpretation of explanation that is *accepted* by the patient is the one that may have some positive therapeutic impact' (1990: 276). Others, for example Silberchatz and Curtis (1986), argue that the interpretations which are important are those which are consistent with the client's unconscious plan for therapy rather than those relating, for example, to the transference. However, the story is incomplete as much of this work so readily lends itself to further research using more qualitative methods. For example, investigations into the mechanism of insight in psychological therapies have been progressed by intensive qualitative study of insight events in both psychodynamic interpersonal and cognitive behavioural therapy (e.g., Elliott et al., 1994). It is an area where there is considerable merit in harnessing both quantitative and qualitative methods.

What role does the therapeutic alliance have?

Context

Process research has often been viewed as a dichotomy comprising common factors and specific techniques. As indicated above, research interest has moved from the facilitative conditions to investigating the therapeutic alliance. While the facilitative conditions have been viewed as a possible mechanism of change, the therapeutic alliance is best viewed as a mechanism which enables the client to remain in and comply with treatment (Bordin, 1979; Sexton and Whiston, 1994).

Methodological issues

This area of research has led to the development of a range of measures which tap the client–counsellor relationship. Primary candidates include the Working Alliance Inventory (WAI; Horvath and Greenberg, 1989) and the CALPAS (CALifornia Psychotherapy Alliance Scales; e.g., Gaston, 1991). However, different definitions have resulted in different measures of the alliance such that it is unclear whether any two measures are tapping the same phenomenon. There are also some quite important conceptual problems. One example is the potential confusion between items relating to the status of the client–therapist relationship with items asking about the client's progress in therapy. If an alliance measure asks a client about the latter, then this is tapping early outcome and it would then not be surprising to find positive associations between alliance and outcome. Another example concerns the extent to which items tap aspects of the client alone rather than the relationship between client and therapist. As client measures tend to be more highly correlated with outcome than therapist measures, it would not be surprising that a measure which taps more into the client's world rather than that of the client–therapist relationship should be highly correlated with outcome. Indeed, there are those who argue that the definition of the alliance should be limited to client contributions (e.g., Frieswyk et al., 1986) on the basis that this facilitates research. Others (e.g., Henry and Strupp, 1994) argue for an interpersonal approach. The point here is to ensure that any measure of the client–therapist relationship is tapping what it purports to measure. A thorough conceptual review of the client–counsellor relationship has been carried out by Gelso and Carter (1994), with replies by prominent researchers.

Substantive findings

Sexton and Whiston (1994) reviewed the research literature on the client–therapist relationship since 1985 using three domains: the 'real' relationship, the transference and the working alliance. Findings summarized here focus on the last of these: the working alliance. A meta-analytic review of 24 studies (Horvath and Symonds, 1991) found that the working alliance was positively related to outcome and that client and observer ratings were better predictors of outcome than therapist ratings. However, the overall effect size only approached medium size and it appears that findings from individual studies are affected by such factors as when the alliance was assessed and the particular outcome index used. Overall though, from the available evidence, it appears the therapeutic alliance might account for upwards of 45 per cent of outcome variance (Horvath and Greenberg, 1989).

The perspective taken by the rater influences the results and it is invariably the client's ratings of the alliance that are most predictive of outcome. Further, if client change is the criterion for measuring outcome, then client ratings of process are the best judges. There is also evidence that clients have predispositions to the quality of the alliance they might develop. Horvath and Greenberg (1994) cite work suggesting that clients who have difficulty in maintaining their social relationships or have experienced relatively poor family relationships prior to therapy are less likely to develop strong alliances. However, severity of presenting symptoms did not appear to impact on the quality of the alliance.

In terms of the temporal nature of the therapeutic alliance, research findings are equivocal, with some researchers (e.g., Eaton et al., 1988) finding that it is constant while others (e.g., Klee et al., 1990) have suggested the opposite. This is an area requiring further research as it relates to the development and maintenance of the client–therapist relationship.

Comment

While there has been considerable effort in terms of measure development for the therapeutic alliance, there has been 'greater emphasis on interrater reliability and predictive validity and less emphasis on issues of dimensionality and convergent and discriminate validity' (Marmar, 1990). Thus, it is not clear that equivalent emphasis has been placed on furthering our understanding of what are the actual components of this 'umbrella' concept.

Focusing on the individual client

Context

At the beginning of this chapter reference was made to the relative paucity of single-case studies in counselling psychology, a discipline which purports to 'revere the individual'. Two publications (or series of publications) drew attention to the single case within counselling and psychotherapy: Hill et al.'s (1983) publication and Strupp's series of four individual case studies (1980a, b, c, d). More recently, there has been a special section of the *Journal of Consulting and Clinical Psychology* (see Jones, 1993) devoted to single-case research in psychotherapy. While single-case methodology has applications across many disciplines (especially in more behaviourally oriented approaches), it might be expected that counselling psychology could frame a particularly human approach using this modality.

Methodological issues

Hill et al. (1983) presented four arguments justifying the use of single-case methodology. First, it describes more adequately what happens between counsellor and client; secondly, positive and negative outcomes can be understood in terms of process data; thirdly, both the client–counsellor relationship and the change process can be highlighted; and fourthly, the outcome measures used can be specifically chosen given the client's presenting problems. More recently, Kirschner, Hoffman and Hill used a single-case approach in career counselling stating: 'Case studies enable researchers to investigate the counselor–client interaction by allowing for the specification of techniques and the isolation of specific change mechanisms that might be unique to a specific dyad' (1994: 216).

Many of the salient issues in using a single-case methodology both in process and outcome work have been summarized by Hilliard (1993). Largely, the problems arise in non-behavioural interventions where the manipulations cannot be readily reversed (for example, a client cannot 'unlearn' an insight) and particular domains of functioning (cognitions and emotions, for example) are intrinsically interdependent. These give rise to problems of internal validity which are not easily addressed. Beyond these problems, there is the enduring issue of selection. Should the individual selected be an 'exemplar' of a particular process (such as a highly successful case), or should they be 'representative'? It probably happens that each is appropriate in differing situations. There is considerable merit in selecting, for example, a highly successful case if one has reason to suppose that putative processes will be more evident in good outcome cases (that is to say, good outcome cases are the place to be looking).

However, if the presence of a process is hypothesized to be associated with a good outcome, it might then be appropriate to test for its absence in a poor outcome case. If it is also present in the poor outcome case to the same degree, then such a finding would argue against its having a specific role in facilitating good outcome. Selecting 'representative' cases might then be followed as a strategy to enhance generalizability of results.

Substantive findings

Given that this is a methodological approach, 'findings' has a rather different connotation. Since the publication of Hill et al.'s report in 1983, several further single cases have been published in the *Journal of Counseling Psychology*. For example, Kirschner et al. (1994) employed the single-case approach in career counselling. Findings indicated that the client found insight and challenge most helpful, suggesting that learning something new and having her perceptual world 'shaken up' was beneficial. In another study, Field, Barkham, Shapiro and Stiles (1994) combined both quantitative and qualitative methodologies in an investigation of one particular model of the change process in a good outcome case (Stiles et al., 1990). Findings supported the theory that in order to resolve a particular problematic experience, a client progresses through specific stages: in this particular case from vague awareness, through problem clarification, towards insight and application/working through.

Comment

High-quality research based on a single-case methodology is still the exception rather than the rule, supporting Galassi and Gersh's (1993) judgement that counselling psychology 'virtually eschews single-case designs'. There are obviously problems with the individual case study in terms of the extent to which internal validity can be assured. However, it is a challenge for counselling psychology research to devise and inform the scientific community regarding methods which are inherently rigorous but which allow greater consideration for the individual.

Future generations

Overall, what might be considered to be the areas that will feature in future research generations? Hill and Corbett suggest an overall goal for process and outcome research in counselling psychology for the future: 'to develop new theories of therapy, to provide information for practitioners about how to intervene with clients at different points in therapy, and to develop training programs based on the empirical results of what works in therapy' (1993: 16). In addition, they identify a number of areas for development. First, to test the 'entire model . . . of pretherapy characteristics . . ., process variables . . ., immediate outcome . . ., extra-therapy variables . . ., and long-term outcome' (p. 16). Secondly, to address issues relating to 'timing, quality, and competence'. Thirdly, Hill and Corbett suggest that research should determine the effective components of therapy and then the treatment approach can be built (rather than vice versa as is currently the case). And fourthly, the content of therapy work needs to be rekindled. These are huge and challenging tasks.

As a final comment, it is worth noting how much the present chapter, like those chapters in other texts of 'counselling' and 'counselling psychology', draws on the mainstream 'psychotherapy' literature. Whilst accepting that no single discipline (or professional division) has a monopoly on any one research tradition or scientific method – hence the commonality – it is clear that counselling psychology research needs to build and extend its current research activities in the area of everyday/normal functioning and to utilize research approaches which harness its emphasis on the individual.

References

Andrews, G., Guitar, B. and Howie, P. (1980) 'Meta-analysis of the effects of stuttering treatment', *Journal of Speech and Hearing Disorders*, 45: 287–307.

Aveline, M. and Shapiro, D.A. (eds) (1995) *Research Foundations for Psychotherapy Practice*. Chichester: Wiley.

Barker, C., Pistrang, N. and Elliott, R. (1994) *Research Methods in Clinical and Counselling Psychology*. Chichester: Wiley.

Barkham, M. and Shapiro, D.A. (1986) 'Counselor verbal response modes and experienced empathy', *Journal of Counseling Psychology*, 33: 3–10.

Barkham, M. and Shapiro, D.A. (1990) 'Brief prescriptive and exploratory therapy for job-related distress: a pilot study', *Counselling Psychology Quarterly*, 3: 133–47.

Barrett-Lennard, G.T. (1962) 'Dimensions of therapist response as causal factors in therapeutic change', *Psychological Monographs*, 76 (43, Whole No. 562).

Beck, A.T., Ward, C.H., Mendelson, M., Mock, J. and Erbaugh, J. (1961) 'Inventory for measuring depression', *Archives of General Psychiatry*, 4: 561–71.

Bergin, A.E. (1971) 'The evaluation of therapeutic outcomes', in A.E. Bergin and S.L. Garfield (eds), *Handbook of Psychotherapy and Behavior Change*. New York: Wiley. pp. 217–70.

Bergin, A.E. and Garfield, S.L. (eds) (1994a) *Handbook of Psychotherapy and Behavior Change*, 4th edn. New York: Wiley.

Bergin, A.E. and Garfield, S.L. (1994b) 'Overview, trends, and future issues', in A.E. Bergin and S.L. Garfield (eds), *Handbook of Psychotherapy and Behavior Change*, 4th edn. New York: Wiley. pp. 821–30.

Bergin, A.E. and Lambert, M.J. (1978) 'The evaluation of therapeutic outcome', in S.L. Garfield and A.E. Bergin (eds), *Handbook of Psychotherapy and Behavior Change*, 2nd edn. New York: Wiley. pp. 139–90.

Bordin, E.S. (1979) 'The generalizability of the psychoanalytic concept of the working alliance', *Psychotherapy: Theory, Research and Practice*, 16: 252–60.

Brockman, B., Poynton, A., Ryle, A. and Watson, J.P. (1987) 'Effectiveness of time-limited therapy carried out by trainees: comparison of two methods', *British Journal of Psychiatry*, 151: 602–10.

Brown, S.D. and Lent, R.W. (eds) (1992) *Handbook of Counseling Psychology*. New York: Wiley.

Butler, E.R., Rice, L.N. and Wagstaff, A.K. (1962) 'On the definition of variables: an analogue of clinical analysis', in H.H. Strupp and L. Luborsky (eds), *Research in Psychotherapy*, vol. 2. Washington, DC: American Psychological Association. pp. 178–205.

Carkhuff, R.R. and Berenson, B.G. (1967) *Beyond Counseling and Therapy*. New York: Holt, Rinehart and Winston.

Cohen, J. (1977) *Statistical Power Analysis for the Behavioural Sciences*, 2nd edn. Hillsdale, NJ: Erlbaum.

Crits-Christoph, P., Cooper, A. and Luborsky, L. (1988) 'The accuracy of therapists' interpretations and the outcome of dynamic psychotherapy', *Journal of Consulting and Clinical Psychology*, 56: 490–5.

Eaton, T.T., Abeles, N. and Gutfreund, M.J. (1988) 'Therapeutic alliance and outcome: impact of treatment length and pretreatment symptomatology', *Psychotherapy*, 25: 536–42.

Elkin, I. (1994) 'The NIMH Treatment of Depression Collaborative Research Study', in A.E. Bergin and S.L. Garfield (eds), *Handbook of Psychotherapy and Behavior Change*, 4th edn. New York: Wiley, pp. 114–39.

Elkin, I., Shea, M.T., Watkins, J.T., Imber, S.D., Sotsky, S.M., Collins, J.F., Glass, D.R., Pilkonis, P.A., Leber, W.R., Docherty, J.P., Fiester, S.J. and Parloff, M.B. (1989) 'National Institute of Mental Health Treatment of Depression Collaborative Research Program: general effectiveness of treatment', *Archives of General Psychiatry*, 46: 971–82.

Elliott, R., Hill, C.E., Stiles, W.B., Friedlander, M.L., Mahrer, A.R. and Margison, F.R. (1987) 'Primary therapist response modes: a comparison of six rating systems', *Journal of Consulting and Clinical Psychology*, 55: 218–23.

Elliott, R., Shapiro, D.A., Firth-Cozens, J., Stiles, W.B., Hardy, G.E., Llewelyn, S.P. and Margison, F. (1994) 'Insight in interpersonal-dynamic therapy: a comprehensive process analysis', *Journal of Counseling Psychology*, 41: 449–63.

Eysenck, H.J. (1952) 'The effects of psychotherapy: an evaluation', *Journal of Consulting Psychology*, 16: 319–24.

Eysenck, H.J. (1961) 'The effects of psychotherapy', in H.J. Eysenck (ed.), *Handbook of Abnormal Psychology*. New York: Basic Books.

Eysenck, H.J. (1966) *The Effects of Psychotherapy*. New York: International Science Press.

Eysenck, H.J. (1992) 'The outcome problem in psychotherapy', in W. Dryden and C. Feltham (eds), *Psychotherapy and Its Discontents*. Buckingham: Open University Press. pp. 100–24; 131–4.

Field, S.D., Barkham, M., Shapiro, D.A. and Stiles, W.B. (1994) 'Assessment of assimilation in psychotherapy: a quantitative case study of problematic experiences with a significant other', *Journal of Counseling Psychology*, 41: 397–406.

Frieswyk, S.H., Allen, J.G., Colson, D.B., Coyne, L., Gabbard, G.O., Horowitz, L. and Newsom, G. (1986) 'Therapeutic alliance: its place as a process and outcome variable in dynamic psychotherapy research', *Journal of Consulting and Clinical Psychology*, 54: 32–8.

Galassi, J.P. and Gersh, T.L. (1993) 'Myths, misconceptions, and missed opportunity: single-case designs and counseling psychology', *Journal of Counseling Psychology*, 40: 525–31.

Garfield, S.L. (1990) 'Issues and methods in psychotherapy process research', *Journal of Consulting and Clinical Psychology*, 58: 273–80.

Garfield, S.L. and Bergin, A.E. (1994) 'Introduction and historical overview', in A.E. Bergin and S.L. Garfield (eds), *Handbook of Psychotherapy and Behavior Change*, 4th edn. New York: Wiley. pp. 3–18.

Gaston, L. (1991) 'Reliability and criterion-related validity of the California Psychotherapy Alliance Scales – patient version', *Psychological Assessment: a Journal of Consulting and Clinical Psychology*, 3: 68–74.

Gelso, C.J. and Carter, J.A. (1994) 'Components of the psychotherapy relationship: their interaction and unfolding during treatment', *Journal of Counseling Psychology*, 41: 296–306.

Gurman, A.S. (1973) 'Instability of therapeutic conditions in psychotherapy', *Journal of Counseling Psychology*, 20: 16–24.

Gurman, A.S. (1977) 'The patient's perception of the therapeutic relationship', in A.S. Gurman and A. Razin (eds), *Effective Psychotherapy: a Handbook of Research*. Oxford: Pergamon Press, pp. 503–43.

Henry, W.P. and Strupp, H.H. (1994) 'The therapeutic alliance as interpersonal process', in A.O. Horvath and L.S. Greenberg (eds), *The Working Alliance: Theory, Research, and Practice*. New York: Wiley. pp. 51–84.

Hill, C.E. (1989) *Therapist Techniques and Client Outcomes: Eight Cases of Brief Psychotherapy*. Newbury Park, CA: Sage.

Hill, C.E. (1990) 'Exploratory in-session process research in individual psychotherapy: a review', *Journal of Consulting and Clinical Psychology*, 58: 288–94.

Hill, C.E. (1991) 'Almost everything you ever wanted to know about how to do process research on counseling and psychotherapy but didn't know who to ask', in C.E. Watkins, Jr and L.J. Schneider (eds), *Research in Counseling*. Hillsdale, NJ: Lawrence Erlbaum Associates. pp. 85–118.

Hill, C.E. and Corbett, M. (1993) 'A perspective on the history of process and outcome research in counseling psychology' *Journal of Counseling Psychology*, 40: 3–24.

Hill, C.E., Carter, J.A. and O'Farrell, M.K. (1983) 'A case study of the process and outcome of time-limited counseling', *Journal of Counseling Psychology*, 30: 3–18.

Hill, C.E., Helms, J.E., Tichenor, V., Spiegel, S.B., O'Grady, K.E. and Perry, E.S. (1988) 'Effects of therapist response modes in brief psychotherapy', *Journal of Counseling Psychology*, 35: 222–33.

Hilliard, R.B. (1993) 'Single-case methodology in psychotherapy process and outcome research', *Journal of Consulting and Clinical Psychology*, 61: 373–80.

Horvath, A.O. and Greenberg, L.S. (1989) 'Development and validation of the Working Alliance Inventory', *Journal of Counseling Psychology*, 36: 223–33.

Horvath, A.O. and Greenberg, L.S. (1994) (eds) *The Working Alliance: Theory, Research, and Practice*. New York: Wiley.

Horvath, A.O. and Symonds, D.B. (1991) 'Relation between working alliance and outcome in psychotherapy', *Journal of Counseling Psychology*, 38: 139–49.

Horvath, A.O., Marx, R.W. and Kamann, A.M. (1990) 'Thinking about thinking in therapy: an examination of clients' understanding of their therapists' intentions', *Journal of Consulting and Clinical Psychology*, 58: 614–21.

Howard, K.I., Kopta, S.M., Krause, M.S. and Orlinsky, D.E. (1986) 'The dose–effect relationship in psychotherapy', *American Psychologist*, 41: 159–64.

Jacobson, N.S. and Truax, P. (1991) 'Clinical significance: a statistical approach to defining meaningful change in psychotherapy research', *Journal of Consulting and Clinical Psychology*, 59: 12–19.

Jones, E.E. (1993) 'Special section: single-case research in psychotherapy', *Journal of Consulting and Clinical Psychology*, 61: 371–430.

Karl, N.J. and Abeles, N. (1969) 'Psychotherapy process as a function of the time segment sampled', *Journal of Consulting and Clinical Psychology*, 33: 207–12.

Kazdin, A.E. (1994) 'Methodology, design, and evaluation in psychotherapy research', in A.E. Bergin and S.L. Garfield (eds) *Handbook of Psychotherapy and Behavior Change*, 4th edn. New York: Wiley, pp. 19–71.

Kiesler, D.J. (1966) 'Basic methodological issues implicit in psychotherapy research', *American Journal of Psychotherapy*, 20: 135–55.

Kirschner, T., Hoffman, M.A. and Hill, C.E. (1994) 'Case study of the process and outcome of career counseling', *Journal of Counseling Psychology*, 41: 216–26.

Klee, M.R., Abeles, N. and Muller, R.T. (1990) 'Therapeutic alliance: early indicators, course, and outcome', *Psychotherapy*, 27: 166–74.

Klein, M.H., Mathieu, P.L., Gendlin, E.T. and Kiesler, D.J. (1970) *The Experiencing Scale: a Research and Training Manual*, vols 1 and 2. Madison, WI: Winconsin Psychiatric Institute.

Koss, M.P. and Shiang, J. (1994) 'Research on brief psycheotherapy', in A.E. Bergin and S.L. Garfield (eds), *Handbook of Psychotherapy and Behavior Change*, 4th edn. New York: Wiley. pp. 664–700.

Krumboltz, J.D. (1966) *Revolution in Counseling: Implications of Behavioral Science*. Boston: Houghton Mifflin.

Lambert, M.J. and Bergin, A.E. (1994) 'The effectiveness of psychotherapy', in A.E. Bergin and S.L. Garfield (eds), *Handbook of Psychotherapy and Behavior Change*, 4th edn. New York: Wiley. pp. 143–89.

Lambert, M.J. and Hill, C.E. (1994) 'Assessing psychotherapy outcomes and processes', in A.E. Bergin and S.L. Garfield (eds), *Handbook of Psychotherapy and Behavior Change*, 4th edn. New York: Wiley. pp. 72–113.

Llewelyn, S.P., Elliott, R., Shapiro, D.A., Hardy, G.E. and Firth-Cozens, J. (1988) 'Client perceptions of significant events in prescriptive and exploratory periods of individual therapy', *British Journal of Clinical Psychology*, 27: 105–14.

Luborsky, L., Singer, B. and Luborsky, L. (1975) 'Comparative studies of psychotherapies: is it true that "everyone has won and all must have prizes"?', *Archives of General Psychiatry*, 32: 995–1008.

Marmar, C.R. (1990) 'Psychotherapy process research: progress, dilemmas, and future directions', *Journal of Consulting and Clinical Psychology*, 58: 265–72.

McLeod, J. (1993) *An Introduction to Counselling*. Buckingham: Open University Press.

McLeod, J. (1994) *Doing Counselling Research*. London: Sage.

Meltzoff, J. and Kornreich, M. (1970) *Research in Psychotherapy*. Chicago: Aldine Publishing Company.

Mitchell, K., Bozarth, J.D. and Krauft, C.C. (1977) 'A reappraisal of the therapeutic effectiveness of accurate empathy, nonpossessive warmth, and genuineness', in A.S. Gurman and A. Razin (eds), *Effective Psychotherapy: a Handbook of Research*. Oxford: Pergamon Press. pp. 482–502.

Nietzel, M.T., Russell, R.L., Hemmings, K.A. and Gretter, M.L. (1987) 'Clinical significance of psychotherapy for unipolar depression: a meta-analytic approach to social comparison', *Journal of Consulting and Clinical Psychology*, 55: 156–61.

Norcross, J. (ed.) (1986) *Handbook of Eclectic Psychotherapy*. New York: Brunner/Mazel.

Norcross, J.C. (ed.) (1993) 'Research directions for psychotherapy integration: a roundtable', *Journal of Psychotherapy Integration*, 3: 91–131.

Norcross, J.C. and Goldfried, M.R. (eds) (1992) *Handbook of Psychotherapy Integration*. New York: Basic Books.

O'Farrell, M.K., Hill, C.E. and Patton, S. (1986) 'Comparison of two cases of counseling with the same counselor', *Journal of Counseling and Development*, 65: 141–5.

Orlinsky, D.E., Grawe, K. and Parks, B.K. (1994) 'Process and outcome in psychotherapy – Noch einmal', in A.E. Bergin and S.L. Garfield (eds), *Handbook of Psychotherapy and Behavior Change*, 4th edn. New York: Wiley. pp. 270–376.

Orlinsky, D.E. and Howard, K.I. (1986) 'Process and outcome in psychotherapy', in S.L. Garfield and A.E. Bergin (eds), *Handbook of Psychotherapy and Behavior Change*, 3rd edn. New York: Wiley. pp. 311–81.

Orlinsky, D.E. and Russell, R.L. (1994) 'Tradition and change in psychotherapy research: notes on the fourth generation', in R.L. Russell (ed.), *Reassessing Psychotherapy Research*. New York: Guilford Press. pp. 185–214.

Parry, G. and Watts, F.N. (in press) *Behavioural and Mental Health Research: a Handbook of Skills and Methods*, 2nd edn. Hove: Lawrence Erlbaum Associates.

Paul, G. (1967) 'Strategy in outcome research in psychotherapy', *Journal of Consulting Psychology*, 31: 109–18.

Porter, E.H. Jr (1943) 'The development and evaluation of a measure of counseling interview procedures', *Educational and Psychological Measurement*, 3: 105–26.

Quality Assurance Project (1984) 'Treatment outlines for the management of schizophrenia', *Australian and New Zealand Journal of Psychiatry*, 18: 19–38.

Rachman, S. (1971) *The Effects of Psychotherapy*. Oxford: University Press.

Rice, L.N. and Greenberg, L.S. (eds) (1984) *Patterns of Change*. New York: Guilford Press.

Robinson, L.A., Berman, J.S. and Neimeyer, R.A. (1990) 'Psychotherapy for the treatment of depression: a comprehensive review of controlled outcome research', *Psychological Bulletin*, 108: 30–49.

Rogers, C.R. (1942) *Counseling and Psychotherapy*. Boston: Houghton Mifflin.

Rogers, C.R. (1951) *Client-Centered Therapy: Its Current Practice, Implications, and Theory*. Boston: Houghton Mifflin.

Rogers, C.R. (1957) 'The necessary and sufficient conditions of therapeutic personality change', *Journal of Consulting Psychology*, 21: 95–103.

Rogers, C.R. and Dymond, R.F. (eds) (1954) *Psychotherapy and Personality Change*. Chicago: University of Chicago Press.

Rogers, C.R., Gendlin, E.T., Kiesler, D.J. and Truax, C.B. (1967) *The Therapeutic Relationship and Its Impact: a Study of Psychotherapy with Schizophrenics*. Madison, WI: University of Wisconsin Press.

Rosenthal, R. and Rosnow, R.L. (1991) *Essentials of Behavioral Research: Methods and Data Analysis*, 2nd edn. New York: McGraw-Hill.

Ryle, A. (1990) *Cognitive-Analytic Therapy: Active Participation in Change*. Chichester: Wiley.

Sexton, T.L. and Whiston, S.C. (1994) 'The status of the counseling relationship: an empirical review, theoretical implications, and research directions', *The Counseling Psychologist*, 22: 6–78.

Shapiro, D.A. (1989) 'Outcome research', in G. Parry and F.N. Watts (eds), *Behavioural and Mental Health Research: a Handbook of Skills and Methods*. Hove: Lawrence Erlbaum Associates. pp. 163–87.

Shapiro, D.A., Barkham, M., Rees, A., Hardy, G.E., Reynolds, S. and Startup, M. (1994) 'Effects of treatment duration and severity of depression on the effectiveness of cognitive-behavioral and psychodynamic-interpersonal psychotherapy', *Journal of Consulting and Clinical Psychology*, 62: 522–34.

Shapiro, D.A., Barkham, M., Reynolds, S., Hardy, G.E. and Stiles, W.B. (1992) 'Prescriptive and exploratory psychotherapies: toward an integration based on the assimilation model', *Journal of Psychotherapy Integration*, 2: 253–72.

Shapiro, D.A., Rees, A., Barkham, M., Hardy, G.E., Reynolds, S. and Startup, M. (1995) 'Effects of treatment duration and severity of depression on the maintenance of gains following cognitive-behavioral and psychodynamic-interpersonal psychotherapy', *Journal of Consulting and Clinical Psychology*, 63: 378–87.

Silberschatz, G. and Curtis, J.T. (1986) 'Clinical implications of research on brief dynamic psychotherapy: 2. How the therapist helps or hinders therapeutic progress', *Psychoanalytic Psychology*, 3: 27–37.

Sloane, R.B., Staples, R.F., Cristol, A.H., Yorkston, N.J. and Whipple, K. (1975) *Psychotherapy versus Behavior Therapy*. Cambridge, MA: Harvard University Press.

Smith, M.L. and Glass, G.V. (1977) 'Meta-analysis of psychotherapy outcome studies', *American Psychologist*, 32: 752–60.

Smith, M.L., Glass, G.V. and Miller, T.I. (1980) *The Benefits of Psychotherapy*. Baltimore, MD: Johns Hopkins University Press.

Snyder, W.U. (1945) 'An investigation of the nature of nondirective psychotherapy', *Journal of General Psychology*, 33: 193–223.

Steinbrueck, S.M., Maxwell, S.E. and Howard, G.S. (1983) 'A meta-analysis of psychotherapy and drug therapy in the treatment of unipolar depression with adults', *Journal of Consulting and Clinical Psychology*, 51: 856–63.

Stiles, W.B., Elliott, R., Llewelyn, S.P., Firth-Cozens, J.A., Margison, F.R., Shapiro, D.A. and Hardy, G.E. (1990) 'Assimilation of problematic experiences by clients in psychotherapy', *Psychotherapy*, 27: 411–20.

Stiles, W.B., Shapiro, D.A. and Elliott, R. (1986) 'Are all psychotherapies equivalent?', *American Psychologist*, 41: 165–80.

Strupp, H.H. (1980a) 'Success and failure in time-limited psychotherapy. A systematic comparison of two cases: Comparison 1', *Archives of General Psychiatry*, 37: 595–604.

Strupp, H.H. (1980b) 'Success and failure in time-limited psychotherapy. A systematic comparison of two cases: Comparison 2', *Archives of General Psychiatry*, 37: 708–16.

Strupp, H.H. (1980c) 'Success and failure in time-limited psychotherapy. With special reference to the performance of a lay counselor', *Archives of General Psychiatry*, 37: 831–41.

Strupp, H.H. (1980d) 'Success and failure in time-limited psychotherapy. Further evidence (Comparison 4)', *Archives of General Psychiatry*, 37: 947–54.

Taube, C.A., Burns, B.J. and Kessler, L. (1984) 'Patients of psychiatrists and psychologists in office-based practice: 1980', *American Psychologist*, 39: 1435–7.

Truax, C.B. (1961) 'A scale for the measurement of accurate empathy', *Psychiatric Institute Bulletin* (Wisconsin Psychiatric Institute, University of Wisconsin) 1: 12.

Truax, C.B. and Carkhuff, R.R. (1967) *Toward Effective Counseling and Psychotherapy: Training and Practice*. Chicago: Aldine.

Truax, C.B. and Mitchell, K.M. (1971) 'Research on certain therapist interpersonal skills in relation to process and outcome', in A.E. Bergin and S.L. Garfield (eds), *Handbook of Psychotherapy and Behavior Change*. New York: Wiley. pp. 299–344.

Wampold, B.E. and Poulin, K.L. (1992) 'Counseling research methods: Art and artifact', in S.D. Brown and R.W. Lent (eds), *Handbook of Counseling Psychology*, 2nd edn. New York: Wiley. pp. 71–109.

Watkins, C.E. Jr and Schneider, L.J. (1991) *Research in Counseling*. Hillsdale, NJ: Lawrence Erlbaum Associates.

Whitehorn, J.C. and Betz, B. (1954) 'A study of psychotherapeutic relationships between physicians and schizophrenic patients', *American Journal of Psychiatry*, 3: 321–31.

Wolfe, B. and Goldfried, M.R. (1988) 'Research on psychotherapy integration: recommendation and conclusions from an NIMH workshop', *Journal of Consulting and Clinical Psychology*, 56: 448–51.

3

Qualitative Research Methods in Counselling Psychology

John McLeod

As an academic discipline, psychology has shown a historic tendency to identify with the methods and values of the 'hard', natural sciences. Any graduate of a psychology degree course will be aware of the importance of measurement, experimentation and statistics in achieving valid knowledge. Nevertheless, many psychologists will also be aware that there exists an alternative to the traditional positivist approach. This alternative is often known as 'qualitative' research, and occupies a niche within the 'soft' end of psychology concerned with topics such as personality and social psychology. The most recent eruption of qualitative methodology has been the popularity of discourse analysis in social psychology (Potter and Wetherell, 1987) and the emergence of feminist approaches to psychological inquiry (Burman, 1989; Hollway, 1989). Before that, anti-positivism in the 1970s and 1980s was represented by the 'new paradigm' approach advocated by Reason and Rowan (1981) and supported by the philosophical critique developed by Harré and Secord (1972) and Shotter (1975).

However, it is important to recognize that qualitative research has in fact been a part of psychology from the very beginning. The founding figures of psychology, Wundt and Dilthey, both argued that a true 'human science' could only be based on the analysis and interpretation of meaning, and that the role of experimental methods should be confined to areas such as perception, neuropsychology and memory (Rennie, 1994e). Another of the early psychologists, William James, wrote a book on the *Variety of Religious Experience* based on qualitative accounts of spiritual experience. Phenomenological psychology, which evolved from the work of nineteenth-century philosophers such as Brentano and Husserl, continues to generate research (Valle and Halling, 1989). Finally, psychoanalysis, the starting point for so much of counselling and psychotherapy, is built on the study of qualitative single case studies.

Over the past decade, there has been an increase in the interest in and acceptability of qualitative methods in the social sciences in general. The productivity of qualitative researchers in disciplines such as anthropology, sociology, criminology, education, social work, management, organizational studies, cultural studies and nursing is demonstrated in the *Handbook of Qualitative Research*, edited by Denzin and Lincoln (1994a). The impact on counselling psychology of this trend can be observed in the increasing emphasis given to qualitative research in methods textbooks such as Heppner et al. (1992), McLeod (1994) and Watkins and Schneider (1991), and in the devotion of a special edition of the *Journal of Counseling Psychology* to qualitative studies (Polkinghorne, 1994). In the recent edition of the *Handbook of Psychotherapy and Behavior Change*, Bergin and Garfield, anticipating future trends in psychotherapy research, predicted that:

> the growing endorsement of narrative, descriptive and qualitative approaches represents a rather significant shift in attitude that is likely to become more and more manifest in the conduct and reporting of inquiries. (1994: 828)

Qualitative research is generally defined as research built around the collection and analysis of the accounts or stories that people offer regarding their experience. The data of qualitative research is therefore 'words' rather than 'numbers'. However, to describe qualitative research merely in terms of an *absence* of quantification and statistics is to miss the point. At a more fundamental level, the aim of qualitative research is to illuminate and clarify the *meaning* of social actions and situations. The outcome of qualitative research is understanding rather than explanation. Qualitative research is therefore part of a broad interpretive or hermeneutic tradition in social science and the humanities (Messer et al., 1988; Taylor, 1979). Good qualitative studies rely on detailed descriptive accounts of the phenomena being researched, with theoretical formulations arising inductively from this material. Some branches of qualitative research also aim to be reflexive, with priority given to the role of the researcher in the creation of meaning, or may strive to be participative, with the goal of involving and empowering research informants as 'coresearchers'. Qualitative research is often 'discovery-oriented' or 'heuristic' in nature.

Qualitative research is based in a 'social constructionist' perspective on knowledge (Gergen, 1985), which assumes that, in the sphere of social and psychological inquiry, there is no fixed external reality to be 'objectively' known but a fluid 'social reality' which is co-constructed. The task of the researcher is therefore to construct (or deconstruct) versions of this social reality. One of the implications of this philosophical position is that qualitative researchers do not claim to generate 'universal' truths or scientific laws, but rather are striving to build meaningful 'local knowledges'.

This chapter introduces the main principles of qualitative research, and explores the ways in which these techniques can be used in research into counselling and psychotherapy. The chapter will primarily focus on the following topics: methods of gathering qualitative data, approaches to the analysis of qualitative data, criteria for assessing the validity of qualitative studies and the application of these ideas within counselling psychology.

Methods of gathering qualitative data

The process of doing qualitative research involves finding appropriate informants, the collection of detailed descriptive material, and then codification, categorization and interpretation of data. There are a range of different approaches to gathering qualitative data, and many researchers intentionally build into their research design the possibility of combining types of data, to enable 'method triangulation' by checking the extent to which different types of information generate the same themes or meanings. For example, face-to-face interviews are always to a greater or lesser extent **reactive**, with the attitudes and personality of the interviewer shaping what the informant will say. If interview data are combined with personal diaries kept by informants, the researcher can examine the degree to which informants say the same kinds of things in both media.

In designing qualitative studies, it is necessary to be aware that principles and assumptions about **sampling** are quite different from those relevant to quantitative research. Qualitative research is **intensive**, with single or small numbers of cases being explored in depth. It is impossible to carry out effective qualitative research with very large samples of people, since as *n* increases, so does the difficulty of doing justice to the mass of qualitative material that is produced. In qualitative research, informants or cases are selected on the basis of their theoretical significance rather than in accordance with rules of randomized or stratified sampling (see Strauss and Corbin, 1990, and Yin, 1989, for more detailed discussion of sampling issues).

Interviews

The most widely used method for gathering qualitative data is the **research interview**. Interviews can be constructed around schedules of questions (Lofland and Lofland, 1984) or can be more open-ended in nature (Kvale, 1983). The advantage of the face-to-face interview is that it represents a flexible technique for gathering accounts of experience. The researcher can readily monitor whether the informant is understanding the meaning or wording of questions, and can check out his or her own understanding of what the informant has disclosed by reflecting back at regular intervals. However, the time required for setting up and conducting an interview may be a problem for both researcher and participant. Also, the time involved in transcribing interview tapes is considerable. Variants on the standard one-to-one research interview are the telephone interview and the group interview. In market research, for example, **focus groups** (Krueger, 1988; Stewart and Shamdasani, 1990) are often used to generate rich qualitative data on consumer perceptions of products. The issues involved in using all kinds of qualitative research interviews are critically reviewed by Fontana and Frey (1994).

Open-ended questionnaires

Many qualitative researchers find that the use of the **open-ended questionnaire** represents a practicable alternative to the interview. Although questionnaires are less flexible and sensitive than interviews, the researcher can potentially reach a much greater number of informants, and the time needed for data analysis is reduced by eliminating the necessity to transcribe tapes. In some situations, informants may find it easier to disclose confidential or sensitive material through an anonymous questionnaire than in a personal interview. Examples of open-ended questionnaires in research in counselling psychology have been studies where clients have been asked to describe the 'most helpful' or 'least helpful' aspects of a session.

Stimulated recall techniques

Interviews and questionnaires are generally used to explore events that have happened some time in the past, and it is reasonable to suppose that informants may not remember significant aspects of what they actually experienced at the time of the event itself. Elliott (1986) and other psychotherapy researchers have developed the use of **stimulated recall** methods to overcome this problem. The main technique in this area, **Interpersonal Process Recall** (IPR), was devised by Kagan (1984) as a training technique. An audio or video tape was made of a counselling session, and the trainee counsellor was invited to play the tape back, stopping whenever he or she recalled what they had been feeling or thinking during the original counselling session. In becoming more aware of his or her momentary reactions to the client, and range of behavioural intentions, the trainee counsellor was helped to evolve a wider repertoire of therapeutic responses. Elliott (1986), Rennie (1990) and others have adapted this approach to explore the in-session experiences of both clients and therapists for research purposes.

Projective techniques

Implicit in the use of stimulated recall is an assumption that informants may frequently 'know more than they can tell' (Nisbett and Wilson, 1977), and consequently require some assistance from researchers in retrieving experiential material that is transient or pre-verbal. The same assumption lies behind the use of **projective techniques** in qualitative research. Methods such as making up fantasy stories, finding images, creative drawing and finishing off incomplete sentences are all ways in which informants can be helped to express themselves through meta-phoric and figurative language. The data from projective techniques can be difficult to interpret at times, but can add a valuable dimension to interview or questionnaire-based studies (Branthwaite and Lunn, 1985).

Documentary sources

All the qualitative data gathering methods described so far require active initiation on the part of the researcher, and as a result evoke some sort of reactivity on the part of the informant. Inevitably, informants will wonder why a particular question is being asked, or how much they can trust a researcher with a particular piece of information. The use of qualitative data gained from **personal and official documents** is therefore of special interest to researchers. Diaries, letters, memos and case notes may yield material that might never be disclosed in an interview.

Participant observation

Within disciplines such as sociology and anthropology, one of the principal modes of qualitative data gathering is through **participant observation**. Ethnographic studies that aim to capture the rituals or way of life of a group or culture rely on months or years of painstaking observation conducted by researchers who participate in the day-to-day activities of the people being studied. Participant observation offers a uniquely detailed and intimate type of knowledge. Unfortunately, ethical and practical difficulties inhibit the use of participant observation in counselling and psychotherapy research. For example, who would tolerate the presence of a researcher sitting in on therapy sessions, or accompany-ing a client home to observe how his or her behaviour toward family members changed following that session?

Inquiry groups

The final approach to generating qualitative research data is through the **human inquiry group**. This is a technique devised by those within the 'new paradigm' research tradition (Reason, 1988; Reason and Rowan, 1981) to reflect the distinctive values of their radically humanistic approach to human inquiry. The human inquiry group consists of a group of co-researchers who meet to examine their own experience of a phenomenon. The group itself decides on how data will be collected, and how the authenticity and validity of material will be evaluated. This is a research method that places a significant emphasis on the human capacity for reflexivity.

Approaches to the analysis of qualitative data

There are a number of approaches that can be taken to the analysis of qualitative research data. It is quite possible to gather qualitative material, such as transcripts of therapy sessions, and then apply quantitative techniques such as coding or content analysis at the analysis stage of the study. Usually, however, the term 'qualitative research' is reserved for studies that apply a more open-ended, interpretive style of data analysis. Although the field of qualitative research is fragmented, with a huge diversity of analytic techniques and procedures used by different researchers, it is nevertheless possible to identify four main schools of qualitative analysis: phenomenology, grounded theory, narratology and discourse analysis. In qualitative research, data collection and analysis tend not to form discrete stages of a piece of research, with all the data being gathered and then, once that stage is complete, being subjected to analysis. Instead, qualitative researchers will often move back and forward between data gathering and analysis in a cyclical process, deliberately using the analysis of early data to guide the choice of new cases, informants or research sites.

Phenomenological methods

The aim of phenomenological research is to achieve an authentic and comprehensive description of the way in which a phenomenon is experienced by a person or group of people. Phenomenological studies tend to use data based on informants' written or spoken accounts of their experience. The task of the researcher is to immerse himself or herself in this material until the 'essence' of what it means, its essential meaning, becomes clear. In this process of immersion, the researcher needs to 'bracket off' his or her assumptions about the phenomenon. The researcher is in effect suspending his or her 'natural' or 'taken-for-granted' attitude toward the phenomenon, in the search for new and underlying meanings. Each set of meanings that is 'bracketed' in this way becomes part of the final descriptive representation of the phenomenon. This ultimate representation can be seen as comprising ever widening 'horizons' of meaning. It is a mistake to imagine that this process can ever reveal any ultimate 'true' meaning. The methodology is, instead, intended to enable the researcher to open up an area of human experience, not to arrive at a once-and-for-all definition of it. The similarities between phenomenological inquiry and the work of the therapist, particularly therapists within the client-centred or person-centred tradition, should be obvious. The contrast between the inductive and open-ended nature of phenomenological research and the attempts by Rogers and his colleagues to develop 'operationalized' phenomenological measures such as the self–ideal self Q-sort will also be apparent.

In practice, phenomenological research is difficult to do, requiring sufficient self-belief to be willing to suspend normal 'ways of seeing', and also making great demands on the ability of the researcher to construct a readable account of what he or she has done. Further information about the use of phenomenological methods in psychological research is available in Becker (1992), Moustakas (1994) and Osborne (1990). Although relatively little 'pure' phenomenological research has been carried out in the field of counselling and psychotherapy, it is essential to recognize that all other approaches to qualitative research draw heavily on the phenomenological tradition.

Grounded theory analysis

Grounded theory was devised by two sociologists, Barney Glaser and Anselm Strauss, in the 1960s (Glaser and Strauss, 1967). Their aim was to develop a form of research that would allow theoretical statements to be clearly 'grounded' in experiential data. So, from their point of view, phenomenological research, in restricting itself to description rather than model-building, did not go far enough. Conversely, traditional quantitative methods erred in the opposite direction by imposing pre-decided categories and variables on the data, and therefore sacrificing the potential to generate new ideas and concepts by listening closely to what informants actually have to say about their lives. Grounded theory studies typically use observational, documentary or transcribed interview data, to which the researcher applies a systematic step-by-step analysis. First, the material is segmented into 'meaning units', which may be as short as a word or phrase or as long as a paragraph or page. Then, the researcher attempts to code the meaning of these units in as sensitive and open a manner as possible. Rather than just assigning one meaning to each segment, the researcher will strive to imagine all the different meanings that might be applied. A careful record is kept of each meaning or 'concept' that arises, along with its corresponding piece of text. The researcher goes on to explore similarities and differences between the concepts that have been produced in this way, and merges similar concepts into 'categories'. The accuracy and generality of these categories is checked by tracking through all the data, looking for counter-instances. Finally, the researcher finds a smaller set of 'main categories' that effectively capture the meaning of the material as a whole, and is then able to construct a model, or theoretical framework, for understanding the phenomenon being studied. This description of grounded theory analysis is, for reasons of space, somewhat over-simplified, and the reader is urged to consult Glaser and Strauss (1967), Glaser (1978), Strauss and Corbin (1990) or Rennie, Phillips and Quartaro (1988) for fuller accounts of what is involved in using this method.

The attraction of grounded theory is that it offers qualitative researchers an explicit, practicable set of steps to follow when dealing with qualitative data. However, some observers have argued that the practice of grounded theory analysis is an art that relies on intuition and creativity that must be learned through apprenticeship rather than acquired by following a book (Stern, 1994).

Narrative analysis

A third tradition in qualitative research involves close attention to stories and conversations. In phenomenological or grounded theory analysis, informant narratives tend to become transformed into more general themes or categories. There is therefore a tendency to lose sight of individual built-up sequences of meaning (stories for example) in the search for the underlying content of what the stories are *about*. With the various forms of narrative analysis, by contrast, it is assumed that the structure of the actual story or conversation sequence serves as an important vehicle for meaning. Narrative analysis, or 'narratology', is an approach that:

> examines the informant's story and analyses how it is put together, the linguistic and cultural resources that it draws on, and how it persuades a listener of authenticity. Analysis in narrative studies opens up the forms of telling about experience, not simply the content to which language refers. We ask, why was the story told *that* way? (Riessman, 1993: 2).

Narrative approaches to qualitative research have been developed from a variety of different analytic perspectives. One widely used approach takes as its focus the ways in which self and personal identity are expressed in narrative and conversation (Josselson and Lieblich, 1993; Riessman, 1993; Rosenwald and Ochberg, 1992). Another quite different approach is taken by the proponents of **discourse analysis**, who place their main emphasis on the social functions of language. The aim of this type of study is to gain an understanding of the pre-existing linguistic resources or social discourses which speakers draw upon in making any statements (Wetherell and Potter, 1988).

The common ground between different styles of narrative analysis is the close attention that it pays to the subtle and complex ways in which people construct meaning, and also to the influence of context on the kinds of stories that people tell. These intricacies can only be captured by looking in detail at samples of conversation, and it is usual in narrative research to include segments of transcript material in the text of the research article. Typically, narrative researchers might interview several informants to gain a general sense of the phenomenon in which they are interested, but then present their conclusions through the vehicle of an in-depth analysis of a single case. For example, in her research into marital violence, Riessman (1994) uses the words of one woman to represent the experience of deciding to leave a violent marriage. In the paper, the informant is allowed to tell the reader directly how it was for her, while the commentary provided by the researcher points to some of the wider cultural meanings of her words.

The qualitative researcher as *'bricoleur'*

These three qualitative research approaches – phenomenology, grounded theory and narratology – have been selected as the forms of data analysis most applicable to topics in the field of counselling psychology. However, it is misleading to take the view that any of these methods represent analytic procedures that can be followed mechanistically in the hope of producing acceptable qualitative returns. The practice of qualitative research involves personal engagement with the phenomena being studied, and the employment of *any* tools likely to facilitate understanding. One of the features of qualitative research has been the creativity and innovation with which investigators have developed new analytic and data presentation techniques. The vast range of analytic strategies that have been invented are reviewed in Miles and Huberman (1994) and Bryman and Burgess (1992). Denzin and Lincoln (1994b) have suggested that it is helpful to see qualitative research as a *bricolage* (a pieced-together solution to a specific problem in a concrete situation), and the qualitative researcher as *bricoleur* (a kind of professional do-it-yourself person). They write that:

> The *bricoleur* is adept at performing a large number of diverse tasks, ranging from interviewing to observing, to interpreting personal and historical documents, to intensive self-reflection and introspection. The *bricoleur* reads

widely and is knowledgeable about the many interpretive paradigms (feminism, Marxism, cultural studies, constructivism) that can be brought to any particular problem. . . . The *bricoleur* understands that research is an interactive process shaped by his or her personal history, biography, gender, social class, race and ethnicity, and those of the people in the setting . . . . The product of the *bricoleur's* labour is a bricolage, a complex, dense, reflexive, collage-like creation that represents the researcher's images, understandings, and interpretations of the world or phenomenon under analysis. (Denzin and Lincoln, 1994b: 2–3)

The metaphor and image of the *bricoleur* captures the complexity, difficulty and also excitement of qualitative research. It also illuminates the attraction of qualitative research for many counselling psychologists, since the effective therapist is similarly required to integrate under-standings of the personal, cultural and historical, and find meaning in complexity.

Applications of qualitative methods in counselling psychology research

It has been argued by Mishler (1990) that in practice most researchers tend not to construct studies according to abstract principles of research design and philosophy of science. Instead, researchers are influenced by 'exemplar' studies, investigations that have applied a particular technique and have produced credible new knowledge. In this section, some exemplar qualitative studies in the field of counselling psychology are introduced and discussed.

The client experience of the therapy hour

The work of Rennie (1990, 1992) embodies one of the most rigorous and sustained applications of qualitative methodology within psychotherapy research. Working within the person-centred tradition, the aim of this programme of research has been to construct a detailed and compre-hensive understanding of the client's experience of a therapy session. These studies have involved the use of Interpersonal Process Recall (IPR) interviews carried out with 14 therapy clients. During the recall interview, a tape recording of the session is played to the client, who is invited to stop the tape whenever he or she has any comment to make about what he or she was experiencing at that moment of the therapy session. These IPR interviews are transcribed, and then analysed according to the procedures of grounded theory. A full account of the data gathering and analysis process can be found in Rennie (1994d). This method enabled Rennie (1990, 1992) to construct a general representation of the client's experience of the therapy hour, built around three main categories: the client's *relationship with personal meaning*, the client's *perception of the relationship with the therapist*, and *awareness of outcomes*. In further, more fine-grained thematic explorations of the same material, Rennie has examined the client's experience of processes of resistance (Rennie, 1994c), story-telling (Rennie, 1994b), and deference (Rennie, 1994a). Angus and Rennie (1988, 1989) used a similar technique to explore client experiences of the use of metaphor in therapy sessions. This set of studies illustrates the systematic use of IPR and grounded theory in the service of developing a convincing and practically valuable model of therapeutic process.

Client evaluations of family therapy

Howe (1989) was invited by a family therapy team in a British social services department to carry out an evaluation of their therapeutic work with families. In this study, members of 33 families were interviewed. Twenty-two of the families had received therapy and ten had turned down the offer of this type of help. Open-ended interviews were carried out between four and seven weeks after the completion of treatment, and again after one year. Case notes and agency files were also examined. This mass of qualitative data was analysed in an 'interpretive' style loosely based on grounded theory. Howe presented his account of the clients' experiences of family therapy in terms of three main categories: 'to be engaged', 'to understand' and 'to be understood'. These themes converged in a discussion of client 'verdicts' on their treatment. In this study, Howe found strikingly low levels of client satisfaction. He noted that 'the overwhelming verdict was captured in a phrase that cropped up in almost all interviews with those families that felt dissatisfied: "it was a waste of time"' (1989: 77). In fact, only three families felt that the therapy had helped them. The kind of analysis undertaken by Howe (1989) in this research allows the creation of a comprehensive and well-rounded account of what these clients felt and thought about the therapeutic help they had received. It yields an estimate of overall success rates that stands comparison with the type of data produced by traditional quantitative outcome studies, but has the advantage of being able to place these evaluations in the context of a framework for understanding why and how these effects were generated.

Patterns of client change in short-term counselling

The study by Cummings, Hallberg and Slemon (1994) demonstrates one of the ways in which open-ended questionnaires can be used along with narrative analysis in counselling research. Ten clients engaged in time-limited (8–11 sessions) counselling were asked after each session to write in response to five open-ended questions: 'What was the most important thing that happened in this session?'; 'Why was it important and how was it helpful or not helpful?'; 'What thoughts and feelings do you recall experiencing/having during the session?'; 'What did you find yourself thinking about or doing during the time in between sessions that related in any way to the last session?'; and, 'Are you experiencing any change in yourself, and if so, what?' The researchers read through these written accounts, and constructed a narrative summary of what the client had reported. Other independent judges compared the original data with the narratives to check for bias or inaccuracy. The set of narratives produced by each client was analysed to identify the pattern of change that had occurred for that individual. Over the sample of ten cases, three different change patterns were found: consistent change, interrupted change and minimal change. Although clients categorized as showing 'consistent' and 'interrupted' change both appeared to gain from counselling, these contrasting patterns were associated with distinct sets of client experiences and needs. This small-scale study contributes to an understanding of change processes, by offering the reader vivid examples drawn from participants' written accounts, while at the same time raising important theoretical issues relevant to any assumption that the change process is the same for all clients.

The process of problem formulation in therapy

The research by Davis (1986) represents an effective application of discourse analysis in the field of psychotherapy research. The aim of the study was to explore the way in which the stories that clients tell about their 'troubles' become transformed into 'problems' suitable for psychotherapeutic intervention. The background to the study is given by Davis (1986) as arising from feminist critiques of psychotherapy. From a feminist perspective, when women go to see a psychotherapist, their problems are taken out of their social context and individualized. The woman is therefore pathologized, with 'problems which many women have in common and which are related to the oppressive exigencies of their living and working conditions [being] shorn of all political significance' (Davis, 1986: 46). However, as Davis (1986) pointed out, there had been no research that examined just *how* this happened within therapy sessions. Davis selected a video of a first session with a woman client and an expert, 'highly respected' male therapist. The video had been employed for teaching purposes, and was used because it could be regarded as an example of good practice. The conversation between therapist and client was transcribed, and a detailed analysis of conversation sequences was carried out. Davis (1986) concluded that, during the course of the session, the therapist carried out a *reformulation* of the client's problems, offered the client *documentation* of the reformulation through examples drawn not only from her initial statements but also from her in-session behaviour, and finally achieved the client's *consent* to his views. In the particular session analysed by Davis the client began by describing a set of difficulties relating to her role as a full-time housewife and mother who was pregnant. The formulation offered by the therapist was that these difficulties arose from not being able to express her emotions openly, and striving to keeping up a façade of control. Davis observes: 'more than half of the therapy session is devoted to persuading the client that the façade-problem is what she needs to work on' (1986: 65). This piece of research is inevitably limited in its generalizability (for example, would other therapists act in a similar fashion?). However, a significant strength of this approach is that a fair amount of the session transcript is included in the paper, so the reader can independently assess the plausibility of the analyses made by the author.

Lesbian self-disclosure of sexual orientation to health professionals

A study by Hitchcock and Wilson (1992) explores the processes and issues surrounding the decision of lesbian health care clients to disclose their sexual orientation to health professionals. This paper has broad terms of reference, in looking at disclosure to all kinds of health professionals, and not just psychotherapists. However, it is nevertheless relevant to counselling psychologists, in focusing on a significant issue and also in acting as an example of the use of grounded theory methods. Hitchcock and Wilson carried out interviews with 33 self-identified lesbians. Each interview was tape recorded and transcribed, and 'in keeping with conventions associated with the discovery of grounded theory method, data collection and analysis took place simultaneously and in a nonlinear fashion' (1992: 179). This material was coded, with a multiplicity of codes then condensed into more general categories, and finally a set of core concepts emerged. This process continued until no new meanings appeared in the data. The analysis Hitchcock and Wilson carried out revealed that lesbian health care users shared a *fear* of disclosure, and attempted to cope with this feeling through a process of *personal risking*. On first contact with a health professional, for example, many of these informants engaged in *scouting out*: 'collecting information about health care providers before deciding whether they are safe' (1992: 180). Following this initial information gathering, the lesbian client takes one of four possible stances on whether or not to let the health professional know about her sexual orientation: *passive disclosure, passive non-disclosure, active disclosure* and *active non-disclosure*. The decision to disclose is also affected by factors such as relationship status (that is, whether or not in a primary relationship), past experience with health professionals, and relevance of sexual orientation to the health problem. This study offers a detailed appreciation of the experiences of lesbian clients. The message comes through strongly that lesbian clients feel it is risky to disclose any information about their sexuality, and take every precaution to do so as carefully as possible. It is of particular interest that this study was carried out in the San Francisco Bay area, a region with a tradition of tolerance of lesbian and gay people. The degree of fear and risk might well be assumed to be much higher in other places.

The experience of 'schizophrenia'

The research carried out in the late 1950s by the psychiatrist R.D. Laing and reported in *The Divided Self* (Laing, 1960) and *Self and Others* (Laing, 1961) remains a powerful example of the application of the phenomenological method. Laing's aim in this work was to understand the experience of being 'schizophrenic', to 'reconstruct the patient's way of being himself in his world' (Laing, 1960: 25). In achieving this aim he needed to undertake a great deal of 'bracketing-off' of assumptions. His own training as a doctor and psychiatrist, for example, had given him a language that acted as a barrier to an appreciation of what patients might be experiencing. Laing (1960: 18) wrote that 'as a psychiatrist, I run into a major difficulty at the outset: how can I go straight to the patients if the psychiatric words at my disposal keep the patient at a distance from me?' It was therefore necessary for him to 'deconstruct' the meaning of psychosis by developing a critique of the ways that 'psychiatric words' were used in practice. Having done this, he was able to explore the experiential world of 'schizophrenic' people from a fresh perspective. His phenomenological investigation of this way of 'being-in-the-world' resulted in two kinds of research output. First, there was a series of sensitive case studies of individual patients. Second, the recurring themes in these case studies were conceptualized in existential-phenomenological terms through ideas such as *ontological insecurity, engulfment, implosion, petrification, pretence* and *elusion*. Taken as a whole, this set of studies introduced the possibility of understanding the lives and experiences of people who are 'mad'. Unfortunately, the subsequent career of R.D. Laing progressed in directions that became increasingly difficult to reconcile with the world of research, even phenomenological research, and as a result these early studies have been neglected and discredited.

The history and organization of a counselling agency

In their book *Whom God Hath Joined Together: the Work of Marriage Guidance*, Lewis, Clark and Morgan (1992) present a historical account of the development of the National Marriage Guidance Council, the leading British agency dealing in couples counselling. In this study, Lewis et al. draw together data from a variety of sources: interviews, personal and official documents, and observation. Their investigation provides a good example of the use of **triangulation**: using agreement between data from different sources as a check on validity. They also attempted to establish the accuracy of their data and analysis by asking a member of the agency to comment on a draft of their report.

Exemplar studies of the use of qualitative methods in counselling psychology research: some conclusions

These examples illustrate what can be done with qualitative methods. The same set of general research approaches and techniques could in principle be applied to a large number of questions of interest to counselling psychologists. It is perhaps worth noting a number of features of the qualitative research paradigm. First, it requires intense personal involvement on the part of the researcher. In the studies by Rennie, for example, the task of coding and categorizing interview transcripts took years of careful work. In other exemplar studies, good-quality data could only be obtained through a capacity to form genuine relationships with informants, in which they felt safe enough to disclose sensitive personal information. Secondly, reflexive self-awareness on the part of the researcher is necessary. Davis (1986), for instance, was clear about the feminist values informing her approach. Laing has written in many places about his own understanding of schizophrenia and his personal experiences in relation to this topic. If a qualitative research report is a 'construction' of a segment of social reality, it is important to know the ways in which the personal beliefs and values of the researcher have played a part in the inquiry process. Thirdly, good qualitative research is challenging. A qualitative study that merely presents a version of what is 'obvious' is not very interesting. The studies reviewed earlier each go beyond the obvious and reveal new aspects of phenomena, new horizons of meaning. Rennie describes the ways in which clients 'defer' to their therapists, keeping quiet when the therapist has misunderstood the client or said something unhelpful. Many health professionals who would see themselves as accepting of gay and lesbian clients might well feel uncomfortable on reading the study by Hitchcock and Wilson (1992). The three core values exhibited in these exemplar studies – authentic personal involvement, reflexivity and challenge – embody the core of the qualitative approach to research.

Criteria for evaluating the validity of qualitative studies

The criteria used in assessing the quality of a piece of qualitative research are quite different from those employed in traditional, experimental, positivist psychology. For example, concepts such as predictive or construct validity, inter-rater or test–re-test reliability are defined through, and depend on, statistical operations. The assumption that underpins these traditional concepts of validity is that there does exist an objective reality, and that the methods of science can be used to gain ever more accurate models of that reality. Qualitative research, by contrast, is built on an assumption that the world of persons is a co-constructed social reality (Gergen, 1985). Different participants in a social world will, therefore, each possess a somewhat different version of what is 'real' or 'true'.

The fundamental criterion for evaluating the products of this type of human science was described by Weber and Dilthey as *Verstehen*, or a 'sense of understanding', close to the counselling notion of **empathy**. In practice, this concept has at least two sides to it. First, readers must recognize the 'world' or set of experiences that the researcher is describing as authentic and credible. Secondly, the analysis, interpretation or conceptualization carried out by the researcher should lead to new insights into the object of study. It is clear that these criteria are highly subjective. Readers may well differ in the degree to which they regard a research account as authentic or providing insight. As a result, a number of attempts have been made to elaborate a more specific set of quality control criteria for qualitative research (Henwood and Pidgeon, 1992; Kirk and Miller, 1986; Lincoln and Guba, 1989; Stiles, 1993). These efforts have been motivated in part by a desire on the part of qualitative researchers to see their work published in mainstream psychology journals. In the past, journal editors and reviewers unfamiliar with qualitative research have not known how to evaluate the merit of qualitative papers submitted to them, and have often refused to publish such work.

In relation to qualitative research in the field of counselling psychology, some of the central issues in assessing the validity of a study are: adequacy of information given about the context of the study and procedures employed, the extent to which conceptualization is explicitly grounded in data, the credibility of the researcher, the degree to which research participants have been empowered by their involvement in the study, and the success with which conclusions have been 'triangulated' against different sources of data. More detailed discussion of these issues can be found in McLeod (1994) and Stiles (1993). Many of these issues have been most clearly identified and addressed by feminist researchers (Finch, 1984; Mies, 1983; Oakley, 1981). A central theme in this area concerns the role of researcher **reflexivity** (Berg and Smith, 1988; Steier, 1991). In qualitative research, the personal experience of the researcher is an important source of data. The researcher may often, for example, choose to include in a research report an account of his or her reflexive involvement in the research process (Wolcott, 1990).

Qualitative research in counselling psychology – future directions

It is necessary to be aware of some of the limitations of qualitative research in counselling psychology. For example, there has been very little qualitative research carried out in the field of outcome research. Although the studies by Howe (1989) and Cummings et al. (1994) demonstrate that therapy can be evaluated using qualitative methods, it is not clear how or whether it would ever be possible to compare effectiveness rates across studies or carry out meta-analyses using **'effect sizes'** (see Chapter 2) from a qualitative perspective. One solution to this problem might be to develop 'mixed' or 'pluralist' studies in which qualitative and quantitative methods are combined. However, the different epistemological assumptions underlying the two approaches can make it difficult to integrate data from these two very different sources (Brannen, 1992: McLeod, 1994).

Another limitation of qualitative research arises from the amount of time and effort required to accomplish a satisfactory qualitative study. Basic qualitative research tasks such as interviewing, transcribing tapes and coding data are very labour-intensive. Also, the art or craft of writing reports based on qualitative data can be highly demanding. The rapidly advancing availability of personal computer software for analysing qualitative data (Fielding and Lee, 1991; Richards and Richards, 1994) may eventually attenuate these difficulties.

A third limitation or dilemma arising from the use of qualitative methods is that these approaches have been generally used in a 'discovery-oriented' or 'heuristic' manner. In other words, qualitative researchers enter the field with relatively few presuppositions about what they might find, and are primarily interested in developing *new* insights or models. It is not clear whether qualitative methods are equally applicable during a verification or theory-testing phase of a research programme. On the whole, qualitative researchers take the view that concepts or categories should emerge inductively from the data that is gathered. If a researcher began a study with a well-defined set of concepts (for example, derived from psychodynamic or person-centred theory) this inductive or naturalistic process could not occur in the same manner.

It is also important to recognize that qualitative research in counselling psychology is in its infancy. Up to now, relatively few qualitative studies have been carried out in this area. Nevertheless, it is apparent that this style of research has an important contribution to make. Some of the advantages of qualitative research are that it respects the complexity of the phenomenon being studied, invites the active participation of informants, and takes as its goal the enhancement of understanding. Qualitative research is, therefore, highly consistent with many of the values of counselling psychology, and is therefore more likely to be perceived as credible and relevant by practitioners. In addition, doing qualitative research is similar to doing therapy. The good qualitative researcher uses empathy, genuineness and acceptance in developing relationships with informants (Mearns and McLeod, 1984). As a result, it is possible that qualitative research may be a style of inquiry that many counselling psychologists are able to do well.

In a review of the evolution of psychotherapy research, Orlinsky and Russell (1994) argue that this field of research has entered its fourth major phase. The first phase was characterized by the need to establish the legitimacy of scientific research into therapy. The second phase was marked by a search for greater rigour. The third phase represented the expansion and consolidation of the field. They regard the fourth, current, phase, which began in the mid-1980s, as encompassing a powerful sense of dissatisfaction with prevailing research methods and an increasing openness to a radical reformulation of research practice. Qualitative research and human science are essential elements of this new movement.

References

Angus, L.E. and Rennie, D.L. (1988) 'Therapist participation in metaphor generation: collaborative and noncollaborative styles', *Psychotherapy*, 25: 552–60.

Angus, L.E. and Rennie, D.L. (1989) 'Envisioning the representational world: the client's experience of metaphoric expressiveness in psychotherapy', *Psychotherapy*, 26: 373–9.

Becker, C.S. (1992) *Living and Relating: an Introduction to Phenomenology*. London: Sage.

Berg, D.N. and Smith, K.K. (eds) (1988) *The Self in Social Inquiry: Researching Methods.* London: Sage.

Bergin, A.E. and Garfield, S.L. (1994) 'Overview, trends and future issues', in A.E. Bergin and S.L. Garfield (eds), *Handbook of Psychotherapy and Behavior Change*, 4th edn. New York: Wiley.

Brannen, J. (ed.) (1992) *Mixing Methods: Qualitative and Quantitative Research.* Aldershot: Avebury.

Branthwaite, A. and Lunn, T. (1985) 'Projective techniques in social and market research', in R. Walker (ed.), *Applied Qualitative Research.* Aldershot: Gower.

Bryman, A. and Burgess, R.G. (eds) (1994) *Analyzing Qualitative Data.* London: Routledge.

Burman, E. (ed.) (1989) *Feminists and Psychological Practice.* London: Sage.

Cummings, A.L., Hallberg, E.T. and Slemon, A.G. (1994) 'Templates of client change in short-term counseling', *Journal of Counseling Psychology*, 41(4): 464–72.

Davis, K. (1986) 'The process of problem (re)formulation in psychotherapy', *Sociology of Health and Illness*, 8(1): 44–74.

Denzin, N.K. and Lincoln, Y.S. (eds) (1994a) *Handbook of Qualitative Research.* London: Sage.

Denzin, N.K. and Lincoln, Y.S. (1994b) 'Introduction: entering the field of qualitative research', in N.K. Denzin and Y.S. Lincoln (eds), *Handbook of Qualitative Research.* London: Sage.

Elliott, R. (1986) 'Interpersonal Process Recall (IPR) as a psychotherapy process research method', in L.S. Greenberg and W.M. Pinsof (eds), *The Psychotherapeutic Process: a Research Handbook.* New York: Guilford Press.

Fielding, N.G. and Lee, R.M. (eds) (1991) *Using Computers in Qualitative Research.* London: Sage.

Finch, J. (1984) '"It's great to have someone to talk to": ethics and politics of interviewing women', in C. Bell and H. Roberts (eds), *Social Researching: Politics, Problems, Practice.* London: Routledge.

Fontana, A. and Frey, J.H. (1994) 'Interviewing: the art of science', in N.K. Denzin and Y.S. Lincoln (eds), *Handbook of Qualitative Research.* London: Sage.

Gergen, K. (1985) 'The social constructionist movement in modern psychology', *American Psychologist*, 40(3): 266–75.

Glaser, B.G. (1978) *Theoretical Sensitivity: Advances in the Methodology of Grounded Theory.* Mill Valley, CA: The Sociology Press.

Glaser, B.G. and Strauss, A. (1967) *The Discovery of Grounded Theory.* Chicago: Aldine.

Harré, R. and Secord, P.F. (1972) *The Explanation of Social Behaviour.* Oxford: Blackwell.

Henwood, K.L. and Pidgeon, N.F. (1992) 'Qualitative research and psychological theorising', *British Journal of Psychology*, 83: 97–111.

Heppner, P.P., Kivlighan, Jr, D.M. and Wampold, B.E. (1992) *Research Design in Counseling.* Pacific Grove, CA: Brooks/Cole.

Hitchcock, J.M. and Wilson, H.S. (1992) 'Personal risking: lesbian self-disclosure of sexual orientation to professional health care providers', *Nursing Research*, 41(3): 178–83.

Hollway, W. (1989) *Subjectivity and Method in Psychology: Gender, Meaning and Science*. London: Sage.

Howe, D. (1989) *The Consumers' View of Family Therapy*. Aldershot: Gower.

Josselson, R. and Lieblich, A. (eds) (1993) *The Narrative Study of Lives*. London: Sage.

Kagan, N. (1984) 'Interpersonal Process Recall: basic methods and recent research', in D. Larsen (ed.) *Teaching Psychological Skills*. Monterey, CA: Brooks Cole.

Kirk, J. and Miller, M.L. (1986) *Reliability and Validity in Qualitative Research*. London: Sage.

Krueger, R.A. (1988) *Focus Groups: a Practical Guide for Applied Research*. London: Sage.

Kvale, S. (1983) 'The qualitative research interview: a phenomenological and hermeneutical mode of understanding', *Journal of Phenomenological Psychology*, 14(2): 171–96.

Laing, R.D. (1960) *The Divided Self: an Existential Study in Sanity and Madness*. London: Tavistock.

Laing, R.D. (1961) *Self and Others*. London: Tavistock.

Lewis, J., Clark, D. and Morgan, D. (1992) *Whom God Hath Joined Together: the Work of Marriage Guidance*. London: Routledge.

Lincoln, Y.S. and Guba, E.G. (1989) 'Judging the quality of case study reports', *Qualitative Studies in Education*, 3: 53–9.

Lofland, J. and Lofland, L. (1984) *Analyzing Social Settings: a Guide to Qualitative Observation and Analysis*, 2nd edn. Belmont, CA: Wadsworth.

McLeod, J. (1994) *Doing Counselling Research*. London: Sage.

Mearns, D. and McLeod, J. (1984) 'A person-centred approach to research', in R. Levant and J. Shlien (eds), *Client-Centered Therapy and the Person-Centered Approach: New Directions in Theory, Research and Practice*. New York: Praeger.

Messer, S.B., Sass, L.A. and Woolfolk, R.L. (eds) (1988) *Hermeneutics and Psychological Theory: Interpretive Perspectives on Personality, Psychotherapy and Psychopathology*. New Brunswick, NJ: Rutgers University Press.

Mies, M. (1983) 'Towards a methodology for feminist research', in G. Bowles and R.D. Klein (eds), *Theories for Women's Studies*. London: Routledge and Kegan Paul.

Miles, M. and Huberman, A. (1994) *Qualitative Data Analysis: a Sourcebook of New Methods*, 2nd edn. London: Sage.

Mishler, E.G. (1990) 'Validation in inquiry-guided research: the role of exemplars in narrative studies', *Harvard Educational Review*, 60(4): 415–42.

Moustakas, C. (1994) *Phenomenological Research Methods*. London: Sage.

Nisbett, R.E. and Wilson, T.D. (1977) 'Telling more than we can know: verbal reports on mental processes', *Psychological Review*, 84: 231–59.

Oakley, A. (1981) 'Interviewing women: a contradiction in terms', in H. Roberts (ed.), *Doing Feminist Research*. London: Routledge and Kegan Paul.

Orlinsky, D.E. and Russell, R.L. (1994) 'Tradition and change in psychotherapy research: notes on the fourth generation', in R.L. Russell (ed.), *Reassessing Psychotherapy Research*. New York: Guilford Press.

Osborne, J.W. (1990) 'Some basic existential-phenomenological research methodology for counsellors', *Canadian Journal of Counselling*, 24(2): 79–91.

Polkinghorne, D.E. (1994) 'Reaction to Special Section on qualitative research in counseling process and outcome', *Journal of Counseling Psychology*, 41(4): 510–12.

Potter, J. and Wetherell, M. (1987) *Discourse and Social Psychology: Beyond Attitudes and Behaviour*. London: Sage.

Reason, P. (ed.) (1988) *Human Inquiry in Action: Developments in New Paradigm Research*. London: Sage.

Reason, P. and Rowan, J. (eds) (1981) *Human Inquiry: a Sourcebook of New Paradigm Methods*. Chichester: Wiley.

Rennie, D.L. (1990) 'Toward a representation of the client's experience of the psychotherapy hour', in G. Lietaer, J. Rombauts and R. Van Balen (eds), *Client-Centered and Experiential Therapy in the Nineties*. Leuven: University of Leuven Press.

Rennie, D.L. (1992) 'Qualitative analysis of the client's experience of psychotherapy: the unfolding of reflexivity', in S.G. Toukmanian and D.L. Rennie (eds), *Psychotherapy Process Research: Paradigmatic and Narrative Approaches*. London: Sage.

Rennie, D.L. (1994a) 'Clients' deference in psychotherapy', *Journal of Counseling Psychology*, 41(4): 427–37.

Rennie, D.L. (1994b) 'Storytelling in psychotherapy: the client's subjective experience', *Psychotherapy*, 31: 234–43.

Rennie, D.L. (1994c) 'Clients' accounts of resistance in counselling: a qualitative analysis', *Canadian Journal of Counselling*, 28: 43–57.

Rennie, D.L. (1994d) 'Strategic choices in a qualitative approach to psychotherapy process research: a personal account', in L. Hoshmand and J. Martin (eds), *Method Choice and Inquiry Process: Lessons from Programmatic Research in Therapeutic Practice*. New York: Teacher's College Press.

Rennie, D.L. (1994e) 'Human science and counselling psychology: closing the gap between research and practice', *Counselling Psychology Quarterly*, 7: 235–50.

Rennie, D.L., Phillips, J.R. and Quartaro, J.K. (1988) 'Grounded theory: a promising approach for conceptualization in psychology?', *Canadian Psychology* 29: 139–50.

Richards, T.J. and Richards, L. (1994) 'Using computers in qualitative research', in N.K. Denzin and Y.S. Lincoln (eds), *Handbook of Qualitative Research*. London: Sage. pp. 445–62.

Riessman, C.K. (1993) *Narrative Analysis*. London: Sage.

Riessman, C.K. (1994) 'Making sense of marital violence: one woman's narrative', in C.K. Riessman (ed.), *Qualitative Studies in Social Work Research*. London: Sage.

Rosenwald, G.C. and Ochberg, R.L. (eds) (1992) *Storied Lives: the Cultural Politics of Self-Understanding*. New Haven, CT: Yale University Press.

Shotter, J. (1975) *Images of Man in Psychological Research*. London: Methuen.

Steier, F. (ed.) (1991) *Research and Reflexivity*. London: Sage.

Stern, P.N. (1994) 'Eroding grounded theory', in J.N. Morse (ed.), *Critical Issues in Qualitative Research Methodology*. London: Sage.

Stewart, D.W. and Shamdasani, P.N. (1990) *Focus Groups: Theory and Practice*. London: Sage.

Stiles, W.B. (1993) 'Quality control in qualitative research', *Clinical Psychology Review*, 13: 593–618.

Strauss, A. and Corbin, J. (1990) *Basics of Qualitative Research: Grounded Theory Procedures and Techniques*. New York: Sage.

Taylor, C. (1979) 'Interpretation and the science of man', in P. Rabinow and W. Sullivan (eds), *Interpretive Social Science: a Reader*. Berkeley, CA: University of California Press.

Valle, R.S. and Halling, S. (eds) (1989) *Existential-Phenomenological Perspectives in Psychology: Exploring the Breadth of Human Experience*. New York: Plenum.

Watkins, Jr, C.E. and Schneider, L.J. (eds) (1991) *Research in Counseling*. Hillsdale, NJ: Lawrence Erlbaum.

Wetherell, M. and Potter, J. (1988) 'Discourse analysis and the identification of interpretive repertoires', in C. Antaki (ed.), *Analysing Everyday Explanation: a Casebook of Methods*. London: Sage.

Wolcott, H.F. (1990) *Writing up Qualitative Research*. London: Sage.

Yin, R.K. (1989) *Case Study Research: Design and Methods*. London: Sage.

4

Evaluating Counselling Psychology Practice

Michael Barkham and Chris Barker

This chapter aims to set out the central concepts of evaluation research and to give some practical suggestions for counselling psychologists who wish to evaluate their own practice. We wish to emphasize the continuity between evaluation and other forms of research, and accordingly have drawn upon the previous two chapters (Chapters 2 and 3) in their accounts of research methods and substantive findings. Knowledge of a broad range of research methods is fundamental to the task of evaluation and the acquisition of such knowledge is an essential aspect of counselling psychology training. We regard well-conducted evaluation and research to be fundamental to the development of the profession of counselling psychology and concur with Barker, Pistrang and Elliott's view that 'evaluation should be a routine part of applied psychology: much clinical and counselling work is based on custom and practice rather than any formal knowledge base, and evaluating it is a way of seeing whether or not it lives up to its claimed benefits' (1994: 196–7).

This chapter has six parts. The first summarizes the key concepts and definitions used in evaluation research, and the second presents some preliminary issues which counselling psychologists need to consider before setting up an evaluation. The third part looks at the central issues of measurement, the fourth looks at design, and the fifth gives examples of evaluation studies. The sixth part examines how to assess the significance of the findings and how to communicate them to others.

General concepts and definitions in evaluation research

'Evaluations are concerned with whether or not programs or policies are achieving their goals and purposes' (Berk and Rossi, 1990: 15). In this context a programme can refer to something large, like the service provided by a national institution such as Relate (a British organization that provides low-cost couples counselling), medium-sized, such as a student counselling service at a particular university, or small, such as the work of an individual counselling psychologist. We assume that many readers of this chapter may be working on their own and are looking for ways to monitor their own work. We argue that the central principles of evaluation apply to all types of service, including one-person operations.

Evaluation research addresses issues that are contained within the current 'policy space': that is, it aims to address issues that particular policy-makers (or 'stakeholders') consider to be important. A major factor in determining the nature of the evaluation is whether the impetus for it derives from the counselling psychologist(s) or from external stakeholders such as funding agencies or users' groups. An evaluation driven by a counselling psychologist's own desire to look at his or her work imposes little restriction. By contrast, an evaluation driven by external demands needs to attend to the requirements of the different stakeholders.

Research is sometimes divided into pure research (often referred to as basic or scientific research) and applied research (or evaluation). Pure research is that which addresses fundamental psychological processes (for example, the role of cognitive biases in explaining one's own behaviour) whereas applied research or evaluation addresses a particular service at a particular time (such as the effectiveness of a student counselling service based on cognitive-behavioural principles). However, it is usually better to think of the pure–applied distinction as a continuum rather than a dichotomy, with most examples of research falling somewhere in the middle. Since counselling psychology is an applied discipline, counselling research always has an element of the applied in it (see Barker et al., 1994).

Because it is applied and policy-oriented, there is a tendency to view evaluation as less rigorous than traditional scientific research. Indeed, several characteristics of evaluation research appear to create potential tensions between it and the scientific basis of research (Cowen, 1978). Service settings are often organizationally messy, politicized, chaotic and pressured: an environment that may be hard to reconcile with one's noble ideals of dispassionately evaluating one's own work. However, our view is that the fundamental principles of scientific research apply equally well to evaluation research, but that evaluation researchers must also be adept at the art of compromise and knowing how to do the best that they can under adverse circumstances.

In evaluating counselling practice, three particular descriptions of activities are most commonly used: service audit, quality assurance and evaluation (see Parry and Watts, in press: b). We describe features of each of these.

Service audit refers to an examination of some aspect of a service delivery system. Recent writers, for example Crombie, Davies, Abraham and Florey (1993), have focused on a comparison with an agreed standard. Hence, an audit of a counselling service in a general medical practice may be based on a standard of 90 per cent of clients being seen within a month of referral. However, preliminary research may need to be carried out to determine what is a reasonable standard initially, although this may not strictly be considered as audit. The standard ought to be based upon several criteria. For example, it ought to be a balance between psychological knowledge (that is, presumably the sooner clients are seen the better, but is a four-week delay twice as bad as a two-week delay?), and pragmatism (that is, it is unrealistic to expect that all clients be seen within two weeks). Variants of the term 'service audit' include 'medical audit' in which the audit is carried out by doctors, and 'clinical audit' in which the audit is carried out by a multiprofessional team.

Quality assurance refers to instituting procedures that help maintain a high standard of service. Cape (1991) outlines four types of procedure. One is clinical audit (see above) and another is consumer surveys (discussed below). The third procedure is guidelines and standards which refer to quality targets (for example, 'all counselling sessions will occur in a quiet, comfortable and private location', 'after the first or second interview, counsellors will discuss with the client their formulation of the client's presenting problems and their opinion about which intervention would be most helpful'). Thus they are respectively equivalent to aims and objectives, which we discuss below. The fourth method, peer review, refers to members of the service meeting together regularly to examine the service that is delivered, such as when psychotherapists use peer group supervision to monitor the quality of therapy. Peer review may be formalized by having explicit criteria for case selection. Examples include cases involving long-term counselling, clients from a particular ethnic group, or clients at risk of suicide.

Evaluation has been classified into two categories: 'formative' and 'summative' (Scriven, 1972). Formative evaluations feed back continuously to inform and modify the service as it develops and are particularly appropriate for enhancing the design and implementation of new services. In contrast, summative evaluations provide a more definitive evaluation of an already existing service. Both audit and evaluation are retrospective in that the information they provide can then be fed back into the system and change made accordingly. This feedback system becomes one of a 'quality cycle' or 'audit loop' (Firth-Cozens, 1993; Shaw, 1986). In contrast, quality assurance attempts to be prospective in setting up standards and procedures to ensure that no problems arise in the system (although strictly speaking this is on the basis of evaluating past performance).

Having looked at some of the background concepts, we will now turn to the issues involved in putting evaluation into practice. Fortunately, there is a large evaluation literature to draw on (e.g., Cook and Campbell, 1979; Cronbach, 1982; Milne, 1987; Rossi and Freeman, 1989; Weiss,

1972). We look first at preparatory issues in building evaluation into counselling psychology services, and then at some of the choices that need to be made about which research methods to employ.

Preliminary issues in evaluating a service

Much groundwork needs to be done before evaluation can be successfully conducted. Some of these tasks are socio-political, having to do with the organization in which the evaluation is being carried out, others are conceptual, having to do with thinking clearly about what the service is trying to do and what is the rationale behind its operations.

Socio-political issues

One major issue is the impact of evaluation on the organization or system being evaluated. Let us take a simple example at the level of the individual counselling psychologist. An increasingly important component in ensuring the delivery of good therapy is peer group supervision (Cape, 1991). One way to ensure that the supervision is based on what actually was said rather than the therapist's recall of what was said is to ensure that tape recordings are made of therapy sessions (Barker, 1985). For counsellors who are not used to taping their sessions, this can be a threatening experience, and there is a small literature on the kinds of things which psychologists have done to avoid taping their sessions (such as saying 'my clients would be too uncomfortable with a tape recorder' or forgetting to turn on the machine). The point is that the threat felt by many people at this individual level can become considerable when the evaluation is being made of a system or organization.

When evaluating a larger organization, counselling psychologists need to employ their skills of empathizing with and accepting people's fears, and disclosing their own intentions and needs (Barker et al., 1994). An example of a project in which this issue has been addressed is in the recent evaluation of Relate counselling, in which Shapiro and Barkham (1993) addressed head-on the range of 'hopes' and 'fears' that would likely be encountered by members of the organization. This was achieved by running sessions facilitated by an external consultant (that is, one of the researchers) in which members of the organization were able to list both their 'hopes' and their 'fears' relating to the evaluation which was planned. Such a task enables issues arising from an evaluation procedure to be addressed more productively by focusing on them rather than on specific individuals.

Conceptual issues

Before the evaluation proper can be conducted, it is important to be clear about what the service is intending to do and how it is intending to go about it. This task can usefully be broken down into a series of sequential steps. Rossi and Freeman (1989), whose text is a key reference on evaluation research methods, set out six stages:

1 formulating the service's aims and objectives;
2 specifying the impact model;
3 specifying the target population;
4 estimating the extent of the target problem in the target population;
5 assessing the need for the service;
6 specifying the delivery system design.

We will address each of these stages in turn.

Aims and objectives Aims can be defined as overall statements of the desired outcomes of the service. These are often stated in a relatively idealized manner. For example, the aims of a counselling service in a health centre might be as follows: 'To provide an efficient service that reduces the psychological distress of patients who are referred to it', 'To reduce the number of inappropriate consultations with GPs for psychological problems', and 'To raise the level of psychological well-being in the local community'. In order to address such aims, objectives need to be set up which specify how these aims are going to be achieved. For example, one objective related to the second and third aims above might be to provide a monthly anxiety management workshop that is open to everyone in the local community.

The impact model The impact model is a way of specifying the rationale behind what the service is trying to do to meet its objectives. 'An impact model takes the form of a statement about the expected relationships between a program and its goal, setting forth the strategy for closing the gap between the objectives set during the planning process and the existing behavior or condition' (Rossi and Freeman, 1989: 129). The impact model comprises three types of hypotheses: a causal hypothesis, an intervention hypothesis, and an action hypothesis. The causal hypothesis describes what causes or maintains the target problem which the service is seeking to address (for example, the hypothesis is that patients use doctors inappropriately because they have no one else to tell their troubles to). The intervention hypothesis specifies how the proposed intervention will affect the causal determinant (for example, that the counselling service will provide an alternative, more appropriate place for patients to discuss

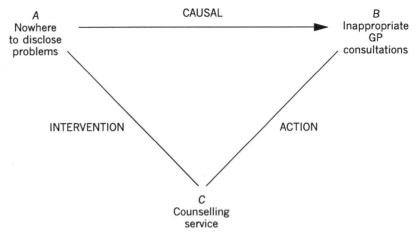

Figure 4.1   *The impact model*

their psychological problems). Finally, the action hypothesis specifies that the intervention will reduce the target problem (for example, that the existence of the counselling service will reduce the number of inappropriate GP consultations). The model, together with the above examples, is depicted in Figure 4.1. The purpose in specifying the impact model is to make the rationale for the service's actions as explicit as possible and to subject them to empirical test, although it is not always feasible, or desirable, to test all three components.

The target population   The target population is those people at whom the service is aimed. There are two types of targets: direct and indirect. Direct targets are the people for whom the intervention is designed. In effect, this becomes the unit of analysis for any statistical work carried out later. Often the unit of analysis will be 'the individual' (such as people attending a clinic). However, for marital work the unit of analysis may more appropriately be the couple, where the aim of the counselling is to see if the relationship between the two people can be sustained. Similarly, work focused on families may adopt 'the family' as the unit of analysis in the same way that group work may adopt 'the group' as the appropriate unit of analysis. Of course, given the interactive way in which people live, there will usually be effects experienced by others as a result of one person experiencing change. Consequently, the indirect targets consist of those other people who will benefit from the service (such as the parents of adolescents who attend a counselling service).

The extent of the target problem   The next task is to estimate the extent of the problem in the target population. Three terms from epidemiology are useful. 'Incidence' refers to the number of new cases occurring during a specified time period (e.g., one year). 'Prevalence' is the number of existing cases either at a particular point in time (termed point prevalence) or during a short time period (e.g., three-month prevalence). 'Population at risk' refers to a subset of the general population who are at greater risk for the problem under evaluation (e.g., gay men are a population at risk for HIV infection). Rossi and Freeman (1989) identify some methods for estimating the extent of the target problem in the target population. First, surveys and censuses of the target population, which provide direct estimates of the size and severity of the problem. Secondly, rates under treatment in similar services elsewhere can be used to estimate the size of the problem, although often the number of people using a service is a small fraction of people who are suffering from the problem that the service addresses. For example, only one in six people with severe depression seek psychological or psychiatric services (Weissman, 1987). Finally, there is the method of key informants, in which members of the community are interviewed to gain their estimates of the size of the problems.

Assessing the need for the service   As suggested above, it is important not to assume that the extent of the target problem corresponds to the need for the service. Health planners (e.g., Stevens and Gabbay, 1991) make the useful distinction between need (as seen from a professional perspective, demand (what people ask for), and supply (what is available). For example there is a need for reducing smoking amongst teenage girls (because of its adverse health risks), but there may not be a demand for counselling services designed to prevent girls smoking (because smoking may be perceived as glamorous or daring). So when designing a service, one must take account of demand and need, as well, of course, as supply, which depends on the available resources.

Delivery system design   Having gone through all these preliminary steps, you are then in a good position both to design a service that is matched to the size, needs and demands of the target population and also to evaluate the extent to which the service's aims and objectives are met. In the next section we look at the selection of research methods that can be used to carry out such an evaluation. Before we do, it is important to reiterate the point that in carrying out an evaluation of counselling practice, the researcher is continually weighing up various options and trying to make decisions which are defensible but not necessarily ideal. When planning any study, it is useful to distinguish between measurement and design (Barker et al., 1994). Measurement consists of specifying the concepts or variables that you will be studying (depression, well-being, safe sex, etc.) and how you will be measuring them (self-report or observation, qualitative or quantitative methods). Design consists of when you will be assessing them (at one moment in time or several, whether or not there is a control or comparison group, etc). We will look first at measurement, then design.

Measurement

The measures used in an evaluation study should be derived from the aims and objectives of the programme. Well-formulated aims and objectives will have direct implications about what to measure and in turn will determine the programme's success or failure. However, it is sometimes useful to have a classification scheme as a way to think about which aspects of a service to measure. One widely adopted taxonomy is Maxwell's (1984) list of six criteria for quality assessment:

1 access to services;
2 relevance to need;
3 effectiveness;
4 equity;
5 social acceptability;
6 efficiency/economy.

Parry (1992) uses this taxonomy in order to look at research evaluating psychotherapy services. Firth-Cozens (1993) expands these six quality areas and combines them with Donabedian's (1980) distinction between structure, process and outcome, which we will term 'levels'. This combination creates a matrix (see Table 4.1) which identifies the differing tasks that need to be addressed within each quality area at each of the three levels. Although the language used in the table is more medically oriented, it provides a useful basis for thinking about which variables to examine in evaluation.

In terms of Donabedian's (1980) three levels, structure is the measure of the physical resources available to the service: the physical environment and location of the service. Although less interesting psychologically, structural issues are often important to clients. Their views about structural (and all other) aspects of a service can usefully be assessed via client satisfaction surveys. However, client satisfaction surveys tend to produce positive results: often around 80 per cent of clients say that they were satisfied with the service they received (Lebow, 1983), so it is usually better to probe directly about client *dis*satisfaction and suggestions for improvements in the service.

Measures of process concern how the service is being delivered. One set of measures assesses which clients come to the service: whether they

	Structure	Process	Outcome
Equity and access	Availability of psychotherapy service. Day hospital relief for carers. Standards set for level of community staff. Condition in community homes	Minority languages catered for in terms of interpreters, bilingual professional. Waiting times for assessment, outpatients. Patient's Charter.	Does 'Did not attend' (DNA) rate reduce when interpreters available?
Acceptability and responsiveness	Patient satisfaction with wards, community homes, access to senior staff. Are the services offered reflecting patient needs?	Patient and carer's satisfaction with communication, responsiveness to needs, frequency of appointments, etc.	Was outcome acceptable in terms of quality of life, satisfaction, family dynamics, etc?
Appropriateness	Do we still have appropriately trained staff for the patients we see? Survey of security arrangement of rooms used by psychiatrists to assess emergency referrals. Conditions of consulting rooms	Are our physical investigations appropriate? Are we giving CBT, psychotherapy, OT, play therapy, group therapy, etc., when appropriate? Are particular patient groups seeing appropriate levels and types of professional? Are patients receiving appropriate psychometric testing? OT and nursing assessment	Does drop-out reduce when appropriate assessments are conducted?
Communication	Are our notes maintained in an acceptable manner? Do we have easy access to information for patients? Are our confidentiality procedures adequate?	Do letters to GPs have sufficient information? Are our communications to each member of the team acceptable? Do we make it clear to patients' relatives the treatment options that are possible/ available?	Is outcome communicated sufficiently well to patients/relatives, GPs and other community staff?
Continuity	Where continuity of care is not possible, are notes maintained to ensure similar care?	Do patients have continuity of care from one person where that is called for? Follow-up of patients referred from general hospital to addiction unit	Is there continuity in aftercare? Respite care

continued overleaf

	Structure	Process	Outcome
Effectiveness	Are wards/hostels, etc. sufficiently clean?	Is alcohol/drug dependency 'absent' at each appointment? Are we maintaining patient compliance in drug therapy? Are community patients competent in necessary life skills? Is our proportion of bedsores meeting national standards?	Are our outcomes in short-term therapy as good as they should be? What are our long-term outcomes for substance abuse, truancy, carers' health, marital discord, sexual abuse, independence, etc? Is our relapse/readmission rate meeting our standards?
Efficiency	Procedure for reducing non-attendance is being followed	Are tests, procedures, seclusions, drugs, therapies given only when indicated? Time spent travelling	Is the length of therapy no longer than is necessary according to research?

Source: Firth-Cozens, 1993, by kind permission of Lawrence Erlbaum Associates Ltd, Hove, UK

Table 4.1 *Matrix of levels and quality areas involved in developing an audit*

are representative of the intended target population. The important issue here is the extent of potential bias (Rossi and Freeman, 1989), that is, the tendency of a service to address a small and unrepresentative subsection of the population, such as Schofield's (1964) well-known acronym of the YAVIS psychotherapy client: Young, Attractive, Verbal, Intelligent and Successful. Another important source of bias is along ethnic lines. Members of minority ethnic groups are often poorly served by established psychological services. It is obviously important to monitor service delivery to see that such biases do not occur and correct them if they do. The other set of process measures concerns what service is being delivered. How many sessions do clients typically come for? If there is a structured service being given, such as in HIV pre-test counselling, to what extent do counsellors adhere to the protocol for that service? Otherwise, what happens in counselling sessions? Post-session reports or tape recordings of sessions are useful ways to address this.

Measures of outcome

Donabedian's third level for evaluation – outcome – raises the crucial question: do clients benefit from the service? There is an enormous literature on psychotherapy outcome research to draw upon here (see Chapters 2 and 3). We have compiled a list of seven criteria which provide a benchmark against which to evaluate any outcome measure. First, it should be easy to use (that is, it should not require specialist professional skills). Secondly, it should be relatively short. Many measures are developed in research settings where participants may be more tolerant of completing long questionnaires than in standard service settings. In addition, an evaluation may want to tap a wide range of variables, hence requiring more than one measure. Thirdly, the measure should be clinically sensitive in that it will detect change when it has occurred. Fourthly, it should be psychometrically sound in terms of standard parameters (test–retest reliability, internal consistency, etc.). Fifthly, there should exist normative data on the measure. Ideally, there should be norms for differing populations (such as client and non-client populations) as well as for differing cultures if that is appropriate. These should be contained in manuals which provide standard guidance on the implementation of a measure. Without this, considerable discrepancy can be introduced unwittingly. An aspiration is that there should be appropriate versions of the measure for ethnic minorities. Sixthly, the measure should be atheoretical. At first, this may appear inconsistent with psychologists' constant search for theory. However, if the measure is based on a specific theory, then it becomes a test of that one theory rather than being a more generic measure of change derived from an empirical base. And finally, the measure should be cheap or, more preferably, in the public domain.

While the above is a comprehensive list, and probably no measure satisfies all of the criteria, any measure should meet as many of them as possible. A critical problem in evaluation is not only the diversity of measures but also the large number of one-off measures. For example, Lambert and Hill (1994) report on a study which reviewed 348 outcome studies in 20 selected journals from 1983 to 1988 and identified 1,430 outcome measures, of which 840 were used just once. This makes comparisons with other studies very difficult and fails to contribute to the overriding need for comparative (i.e., normative) data. However, there is an increasingly recognized pool of measures of which the interested practitioner should be aware, and some initial sources for these are listed in the Appendix. It is usually better not to rely solely upon one outcome measure. Although adopting more than one outcome measure will increase the burden of evaluation on both the participants and the investigator, if only one measure is used, then outcome and the constraints of that single measure are inextricably bound together and partly reflect its over-specificity and unreliability. In addition, data from another measure can be viewed as concurrent replication.

One central issue relating to evaluation measures is that it is probably easier to show change arising from a reduction in symptomatology than a rise in personal well-being. This reflects the fact that reductions in symptomatology may be tapping effect sizes which are medium or large. In contrast, raising levels of personal well-being in people already functioning within 'normal' ranges will be tapping a small effect size and will be appreciably harder to detect reliably.

A further issue arises from what has been referred to as the 'bandwidth-fidelity' dilemma. While researchers are keen to use measures with proven psychometric qualities (i.e., high fidelity) which often entails their focusing on narrowly defined constructs, practitioners wish to tap a broad range of issues (i.e., broad bandwidth): for example, general functioning, levels of subjective distress, quality of life, interpersonal issues, etc. Hence, practitioners wish to tap 'bandwidth' and accordingly require 'good-enough' measures rather than pure (fidelity) measures which researchers might adopt. This is a pervasive issue in evaluation research and in counselling psychology and psychotherapy research in general.

While the practitioner needs to take into account all the above considerations when deciding on the selection of measures, they also need a guiding strategy through the selection of measures. We identify three areas of measurement: outcome, process and change processes. In providing some initial guidance within each of these three areas, we acknowledge that the actual area which has priority for the practitioner will vary and depend very much on what question is being asked. At the level of outcome, practitioners may select a *global* standardized measure, for example, the Symptom Checklist-90-R (SCL-90-R; Derogatis, 1993) or a standardized measure targeting a *specific* presenting problem, for example, the Beck Depression Inventory for depression (BDI; Beck, Steer and Garbin, 1988). They might then add an *individualized* measure which is idiographic (that is, it has items identified by the client) rather than nomothetic (that is, where the items are invariant across clients). Examples include variants of the Personal Questionnaire (Phillips, 1986). At the level of process, practitioners need to decide between either asking clients to complete session-based measures of aspects of the process, or obtaining audiotapings of the sessions and having these rated at some future date. Of course, both can be done but the practitioner may not wish to overload themselves with material. Examples of session-based measures include those tapping the therapeutic alliance (e.g., Working Alliance Inventory; Horvath and Greenberg, 1994) or impressions of the session itself (e.g., Session Evaluation Questionnaire and Session Impacts Scale; Stiles et al., 1994). At the level of change processes, practitioners can utilize a combination of the other two levels in order to set the context and then employ a strategy of interviewing the client or carrying out detailed analysis on the audio recordings. In particular, there is considerable merit in focusing on significant events within sessions as these are likely to be a cost-effective means to advancing practitioners' understandings about what specifically leads to change. More detailed information on these three levels can be found in Barker et al. (1994).

Effectiveness and efficiency

The final two quality areas in Table 4.1 denote effectiveness and efficiency. There has been a recent move towards not just assessing outcome, which looks at absolute change, but effectiveness, which looks at relative change. Berk and Rossi (1990) make the point that effectiveness must always address the issue 'compared with what?' They identify three forms of effectiveness:

1 Marginal effectiveness, where the issue is one of dosage, where the evaluator is making a judgement concerning more or less of some intervention.
2 Relative effectiveness, where the comparison is between an active treatment versus no-treatment, or between two or more active treatments.
3 Cost-effectiveness, where comparisons are made in terms of units or outcome per units of expenditure (e.g., pound or dollar).

A further task may be required, namely to evaluate efficiency. Efficiency can be construed as effectiveness but expressed in terms of financial or other resources. There is a potential tension here between practitioners devising models of intervention which are effective, versus managers seeking to address the question of efficiency. For example, a particular intervention may be shown to be effective but at such a large financial cost that it raises questions about its efficiency. Clearly, it is a matter of balancing these two issues.

Design

Design refers to when and how the measures are collected: design issues can usefully be thought of independently of measurement issues. (The term design is sometimes used in a broader sense to encompass measurement as well; however, we will adhere to the more precise usage.) Design is an enormous topic, that we can only touch on briefly here; more extended treatments are given in texts on research methods (e.g., Barker et al., 1994; Cook and Campbell, 1979; Kazdin, 1994; Parry and Watts, in press:a; Rossi and Freeman, 1989). There is no one best design for all purposes; the type of design is determined by the aims of the evaluation. We will look at three key design issues here:

1 whether one or more groups are studied (for example, whether a control or comparison group is used);
2 whether a single case or a larger sample size is used; and
3 the number of assessment points over time.

Control or comparison groups

Psychologists are often socialized into believing that they must have a control or comparison group in order to be doing good research. Of course, control and comparison groups are vital for addressing certain research questions, mainly those which address the explanations for change processes or questions of relative effectiveness. However, evaluations are frequently not concerned with explanations, they simply seek to establish that a service is beneficial: why it is beneficial, or whether it is more beneficial than other services, can be left to subsequent inquiry. Thus it is often sufficient to adopt a one-group design in which a single group of clients, perhaps receiving a specific form of counselling for a specific presenting problem, are studied. (Note that the word 'group' here is a technical design term: we are not implying that group rather than individual work is being evaluated.) For example, 40 clients who come to a university counselling centre for help with relationship difficulties may be assessed before and after brief psychodynamically-oriented counselling.

Single-case designs

The extreme example of a one-group design is a N of 1, or single-case design, which looks at the work of one counselling psychologist with a single client. They are congenial designs for practitioners who wish to evaluate the effectiveness of their own counselling. One or more measures can be administered to clients at frequent intervals. For example, a client's anxiety may be assessed weekly, or a married couple may record the quality of their interactions every day. In this way the counsellor can look closely at improvement as it occurs over time. The type of improvement is usually obvious from a simple graphical inspection of the data, but statistical methods can also be used. A good example of a single-case study is Parry et al.'s (1986) case of the 'anxious executive'. It used the Personal Questionnaire method (Mulhall, 1976) in which the client selected items to capture his problems and rated them throughout the course of therapy. These ratings were supplemented by data on the therapist's views of themes and the client's views of helpful and unhelpful events within the sessions. The data set thus provided frequent measures across therapy on the processes of change for a range of issues salient to the client.

One advantage of this form of evaluation is that it can be readily extended to other clients, and thereby become what is known as a clinical replication series (Barlow et al., 1984). Such a procedure enables practitioners to become informed about possible important variables. For example, suppose a practitioner carries out a simple evaluation in which the first series of clients can be described as 'young' (say, under 35 years old) and these cases are deemed successful. The practitioner then evaluates a series of clients who might be described as 'older' (over 50) and these cases are not so successful. The practitioner then sees another series of younger clients for whom the outcome is successful. Such data may begin to inform the practitioner about those clients with whom he or she is more successful. Clearly, he or she must consider other variables which might co-vary with age (such as social support network). However, it provides the practitioner with a means for evaluating their practice by testing competing hypotheses. In this design, it is the approach which is dominant. That is to say, the practitioner might employ any given instrument or instruments; the power of the design lies in the replication with a series of clients.

Number of assessment points

In both group designs and single-case designs, the number of assessment points over time is determined by the aims and objectives of the evaluations. In some cases (for example, evaluating clients' satisfaction with the structure or process of the service), a single time point may suffice. However, in other cases, usually concerned with evaluating outcome, several measurement points are valuable. While there is much interest in the interactive nature of process and outcome in psychotherapy and counselling psychology (e.g., Greenberg, 1986), it is hard to argue against the inclusion of a pre–post evaluation of a psychological intervention. Here the question being asked is, 'At the end of an intervention, has something changed as compared with the beginning of the intervention?' The change which is being monitored could be, for example, a fall in the client's level of distress or a rise in the client's sense of personal well-being or quality of life.

Assessing clients prior to an intervention is essential in order to describe their severity of presenting problems. In evaluating the intervention, it then becomes essential to determine their well-being after the intervention. This is the logic which leads to pre–post assessments, which are necessary but not sufficient for evaluating change. The critical point is the nature and psychological process of change. Data at two points in time may tell us that initially a client's score was high (that is, it reflected poor psychological functioning) and then improved after the intervention. If we are only interested in end-point analyses, then this might be sufficient. However, there is a range of problems. First, many psychological experiences run in cycles, hence the post-assessment may well reflect improvement, but this ignores the naturally occurring increase a few months later. Secondly, two data points gives only two shots at tapping any psychological process, and this is not particularly stable. More data points provide more stable data; post-counselling change needs to be followed up. And thirdly, only a straight line can be drawn between two data points, and it seems unlikely that a straight line reflects the only change process. Thus we suggest measurement points halfway through counselling and at three-month follow-up if possible.

These problems notwithstanding, it may now be appropriate to consider some evaluation studies.

Evaluation studies: examples

At the beginning of this chapter, we stated that evaluation could be carried out on large and medium-sized organizations as well as at the level of the individual counselling psychologist. This section summarizes examples of evaluation studies. The first is a study of part of a large national organization (i.e., Relate). The remaining studies are of medium-sized organizations (e.g., university counselling service, clinical psychology services) which include more direct examples of audit. Published examples of studies carried out at the individual level are rare.

National organization

Shapiro and Barkham (1993) present a report of an evaluation of one region within the Relate organization. Clients completed the 12-item version of the General Health Questionnaire (GHQ-12; Goldberg and Williams, 1988) and questionnaires about their relationship with their partner (as improving this is a natural aim of counselling). The pre-counselling data set was drawn from 352 clients and suggested that a very high percentage (83 per cent) met a definition of 'caseness'. Similarly, the measure of relationship difficulties indicated that 51 per cent of clients reported 'severe' or 'very severe' difficulties, a figure twice what would be expected according to the measure used. A sub-sample of 101 clients who completed pre- and post-counselling questionnaires was analysed further. The GHQ-12 revealed a pre–post effect size for change of 1.01 standard deviation units, which was probably an underestimate due to the large number of clients obtaining maximum scores pre counselling and minimum scores post counselling. However, there are issues concerning whether GHQ data can be used to determine change (Firth-Cozens, 1993). Change on the relationship measure was less, with the pre–post effect size of 0.54 standard deviation units (compared with an expected change of 0.85 standard deviation units). Hence, clients showed substantial benefits in their general well-being but this did not have an equivalent effect on their relationships. The study found high satisfaction rates, with over 80 per cent of clients having 'most' or 'almost all' of their needs met, and 97 per cent of clients were 'mostly' or 'very' satisfied.

Medium-sized organizations

Mathers, Shipton and Shapiro (1993) present an evaluation of short-term counselling in a university setting. The period of evaluation was 14 months, during which ten counsellors saw a total of 401 clients. Of this total, 142 were attending for their initial appointment and were the focus of the study. The scores of 45 clients were compared pre and post counselling using the GHQ-12 and showed a significant reduction from pre to post counselling (mean pre = 23.1; mean post = 13.8). Skaife and Spall (1995) report on an evaluation of a clinical psychotherapy service and place importance on the independence of the person carrying out the evaluation (in this case an audit). They sampled 44 discharged clients who were selected randomly and mailed a questionnaire. Responses were returned by 20 clients. Information was obtained in the areas of clients' introduction to the department, the process of therapy, outcome and suggestions for improvements in the service. What is of note in this report is that the authors presented an 'action' plan based on the results and organized under Donabedian's (1980) three levels: 'structure', 'process' and 'outcome'. In terms of structure, consideration was given to moving the psychology department to the district hospital. At the level of process, a leaflet focusing on details of the service clients would receive was prepared and sent to clients. At the level of outcome, it was decided that the most sensible use would be a baseline against which to compare subsequent data.

A study of therapist and client evaluations within the psychology department of a large Scottish psychiatric hospital was carried out by Neilson (1994). The sample comprised seven clinical psychologists and 36 clients. Interestingly, measures of process and outcome were used, being completed by therapists and clients. Results suggested that therapists were less positive in their evaluation of therapy than clients, a finding repeatedly observed in outcome studies. In general, therapists may have been more guarded than clients in their evaluations because they held a more long-term model of the impact of change. However, it might also be influenced by how outcome was evaluated in this study. Rather than basing the evaluation on clients' and therapists' ratings of current 'state', questions were asked about the amount of improvement achieved and whether therapy had been successful or not. This procedure 'collapses' the evaluation of change into a single judgement rather than it being determined by calculating the difference between clients' degree of distress at pre-therapy and then at any point subsequently. Where there is no pre-therapy data available, this is the only option. However, as stated earlier, it is less satisfactory than building in evaluation from the beginning of a client's contact with the service and then administering subsequent measures in order to obtain data on whether clients have improved or not. The study also found that all clients were satisfied with the service provided. This finding, whilst initially gratifying to those in the service, supports our point made earlier that more information may be obtained by asking clients about their *dis*satisfactions with the service.

Weighing up and communicating the findings

Having collected the data, how can you determine that meaningful change has occurred? Let us consider three broad approaches to how 'change' can be determined: criterion, statistical and clinical.

Determining change

Criterion change A criterion approach makes comparisons with categorical levels of a particular behaviour. Hence, if a target is set, say of all clients being offered an initial appointment within three weeks of seeking help, then when this has been achieved the criterion can be said to have been met. At the level of the individual client, suppose a client presents with a social phobia, then a criterion approach would be that the counselling is considered successful if the client's behaviour at the end of counselling meets certain criteria agreed upon at the beginning of counselling; for example, she is able to feel relaxed at social gatherings, is able to initiate social relationships, and so on.

Statistical change Traditionally, researchers have tended to adopt the statistical change approach, which aims to establish whether the observed change could reasonably have been expected to occur by chance. The level of 0.05 has become established as the norm: if the probability is less than 1 in 20 that the change happened by chance, then it is deemed statistically significant. However, there are many issues raised by this approach, the most important of which can be highlighted by the following example. Suppose 25 people who weigh between 125 and 165 kg take part in a programme to reduce weight because they are deemed to be at a heightened risk of a heart attack. Suppose they all lose 5 kg by the end of the programme. This pre–post change will be significant, but with their weights now being 120–160 kg respectively, it is unlikely that they are at any appreciably less risk of a heart attack. The same principle applies to scores reflecting psychological well-being, in that a group of clients' scores on a measure may show a statistically significant reduction and yet their psychological state may still be very distressed.

Reliable and clinically significant change   Recent approaches have tended to look not just at statistical significance but also at reliable and clinical significance (Jacobson and Truax, 1991). Reliable and clinically significant change comprises two components, which can be phrased as separate questions. First, is the change which has occurred 'reliable'? This question can usually be operationalized as 'Is the client's movement from when they were previously tested greater than the measurement error of the instrument?' Consider the difference between measuring someone's weight and their psychological well-being. While there will be variability in a person's weight and psychological well-being at two points in time, it is likely that there will be considerably more measurement error in psychological well-being than weight. That is, the instruments for determining weight are relatively precise, compared with asking a client to complete a self-report measure on well-being. In order to take account of the fact that some change measures are more reliable than others, Jacobson and Truax (1991) propose the use of a reliable change index, which, broadly speaking, requires demonstrated change on a measure to be greater than the error arising from its unreliability of measurement.

The second component can be phrased in the form 'Where has the client moved to on the measure of interest?' This question focuses on the stage or level to which the client has moved rather than the actual amount of change. Questions of clinical significance ask about the meaning of a client's state at the end of counselling. Do their scores on various measures represent a return to functioning within the normal range, or at least a move out of the range of a dysfunctional group? The various criteria by which these notions might be encapsulated are summarized by Jacobson and Truax (1991). Generally, they focus on whether a practitioner wishes to identify as 'improved' a client whose score moves out of the dysfunctional range (that is, the client no longer belongs to the dysfunctional population but equally cannot be said to belong to the normal population) or whether a client's score has to enter the normal range (that is, the client is a member of the normal population rather than any other population). A final criterion enables the practitioner to state whether a client is nearer to one population than to another.

Presenting data to stakeholders

In presenting data to a stakeholder, it is important to consider its impact: data presented to one party may not be appropriate to present to another party. There is a considerable variety of ways of presenting data to stakeholders (e.g., see Barkham, 1992). Let us consider the issue of presenting data concerning client follow-up. A manager will be interested in the number of clients who can be identified as likely not to need further services. One method which might be seen as the most stringent would be to set a criterion on a primary outcome measure which was equivalent to clients being asymptomatic. Using a definition based upon either a specific criterion or on reliable and clinically significant change, it is possible to determine the percentage of clients who meet such criteria. This approach carries with it the advantage of 'specificity': a specified percentage of clients are being stated as improved. However, serious consideration needs to be given to espousing a criterion which may be unrealistic. Identifying criteria which are met and which indicate a real improvement in the quality of clients' lives may be as, if not more, appropriate. For example, in evaluating people who have developed a fear of leaving their house, it might be reasonable to apply the following criterion: 'Is able to leave the house alone'. This presents a real improvement. However, we also know that such improvement can also carry with it other difficulties in terms of family dynamics. Hence, a stringent criterion which includes addressing the family dynamic may show no change and the service might not be seen as achieving the real gains made by the client.

Conclusion

We conclude that evaluation is central to the process of quality control in any service delivery system. However, the scope of the evaluation very much depends on the resources available and the interested stakeholders. The former can be increased by bidding to appropriate funding agencies and stakeholders for support money. In this chapter we have hopefully provided a picture of the wide range of methods available to interested practitioners. Certainly it is our view that there is a sufficient range of methods to match the resources, interests and values of most practitioners.

References

Barker, C. (1985) 'Interpersonal Process Recall in clinical training and research', in F.N. Watts (ed.), *New Developments in Clinical Psychology*. Chichester: Wiley. pp. 154–69.

Barker, C., Pistrang, N. and Elliott, R. (1994) *Research Methods in Clinical and Counselling Psychology*. Chichester: Wiley.

Barkham, M. (1992) 'Understanding, implementing and presenting counselling evaluation', in R. Bayne and P. Nicolson (eds), *Counselling and Psychology for Health Professionals*. London: Chapman & Hall. pp. 65–83.

Barlow, D.H., Hayes, S.C. and Nelson, R.O. (1984) *The Scientist-Practitioner: Research and Accountability in Clinical and Educational Settings*. New York: Pergamon Press.

Beck, A.T., Steer, R.A. and Garbin, M.G. (1988) 'Psychometric properties of the Beck Depression Inventory: twenty-five years of evaluation', *Clinical Psychology Review*, 8: 77–100.

Berk, R.A. and Rossi, P.H. (1990) *Thinking about Program Evaluation*. Newbury Park, CA: Sage.

Cape, J. (1991) 'Quality assurance methods for clinical psychology services', *The Psychologist*, 4: 499–503.

Cook, T.D. and Campbell, D.T. (1979) *Quasi-Experimentation: Design and Analysis for Field Settings*. Chicago: Rand McNally.

Cowen, E.L. (1978) 'Some problems in community program evaluation research', *Journal of Consulting and Clinical Psychology*, 46: 792–805.

Crombie, I.K., Davies, H.T.O., Abraham, S.C.S. and Florey, C.du V. (1993) *The Audit Handbook: Improving Health Care through Clinical Audit*. Chichester: Wiley.

Cronbach, L.J. (1982) *Designing Evaluations of Educational and Social Programs*. San Francisco: Jossey Bass.

Derogatis, L.R. (1993) *SCL-90-R: Administration, Scoring and Procedures*, 3rd edn. Minneapolis: National Computer Systems.

Donabedian, A. (1980) *The Definition of Quality and Approaches to its Assessment*. Ann Arbor, MI: Health Administration Press.

Firth-Cozens, J. (1993) *Audit in Mental Health Services*. Hove: Lawrence Erlbaum.

Goldberg, D. and Williams, P. (1988) *A User's Guide to the General Health Questionnaire*. Windsor: NFER-Nelson.

Greenberg, L.S. (1986) 'Change process research', *Journal of Consulting and Clinical Psychology*, 54: 4–9.

Horvath, A.O. and Greenberg, L.S. (eds) (1994) *The Working Alliance: Theory, Research, and Practice*. New York: Wiley.

Jacobson, N.S. and Truax, P. (1991) 'Clinical significance: a statistical approach to defining meaningful change in psychotherapy research', *Journal of Consulting and Clinical Psychology*, 59: 12–19.

Kazdin, A.E. (1994) 'Methodology, design, and evaluation in psychotherapy research', in A.E. Bergin and S.L. Garfield (eds), *Handbook of Psychotherapy and Behavior Change*, 4th edn. New York: Wiley. pp. 19–71.

Lambert, M.J. and Hill, C.E. (1994) 'Assessing psychotherapy outcomes and processes', in A.E. Bergin and S.L. Garfield (eds), *Handbook of Psychotherapy and Behavior Change*, 4th edn. New York: Wiley. pp. 72–113.

Lebow, J.L. (1983) 'Research assessing consumer satisfaction with mental health treatment: a review of findings', *Evaluation and Program Planning*, 6: 211–36.

Mathers, N., Shipton, G. and Shapiro, D.A. (1993) 'The impact of short-term counselling on General Health Questionnaire scores', *British Journal of Guidance and Counselling*, 21: 310–18.

Maxwell, R.J. (1984) 'Quality assessment in health', *British Medical Journal*, 288: 1470–2.

Milne, D. (1987) *Evaluating Mental Health Practice: Methods and Applications*. Beckenham: Croom Helm.

Mulhall, D. (1976) 'Systematic self-assessment by PQRST', *Psychological Medicine*, 6: 591–7.

Neilson, J. (1994) 'Therapist–client concordance on therapy process and outcome and its implications for service evaluation', *Clinical Psychology Forum*, 73: 5–7.

Parry, G. (1992) 'Improving psychotherapy services: applications of research, audit and evaluation', *British Journal of Clinical Psychology*, 31: 3–19.

Parry, G. and Watts, F.N. (in press:a) (eds) *Behavioural and Mental Health Research: a Handbook of Skills and Methods*, 2nd edn. Hove: Lawrence Erlbaum.

Parry, G. and Watts, F.N. (in press:b) 'Service evaluation and audit methods', in G. Parry and F.N. Watts (eds) *Behavioural and Mental Health Research: a Handbook of Skills and Methods*, 2nd edn. Hove: Lawrence Erlbaum.

Parry, G., Shapiro, D.A. and Firth, J. (1986) 'The case of the anxious executive: a study from the research clinic', *British Journal of Medical Psychology*, 59: 221–33.

Phillips, J.P.N. (1986) 'Shapiro Personal Questionnaire and generalized personal questionnaire techniques: a repeated measures individualized outcome measurement', in L.S. Greenberg and W.M. Pinsof (eds), *The Psychotherapeutic Process: a Research Handbook*. New York: Guilford. pp. 557–89.

Rossi, P.H. and Freeman, H.E. (1989) *Evaluation: a Systematic Approach*, 4th edn. Newbury Park, CA: Sage Publications.

Schofield, W. (1964) *Psychotherapy: the Purchase of Friendship*. Englewood Cliffs, NJ: Prentice Hall.

Scriven, M. (1972) 'The methodology of evaluation', in C.H. Weiss (ed.), *Evaluating Action Programs*. Boston, MA: Allyn and Bacon.

Shapiro, D.A. and Barkham, M. (1993) *RELATE: Information Needs Research. Final Report to Department of Social Security*. Rugby: Research and Policy Unit, Relate Marriage Guidance.

Shaw, C. (1986) *Introducing Quality Assurance*. London: King's Fund Centre.

Skaife, K. and Spall, B. (1995) 'An independent approach to auditing psychology services for adult mental health clients'. *Clinical Psychology Forum*, 77: 14–18.

Stevens, A. and Gabbay, J. (1991) 'Needs assessment needs assessment', *Health Trends*, 23: 20–3.

Stiles, W.B., Reynolds, S., Hardy, G.E., Rees, A., Barkham, M. and Shapiro,

D.A. (1994) 'Evaluation and description of psychotherapy sessions by clients using the Session Evaluation Questionnaire and the Session Impacts Scale', *Journal of Counseling Psychology*, 41: 175–85.

Weiss, C.H. (1972) *Evaluation Research*. Englewood Cliffs, NJ: Prentice Hall.

Weissman, M.M. (1987) 'Advances in psychiatric epidemiology: rates and risks for major depression', *American Journal of Public Health*, 77: 445–51.

Appendix

Academic texts on assessment and related issues

Anastasi, A. (1988) *Psychological Testing*, 6th edn. New York: Macmillan.

Bowling, A. (1991) *Measuring Health: a Review of Quality of Life Measurement Scales*. Buckingham: Open University Press.

Buros, O.K. (various dates) *Mental Measurements Yearbooks*. University of Nebraska Press.

Ciminero, A.R., Calhoun, K.S. and Adams, H.E. (eds) (1986) *Handbook of Behavioural Assessment*, 2nd edn. New York: Wiley.

Goldstein, G. and Hersen, M. (eds) (1990) *Handbook of Psychological Assessment*, 2nd edn. Oxford: Pergamon.

Groth-Marmat, G. (1990) *Handbook of Psychological Assessment*, 2nd edn. New York: Wiley.

Karoly, P. (ed.) (1985) *Measurement Strategies in Health Psychology*. New York: Wiley.

McDowell, I. and Newell, C. (1987) *Measuring Health*. Oxford: Oxford University Press.

Nelson, R.O. (1981) 'Realistic dependent measures for clinical use', *Journal of Consulting and Clinical Psychology*, 49: 168–82.

Peck, D.F. and Shapiro, C. (1990) *Measuring Human Problems: a Practical Guide*. Chichester: Wiley.

Spreen, O. and Strauss, E. (1991) *A Compendium of Neuropsychological Tests: Administration, Norms and Commentary*. Oxford: Oxford University Press.

Streiner, D.L. and Norman, G.R. (1991) *Health Measurement Scales: a Practical Guide to Their Development and Use*. Oxford: Oxford University Press.

Sundberg, N.D. (1977) *Assessment of Persons*. Englewood Cliffs, NJ: Prentice Hall.

Thompson, C. (ed.) (1989) *The Instruments of Psychiatric Research*. Chichester: Wiley.

Woody, R.H. (ed.) (1980) *Encyclopedia of Clinical Assessment*, 2 vols. San Francisco: Jossey Bass.

Commercial organizations:

NCS (National Computer Systems) Assessments, c/o Afterhurst Ltd, 27 Church Road, Hove, East Sussex, BN3 2FA, UK.

NFER-Nelson, Darville House, 2 Oxford Road East, Windsor, Berkshire, SL4 1DF.

Oxford Psychologists Press, Lambourne House, 311–321 Banbury Road, Oxford OX2 7JH, UK.

Psychological Assessment Resources, Inc., PO Box 998, Odessa, Florida 33556, USA.

The Psychological Corporation, Harcourt Brace & Co. Ltd, 24–28 Oval Road, London, NW1 1YA, UK.

Part Three

Perspectives on Practice

5

The Psychodynamic Paradigm

Michael Burton and Tom Davey

Majority does not mean great number but great fear.   JEAN-FRANCOIS LYOTARD

... the neurotic is one who refuses the loan of life in order not to pay the debt of death.
OTTO RANK

Psychodynamic counselling is a broad church and different versions derive inspiration from selective readings of Freud, Jung and a wide range of later theorists. There is no obvious ascendant core text or belief system although there are some broad separations geographically in terms of the influence of American self or ego psychology, British object relations including Klein, and European traditions including Freud, Lacan and postmodern theorists. Other influences include psychology, feminism, cognitive sciences and humanism. The term counselling rather than psychotherapy seems to be used in reference to the following dimensions:

- Cost and length of training
- Relative weighting of experimental versus clinical evidence
- Low dosage
- Focus of aims
- Degree of regression
- Use of transference
- Symptom relief versus insight
- Conscious versus unconscious
- Low intensity
- Fantasy versus reality.

In comparing psychodynamic counselling with short-term psychodynamic psychotherapy it is difficult to sustain any of these differences as crucially discriminative and issues of power, authority and money (training cost) appear to play as important a role in this debate as practice (see Steenbarger, 1992, for a discussion of the issues involving brief therapy and Henry et al., 1994, for a thorough review of the psychoanalysis/ psychotherapy debate).

> Equating longer therapy with deeper or more substantive change, therapists frequently resist the use of brief treatments even when these have been

113

demonstrated to be effective and underestimate the effects of those brief interventions they do undertake. (Steenbarger, 1992)

The counselling psychologist represents a third position in this debate with respect to the application of the techniques of social science to assess the truth claims of particular hypotheses. The problem as both Frosh (1987) and Elliot (1994) discuss is that such social science positioning may assume particular philosophical and political premises; specifically the pathologizing that may occur from normative, behavioural and theoretical assumptions. However one contribution of counselling to psychology has been to develop and buttress the importance of the individual's sense of meaning (Mair, 1989). Frosh (1987) and Elliot (1994) discuss the very different philosophical and political premises from which particular brand loyalties derive. These loyalties typically turn upon the particular influences which are believed to underlie the formation and/or representation of self or subjectivity. The interested reader is referred to Elliot (1994). It is an amalgam of ideas from these theories as well as influences from brief intervention psychotherapy that have provided the basis for most ideas that are currently packaged as psychodynamic counselling in Britain (see Jacobs, 1988; Noonan, 1983). In this chapter we will attempt to represent these contrasts by considering how proponents of particular theories respond to core concepts in the psychodynamic field. In the best traditions of British liberal egalitarianism, psychodynamic counselling in Britain has often sought to present aspects of many positions, sometimes resulting in inconsistency and incoherence but also generating a richness and critical stance lacking in many psychodynamic therapy trainings. If, as we will argue, part of the counselling process is an appreciation of the multiplicity of narratives by which our lives may be represented an appreciation of the plurality of influences is an important part of counselling training. It is often reckoned that a field comes of age when it has its own journal, and psychodynamic counselling arrived in late 1994. It will be a matter of interest to see what influences are expressed within it.

In terms of importance (at least in terms of numbers of practising counsellors in the USA in particular) perhaps the most prevalent of the practices of psychodynamic counselling is what is called **psychoanalytic counselling** (see Patton and O'Meara, 1992, for review). This takes its sources from the work of Freud's daughter Anna, whose work highlighted the role of early interpersonal relationships via the mechanisms of ego growth and defence. It was left to Hartmann to attempt to describe the psychic structure of the ego and to argue that its development could result in a conflict-free adaptation to social reality. These ideas were taken up by the self psychologists Kohut and Kernberg, who argued that the child is symbiotically linked with adults and their experience and in effect initially borrows and subsequently internalizes notions of an object world from them in the form of self objects. This shifts the entire emphasis of psychodynamic thinking away from the fundamental impossibility of knowing represented by Freud's notion of the unconscious towards a vision of adaptation, social integration and normalcy (see Elliot, 1994). In this reading the task of both development and cure is fundamentally an educative one related to the development of a conscious ego and this leads to considerable overlap with cognitive therapy in, for instance, the work of Horowitz (1988) and Ryle (1982).

Psychodynamic counselling in Britain as represented by, for instance, the published texts of Noonan (1983) and Jacobs (1988), draws on Freud and the object relation theorists, in particular the work of Klein and Winnicot (see Elliot, 1994, for discussion). Emphasis is given to the vicissitudes of early development and the crucial role of early parenting in the formation of a sense of self and the other. In this vision human beings are relationship- or object-seeking, rather than as in Freud's vision of development, largely self-organized in terms of the satisfaction of libidinal drives. This leads to considerable interest by the counsellor in the difficulties of early childhood relationships with significant others, particularly the mother. In some hands this can become a narrative of the patient in terms of being a victim of parental oppression (see Alice Miller, 1983) and offers as a vision of cure the possibility of a reparative relationship with the therapist as the 'good enough' mother. The positioning of the counsellor can easily become deeply seductive (for both parties) and the problems for such an approach in practice centre on issues of separation and loss when the mutual fantasy comes to an end or is challenged by discussion of the end. Some brief therapists would argue that such an outcome, sometimes called a transference neurosis, can be avoided by structuring therapy in such a way as to minimize such regressive or symbiotic invitations. Clients are seen seated, not on the couch, the time limitations are spelt out from the beginning, and therapy is conducted at low intensity. The logical extension of this has been to reduce therapy to a single or double encounter, see Barkham (1989). None the less, there are many who would argue that within such a relationship the mix of supportive and challenging elements provides a perfect setting in which to rework the dysfunctional interpersonal dramas of childhood, and that surviving ending and frustration are fundamental to leading a full life in a postmodern world.

The third reading derives from an existential/phenomenological tradition and a re-reading of Freud which emphasizes the essential unknowability of the unconscious and the fragmented and incoherent conscious 'I' that seeks to deny this essential alienation by placing itself at the centre as speaking subject. In this the patient is encouraged to recognize that he or she is, in Heidegger's words, 'neurotic because they are in love with the truth', and that essential to existence in a post-modern world is toleration of difference, unknowability and the internal inconsistency of a self which is resultant from a multitude of influences. Although in the hands of Lacan the truth claims are meant to be universal, later exponents see it much more as description of particular socio-cultural angsts of the late twentieth century (see Grosz, 1990, for a review). In this view the parental drama is an important mythology of the late twentieth century which has extensive narrative power but which also easily entraps people into a victim position. Consistent with this view is the psychological evidence of the inconsistent predictive power of early traumas in later pathology, the importance of other family members, and feminist critiques of the positioning of women in the vision of the maternal. Phillips (1994) offers a more extended discussion and quotes a contemporary of Freud's, Karl Kraus, as describing Freud's acolytes as 'lustful rationalists' creating 'psychoanalysis', which with its truth claims, was 'the disease it sought to cure'.

A fourth influence comes from brief therapy where economic and situational (often military or related to emergencies) pressures have led to the development on all continents of psychodynamic therapeutic systems based on limited numbers of sessions (Peake et al., 1988; Koss and Shiang, 1994, who list 21 different variants for a full review). Early innovators, such as Ferenczi and indeed Freud himself, were concerned at the general inflationary spiral that has characterized psychoanalysis and sought via a more active role by the analyst to shorten the process. There has always been a considerable tension between what many analytic therapists might deem appropriate and what many patients are able to afford, tolerate or indeed want.

However, some analytic therapists have seen in the constraints of short-term working a reality-based discipline that permits a profound exploration of the transient and yet important aspects of human relations permitting 'experiential learning' or 'corrective emotional experiences', or 'core conflictual relationship themes' to be enacted and explored (Luborsky, 1993). Others have emphasized the motivational aspects of brief work and the anxiety-rousing quality of realizing that the offer is of strictly limited duration (Mann, 1982). Yet others have gone on to argue that anxiety constitutes an arena for change which should be generated both by situational factors and by therapists' confrontation of patients' patterns. Davanloo took this to its logical conclusion in arguing that it is possible in the dynamic interaction between patient and therapist to unlock unconscious patterns by relentlessly challenging patterns of defence, resistance and relating, although many have found the level of challenge and coercion hard to stomach (see Flegenheimer, 1982, for a review).

The particular melding of sources in counselling psychology training courses often seems motivated by a desire for an accommodation between counsellors and the psychotherapists (who often teach them), in which the long-term, deep, regressive and intensive is ceded to the experienced therapist and the short-term, low intensive (one or two sessions a week), focused crisis response is ceded to counsellors. A number of problems arise concerning this consensus, principal amongst which are: that research studies appear to show little difference between long- and short-term interventions; that maximal gains occur in the first eight sessions; that working in the short term in a focused way is considerably more tiring and demanding than 'long-term' therapy (Malan, 1979).

This notion that there might be particular demands or skills involved in brief therapy has been explicitly taken up by many authors, particularly those who have emphasized the planned ending or contract as an important reality-based element in containing and interpreting the fantasized elements of understanding and support (see Steenbarger, 1992). This raises a central issue for dynamic therapy in the notion of death and mortality where every ending is seen to signify the larger ending that awaits us all, and close attention is therefore given to the termination of sessions and the therapy as a whole as revealing of the kinds of defensive structures that patients mobilize to defend themselves against an awareness of mortality. Some would argue that it is only in a recognition of these defences that we can be truly alive, as is demonstrated by the quotation from Rank at the opening of this chapter.

The underlying theory of personality and motivation

Freudian theory attempted to resolve a considerable range of philosophical and psychological problems within a biological and positivistic framework, and as we have suggested above, component sub-theories have been taken up by the various theorists to the extent to which they meet their philosophical, political and emotional ends. Thus within the Freudian opus can be found theories of the structure and function of mind, the nature of child development, the development of gender differences, the nature of socialization. The exact relationship between these theories was a matter of concern to Freud and all those who have followed him. As with any prolific writer, Freud was often more concerned with developing new ideas rather than integrating them with the old, but he might also have warned against assuming that any singular theory of personality could catch the multiply determined motives – conscious and unconscious – of the human subject.

Thus a radical critique of this section heading might question the assumption concerning the singularity and predictability of traits or types, and the unitary self of psychology, and the power that derives from the normative assumptions of psychology (Foucault, 1961). A more radical psychodynamic reading would wish to challenge the centrality of the unitary self or *subject* and present such assumptions as a core and delusional construct of consciousness in which constructs of mastery and narrative coherence consistently attempt to present the world, self and others, as predictable and known. Motivation in this view derives from a desire to reimpose a sense of primordial singularity that derives from the human infant's loss of early fusion with its mother (Benvenuto, 1989) and anything that appears to hold out such a prospect is seen to be salient and desirable. In this view, then, an initial alienation leads to a life-long search for unity, and motivation is seen as an implicit function of the knowledge-seeking organism casting its neutral net over William James's sea of confusion. This contrasts with the alternative reading of drive theory where cognitive development is seen as a resultant of motivation. A fundamental challenge to most current therapeutic theories is to resolve the relative priorities to give to cognition and motivation. A more radical challenge might question the attempt to formulate such theories as a defence against the absurdity or uncertainty of human existence and thus as part of the construction of technological social myths of the late twentieth century.

If our categorization of the world is both learnt and hierarchical, the child (and its socialization) is seen by most psychodynamic theorists to be the author of the adult personality. In as far as this implies an entry into a public domain and shared language, developmental tasks are fundamentally about the repression of difference and conflict. Notions of personality may serve to map out the trajectory and history of these losses. This is not to deny the importance of development but rather to emphasize that what is of interest to the therapist is the utility in the patient's current drama that their recollections and responses play. The stage on which such recollections and responses will be marshalled and played out may well depend on the particular cognitive style and developmental achievements, but whether these constitute stable types or more transient adaptive traits is unclear in psychodynamic theory, although it is worth noting that tests such as Myers-Briggs or Eysenck draw on concepts that at least share a common signifier with those in Jungian and Freudian theories (see Deary and Matthews, 1993, for a review). Although it is difficult to define any general theories of personality or motivation which are common to all those who might describe themselves as psychodynamic, some terms do seem to be used in common parlance.

The notion of **depth** which often appears to equate with the hypothesized age of developmental arrest or difficulty is fundamental to both object relations and ego psychology. This raises a further shibboleth of much psychoanalytic thinking in the concept of **transference** in which early patterns of fantasy and behaviour (classically unconscious but latterly in some schools both conscious and unconscious) are re-enacted with the therapist and are dealt with by interpretation of the underlying conflicts which led to the arrest in development and which are being re-experienced in the current relationship. There is some consensus amongst object relations-influenced therapists that transference interpretations are not as helpful in short-term work and that sustaining a focus on present behaviour and minimizing regressive invitations and negative transference is preferable, although others would prefer to structure the session around the client rather than the theory. Further, for research purposes so many complex aspects of interpersonal relatedness have become compressed into the single term transference that it has lost much of its utility. It has therefore been replaced by more specific terms (see below).

The notions of depth and transference in the hands of many counsellors become comforting theoretical crutches in the formulation of the relationship and enable the counsellor to treat the client as an arrested infant, avoiding those elements of the interaction between two adults, such as sexuality, power, money and professional convenience, which appear to trouble most therapists (see Langs, 1986, for a discussion of the defensive potential of these terms in protecting the therapist's position and power). The complex inter-relationship between unconscious intra-personal modes of relating and conscious, external, interpersonal, collaboration is an area which separates many analytic therapists, who emphasize the primacy of the former, from psychodynamically oriented counsellors, who tend to work with an amalgam of both.

This raises a second key concept, that of the **unconscious**, and with it notions of **repression** and psychodynamic theories of memory. There is fundamental agreement that people are often unable to recall aspects of their past or current behaviour. The particular claims of psychoanalysis are that this forgetting is motivated (it is not simply that painful things are forgotten but that even the forgetting is forgotten) and that repressed memories are subject within the unconscious to mechanisms of displacement and deferral characterized by metaphoric and metonymic (primary) processes different from the inductive and deductive logic of conscious awareness (secondary process), particularly in relationship to traumatic or conflicted events (see Erdelyi, 1984). Many of these claims have been assessed experimentally and the picture that emerges appears rather more complex. Generally trauma *per se* does not cause amnesia, although adults and children will often actively attempt to avoid discussing it. These processes appear more akin to denial or disavowal than repression. What does seem clear from experiment is that memory is radically reconstructive in the light of current salient meanings, rather than veridical (Laplanche, 1992). This has raised particular anxieties with respect to **false memory syndrome** where patients or their relatives have claimed that memories of abuse or childhood trauma are fabrications encouraged by the therapist. In many respects the controversy has echoes of the earlier one where Freud decided that the reports of infantile sexual abuse by his female patients generally represented not actual abuse but the operations of imagination and fantasy in the face of unresolved childhood internal conflicts. The jury is still out but it is experimentally possible to generate false memories and hypnotists (Wagstaff, 1981) have long known of the confabulatory potential of patients to suggestion. What is important to the psychodynamic vision is not that it has a dogmatic position but rather that it invites us to consider how our current narratives and recollections act to serve a particular, singular and ultimately entrapping vision of ourselves. It also throws into question the function of rationality; there seems increasing evidence that we construct a world of meaning based upon saliency and convenience but then report its construction as representing the processes of logic (see Sutherland, 1992, for review).

In psychodynamic terms, entrapping responses are termed **defences**.

> An overall definition of a defence is an individual's automatic psychological response to internal or external stressors or emotional conflict. Defences generally act automatically, that is without conscious effort. . . . Character traits are in part made up of specific defences which individuals use repetitively in diverse situations. Individuals tend to specialize using a prototypical set of defences across a variety of stressors . . . defences affect adaptation . . . there is a clear hierarchy of defences in relation to the overall adaptiveness of each one . . . the least adaptive protect the individual from awareness of stressors and/or associated conflicts at the price of constricting awareness, freedom to choose and flexibility in maximising positive outcomes. When defences are most adaptive, they maximise the expression and gratification of wishes and needs, minimise negative consequences, and provide a sense of freedom of choice. (Perry, 1993)

Symptoms in this account are compromises which serve to express some aspects of the original conflict whilst keeping others at bay. Freud's idea of defences was developed by a number of workers to include responses to external as well as internal stimuli, and to incorporate the idea that it was the fantasy induced by a stimulus not the stimulus itself that was crucial.

One important concept that emerges from the idea of defence is that of patient **compliance**. As we have hinted extensively in this prologue, although psychodynamic theorists have not always been as aware of it as Freud was, this issue is crucial to an understanding of the possibilities of

120

cure and the extent to which the task of therapy is compliance to the normalizing authority of the therapist. If what ails people is precisely how the demands of society impact upon their lives to define them in ways that deny their difference and diversity it may well be that the body and symptoms become a method of both expressing dis-ease but at the same time of distancing the self from its implication by declaring one's problems medical. Psychodynamics is often torn between a desire to hitch-hike on the status and esteem of the medical model of mental illness and the more radical deconstructive challenge that suggests that we are trapped precisely by a vision of ourselves that splits off unacceptable parts or declares them alien from our being. Whilst the record of psychodynamic therapy is no better than any other therapeutic system in terms of cure, we might suggest that its ability consistently to reopen and challenge the premises of illness and symptom places it in a unique position: as one therapist when faced by a long re-iteration of symptoms said, 'Talk about something else'. The problem is that considerable career investment by both patients and physicians in a medical system is profoundly challenged by such a suggestion. Not surprisingly, if the measures of success are to do with symptom reduction, social acceptance or compliance, psychodynamics can show no particular benefit and the benefits it might show lie outside the arena of conventional psychological and medical variables.

The assessment process

The process of analytic therapy presupposes the ability to engage in a certain kind of reflexive conversation, involving both the ability to recognize the 'as if' quality, as in 'it is as if you are my father, etc.', and to tolerate the imposition by the therapist of boundaries concerning time, attendance, payment and the like. In addition it may require the ability to tolerate levels of anti-social behaviour on the part of the therapist in not answering or in failing to respond politely but rather in insisting that all the patient's comments intended or otherwise can be understood to be relational and positional. Not surprisingly high drop-out rates have been widely reported and short-term interventions in this view are appropriate to only a limited group of relatively 'robust' clients (Malan, 1979). Other schools have emphasized the notion of depth and claim a continuum with counselling and short-term therapy best addressing issues that derive from relatively late on in childhood development of an Oedipal nature (Yorke, 1988). This notion of developmental arrests has led some workers to propose, after Klein, that particular periods of childhood are characterized by different cognitive coping processes and that these arrests are

Psychotic	Immature	Image distorting	Neurotic	Mature
Delusional projection	Avoidance	Splitting of others' images	Displacement	Sublimation
	Acting out		Dissociation	Altruism
Psychotic denial distinction	Neurotic denial	Splitting of self-images	Asceticism	Humour
	Fantasy	Devaluation	Reaction formation	Anticipation
	Projection	Omnipotence		Suppression
			Repression	
	Hypochondriasis	Manic denial	Rationalization	
	Passive aggression	Bland denial	Undoing	
		Projective identification	Isolation	
			Intellectualization	
		Primitive idealization		

Figure 5.1 *Taxonomy of Defences (Perry, 1993)*

represented in adult life by particular defences. Some 42 possible mechanisms of defence have been described.

This has led to the formulation of hierarchies of defences based on developmental models and to the assessment and categorization of patients in terms of the defences manifested in presenting sessions. In as far as these categorizations turn upon particular theories they are subject to all the caveats described so far. They do represent a bridge between psychiatric and psychodynamic classificatory systems and the terms psychotic, neurotic, borderline, mature and immature that derive from them have very much entered popular parlance, albeit that in practice they seem less easy to apply.

The view that ego mechanisms are hierarchically organized, proposed originally by Semrad, has been tested in a number of studies that group defences into four (or five if we include image distorting which subsumes both borderline and narcissistic) categories along a dimension from least to most adaptive – psychotic, immature, neurotic and mature. These categories are characterized by specific defences (Figure 5.1) and inversely correlated with measures of global health from psychotic to mature (see Perry, 1993). The problem for such categorical schemes with their medical overtones is that they label the patient and offer the marginalized prospect of a career as a patient and position the counsellor or therapist as expert.

In our experience the issues of assessment turn not so much on any hypothesized madness in the patient but on the ability of the therapist and organization to tolerate certain kinds of behaviour or defence, specifically impulsive or violent behaviour, failure to attend or to attend in a fit state (focused around addictive behaviours of a variety of kinds) and the production of discourses that profoundly challenge or ignore the therapist. Such people have often been termed psychotic, borderline or narcissistic. Interestingly these are precisely the 'heart-sink' patients who are often allocated to neophyte counsellors in public sector settings, on the grounds that more experienced therapists and physicians prefer not to work with them!

What does change mean and how is it brought about?

As with all matters psychodynamic, there are considerable disagreements as to what might constitute change and as to how such change is to be achieved. There seems some consensus that early difficulties in parenting lead to developmental arrests that in turn lead to currently inappropriate modes of responding and thinking. Major differences arise as to whether these problems of thought, speech or response are best addressed directly as symptoms, or whether constitutive elements of early learning need to be addressed first or as well. Many dynamic therapists would argue that correction or re-education alone is not enough for lasting change; what is required is a reparative experience with the therapist in terms of reparenting, or of enacting previously learnt behaviours under similar affective conditions but achieving a different cathartic outcome. This raises an important debate between the ideas of enactment and analysis. In the latter the task is to bring into consciousness by interpretation repressed material and to thus allow new and more adult defensive structures to be mobilized and in turn analysed. In this vision the client's responses and use of the therapist, in the absence of knowledge or information concerning the therapist, allows both parties to hypothesize as to the structure of the client's inner world. This vision of the therapist as somewhat distant is, as already discussed, mostly a fiction and supportive comments seem part of all therapeutic practices. None the less the notions of therapy as anxiety-inducing, different and fundamentally unknowable are common to many theories of short-term work as a motivating factor in uncovering buried conflicts and unconscious processes.

What these approaches take for granted is the nature of the subject of self that is to be the end project of the therapeutic enterprise, thus considerable bodies of research exist in short-term dynamic therapy concerning client and therapist variables that are prognostic of good outcome (see below).

The nature of the relationship between counselling psychologist and individual client

The pressures of training courses and developments in the registration of counsellors, counselling psychologists and psychotherapists have led to an intense interest in the defining and discriminating factors that separate and demarcate different schools of therapy. The academization of therapy has also led to increasing intellectual scrutiny of the counselling process which has in turn led to attempts to formulate counselling psychology in terms of identifiable skills and practices. Much of this work in the arena of psychodynamic counselling psychology has been conducted in America where the premises of ego psychology, and in particular the idea of a reality-based collaboration between counsellor and client, the so-called ego or working alliance, have been more acceptable. In Britain the idea of such a collaboration has more often been seen as an example of unresolved positive transference resulting from the unconscious projection of the client's idealizing fantasy and therefore to be interpreted rather than studied or encouraged.

Attempts to study the working or ego alliance have led to the development of a number of research instruments (see Horvath et al., 1993, for a review), and a good deal of work has been done attempting to map the changes in client and counsellor perceptions across a series of sessions. It is probably premature as yet to come to anything more than tentative conclusions but some of the results seem to fly in the face of popular beliefs. Studies by Bordin (1976) and by Luborsky et al. (1975) appeared to show that what was crucial was not the therapist's attitude but the client's perception of it. Subsequent studies by Safran et al. (1990) and others suggested that this conclusion needed to be modified to track the changes that occurred across sessions and that the working alliance and client therapist attitudes might follow a cyclic form. Thus Horvath et al. (1993) suggest that there may be an initial honeymoon phase peaking at or around session three where the client develops attitudes toward the therapist based upon the client's perceptions of the relevancy and potency of the interventions offered. This involves the therapist being able to communicate to the client the important link between therapy-specific tasks and the overall goals of treatment and to maintain an awareness of the client's commitment to these activities, and to intervene effectively if resistance is present. A major difficulty here is the disparity between the client's desire for relief from pain and symptoms in the shortest possible order and the therapist's awareness of the longer-term plan of therapy and the necessity of delayed gratification.

In the second phase after alliance building the presence of dysfunctional interpersonal relationship schemas reactivated in therapy needs to be challenged by the therapist, which leads to an increase in the client's perception of having sympathy withdrawn and an increase in negative feelings about the therapy and therapist. If these issues are taken up, the argument is that the therapeutic alliance can be repaired ready for another cycle of challenge. There seems to be some evidence to support this contention in that skilled therapists appeared more attentive to timing of interpretations and were better at retaining clients. Equally strength of commitment to the shared goals of therapy appears to be a good predictor of positive outcome. Interestingly there was little evidence that interpretation *per se* or reference to the relationship improved outcome; what seemed critical was a close attention to the client's best interest, although relationships in which no challenge occurred would be simply collusive with the dysfunctional schema of the patient. The problem with all such generalizations is that they assume patients are in a common presenting state whereas the evidence on diagnosis suggests that for some patients a very extended period of alliance building may be necessary before any challenge can be tolerated. It is a fine calculation as to when collaboration shades into collusion.

Common to a number of recent formulations, then (Luborsky, 1993; Steenbarger, 1992), is the idea that counsellor behaviour may have to change to meet certain client and situational demands. Thus Steenbarger attempts to integrate research findings on brief therapy proposing a three-stage process and a changing pattern of counsellor behaviour as a result. To put the claim in simple common-sense terms, initially you have to listen carefully to understand what is being said and this induces a sense of understanding and concern in the other. During this process certain discrepancies and inconsistencies or repetitions become clear which can be discussed and challenged. This makes demands on the client to be different which they respond to more or less positively, posing problems as to how to integrate these changes into their own and others' visions of them, especially in the absence of the therapist's support. Not surprisingly many of the processes of change can be shown to go on after the cessation of therapy, which places the notion of short-term therapy into a different perspective. Despite claims to the contrary these changes can be shown to hold up for sustained periods after therapy has ceased but appear to do so most effectively where the ending has been planned and the problems of isolation discussed. Clients commonly discuss carrying an internalized model of the therapist within them.

An alternative view often described as phenomenological or existential is that counselling is fundamentally an ethical activity in which the therapist seeks to 'meet with' the other as profoundly as possible by entering into an ethical relationship (Gans, 1988). What is in question is the understanding and experience of what is relationally possible between two people. The therapist's offer is to monitor and report whenever they sense that this relating is checked by the therapist's inability or difficulty, and consistently to wonder as to the particular forms and practices being mutually employed. What this poses is a radical challenge to the expertise of the therapist which is profoundly uncomfortable to the patient because of the challenge to the projection of authority. It challenges both patient's and therapist's notions of expertise and questions the moral force of the particular value systems both may espouse and is therefore radically uncomfortable for anyone seeking the comfort of received authority or wisdom. It does acknowledge the extraordinary complexity of the human mind and our endless pursuit of a knowing which seeks to make the world predictable; this all too often leads to an ossification of meanings in which we become trapped within our own narrative closure.

Family, group and organizational applications

Although psychodynamic theories are fundamentally about the formation of singular selves, both Freud and Jung included the collective group unconscious in their formulations (de Mare, 1972). There is a large body of literature devoted to what happens when aggregations of selves collide in differing contexts. Broadly speaking, family, group and organizational applications of psychodynamic theory have become entities in their own right and have not been subsumed into counselling psychology, at least not in this country. Indeed to some extent these applications remain opposed to individual ways of working as they represent a different view: of society as a single entity as opposed to an aggregation of individual selves that is often assumed in individual work. If one believes in the multiplicity of narratives running through human discourse, family, group and organizational applications of psychodynamic theory offer arenas for airing these narratives and therefore the registration of difference. Although the validity of extrapolating models of early development to generalized models of society is open to question, these applications challenge individual counselling's assumption of the primacy of singular selves with an alternative vision from sociology, of society as singular, which has echoes in the deconstructive movement. In emphasizing the homeostatic and causal feedback loops between the internal and external, and between the individual and the group, family, group and organizational therapists have often emphasized the circularity of cause and effect and criticized the linear formulations of individual psychotherapists. However, in Freud's notion of the idea of primary and secondary gains the idea certainly exists that symptoms can serve not merely as the representation of repressed material, but are also socially functional. This leads to a new class of question concerning what may be obscured by virtue of an individual's or group's obsession with a particular issue. Such a view may offer a radical critique of the current obsession with 'symptom' support groups (anorexia, alcohol, etc.) in that whilst it may mobilize people's political power it may also serve to obscure in silence issues of difference. In the group analytic tradition of Foulkes (1964) where the group itself is seen to be its own psychotherapist such a selection would be seen as contra-indicated in creating a monologic and obsessed therapist. The counselling psychologist in espousing belief in the importance of the falsification of theories may be uniquely placed to recognize the heuristic utility of identification and group compliance in creating an identity, but also to see the loss that may result from the failure to address issues of difference. The effectiveness of these two modes of symptom reduction versus individuation is a subject for empirical testing, but is also a function of personality and developmental issues.

This raises an important contribution of counselling psychology as it brings to the debate on individuation a raft of empirical research. It is perhaps one of the ironies of psychodynamic practice that it has in its family, group and organizational applications emphasized the importance of context and group fantasy which are often invaluable insights into understanding the ways that institutional influences are encoded in the work of the counselling psychologist.

For reviews of these applications see: Hoffman (1981) for family therapy applications; de Mare (1972) for group therapy applications; Hinshelwood (1979) for organizational applications.

Research evidence about effectiveness

Research on the outcome of psychodynamic therapy has been reviewed in two celebrated papers by Luborsky and his associates (Luborsky et al., 1975; Luborsky et al., 1993) which take their title from the caucus race in *Alice in Wonderland* of which the dodo says: 'Everyone has won and all have won prizes'. This refers to the number of celebrated meta review studies which show that no particular method or theoretical stance is particularly advantaged with respect to any other (see Miller et al., 1993, for review). Luborsky summarizes his own study of research rigorously assessed to meet 19 criteria as follows: 'group versus individual; time-limited versus time-unlimited; client-centred versus other psychotherapies; behaviour therapy versus other therapy; and dynamic therapy versus other therapies . . . the main trend is the non-significant difference effect' (Luborsky et al., 1975). There was a tendency for psychotherapies with

	Measured at termination	Measured at follow-up
Dynamic therapies better	1	1
Non-significant difference	14	5
Other psychotherapies better	2	2

Source: Adapted from Luborsky et al., 1993

Table 5.1   *Results of meta analysis*

medication to be better than therapy alone, and an overwhelming superiority for psychotherapy versus no psychotherapy.

In its psychoanalytic incarnation psychodynamic therapy proposes five or six times a week therapy for several years as constituting a minimum commitment, with an investment of tens of thousands of pounds. The prospect that a few sessions of cognitive analytic therapy can achieve the same result invites at best a sharp intake of breath and at worst an action under the Trades Descriptions Act! As we have argued, psychodynamic counselling makes no such time or frequency demands, but there is in the field a creeping tendency toward the belief that more is better and, as we have seen, deeper. There are a few studies that address this issue although the vast majority of studies have been reported as short-term work whether it be five or fifty sessions.

Table 5.1 summarizes Luborsky's results. It offers no satisfaction to any claim of the superiority of dynamic treatment versus any other kind and it would seem that the dodo was correct, as least in this race. Smith, Glass and Miller (1980) summarized their finding by saying that 'A typical therapy client is better off than 75% of untreated individuals'.

A variety of explanations are offered for these results. The most obvious argument proposed by protagonists of the psychodynamic view is that these results are relevant only to short-term therapy and that studies of longer-term therapy would be more impressive. Bacharach et al. (1991) summarized the results from six studies of psychoanalysis with a total N of over 500 and claimed improvements were in the 60–90 per cent range which appears to be comparable to but not better than other treatments, although these were not comparison studies. There is some evidence to show that psychotherapy plus a medical treatment does better than medicine alone in a variety of psychosomatic treatments and that this reduces calls on medical resources; panic attacks may be best dealt with by cognitive therapies and mild phobias by behaviour therapy, whilst schizophrenics benefit from family therapy and social skills training.

There are numerous caveats in a field plagued by methodological difficulties, but there it may well be that if psychodynamic therapy is to make claims for any special status it will have to look elsewhere than to empirical research and outcome studies to justify them.

Whilst valuable contributions have been made by research in removing some of the mystique of the counselling process – it has, for instance, been possible to produce training protocols that pay attention to research findings and that improve the therapeutic outcomes for counsellors who previously seemed to lose clients and to produce rather low working alliance ratings – a danger is that a skills-based approach may assist counsellors to improve client retention in the short term at the cost of development in later stages of expertise (see Skovholt and Ronnestad, 1992, for discussion). Thus computer instanciations of expert systems have gone some way to emphasize the importance of tacit of fuzzy logic calculations. It is our concern that to be human is to be able to tolerate enormous confusion and to make and correct huge inductive and deductive leaps. The question therefore is not one of learning to act the part but of being it. But what might it mean to be human? There have been countless attempts to specify the critical processes in operational terms but a brief examination of English literature might suggest that the complexity of an answer continues to provide a creative source for generation after generation.

Rather than further review research attempts to specify the crucial processes in therapy, we wish to suggest that the therapeutic task is to be able to sustain without panic, and even with it, the unknown or painfully familiar feelings that are engendered by the presence of the *other*, to come to accept that we are always at the mercy of the other because we are created by them and not vice versa. This view is so subversive to the *subject* of much psychological investigation, and to the rationalist and positivistic positions prevalent in the West, that it tends to engender powerful opposition. To be other than is desired by the client, to frustrate their demands to make us into what they want, is so contrary to the notions of ethical committees and customer's charters that it is often far simpler for both parties to talk about symptoms, or lapse into reparative fantasies of reparenting or take up the authoritative stance of the healer. The phrases 'to give people the space to start experiencing themselves', 'to slouch toward Bethlehem with them' are ways people have tried to articulate this in the literature. But what this means operationally is presumably to emphasize the uniqueness of the relationship, which can only be unique if counsellor and counsellee can both bear the feelings that acknowledging difference involves. What claims such an enterprise can expect to make upon the public purse is unclear; there is little room in our current visions of efficiency and cure for not knowing. It is relevant that the authors have racked up at least ten years of personal therapy between them and regard it as time and money well spent. But in the celebrated words of Mandy Rice Davis, 'they would say that wouldn't they'.

Psychology has always struggled with such ideographic data to say something of generality, failing often to recognize the essential paradox inherent in doing so. The situation often seems not dissimilar to the training of Buddhist monks who demand of the master that he tells them the secret of mastery. He tolerates but never answers until the monks cease finally to question and can accept there is no answer other than the process of living itself, albeit reflexively. In an age of technological fixes this is never likely to be an attractive proposition in the West but we believe it should find some room for articulation in the processes of counselling and training.

In the words of one researcher, Luborsky, after summarizing all the current studies and showing no conclusive difference in therapeutic outcome between different therapeutic interventions:

> *Question*: Don't you feel, despite all the evidence for the non-significant difference effect, that dynamic therapies have some special virtues to offer that are still not well enough recognised?
> *Answer*: . . . Yes. The studies have not yet dealt with possible long-term benefits, nor . . . with the distinction between changes in symptoms and changes in general adjustment. (Luborsky et al., 1993: 511)

Or in the words of Alan Bennett, 'there is always a little bit in the corner that you can't get out'. It may well be that one can achieve the same behavioural outcome via a range of means, most parents of small children will have run the gamut from bribery, through seduction to coercion, to diversion many times in an average day and will report varied degrees of success with each of these methods. The choice of method will be seen to turn on the familial dynamics, social context and the personalities of the participants. One explanation of the widespread adherence to psychodynamic methods as at least part of an eclectic mix is that it fits well into the dominantly, white, middle-class presuppositions of its protagonists. We would argue that there is nothing inherently wrong with therapist comfort other than that it requires an awareness of the counsellor's positioning, power and needs in its exercise. Psychodynamic counselling in its dogmatic claims is as authoritarian and wrong-headed as any 100-year-old piece of positivism is likely to be; in its radical and subversive deconstruction of the unitary subject it profoundly challenges many of the sacred cows of late twentieth-century Western mythology. As such it deserves to be part of the armoury of any therapist. We may in the face of the other's pain and need decide to accept the offer of authority and cure them, but at least we can seek to defend ourselves against the seductions of expertise and charisma inherent in the process, and hope to be braver tomorrow.

References

Bacharach, H., Galatzer-Levy, R., Slolnikoff, A. and Waldron, S. (1991) 'On the efficacy of psychoanalysis', *Journal of the American Psychoanalytic Association*, 39: 871–916.

Barkham, M. (1989) 'Exploratory therapy in two plus one sessions, rationale for a brief psychotherapy model', *British Journal of Psychotherapy*, 6: 79–86.

Benvenuto, B. (1989) 'Once upon a time: the infant in Lacanian theory', *British Journal of Psychotherapy*, 5(3): 409–22.

Bergin, A.E. and Garfield, S.L. (1994) *Handbook of Psychotherapy and Behavior Change*, 4th edn. New York: Wiley.

Bordin, E.S. (1976) 'The generalizability of the psychoanalytic concept of the working alliance', *Psychotherapy: Theory, Research and Practice*, 16: 252–60.

Deary, I.J. and Matthews, G. (1993) 'Personality traits are alive and well', *The Psychologist*, 6: 299–311.

Elliot, A. (1994) *Psychoanalytic Theory*. Oxford: Blackwell.

Erdelyi, M.H. (1984) *Psychoanalysis: Freud's Cognitive Psychology*. San Francisco: W.H. Freeman.

Flegenheimer, W.V. (1982) *Techniques of Brief Psychotherapy*. London: Jason Aronson.

Foucault, M. (1961) *Madness and Civilization*. London: Tavistock.

Foulkes, S.H. (1964) *Therapeutic Group Analysis*. London: Allen and Unwin.

Frosh, S. (1987) *The Politics of Psychoanalysis*. London: Macmillan.

Gans, S. (1988) 'Levinas and Pontalis: meeting the other as in a dream', in R. Bernasconi and D. Wood (eds), *The Provocation of Levinas*. London: Routledge.

Grosz, E. (1990) *Jacques Lacan. A Feminist Introduction*. London: Routledge.

Henry, W.P., Strupp, H.H., Schacht, T.E. and Gaston, L. (1994) 'Psycho-dynamic approaches', in A.E. Bergin and S.L. Garfield (eds), *Handbook of Psychotherapy and Behavior Change*, 4th edn. New York: Wiley.

Hinshelwood, R. (1979) *Therapeutic Communities*. London: Routledge and Kegan Paul.

Hoffman, L. (1981) *Foundations of Family Therapy*. New York: Basic Books.

Horowitz, M.J. (1988) *Introduction to Psychodynamics*. New York: Basic Books.

Horvath, A., Gaston, L. and Luborsky, L. (1993) 'The therapeutic alliance and its measures', in N.E. Miller et al. (eds), *Psychodynamic Treatment Research*. New York: Basic Books.

Jacobs, M. (1988) *Psychodynamic Counselling in Action*. London: Sage.

Koss, M.P. and Shiang, J. (1994) 'Research on brief psychotherapy', in A.E. Bergin and S.L. Garfield (eds), *Handbook of Psychotherapy and Behavior Change*, 4th edn. New York: Wiley.

Langs, R. (1986) *Madness and Cure*. New York: Jason Aronson.

Laplanche, J. (1992) 'Interpretation between determinism and hermeneutics: a restatement of the problem', *International Journal of Psycho-Analysis*, 73: 429–45.

Luborsky, L. (1993) 'How to maximise the curative factors in dynamic psychotherapy', in N.E. Miller et al. (eds), *Psychodynamic Treatment Research*. New York: Basic Books.

Luborsky, L., Singer, B. and Luborsky, E. (1975) 'Comparative studies of psychotherapies: is it true that everybody has won and all must have prizes?', *Archives of General Psychiatry*, 32: 995–1008.

Luborsky, L., Diguer, L., Luborsky, E., Singer, B., Dickter, D. and Schmidt, K.A. (1993) 'The efficacy of dynamic psychotherapies: is it true that everybody has won and all must have prizes?', in N.E. Miller et al. (eds), *Psychodynamic Treatment Research*. New York: Basic Books.

Mair, M. (1989) *Between Psychology and Psychotherapy: a Poetics of Experience*. London: Routledge.

Malan, D. (1979) *Individual Psychotherapy and the Science of Psychodynamics*. London: Butterworth.

Mann, J. (1982) *A Casebook in Time-limited Psychotherapy*. New York: McGraw-Hill.

de Mare, P.B. (1972) *Perspectives in Group Psychotherapy*. London: George Allen and Unwin.

Miller, A. (1983) *For Your Own Good*. London: Virago.

Miller, N.E., Luborsky, L., Barber, J.P. and Docherty, J.P. (eds) (1993) *Psychodynamic Treatment Research*. New York: Basic Books.

Noonan, E. (1983) *Counselling Young People*. London: Methuen.

Oatley, K. (1992) *Mind the Slip*. Cambridge: Cognitive Theories of the Emotions.

Patton, M.J. and O'Meara, N.M. (1992) *Psychoanalytic Counselling*. New York: Wiley.

Peake, T.H., Borduin, C.M. and Archer, R.R. (1988) *Brief Psychotherapies*. London: Sage.

Perry, J.C. (1993) 'Defences and their effects', in N.E. Miller et al. (eds), *Psychodynamic Treatment Research*. New York: Basic Books.

Phillips, A. (1994) *On Flirtation*. London: Faber.

Ryle, A. (1982) *Psychotherapy: a Cognitive Integration of Theory and Practice*. London: Academic Press.

Safran, J.D., Crocker, P., McMain, S. and Murray, P. (1990) 'The therapeutic alliance rupture as a therapy event for empirical investigation', *Psychotherapy*, 27: 154–65.

Skovholt, T.M. and Ronnestad, M.H. (1992) *The Evolving Professional Self: Stages and Themes in Therapist and Counsellor Development*. Chichester: Wiley.

Smith, M.L., Glass, G.V. and Miller, T.I. (1980) *The Benefits of Psychotherapy*. Baltimore, MD: Johns Hopkins University Press.

Steenbarger, B.N. (1992) 'Toward science – practice integration in brief counseling and therapy', *The Counselling Psychologist*, 20(3): 403–50.

Sutherland, S. (1992) *Irrationality, the Enemy Within*. London: Constable.

Wagstaff, G.F. (1981) *Hypnosis Compliance and Belief*. Brighton: Harvester.

Yorke, C. (1988) 'Some thoughts on pre-Oedipal development – a "contemporary Freudian" view', *British Journal of Psychotherapy*, 4(3): 436–45.

6

The Humanistic Paradigm

John McLeod

The use of the concept of 'paradigm' to describe different approaches in counselling psychology derives from the work of the philosopher of science Thomas Kuhn (1962), who argued that knowledge is created through the collective activity of communities of scientists. A 'scientific community' comprises not only theory and concepts, but also a wide range of shared experiences such as exposure to similar types of training, readership of a common set of books and journals, and participation at conferences. This notion of a community of like-minded inquirers matches very well the conditions surrounding the origins of humanistic psychology. In the early 1950s, particularly in North America, academic psychology was dominated by behaviourism, and psychotherapy was dominated by psychoanalysis. However, at the same time, a growing number of psychologists were becoming convinced that neither behaviourism nor psychoanalysis could adequately account for the key questions of human experience. Many of these psychologists had been influenced by the European philosophical traditions of phenomenology and existentialism (Misiak and Sexton, 1973). Gradually, members of this group began to develop a new professional and academic identity: humanistic psychology.

The standard-bearers of the humanistic psychology movement were the Association for Humanistic Psychology, founded in 1962, and the *Journal for Humanistic Psychology*, founded in 1961. The intellectual scope and aims of humanistic psychology were summarized in the first editorial of that journal in the following terms:

> The *Journal of Humanistic Psychology* is being founded by a group of psychologists and professional men and women from other fields who are interested in those human capacities and potentialities that have no systematic place either in positivistic or behavioristic theory or in classical psychoanalytic theory, e.g., creativity, love, growth, organism, basic need-gratification, self-actualization, higher values, ego-transcendence, objectivity, autonomy, identity, responsibility, psychological health, etc. This approach can also be characterised by the writings of Goldstein, Fromm, Horney, Rogers, Maslow, Allport, Angyal, Buhler, Moustakas, etc., as well as by certain aspects of the writings of Jung, Adler, and the psychoanalytic ego-psychologists. (Sutich, 1961: viii–ix)

This definition captures the central themes of the humanistic paradigm. First, it is an approach that is not based solely in psychology but also draws significantly from the 'other fields' of humanism such as literature, the arts and philosophy. Secondly, there is an emphasis on optimal functioning rather than pathology. Thirdly, there is a conceptualization of the person as an individual 'self'. Fourthly, it does not employ a single clear theoretical focus, but instead relies on a loosely connected network of ideas. Finally, there is a sense of a set of ideas and practices that exist in opposition to the mainstream, that find their identity through *not* being psychoanalysis or behaviourism rather than constituting a positive alternative that might seek to replace them.

The period since the inauguration of the 'third force' of humanistic psychology has seen major fluctuations in its popularity and influence. In the 1960s and 1970s, humanistic psychology was in tune with the spirit of economic expansion and personal freedom. The economic recession of the 1980s, accompanied by a demand for counselling and psychotherapy to be more accountable and problem-focused, resulted in a lessening of interest in humanistic approaches. Smith (1982) and Giorgi (1987) described this period as representing a crisis in humanistic psychology. More recently, however, there has been a resurgence in the humanistic orientation, with a steady growth in training opportunities, theoretical development and research activity.

The humanistic paradigm can be characterized as consisting of a number of discrete approaches to counselling psychology, each of which represents a distinct domain of theory, research and practice, but nevertheless draws on a core set of philosophical and psychological assumptions. The most important of these approaches are client-centred or person-centred counselling and psychotherapy, Gestalt therapy, and experiential psychotherapy. There are several other therapeutic approaches, such as existential therapy and the various transpersonal theories, that overlap significantly with humanistic psychology and therapy. Well-known and widely used models such as transactional analysis and rational-emotive therapy have also been informed and influenced by humanistic theory and practice. However, for the purpose of this chapter, the humanistic paradigm will be discussed through examples drawn from the three approaches that most faithfully reflect the philosophy of humanism: person-centred, Gestalt and experiential.

The humanistic approach, as a relatively recent addition to the field of psychological therapies, has been dominated by the theories and teachings of two major figures: Carl Rogers, the founder of client-centred therapy, and Fritz Perls, founder of Gestalt therapy. The key ideas of these 'first generation' humanistic writers are well known and widely available (see Clarkson, 1989; Clarkson and Mackewn, 1993; Mearns and Thorne,

1988; Thorne, 1992). While acknowledging the enormous contribution made by Rogers and Perls, it is also important to recognize that in recent years a 'second generation' of humanistic theorists has emerged, represented by Goff Barrett-Lennard, Eugene Gendlin, Les Greenberg, Erving Polster, David Rennie and Laura Rice.

In practice, humanistic therapy usually takes place either in one-to-one, hour-long sessions, or in groups led by a facilitator. Most humanistic practitioners rely on dialogue as a means of helping clients to explore the meaning of their troubles, although some will also employ enactments (such as Gestalt two-chair work), exercises (such as guided fantasy) or expressive media (clay, paint, voice, dance) to facilitate the therapeutic process. Humanistic counselling and psychotherapy has been used effectively in time-limited mode, and with couples and families.

The underlying theory of personality and motivation

Any counselling psychologist applying a humanistic approach in work with clients will draw upon a set of core theoretical assumptions and therapeutic principles. The basic theory of the humanistic approach, its theory of personality or concept of the person, constitutes what Maddi (1989) has called a **fulfilment** model. The 'root metaphor' of the paradigm is that of **growth**. The person is seen as striving to create, achieve or become. The need for fulfilment, actualization or transcendence is regarded as a fundamental human motive. This image of the person stands in contrast to the conflict model implicit in psychodynamic theory, and the problem-management or coping model implicit in behaviourism. Fulfilment and growth, from a humanistic point of view, are achieved through the search for meaning in life. The centrality of meaning-making and meaning-creation in humanistic psychology places it in the constructionist movement in social science (Gergen, 1985). The aims and scope of humanistic psychology are exemplified in the book of readings edited by Bugental (1967).

Within the broad framework supplied by the fulfilment model, humanistic theory makes sense of human experience through concepts of **process, reflexivity, self, organism** and **experiencing**. These concepts represent the fundamental assumptions underpinning any humanistic approach to counselling psychology, and can be viewed as a philosophical or value position adopted by humanistic counsellors and psychotherapists, an attitude towards the person.

One implication of the humanistic image of the person as actively seeking meaning and fulfilment is to give central emphasis to the concept of **process**. Actualization or fulfilment is not an end-state to be attained, but a continual challenge or journey to be experienced. Humanistic counselling and psychotherapy views the client, and what happens during therapy, as a set of processes. From this perspective, any attempt to categorize or label the client, for example by using a psychiatric diagnosis or personality test, can be seen as inappropriate and unhelpful, a misunderstanding of the true nature of persons. The humanistic conception of the person implies that change or becoming is inherent in the experience of being human. Humanistic therapists do not initiate or engineer change, but give attention to the internal or external factors that prevent change from occurring. This is an essential aspect of the philosophical stance of humanistic counsellors and psychotherapists. Therapeutic change is not attributed to the actions, interventions or expertise of the therapist. It is not the interpretation of the therapist, or his or her use of behavioural techniques, that is responsible for change. People, and the systems in which they live, are systems that are inherently capable of evolving and renewing themselves, and the job of the therapist is to facilitate these processes.

The concept of **reflexivity** refers to the human capacity to monitor reactions to situations, actions and inner feelings. Humanistic theory, drawing on the older traditions of existentialism and phenomenology, stresses the importance of viewing persons as capable of reflecting on experience. The possibility of choice arises from reflexivity, since the person does not respond automatically to events but acts intentionally based on an awareness of alternatives. The existence of choice also brings with it the necessity to examine the values upon which choices are based. It is associated with an appreciation of the role of moral responsibility in intentional human action. Humanistic approaches consider value and responsibility issues to be central to therapy, for example through the Rogerian concept of 'internal' and 'external' locus of evaluation, or through the use of notions of authenticity and genuineness.

Another key concept in humanistic theory is that of **self**. One consequence of the human capacity for reflexivity is the possibility of gaining a sense of 'who am I?' through reflecting on the totality of personal experience. The concept or definition of self possessed by a person is a product of both personal reflection and also of social interaction, as others attribute qualities and characteristics to self. The effort to reconcile the senses of self derived from the dialectic between an active, experiencing 'I' and a reactive, socially defined 'me' constitute much of the territory of humanistic therapy. The issue of how to understand the scope and domain of the self has been a recurring issue in humanistic psychology. For example, various writers have argued that any adequate definition of self must include its spiritual and political as well as interpersonal aspects.

Humanistic theory regards people as **organismic** beings, as embodied.

This is not an attempt to reduce human experience to biology and genetics, but represents instead an awareness of the fact that the sense that people have of the world is usually experienced at a visceral, feeling level.

The final core concept of the humanistic paradigm in counselling psychology is that of **experiencing**. Indeed, some writers would describe all humanistic therapies as fundamentally experiential in nature. The concept of experiencing employed in humanistic psychology is fundamentally anti-reductionist in nature. Being a person is not reduced either to cognition or to emotion, nor are these two concepts conceived as polar opposites. Instead, life is apprehended through experiencing, which always involves an interplay of thought and feeling (Bohart, 1993). Similarly, current actions are not determined by past events or memories, since action is carried out with reference to experiencing, which always includes threads of meaning that relate to the sense the person has of their past, present and future. Moreover, experiencing is coloured by a sense of purposefulness or intentionality.

Limitations of space make it difficult to do justice to the philosophical basis of humanistic psychology. However, this brief overview should be sufficient to demonstrate that the paradigm represents a way of understanding persons that is coherent and distinctive.

The assessment process

Differences exist between the humanistic approach and other paradigms in counselling psychology in relation to the practice of assessing clients. In emphasizing the sense of person-in-process, and in seeking to understand the person from within his or her frame of reference, humanistic therapists and researchers find little value in conventional approaches to psychological assessment. For example, any attempt to fit a diagnostic label to the client is seen as likely to intrude into the relationship between client and therapist, and interfere with the task of understanding the client's experience from his or her own point of view. Identification of target problems or behavioural repertoires, as in behaviour therapy, would similarly represent a distraction from the aim of exploring the experiential dimensions of these behaviours. In either case, assessment procedures could well introduce into the therapeutic relationship an image of therapist as expert and authority figure, which would run counter to the intention of encouraging the growth of an internal locus of evaluation in the client. In humanistic work, therapist interventions are not initiated in response to global categorizations of the client (e.g. 'borderline') but are made in reaction to in-session events and are negotiated with the client.

The one area in which assessment occurs in humanistic counselling is in relation to the decisions made by both therapist and client to make a commitment to working together. Usually, a humanistic therapist will meet with a prospective client before beginning therapy, to enable a process of mutual decision-making to take place. From the point of view of the client, it is important to check out the credibility and humanity of the therapist. From the perspective of the counsellor or psychotherapist, there are two main objectives. First, the therapist is interested in the readiness and willingness of the client to engage in therapy (see Mearns and Thorne, 1988). Secondly, the therapist reflects on his or her own personal reactions to the client in order to discover whether there will be any personal barriers to being able to enter into an accepting and congruent relationship with them. To do this effectively, the therapist must have the capacity to trust his or her own feelings about the client. This kind of assessment therefore relies on interpersonal skills and awareness rather than on history-taking or the use of questionnaires or other psychometric instruments. Where such standard measures are employed, the meaning of the data that is generated will be determined by the client.

Researchers working within the humanistic paradigm have also found it necessary to confront the issue of client assessment. Clearly, a great deal of published psychotherapy research relies on the administration of standardized assessment instruments. In the early years of research into the humanistic therapies, efforts were made to develop questionnaire measures of humanistic concepts such as self-actualization, self-esteem, self-disclosure and experiencing. Rogers and his colleagues (Rogers and Dymond, 1954) developed Q-technique as a tool for assessing self-acceptance in a way that was consistent with a phenomenological perspective. More recently, researchers have begun to explore the process of therapy using Interpersonal Process Recall (Elliott, 1986; Rennie, 1992), a method that calls on the active participation of the client and is highly sensitive to the nuances of the experiential world of the client.

Much of the impetus behind the construction of psychological tests, from the invention of the first intelligence tests, has arisen from the wish to screen or detect people with severe problems so that they can be directed towards special forms of help or control. However, the concept of psychopathology or 'abnormal' psychology does not sit easily with the philosophical and ideological assumptions of the humanistic paradigm. The few humanistic measures that have been constructed have emphasized aspects of mental 'health' (for example, self-actualization) rather than 'illness'. Nevertheless, the practical demands of dealing with clients, some of whom may indeed by highly disturbed, and the requirement to communicate with therapists and mental health professionals of other orientations, has led some humanistic psychologists to begin to evolve a set of classifications of disorders compatible with their approach (see Mearns, 1994; Melnick and Nevis, 1992).

The reluctance on the part of humanistic practitioners to participate in assessment of clients has denied them one of the most important means of professional influence and control. In the realm of service provision, counselling and psychotherapy are increasingly becoming assimilated into systems of managed patient care that require categorization of clients and demonstrable therapist competency in relation to specific presenting disorders. In research, there has been a trend toward the evaluation of specific interventions targeted on specific problems. In practice, this quest for specificity is made possible through the use of standardized assessment techniques. In their unwillingness to employ bureaucratized and de-personalized methods of assessment that result in the disempowering of persons, humanistic practitioners have taken a stance that has political implications as well as possessing theoretical consistency.

What does change mean and how is it brought about . . . what psychological theory of learning is being employed?

Given the philosophy and concept of the person outlined above, how does a humanistically oriented counselling psychologist work with clients? What are the basic change processes occurring in humanistic therapy? Taking the humanistic therapy literature as a whole, it is possible to identify three core therapeutic principles: heightened awareness, carrying forward and 'meeting as healing'. Within the different schools of humanistic practice different aspects of these themes are given greater of lesser emphasis. For example, the person-centred approach has tended to give greater prominence to the way that a productive therapeutic relationship (as a healing encounter) can be facilitated through the 'core conditions' of empathy, acceptance and congruence. The Gestalt tradi-tion, on the other hand, has given priority to the here-and-now awareness of the client.

Awareness

Working with **awareness** in humanistic counselling or psychotherapy can take many forms. The assumption in humanistic therapy is that whatever is troubling the client is exhibited in the quality of their here-and-now awareness. The healthy or fully-functioning person (Rogers, 1961) is open to experience or in a state of 'flow', whereas the person who is

The phenomenological stance of the therapist
Reflection of meanings and feelings
Therapist resonance
Therapist sensitivity to the client's 'edge of awareness'
Experiential focusing
Use of expressive media – art, movement, voice
Exploring the awareness continuum
Expressing aspects of experience through action and dialogue (e.g., Gestalt two-chair work)
Meditation

Table 6.1   *Strategies for working with awareness in humanistic therapy*

troubled and seeking help is engaged in denying or distorting their awareness of self and others in order to avoid unacceptable or frightening areas of feeling or experiencing. From a Gestalt therapy perspective, awareness is an indicator of the quality of the contact between the person and his or her environment. Awareness that is reduced or constricted is associated with an impeded ability to interact with the environment, for example to perceive the wishes of others accurately.

There are significant similarities and differences between the humanistic understanding of the role of awareness in therapy and the psychodynamic understanding of the operation of unconscious phantasy and defence mechanisms. The similarity lies in an agreement that the current conscious awareness of the client may exclude essential data that he or she needs in order to resolve whatever life difficulties he or she may be experiencing. There are, however, two main differences between the humanistic and psychodynamic views on how to help the person in this situation. From a psychodynamic point of view, the client must gain insight into the buried or repressed unresolved childhood events that lie behind the present disturbance, so the primary task of the therapist is to offer interpretations of the links between present problems and past experience. From a humanistic perspective, by contrast, the primary task is to explore the ways in which the client is denying aspects of his or her *current* awareness, and to try out, or experiment with, strategies for becoming more aware. Some of the awareness strategies employed by humanistic therapists are listed in Table 6.1. Using these strategies may have the consequence, in some cases, of opening up areas of buried childhood experience, but uncovering this type of material is not considered necessary for effective therapy to occur. The second important difference between psychodynamic and humanistic conceptions of awareness arises from the question of the extent to which awareness or consciousness can be viewed as intentional. For a psychodynamic therapist, defences are *mechanisms* caused by childhood events, and the client has little control over whether and how these mechanisms operate.

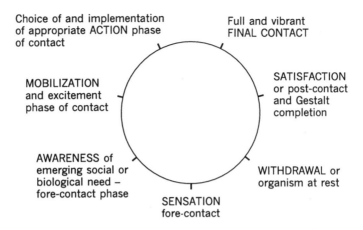

Figure 6.1 *The awareness cycle (Clarkson, 1989)*

Humanistic therapists, on the other hand, assume that the person has a substantial degree of choice over his or her attention and awareness. The implication is that the person can choose to be more aware. An example of how this assumption might be applied in practice would be the Gestalt technique of inviting the client to use more direct language, such as 'I feel' rather than 'it feels'.

Exploration of client awareness is facilitated by a rigorous *phenomenological stance* taken by the therapist. The aim of the therapist is to become sensitive to as many of the client's horizons of meaning as possible, to gain as complete an understanding of the experiental world of the client as can be achieved. This process is similar to that of 'phenomenological reduction', in which any assumptions or interpretations about an experience are systematically 'bracketed off' in an endeavour to reach the core or essence of the phenomenon. The task for the humanistic therapist is to work with the client to open up the many facets of meaning implicit in an issue or problem, without imposing an externally derived or 'expert' interpretation of what the client is feeling. The rule of humanistic therapy is that the client is always the expert on his or her experience. The aim of the therapist is to accept and give value to the meaning or content of whatever the client is exploring, while actively facilitating the process of exploration. The slogan for therapists coined by Greenberg, Rice and Elliott (1993) is to 'direct process not content'.

Perhaps the clearest articulation of the humanistic sense of awareness as an active process of experiential processing can be found in the notion of the **awareness cycle** that has been developed in Gestalt therapy (Figure 6.1). This model of awareness provides a way of making sense of how the on-going flow of living and relating can be blocked in a number of different ways. For example, a client working on a relationship problem could be open to the feelings he has about the situation, but may be stuck at the stages of mobilizing energy and taking action that would bring about change. The awareness cycle model can be useful for the therapist in helping him or her to focus on the tasks the client might need to complete in order to re-establish a healthy flow of experiencing.

Carrying forward

The second fundamental principle of humanistic therapy can be described as **carrying forward**. This principle is based on the philosophical assumption that some kind of search for fulfilment or 'growth' is intrinsic to being human, and that as a result there is always a sense of movement, emergence, direction or intentionality in attempts by clients to resolve difficult life dilemmas. The idea of carrying forward can be observed in the Awareness Cycle model, which is based in an assumption that the 'natural' state of affairs is continuous movement through these phases of experiencing. The writings of Gendlin (1984) on experiential focusing convey a similar perspective.

Bozarth has argued that the central task in client-centred or person-centred therapy is 'going with the client's direction, at the client's pace, and with the client's unique way of being' (1990: 63). Rennie (1990), in his research into the experiences of therapy clients, reports that they are frequently aware of a sense of direction, which he refers to as the client's 'track', in what they are working on:

> clients . . . increasingly have a sense of being on a path, or train of thought (client's track). There is a compellingness to the track: clients feel that they are on the edge of their experience; there is uncertainty whether words can be found to express what they are sensing. (1990: 160)

The therapeutic principle of experiential carrying-forward is also evident in the use of process models of therapeutic change. The original global model of therapeutic process developed by Rogers (1961) described a series of seven stages though which successful client-centred therapy would proceed (Table 6.2). More recently, more specific micro-process change models have been constructed, identifying stages in effective empathic responding (Barrett-Lennard, 1981), focusing on a problem (Gendlin, 1981) and experiential processing of various kinds of emotional problems (Greenberg et al., 1993). The research carried out by the group led by Greenberg and Rice has been instrumental in developing a perspective on experiential processing that combines key elements of both person-centred and Gestalt practice. From Gestalt, they have

Stage 1
Communication is about external events. Feelings and personal meanings are not 'owned'. Close relationships are construed as dangerous. Rigidity in thinking. Impersonal, detached. Does not use first-person pronouns

Stage 2
Expression begins to flow more freely in respect of non-self topics. Feelings may be described but not owned. Intellectualization. Describes behaviour rather than inner feelings. May show more interest and participation in therapy

Stage 3
Describes personal reactions to external events. Limited amount of self-description. Communication about past feelings. Beginning to recognize contradictions in experience

Stage 4
Descriptions of feelings and personal experiences. Beginning to experience current feelings, but fear and distrust of this when it happens. The 'inner life' is presented and listed or described, but not purposefully explored

Stage 5
Present feelings are expressed. Increasing ownership of feelings. More exactness in the differentiation of feelings and meanings. Intentional exploration of problems in a personal way, based in processing of feelings rather than reasoning

Stage 6
Sense of an 'inner referent', or flow of feeling which has a life of its own. 'Physiological loosening' such as moistness in the eyes, tears, sighs, muscular relaxation accompanies the open expression of feelings. Speaks in present tense or offers vivid representation of past

Stage 7
A series of felt sense connecting the different aspects of an issue. Basic trust in own inner processes. Feelings experienced with immediacy and richness of detail. Speaks fluently in present tense

Sources: Klein et al., 1986; Rogers, 1961

Table 6.2   *The process of change*

taken the idea that it is possible to identify discrete change events within each therapy session. These events are triggered by the client expressing a dilemma or emotion that acts as a 'marker' to initiate a distinctive set of experiential processing tasks. From the person–centred approach, they have identified the therapeutic relationship as a whole, and therapist empathy in particular, as critical factors in enabling the client to carry out processing tasks effectively.

From a humanistic point of view, learning is always **experiential** in nature and is always a **process** that occurs in a **relational** context (Kolb, 1981; Rogers, 1969). Whereas other orientations would stress the cognitive (for example, insight or reframing), behavioural or emotional/cathartic elements in therapeutic learning, from a humanistic perspective all these elements are seen as facets of one experiential process. Working experientially involves taking account of the interplay between thoughts, action and feelings rather than attending rigidly to any one of these modes in isolation.

The nature of the relationship between counselling psychologist and individual client

The third element of the humanistic approach to enabling therapeutic change is based in an acceptance of the healing power of the relationship between therapist and client. In humanistic therapy, the practitioner strives to meet the client as a person, in as genuine a manner as possible. The therapist does not assume that the feelings that the client has towards him or her are necessarily due to some kind of reproduction of what was felt in previous relationships (with parents for example), but is a real relationship between two people who are each reacting to the other in the here-and-now. The discussion by Shlien (1984) of the Freudian concept of transference makes this clear. Shlien (1984) acknowledges that clients may love or hate their therapist, but he disputes the view that this phenomenon must be seen as a repetition of previous patterns of relating. For Shlien, such feelings are expressed by the client in response to whether they feel themselves to be accepted and understood by the therapist:

> the therapist is responsible for two fundamental behaviors – understanding and misunderstanding – which account for love, or for hate, and their associated affects. These, as well as other behaviors and the situation and personality of the therapist, may account – should first be held accountable – for the whole of what passes for transference. (Shlien, 1984: 177)

In his analysis of the origins of the concept of transference in the early work of Freud and Breuer, Shlien argues that: '"transference" is a fiction, invented and maintained by the therapist to protect himself from the consequences of his own behaviour' (1984: 153).

The formulation by Rogers (1957) of the 'necessary and sufficient conditions' for therapeutic change, which has subsequently become known as the **'core conditions'** model, suggests that effective therapy can only occur within a relationship between therapist and client in which the latter perceives the former as being accepting, empathic and congruent. Within Gestalt therapy, notions of therapist–client **contact** and **merger** are used to refer to the same kind of relationship qualities. Although much of the published work of Fritz Perls appears to depict a version of Gestalt therapy in which an on-going relationship with the client is not given any great emphasis, recent developments in Gestalt have tended to favour the more relational version of the approach attributed to Laura Perls (Perls, 1992; Serlin, 1992).

The kinds of therapeutic processes already described, involving the deepening of awareness and the carrying-forward of experiencing, are more likely to occur in the context of a relationship in which the client feels enough trust and safety to take risks and be open. However, the view in humanistic psychology is that participation in a close, authentic relationship with another person is healing in itself. The therapeutic alliance or relationship is not merely a means to a set of therapeutic ends, but is empowering and valuable in its own right. People are seen as becoming anxious, depressed or confused because they lack relationships that are affirming and supportive. The humanistic therapist aims to achieve authenticity and **transparency** (Jourard, 1971) in relation to the client. In practice, this means that the therapist is more willing to be known, for example being more open about his or her personal values or feelings, than would practitioners from other orientations. Van Balen (1990) and Friedman (1992) represent an important strand of humanistic thinking, influenced by the work of the philosopher Martin Buber, with their proposal that therapists should aim to enter into a **dialogue** with their clients, and accept the implication that to do so will involve a degree of **mutuality** in the relationship: 'we come to awareness of ourselves not just through our individuality . . . but in our dialogue with other selves – in their response to us and in the way they call us into being' (Friedman, 1992: 5).

These relationship qualities are actively constructed by humanistic therapists. For example, therapist transparency and genuineness can be communicated to the client through the use of **meta-communication**. Rather than merely responding directly to the client, the counsellor may make reference to the feelings, intentions and understandings that lie behind his or her response. The therapist response may be offered in a tentative manner, to allow the client every opportunity to disagree with or correct the therapist's understanding of the situation. This style of communicating with the client has a number of advantages. It conveys the message that the client is in control, it encourages the use of the internal locus of evaluation of the client, and minimizes the likelihood of the therapist intruding on the internal processing or 'track' (Rennie, 1990) being pursued by the client. It also models for the client a means of dealing with the pervasiveness of meta-perspectives in everyday interactions. A further use of meta-communication is suggested by Kiesler (1988), who views it as a way of providing the client with feedback on his or her style of relating to others.

A final dimension of the counsellor–client relationship from a humanistic perspective concerns professionalization. Humanistic practitioners have generally done their best to reduce the status and power differences existing between client and helper. For example, while other approaches to counselling and psychotherapy have fought hard to fashion strong professional identities, there has been some ambivalence within the humanistic paradigm over this issue. The elements of professionalization put in place by members of other therapeutic orientations have included:

professional associations with licensing and disciplinary powers, exclusion from practice of non-professionals, a significant presence in university-based training, a strong emphasis on research, representation in national professional bodies and a wide range of publishing outlets. Although the humanistic paradigm includes, in some form, all of these elements of professionalization, the commitment and energy with which these professional goals have been pursued has not matched that exhibited by other approaches to therapy. To some extent this ambivalence over professional status reflects the origins of the humanistic paradigm as a 'third force' protest movement. The social philosophy or politics implicit in the humanistic paradigm has influenced adherents of this approach to be cautious about the increasing trend toward viewing counselling and psychotherapy as professional specialisms.

Traditionally, humanistic psychology has been developed either by individuals or by non-hierarchical, non-bureaucratic collectives. Key figures in humanistic psychology such as Fritz Perls, Sidney Jourard or Sheldon Kopp worked largely alone or in temporary collaborations with small groups of colleagues. The most important organizational centre during the early years of humanistic psychology, the Counselling Centre at the University of Chicago, was led by Rogers but was characterized by 'maximum participation by all staff members in matters which concern the total group' (Gordon, 1951: 322). It is significant that, despite the dominant position in psychotherapy training and research held by the Chicago group during the 1950s, they did not establish a specialist journal or professional association for client-centred therapy.

It would be easy to attribute this ambivalence over professionalization to an individualism inherent in the humanistic approach. Holland (1977) and Masson (1988), for example, have criticized humanistic psychology for constructing an image of the person detached from any social or political context. It is certainly true that there exist some strands of extreme masculine individualism within humanistic writing. Nevertheless, there has also been a strong communitarian movement within the humanistic approach, a deep appreciation of collective experience, expressed through the writings of Rogers (1969) on the 'healing capacity' of the group (see also Barrett-Lennard, 1994; Wood, 1984). This sense of collective life has been rooted in experience in temporary community groups (up to about 100 members) that meet face-to-face and share a commitment to authentic dialogue. It is probably reasonable to conclude that people who have been exposed to this type of community group experience have a distrust of the operation of larger, more formal organizational groupings and institutions.

Although humanistic psychology grew out of the European philosophical traditions of existentialism and phenomenology, it took root originally in the USA, and as a result has assimilated American values around self-help and mistrust of experts (Sollod, 1978). Humanistic approaches in counselling have therefore been in the vanguard of the psychology that has been 'given away' so that it can be used by ordinary people. The humanistic paradigm includes many applications within self-help groups and counselling agencies staffed by non-professional helpers (for details see Larson, 1984). In addition, a number of books written by humanistic psychologists have been aimed at the popular market rather than merely at a readership of mental health professionals.

Family, group and organizational applications

The humanistic approach to counselling psychology has been applied in most of the major areas of counselling psychology practice. The emphasis of the approach on personal growth and empowerment has resulted in wide usage within student counselling and private practice. The reliance on personal qualities and the ability of the counsellor to form a healing relationship, rather than on his or her ability to master abstract theory or complex technique, has led to extensive adoption of the approach in voluntary agencies. The humanistic-experiential model has also been implemented in work with families, couples and children, and with highly disturbed clients (see Lietaer et al., 1990, for examples of recent developments in these areas). Many models of groupwork and organizational development have drawn heavily on humanistic theory. Finally, humanistic ideas have been applied to a range of social and political problems (e.g. Rogers, 1978).

Research evidence about effectiveness

Some of the earliest controlled outcome studies of counselling and psychotherapy were carried out by Rogers and his colleagues at Ohio and Chicago in the 1940s (Cartwright, 1957; Rogers and Dymond, 1954). These studies provided evidence for the effectiveness of client-centred therapy in bringing about positive changes in client self-acceptance, self-awareness, confidence, emotional maturity and adjustment. However, subsequent research into humanistic therapy has placed less emphasis on the issue of outcome. Partly, this can be attributed to a realization that, from a phenomenologically informed perspective, any definition of outcome is complex and ambiguous:

> We have come to the conclusion that 'success', no matter how it is phrased or described, is not a usable or useful criterion for research in psychotherapy . . . in every meaningful way we have given up the concept of 'success' as the

criterion against which our research measurements will be compared. (Rogers and Dymond, 1954: 29)

In the 1960s and 1970s, therefore, the attention of humanistic researchers was drawn more toward the question of therapy process, in particular to testing Rogers's (1957) 'necessary and sufficient conditions' process model. Reviews of the findings obtained by this programme of research can be found in Watson (1984) and Cramer (1992). Other factors contributing to the decline of outcome studies of humanistic counselling and psychotherapy were the failure of the approach to maintain its presence in the academic world, and also a general sense that the methods of empiricist psychology were not consistent with the values and philosophy of humanism (Giorgi, 1987).

Despite these constraints, a number of outcome studies of humanistic counselling and psychotherapy have been carried out in recent years. In an authoritative review, Greenberg et al. (1994) found 37 studies published between 1978 and 1992, involving 1,272 clients. Fifteen of these studies included comparisons with no-treatment or waiting-list groups, and 26 studies compared humanistic therapy with another therapeutic orientation. Taken as a whole, the results of these studies provide strong evidence for the general efficacy of humanistic therapy, with a mean effect size (ES) of 1.30, which means that the average client would move from the 50th to the 90th percentile in relation to the pre-therapy sample. When compared with other forms of active intervention, humanistic therapy proved to be no more or no less effective than any other approach. It is of some interest that many of these studies were carried out by researchers employing client-centred therapy as a kind of a placebo control. This circumstance would tend to lower expectation of positive outcomes, and would be consistent with the view that the research does not over-estimate the effectiveness of humanistic therapy.

The relatively small number of studies carried out makes it difficult to estimate the efficacy of humanistic-experiential counselling and psychotherapy with reference to particular client groups. Greenberg, Elliott and Lietaer (1994) observe that there is some evidence to suggest that clients who are interested in their inner experience, have good social skills and a high need for intimacy are best suited for humanistic-experiential work. More favourable outcomes were obtained with clients with relationship problems, anxiety or depression, with less impressive results for more chronic or severe problems such as schizophrenia. These trends are similar to those found with other forms of therapy. Greenberg, Elliott and Lietaer conclude that 'there is as yet no clear evidence for selecting or deselecting experiential therapy in treating any specific disorder' (1994: 518).

To sum up, it is perhaps reasonable to comment that much more research needs to be carried out to evaluate the effectiveness of humanistic therapy with different client groups. By contrast, humanistically oriented studies of psychotherapy process have been at the leading edge of psychotherapy research. The development by Elliott (1986) of Inter-personal Process Recall as a research tool, the studies by Rennie (1990, 1992) into the experience of the client, and the introduction by Greenberg (1984) of task analysis methods have been instrumental in advancing studies of the 'interior' of the therapy hour. It is perhaps worth noting that these developments in process research have been carried out in North America and have relied on various qualitative approaches to research that are broadly consistent with the philosophy and values of the originators of humanistic psychology, whereas many of the more recent outcome studies, which have used traditional research designs, have been carried out in Europe. There has been no British research of any significance into humanistic therapy.

Conclusions

In the conclusion to this chapter, the current status of the humanistic paradigm will be evaluated by considering the strengths and weaknesses of the approach, and identifying some of the directions in which it appears to be moving. For an alternative perspective on the same topics, the reader is recommended to consult Rice and Greenberg (1992).

The weaknesses of the humanistic approach to counselling and psychotherapy are obvious to most psychologists. Historically, psychology has worked hard to legitimize its status as a scientific discipline by using research to distance it from the domain of common-sense belief and folk psychology. In the field of humanistic psychology, however, there has been a marked lack of research, not merely into the processes and outcomes of humanistic therapy, but into the personality theory and concepts that underpin it. Despite the influence of Rogers, a leading figure in psychotherapy research, there has evolved what could be described as an anti-intellectual bias in much humanistic writing and training. The leading journals, *Journal of Humanistic Psychology* and *Self and Society*, contain very little research material. There are few discoveries or theoretical advances being made in humanistic psychology. There is no humanistic developmental psychology, or humanistic cognitive psycho-logy. This absence of research activity places humanistic counselling psychologists at a growing disadvantage in a market place that increasingly demands accountability and evidence of effectiveness in relation to tightly defined client groups or presenting problems.

From a sociological perspective, humanistic therapy can be viewed as very much a product of a particular era in which the prosperity of Western industrial societies allowed a greater than usual expression of individual creativity and freedom. It can be argued that humanistic therapy embodies a 'monocultural' image of the person (Holdstock, 1993) which has little relevance outside of this specific time and place. Even within the cultural milieu in which it has evolved, humanistic psychology is silent on many critically important issues. For example, there has been no systematic attempt within humanistic therapy to assimilate the lessons of feminism or to confront the experience of racism and colonialism. It would be difficult to characterize psychoanalysis as a politically radical movement, but these debates have not been opened up in humanistic psychology to the extent they have within psychoanalysis. It is certainly true that individual humanistic practitioners have addressed these issues at a local level, but there has been little attempt to integrate what they have learned into the paradigm as a whole. On the other hand, there are those within the humanistic approach who would argue that its strong emphasis on authenticity and acceptance in relationships mitigates against systematic discrimination in the form of racism, sexism or ageism, and that equality of value for persons lies at the core of a humanistic orientation.

The issues being discussed here can be seen as representing significant gaps in the humanistic paradigm, and their existence can be attributed to a number of factors. The emergence of humanistic psychology as a protest movement in psychology in the 1950s has had the effect of 'humanizing' much of mainstream psychology, so that writers such as Wertheimer (1978) and Smith (1982) can claim that much of psychology as a whole is humanistic in nature. The more radical humanistic theorists and practitioners, those who have continued to argue for a distinctive humanistic agenda, have found little welcome within the academy. Most have made their living as practitioners, with limited time for scholarship and research. Those who have worked in universities have found it difficult to secure funding for humanistic research programmes. There is, however, a more basic difficulty that underlies the lack of advance in humanistic thought: the lack of a credible humanistic research method. The pioneering research into client-centred therapy carried out by Rogers and his colleagues attempted to accommodate phenomenological ideas within a traditional empiricist approach, without acknowledging the epistemological tensions implicit in this endeavour. On the other hand, research based on a rigorous application of phenomenological methods (see Valle and Halling, 1989) has had limited impact. Mainstream psychologists have been able to apply experimental methods to a wide array of research problems. Likewise, psychoanalytic scholars have been able to rely on an interpretive approach to research topics. By contrast, humanistic psychologists have not possessed a methodology for doing research that is consistent with the broader aims and values of the paradigm.

Nevertheless, humanistic approaches to counselling psychology also possess a number of significant strengths. The humanistic paradigm is built on a distinctive concept of the person, viewed as an active, aware, contextualized and intentional agent who must be understood as a complex whole. This way of seeing self and others is experienced by many people as affirming and facilitative. There exists a set of basic principles concerning the application of this concept of the person within therapy, through the creation of a helping or healing relationship. It is a flexible approach, and one that can be readily learned. It is a way of working with people that can be used in many different settings.

The humanistic paradigm in psychology is emerging from a period in which it was dominated by a handful of major figures such as Rogers and Perls. It is also emerging from a period in which its aims and values have not been favoured by the prevailing political and economic conditions. There are four trends that can be detected within the paradigm that represent possibilities for significant future advances in this approach. These trends are:

1   integration of ideas from cognitive psychology;
2   development of a distinctive research methodology;
3   theoretical assimilation of concepts of spirituality;
4   re-establishing links with broader humanistic traditions in literature and the arts.

Given that humanistic psychology is centrally concerned with the process of meaning-making, the relevance of cognitive psychology has always been clear. Indeed, Gestalt therapy, which in many ways draws upon existential and biological/organismic concepts, was named in recognition of its debt to early cognitive psychologists such as Koffka, Kohler and Wertheimer. The connection between client-centred therapy and cognitive psychology can be seen in the collection of papers in Wexler and Rice (1974). However, as Greenberg, Rice and Elliott (1993) observe, there has been substantial progress made in cognitive psychology in recent years. Their own work has had the objective of developing an experiential psychotherapy which explicitly draws on contemporary cognitive theory and research in areas such as attention, memory and parallel processing. Their model is based on the idea that problems in living are associated with the operation of dysfunctional emotional schemes. This kind of careful, well-informed use of insights from cognitive psychology in the context of a humanistic model of therapy (Greenberg et al., 1993) provides a powerful model for future developments in the field. The work of Toukmanian (1992) has also made a significant contribution to this trend.

The second important area of new thinking within humanistic psychology is related to the question of finding an appropriate research methodology. The increasing acceptance of qualitative methods in the counselling and psychotherapy research community (see Chapter 3) has resulted in the refinement of research approaches that are consistent with the underlying philosophical assumptions of humanistic psychology. These methods involve collaboration with informants or co-participants, along with sensitive strategies for gaining access to experiential material. The researcher is expected to be aware of his or her own role in the inquiry process, and to adopt a reflexive stance toward the data. The research strategies most widely used to achieve these aims are the **human inquiry** approach (Reason, 1988; Reason and Rowan, 1981), the analysis of narrative and discourse (Riessman, 1993) and the use of **grounded theory** analysis (Rennie, 1990). This movement has been characterized by Rennie (1994) as representing a return to Dilthey's conception of a human science.

A third challenge for the future of humanistic psychology lies in the area of spiritual experience. Despite research findings showing that at least one-third of people have at some point undergone a significant spiritual experience in their lives, counselling and psychotherapy have evolved as mainly secular activities which have tended to deny or ignore this area of human experience. Humanistic psychology, with its emphasis on meaning and higher-order needs, and its openness to ideas from Eastern religions, has always allowed a place for spiritual experience. However, although in the past the real concern for spiritual issues has been shown mainly in transpersonal therapies, there is an increasing interest in finding ways of assimilating this dimension into more widely used humanistic therapies such as the person-centred approach (Thorne, 1992).

Finally, there are signs of a renewed willingness in humanistic psychology to draw upon the much wider and deeper tradition of humanism found in the arts and literature. Many of the founders of humanistic psychology, such as Jacob Moreno, Erich Fromm and Henry Murray, were highly active in exploring the relevance for psychology of fiction and drama. The appreciation of this enormous cultural resource became lost as humanistic psychology became identified as a model of therapy rather than as an approach to psychology. The rediscovery of fiction by writers such as Polster (1987), and the powerful statement by Bruner (1986) of the importance of narrative ways of knowing, signify a return to this fundamental tradition in the humanistic approach. Perhaps there is now an opportunity to look in a fresh way at the roots of the humanistic approach, at those areas of human experience that Sutich (1961) characterized as the 'human capacities and potentialities that have no systematic place either in positivistic or behavioristic theory or in classical psychoanalytic theory, e.g., creativity, love [and] growth'.

References

Barrett-Lennard, G.T. (1981) 'The empathy cycle: refinement of a nuclear concept', *Journal of Counseling Psychology*, 28: 91–100.

Barrett-Lennard, G.T. (1994) 'Toward a person-centered theory of community', *Journal of Humanistic Psychology*, 34(3): 62–86.

Bohart, A.C. (1993) 'Experiencing: the basis of psychotherapy', *Journal of Psychotherapy Integration*, 3(1): 51–67.

Bozarth, J.D. (1990) 'The essence of client-centered therapy', in G. Lietaer, J. Rombauts and R. Van Balen (eds), *Client-Centered and Experiential Therapy in the Nineties*. Leuven: University of Leuven Press.

Bruner, J. (1986) *Actual Minds, Possible Worlds*. Cambridge, MA: Harvard University Press.

Bugental, J. (ed.) (1967) *Challenges of Humanistic Psychology*. New York: McGraw-Hill.

Cartwright, D.S. (1957) 'Annotated bibliography of research and theory construction in client-centered therapy', *Journal of Counseling Psychology*, 4(1): 82–100.

Clarkson, P. (1989) *Gestalt Counselling in Action*. London: Sage.

Clarkson, P. and Mackewn, J. (1993) *Fritz Perls*. London: Sage.

Cramer, D. (1992) *Personality and Psychotherapy: Theory, Practice and Research*. Buckingham: Open University Press.

Elliott, R. (1986) 'Interpersonal Process Recall (IPR) as a psychotherapy process research method', in L.S. Greenberg and W.M. Pinsof (eds), *The Psychotherapeutic Process: a Research Handbook*. New York: Guilford Press.

Friedman, M. (1992) *Dialogue and the Human Image: Beyond Humanistic Psychology*. London: Sage.

Gendlin, E.T. (1981) *Focusing*. New York: Bantam Books.

Gendlin, E.T. (1984) 'The client's client: the edge of awareness', in R.F. Levant and J. Shlien (eds), *Client-Centered Therapy and the Person-Centered Approach: New Directions in Theory, Research and Practice*. New York: Praeger.

Gergen, K.J. (1985) 'The social constructionist movement in modern psychology', *American Psychologist*, 40(3): 266–75.

Giorgi, A. (1987) 'The crisis of humanistic psychology', *The Humanistic Psychologist*, 15(1): 5–20.

Gordon, T. (1951) 'Group-centered leadership and administration', in C.R. Rogers (ed.), *Client-Centred Therapy*. London: Constable.

Greenberg, L.S. (1984) 'Task analysis: the general approach', in L.N. Rice and L.S. Greenberg (eds) *Patterns of Change: Intensive Analysis of Psychotherapy Process*. New York: Guilford Press.

Greenberg, L.S., Elliott, R.K. and Lietaer, G. (1994) 'Research on experiential psychotherapies', in A.E. Bergin and S.L. Garfield (eds), *Handbook of Psychotherapy and Behavior Change*, 4th edn. New York: Wiley.

Greenberg, L.S., Rice, L.N. and Elliott, R. (1993) *Facilitating Emotional Change: the Moment-by-Moment Process*. New York: Guilford Press.

Holdstock, L. (1993) 'Can we afford not to revision the person-centred concept of self?' in D. Brazier (ed.), *Beyond Carl Rogers*. London: Constable.

Holland, R. (1977) *Self and Social Context*. London: Macmillan.

Jourard, S.M. (1971) *The Transparent Self*, 2nd edn. New York: Van Nostrand Reinhold.

Kiesler, D. (1988) *Therapeutic Metacommunication: Therapist Impact Disclosure as Feedback in Psychotherapy*. Palo Alto, CA: Consulting Psychologists Press.

Klein, M.H., Mathieu-Coughlan, P. and Kiesler, D.J. (1986) 'The Experiencing Scales', in L.S. Greenberg and W.M. Pinsof (eds), *The Psychotherapeutic Process: a Research Handbook*. New York: Guilford Press.

Kolb, D. (1981) *Experiential Learning*. New York: Wiley.

Kuhn, T.S. (1962) *The Structure of Scientific Revolutions*. Chicago: University of Chicago Press.

Larson, D. (ed.) (1984) *Teaching Psychological Skills: Models for Giving Psychology Away*. Monterey, CA: Brooks/Cole.

Lietaer, G., Rombauts, J. and Van Balen, R. (eds) (1990) *Client-Centered and Experiential Therapy in the Nineties*. Leuven: University of Leuven Press.

Maddi, S. (1989) *Personality Theories: a Comparative Analysis*, 5th edn. Pacific Grove, CA: Wadsworth.

Masson, J. (1988) *Against Therapy*. Glasgow: Collins.

Mearns, D. (1994) *Developing Person-Centred Counselling*. London: Sage.

Mearns, D. and Thorne, B. (1988) *Person-Centred Counselling in Action*. London: Sage.

Melnick, J. and Nevis, S.M. (1992) 'Diagnosis: the struggle for a meaningful paradigm', in E.C. Nevis (ed.), *Gestalt Therapy: Perspectives and Applications*. New York: Gardner Press.

Misiak, H. and Sexton, V.S. (1973) *Phenomenological, Existential and Humanistic Psychologies: a Historical Survey*. New York: Grune and Stratton.

Perls, L. (1992) 'Concepts and misconceptions of Gestalt therapy', *Journal of Humanistic Psychology*, 32(3): 50–6.

Polster, E. (1987) *Every Person's Life is Worth a Novel*. New York: Norton.

Reason, P. (ed.) (1988) *Human Inquiry in Action: Developments in New Paradigm Research*. London: Sage.

Reason, P. and Rowan, J. (eds) (1981) *Human Inquiry: a Sourcebook of New Paradigm Research*. Chichester: Wiley.

Rennie, D.L. (1990) 'Toward a representation of the client's experience of the psychotherapy hour', in G. Lietaer, J. Rombauts and R. Van Balen (eds), *Client-Centered and Experiential Therapy in the Nineties*. Leuven: University of Leuven Press.

Rennie, D.L. (1992) 'Qualitative analysis of the client's experience of psychotherapy: the unfolding of reflexivity', in S.G. Toukmanian and D.L. Rennie (eds), *Psychotherapy Process Research: Paradigmatic and Narrative Approaches*. London: Sage.

Rennie, D.L. (1994) 'Human science and counselling psychology: closing the gap between research and practice', *Counselling Psychology Quarterly*, 7: 235–50.

Rice, L.N. and Greenberg, L.S. (1992) 'Humanistic approaches to psycho-therapy', in D.K. Freedheim (ed.), *History of Psychotherapy: a Century of Change*. Washington, DC: American Psychological Association.

Riessman, C.K. (1993) *Narrative Analysis*. London: Sage.

Rogers, C.R. (1957) 'The necessary and sufficient conditions of therapeutic personality change', *Journal of Consulting Psychology*, 21: 95–103.

Rogers, C.R. (1961) *On Becoming a Person*. London: Constable.

Rogers, C.R. (1969) *Freedom to Learn*. Columbus, OH: Charles E. Merrill.

Rogers, C.R. (1978) *Carl Rogers on Personal Power: Inner Strength and its Revolutionary Impact*. London: Constable.

Rogers, C.R. and Dymond, R.F. (eds) (1954) *Psychotherapy and Personality Change: Co-ordinated Research Studies in the Client-Centered Approach*. Chicago: University of Chicago Press.

Serlin, I.A. (1992) 'Tribute to Laura Perls', *Journal of Humanistic Psychology*, 32(3): 57–66.

Shlien, J.M. (1984) 'A countertheory of transference', in R.F. Levant and J. Shlien (eds), *Client-Centered Therapy and the Person-Centered Approach: New Directions in Theory, Research and Practice*. New York: Praeger.

Smith, M.B. (1982) 'Psychology and humanism', *Journal of Humanistic Psychology*, 22(2): 44–55.

Sollod, R.N. (1978) 'Carl Rogers and the origins of client-centered therapy', *Professional Psychology*, 9: 93–104.

Sutich, A. (1961) 'Introduction', *Journal of Humanistic Psychology*, 1(1): vii–ix.

Thorne, B. (1992) *Carl Rogers*. London: Sage.

Toukmanian, S.G. (1992) 'Studying the client's perceptual processes and their outcomes in psychotherapy', in S.G. Toukmanian and D.L. Rennie (eds), *Psychotherapy Process Research: Paradigmatic and Narrative Approaches*. London: Sage.

Valle, R.S. and Halling, S. (eds) (1989) *Existential-Phenomenological Perspectives in Psychology: Exploring the Breadth of Human Experience*. New York: Plenum.

Van Balen, R. (1990) 'The therapeutic relationship according to Carl Rogers: Only a climate? A dialogue? Or both?' in G. Lietaer, J. Rombauts and R. Van Balen (eds), *Client-Centered and Experiential Therapy in the Nineties*. Leuven: University of Leuven Press.

Watson, N. (1984) 'The empirical status of Rogers's hypotheses of the necessary and sufficient conditions for effective psychotherapy', in R.F. Levant and J. Shlien (eds), *Client-Centered Therapy and the Person-Centered Approach: New Directions in Theory, Research and Practice*. New York: Praeger.

Wertheimer, M. (1978) 'Humanistic psychology and the humane but tough-minded psychologist', *American Psychologist*, 33: 739–45.

Wexler, D.A. and Rice, L.N. (eds) (1974) *Innovations in Client-Centered Therapy*. New York: Wiley.

Wood, J.K. (1984) 'Communities for learning: a person-centered approach', in R.F. Levant and J. Shlien (eds), *Client-Centered Therapy and the Person-Centered Approach: New Directions in Theory, Research and Practice*. New York: Praeger.

7

The Cognitive-Behavioural Paradigm

Michael J. Scott and Windy Dryden

The theoretical origins of cognitive-behaviour therapy can be traced back to the Stoic philosopher Epictetus, who in the first century AD observed that 'People are disturbed not so much by events as by the views which they take of them'. The implication of this observation is that situations (like objects in the visual world), are better viewed from some angles than from others and that, at least in principle, people choose their orientation. However a person's 'orientation' is itself influenced by his beliefs about himself in relation to the world. Thus if I believe myself to be a football referee I will watch the football match from a different 'angle' from that used if I believe myself to be a football spectator. The task of cognitive-behaviour therapy is to relieve emotional disturbance by helping people change their maladaptive beliefs and behaviours.

Underlying Theory of Personality and Motivation

From a cognitive-behavioural perspective human experience is viewed as a product of four interacting elements – physiology, cognition, behaviour and emotion (Figure 7.1). Thus if I am tense (physiology) when I come to write an essay this may lead me to think 'I am not going to write a good essay' (cognition), which in turn might lead me to feel anxious (emotion) and that might lead me to put my pen down and go for a walk (behaviour). The effect of going for a walk might be to reduce my tension (back to physiology), I may then be more inclined to think 'in reality I actually do quite well on essays' (cognition) and this may make me feel in turn more relaxed (emotion). In this instance a behaviour (going for a walk) has broken down the negative chain reaction. This behaviour itself may have been energized by my general knowledge (cognition) that going for walks lifts my mood. Within the cognitive-behavioural tradition, the primary emphasis is on breaking out of negative chains via the cognitive and behavioural ports of entry. It should be noted, however, that it is perfectly possible in principle to break negative cycles via the physiological port, for example a relaxation exercise involving tensing and relaxing each muscle group in turn, or via the

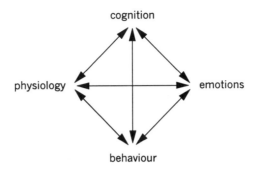

Figure 7.1   *The cognitive-behavioural model*

emotional port, for example playing a favourite music tape. Whilst the cognitive-behavioural approach to anxiety and depression and other emotional disorders has concentrated on changing cognitions and behaviours there has been a shift to include emotions as a port of entry when it comes to the treatment of personality disorders. To return to our example, if I thought that 'I am not going to write a good essay' but also that 'I am a stupid person and worthless', such a belief might sabotage all my efforts. Thus, I may not even go for a walk in the first place. This distinction between thoughts and beliefs becomes more apparent if we use Persons' (1989) method of conceptualizing clients' difficulties. She has a two-level model. The first level is one of overt difficulties, with cognitions, emotions and behaviour reciprocally interacting (Figure 7.2). The second level is one of covert difficulties, and it is at this level that core beliefs operate, for example, 'I am stupid'. Core beliefs are the tacit beliefs people have about themselves and their relationship to the world. The core beliefs are rarely verbalized and usually operate at the edge of a person's awareness. They are inferred beliefs from a person's responses to a wide range of situations. The core beliefs are moulded in childhood.

There are reciprocal interactions between levels one and two. My belief that 'I am stupid' may make it more likely that I will automatically think 'I am going to make a mess of something' when confronted with a task. But if I can change such automatic thinking (what are called automatic thoughts) across a range of similar situations then I may eventually change the core beliefs. With disorders such as anxiety and depression, that is the Axis 1 disorders in the *Diagnostic and Statistical Manual* 4th Edition (DSM IV; APA, 1994), automatic thoughts tend to be the target whereas with Axis 2 disorders in DSM IV, the personality disorders, the core beliefs are the more direct focus. Individuals differ in their core beliefs and it is the omnipresence of an individual's core beliefs

157

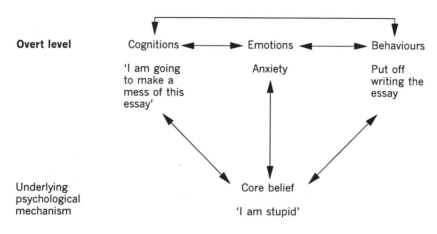

Figure 7.2 *Person's (1989) model of client difficulties*

that makes his or her behaviour relatively predictable and confers on that individual a particular personality. Beck et al. (1983), for example, have made the distinction between autonomous and sociotropic personalities. The autonomous personality bases his sense of self-identity on his achievements and would have a core belief of the form 'if I am not the top then I am a flop'. The sociotropic personality on the other hand believes that he needs the approval of others. His core belief is of the form 'I am nothing if I do not always have other people's approval'.

Within a cognitive-behavioural paradigm the motivation of an individual is held to be a product of two sets of beliefs – self-efficacy and outcome expectancies (Bandura, 1982). Self-efficacy relates to a person's belief in their ability to perform an action, whilst outcome expectancies relate to their belief in whether the outcome is worthwhile.

The assessment process

Cognitive-behavioural approaches have been developed differently for various disorders. It is therefore important to be able to identify and distinguish the different disorders. To diagnose patients use is made not only of a clinical interview but also of self-report measures. For example, the primary theme that emerges when interviewing depressed clients is one of loss, of life having lost its flavour, whereas the main theme permeating an interview with an anxious client is one of threat. A self-report measure such as the Hospital Anxiety and Depression (HAD) Scale (Zigmond and Snaith, 1983) is useful to distinguish the two conditions;

Anxiety	Depression
Feeling tense or wound up	Not enjoying things the way you used to
Getting a sort of frightened feeling as if something awful is about to happen	Being unable to laugh and see the funny side of things
Having worrying thoughts going through your mind	Not feeling cheerful
Inability to sit at ease and relax	Feeling as if you are slowed down
Getting a sort of frightened feeling like butterflies in the stomach	Losing interest in your appearance
Feeling restless as if you have to be on the move	Not looking forward with enjoyment to things
Getting sudden feelings of panic	Being unable to enjoy a good book or radio or television programme

Figure 7.3   *Indicators of anxiety and depression from Zigmond and Snaith's (1983) HAD Scale*

clients are asked to report the severity of each of the symptoms in Figure 7.3 on a scale of 0 to 3, and a score of greater than 8 on either sub-scale has been found to most reliably distinguish clinical cases of a disorder from non-cases.

A client's response to a question on the HAD can be an important discussion point in the assessment process. For example, a response of 'quite often' to the question on the frequency of panics should lead to further questioning as to whether the client actually experiences discrete panic attacks (usually 5–10 minutes' duration), so that a diagnosis of panic disorder would be warranted rather than for example generalized anxiety disorder. Different CB treatments have been elaborated for panic disorder (Clark, 1989), generalized anxiety disorder (Butler et al., 1987) and depression (Beck et al., 1979). Nevertheless there is some overlap in the treatment because of co-morbidity, the fact that many depressed clients are also highly anxious and that many panic disorder clients are often at least mildly depressed. The counselling approach used has to take account of any co-morbidity whilst at the same time having a primary focus on that disorder which is most debilitating for the individual. A differential diagnosis indicates the major and minor targets in the client's condition. Having specific criteria for different conditions provides a basis for answering the fundamental research question of 'which treatment works best for which client' (Paul, 1967).

Within the cognitive-behavioural paradigm it is suggested that each of the emotional disorders has a particular cognitive content, which can be assessed with self-report measures with varying degrees of established reliability. For example, for depression, the Dysfunctional Attitude Scale

(Weissman, 1979) is an often used and well-validated instrument; respondents are asked to register their agreement on a 7-point Likert Scale to statements such as 'My happiness depends more on other people than it does on me' and 'I can reach important goals without slave driving myself'. The cognitive content of a client's panic disorder can be made explicit using Greenberg's (1989) questionnaire, which contains items such as 'a panic attack can give me a heart attack' and 'I have to escape the situation when I start having symptoms or something terrible could happen'.

A cognitive-behavioural assessment requires not only an identification of cognitive content but also of the typical distorted cognitive processes of the client. Burns (1980) has listed what seem to be the ten most common self-defeating thought processes.

1 **All or nothing thinking** – seeing everything as black and white, e.g. 'if I am not in complete control, I will lose all control'.
2 **Over-generalization** – where it is concluded from one negative event that other negative events are thereby likely, e.g. 'I wasn't successful at that and now everything is probably going to fall apart'.
3 **Mental filter** – seizing on a negative fragment of a situation and dwelling on it, omitting consideration of any positive feature, e.g. 'town was crowded, it was awful, . . . oh yes I did get some great bargains and bump into some old friends . . . but it was so bad in town'.
4 **Automatic discounting** – a sensitivity to absorbing negative information and summarily discounting positive information, e.g. 'yes I was complimented, but he is nice to everyone'.
5 **Jumping to conclusions** – where a conclusion is inferred from irrelevant evidence, e.g. 'everyone stared at me because my stomach was bloated'. This often involves 'mind reading'.
6 **Magnification and minimization** – magnifying imperfections and minimizing positive attributes.
7 **Emotional reasoning** – using feeling as evidence of the truth of a situation, e.g. 'I feel guilty therefore I must have done something bad'.
8 **Should statements** – an overdose of moral imperatives, 'shoulds', 'musts', 'have to's' and 'oughts'.
9 **Labelling and mislabelling** – emotional reactions are in large measure a product of the label a person attaches to a phenomenon. An inappropriate label can produce a distressing reaction.
10 **Personalization** – egocentric interpretation of interpersonal events relating to the self, e.g. 'two people laughed and whispered something to each other when I walked by, they were probably saying I look odd'.

Paranoid personality
  I am disliked by others
  Life is a competitive struggle against external enemies
  Therefore, I will excuse myself from blame and failure by attributing blame to others

Schizoid personality
  I am a misfit
  Life is a difficult place and human relationships are troublesome
  Therefore, it is better for me to keep my distance and maintain a low profile

Anti-social personality
  I am entitled to what I want
  Life is a jungle where dog eats dog
  Therefore, I will eat before I am eaten and defy their efforts to tame me

Obsessive-compulsive personality
  I am liable to be held responsible for what goes wrong
  Life is unpredictable
  Therefore, I have to be on guard against anything that might go wrong

Figure 7.4   *Core rubrics for personality disorders*

These distorted cognitive processes can be found across the full range of emotional disorders and any one client will probably be particularly prone to a few of these processes. There is some overlap between the processes, it is not suggested that each self-defeating thought pattern is in a water-tight container.

In recent years the attention of cognitive-behaviourists has shifted to a focus on personality disorders, partly because these disorders may co-exist with an emotional disorder such as depression or anxiety and make it more difficult to treat the latter. Forgus and Shulman (1979) have provided a framework for examining the cognitive content of the personality disorders by asking clients to perform the sentence completion exercise below.

1   I am . . .
2   Life is . . .
3   So I . . .

Whilst each individual's response will be unique to them, it is argued that there are families of responses that typify the personality disorders. Completion of the above sentences by a client would give a brief summary (rubric) of that client in relation to others and the strategies he or she uses. Certain rubrics are held to be prototypical of particular personality disorders; these are called core rubrics (Figure 7.4).

To meet the diagnostic criteria for a personality disorder the client would not only have to manifest the criteria at the time of assessment but would also have to have exhibited such traits by early adulthood. It follows that the personality disorderd client will have exhibited the same view of themselves (I am), view of the world (Life is) and strategies

(Therefore), in early adulthood. Within the cognitive-behavioural frame-work the genesis of personality disorders is held to lie in the acquisition of maladaptive beliefs in childhood. These beliefs were probably functional in the context in which they originated but are maladaptive in the current adult situation. To trace the aetiology of personality disorder it is also useful to ask clients to complete the framework as if they were in childhood. Where the truthfulness of a client might be in question (for example, a client with a suspected anti-social personality disorder), evidence would need to be collected from significant others and 'slotted' into the framework. In moving from the treatment of emotional disorders to personality disorders there is a shift to a more historical focus with a greater emphasis on childhood material. Beck, Freeman and Associates (1990) have developed a similar framework to Forgus and Shulman (1979) using the headings View of self, View of others (a greater emphasis than in Forgus and Shulman on the interpersonal), Strategies and Main Beliefs, and have applied it to elaborate each of the personality disorders except for borderline personality disorder (BPD). Beck, Freeman and Associates were unable to explicate the specific thought content of BPDs and suggest that it is more their thought processes such as all or nothing thinking that are the primary problem. In addition they suggest their compulsiveness and low frustration tolerance complicate matters. Beck, Freeman and Associates also suggest that their chronically low self-esteem has to be a prime therapeutic target.

Young (1990) contends that dysfunctional experiences with early socializing agents and peers can lead to the formation of Early Maladaptive Schemas (EMS). He defines EMS as 'extremely stable and enduring themes (regarding oneself and one's relationship with others) that develop during childhood and are elaborated throughout an individual's lifetime. These schemas serve as templates for the processing of later experiences' (1990: 9). They are most in evidence when the person shows high levels of affect and overreacts to situations. He identifies 16 maladaptive schemas grouped under five headings.

1 **Impaired autonomy** – expectations about oneself and the environment that interfere with one's perceived ability to separate, survive and function independently.
2 **Disconnection** – expectation that one's need for nurturing, stable, trustworthy and empathetic relationships – social or intimate – will not be met in a predictable manner.
3 **Undesirability** – the expectation that one will not be desirable to other people in terms of any of the following: physical attractiveness, social skills, inner worth, moral integrity, interesting personality, career accomplishment, etc.

4　**Restricted self-expression** – inordinate restriction or suppression of one's emotions, impulses, natural inclinations or daily preferences in order to gain the respect of others or avoid guilt.

5　**Insufficient limits** – excessive personal wants that lead to difficulty meeting others' expectations or one's personal goals.

Young educates clients on how they use schema maintenance strategies (for example, look for information that supports their schema and discount information that contradicts the maladaptive schema). He also introduces the notion of schema avoidance, where the client will not think about certain material because it is highly affect-laden; this seems consistent with defensive notions such as denial. The third process he highlights is schema compensation: engaging in behaviour to compensate for an activated maladaptive schema (for example, a person who proves to himself and others how strong he is to compensate for an activated 'weakness' schema). The focus of therapy is schema change. This is done by the counsellor identifying and labelling the client's schemas and challenging them. Extensive use is made of imagery to evoke memories and feelings.

What does change mean and how is it brought about?

Change within the cognitive-behavioural paradigm is often synonymous with symptom reduction and behaviour change. Thus success with an anxious client would be gauged by say a reduction in the number of and intensity of the symptoms on the anxiety sub-scale of the Hospital Anxiety and Depression Scale described earlier. If the anxious client had also shown agoraphobic avoidance his/her improvement would also be assessed by his/her ability to venture forth alone. However, for some conditions such as depression, lasting symptom reduction, that is to say relapse prevention, is postulated to depend on the modification of core beliefs. Counselling psychologists are likely to consult not only with clients who might merit a diagnostic label on DSM IV but also with clients with problems in living; for both categories attention has been paid to the question of what constitutes clinical change. (This is an important question not only from the point of view of whether what the counselling psychologist does makes any 'real' difference to the client's life but also from the point of view of the audits demanded of employers of counselling psychologists. Jacobson and Truax (1991) have suggested three ways to operationalize clinically significant change:

1　When the post-test mean score of a client falls beyond the mean of a comparative dysfunctional group by two or more standard deviations.

2　When the post-test mean score of a client falls within two standard deviations of a normative group's mean.

3   When the post-test mean score of a client is more likely to have been
    drawn from the normative rather than the dysfunctional group's
    distribution.

For depression, norms for normal and dysfunctional groups are readily
available (Nietzel et al., 1987), making the determination of clinically
significant change easier than for other disorders where comparative data
have yet to be assembled. Cognitive-behaviour therapy is not a single
therapy and it may be that some cognitive-behaviour therapies turn out to
be better than others at bringing about change with some disorders. They
can be categorized under four main headings: coping skills, problem-
solving, cognitive restructuring and structural cognitive therapy. First the
similarities of the cognitive-behaviour therapies are described and then the
differences. The family members share the following characteristics.

1   Therapy begins with an elaborate, well-planned rationale. This
provides clients with an explanation of their disturbance and of the steps
that they will be guided through to help them overcome their difficulties.
In practice this means explaining that it is the interpretation and evaluation of an event (B) that is the major influence on emotional response
(C), rather than the event/stimulus (A) *per se*. Analogies are useful to
convey this message. For example 'the mind is like a camera, it depends
on the settings and the lenses you choose as to what sort of photographs
of events you take. It is possible to teach people to choose the settings
and lenses so that you get a more realistic picture of the situation than the
ones that you are typically disturbed about.'

The rationale for the behavioural dimension of therapy is usually
explained in terms of activity as a prerequisite for a sense of mastery or
pleasure. It is therefore necessary to overcome the inertia that emotional
distress can produce.

The cognitive and behavioural dimensions overlap considerably. For
example, a client may refuse to go to the theatre, something he once used
to enjoy; that is, he resists the behavioural task on the cognitive grounds
that 'I know I am not going to enjoy it, so why bother?' This roadblock
would be tackled cognitively by suggesting that the thought he would
not enjoy the play was a hypothesis; he does not have a crystal ball and as
such he needs to conduct an experiment to assess the veracity of his
prediction. At the start of therapy it is also important to outline the time
scale of therapy, the likelihood of success and the importance of
homework assignments.

2   Therapy provides training in skills that the client can utilize to
increase his effectiveness in handling his daily life.

Clients are asked to record events between sessions that they experience as upsetting. These may be external events such as being criticized

by a spouse or internal events, for example a sudden change of mood looking out of the window watching the traffic go by. Having identified the triggering events and the emotional responses to these events, clients are asked to record what they might have said to themselves to get so upset, that is, to find the Bs of the ABC model. Clients may have greater or less access to the B depending on whether it is at the forefront of their mind or at the edge of awareness. Part of the counselling psychologist's therapeutic skills lies in making the Bs explicit and then helping the client challenge whether or not they are valid and useful and by whose authority they are held. For example, a client who experiences a down-turn in mood watching the traffic go by may have been saying to himself: 'Life is just passing me by, I'm always getting myself into a bad mood, I'll always be this way, I'm a failure.' A more rational response might have been, 'I am only 40, life begins at 40, some things I have done well, some badly. Join the human race.'

3   Therapy emphasizes the client making independent use of cognitive-behavioural skills outside of the therapy context.

If in the therapy session the therapist had, for example, drawn a client's attention to a constant theme of failure in his Bs, the client would be alerted that such thoughts could well be triggers for a lowering of mood outside the therapy session. Consequently the client would be given a mood monitoring exercise to conduct outside of therapy. First the client might be instructed to pause when she noticed the first signs of emotional distress. Then she would have to review her self-defeating talk for themes of failure. Having identified which theme or themes were operative, she would then apply the alternative rational response which had been selected and practised in therapy in order to behave in a way that could enhance her sense of mastery or pleasure.

4   Therapy encourages the client to attribute his improvement in mood more to his own increased skilfulness than to the therapist's endeavours.

If the client sees his improvement in mood as a product of his own change in thinking habits and behaviour and can continue using these skills, the therapist will be able to terminate therapy. Clients can be prepared to make such attributions by the therapist's constant emphasis on the importance of homework assignments. Essentially clients are being taught a skill for their independent use, and the more they practise it the more skilful they will become.

The cognitive-behaviour therapies can be categorized under four main headings, although there is some overlap between them.

Coping skills   A coping skill has two components: a self-verbalization or instruction and a resultant behaviour. A client's difficulty in managing particular situations may be due to a deficiency in a coping skill. For example, a depressed client's inability to be assertive, may be due to a belief that they should never express their own needs, and a consequent 'mumbling' at a time that they should express their needs. The Stress Inoculation Training (SIT) of Meichenbaum (1985) addresses both the cognitive and behavioural aspects of coping skills and is the most well-known therapy in this category. SIT is aimed at the reduction and prevention of stress. Stress is viewed as an interaction between the individual and the environment. Both need to be targeted for change. At an individual level clients may be taught what to say to themselves and how to respond in situations that they find difficult. At an environmental level the client might be encouraged to organize with others, say, a change in their shift pattern that was more conducive to the workers' interests.

Problem-solving The problem-solving therapies suggest that it is clients' deficiencies in problem-solving that lead to the development and maintenance of their disturbance. Problem-solving therapy (Nezu et al., 1989) has been the most widely applied therapy in this category. Problem-solving is conceptualized as involving the following stages:

(a) problem orientation, i.e. 'locking on' to a problem;
(b) precise definition of the problem;
(c) the generation of as many alternative solutions as possible;
(d) choosing the best solution;
(e) planning implementation of the solution;
(f) reviewing progress.

If the chosen solution has not remedied the problem or only partially so, another 'solution' is chosen, implemented and subsequently reviewed. This approach can be applied to both impersonal and interpersonal problems.

Cognitive restructuring The two main therapies under this category are rational emotive behaviour therapy (REBT; Dryden, 1990) and cognitive therapy (CT; Beck et al., 1979).

REBT contends that irrationality is a major determinant of emotional disorder. Ellis (1962) has suggested that much of the neurotic person's thinking is dominated by 'musts', 'shoulds', 'oughts' and 'have to's'. From the inappropriate use of these moral imperatives, three beliefs may develop:

1 'Awfulizing', which is the tendency to make grossly exaggerated evaluations of negative events.

2 'Low Frustration Tolerance', which is the tendency to believe that uncomfortable situations are impossible to bear.
3 'Damnation', which is the tendency to evaluate as 'bad' the essence or human value of self and/or others as a result of the individual's behaviour.

In CT it is maladaptive interpretations of situations that are viewed as exercising a pivotal role with regard to emotional distress rather than irrational beliefs. Beck, Freeman and Associates (1990) contend for example that an interpretation of a situation that was adaptive in childhood may become maladaptive in adulthood. For example, an abused child may well conclude on the basis of his/her experiences that adults should be approached with great caution, and this may lead to an unnecessary timidity with other people when he or she becomes an adult.

In CT clients are asked to collect data on their current maladaptive interpretations of situations. These interpretations are then cross-examined and if possible tested out empirically. Thus the counselling psychologist may, say, seek to lift a depressed client's mood by tackling the latter's inactivity. However, the client might protest that there is little point in activity because there will be no enjoyment. Rather than get into an argument with the client as to whether he will or will not enjoy the activity, in a spirit of what Beck terms collaborative empiricism, the counselling psychologist might suggest trying the activity as the only sure way of finding out how it influences mood.

Structural cognitive therapy In structural cognitive therapy (Liotti, 1986) the concern is with 'deep' structures. Three levels of cognitive organization are posited:

1 **Core level** – beliefs (schemata) of the individual that have been formed, usually during childhood and adolescence, and that are tacitly held by the individual as unquestionable assumptions about some important aspect of self and reality.
2 **Intermediate level** – verbalizable, explicit descriptions of the self, other people and the world.
3 **Peripheral level** – the plans of action and problem-solving strategies that each individual is able to develop in the day-to-day confrontation with the environment.

A primary concern in structural cognitive therapy is to make explicit the core level. The treatment, for example, of an agoraphobic client would begin with behavioural strategies of helping the client to try going gradually greater distances alone but therapy would not be terminated when the client had learnt to travel alone. Therapy would also explore deeper issues such as 'who am I getting out and about for anyway?' In addition, developmental origins of the disorder would be explored; for example, an adult agoraphobic may have had a very unwell mother as a child and found that he regularly had to leave her behind to stay with a variety of relatives.

The time scale for the application of the first three categories of CBT is brief compared to traditional psychotherapy, typically involving weekly sessions over three to four months. However, the time scale for the fourth category, structural cognitive therapy, is considerably longer, typically 18 months, because its goal is to achieve such fundamental changes in the individual. In many ways structural cognitive therapy reflects the recently evolved cognitive-behavioural approach to personality disorders. It is well established that if clients not only have an Axis 1 disorder, such as depression, but also an Axis 2 personality disorder, then they are less likely to respond to psychotherapy. As between one-third and two-thirds of clients presenting with anxiety and depression have a co-existing personality disorder it has been important to develop treatment strategies to take account of this (Scott et al., 1995).

Pretzer and Fleming (1989) have suggested the following guidelines for treating clients with personality disorders. (It should be emphasized, however, that none of the CB approaches for treating personality disorders has yet been empirically evaluated.)

1 Interventions are most effective when based on an individualized conceptualization of the client's problems.
2 It is important for the therapist and client to work collaboratively towards clearly identified shared goals.
3 It is important to focus more than usual attention on the therapist–client interaction.
4 Consider interventions that do not require extensive client self-disclosure.
5 Interventions which increase the client's sense of self-efficacy often reduce the intensity of the client's symptomatology and facilitate other interventions.
6 The therapist should not rely primarily on verbal interventions.
7 The therapist should try to identify and address the client's fears before implementing changes.
8 The therapist should anticipate problems with compliance.
9 The therapist should not assume that the client exists in a reasonable or functional environment.
10 The therapist must attend to his or her emotional reactions during the course of therapy.

11 The therapist should be realistic regarding the length of therapy, goals for therapy and standards for self-evaluation.

The CB approaches to personality disorders are an expression of four trends in cognitive-behaviour therapy, that make dialogue and perhaps integration with other psychotherapies more feasible than hitherto.

1 **Inclusion of non-conscious processes**. There is an acceptance that schemata and personal rules are inferred constructs and not observable behaviours which operate covertly and without awareness, though this does not go as far as acceptance of the notion of a Freudian unconscious.
2 **Emphasis on interpersonal process**. The salient cognitions to tackle in the personality disorders are thought to be those concerned with the view of self in relation to others.
3 **Concern for emotional processes**. Whilst cognitive-behaviour therapists have long accepted the interdependence of cognition and affect there is increasing attention being given to affect as conveying information, and as an action disposition. Affect is given the same status as cognition as a therapeutic means by which the client can become less disturbed.
4 **The importance of the therapeutic relationship**. Whilst a good therapeutic relationship has always been held to be a necessary part of teaching clients the various cognitive-behavioural skills, it is only recently in the treatment of personality disorders that it is coming to be understood as a possible laboratory or microcosm of the client's difficulties.

The nature of the relationship between counselling psychologist and client

Within cognitive-behaviour therapy the therapeutic relationship has received much less attention than the technical aspects of counselling. This has not been because the therapeutic relationship was thought unimportant but rather that it was taken for granted that a good therapeutic relationship was a necessary but not sufficient condition for client change. The cognitive-behaviour therapist would insist that both technical and relationship skills are necessary for client change, whilst some other schools of counselling see only the necessity for the relationship to be considered. The Therapist Client Rating Scale (TCRS; Bennun et al., 1986) has been used to assess the client's view of therapy sessions and also the counsellor's view. The client form consists of three scales:

1   Positive regard/interest
2   Competency/experience
3   Activity/guidance.

The counsellors form also consists of three scales:

1   Positive regard
2   Self-disclosure/engagement
3   Cooperation/goal orientation.

Both forms are made up of 29 items with each item scaled 1 to 6 (e.g. 1 = very talkative to 6 = very quiet). The instrument has been used with phobic and obsessive–compulsive clients and a significant positive correlation was found between the client factor 'positive regard' and outcome of therapy.

Counsellors providing cognitive therapy for depression are assessed in research trials using the Cognitive Therapy Scale. The scale has three parts. Part 1, General Therapeutic Skills, and Part 2, Conceptualization, Strategies and Techniques, are of equal depth reflecting the equal weighting given to the personal and technical in cognitive therapy. Part 3 is a brief section in which the rater indicates any additional considerations, for example a particularly difficult client, to be taken into account when rating the quality of the interview. The headings from Part 1 of the Cognitive Therapy Scale are shown below and the extent to which the counsellor met the goal for each heading on a scale 0 to 6 indicated: 0 = poor; 1 = barely adequate; 2 = mediocre; 3 = satisfactory; 4 = good; 5 = very good; 6 = excellent.

Cognitive Therapy Scale

Part 1   General Therapeutic Skills

1 Agenda (0–6)
Therapist worked with client to set an appropriate agenda with target problems suitable for available time. Established priorities then followed agenda.

2 Feedback (0–6)
Therapist was especially adept at eliciting and responding to verbal and non-verbal feedback throughout the session, e.g., elicited reaction to session, regularly checked for understanding and helped summarize main points at end of session.

3 Understanding (0–6)
Therapist seemed to understand the client's internal reality thoroughly

and was adept at communicating this understanding through appropriate verbal and non-verbal responses to the client, e.g. the tone of the therapist's response conveyed a sympathetic understanding of the client's 'message'. Excellent listening and empathic skills.

4 Interpersonal effectiveness (0–6)
Therapist displayed optimal levels of warmth, concern, confidence, genuineness and professionalism appropriate for this particular client in this session.

5 Collaboration (0–6)
Collaboration seemed excellent. Therapist encouraged client as much as possible to take an active role during the session, for example by offering choices, so they could function as a team.

6 Pacing and efficient use of time (0–6)
Therapist used time very effectively by tactfully limiting peripheral and unproductive discussion and pacing the session as rapidly as was appropriate for the client.

Thus in the treatment of Axis 1 disorders the therapeutic relationship has been an important, albeit infrequently discussed, aspect of the counselling process. With regard to the counselling of Axis 2 personality disorders the role of the therapeutic relationship assumes an even greater importance. For example, if a client has an avoidant personality disorder, the key feature of the disorder is that others are seen as critical and demeaning; the therapeutic implication of this is that the counsellor can very easily be cast as 'just like all the others' and special care has to be taken to elicit from the client whether anything has been said or done by the therapist that has upset them. By contrast, a less solicitous stance would be needed with a client with a dependent personality disorder, where the key feature is a belief that they cannot function independently. Thus the counsellor's approach to the relationship is not uniform across the personality disorders.

Family, group and organizational applications

The reciprocal interaction of cognitions, emotions, behaviours and physiology, shown in Figure 7.1 above, takes place in an environment which may to varying degrees be toxic. The individual may 'inhale' the fumes through any or a combination of the four ports of entry – cognitions, emotions, behaviours and physiology. The cognitions port is always implicated in emotional distress, though the cognition need not necessarily be conscious, as it is now well established in cognitive psychology that people do process information outside of conscious awareness.

The environments which have so far been given consideration in cognitive-behaviour therapy are current partner or family and the organizational environment at work. These are now considered in turn.

Current partner and family

In some instances it is recognized that it may be more appropriate to target the faulty cognitions in the environment rather than the individual. For example, a depressed child might be better helped by the counsellor challenging maladaptive family constructs (i.e. family-held beliefs) with his/her parents and perhaps siblings. So that though the target for change is the child's symptoms, the most efficient way forward might be to challenge the reasonableness of the parents' expectations of him/her and what they communicate to him/her about his/her worth. Cognitive family therapy may in such circumstances be the best way forward. Even in instances of adult depression, marital therapy may be the counselling modality of choice rather than individual therapy. It has been found that 50 per cent of women with depression have severe marital problems, and that the provision of cognitive-behavioural marital therapy, to couples willing to participate, not only improves marital satisfaction but also lifts depression. By contrast, providing individual cognitive therapy to depressed women whilst lifting the depression does not improve marital satisfaction (O'Leary and Beach, 1990).

Cognitive-behavioural marital therapy involves behaviour exchange contracts, practice in communication skills and the challenging of beliefs that disrupt relationships (see Scott, 1989). The beliefs targeted for change in cognitive-behavioural marital therapy tend to cluster under five headings.

1 **Disagreement is destructive**: 'When my partner and I disagree, I feel like our relationship is falling apart.'
2 **Mindreading is expected**: 'People who have a close relationship can sense each other's needs as if they could read each other's minds.'
3 **Partners cannot change**: 'Damage done early in relationships probably cannot be reversed.'
4 **The sexes are different**: 'Misunderstandings between partners generally are due to inborn differences in the psychological make-up of men and women.'
5 **Sexual perfectionism**: 'I get upset if I think I have not completely satisfied my partner sexually.'

Organizations

The most popular model of stress is a transactional one, that is, stress resides neither in the individual nor in the environment, but arises when there is a poor fit between the individual and the environment. Within the work context, stress can arise at the individual (I)/organization (O) interface. By organization is meant the immediate line managers of the individual, who may act as conduits of the organization's belief system. Richman (1988) has contended that individuals may possess vocational irrational beliefs (VIBS) and that the nature of these will be different at various points of the career cycle. Similarly, organizations may be purveyors of VIBS. A list, by no means exhaustive, of I/O VIBS is shown below.

Vocational Irrational Beliefs (VIBS)

At entry

1 'I have to show my boss I can do an excellent job or I will be a failure.'
2 'If I do not like the post right away I will never find a post that is for me.'
3 'I am bright and talented and therefore should not have to do the mundane jobs.'
4 'I cannot stand not using my potential.'

VIBS of a demoralizing boss

1 'New recruits must learn the job slowly, going through every single step.'
2 'New recruits cannot have anything to contribute and therefore should not have their views considered.'
3 'Beginning recruits should do as we say and not ask questions or expect feedback unless we choose to give it.'
4 'New recruits should be given the easiest tasks.'
5 'New recruits should be tested out by being assigned to do the most difficult tasks right away.'

Mid–career

1 'I should have achieved a higher position by this age in my life.'
2 'I cannot stand that I may never accomplish my career goals.'
3 'I am worthless as a person because others of my age have gone further.'
4 'I cannot stand looking after younger workers who may move up beyond my position.'

5 'I should not level off in my career or redefine my goals because this will mean I am weak and not ambitious enough.'

Organizational VIBS

1 'He/she has done well enough in their specialism, they should not want to make any kind of change.'
2 'He/she has too many concerns about their family, they can no longer be trusted as a committed member of the Company.'
3 'He/she should not suddenly try to make a name for themselves at this stage in their career.'
4 'I should not offer him/her any growth opportunities since their time here is limited.'
5 'Mid-career workers seem too conflicted and unmotivated to be given any challenging assignments.'

Resolving many of the so-called 'personality clashes' within industry is actually about identifying and modifying individual and organizational VIBS.

Group

The cognitive-behavioural approaches that have been described for Axis 1 disorders are essentially psycho-educational and lend themselves easily to group treatment. The intent in group cognitive-behaviour therapy, it should be noted, is different from other group psychotherapies where the focus is on group processes and dynamics. The group cognitive-behavioural approach is commended because it is seen as a cost-effective way of bringing about change. For example, Scott and Stradling (1990) have demonstrated that group cognitive therapy for depression produces as much change as individual cognitive therapy. Group cognitive-behavioural programmes have also been described for anxiety and bulimia. Given the scarcity of counsellor resources and long waiting lists in the UK, group cognitive-behavioural approaches are likely to become more common-place, with counsellors having difficulty making time for the lengthier individual CBT treatments of personality disorders developed primarily in the United States.

Research evidence about efficacy

There is now no disorder to which cognitive-behaviour therapy has not been applied, including teaching psychotic clients to control their symptoms. But this is not to say that CBT is of demonstrated efficacy for all disorders; with many disorders systematic evaluations have only just begun. At least, however, with regard to CBT a beginning has been made to answer the basic research question posed by Paul (1967), 'What treatment works best, with which clients, under what circumstances, delivered by whom?' The most numerous outcome studies at present relate to depression and anxiety, and the results of these are briefly summarized now.

Depression is the most extensively researched disorder to which CBT has been applied. An analysis of 29 randomized controlled trials (Depression Guideline Panel, 1993) suggested that in acute treatment the efficacy of cognitive therapy was 47 per cent, of interpersonal therapy was 52 per cent (based on one trial only) and of brief dynamic psychotherapy was 35 per cent. However, there was a trend for cognitive therapy to have a lower relapse rate than interpersonal therapy (Shea et al., 1992). Indeed, cognitive therapy appears to have approximately half the relapse rate of antidepressant medication (Evans et al., 1992).

Numerous studies have attested to the efficacy of exposure treatment for agoraphobia, and it has been shown to be superior to a variety of credible 'placebo' interventions (Mathews et al., 1981). Though the graded exposure to feared situations is overtly a behavioural strategy, there are implicit cognitive strategies, about for example the conceptualization of 'failure' experiences. The typical finding is that two-thirds of clients are substantially improved, though even in these some disability remains.

Most clients with agoraphobia also experience some episodes of panic, and panic disorder has become a focus of treatment in its own right. The key elements in the treatment of panic are:

1 Systematic exposure to somatic sensations associated with panic (for example, those associated with hyperventilation, overbreathing).
2 Challenging catastrophic misinterpretations of bodily symptoms.
3 (Usually) breathing retraining.

For panic disorder clients who do not have severe agoraphobic avoidance, that is mild/moderate agoraphobic avoidance, the typical finding is that 90 per cent become panic free after 12 one-hour sessions of cognitive therapy, whereas the comparable figures for applied relaxation training are 50–55 per cent, and for clients on a waiting list 5 per cent. These changes have been found to be maintained at one-year follow-up. For panic disorder clients with only mild agoraphobic avoidance, applied relaxation training and cognitive therapy seem to be roughly comparable. In one study (Telch et al., 1993), involving a comparison of 12 sessions of group cognitive-behaviour therapy for panic disorder over an eight-week period with a delayed treatment control, at six-month follow-up 63 per cent of the treated patients had recovered compared to 9 per cent of controls.

For generalized anxiety disorder Butler et al. (1987) have developed a treatment package that consists of:

(a) information about the nature of anxiety and what to expect from treatment;
(b) a cognitive component to address specific anxiety-producing thoughts;
(c) distraction and relaxation techniques for anticipating anxiety;
(d) *in vivo* exposure to avoided situations; and
(e) a component focusing on increasing self-confidence, which includes identification of the client's strengths and areas of competence and identification of and increase in enjoyable activities.

They found their anxiety management programme superior to a waiting-list control condition at post-test and clinically significant gains were maintained at follow-up. However, in trials where such programmes have been conducted but without the *in vivo* exposure component, the anxiety management clients have only fared as well as those given non-directive counselling.

Counselling psychologists can become dismayed that their clients may not seem to do as well as those in published controlled trials. One of the reasons for the 'apparent failure' is that clients with a mixed diagnosis are deliberately screened out from trials. For example, a depressed client with a drink problem would be excluded from a controlled trial of depression. As such the exclusion criteria of controlled trials have to be carefully examined. They may, for example, exclude panic patients who are housebound or those with a personality disorder. Nevertheless, in a consecutive series of 100 referrals the first author found that in primary care, 67 per cent met inclusion criteria, depression (23 per cent), generalized anxiety disorder (25 per cent) and panic disorder (19 per cent). It is then possible to use the results of outcome studies to evaluate the majority of cases seen by a counselling psychologist. There is, however, another difference between controlled trials and counselling psychology in practice that has to be taken into account, which is of ensuring that the client has an adequate 'dose' of counselling. In a controlled trial 'the dose of therapy' is guaranteed: however, the counselling psychologist in practice has to contend with the pressures of the waiting list and may often be only able to deliver one-half the number of sessions delivered per patient in trials. Accordingly the degree of change expected has to be scaled down. It may be that the norm for depressed patients by the seventh session should be a 25 per cent reduction in Beck

Depression Inventory score. (This can also serve as a marker for progress when it is possible to provide more sessions.) For generalized anxiety disorder a 25 per cent reduction in Beck Anxiety Inventory score by the seventh session may be the appropriate norm.

The continued existence of counselling psychology will probably depend on its ability to produce demonstrable change and establish an adequate methodology of audit. One of the advantages of the cognitive-behavioural approach in this connection is the careful explanation of procedures and the many areas in which it is already of demonstrated efficacy.

References

APA (American Psychiatric Association) (1994) *Diagnostic and Statistical Manual of Mental Disorders*, 4th edn. Washington, DC: APA.

Bandura, A. (1982) 'Self-efficacy mechanism in human agency', *American Psychologist*, 37: 122–47.

Beck, A.T., Epstein, N. and Harrison, R. (1983) 'Cognition, attitudes and personality dimensions in depression', *British Journal of Cognitive Psychotherapy*, 1: 1–16.

Beck, A.T., Freeman, A. and Associates (1990) *Cognitive Therapy of Personality Disorders*. New York: Guilford Press.

Beck, A.T., Rush, A.J., Shaw, B.F. and Emery, G. (1979) *Cognitive Therapy of Depression*. New York: Wiley.

Bennun, I., Hahlweg, K., Schindler, L. and Langotz, M. (1986) 'Therapists' and clients' perceptions: the development and cross-cultural analysis of an assessment instrument'. *British Journal of Clinical Psychology*, 25: 275–85.

Burns, D. (1980) *Feeling Good: the New Mood Therapy*. New York: New American Library.

Butler, G., Cullington, A., Hibbert, G. et al. (1987) 'Anxiety management for persistent generalised anxiety', *British Journal of Psychiatry*, 151: 535–42.

Clark, D.M. (1989) 'Anxiety states: panic and generalised anxiety', in K. Hawton et al. (eds), *Cognitive-Behaviour Therapy for Psychiatric Problems*. Oxford: Oxford University Press.

Depression Guideline Panel (1993) *Depression in Primary Care: Treatment of Major Depression*. Washington, DC: US Department of Health and Human Services.

Dryden, W. (1990) *Rational-Emotive Counselling in Action*. London: Sage.

Ellis, A. (1962) *Reason and Emotion in Psychotherapy*. New York: Lyle Stuart.

Evans, M.D., Hollon, S.D., DeRubeis, R.J. et al. (1992) 'Differential relapse following cognitive therapy and pharmacotherapy for depression', *Archive of General Psychiatry*, 49: 802–8.

Forgus, R. and Shulman, B. (1979) *Personality: a Cognitive View*. Englewood Cliffs, NJ: Prentice Hall.

Greenberg, R.L. (1989) 'Panic disorder and agoraphobia', in J. Scott, J. Mark,

G. Williams and A.T. Beck (eds), *Cognitive Therapy in Clinical Practice: an Illustrative Casebook*. London: Routledge.

Jacobson, N.S. and Truax, P. (1991) 'Clinical significance: a statistical approach to defining meaningful change in psychotherapy research'. *Journal of Consulting and Clinical Psychology*, 59: 12–19.

Liotti, G. (1986) 'Structural cognitive therapy', in W. Dryden and W. Golden (eds), *Cognitive-Behavioral Approaches to Psychotherapy*. London: Harper and Row.

Mathews, A.M., Gelder, M.G. and Johnson, D.W. (1981) *Agoraphobia: Nature and Treatment*. New York: Guilford Press.

Meichenbaum, D. (1985) *Stress Inoculation Training*. New York: Pergamon Press.

Nezu, A.M., Nezu, C.M. and Perri, M.G. (1989) *Problem Solving Therapy for Depression*. New York: Wiley.

Nietzel, M.T., Russell, R.L., Hemmings, K.D. and Gretter, M.L. (1987) 'Clinical significance of psychotherapy for unipolar depression: a meta-analytic approach to social comparison', *Journal of Consulting and Clinical Psychology*, 55: 156–61.

O'Leary, K.D. and Beach, S.R.H. (1990) 'Marital therapy: a viable treatment for depression and marital discord', *American Journal of Psychiatry*, 147: 183–6.

Paul, G.L. (1967) 'Strategy of outcome research in psychotherapy', *Journal of Consulting Psychology*, 31: 109–18.

Persons, J.B. (1989) *Cognitive Therapy in Practice: a Case Formulation Approach*. New York: Norton.

Pretzer, J. and Fleming, B. (1989) 'Cognitive-behavioral treatment of personality disorders', *The Behavior Therapist*, 12: 105–9.

Richman, D.R. (1988) 'Cognitive psychotherapy through the career cycle', in W. Dryden and P. Trower (eds), *Developments in Cognitive Psychotherapy*. London: Sage.

Scott, M. (1989) *A Cognitive-Behavioral Approach to Clients' Problems*. London: Tavistock/Routledge.

Scott, M.J. and Stradling, S.G. (1990) 'Group cognitive therapy for depression produces clinically significant reliable change in community-based settings', *Behavioural Psychotherapy*, 18: 1–19.

Scott, M.J., Stradling, S.G. and Dryden, W. (1995) *Developing Cognitive-Behavioural Counselling*. London: Sage.

Shea, T.M., Elkin, I., Imber, S.D., Sotsky, S.M., Watkins, J.T., Collins, J.F., Pilkous, P.A., Bickham, E., Glass, D.R. Dolan, R.T. et al. (1992) 'Course of depressive symptoms over follow-up: findings from the NIMH Treatment of Depression Collaborative Research Programme', *Archives of General Psychiatry*, 49: 782–7.

Snaith, P. (1993) 'Measuring anxiety and depression', *The Practitioner*, 237: 554–9.

Telch, M.J., Lucas, J.A., Schmidt, N.B., Hanna, H.H., Jaimez, T. LaNae. and Lucas, R.A. (1993) 'Group cognitive-behavioural treatment of panic disorder', *Behaviour Research and Therapy*, 31: 279–87.

Weissman, A.N. (1979) 'The dysfunctional attitude scale: a validation study', PhD Dissertation, University of Pennsylvania.

Young, J. (1990) *Cognitive Therapy for Personality Disorders: a Schema Focussed Approach*. Sarasota, FL: Professional Resource Exchange.

Zigmond, A. and Snaith, R.P. (1983) 'The Hospital Anxiety and Depression Scale', *Acta Psychiatrica Scandinavica*, 67: 361–70.

8

The Existential-Phenomenological Paradigm

Ernesto Spinelli

The existential-phenomenological model of counselling psychology presents a radical challenge to many of the fundamental assumptions brought to both the practice of counselling psychology and to psychological research focused upon the analysis of the central features of the counselling process and their influences upon its outcomes. Much of this challenge derives from the explicitly philosophical origins of existential-phenomenological psychology that have remained central to its approach and which provide the model with its primary critiques of the natural science framework that underlies currently dominant trends in psychological theory and research.

Phenomenology refers to the study of phenomena (or 'the appearance of things') in order to clarify how the object-world is humanly experienced and presents itself to our consciousness. As such, phenomenology attempts to understand more adequately the human condition as it manifests itself in lived experience. The **existential** focus of phenomenology takes as its fundamental starting point the idea that the substance of human beings is their existence which, properly understood, reveals an inevitable relational process or movement of being ultimately leading to non-being. Taken within the context of psychology, 'existential-phenomenological psychology . . . has become that psychological discipline that seeks to explicate the *essence, structure,* or *form* of both human experience and human behavior as revealed through essential *descriptive* techniques including disciplined reflection' (Valle et al., 1989: 6, original emphasis).

Phenomenology, as a philosophical system, arose in the early years of this century. Its founder, Edmund Husserl (1859–1938), initially a student of mathematics and the natural sciences, sought to establish phenomenology as the fundamental philosophy for all scientific investigation (Husserl, 1977). In attempting such, Husserl confronted the bedevilling 'dualistic split' between subject and object upon which natural science is based, argued this to be the source of serious error and, instead, suggested a fundamental unity founded upon the phenomena of consciousness that phenomenology sought to expose and clarify (Husserl, 1977). Husserl's principal assistant, Martin Heidegger (1889–1976) both extended and 'slanted' such investigations so that they focused upon the issue of human existence, hence providing the principal spur to the development of existential-phenomenology.

Whereas dominant views of philosophy, psychology and therapy impose a separateness or distinction between individuals and the world (or between 'self and other' or 'subject and object'), the existential-phenomenological model denies this distinction and proposes, in its place, a co-constituted view of existence which argues that everything that we are, or can be, aware of, all that we reflect upon, define or distinguish is relationally derived. The very experience of 'being', for instance, is only opened to conscious reflection when it is placed in the contextual relationship of being-in-the-world (or '*Dasein*'). In this way, the reflecting being and the focus, or object, of reflection are each fundamentally defined, or co-constituted, through their various existential relations (Heidegger, 1962).

The structural tendency, or 'given' through which relations emerge has been termed by existential-phenomenological theory as **intentionality**. Intentionality refers to the fundamental, simultaneous and inseparable relationship between human consciousness and the world (that is to say, our consciousness is always *of* some 'thing') from which 'reality', as humanly experienced, is shaped, or interpreted. When viewed from the standpoint of 'being', intentionality reveals that through the process of re-constructing the meaning-possibilities of those 'things' that we are in relation with, we also re-construct the meaning-possibilities of the 'thing-constructing' being (i.e. ourselves). As such, the notion of intentionality reveals that both 'self' and 'other' (or, 'the world') are made meaningful, or 'come into being' through their interdependent, co-constitutional relations. One of the important consequences of this argument is that each of us is actively involved, or *implicated* in construing, or attempting to make meaningful, our experience of the world – which includes our experience of ourselves, of others, and of all those features, objects and mental processes that make up our lived reality.

This view stands in stark opposition to the naive assumption of the natural scientific view that posits that we can speak with impersonal certainty about the true, or objective, nature of reality. Instead, the existential-phenomenological model argues that we can never know the real world, only the interpreted world – the world that emerges through our reflections upon it. As such, all our statements about the world, or any aspect of the world – including, of course, ourselves – are, at best, approximations. We can never truly speak of 'facts' or with any final certainty because all our statements reveal limitations and assumptions that impede our ability to describe or understand things as they really are.

Some, perhaps many, or these limitations and assumptions can be made explicit, even set aside. But even so, some will always remain because they are imposed upon us by our very make-up as a species. Any number of biological, neuro-physiological, and even psychic limitations, which cannot be removed or set aside, will always be contained within any reflected statement we made about the world or ourselves. The discovery and elucidation of these givens (or interpretative limits) of our experience forms one major aspect of existential-phenomenological inquiry, just as the attempt to set aside socio-culturally and psychologically derived biases and assumptions forms the second, equally significant, concern.

The main means through which the existential-phenomenological model explores and clarifies questions of essence and existence is via a particular method that enjoins investigators to seek (1) to suspend, or **bracket** their biases and presuppositions in order to allow an openness to one's experience; (2) to remain at a **descriptive level of interpretation** in order to focus upon the immediate, or primary, data of experience; and (3) to **horizontalize** the items of description by avoiding placing any immediate hierarchies of importance or significance upon them – particularly during the early stages of investigation (Spinelli, 1989). While this method must always remain an attempt that can never be final or complete, it serves to make explicit with increasing adequacy those biases and assumptions – both (at least partially) 'bracketable' and 'given' (or invariable) – that we bring to any encounter with the world.

Underlying theory of personality

According to the existential-phenomenological model, human existence reveals

> the total, indissoluble unity or interrelationship of the individual and his or her world . . . In the truest sense, the person is viewed as having no existence apart from the world and the world as having no existence apart from persons . . . (Valle et al., 1989: 7)

When applied to life sciences such as psychology, the existential-phenomenological model approaches the question of human nature from the assumption that it is open-ended, and capable of an enormous range of experience (van Duerzen-Smith, 1988). Such a view eschews the trend in modern personality theories which seeks to categorize or 'typologize' individuals or which attempts to divide and reduce people in terms of various 'parts' or components. Instead, it aims to remain at a descriptive and open-ended level of analysis of human experience that simultaneously acknowledges both the uniqueness of each 'being-in-the-world' and the

species-shared transcultural 'givens' of being human that set the boundaries – or invariant givens – for the possibilities of our experience.

As such, the human senses that provide the basis for the information
received and perceptually translated by our brains are species-based and
limited. While they allow us to experience consciously the stimuli of the
world, their very limitations would make it at least hypothetically feasible
to argue that not *all possible* stimuli are received through them. Unlike
other living organisms whose sensory characteristics may be different, or
attuned in differing ways, human beings are governed by certain fixed
'invariants' which exist at the species level. In addition, however, all
manner of other biasing influences exist at a socio-cultural level that
further affect both the way that we process our perceptions and the
meanings we provide for the interpreted objects of our perceptions.
Psychologists interested in perceptual processes have pointed out a
substantial number of such invariants – both at the species and socio-
cultural levels (Spinelli, 1989). Furthermore, there also exist biasing
influences that are individually derived – that is to say, that are formed
from the unique experiences and interactions each of us has with the
world. All such limitations lead to the conclusion that, as humans, we
interpret the world within the 'givens' of our species-possibilities, from
biases and perspectives derived from socio-cultural influences, and from
the influences of our own unique development.

For instance, while it appears to be a 'given' of our species to perceive
reality in a 'thing'-like manner, 'the specifically labelled, or named,
"thing" that each of us experiences, and the manner or mode by which
we experience it, is dependent upon various linguistic, socio-culturally
derived influences as well as influences from our own personal experience
that dispose, or bias, us to perceive it in the way that we do' (Spinelli,
1994: 293).

This stance provokes a deeply unsettling perspective since, in one
stroke, it places human personality and experience in an uncertain,
relativistic realm of being wherein whatever meaning we may 'find' for
ourselves can no longer be seen to be certain in that it has no fully
independent, or external, basis. Further, the possibilities of human
experience are bounded, and shaped, by a number of invariants through
which each being-in-the-world interprets experience in a unique manner.
In addition, because existence is co-constituted, then each 'being-in-the-
world' is characteristically open-ended, in constant flux, or plastic, rather
than fixed or fully definable. If we consider this conclusion further,
however, we can understand that, as well as being unique and plastic,
existence is also never fully shareable since the variables that make up
each human being's experience of the world are not accessible, in any
complete or final manner, to any other human being. At best, what

attempts one might make to provide another with some sense of his or her experience of the world, can be seen to be increasingly adequate but never total or complete. Viewed from the standpoint of existential-phenomenological psychology, this view concludes that each of us is alone in our experience of reality. 'And yet, paradoxically, this "aloneness" emerges precisely because we are *in relation* to one another' (Spinelli, 1994: 294, original emphasis).

Not surprisingly, if we attempt to take in the full impact of all these ideas, we are confronted with the meaninglessness of existence, in that it has no intrinsically independent meaning. In this way, 'meaning', too, is a relative and plastic concept which emerges from co-constitutionality. Nevertheless,

> Our need to make things meaningful (by defining, or distinguishing, or 'bounding' them) appears to be another 'given' of our species. Our intolerance of meaninglessness seems to be deep-rooted, even fundamental, to our make-up. Meaninglessness instils us with *anxiety* – something seemingly meaningless disturbs us, such that we refuse to accept it and attempt to find ways to make it meaningful – usually by *likening* it to an other object whose meaning is known to us and with which the foreign object seems to share some characteristics, or by imposing some sort of functional purpose upon the foreign object which, again, places it in a 'meaningful' context derived from our experience. (Spinelli, 1994: 294–5, original emphasis)

The existential-phenomenological model employs the term **angst** to refer to the inevitable existential anxiety of being. It is the anxiety that comes with the acceptance that there are no meanings in the world apart from the relative ones that we create, that we cannot rely upon the certainty of facts, or of purpose, that we cannot know what happens to us when we are thrown out of the world, when we cease to be as humans. This temporality, which expresses our eventual nothingness, is viewed to be our most fundamental source of *angst* (van Deurzen-Smith, 1988; Heidegger, 1962; Yalom, 1980).

Nothingness, meaninglessness and aloneness are the price we must pay for our freedom, or, as some call it, our attempt to be **authentic** as human beings (Heidegger, 1962). In our efforts to avoid the experience of *angst* we 'de-humanize' ourselves. We become passive, irresponsible, seemingly determined by the will and whim of others, and seek out the security of external truths, permanent meanings, statements from on high concerning the true point and purpose to our lives. This stance towards life has been referred to as **inauthenticity** (Heidegger, 1962) or **bad faith** (Sartre, 1956), and its appeal lies precisely in that it allays the unease and uncertainty of being-in-the-world.

This 'deception' or denial of being can be seen as the central focus for the application of the existential-phenomenological model to the practice of counselling psychology since many of the issues that clients present reveal their attempts to avoid *angst* in any number of ways. For instance, clients might express a view of themselves, or their identity, as defined by certain fixed characteristics, attitudes, patterns of thought and so forth, and, when experientially confronted with evidence to the contrary, or with experiences that expand the 'meaning' they have given themselves, they reject, or disown, the evidence in order to maintain their fixed meaning rather than accept the evidence and re-shape or extend their meaning of themselves. In doing so, such individuals deny the possibilities of experiential freedom, or *choice*, that they have available to them.

'The existential-phenomenological idea of choice has often been mis-understood to suggest that we possess unlimited freedom to choose how and what "to be". This view, quite simply, is wrong' (Spinelli, 1994: 295). The choices that we are free to make arise within a *situated* freedom, which is to say that freedom whose boundaries lie within the intentional relationship through which each of us, as a 'being-in-the-world' is co-constituted. Rather than being free to choose what we want, we are, rather, free to choose how to respond to the unavoidable and unpredictable 'stimuli' of the world. In fact, more accurately speaking, 'we are *condemned* to choose' (Sartre, 1956, emphasis added). As such, our choice is *interpretational*, not at the event – or stimulus – level.

'Equally, choice, should not be understood to be solely at the level of "choosing between optional stimuli" or even between "optional meanings of stimuli"' (Spinelli, 1994: 296). Even if we may have sedimented particular meanings so that no optional alternative seems available, we remain free to choose to acknowledge or accept that one sedimented meaning. While this point may strike some readers as a trick of logic so that the view that we always choose can be maintained, on reflection it should prove to be not the case at all. For instance,

> Many of the problems and issues that clients bring to therapy originate through this self-same 'unwillingness to choose the one choice available'. In this stance . . . clients . . . place themselves in the position of 'passive victims of circumstance'. The one choice may remain the same regardless of the position I adopt toward it, but the experience of 'being' varies significantly depending on whether I choose to accept its presence in my relational world or whether I deceive myself by denying its presence (and, at times, further deceive myself by believing that another choice option is available). (Spinelli, 1994: 296–7)

In this way, it can be understood that existential choice emerges *through* the acceptance of the uncertainties that life presents us with. *Angst*, then, is not, properly speaking, a disturbing aspect of life which counselling psychologists must assist clients in alleviating, removing or resolving. Rather, *angst* exposes us to the possibilities and responsibilities of being — be they joyous or despairing, life-enhancing or confrontative of our eventual nothingness.

The assessment process

While it is highly unusual for existential-phenomenological counselling psychologists to employ any formal assessment procedures or diagnostic tests, they do, however, expect that clients express an honest and open commitment to scrupulous and focused personal disclosure of their various world-views and relations.

Emmy van Deurzen-Smith has suggested that existential-phenomenological counselling is particularly suitable for clients who critically question their own and others' opinions, who demonstrate a willingness to form their own views and who approach their problems and issues from a stance which views them as disturbances related to the dilemmas of life rather than as aspects of pathology. In addition, she has argued that this model is most effective with persons who experience themselves as alienated from the mores and demands of their society or who are at points of crisis such as confronting death or experiencing meaninglessness and isolation, who have lost their sense of relatedness to themselves, 'significant others' and/or to the world in general or who are attempting to cope with sudden and dramatic changes in a variety of personal circumstances. Similarly, she has indicated that the existential-phenomenological model is beneficially applicable to those who inhabit a foreign culture or who are members of a minority group within a dominant culture and society (van Deurzen-Smith, 1988).

While often incorrectly represented as a 'highly intellectual' model, the existential-phenomenological approach is more properly concerned with clients' willingness and ability to express their attitudes, views and feelings concerning their lives. As such, clients' capacity to verbalize their experiences directly, openly and bluntly is considered far more significant than their linguistic or intellectual abilities.

In keeping with its emphasis upon the notion of encounter, the question of assessment within the existential-phenomenological model must also address the qualities of counselling psychologists who wish to work effectively within this standpoint. As well as expecting counselling psychologists to demonstrate sound and wide-ranging theoretical knowledge and professional training, existential-phenomenological counselling psychologists should demonstrate suitable maturity and life-experience that infuses their ability to confront and deal with their own existential dilemmas. Critical self-reflection, wide-ranging engagement with various cultures, environments and work-related situations, an ability to express and acknowledge the humour, tragedy and absurdity of living, and an on-going curiosity about, and tolerance for, the different ways people opt to 'be-in-the-world' are considered to be essential features of effective existential-phenomenological counselling psychologists.

The question of change

The existential-phenomenological model views the person as constantly self-disclosing through his or her on-going relations with the world. Grounded in philosophy, its stance regarding counselling psychology is concerned with the exploration and clarification of the various relational orientations that define and provide meaning for persons at all levels of their existence. Further, it seeks to facilitate a process whereby these relations may be clarified and confronted in ways that promote an attitude of openness to the possibilities and limitations of human existence.

The problems and issues that people bring to the counselling psychologist are seen as being, first and foremost, problems in living which reflect their attempts to avoid the uncertainty and *angst* of living. As such, the challenge for the existential-phenomenological counselling psychologist does not lie in assisting people to remove or evade anxiety but, rather, to confront, clarify and face it as a 'given' of existence.

In this way, the question of change is viewed as an inevitable and on-going feature of life. The task of the existential-phenomenological counselling psychologist, more often than not, is to aid persons in recognizing their resistances to, and attempts to control, the changes in their lives rather than guide them in any direct manner towards novel ways of change. Paradoxically, it is via the very process of clarifying and challenging peoples' stance towards change that the benefits of 'therapeutic change' can be seen to occur.

While it acknowledges the integrity and experiential freedom of human beings, this model eschews any notions of 'self-actualization', or 'inner growth', and the 'innate positive nature' of human beings and, instead, emphasizes the underlying uncertainties, dilemmas and anxieties of living which challenge the person's attempts to establish and maintain a secure foundation. Similarly, while it addresses all possible dimensions of experience (such as the personal, social, physical and ideal/spiritual dimensions), it avoids any assumptions regarding the meaning, purpose, or independent truth or reality of such dimensions. Equally, while it accepts the significance of the past in persons' lives, it abstains from imposing any direct causal determinism between past events and current experience and, instead, promotes the view of persons as *active interpreters* of their past from the standpoint of their current relations and future goals and aspirations.

In adopting this stance, the existential-phenomenological model avoids bestowing upon the counselling psychologist the role of superior, objective instructor who distinguishes for the client those beliefs, attitudes and behaviours which are assumed to be 'irrational' and who attempts to replace them with 'rational' ones. Similarly, rather than present themselves as 'symptom-removers', 'treatment-providers', 'directive educators' or 'professional helpers', existential-phenomenological counselling psychologists seek to *attend to* their clients in that, through descriptively focused interpretations, they attempt to clarify their clients' meaning-world with them, thereby providing them with the experience of being heard – and hearing themselves – in a manner that is non-judgemental and accepting of the stance they maintain.

This neutrality promotes the possibility of the clients' greater willingness and courage to confront the fixed, or sedimented, biases and assumptions they hold with regard to their relations with themselves, others and the world in general, and how these sedimented stances may themselves have provoked their current 'problems in living'. It must be noted, however, that in order to approach this neutral perspective, existential-phenomenological counselling psychologists must, themselves, apply the basic method (as outlined above) which seeks to bracket those views, biases, assumptions, theoretically derived or lived perspectives from their own personal experience so that they may open themselves, as adequately as possible, to the experience of the client as it is being lived.

As the existential-phenomenological model urges counselling psychologists to maintain a flexible approach and attitude towards their therapeutic 'style', it is characteristically critical of any emphasis upon a specific technique or set of 'doing' skills. Instead, it emphasizes the personal or 'being' qualities of the therapist as essential components of the therapeutic encounter. Most significantly, the existential-phenomenological model bestows an undisputed centrality upon the relationship between counselling psychologist and client because it is through this relationship itself that the client's issues are manifested or 'brought forth' for examination. In other words, the therapeutic relationship is seen to be the 'microcosm' through which the 'macrocosm' of the client's lived reality is expressed and opened to inquiry.

But, equally, in order for this enquiry to reflect 'microcosmically' the 'macrocosmic' experience of the client in a suitably adequate, or 'good enough' fashion, existential-phenomenological counselling psychologists must be both willing and able to 'place' themselves into the relationship.

This notion of **encounter** requires both the counselling psychologist and the client to be present in a manner that acknowledges their co-constitutionality.

The nature of the relationship between counselling psychologist and client

It is the case that virtually all psychological research upon the therapeutic process – whether it be process- or outcome-oriented – has concluded that the *relationship* within the therapeutic process is the primary recurring variable to be singled out by both counselling psychologists and clients as being essential to the success of therapy – however 'success' might be defined or measured (Spinelli, 1994).

Nevertheless, what there might be about this particular relationship that is so significant – or, indeed, 'particular' – remains largely unclear. Psychological analyses of therapeutic models have noted two distinct emphases, or tendencies, within therapists' understanding of the relationship – tendencies that stress either the 'doing' or the 'being' elements or qualities that counselling psychologists bring to the relationship and how an emphasis upon one or the other significantly affects not only the structure of the therapeutic process but also the direction it will probably take and the specific exploratory possibilities it will allow to both the client and the counselling psychologist (Spinelli, 1994). Placed in this context, the existential-phenomenological model of counselling psychology takes the position that the very enterprise of therapy is principally dependent upon the establishment and maintenance of a relationship which both expresses and promotes the exploration of the possibilities of *being*. Via this stance, it once again reveals its implicit critique of the dominant 'natural science' model of counselling psychology which concentrates upon what counselling psychologists *do* (partly because these factors can be measured, taught and assessed, at least to some extent). It should be clear that the situation is not necessarily an 'either/or' one in that, ideally, one would hope to find in one's therapist both sufficient professional expertise and personal qualities that will allow suitable attendance.

Nevertheless, the existential-phenomenological model of counselling psychology expresses the view that if alienated from the 'being qualities' of the counselling psychologist, the 'doing' of counselling psychology becomes 'technologized' to such an extent that it distorts the therapeutic relationship in serious ways (raising, among other issues, the question of unnecessary power imbalances weighed heavily in favour of the counselling psychologist) which may well be deeply antagonistic to its fundamental aims and possibilities (van Deurzen-Smith, 1988; Spinelli,

1989, 1994). As such, while by no means dismissing the value of learned skills or knowledge, what is being argued is that these should be placed within a perspective that emphasizes 'doing' as an extension of, and not a substitute for, the therapist's 'being' in the relation. In this way, what counselling psychologists 'do' should be always understandable within, and an expression of, their attempts to acknowledge and enter into the client's world-view rather than be the means of emphasizing their 'taking charge' of the therapeutic encounter.

One existentially informed theorist who emphasized these points and pointed out that they may well contain within them the very key to the clarification of many of the issues that clients express as deeply problematic was R.D. Laing. Throughout his writings, Laing argued that mental distress and disturbances, rather than being primarily a form of 'illness' best dealt with via medical models of treatment, could be more adequately understood as expressions of deep **ontological insecurity** – that is to say, serious unease, conflict and fragmentation of various facets of one's experience of one's own being as expressed through one's relations with oneself and with others (Laing, 1960). Further, Laing, together with his colleague Aaron Esterson, argued the case that ontological insecurity arises precisely when the distinction between who one is and what one does (or must/mustn't be or do) remains unclear or indistinguishable through one's relations (Laing and Esterson, 1964; Spinelli, 1989, 1994).

An important implication of a 'being' focus in counselling psychology is that it allows counselling psychologists to acknowledge themselves as changing beings whose current manner of existence is expressed through their interactive relationship with their clients. As such, it concedes to counselling psychologists a far greater range of possibilities of relating to clients in differing, if apposite, ways. This in itself is a freeing process that would be far less possible if counselling psychologists were to emphasize 'doing skills' that, in contrast, would more likely demand the maintenance of a similar stance or 'way of being' regardless of the situation or relationship encountered.

While this stance might initially – if mistakenly – suggest a *laissez-faire* attitude to the therapeutic process, in fact it requires existential-phenomenological counselling psychologists to *be with* and *be for* their clients. While closely related, and mutually inclusive, these two stances point out emphases whose implications are worth more detailed consideration.

In 'being with' the client, existential-phenomenological counselling psychologists

> acknowledge the interdependence in the therapeutic relationship, and place
> an emphasis on those qualities of being that seek to promote an attitude that

does not, initially at least, seek to confirm the 'objective truth' of the client's statements, or whose aim is to present disconfirmations, rebuttals, contradictions, alternative possibilities and so forth, but, rather, which *stays with the experienced truths of the client as they are being related* in order that they, and whatever implications such truths may hold, may be exposed to further investigation and clarification by both the [counselling psychologist] and the client. In this way, the process of 'being with' the client allows the focus of the relationship to remain firmly on the client's experientially-based statements (be they verbal or non-verbal) so that they can be 'opened up' with regard to the meaning or meanings that the client . . . perceives them to hold. (Spinelli, 1994: 315, original emphasis).

'Being for' the client seeks to remind existential-phenomenological counselling psychologists that within the confines of each sessional encounter, they are there to attempt to 'enter' the experiential world of the client for the sole reason of allowing the client a specific form of encounter with *another who seeks to be the self.* This process can be seen once again to subvert the likelihood that the existential-phenomenological counselling psychologist will perceive his or her role as being that of '"truth-bringer", "healer" or "helper" in any purposive or direct manner' (Spinelli, 1994: 317) regardless of whether the client assumes it to be such.

The notion of 'being for' the client urges existential-phenomenological counselling psychologists

neither to lead the client in various directions which they think to be of important, *nor to be led by the client* into avenues of thought or affect that remain unclear or disconnected to both or either participants, *but to seek to keep up with them side-by-side* (to pursue the analogy) so that the client's path becomes the therapist's path and an approximate symmetry of thought and assumption becomes possible. (Spinelli, 1994: 317, original emphasis)

The distinction between 'being with' and 'being for' can be seen to be both subtle and significant. While the notion of 'being with' the client focuses on the existential-phenomenological counselling psychologist's willingness to accept the experiential reality of the client, the notion of 'being for' the client urges the counselling psychologist to attempt an entry into the client's lived reality in order that the counsellor may experience that reality in a manner that approaches the client's way of being.

The injunctions to 'be with and for' the client are by no means easy ones for counselling psychologists to adhere to (not least because the experience may be disturbing, destabilizing and even frightening), nor is it possible for them ever to be fully completed.

Equally, explanations regarding this attempt which employ terms such as 'transference and counter-transference' have been criticized by the existential-phenomenological model in that, rather than point out important areas of unconscious conflict in either the client or the therapist (as these latter terms would imply), the difficulties encountered may more accurately reflect an unwillingness to engage in this kind of 'being' encounter. Indeed, such explanations may in themselves be seen to be defensive and protective barriers or obstacles which serve to distance both the counselling psychologist and the client from the acknowledgement and exploration of the direct experience each has of themselves, the other, and of themselves-in-relation-to-the-other (May, 1983; Spinelli, 1994).

In a similar fashion, it would be erroneous to assume that the project of 'being with and for' the client equates with the person-centred model's notion of 'mirroring' or 'reflecting back' (Kirschenbaum and Henderson, 1990). Rather than seek to present themselves as 'reflective screens', existential-phenomenological counselling psychologists explicitly acknowledge their own input to the relationship via descriptively focused interpretations that seek to clarify and challenge both the overt and tacit meanings and assumptions suggested within clients' statements so that their significance to and implications for the client's lived reality can be disclosed and considered. Secondly, the project of 'being with and for' the client makes clear that existential-phenomenological counselling psychologists are not being asked to 'be themselves' (in the sense of the 'real self' as the person-centred model would suggest) but, rather, that the 'self' that the counselling psychologist is attempting to be is a *self-in-relation*, whose focus resides in 'the other' (that is, the client).

Briefly, the existential-phenomenological model's focus upon the various issues of 'being' allows the counselling psychologist to approach the world of the client from the standpoint of openness and in the spirit of discovery regarding the constructed meanings that express his or her stances towards the world. In this way, through challenges and clarifications that focus upon the 'what and how' of the client's experience, and hence remain at a descriptive level of the client's current orientation, the existential-phenomenological counselling psychologist is better able to assist the client in making explicit a number of underlying themes and sedimented assumptions that are contained within the client's stances but which are likely to have remained implicit or unexamined. The clarification of these is seen to be, in itself, a major means for the client to gain a more substantial, and often novel, awareness of the presenting problems (van Deurzen-Smith, 1988; Spinelli, 1994).

While some existential-phenomenological counselling psychologists approach the exploration of clients' themes and assumptions through the examination of the clients' relations to the *fourfold world* which expresses the physical, social, psychological and ideal or spiritual dimensions of human existence (Binswanger, 1963; van Deurzen-Smith, 1988), others prefer to bring into focus clients' *sedimented self-structures* which can serve to reveal experiences of 'splitness' or dissociation as expressions of anxiety of being as presented via the various self-self, self-other and self-and-other relational conflicts (Spinelli, 1994). In either case, such explorations assist in the disclosure of clients' resistances to the uncertainties and anxieties of living and the limitations they impose upon their experience of being-in-the-world.

In taking such stances, existential-phenomenological counselling psychologists focus upon clients' *conscious* experience of themselves-in-relation. Again, while not denying that much of experience remains *unreflected*, in that it is not properly clarified and attended to, it need not be the case that this can be understood solely (or even primarily) in terms of unconsciously repressed material. Again, while some existential-phenomenological counselling psychologists retain the notion of the unconscious in so far as it expresses the idea of potential awareness that persons cannot, or will not, allow themselves to reflect consciously upon (May, 1979), others have re-stated the question of the unconscious from the standpoints of dissociation and sedimentation of self-constructs (Spinelli, 1993, 1994). In either case, while by no means denying the experiential features and variables associated with bringing to conscious reflection that which has been previously distorted, denied or unreflected upon, the existential-phenomenological model demystifies the underlying ideas associated with psychoanalytic notions of the unconscious and remains deeply sceptical, if not highly critical, of any attempts on the part of counselling psychologists to impose theoretically derived analytical interpretations that seek to re-formulate the client's experience in terms of 'repressed', 'hidden' or 'latent' meanings that are assumed to require 'decoding'.

As such, the existential-phenomenological model allows clients to focus upon their current experiences of conflict, anxiety and denial not only with regard to how these both express and protect them from the vagaries and uncertainties of existence, but also, from the standpoint of how they present themselves within the encounter with the counselling psychologist. In this way, the encounter itself becomes the central means of exposing and exploring clients' stances toward their various relational experiences (van Deurzen-Smith, 1988; May, 1979; Spinelli, 1994).

It must be said that the adoption of this model asks a great deal of counselling psychologists. For, not only does it remove from them much of their professional mystique, and a good deal of the power that comes with this, it also confronts counselling psychologists with their sense of their own 'being-in-relation' by continually challenging their theoretical and personal beliefs, their sedimented stances toward themselves and others in their lives, and their willingness to attend to clients whose issues may provoke all too painful reminders of their own deceits and anxieties. At the same time, the willingness to encounter another in this fashion may also remind counselling psychologists of the immeasurable wonder and joy that is possible when beings encounter themselves through one another.

Family, group and organizational applications

In line with the above, the existential-phenomenological model does not merely tolerate, but, more correctly, values and embraces the diversity of living as expressed in terms of culture, race, gender and sexual orientation. Concerned as much with the 'universals' of human experience as it is with individual uniqueness, the existential-phenomenological model has been shown to be of particular value to the clarification of various psychological factors relevant to multi-cultural counselling (van Deurzen-Smith, 1988; Eleftheriadou, 1993) and its effectiveness as a model for psychotherapy provided by and for members of the Black community in the UK has recently been espoused (Asmall, 1994). The existential-phenomenological model has also been successfully applied in the fields of nursing and health care (Becker, 1992). With regard to the on-going debates concerning sexuality and sexual orientation, existential-phenomenological authors such as Maurice Merleau-Ponty (1962) and J.H. van den Berg (1972) have provided highly innovative contributions.

While most existential-phenomenological counselling psychologists tend to work with clients on a one-to-one basis, couple therapy and, less commonly, family therapy, is by no means unfeasible. Hans W. Cohn's pioneering contributions to existential-phenomenological group therapy have revealed this model's unique expertise in the analysis and exploration of the individual's experience of relational encounters within various group settings (Cohn, 1993).

Research

The existential-phenomenological model has often been presented as being antagonistic to, or disinterested in, psychological research. This contention is far from the truth. Rather, it has played a major role in the development of qualitatively focused approaches to research (Karlsson, 1993). At the same time, the existential-phenomenological model's view of suitable counselling psychology research stands in direct contrast to the natural scientific viewpoint and its underlying assumptions principally because the questions it poses and the methods it employs are grounded in a carefully articulated, but undeniably different, set of philosophical assumptions.

First, unlike traditional natural science psychological research models, the existential-phenomenological approach denies the possibility of truly objective observation and analysis. Rather, it assumes an indissoluble interrelationship between observer and observed. As this view is the foundational basis of its underlying method, the starting point to any existential-phenomenological investigation lies in the clarification of the researcher's own involvement, biases and aims in order to make explicit his or her personal inclinations and predispositions.

A second major divergence rests on the notion of consciousness. In the typical psychological research model the nature of consciousness, *per se*, rarely surfaces as an issue. From the standpoint of existential-phenomenological psychological research, consciousness or more accurately conscious experience, is central to all inquiry since the primary aim of existential-phenomenological investigation is to approach as adequately as possible direct and immediate experience. As a clarificatory example of what is being argued here, consider the following example originally presented by Valle, King and Halling (1989). Imagine that you are transcribing the musical notes that make up the melody from the first movement of Tchaikovsky's Fifth Symphony. If you the re-write this melody as transposed by one octave, you will transcribe a quite different set of musical notes. Though the two notations reveal surface distinctions from one another, their underlying melody remains the same. While natural science psychological research typically focuses on the notes, existential-phenomenological psychological research seeks to disclose the melody – that is, more broadly speaking, the foundational structure of conscious experience.

Thirdly, existential-phenomenological psychological research rejects the common notion of causality in its linear form as being valid for the subject matter it investigates. Therefore, individuals are not studied or understood in a manner that would suggest the assumption that something that happened in their past is a direct cause of their later behaviour. While by no means denying the importance of the past as 'meaning-giver' to one's experience, existential-phenomenological psychology sees the importance of past events principally in terms of how they are currently understood, weighted and interpreted by the individual. In this way, it construes the past as being far more plastic and dependent upon the present (as well as future expectations) than do most other forms of psychological inquiry. This view expresses the existential-phenomenological stance of 'the-past-as-presently-lived-and-future-directed' since any statement of the past depends upon our current, or present biased perceptions, as well as, of course, our future-directed aims and expectations. It should be evident, therefore, that this stance rejects standard research notions of control groups, dependent and independent variables, preliminary hypotheses, and so forth, since these all suggest and rely upon, to a greater or lesser degree, the notion of linear causality.

Fourthly, as Romanyshyn, among others, has pointed out, while existential-phenomenological psychology, too, initiates its investigations from a naive realism, or natural attitude, it takes as its principal task the elucidation and investigation of this self-same natural attitude and 'seeks to describe the advent of experience's meaning prior to any commitment to philosophical positions of realism or idealism' (Romanyshyn, 1978: 27).

Fifthly, existential-phenomenological research is principally *qualitative-interpretative*, focusing upon descriptive methodologies which focus on questions of *what* and *how* something is, rather than *why* it is. In so doing, it seeks to retain an inside perspective which attempts to remain as faithful as possible to the data of experience. In other words, it seeks to understand rather than to explain. It searches for meaning rather than seeks to collect facts. As Gunmar Karlsson has clarified this distinction:

> Facts are conceived of as objective and independent of consciousness, while meaning is considered subjective and idiosyncratic. In line with logical empiricism, traditional psychology neglects to study meaningful experience in a 'direct' way. Instead, one *operationalizes* variables so as to turn them into observable facts. [Existential-phenomenology] rejects the idea that there exist objective facts, *independent* of a subject or a subjective consciousness. The 'objectively' given fact is always present in relation to . . . a constituting and meaning-imbuing subject . . . . (Karlsson, 1993: 16, original emphasis)

In a similar fashion, David Rennie (1994) has discussed a model for human science research which closely parallels the principal characteristics of existential-phenomenological research in that it emphasizes the researcher's striving to remain as open as possible to the emergent data rather than testing the potential accuracy of an hypothesis. In doing so, Rennie has pointed out the necessity of clarifying the philosophical foundations for human science research and has concluded that the natural science model typical of psychological research methodology is unsuitable to its subject matter. I state the obvious when I say that this important emphasis is a corner-stone of existential-phenomenological theory and research.

Generally speaking, existential-phenomenological counselling research begins with the investigator's clarification of his or her own involvement, biases and aims. He or she must first clarify how his or her personal inclinations and predispositions influence the 'how and what' elements that form the focus of investigation, thereby explicitly acknowledging the investigator's role in the research. In addition, however, this self-same process allows the investigator to refine the focus of inquiry so that he or she can construct a formal statement which will provide the preliminary basis with which to formulate research questions. The success of such questions will depend upon how well they are able to 'tap into' the co-researchers' (that is, the 'subjects") experience so that they can describe and clarify it concretely.

Once the responses have been obtained (usually via face-to-face interviews or written questionnaires), the researcher must read the responses carefully so that significant statements can be extracted from them. From these significant statements the researcher typically extracts general, or foundational meanings, clusters of themes and idiosyncratic statements – all of which are integrated into an adequately reflective description of the investigated phenomenon in as unequivocal a statement of identification of its formal structure as is possible. In most instances, this statement is discussed with each co-researcher in order to ascertain its adequacy in conveying the co-researcher's experience and, possibly, bringing to light previously unexplored, misunderstood or inadequately expressed experiential variables. In this way, the aim of existential-phenomenological research can be seen to be that of providing descriptive statements whose adequacy is measured on the basis of their ability to express and contain the richness and diversity, as well as the invariant elements, of a given focus-experience. This approach stands in direct contrast to the more typical attempts on the part of psychological research to reduce, deny, denigrate or transform experience into a form of operationally defined behaviour.

As valuable and original as its contributions to counselling psychology (and general psychology) are, it remains evident that owing to the relatively limited amount of existential-phenomenological impact upon counselling psychology (which, in turn, reflects the small number of active researchers and practitioners who employ this model), there remains a great deal of research to be done. Recent and current developments, however, suggest that both interest in, and reliance upon, the existential-phenomenological model for research in both general and counselling psychology are increasing significantly. Valle and King's *Existential-Phenomenological Alternatives for Psychology* (1978), May's *Psychology and the Human Dilemma* (1979), Giorgi's *Phenomenology and Psychological Research* (1985), Valle and Halling's *Existential-Phenomenological Perspectives in Psychology* (1989) and the present author's own text, *The Interpreted World: an Introduction to Phenomenological Psychology* (Spinelli, 1989), all provide wide-ranging explorations, critiques and research studies focusing on many of the major areas of experimental and applied psychology. Equally, the *Review of Existential Psychology and Psychiatry* and the *Journal of the Society for Existential Analysis* regularly publish articles and papers relevant to counselling psychology research and practice.

With regard to research evidence for the effectiveness of the existential-phenomenological model, it must be acknowledged that few studies currently exist which are specific to this issue. Irvin Yalom has noted that the effectiveness of this model is 'as rational, as coherent, and as systematic as any other' (Yalom, 1980: 5). Nevertheless, it remains the case that researchers associated with the existential-phenomenological model remain highly critical of much of the research focused upon outcome studies that has been carried out, pointing out that the natural science approach typically adopted to analyse and measure the effectiveness of therapeutic interventions is at best limited and often unsuitable to the subject matter (Rennie, 1994; Spinelli, 1994) and that models incorporating new paradigm research such as those advocated by Reason and Rowan (1981), and human science research favoured by Rennie (1994), are far more likely to provide more suitable means for exploring the effectiveness of this, or any other, model relevant to counselling psychology.

Concluding statements

While it is hoped that this brief overview of the existential-phenomenological model has convinced readers of its specific and unique paradigm characteristics and contributions to counselling psychology, it would be misleading to suggest that, as a model, it seeks to present itself solely as a separate and independent approach to counselling psychology research and practice. While it undoubtedly fulfils these requirements, an equally significant 'thrust' of the model lies in its attempts to demonstrate its relevance to other counselling psychology models in that, via its principal method of investigation, it provides an original and important means of exposing and clarifying the underlying, often implicit, assumptions contained in *all* theoretical models and their applications. Via the critical stance that it advocates, its inclination towards the suspension of judgement, and in its questioning of assumed truths, facts and the soundness of inferences that all models adopt, the existential-phenomenological model reveals a healthy scepticism that is much needed in the psychological investigation of counselling and psychotherapeutic theories and practices.

In this latter sense, the existential-phenomenological model can be more accurately seen to be an *attitude* or stance taken towards thinking about and 'doing' counselling psychology. Such input will serve both to delineate the boundaries of counselling psychology and to clarify its unique place and contributions to psychological theory and research in general.

References

Asmall, I. (1994) 'Existential therapy in a non-Western cultural context'. Paper delivered to the Forum of the Society for Existential Analysis, June.

Becker, C.S. (1992) *Living and Relating: an Introduction to Phenomenology.* London: Sage.

Binswanger, L. (1963) *Being-in-the-World: Selected Papers of Ludwig Binswanger.* (S. Weedleman, ed.) New York: Basic Books.

Cohn, H.W. (1993) 'Matrix and intersubjectivity: phenomenological aspects of group analysis', *Group Analysis*, 26: 481–6.

Deurzen-Smith, E. van (1988) *Existential Counselling in Practice.* London: Sage.

Eleftheriadou, Z. (1993) 'Applications of a philosophical framework to transcultural therapy', *Journal of the Society for Existential Analysis*, 4: 116–23.

Giorgi, A. (1985) *Phenomenology and Psychological Research.* Pittsburgh: Duquesne University Press.

Heidegger, M. (1962) *Being and Time* (trans. J. Macquarrie and E. Robinson). Oxford: Basil Blackwell.

Husserl, E. (1977) *Phenomenological Psychology.* The Hague: Nyhoff.

Karlsson, G. (1993) *Psychological Qualitative Research from a Phenomenological Perspective.* Stockholm: Almqvist and Wiksell International.

Kirschenbaum, H. and Henderson, V.L. (1990) *The Carl Rogers Reader.* London: Constable.

Laing, R.D. (1960) *The Divided Self.* London: Tavistock Publications.

Laing, R.D. and Esterson, A. (1964) *Sanity, Madness and the Family.* Harmondsworth: Penguin.

May, R. (1979) *Psychology and the Human Dilemma.* New York: W.W. Norton and Co.

May, R. (1983) *The Discovery of Being: Writings in Existential Psychology.* New York: W.W. Norton.

Merleau-Ponty, M. (1962) *The Phenomenology of Perception.* (trans. C. Smith). London: Routledge and Kegan Paul.

Reason, P. and Rowan, J. (1981) *Human Enquiry: a Sourcebook of New Paradigm Research.* Chichester: Wiley.

Rennie, D. (1994) 'Human science in counselling psychology: closing the gap between research and practice'. Paper delivered to the 1st Annual Conference of the BPS Division of Counselling Psychology, May.

Romanyshyn, R.D. (1978) 'Psychology and the attitude of science', in R.S. Valle and M. King (eds), *Existential-Phenomenological Alternatives for Psychology.* New York: Oxford University Press.

Sartre, J.P. (1956) *Being and Nothingness: an Essay on Phenomenological Ontology* (trans. H. Barnes). London: Routledge (1991).

Spinelli, E. (1989) *The Interpreted World: an Introduction to Phenomenological Psychology*. London: Sage.

Spinelli, E. (1993) 'The unconscious: an idea whose time has gone?', *Journal of the Society for Existential Analysis*, 4: 19–47.

Spinelli, E. (1994) *Demystifying Therapy*. London: Constable.

Valle, R.S. and Halling, S. (eds) (1989) *Existential-Phenomenological Perspectives in Psychology*. London: Plenum Press.

Valle, R.S. and King, M. (eds) (1978) *Existential-Phenomenological Alternatives for Psychology*. New York: Oxford University Press.

Valle, R.S., King, M. and Halling, S. (1989) 'An introduction to existential-phenomenological thought in psychology', in R.S. Valle and S. Halling (eds), *Existential-Phenomenological Perspectives in Psychology*. London: Plenum Press. pp. 3–16.

van den Berg, J.H. (1972) *A Different Existence*. Pittsburgh: Dusquesne University Press.

Yalom, I. (1980) *Existential Psychotherapy*. New York: Basic Books.

9

The Feminist Paradigm

Maye Taylor

A great deal remains unknown about the psychology of women, although numerous theories have been generated from which therapeutic interventions have been derived. These theories have rarely been offered as tentative and partial beliefs, but rather put forward as the scientific facts of the day. Generations of women have attempted to conform to prevailing notions of what is right and appropriate for their sex, and the psychological costs have been enormous.

This chapter will explore how a feminist perspective has, and does, serve as a critique for psychological theory and counselling practice and will give centrality to that critique. Given that a feminist perspective is predicated on a rejection of any theory of human behaviour and personality that does not taken into consideration the social context, it will be argued that there can be no deterministic theory of personality. This chapter, of necessity, approaches the issues of the book differently, the structure and organization cannot be tidily arranged, the text will be more discursive as befits the feminist critique, but nevertheless within the text the key issues are addressed. The psychology of women, like this chapter, is a work in progress and adds a small piece to a picture that will continue to be changed and enlarged over time. It is aimed at developing a more useful understanding of women's experience and acknowledges that we are still in the process of formulating the right questions and finding an appropriate language in which to discuss issues of gender. It is not definitive, rather it is a reflection of the feminist spirit of enquiry, the evolution of certain ideas through feminist critical thought.

The chapter challenges the way that theories of female psychology, in particular personality development and motivation, have been reified as truth and viewed as possessing a life of their own apart from any specific context. This chapter argues that any *useful* theory of female development or behaviour must account both for the profound impact of gendered family and work roles and for the psychology of dominant and subordinate groups, perhaps best conveyed by the words of Horney quoted in Burman (1989):

> Like all science and all valuations, the psychology of women has hitherto been considered only from the point of view of men. It is inevitable that man's position of advantage should cause objective validity to be attributed to

his subjective, affective relations to the women, and according to Delius the psychology of women hitherto actually represents a deposit of the desires and disappointments of men.

These themes will be taken up, as the central focus of the chapter is how the social context of women's lives influences their development, choices and goals. It is further acknowledged that there is no necessary homogeneity of women's experiences, since women are divided by the differential positions and power relationships of 'race', class and sexuality. The conceptual shift from 'sex' to 'gender' has involved a revolutionary change in assumptions about the causes of human behaviour and highlights the importance of the shift away from psychological theory of sex differences historically derived from an internally determined or individual difference perspective and thus mutable to the process of change on which counselling is predicated. This shift has profound implications for psychological theories of personality and motivation, as will be demonstrated in this chapter.

Feminist psychologists take as axiomatic the view that biological sex forms the basis of a social classification system, namely gender, and that gender is not just a property of individuals but is a principle of social organization, that is to say it is a pivotal point for the real differences in women's and men's lives. By examining what women and men do, as a result of their roles, statuses and obligations, there is clearly a wealth of difference in their subjective experience (Taylor, 1989a). It is argued that the social milieu has detracted from rather than enhanced the potential for a full and satisfying development of life for women (and men). Thus, feminism challenges the very knowledge base of psychology and counselling and how it is currently conceptualized and practised as well as the way in which counsellors are trained and supervised. Feminist counselling and therapy involve a new perspective, new ways of looking at old problems, whilst at the same time drawing on many of the skills of more 'traditional' approaches.

Counselling psychology could be unique in a focus on and commitment to both individual change and broad social change, and how an awareness and understanding of gender as a process and as an organizer of social relations is crucial to good practice. In psychological counselling the purpose of relevant psychological theory is not just to mirror 'nature' but to present an image of nature that appears useful for understanding individuals.

Personality and motivation viewed from a feminist perspective

Theory is a construction of reality and reflects the understandings that exist at the time of social history in which the theory is developed. Many psychological theories were 'born' during a period in history in which gender was viewed as a dichotomous property of the state of being female or male and observed social arrangements were thus assumed to be rooted in the individual, in other words the 'amputation school of psychology'. This chapter rejects that.

Everyone is different, yet we do have things in common, and coming to terms with human individuality and what makes an individual personality is one of the questions which psychologists have addressed with varying theories from the outset. The ancient Greeks, for example, saw personality as depending on the balance of fluids in the body – blood, phlegm, black bile and yellow bile – believing people characteristically had a higher proportion of one fluid than another which produced different personalities. Darwinian thinkers argued that the brain and the uterus were directly linked and that this, through menstrual blood, produced the 'female' personality. Clearly the model of personality held is crucial for our perception of human beings, it gives us our underlying beliefs about what human beings are really like. Consider this:

- Men are more conceited than women.
- Men overvalue the work they do.
- Men are not as realistic as women in assessing their abilities.
- Men are more likely to accuse and attack others when unhappy, instead of stating that they feel hurt and inviting sympathy.
- Men have difficulty in forming and maintaining relationships.

Tavris (1993) argues that most people will see at once that this way of talking about men is biased and derogatory. It *is* biased and derogatory, but that is the point. Why has it been so difficult (and still is) for psychologists and therapists in particular to accept that this is exactly how we have conceptualized women, talk about women, and how we use powerful negative images, and in particular for our purposes here, how psychology *negatively* conceptualizes women? Some 'typical' findings in psychological research are that:

- Women have lower self-esteem than men do.
- Women do not value their efforts as much as men do.
- Women are less self-confident than men.
- Women are more likely to say they are 'hurt' than to admit that they are angry.
- Women have more difficulty developing 'a separate sense of self'.

The reader can detect that these are the 'other side' of the previous statements on men, statements which appear time and time again in the literature about women. The 'answer' to the question posed lies in the 'habit' of seeing women's behaviour as something to be explained in relation to men, that we are used to seeing women as the problem and to regarding women's differences from men as deficiencies and weaknesses. Indeed it can be argued for instance that the 'hysterical personality' is merely a caricature of stereotypical feminity. In any domain of life in which men have set, and still set, the standard of normalcy, women will be considered abnormal and society will discuss, debate and theorize women's nature and place. This is Weisstein's (1971) argument that 'psychology constructs the female'.

Any discussion about underlying personality and motivation must take place in the wider social context. In conceptualizing personality development from a feminist perspective a constructivist view is central. Personality can be seen as a combination of three elements:

1   The individual's behaviour.
2   The meaning of that behaviour as constructed by other people.
3   The meaning of that behaviour as constructed by the individual herself/himself.

The underlying rationale of this constructivist view is that studying personality outside its social context is bound to give an incomplete account. It is only when 'behaviour' is imbued with social meaning that it becomes 'personality'. The following discussion elaborates on these three elements.

The study of difference is not in itself the problem. Of course people differ; the problem has occurred when one group is considered the norm with others differing from it, thereby failing to 'measure up' to the ideal, superior dominant standard, *and* when the dominant group uses the language of difference to justify its social position and the differential treatment of the other – slipping into the terminology of the 'pathological' and the 'normal'. To illustrate: in *The Mismeasure of Man*, Gould (1981) used the study of race differences in intelligence to illustrate how science has long been used and abused to serve a larger cultural agenda, namely to confirm prejudices that 'blacks, women and poor people occupy their subordinate roles by the harsh dictates of nature' (1981: 74). Examining only two dominant discourses, namely psychiatric Darwinism and psychiatric modernism, exemplified by Freud (Showalter, 1987; Taylor, 1991), demonstrates all too well the lived consequences for women: how women attribute meaning to their own behaviour, and how such discourses found their way into the hearts and minds of the women themselves and inevitably into the mental health treatment of women.

The 'slipping into the language' of the normal and abnormal can be illustrated by three competing versions of this 'mismeasurement' of women which have been identified (Hare-Mustin and Marecek, 1990). One already identified here is that man is the norm, and woman is 'other', opposite, lesser, deficient, 'the problem'. This is the view that has underlain so much research in psychology (and psychiatry) to find out why women are not 'as something' as men – as moral, as intelligent, as rational, as funny, as assertive and so on. Perhaps this is one of the reasons why women turn to counselling and psychotherapy in such larger numbers than men, and consume all those books advising them on how to be more competent, more independent (or dependent!). Men being 'normal' perhaps do not feel the same pressure to 'put themselves right' in corresponding ways. Gilligan (1982) describes this as 'women's place in the men's life cycle'. She cites how Freud built his theory of psychosocial development around the experiences of the male child that culminate in the Oedipus complex. He tried to fit women into his masculine conception, seeing them as envying what they lacked, the 'penis', and conceptualized the persistence of women's pre-Oedipal attachments to their mothers as a developmental difference and crucially saw this as a developmental failure. Chodorow (1978) challenges this and reiterates the social environmental influence on woman's development and her desire for self-actualization and growth, be it through motherhood and/or professional development.

A second version is that man is the norm, and woman is opposite, but better: 'the solution'. This is the perspective of those cultural feminists who have retrieved the qualities associated with women that have for so long been devalued – nurturance, compassion, attachment and so on – and who now claim them to be the source of women's moral superiority. You only have to turn to books such as *Women who Run with the Wolves* (Estes, 1992) to see the liberation in transforming women's 'weaknesses' into strengths. After centuries of trying to measure up, many women, understandably, feel delighted by having their female qualities celebrated. The discovery, now being celebrated by men in mid-life of the importance of intimacy, relationships and care is something that women have known from the beginning. Gilligan argues that because that knowledge in women has been considered 'intuitive' or instinctive', a function of anatomy coupled with destiny, psychologists have neglected to describe its development. She replaces Freud's negative and derivative description of female psychology, arguing that the quality of embeddedness in social interaction and personal relationships that characterizes women's lives in contrast to men's, is not only a descriptive difference but becomes a developmental liability when the milestones of childhood and adolescent development in the psychological literature are markers of increasing separation. Women's 'failure' to separate then becomes by definition a failure to develop and makes attainment of the much lauded mature personality theoretically impossible.

The third view is that there is no problem, because man is the norm and woman is just like him. Tiefer (1992), in her analysis of the assumptions in the DSM in the diagnosis of sexual disorders, observes that in this view, 'men and women are the same, and they're all men'. The massive institutional denial of the existence of real discrimination against women is a collective manifestation of such a view. After all we are told that we now live in a post-feminist era and that equality is on offer – all it needs is for women to take their opportunities. I would be delighted if only that were the case. Feminists argue that many of the problems that women bring to counselling are *unique* and as a result of their socialization and relatively powerless structural position. The two cultures of gender are not equal in power, resources or status. Many behaviours and personality traits thought to be typical of women are instead typical of women – *and men* – who lack power.

As this chapter is about 'work in progress', any theory of personality and motivation needs to acknowledge that we are in a 'transforminist' era and that gender, not sex, is the single most influential factor, and gender is socially constructed. Social constructionism challenges our traditional conception of scientific knowledge and has come to play an essential role in our understanding of how we acquire our sense of self and our identity and how this develops and can change given our understanding of that process. The philosophy of science has largely been replaced by the history and sociology of knowledge. Both these areas challenge the view that there is an 'objective reality' out there to be discovered and that the body of scientific knowledge acquired through the practices of 'scientific endeavours' is either 'true' or rationally superior. Instead, such processes trace the cultural and historical processes that bring certain conceptions of nature into favour while suppressing others. In effect, social construc-tionists argue that what we take to be accurate and objective accounts of 'human nature' and self are, in fact, outgrowths of social processes. To locate this in issues of differences between the sexes, in her very powerful book *The Peaceable Sex*, Mitscherlich (1987) argues that it is unrealistic to hold up, for example, an image of a 'natural' non-aggressive peaceable woman against that of a 'natural' aggressive, bellicose man. Instead we need to concentrate on how aggressive impulses are or are not encour-aged, allowed to be worked through and expressed in society. She argues that the division of labour has resulted in social practice where there is separation into a male mentality of achievement and conquest on one hand and a protective, self-sacrificing mentality for women on the other hand. The necessary ego-constricting effects of this feminine socialization have to be taken into consideration in any discussion of normalcy: we must be ever ready to acknowledge cultural transmission as against biological determinism. Acquired behaviour is mutable, an apposite point in a book on counselling psychology.

Social constructionism plays a vital role in our understanding of gender development, and in challenging the notion of essentialism, biological determinism and the belief in fixed gender roles. Thus many theorists argue (feminist and other) that our notions of 'male' and 'female' are constructions, that masculinity and femininity are constructions which are built around anatomical differences, signifying only because they are given significance in the context of the power relations present in the social environment. Hence, masculinity and femininity are positions and ways of seeing and speaking about what we see. As I argued earlier in terms of personality theory *per se* these positions give 'meaning' to what we perceive. However, in practice gender becomes fixed; additionally power bolsters the 'constructed' to the objective and the traits assigned to 'male' and 'female' become 'concrete' differences which then become valued in different ways. Similarly, Worell and Remer (1992) argue that we construct a reality about gender that represents a shared social agreement about what is 'really' there. The social construction of gender defines our knowledge, attitudes and beliefs about women and men. The characteristics we attribute to gender are not 'true' attributes of females and males, but are socially constructed categories that function to maintain male–female dichotomies and male-dominated power structures.

Summary

Finally, if we can agree upon the position that gender roles are created by the social environment that we exist in, then we need to look at the consequences of this position. For example, if we accept that gender is socially constructed, we need to look at what beliefs are laid down about male and femaleness, and thus what is 'normal' and how these gender beliefs are internalized by males and females and what consequences this internalization, in addition to the consequences of living in a society that lays down particular gender beliefs, has on the individual. This has led to the situation where men have become the 'locus of cultural value' and male, as opposed to female, activities are always recognized as predominantly important, and cultural systems give authority and value to the roles and activities of men. It is a process which finds expression in the development of personality. The social construction of gender creates in us a self-image of who we are as males and females and how we should behave and what we should want. Gender also structures the expectations and behaviour of those with whom we interact. Traditional sex typing encourages women to be kind, sensitive, nuturing, submissive, expressive of feelings and dependent on others; and men to be assertive, achieving, dominant, autonomous, less inclined to display feelings and self-determined. The 'typical' woman is more likely to be described in terms of an 'expressive' cluster of traits – hence, as more emotional, home-orientated, considerate, understanding, excitable and devoted to others, and the competency characteristics of self-confidence, independence and assertiveness are more likely to be attributed to men, in other words an asymmetrical cultural evaluation of what is female and what is male. A central characteristic of the sex-typing process has been an association of female with 'domestic' (the family) and male with 'public' spheres of responsibility, and as in Western society power is most often paired with money one result of the private–public split is that women earn far less than men and pay a high price in loss of personal freedom (Benjamin, 1990; Johnson, 1988). So whilst there is a recognition that men have been the victims of a sexist culture and its rigid patterns of socialization, it is still men who hold the balance of power and receive a disproportionate share of social rewards and privileges (Taylor, 1995), with all that that means for self-concept and mental health as previously argued, hence the gender-differentiated turn to counselling.

The feminist counselling relationship and the meaning and facilitating of change

Given that all counselling is about change, the course of feminist counselling and therapy proceeds like any other, meeting, exploring issues, making a contract, establishing the relationship, fostering insight, working on, and through, the issues with resolution in mind. It is a form of psychological intervention predicated in a feminist perspective in which client and counsellor work *together* to bring about a change in the beliefs and behaviour of the client by assisting them to acquire understanding of their 'predicament' by increased insight and skills. (The word client is used here as a convenient way of discriminating the positions.) What is vital is the feminist emphasis on the *explicit* sharing of power in the therapeutic relationship, and the differential experience of power in society, acknowledging that such power does exist and has to be *consciously* worked with and not denied in counselling. It involves establishing a mutual, reciprocal, respectful and non-authoritarian relationship acknowledging that the way we generate our espoused theory and thus conduct counselling and therapy are never separable from our own gender and family experiences which include unconscious fears, wishes and assumptions about women. Clients *and* counsellors inhabit a demarcated social world. We cannot *not* react out of our gender, class sibling position, ethnic background and personal history (herstory), the choice is whether we do so consciously or unconsciously.

This egalitarian relationship maximizes individual freedom of expression and promotes and encourages a working partnership and thus helps women in particular to identify that they do have choices in their lives, to regain power and control which many of them lost as children and who have had their 'personhood' systematically and inter-personally denied, and to live their lives as they see fit rather than as 'significant others' may wish them to do. Feminist counselling facilitates the addressing of their *own* needs in addition to how well (or not) they serve the needs of others. Women are taught to be nurturing of their families, to put others' needs before their own, yet such nurturance is devalued in a society at large which uses the language of competitiveness to evaluate success. The accusation of 'co-dependency' typically applied to women is a good example of how they are pathologized for doing what they were taught to do! For many women the counselling relationship will be the only relationship where they are not expected to take care of the other person; many women describe the experience as exhilarating and therapeutic in its own right and is over and above the benefits they derive from the content and process of the counselling itself. This is the 'permission to change' bedrock of feminist counselling.

It is important to be explicit in addressing the issue of power, because the very nature of the therapeutic relationship itself is conducive to power distinctions and abuse. Clients visit counsellors and therapists when they are having problems which they cannot cope with themselves. Power is the capacity to produce a change and people coming to therapy usually see themselves as lacking this capacity. The therapist on the other hand simply because he or she is in the position of being able to provide such help and having the skills and knowledge that another needs, is in this sense, in a position of power. The client's feelings of powerlessness can be either maximized or minimized depending upon the power relationship set up by the therapist and *acceded to by the client*, thus bringing the consequences of the internalization of the messages of difference sharply into focus. The political and social influences on the personal and inter-personal lives of people coming into counselling is a proper area of exploration in counselling. Even Rogers (1977) retrospectively acknowledged his own previous naivete and sexism and somewhat belatedly recognized the political nature of counselling.

Family and organizational implications

This feminist view of the vital need constantly to acknowledge this political nature of counselling can be well illustrated by briefly turning attention to the specific context of couples, family and organizational counselling services. Feminists argue that the sexual division of labour in the form of family relations is seen as having developed spontaneously or 'naturally' by virtue of natural predispositions, e.g. physical strength. Female oppression can be viewed as arising out of the ability of males to exploit relative biological strengths. Male dominance over females established in family groups is strengthened and solidified as other layers of social organization have been built on such elementary relations.

In the case of organizations, the 'fundamental gender personality differences' view has greatly influenced them. Over time, a historical process of 'organizational desexualization' has created an increasingly non-expressive rational, emotionally controlled organizational world with pressure placed on people to 'privatize' their feelings and impulses. Family ties have been severed from organizations and replaced with bureaucratic, professional structures. This wiping out of emotionality from organizational life has strengthened the sexist consequences of this in the process by which men became associated (in location) with rationality/instrumentality and women with emotionality/expressiveness. Locale and personality become indistinguishable and this has the effect of filtering women into a narrow range of occupations that tend to mirror assumed 'primary' domestic roles and responsibilities and seriously curtails their ability to flourish and prosper within organizations; *self*-actualization is just not on offer. The organizational culture might well need to be the 'proper' client for counselling . . . .

Furthermore, sexuality is often perceived as a threat to the organization and efforts are made to inhibit the development of sexual or romantic relationships with further costly implications for women. Given that a large percentage of 'affairs' involve higher-placed males with lower-placed females, it is usually the female who is disciplined, often by sacking. However, 'desexualization' should not be taken to assume that 'sexuality' has no part; sexual attractiveness is often used to influence or stress power within organizations. Certain male organizational members may use 'attractiveness' as a criterion in the employment of female subordinates and many men use sexual harassment as a direct means of emphasizing power over female employees. Any Employee Assistance Programme which does not directly address these issues will (simply) collude with the oppression of women.

To turn to couples and families. Feminists argue that counsellors/ therapists, particularly family therapists, are *not* sensitive to power differences within the family *which favour men*. If therapy proceeds with the expectation that each partner should change equally then pre-therapy inequalities remain intact, because the effect of taken-for-granted sexist discourse is that families are rarely able to define their concerns in terms of power imbalances, the family therapist has an ethical responsibility to address observed power dimensions which are contributing to the distress of the woman. Some feminists have extended this further to suggest that the therapist has a responsibility to intervene directly or indirectly in the client's family value system if it reflects patriarchal bias, providing the opportunity to explore and reflect on the social origin and meaning of feelings and behaviour; that is to say it is legitimate to view the cultural and social context of the client's presenting 'symptoms' as a proper concern and part of therapy. Extending this argument further involves enabling all clients to identify, confront and change their own stereotypical behaviour where appropriate and relevant.

Highlighting such issues of change

There has been much debate is psychology about how people should, and do, change. In counselling psychology there is now some agreement that optimal change in counselling and therapy is best facilitated by encouragement of self-exploration, helping clients to clarify their thoughts, encourage self-examination, fostering hope, focusing on current concerns, and offering general support and encouragement. I would argue that this comes very close to the 'consciousness raising' of early feminist approaches to women's condition.

However, given the earlier comments about the 'amputation' school it would be sexist and naive to ignore the fact that consciousness raising must include counsellors as well as clients acknowledging that society is structured in such a way that there are huge demands made of women's emotional and physical energy yet at the same time they remain largely undervalued, isolated and oppressed. Women have long been seen as synonymous with, and defined by, the family. The massive emphasis on 'women's failure to protect' in child abuse by men emphasizes how women are made responsible for men's behaviour using the passive discourse in discussing male sexuality. This contradictory position leads to many problems for women which have been individualized and medicalized, but a feminist analysis leads to a different view of the causes of the problems, the changes necessary, and the means by which they might be made, that is a rejection of the blaming of the victim syndrome. The growth in the turn to counselling and therapy is a pragmatic response to this. The aim in couples and family counselling should be to facilitate an understanding of the distinctions between internal and external realities, the way in which social structures become internalized as inner pain and anguish, and thus to help women see how internalized behaviour patterns have shaped their capacity to take more control over their lives.

Goals of feminist counselling and therapy

In the light of the earlier parts of this chapter the goals of feminist counselling and therapy can be clearly identified and they have been well discussed, see for example, Worell and Remer (1992). We can identify 11 feminist counselling goals, and all counsellors should help all clients to:

1 Become aware of their own sex-role socialization process.
2 Identify their internalized sex-role messages and beliefs.
3 Replace sex-role stereotyped beliefs with more self-enhancing self-talk.
4 Develop a full range of behaviours that are freely chosen not dictated by sex-role stereotypes, i.e. to become a more flexible, competent and less sex-typed person.
5 Evaluate the influences of social factors on personal experiences.
6 Understand how society oppresses women.
7 Understand that individual women's experiences are common to all women.
8 Identify negative and oppressive social practices that negatively affect them.
9 Acquire skills for enacting environmental change.
10 Restructure institutions to rid them of discriminatory practices.
11 Develop a sense of personal and social power.

Offering counselling and therapy with these goals firmly established in practice provides the means whereby women in particular can examine why and how external reality is manifested in internal crisis and then begin to confront society's oppressive power and control.

So, although the social change goals, which are an important part of the feminist paradigm, would appear to be difficult to integrate directly into the individual focus of counselling it *is* possible using this concept of praxis as enshrined in the work of Freire (see Taylor, 1995). The egalitarian principles enshrined in the feminist counselling relationship inform all aspects of the approach: the counselling relationship as it facilitates the pursuit of the goals above can be a *model* of relationships in general. A feminist approach would thus help clients to gain a sense of self-worth and thus believe they have the right to be in egalitarian relationships, both in a therapeutic sense and in their own life generally. The personal can be the political.

Assessment

Assessment in psychotherapy and counselling can serve a variety of purposes, the central ones being linked to diagnosis, that is, identification of the problem, categorization of that problem and an estimate of appropriate therapeutic interventions. In the light of what I have argued in the preceding part of this chapter it will not be surprising that I argue here that therapeutic assessment procedure and diagnostic classifications themselves often ignore the reality of women's lives and thus that sex bias enters into most traditional approaches. Psychological tests, for example, often have sex-biased items. To illustrate the principle – the Minnesota Multiphasic Personality Inventory asks individuals to say whether they have ever been sorry they were a girl. The item is scored in the pathological direction if respondents mark it 'true' for them. Thus a female could be judged unhealthy if she said she never regretted being a female. One of the problems identified in 'diagnosis' is that most diagnostic classifications focus on locating the problems *within* the client component of assessment and ignore the context. Assumptions derived from personal stereotypes can overpower the interpretation of the information collected for assessment purposes and this lack of awareness of how internalized messages about 'gender-appropriate behaviour' can lead to distortion in what symptoms are looked for, in whom the symptoms are found, and how the symptoms are measured.

Although feminist approaches to assessment and diagnosis are still very much in their infancy all feminists agree that sex bias enters into most traditional approaches. They all emphasize strategies that focus on collaboration between therapist and client which empowers the client and such assessments must include appraisals of the environmental/societal contexts. Common goals in feminist assessment therefore are to develop and use assessment and diagnostic procedures that highlight the impact of sexism and oppression in women's lives. Many feminists argue that we need new DSM categories; one example might well be 'abuse disorders' given the extent of violence against women. Assessment must account for the life-time learning experience of living in a sexist, racist, homophobic, ageist and otherwise oppressive cultural context; perhaps another example could be 'oppression disorder'.

This approach to assessment, of necessity, would move assumptions about the locus of 'pathology' from the individual to the environment and involves redefining what is considered mentally healthy. Women's responses to surviving and coping with the sexist environment can be viewed as assets where in most cases both individual and environmental factors can be seen to contribute to client's problems. A feminist approach would also allow for the possibility that no individual/internal factors are contributing to the presenting problem which has brought the woman into counselling/therapy in the first place, that is, it is possible using the feminist critique outlined at the beginning of the chapter to attribute the entire 'problem' to a pathological environment. To repeat, this is not to say that women are passive victims of culture.

213

Given this feminist emphasis on collaboration and participation, it is evident that the issue of assessment for feminist counselling would *not* involve the 'expert knows best' approach. Assessment in its best sense has already happened, with the client identifying this is what they want. The man who approaches the feminist counsellor and asks for help in 'keeping my balls on but being non-oppressive' is indicating an ability to 'split' constructively, a particularly useful process given the nature of the feminist approach incorporating a personal and social analysis. It is a good place to start. Collaboration means active participation in negotiating the start and style of the counselling. The establishment of the counselling relationship incorporates assessment in the sense of both client and counsellor having a look at each other, exploring what is on offer and what the process will involve and thus making a decision to proceed or not. It is a momentous thing to do to choose to take somebody into feminist counselling and therapy. The responsibility is awesome, the ethical requirements stringent but the possibility of change powerful.

Research and evaluation

Gender bias has been identified not only in the theory base and practice of counselling psychology but is evident in research; the extensive body of feminist research on the psychology of women is testimony to this. Feminist psychologists have pointed out that certain beliefs about how to pursue knowledge have made psychology very prone to bias in its conception, execution and interpretation. The methodology promoted in psychology assumes that the causes of events can be determined by breaking down events into their component parts and then studying the relationship of those parts, isolated from their social context – the amputation school of psychology. Examining one striking example of traditional psychological research and theory will illustrate the point. A critique of the assertiveness training research literature reveals the basic assumption that if women learned to act more assertively their reality would be different; this exposes the focus on individual variables to explain human behaviour which characterizes so much traditional psychological theory. Underlying the practice of assertiveness training are values about 'healthy' and 'adaptive' interpersonal behaviours which appear, at the very least, to lack sensitivity to women's actual experiences in society by context-stripping their behaviour. Thus the two prevalent values in assertiveness training are masculine stereotypes as the norm and individualism versus interdependence, and in learning assertive speech and behaviour women are asked to model themselves on men even though women and men live in different social environments. Women for example are much more likely to have massive infringements of their personal rights – be sexually harrassed, raped, curfewed and made to be economically dependent. Perhaps future researchers could reframe dependency as an enhancing rather than a debilitating quality given men's socialized need for power and the problems that creates!

Using feminist approaches to research facilitates this understanding of women's and men's experience, and enables us to see that meaning derives from experience within the societal context. Research needs concepts such as the self-system, reference persons, social power, status and role relationships if we are to be able to understand women and men in their social context. Non-sexist theories of the development of identity and self-concept can then follow.

Hopefully, we have now moved beyond the need to demonstrate that sexism and discrimination against women exist to more sophisticated analyses of gender belief systems and institutional factors associated with gender – and their effect on women's and men's behaviour. Research and evaluation need to incorporate the feminist principles of using alternative methods of inquiry, basing such inquiry in meaningful context and where the research is collaborative, and compare women and men contextually. Following such principles in researching gender and its effect will enable our non-sexist knowledge base to be widened and provide more appropriate evaluation methods than we currently have.

Evaluating the effectiveness of any psychological intervention is fraught with methodological difficulties (Taylor et al., 1994) and in addition the complexity of evaluating outcomes in therapy is compounded by the addition of feminist principles demanding a wider focus than individual change. For example, a major difference between evaluation of traditional interventions and feminist approaches is to be found in the issue of 'desirable' outcomes. In the outcome research literature (see for example Orlinsky and Howard, quoted in Brown and Lent, 1992) desirable outcomes so identified are the remission of pathological symptoms and behaviours, the rating by others of the client's behaviour as 'normal' and evidence of interpersonal or community social competence such as maintaining a household or holding down a job. A feminist criticism of this is that adjustment is thus defined as *behaviour that falls within accepted definitions of social norms* and the discussion which precedes this section has already focused on the problematics of this. Note in particular the argument that it is possible for a woman's presenting problems to lie entirely in her environment.

The broad goals of feminist therapy are empowerment, egalitarianism and change both for the individual and their effective environment. Thus a central component of feminist counselling is helping women to self-direct, to see and believe that there are alternatives and possibilities for their lives that they hitherto have been unable to see and that adjustment to existing oppressive environments is not a valued outcome. Such a research approach has then, by definition, to be qualitative and collaborative given that it is investigating women's subjectivity (Taylor et al., 1994). Research on feminist counselling and therapy as yet is sparse, but one study which has been done conducted research into women's *experience* of feminist therapy and counselling and concludes that at its best it needs to be seen as providing only a partial solution to the problem of securing women's emotional well-being (McLeod, 1994). The gap needs to be identified if feminist approaches are to be developed pragmatically as well as theoretically.

However, Worell and Remer (1992) argue that it is possible to extrapolate from general outcome research by identifying the three basic feminist goals mentioned above and applying traditional research outcomes to these goals. There is, they argue, evidence to suggest that counsellors and therapists who establish clear rules and expectations at the start, that is who state their values are egalitarian and non-stereotypic in sex-role orientation, are empathetic, affirming and collaborative, who encourage client expressions of anger and who reinforce client empowerment through perceptions of personal control, are likely to realize positive outcomes with their women clients. It seems to me that that is feminist counselling.

Conclusion

This chapter has argued that a feminist critique offers counselling psychologists some valuable insights into why women figure highly in the mental health statistics and thus receive a higher proportion of medical and psychological interventions (Taylor, 1991). It offers explanations of how women's socialization provides women with a set of behavioural norms to internalize, which are undervalued, of low status, have little power and encourage women to behave in ways that cause elements of themselves to be suppressed. It rejects the passive image of women that is sometimes conveyed, a picture of the woman as 'merely' at the mercy of cultural forces that surround her. Showalter (1987) chronicles how women throughout the ages have sought to fight the shackles of stereotyping and oppression and have been punished for this challenge (Faludi, 1992). Women have been, and continue to be, a strong and effective force in challenging and changing the traditional notions of femininity and the social construction of their gender. Feminists have contributed a level of critical theory that has enabled us to move to more gender-appropriate analysis and intervention. The chapter has offered a model of the counselling relationship and desirable goals which pays attention to basic feminist principles and it has argued that conventional outcome research has demonstrated that good counselling is that which *does* pay attention to those principles.

References

Benjamin, J. (1990) *The Bonds of Love*. London: Virago.

Brown, S.D. and Lent, R.W. (1992) *Handbook of Counselling Psychology*, 2nd edn. New York: Wiley.

Burman, E. (1989) *Feminists and Psychological Practice*. London: Sage.

Chodorow, N. (1978) *The Reproduction of Mothering*. Berkeley, CA: University of California Press.

Estes, C.P. (1992) *Women who Run with the Wolves*. London: Rider.

Faludi, S. (1992) *Backlash: the Undeclared War Against Women*. New York: Chatto and Windus.

Gilligan, C. (1982) *In a Different Voice*. Cambridge, MA: Harvard University Press.

Gould, S.J. (1981) *The Mismeasure of Man*. New York: Norton.

Hare-Mustin, R.T. and Marecek, J. (1990) *Making a Difference: Psychology and the Construction of Gender*. New Haven, CT: Yale University Press.

Johnson, M. (1988) *Strong Mothers: Weak Wives*. Berkeley, CA: University of California Press.

McLeod, E. (1994) *Women's Experience of Feminist Therapy and Counselling*. Buckingham: Open University Press.

Mitscherlich, M. (1987) *The Peaceable Sex: On Aggression in Women and Men*. New York: Fromm International.

Rogers, C. (1977) *Personal Power*. New York: Chatto and Windus.

Showalter, E. (1987) *The Female Malady. Women, Madness and English Culture*. London: Virago.

Tavris, C. (1993) 'The mismeasure of women', *Feminism and Psychology*, 3(2): 149–69.

Taylor, M. (1989a) 'The problem with psychoanalytical interpretation with women', in E. Burman (ed.), *Feminists and Psychological Practice*. London: Sage.

Taylor, M. (1989b) 'Personal observations', in D. Scott, K. Smithies and M. Taylor (eds), *Using Experience: Learning and Training in Community Groups*. ARVAC Occasional Paper No. 11, Manchester.

Taylor, M. (1991) 'How psychoanalytical thinking lost its way in the hands of men', *British Journal of Guidance and Counselling*, 19: 93–103.

Taylor, M. (1994) 'Gender and power in counselling and supervision', *British Journal of Guidance and Counselling*, 22(3): 319–26.

Taylor, M. (1995) 'The feminist approach', in M. Walker (ed.), *In Search of a Therapist*. Milton Keynes: Open University Press.

Taylor, M. with Bannister, P., Burman, E., Parker, I. and Tindall, C. (1994)

Qualitative Methods in Psychology: a Research Guide. Milton Keynes: Open University Press.

Tiefer, L. (1992) 'Critique of DSM-III-R Nomenclature for Sexual Dysfunction', *Psychiatric Medicine*, 10: 227–45.

Weisstein, N. (1971) *Kinder, Küche, Kirche as Scientific Law: Psychology Constructs the Female*. Boston, MA: New England Free Press.

Worell, J. and Remer, P. (1992) *Feminist Perspectives in Therapy*. Chichester: Wiley.

10

The Constructivist Paradigm

David A. Winter

Constructivism, which has its roots in the writings of such philosophers as Vico and Kant, is a term which is now applied to approaches in numerous fields of knowledge, including economics, biology, mathematics, physics and sociology as well as psychology. This chapter will outline the increasing influence of constructivism in the areas of counselling psychology and psychotherapy. However, before considering how it is applied in this sphere, the essential features of the constructivist approach and of the theories which it encompasses will be described.

The underlying theory of personality and motivation

In psychology, constructivism 'refers to a family of theories that share the assertion that human knowledge and experience entail the (pro)active participation of the individual' (Mahoney, 1988: 2). In other words, the psychological constructivist believes that people actively construct their worlds.

Two other features which Mahoney considers to be shared by constructivist psychological theories are emphases on 'morphogenic nuclear structure' and 'self-organizing development'. The former refers to the view that people are structured in such a way that core processes constrain more peripheral aspects of the person's functioning. The latter essentially means that each of us organizes our development so that our identity and equilibrium are maintained: to quote Guidano (1987: 3), 'the maintenance of one's perceived identity becomes as important as life itself'. As we shall see, both of these characteristics of constructivism are central to its approach to psychological counselling.

Personal construct theory

The basic features of constructivist meta-theory are fleshed out in somewhat different ways in the various constructivist theories. As it is probably the most elaborate of these, and that which has been used most extensively in the field of counselling psychology and psychotherapy, and has generated the most research, George Kelly's (1955) personal construct theory will now be described as an example of the constructivist approach.

Personal construct theory is based upon the philosophical assumption of 'constructive alternativism', which states that 'all of our present interpretations of the universe are subject to revision or replacement' (Kelly, 1955: 15). Therefore, not only do we construct our worlds but, as the client may discover during counselling, we can reconstruct them. Optimally, each of us functions like a scientist, formulating hypotheses, testing them out, and if necessary revising them. This essentially anticipatory nature of human functioning is expressed in the 'fundamental postulate' of personal construct theory: 'A person's processes are psychologically channelized by the ways in which he anticipates events' (Kelly, 1955: 4).

Kelly elaborated his fundamental postulate in 11 corollaries, which detail the process of construing. Central to this is the development by each individual of a system of bipolar personal constructs. Their bipolarity means that each of our constructs presents us with a 'pathway of movement' (Kelly, 1955: 128). For example, Tom, who employed a construct which contrasted being assertive with being reasonable, was resistant to moving down the path of becoming more assertive because of its implication of also becoming more unreasonable. In choosing which pole of a construct to apply to an event, the person will select that option which is most likely to increase his or her capacity to anticipate the world. This notion may make even the most apparently self-destructive behaviour comprehensible, as in Fransella's (1972) finding that stutterers would not trade stuttering for fluency until the latter carried as many implications for them, and therefore possibilities for anticipating their world, as did stuttering. As is evident from these examples, people differ from each other in their personal construct systems. Construing of another person's construction processes is the essence of intimate relationships, or, to use Kelly's term, role relationships.

In Kelly's view, we each organize our constructs in a hierarchical system, such that some constructs are superordinate to others. The particular relationships between constructs in our system determine the predictions which we make about our world. For example, the relationship within Tom's construct system between the constructs 'dislike meeting people – like people's company' and 'unselfish – demanding' implied predictions not only about other people but also about how he might change were he to see himself as more interested in meeting people.

Our predictions may be validated or invalidated by our experiences of subsequent events. Experiences of invalidation may lead to reconstruing, which may take various forms. For example, if Tom were to meet a person whom he construed as liking meeting people and unselfish, he could respond to the invalidation of his prediction by reconstruing the person as selfish. Alternatively, after several such invalidations, he might reverse the relationship between the two constructs; or 'loosen' this relationship, concluding that people who like meeting others may or may not be selfish. More fundamentally, he might decide that the 'dislike meeting people – like people's company' construct is not particularly useful, perhaps developing a new construct to replace it. Finally, he might avoid reconstruing by attempting to force the world to comply with his construction, for example by making such demands on a person who likes meeting others that the person rejects the demands, and as a result is construed as selfish. This latter strategy was equated by Kelly with hostility. The particular response which a person makes to invalidation will depend, amongst other things, on the type of construct which has been invalidated. For example, research indicates that a person's superordinate constructs are particularly resistant to invalidation, perhaps because the number of implications which they carry means that the effects of their invalidation are likely to reverberate through the system much more than the effects of invalidation of a more subordinate construct.

Those superordinate constructs which are central to an individual's identity were termed core constructs by Kelly. They are particularly resistant to change since threat is 'the awareness of imminent comprehensive change in one's core structures' (Kelly, 1955: 489). A subset of core constructs, termed core role constructs, concern one's construing of one's characteristic mode of interaction with others. For Kelly, guilt was the experience of an 'apparent dislodgement from his core role structure' (1955: 502). It is important to note that this does not necessarily involve an individual engaging in behaviour which is bad in a conventional moral sense: for example, in the case of Tom, whose core role involved unassertive behaviour, occasions on which he found himself acting assertively evoked guilt. A further emotion considered by Kelly was anxiety, which he equated with the awareness that one's constructs do not equip one to predict the events with which one is confronted.

Individuals may adopt various strategies in an attempt to avoid anxiety. They may constrict their worlds to those events which they can predict; or alternatively dilate their perceptual fields in the hope that from their new experiences may develop a system of constructs which may be applied to these. As we have seen above, they may loosen their construing to avoid invalidation and the anxiety associated with this; or tighten construct relationships in an attempt to build a system 'designed to be anxiety-tight' (Kelly, 1955: 849). Optimal functioning involves the cyclical interplay of such contrasting strategies as these, whereas in psychological disorder the individual tends to employ a particular strategy exclusively. For example, to use psychiatric nosological categories, there is evidence that people diagnosed as thought-disordered schizophrenics tend to be characterized by loose construing, and those diagnosed as neurotic by tight construing (Winter, 1992). However, the essential characteristic of psychological disorder is that the individual fails to reconstrue despite persistent invalidation of some construction.

As with other constructivists, Kelly took a holistic view of the person, and did not make the traditional distinctions between cognition, affect and conation. As the examples above demonstrate, he equated emotion with the awareness of a transition in one's construing, the nature of the emotion depending upon the particular transition involved. He saw no need for a concept of motivation since he viewed the person as a 'form of motion', not requiring any motivational force to set him or her moving. Nevertheless, Kelly's view of choice, discussed above, does provide an explanation of the individual's direction of movement, and may also be reframed in terms of the individual moving away from the anxiety associated with inability to anticipate events. Finally, although Kelly did not employ a concept of the unconscious, he did acknowledge that an individual's constructions are at different levels of cognitive awareness, and that therefore people may not always be aware of the bases for their choices. Some of the constructs at a low level of awareness are preverbal, their lack of verbal labels often being because they were developed before the person had the use of words.

Guidano and Liotti's approach

Although Kelly did not consider in depth the development of construing, greater attention has been paid to this area by other constructivists, in particular by drawing upon attachment theory. Guidano and Liotti (1983), for example, consider that attachment processes, particularly in the relationship between child and parent, are central to the development of an individual's knowledge of self and the world, or 'personal meaning organization'. Guidano (1987) also considers the developmental process to be one which involves an interplay of cognitive growth and emotional differentiation, the latter including the development of 'emotional schemata' which are employed in assimilating the individual's experiences. Clusters of schemata form 'scenes' portraying aspects of the person's experience, and similar repeated experiences lead to the development of prototypical 'nuclear scenes', each involving cyclical interplay between two clusters of emotional schemata. Rules for the connection of nuclear scenes are developed in the form of 'scripts' which provide a stable and coherent sense of self in the world, and which may be further organized into 'metascripts', which, in effect, provide a programme for the individual's life. The emotional schemata and scripts are at a more tacit level of knowledge than the person's explicit models of self and the world.

Guidano equates normal functioning with a personal meaning organization which is able to develop flexibly and resiliently towards increasing levels of complexity by a dialectical process of assimilating its contradictions. In such a system, there is an 'essential tension between opponent processes', including that between processes of maintenance and change. The dynamic balance that is achieved requires abstract processing which involves a 'decentring' from the world of immediate experience and a 'recentring' on, and commitment to, the self. The individual will tend to attend selectively to data which are consistent with his or her personal identity, but when it is necessary to process experiences inconsistent with the individual's self- or world-view, this will be achieved by a reconstruction of personal identity. However, in 'cognitive dysfunctions' the view of the self is too rigid to permit reconstruction and the individual therefore distorts information which is inconsistent with it, and attributes to external causes, such as illness, the emotional distress which accompanies this information, which often involves change in the view of a significant figure.

In both neurotic and psychotic disorders, there is a too concrete processing of experiences, and the latter disorders are in addition associated with interference in the individual's 'self-synthesizing ability'. Guidano considers that particular patterns of 'closure' of personal meaning organization, resulting from specific developmental pathways, correspond to certain clinical patterns, of which he has identified four major types. The depressive pattern arises from early distressing events perceived as losses or rejections, and involves a personal meaning organization centred upon a sense of loneliness, and emotional schemata oscillating between helplessness and anger. The agoraphobic pattern arises from interference with the individual's exploratory behaviour, and involves an organization of personal meaning in which there is oscillation between a need for protection and that for total independence. The eating disorders pattern arises from stability of the self-perception being dependent upon an enmeshed relationship with another person, and the corresponding personal meaning organization is centred upon a blurred sense of self, and oscillation between need for approval and fear of disconfirmation by significant others. The obsessive–compulsive pattern results from an ambivalent attachment to a parent, and a correspondingly ambivalent sense of self, and involves a personal meaning organization characterized by oscillation between certainty and uncertainty.

Neurolinguistic programming

Another essentially constructivist approach is neurolinguistic programming, which was devised by Bandler and Grinder on the basis of their study of the patterns employed by outstanding therapists. They consider that people construct maps of their worlds by applying various filters, including language, to their perceptions (O'Connor and Seymour, 1990). Experiences are represented internally primarily through the visual, auditory and kinesthetic systems, and each person has a preferred system for constructing such representations as well as a 'lead system' for bringing memories into conscious awareness. There are submodalities within each of these systems (for example, colour and brightness within the visual system), changing which will change the emotional impact of a particular memory.

The assessment process

George Kelly's 'first principle' was that 'if you do not know what is wrong with a person, ask him; he may tell you' (1955: 322–3). Constructivists have devised various ways of asking their clients what is wrong with them, and several of these have been described by G.J. Neimeyer (1993).

The principal concern of constructivist assessment procedures is, of course, the elicitation of the client's view of the world. Moreover, the initial focus will be on the exploration of this view in the client's own terms rather than in terms of a framework imposed by the counselling psychologist. To use one of Kelly's (1955) terms, the counselling psychologist will begin by adopting a 'credulous approach' in his or her assessment, taking what the client says at face value. This does not preclude the subsequent use by the counsellor of a set of diagnostic constructs in attempting to understand the client's situation. The personal construct counselling psychologist may, for example, apply Kelly's emotional constructs or his notions of tight and loose construing or constriction and dilation to material elicited by the assessment process. A counsellor following Guidano and Liotti's approach might frame diagnostic hypotheses in terms of the feelings, patterns of self-deception and developmental courses typically associated with particular personal meaning organizations. While Guidano and Liotti draw to some extent upon the ideas of Piaget, the influence of these ideas is particularly evident in the assessment process in another constructivist approach, Ivey's (1986) 'developmental therapy'. This involves employing Piaget's concepts of developmental stages metaphorically to identify the client's developmental level so that appropriate interventions may be selected.

The constructivist assessment process will be less concerned with identifying the frequency or intensity of beliefs held by the client than with revealing the relationships between the client's constructs, including their hierarchical organization. A major concern will be with assessing the avenues of movement open to the client rather than, as in a traditional psychiatric diagnosis, providing a static description of the client's predicament. Furthermore, the constructivist counselling psychologist will take the view that assessment and therapeutic intervention are closely interwoven. Rather than striving for an assessment process which does not influence the subject of the assessment, the constructivist will accept that assessment always generates change, and may select assessment procedures to facilitate particular types of reconstruing.

Constructivist assessment techniques tend to be idiographic and inter-active, involving either some variant of a structured interview approach or interaction between the subject and him/herself. As R.A. Neimeyer (1993) has described, they may be usefully categorized in terms of whether they primarily focus on the structure or the process of the client's construing.

Structure-oriented assessment techniques

The most well-known structure-oriented constructivist assessment approach is Kelly's repertory grid technique. The counselling psychologist employing this technique will first elicit from the client a set of 'elements', or aspects of his or her experience. Most commonly, these will be names of people supplied by the client to fit certain role titles (e.g. 'a man and woman you like'; 'your partner'), together with aspects of the self (e.g. 'yourself now'; 'your ideal self'; 'how you will be following counselling'). In the typical procedure, the client will then be presented with successive groups of three of these elements, and asked, for each group, how two of the elements are similar and thereby different from the third. In answering this question, the client will reveal one of his or her constructs. The final stage in the procedure is for the client to sort all the elements in terms of all the constructs thus elicited, usually by rating or ranking them.

While some aspects of the client's construing will be evident from visual inspection of a repertory grid, detailed analysis generally requires the use of one of the computer packages devised for this purpose. A variety of measures may be derived from such a package, including those which indicate similarities and differences between the client's construing of different elements (for example, whether the client's partner is con-strued as similar to some other significant figure in his or her life); those which reveal similarities in meaning between constructs (for example, indicating how the client's problem is construed); and measures of the degree of tightness of the construct system.

Although a repertory grid may provide some indication of the

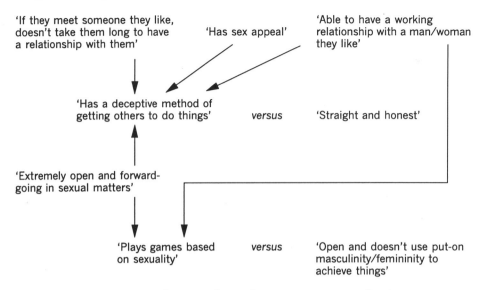

Figure 10.1   *Negative implications of sexual responsiveness in a client's pre-treatment implications grid*

hierarchical relationships between constructs in a client's system, such information may be obtained more directly by two further techniques. In laddering, the client is presented with one of his or her constructs and asked to which pole they would prefer to be assigned, and why. The reason for the client's preference will be a construct more superordinate than the first, and the procedure may be repeated to trace further levels of superordinacy. In the bipolar version of the implications grid (Fransella, 1972), the client is asked, for each of his or her construct poles, which other construct poles would apply to a person so described. Figure 10.1 shows the negative implications of construct poles concerning sexual responsiveness which this procedure revealed in a man who was unable to ejaculate. These implications suggested that were he to be able to be more sexually responsive he would have to see himself in a less favourable light.

Process-oriented assessment techniques

Process-oriented assessment techniques tend to focus upon narrative material since this may reveal something of the flow of a person's construing. One such technique which was developed by Kelly is the self-characterization, in which the client is asked to write a character sketch of himself or herself as if it were written by a sympathetic friend. Variations on this procedure include sketches of the self at different points in time (for example, as a child; if I lost this particular problem). A more extensive written narrative procedure which can provide access to the client's construction and reconstruction processes is for him or her to keep a personal journal. Open-ended interviews may also be employed, as in a procedure developed by Viney and Westbrook (1981: 48) in which the client is asked to 'talk to me for a few minutes about your life at the moment – the good things and the bad – what it is like for you'. Various content analysis scales may be applied to the interview transcript in order, for example, to assess emotions, including anxiety in Kelly's sense of this term. These scales may also be applied to transcripts of counselling sessions to monitor changes in the client.

A further technique which can provide access for both counsellor and client to the client's construing processes is Mahoney's 'stream of consciousness' procedure, in which 'the client is invited to attend to and, as best one can, report ongoing thoughts, sensations, images, memories, and feelings' (1991: 295). The client is not required to share with the counselling psychologist all of this material, and the counsellor will generally be less concerned to provide interpretations of what is reported than to elicit its meaning for the client.

Neurolinguistic programming assessment

Assessment in neurolinguistic programming explores both the structure and process of the client's view of the world. A particular concern is to identify the client's preferred representational system by noting 'accessing cues', such as eye movements, gestures, or speed and tone of speech. For example, if the client's eyes move upwards at some point, or become defocused and look straight ahead, the counselling psychologist will suspect that he or she is visualizing something. The counsellor's interventions may then be matched to the client's preferred system. The psychologist employing this approach will also be concerned to 'calibrate' the client's emotional states by noting the non-verbal expressions of these states. Turning to the client's use of language, the counsellor will employ the 'Meta Model', which involves asking questions to elicit information which, because of omissions, distortions, or generalizations, is not transferred from the client's 'deep structure' to the 'surface structure' of his or her speech. For example, if the client says 'I was hurt', the counselling psychologist might ask 'How and by whom?' Amongst the particular issues which the counsellor will wish to clarify are the client's desired outcomes, and their ecological context, which may be appreciated by asking the client to consider in what way other aspects of his or her life would be affected if each outcome were achieved.

What does change mean and how is it brought about?

Constructivists view therapeutic change as a process of reconstruction. This process may take many forms, as Kelly (1969: 231) described in listing the approaches to their task which a therapist and client might adopt.

1 The two of them can decide that the client should reverse his position with respect to one of the more obvious reference axes.
2 Or they can select another construct from the client's ready repertory and apply it to matters at hand.
3 They can make more explicit those preverbal constructs by which all of us order our lives in considerable degree.
4 They can elaborate the construct system to test it for internal consistency.
5 They can test constructs for their predictive validity.
6 They can increase the range of convenience of certain constructs, that is, apply them more generally. They can also decrease the range of convenience and thus reduce a construct to a kind of obsolescence.
7 They can alter the meaning of certain constructs; rotate the reference axes.
8 They can erect new reference axes.

The earlier items in this list, involving changes in the use of the client's existing constructs, clearly involve more superficial reconstruction than do the later items, involving modification of these constructs or their replacement by new constructs. The level of reconstruction which is attempted may also be viewed in terms of the type of constructs which it involves. For example, counselling may be contrasted with psychotherapy in that it will generally not attempt to produce changes in a client's core constructs.

The variety of possible types of reconstruction is matched by the range of techniques which the counsellor may employ to facilitate these changes. The counselling psychologist will base the selection of the particular type of reconstruing on which to focus, and therefore of the technique to be employed, on his or her assessment of the client's construct system. Of particular concern will be the selection of interventions which are 'ecologically sound', in that they foster the evolution of the client's construct system without disrupting its integrity (Neimeyer and Harter, 1988). For example, there will be a concern not to dismantle some aspect of this system until a viable alternative is available; and not to present a fundamental challenge to a client's core constructs. If the counsellor fails to take such matters into account, the result is likely to be a highly anxious and/or threatened client, who will resist the psychologist's efforts in order to preserve his or her construct system. It is also important to note that, whatever type of reconstruction is aimed for, the constructivist counselling psychologist will not be attempting to persuade the client to adopt some particular view of events, but simply to help the client to discover that it is possible to view events in alternative ways. The client's construing should thereby be set in motion again.

Personal construct psychotherapy

In the personal construct approach, one of the counsellor's first concerns may well be a continuation of the process of elaboration of the client's construct system which is likely to have commenced during the assessment process. This will involve exploring the implications of the client's constructions, initially particularly those relating to the presenting complaint; and identifying, and perhaps resolving, any inconsistencies in his or her construing. This process may be facilitated by the use of the assessment procedures described in the last section, by asking the client to imagine the outcome of alternative courses of action, or by 'casual enactment'. This last approach involves short spells of role-playing by the client and counselling psychologist of situations involving the client and/ or significant or hypothetical figures in his or her life. One of the benefits of enactment is that it may allow the client to experiment with some new behaviour while disengaging core constructs from the experimentation and thereby avoiding the threat which it might otherwise involve.

While enactment is usually employed in a relatively informal way during therapy, Kelly also devised a more formal enactment procedure, known as fixed-role therapy. The counselling psychologist who employs this approach will initially write a sketch of a hypothetical character for the client to enact. In writing this sketch, the counsellor will generally draw upon the client's self-characterization and other assessment material, and will be attempting to describe a person who is orthogonal to, rather than the opposite of, the client. The sketch will also attempt to elaborate some theme which it might be valuable for the client to explore. If the role portrayed in the sketch appears plausible to the client, he or she will be asked to 'become' this character for two weeks, during which there will be frequent rehearsals of the role with the counsellor, focusing on progressively more threatening or anxiety-provoking situations. The aim of the exercise is not to transform the client permanently into the new character, but to provide 'one good, rousing, construct-shaking experience' (Kelly, 1955: 412), which will demonstrate to the client that he or she need not be trapped in one particular role and corresponding set of reactions from other people. The procedure is a good example of the 'invitational mood' in which personal construct counselling is conducted, the client being en- couraged to experiment by approaching events as if some new construction of them were correct. It is, however, only one of many possible ways of facilitating experimentation during this form of counselling.

The personal construct counselling psychologist will at times be concerned either to loosen or tighten a client's construing. Loosening may serve several functions, such as allowing certain aspects of the client's experience to be encompassed by their constructs; setting the stage for realignment of constructs; and facilitating the attachment of a verbal label to a preverbal construct. It may be achieved in various ways, including relaxation, free association of the type employed in psychoanalysis, encouragement of reporting of dreams, and uncritical acceptance of the client's construing. While loosening may be a necessary component of reconstruction, the client's new constructions will need to be tightened if testable predictions are to be derived from them. Many of the techniques used in elaborating a client's construing will have a tightening effect, as will such behavioural procedures as self-monitoring of behaviours or thoughts. A particular set of tightening techniques suggested by Kelly involves 'binding' a construct to the time or person it was initially developed to anticipate. This and other personal construct techniques are illustrated in the following case example.

> In exploring the unfavourable constructions of sexual responsiveness which had been revealed by Rodney's implications grid (see p. 226 above), it became apparent that these had their basis in his childhood experience of a mother who manipulated others with her sexuality. He was therefore encouraged to view these constructions as anachronisms, which had served a useful purpose when first developed but were now inappropriately applied in his adult relationships. Since he had dealt with the inconsistencies in his view of sexuality by constricting his world to exclude sexual experiences, he was encouraged to elaborate his construing in this area to reduce the anxiety which it occasioned. The procedures used included asking him to keep a daily record of his sexual urges; to complete a repertory grid in which the elements were sexual situations; and to experiment with homework tasks designed to enhance his awareness of pleasurable bodily sensations. He eventually reported that he had been able to have his first orgasm, and further grid assessments revealed that this was accompanied by the development of a more favourable construction of sexual responsiveness.

Process-oriented cognitive therapy

The basic features of Guidano's non-rationalistic, process-oriented cognitive therapy are the facilitation of the client's self-awareness and of a flexible response to incongruities so that these may be assimilated into a more abstract self-image. The experience of affect during therapy, particularly in the context of the therapeutic relationship, is considered crucial in prompting reorganization. Therapy, in effect, involves training in self-observation by a 'moviola technique' in which the client is encouraged to 'zoom in and out' on particular scenes from their life, and to view events from both a 'subjective' and 'objective' viewpoint. Homework assignments involve focusing self-observation on particular items between sessions, and techniques borrowed from other therapeutic approaches may be employed to foster experimentation.

The self-observational process in itself, with its emphasis on clients disengaging themselves from their beliefs and viewing these as hypotheses, is likely to modify the client's view of the self and of the events which are being considered. Reorganization of the client's view of the self will also be promoted by explanations offered by the therapist which are discrepant from the client's own explanations, provided that the client is sufficiently emotionally involved in the therapeutic relationship. One such therapeutic explanation will be the therapist's initial reformulation of the client's problem in terms of the personal meaning organization which underlies it. The 'internal' focus of this reformulation will be likely to be inconsistent with the client's view of his or her problem, which may tend to focus on external attributions such as symptoms of illness.

The strategy adopted in therapy is a stepwise one in which the client is only encouraged to move on to a new level of self-observation when stability has been achieved at the level previous to this. During the initial focus on the client's immediate experiences, the client comes to appreciate that emotional states are constructions associated with perceived imbalances in an affective relationship. The next stage is generally a reconstruction of the client's 'affective style' involving analysis of the client's history of affective relationships. Guidano considers that most clients obtain relief from their presenting problems without the necessity for a final stage of analysis of how their developmental pathways led them to arrive at their personal meaning organizations. However, with those who are interested in exploring this area, a self-observational process may again be employed, but with the client being asked to compare their subjective viewpoint of an event with not only their present objective viewpoint but also that from the perspective of the self at the age when the event occurred.

Guidano's (1991) treatment of Sandra, who presented with phobic anxieties concerning both going out and staying at home alone, began with a reformulation of her difficulties as a fear of loss of control which she experienced in situations which she perceived either as constrictive or as not affording her sufficient protection. Focusing self-observation on these experiences, she came to view her fears as 'tests of strength' which she constructed to demonstrate to herself that, since she was liable to lose control, she required her husband to 'keep an eye on her'. Shifting the focus to her marital relationship, it became apparent that, to preserve her sense of self, she had excluded from awareness feelings connected with her husband's affair with another woman and her own subsequent affair with his best friend. These feelings could then only be viewed by her as uncontrollable fears of being alone or losing control which, paradoxically, kept her closer to a husband whom she might otherwise have considered leaving. Exploration of the affective history of her relationships, by focusing on critical scenes from these relationships, allowed the identification of a pattern of oscillation between need for protection and need for freedom and independence. Then, focusing on her early developmental history, it became increasingly apparent that her phobic meaning organization largely derived from inhibition of her exploratory behaviour and autonomy by the ostensibly loving attentions of her mother, the indirectness of this inhibition preventing her from recognizing it at the time. Her reconstrual of her mother was associated with Sandra apparently viewing the world as less threatening and exposing herself to previously avoided situations, such as making a journey by aeroplane.

Developmental therapy

Ivey's developmental therapy aims to help the client progress through a series of stages equivalent to those which Piaget used to characterize child development. If therapy is successful, the client develops into a formal operational thinker, who is able to identify consistently repeating patterns in his or her experiences; or a 'post-formal thinker', who can appreciate that reality is constructed dialectically. For this process to occur, there needs to be an appropriate equilibration between assimilation and accommodation. Ivey (1986: 40) describes the counselling psychologist's task as 'to provide a new environment that provides more useful and accurate environmental feedback and thus returns the client to the process of growth and development'.

Neurolinguistic programming

Neurolinguistic programming tends to be rather more directive than other constructivist approaches in its employment of techniques, some-times facilitated by the use of trance, to modify clients' ways of viewing their worlds. One such technique is the association of certain stimuli, or 'anchors', from different representational systems with some resourceful state which the client wishes to bring to bear in particular problematic situations. By using the anchors (for example, saying a word internally, visualizing an image, and/or making a certain movement) in the situations concerned, the client will then be able to summon up the required resources. Another technique which may be employed to reconstruct some past traumatic event is to ask the client to imagine watching himself or herself watching the event on a screen; and then to ask the client to alter the picture's sub-modalities (such as brightness or size) to change the negative feelings which it brings forth. Next, the client may be asked to join his or her younger self on the screen, bringing resources from the present to cope with the traumatic incident. Finally, the client may be invited, in imagination, to practise coping with similar events in the future. 'Reframing' may also be used in neurolinguistic programming, the counsellor offering alternative meanings of the client's statements. For example, a behaviour which is presented as a problem by a client may be reframed as a strength in certain circumstances, and the client then helped to employ it in only those contexts, and to develop alternative ways of acting in other contexts.

Technical eclecticism

It should now be apparent that constructivist approaches to therapy and counselling psychology are technically eclectic in that they may borrow the techniques of other approaches, but will conceptualize their action in terms of the particular constructivist model concerned rather than the model from which they are derived. For example, both personal construct psychotherapy and the approach of Guidano and Liotti may employ behavioural techniques as aids to experimentation. The latter authors consider that, by changing superficial structures, such techniques may facilitate the identification of the rules which underlie these structures.

The nature of the relationship between counselling psychologist and individual client

Kelly viewed the relationship between therapist or counselling psychologist and client as analogous to that between a research supervisor and student. Guidano and Liotti also use the metaphor of scientific research in describing this relationship, the therapist serving as a model of the scientific attitude for the client. They, like Kelly, emphasize the importance of creating a cooperative, collaborative therapeutic relationship, stressing that this is one which the client can perceive as a 'secure base' from which to explore his or her emotional life and identity. In their view, this requires the therapist to recognize and respect the client's identity, while not confirming its 'basic pathogenetic assumptions'. They

233

also consider that the process of exploration may usefully focus upon the therapeutic relationship itself, and that the client's construing of the therapist, for example, may provide a basis for assessment and change of such aspects of the client's cognitive structures as his or her models of attachment figures. The therapist's own self-awareness is enhanced as he or she attends to the emotions accompanying his or her perceptions of the client, and this increases the therapist's involvement in the therapeutic relationship. Guidano (1991) considers the final stages of therapy as involving a transformation of the therapeutic relationship into one of supervision. He considers that emotions associated with the separation from the therapist should be employed to clarify further the client's bonding style and to renegotiate the 'rules' of the client–therapist relationship.

Taking a credulous, respectful attitude towards the client's view of the world (or 'pacing' the client, to use a term from neurolinguistic programming), the constructivist counselling psychologist will not try to impose his or her own constructions on the client. As Guidano puts it:

> The therapist should try to work only on those areas of experience which have shown themselves to be critical on the basis of a previous reconstruction of the same basic themes of the client's personal meaning, refraining from an exaggerated intervention in other domains despite the fact that one's own conception of life might seem better and more suitable than those exhibited by the client. (1991: 209)

Since the constructivist counsellor in effect 'suspends' his or her own constructions during counselling, the impact on the psychologist's approach of differences between counsellor and client in terms of such areas as gender, race, class, or sexual orientation should be minimal. However, counselling is likely to be more effective if the counselling psychologist is sufficiently familiar with the client's milieu and cultural background to have some awareness of the sources of validation which are available to the client.

Family, group and organizational implications

While the constructivist approaches described above initially focused primarily on the individual's construing of the world, later developments of some of these approaches have demonstrated their applicability to couples, families and broader social groups. For example, Procter (1981) and other post-Kellyan personal construct theorists have developed a family construct psychology, based on the notion that a family (or indeed any social group), may be considered to have a construct system, the properties of which are essentially similar to those of an individual's construct system. Such personal construct assessment techniques as the self-characterization and repertory grid have been adapted for use with couples, families and groups, allowing not only the identification of features of construing shared by the individuals concerned but also indications of the extent to which each individual's construing deviates from this consensus and is understood by other members of the family or group. Similarly, adaptations of methods used in individual personal construct counselling have been employed in marital and family counselling. Their applications in organizational settings have, for example, facilitated conflict resolution and greater awareness by managers and staff of each other's constructions. Neurolinguistic programming has also been fruitfully employed for such purposes, particularly in the business context.

Constructivist counselling may usefully be conducted in a group setting since the group provides an interpersonal laboratory which offers a rich source of validational evidence for clients' constructions. Kelly's (1955) approach to group psychotherapy was based on a view that groups pass through a series of developmental stages, at each of which certain therapeutic techniques are appropriate. One technique of which he and later personal construct therapists have made particular use in groups is enactment. A further personal construct group approach, the Interpersonal Transaction Group, has been devised by Landfield and Rivers (1975) to foster the development of role relationships. Such a group involves brief, non-critical dyadic interactions between group members, who rotate at the end of each interaction until each member has been paired with every other. There is then a plenary discussion of members' experience of the interactions, topics for which are selected for their relevance to the clients' problems.

In addition to applications to couples, families and other groups of constructivist approaches to individuals, several systems theory approaches may themselves be considered essentially constructivist (Feixas, 1992). The methods which they employ are directed towards the elicitation of a family's construing and the promotion of reconstruction. For example, in the Milan group's 'circular questioning' technique (Selvini-Palazzoli et al., 1980), each family member, in front of the others, states his or her construction of some issue, such as the relationship between two other members and the comparison of these with a third. The interactions thus generated may lead constructions to be revised. More precisely, many modern family therapy approaches may be classified as social constructionist (McNamee and Gergen, 1992). Although being similar to the constructivist position in assuming that we construct our worlds, they differ in emphasizing that this construction arises through social interaction and is mediated by language. Family counselling from this perspective may be considered to involve the 'co-construction of realities' by means of conversation between a family and its therapists. This may be facilitated by such devices as allowing a family to observe the family counselling team discussing them, and then to discuss their observations with the team (Andersen, 1987).

Research evidence about effectiveness

There are numerous single-case reports and uncontrolled group studies demonstrating the effectiveness of constructivist counselling or psycho-therapy with a wide range of clients, of all ages, including not only those presenting with psychological disorders but also physically ill people and those with disabilities (see Winter, 1992, for a review of the literature on personal construct psychotherapy and counselling). There are also a few controlled studies of the effectiveness of constructivist techniques, such as fixed-role therapy, employed in the context of another approach or in a modified form which departs significantly from the original. However, controlled outcome studies of relatively 'pure' constructivist approaches are rare. One of the first of these, by Bannister et al. (1975), found only slightly more improvement in thought-disordered schizophrenics treated by personal construct psychotherapy than in a control group. The authors argue that more favourable results might have been achieved had they been able to have more control over the validational fortunes of their clients' construing. Evesham and Fransella (1985) carried out a controlled study of a personal construct psychotherapy treatment method for stutterers which Fransella (1972) had found to produce a significant reduction in disfluencies. Comparing an approach that incorporated this method with one that solely involved training in speech techniques, they found somewhat less change post treatment in the former group but that its clients had a significantly lower relapse rate over the following 18 months. Viney (1990) has investigated personal construct crisis intervention counselling for people hospitalized for medical problems and personal construct psychotherapy for elderly people presenting with psychological problems. In both these client groups, those treated by the personal construct approach not only showed such psychological changes as reductions in anxiety, depression and indirectly expressed anger, and increases in expressed competence, but also greater improvements in physical health than did controls. For example, the hospitalized clients who were counselled spent fewer days on antibiotics and more rapidly returned to normal temperature and to oral food intake. Finally, Jackson (1990) found significant gains in self-esteem in adolescents treated by personal construct group psychotherapy, as compared to a control group, the treated clients also finding each other easier to understand following therapy.

Although the results of most of these investigations are encouraging, there is clearly a need for further controlled outcome research on personal construct and other constructivist approaches to counselling and psychotherapy.

Conclusions

Constructivist counselling psychology, although sometimes sharing techniques with other approaches, offers a distinct, alternative construction of the problems which might lead an individual to seek counselling, and of how these problems might best be addressed. Like a behavioural approach, it is likely to encourage the client to experiment, but unlike such an approach it is primarily concerned with the constructions underlying the client's behaviour. In contrast to rationalist cognitive approaches, it does not consider that there is a correct, rational way of viewing events, and is less concerned with the client's beliefs than with the structures and processes involved in these beliefs. Unlike the psychodynamic approach, it will not necessarily focus upon the client's past, does not generally consider that people should pass through a fixed sequence of developmental stages, and will view interpretation less as providing the client with insight than as demonstrating that an alternative construction of the client's situation is possible. It has greater commonality with those approaches, such as the humanistic and systems paradigms, which reject the deterministic, reductionist assumptions underlying the behavioural, rationalist cognitive and psychodynamic approaches. However, it differs from the humanistic approach in its view of emotions, and in making greater use of diagnostic constructs in assessment of the client's predicament. It differs from some systemic approaches in its less adversarial view of the counsellor–client relationship.

Despite the contrasts between constructivism and traditional versions of many of the other counselling paradigms, there are constructivist trends in several of these paradigms, as in most other areas of human knowledge. Whatever its theoretical base, a counsellor's practice is likely to benefit if he or she takes the view that there are numerous alternative viable constructions of the client's predicament and of a successful outcome of counselling.

References

Andersen, T. (1987) 'The reflecting team: dialogue and metadialogue in clinical work', *Family Process*, 26: 415–28.

Bannister, D., Adams-Webber, J.R., Penn, W.I. and Radley, A.R. (1975)

'Reversing the process of thought disorder: a serial validation experiment', *British Journal of Social and Clinical Psychology*, 14: 169–80.

Evesham, M. and Fransella, F. (1985) 'Stuttering relapse: the effects of a combined speech and psychological reconstruction programme', *British Journal of Disorders of Communication*, 20: 237–48.

Feixas, G. (1992) 'Personal construct approaches to family therapy', in R.A. Neimeyer and G.J. Neimeyer (eds), *Advances in Personal Construct Psychology*, vol. 2. Greenwich, CT: JAI Press.

Fransella, F. (1972) *Personal Change and Reconstruction: Research on a Treatment of Stuttering*. London: Academic Press.

Guidano, V.F. (1987) *Complexity of the Self: a Developmental Approach to Psychopathology and Therapy*. New York: Guilford.

Guidano, V.F. (1991) *The Self in Process: Towards a Post-Rationalist Cognitive Therapy*. New York: Guilford.

Guidano, V.F. and Liotti, G.A. (1983) *Cognitive Processes and Emotional Disorders*. New York: Guilford.

Ivey, A.E. (1986) *Developmental Therapy*. San Francisco: Jossey Bass.

Jackson, S. (1990) 'A PCT therapy group for adolescents', in P. Maitland (ed.), *Personal Construct Theory Deviancy and Social Work*. London: Inner London Probation Service/Centre for Personal Construct Psychology.

Kelly, G.A. (1955) *The Psychology of Personal Constructs*. New York: Norton.

Kelly, G.A. (1969) 'Personal construct theory and the psychotherapeutic interview', in B. Maher (ed.), *Clinical Psychology and Personality: the Selected Papers of George Kelly*. New York: Wiley.

Landfield, A.W. and Rivers, P.C. (1975) 'An introduction to interpersonal transaction and rotating dyads', *Psychotherapy: Theory, Research, and Practice*, 12: 366–74.

McNamee, S. and Gergen, K.J. (1992) *Therapy as Social Construction*. London: Sage.

Mahoney, M.J. (1988) 'Constructive metatheory: I. Basic features and historical foundations', *International Journal of Personal Construct Psychology*, 1: 1–35.

Mahoney, M.J. (1991) *Human Change Processes: the Scientific Foundations of Psychotherapy*. New York: Basic Books.

Neimeyer, G.J. (ed.) (1993) *Constructivist Assessment: a Casebook*. Newbury Park, CA: Sage.

Neimeyer, R.A. (1993) 'Constructivist approaches to the measurement of meaning', in G.J. Neimeyer (ed.), *Constructivist Assessment: a Casebook*. Newbury Park, CA: Sage.

Neimeyer, R. and Harter, S. (1988) 'Facilitating individual change in Personal Construct Therapy', in G. Dunnett (ed.), *Working with People: Clinical Uses of Personal Construct Psychology*. London: Routledge.

O'Connor, J. and Seymour, J. (1990) *Introducing Neuro-Linguistic Programming*. London: Aquarian.

Procter, H.G. (1981) 'Family construct psychology: an approach to under-standing and treating families', in S. Walrond-Skinner (ed.), *Developments in Family Therapy*. London: Routledge and Kegan Paul.

Selvini-Palazzoli, M., Boscolo, L., Cecchin, G. and Prata, G. (1980) 'Hypothesizing–Circularity–Neutrality: three guidelines for the conductor of the session', *Family Process*, 19: 3–12.

Viney, L.L. (1990) 'A constructivist model of psychological reactions to physical illness and injury', in G. Neimeyer and R. Neimeyer (eds), *Advances in Personal Construct Psychology*, vol. 1. New York: JAI Press.

Viney, L.L. and Westbrook, M.T. (1981) 'Measuring patients' experienced quality of life: the application of content analysis scales in health care', *Community Health Studies*, 5: 45–52.

Winter, D.A. (1992) *Personal Construct Psychology in Clinical Practice: Theory, Research and Applications*. London: Routledge.

11

The Systems Paradigm

Robert Bor, Charles Legg and Isobel Scher

For years scientists have grappled with the paradox of trying to explain complex phenomena in the real world in terms of 'fundamental' processes that are, themselves, very simple. One of the most intractable problems has been the explanation of intentionality in terms of simpler, 'mechanistic' processes. Systems theory offers a powerful solution to this conundrum by showing how 'goal directed' behaviour can appear as an emergent property of the systems made up of simple elements that are not, themselves, goal directed. Systems theory in counselling psychology builds on this insight and views 'problems' as an emergent property of social systems, particularly the family, rather than as a property of the individuals who make up that social system.

Systems is both a school of therapy in counselling psychology as well as a meta-theory and it can be used to understand and explain a wide range of therapy approaches and phenomena in therapy. It differs from most of the other theoretical paradigms described in this book in a number of respects. First, there is no underlying theory of personality or motivation. Secondly, the assessment process is an integral part of the therapeutic process and cannot meaningfully be considered separately from it. Thirdly, change is viewed as a change in the functional properties of the system rather than the individual characteristics of any member of the system. Hence, concepts such as the 'theory of learning' are seen as inappropriate. Fourthly, because it is a systems approach, family, group and organizational issues are inherent in the approach and cannot be meaningfully abstracted from this context. Hence, although these issues will be addressed in this chapter, the authors do not view it as appropriate to subdivide the material in this way. This chapter reviews the application of a systems approach in counselling psychology. Drawing on published research, the authors describe the underlying theory, the assessment process, change through therapy and developments in contemporary practice. Systems theory is principally about understanding ideas in the wider social context, and it is appropriate therefore to begin this review with a brief description of the context and historical roots of the paradigm.

Background to the systems paradigm

In 1950, psychotherapy was described by one author as 'an unidentified technique applied to unspecified problems with unpredictable outcomes', for which was recommended 'vigorous training' (Raimy, 1950: 14). It is not surprising, therefore, that a wide range of therapeutic approaches is taught on applied psychology courses in general and counselling psychology courses in particular. The development of different psychotherapeutic approaches has not been a random occurrence. Rather, they are each intimately connected with the social context within which they evolved. Systemic therapy had its origins in post-war research into physics, mathematics, engineering, thermodynamics and organizational psychology, before it was adapted and applied to the behavioural sciences by researchers studying human interactive processes. Systems theory made it possible to conceive of mechanical models of the human brain characterized by interrelatedness of sub-systems, and the whole being greater than the sum of the parts. At this time, research was concerned with describing the functional and structural properties which characterized all systems – both animate and inanimate. The application of systemic ideas to counselling was to come a decade later in the 1960s.

Most counselling models focus on the individual as the unit of analysis and intervention, yet the consequences of psychological and physical problems extend beyond the client and affect many of the people around them. The shift in focus in therapy from the individual to social interaction proposed by systemic theorists brings with it concomitant changes in the focus of therapeutic interventions. This includes changing behaviour and communication patterns between family members, rather than the more traditional psychoanalytic approach of interpreting transference. Problem-solving in therapy replaced exploratory analytic therapy.

Systemic therapy is derived from cybernetics which implies that psychological symptoms should always be viewed within the context of feedback (Keeney, 1983). The information is of a communicational nature, with the relationships and interactions between the elements of the systems facilitating this. A symptom is maintained by particular repetitive patterns of behaviour organized within a troubled social system. An individual orientation leads one to look for indications of problems 'inside' the person and to direct treatment exclusively at the person as the intervention target. This is the traditional medical model of diagnosis. Moving from an individual to a family or systems orientation, one looks to the family system for indications of the problem and focuses on the relationship system as the intervention target. Psychological symptoms can thus be redefined as 'indicators for an entire ecology of relationships' (Keeney, 1983: 124). The changing emphasis in therapy to interactive systems is paralleled by an epistemological shift. The counsellor was not so much concerned with *why* people behave the way they do (cause), but *how* they behave (process) and with what consequences.

The basic tenets of the systems approach can be summarized as follows (see Bor et al., 1992, for a more detailed explanation of these points).

1   Psychological problems need to be understood within a social and political context. Systemic counselling is always contextual.
2   Interaction (reciprocity) is at the heart of all psychological inquiry and counselling practice.
3   Relationships between people (whether they are family members or colleagues) are punctuated by beliefs and behaviours.
4   Problems may occur at particular developmental stages of individuals or families. They may also arise when people deny 'reality'.
5   Problems that present to counsellors are generally expressed in language and in the course of conversation. Systems theory has contributed significantly to insights into the language in counselling.
6   As with most counselling approaches, the systemic counsellor strives to be empathic. Counselling is a collaborative activity with the client.

The underlying theory of the systems paradigm is described below.

Underlying theory

'Personality' and systemic theory

Personality is not a thing, it is a theoretical construct advanced to account for recurrent patterns of human behaviour. Personality-based theories of human action take an essentially ballistic view of the human mind, according to which we are hewn by early experience from the material created by our genetic endowment and then launched into adult life to continue in the trajectory established by these early experiences. Personality-based theories in counselling focus on identifying failures in this process as the source of problems in adulthood and seek to promote change by reversing the damage done in earlier life. Our view is that, when counsellors talk about 'personality', they are really talking about the issue of how psychological and interpersonal problems develop. This section is written in this spirit.

Systemic theorists offer an alternative account of recurrent patterns of behaviour, one that focuses on their maintenance in the present by feedback within the system. It does so by considering the social context of the behaviour rather than the characteristics of the individual displaying that behaviour. The primary social context in systemic therapy is the client and his or her family (Jones, 1993). Ideas about the evolution and resolution of problems in the family system are described below.

Families satisfy the minimum criteria for being a system by definition. There is a series of elements, the family members, and they are interconnected, in that what one member of a family does affects the other members of the family. The elements and the interconnections between them are also enduring. The family is both a biological and a social construct and the two do not need to match. An individual may be defined socially as part of one's family but not biologically, as in the case of adoption. Although the family serves a biological function, the *experience* of an individual as a family member cannot be determined biologically.

How do family processes lead to psychological problems?

What most psychologists view as 'symptoms', systems theorists view as the product of attempted *solutions* to the problems in the family. Those problems can come about for a number of possible reasons. Many theorists focus on problems in communication (Bateson et al., 1956) while others focus on problems stemming from transitions within the family (Andolfi et al., 1983).

Change in the family

As family members age, so the dispositions of the individuals and the appropriateness of particular patterns of care will change. This process of change may result in psychological problems for individuals in the family (Andolfi et al., 1983; Carter and McGoldrick, 1989). According to Andolfi et al. (1983) psychological problems develop either when families *create* inappropriate solutions or when families attempt to resist change while Carter and McGoldrick (1989) argue that problems arise when families attempt to *apply* inappropriate solutions to the problems created by change.

Andolfi et al. (1983) identify two types of family in which a developmental event is translated into individual pathology. One is the 'at risk' family, in which the tensions involved in passing through a major developmental stage are resolved by one member of the family developing symptoms in such a way as to allow the rest of the family to complete its restructuring. The other is the 'rigid' family, in which restructuring is resisted by means of an individual developing symptoms. They give as an example of an 'at risk' family, one in which the maternal grandfather has died and the maternal grandmother has come to live with the family. This is a family coping with two developmental events simultaneously, the death of a member and the acquisition of a new member of a household.

One solution to this problem may be for a child to regress developmentally, as a consequence of which the grandmother may acquire someone to care for, the child, and the parents can focus their anxiety on the child rather than the tensions created by having the grandmother living with them. Rigidity, they suggest, may underlie disorders like depression, where the development of depressive symptoms in the child may remove the need to restructure the family following the child's leaving home.

Andolfi et al. (1983) pointed out that 'rigidity' is not necessarily an inherent property of a family system but something that develops out of the family's attempt to deal with developmental transitions. Thus the distinction between an 'at risk' and a 'rigid' family is that the former changes its organization and the latter does not. Although the necessary modelling has not yet been carried out, there are enough formal similarities between family systems and the simple networks that have been simulated in recent years to suggest that each family may have the potential to apply different solutions to the same developmental event. That is to say, whether or not the family progresses through at the expense of the well-being of one member or gets stuck may be more a function of accidents and incidents occurring during the transition than of the properties of the family prior to the transition. Having said that, there are likely to be pre-existing family structures that make families more prone to maladaptive outcomes than others.

While Andolfi et al. (1983) view the family as being creative, Carter and McGoldrick (1989) view the family as essentially conservative. Following from Bowen they put forward a dual stressor model in which liability to psychological problems is the result of interactions that have persisted across a number of generations. According to this approach, life cycle transitions create psychological problems when the family attempts to apply, inappropriately, the solutions developed by previous generations in the family. For example, if one's parents reacted to the birth of children by panicking then one would be inclined to do the same thing. Carter and McGoldrick's approach is best viewed as an extension of Andolfi et al.'s since it reminds us that, when faced with problems, most people attempt to solve them heuristically, by applying solutions that were used in the past for similar problems. It is incomplete as a model for the development of psychological problems because it lacks an explanation of how family attitudes, taboos and expectations develop.

Psychological assessment in systemic counselling

Systemic counselling differs from other approaches in two ways. The first is in the methods used in the assessment process and the second is in the nature of the hypotheses entertained about the processes underlying the problem. The methods involve asking clients questions about relationships, the choice of operation at any point being guided by the counsellor's current hypothesis about the origins of the client's problems. Typically, the hypotheses revolve around the relationships between the client and their social context, especially the family, rather than intrapsychic processes (Liddle, 1983; Selvini–Palazzoli et al., 1980b; Tomm, 1984).

One of the strengths of the systems approach is that it encourages the counsellor to consider the possibility that the 'problem' is located outside the identified patient. People come to counselling when there is a 'problem' but it would be naive to believe that the individuals who have been referred are always the ones with the problem. Clients may also be referred because of problems with the referring agency or with the relationship between the client and the referring agency (Selvini–Palazzoli et al., 1980a). In these circumstances the aim of the counselling would not be aimed at dealing with the referred problem but at dealing with the relationship between the client and the referring agency.

The referring agency may have a very clear idea of the 'problem', as seen from their point of view, but since the aim of counselling is to work within the framework of the client it is essential to find out what they view as the problem. One of the advantages of working in the family setting is that it will remind the counsellor that there may not be a single problem but there may be as many as there are members of the family, as each family member has a different perspective on the situation. At this stage the aim is to build up a picture of what the family members think the problem is as a prelude to forming a hypothesis about the underlying family dysfunction. In addition to feeding into the hypothesis-forming stage, this stage is vital for engaging the client as it is a means of showing the client that they are being listened to.

The fundamental process in assessment is creating an hypothesis about the presenting problem in the terms of the conceptual framework with which the counsellor operates. An hypothesis directs the counsellor to think about the problem in a particular way and to seek particular types of information from the client. The process of counselling is therefore concerned with the refinement of an hypothesis rather than their gener-ation of one *de novo*.

There are a number of schools of systemic therapy and, according to Liddle (1983), they differ in their approaches to the hypothesis-formation stage. We can divide them into two broad categories; those that attempt to place families along universal dimensions of family function, such as Bowen's approach (see Liddle, 1983), and those that attempt to view the family from within its own frame of reference, such as the Milan team's systemic approach (Selvini–Palazzoli et al., 1980b).

Bowen's approach is to view the family from the outside, collecting data from the parents on a number of aspects of family functioning, including the history of symptom(s) and the interaction between the nuclear family. This information is often organized using a genogram (Liddle, 1983; McGoldrick and Gerson, 1989). The aim of this information gathering is to determine, amongst other things, the family's level of anxiety, the degree of 'differentiation of self' of each family member, the flexibility–rigidity of the family and the family's responsiveness to stress.

Approaches like Bowen's recognize that families act as complex systems but they deal with them by trying to measure high-level system variables that are emergent properties of the system. Such an approach is only possible from a fixed reference point. The variants of the systemic approach (Liddle, 1983; Selvini-Palazzoli et al., 1980b; Tomm, 1984) explicitly deny the possibility of dealing with universal system variables. Instead of viewing the family from the outside inwards, the systemic therapist attempts to view the world from within the frame of reference of the family and thus look outwards from within.

The task of the systems therapist is to construct a model of the family's model of itself. Expressing the problem in this way highlights the point that the therapist can never come to experience the world in exactly the same way as a member of the family, although they may be able to get an idea of what it might be like to be one. The problem is that therapists always view the world through their own sets of constructs, which will not be the same as those of the family members. Most systemic therapists adopt Bateson's approach to information, which holds that:

1 information is a difference; and
2 difference is a relationship (or a change in a relationship).

Thus, information is a relationship, which means that the systemic therapist can concentrate on collecting the details of the relationships (or, more properly, relationships between relationships, since the concern is the relationship between the position someone holds in the family and the way that they behave towards other family members) between family members, using techniques like circular questioning and future-oriented questions (Selvini-Palazzoli et al., 1980b; Tomm, 1984). For many therapists the use of questions constitutes an assessment tool and a therapeutic intervention.

Circular questions (Penn, 1982) are difficult to define individually as their circularity depends upon the context. The essence of the approach is for the counsellor to ask questions that generate feedback to the counsellor that provides the basis for subsequent questions. There are a number of ways that the feedback can be obtained. For example, the counsellor may attend to the non-verbal and paralinguistic cues provided by the client. Used in a family setting, circular questioning links the family members together as one person's answer to a question can be used to generate a question to another family member. Circular questioning may prove a useful tool for elaborating the nature of the problem and getting the family to develop a representation of its own dynamics.

Penn (1985) suggests the technique of challenging the family with future-oriented questions. Instead of asking the family about how they feel and act now and how they felt and acted in the past, Penn proposes asking them about how they will deal with events in the future. This approach has two benefits. The first is that it may enable the client to explore alternative ways of acting that may be more adaptive for the client. By allowing the client to explore them in a environment of 'positive connotation' the counsellor may facilitate the client's adopting these other modes of action in the future. The other advantage is that it allows the counsellor and client to investigate the implicit assumptions, the 'premises', underlying the client's way of adapting to change, and thus to work on those premises. Having identified a premise the counsellor can ask the client to consider what might happen if they violated the assumption in some way.

In all counselling approaches, it is necessary to determine the point at which the relationship should be terminated. This is problematic because it is assumed that the 'problem' extends beyond the symptoms of the identified patient. Furthermore, the identified patient may have a problem, such as a terminal illness or brain damage, that is not susceptible to counselling. Faced with these problems the counsellor has to negotiate the endpoint rather than impose it. As a consequence, this process is intimately related to the process of establishing each person's expectations of therapy. It will be difficult, if not impossible, to negotiate an acceptable endpoint with a family that expects therapy to remove the symptoms of the identified patient without there being a change in themselves or their relationships. Following on from this point, this process must also be viewed as a therapeutic intervention as well as part of the assessment phase since it will involve getting families to think about how their lives might be different following therapy.

Assessment in systemic counselling might be expected to be much more complex than assessment in individual counselling but, in many ways, the systemic counselling context is a liberating one. Not only may systemic counselling allow one to approach problems that are inaccessible to individual methods but it also makes explicit what is implicit in most individual counselling methods, which is that most problems of individual adjustment are influenced, if not determined, by the individual's relationship with their family, and this allows the counsellor to collect information about this relationship from a number of sources, rather than just from the individual client.

The systems approach to the therapeutic relationship

It is impossible to make generalizations about the therapeutic relationship within the systems framework because there are so many different approaches adopted. Clients will experience the different forms of systems-based therapy in different ways. For example, the approach of Selvini-Palazzoli et al. (1980b) recommends maintaining strict neutrality to all family members, a neutrality reinforced by the stylized assessment tools (like circular questioning) advocated by this group. At the other extreme, Andolfi et al. (1983) recommend taking an active part in the family group, even to the extent of appearing to form alliances with particular family members. The narrative approach, which has grown out of the systems approach, favours forming an alliance with the individual client to aid them in forming a new narrative.

Contemporary systemic ideas: the narrative metaphor

Most psychological therapies themselves undergo change as new ideas influence practice and vice versa. Even though the systems approach is very modern in comparison to the longer-established therapies, such as psychodynamic therapy, it is no exception to this. The systems approach was established with the idea that problems emerge from the relationship between an individual and the environment, rather than psychological problems being inherent in the individual. A number of unanswered problems with the approach and unsatisfactory theoretical underpinnings have given rise to new ways of understanding problems, therapy and change within the systems paradigm. The narrative metaphor has emerged from this. Early systemic theory had a narrow view of context (the individual in relation to the family), while the narrative approach has widened the scope of context to include social and political forces (such as gender and sexuality) and how these shape context and experience. The emphasis on problem resolution meant that the background to and history of problems fitted uncomfortably (if at all) with systemic therapy. By way of contrast, the narrative approach takes into consideration both the here-and-now experience of the client as well as history in the aetiology of problems, including the political issues referred to above. The systems approach has not adequately addressed how being a part of a system (such as a family) can have implications for people's behaviour in a variety of contexts. The narrative approach has begun to consider how one's experience of being in a family system creates a story about oneself, which is carried over into other contexts. Finally, the narrative approach considers what is being created by a family system, and what solutions to problems look like. The emphasis in therapy is on language and the construction of reality (ideas). This section describes the background to and basic tenets of the narrative metaphor in the systemic paradigm.

Recent developments (1990 to the present) in systemic counselling approaches reflect a move towards an emphasis on stories and conversation in therapy and away from ideas of theoretical certainties, notions of truth, grand solutions or final answers. Perhaps the main changes in the metaphor of thinking about counselling have been from a cybernetic to a narrative metaphor where the central belief is that narrative structures lives (White and Epston, 1990). As every metaphor presents different implications for how change occurs, this change in metaphor and subsequent shift in thinking has led to new ideas about counselling, clients and ourselves as counselling psychologists. From a narrative metaphor perspective, there is an emphasis on meaning and the importance of language as a mechanism for change. Therapy involves freeing the client from a particular kind of account or 'story', and opening the way to alternatives of greater possibility and promise. This approach looks to the effects of literary traditions, social conditions, cultural values and most importantly, social processes.

This evolution in therapy has been very greatly influenced by ideas of power and knowledge of the French philosopher Michel Foucault (Rabinow, 1984) and from social constructivists (Gergen, 1991). Finally, these ideas are situated in a narrative metaphor and much of the current thinking on narrative has been influenced by Jerome Bruner (Bruner, 1986). Foucault's influence has made systemic therapy more responsive to issues associated with gender, power, sexual orientation and social structure. Until recently, these have not featured prominently in systemic theory and practice. At best the strategic position of the therapist's neutrality towards family process and structures may have inadvertently preserved the status quo in the same systems. At worst, discrimination and injustice within family systems may have gone unquestioned. The narrative approach introduces the idea that it is neither ethical nor therapeutic to omit discussion about these issues in sessions.

Narrative metaphor

In a narrative metaphor people are seen as organizing their experience in the form of stories. According to Lynn Hoffman, 'It is as if reality consists of the tales people tell themselves to make sense of the world and to navigate within it' (Hoffman, 1993: 71). Narrative produces experience, and vice versa, and the relationship between narratives and experience is a circular one. A narrative metaphor proposes that people 'story' their lives and it is through storying that people structure and give meaning to their lives. This is different from saying that people describe their lives by stories; the difference being that stories lend structure to life and provide meaning. The stories by which people conduct their lives also shape them and have real effects on them. The function of narratives may be expressed as follows: 'we tell ourselves stories in order to live' (Didion, 1979: 11). People usually have several stories about their lives, with one story invariably being more dominant and influential. No single story can capture the range of richness of people's experience: 'Life experience is richer than discourse. Narrative structures organise and give meaning to experience, but there are always feelings and lived experience not fully encompassed by the dominant story' (Bruner, 1986: 143).

When individuals and families seek the help of a counsellor, they usually present this dominant story which contains the so-called problem (White, 1989). It may be helpful for the counsellor to think of problems as stories that people have agreed to tell themselves to justify their behaviour, and to understand exceptions or deviations from the customary or ordinary. Within this framework it is assumed that people seek counselling 'when the narratives in which they are "storying" their experience, or in which they are having their experience "storied" by others, do not sufficiently represent their lived experience. In these circumstances, there will be significant aspects of their experience that contradict these dominant narratives' (White and Epston, 1990).

It is important to note that within the narrative metaphor experience is regarded as a primary variable. This shift is part of the evolution in thinking in systemic counselling. Another major shift is the move away from thinking about positive explanations and associated ideas of circular causality. Positive explanation proposes that events take their course because they are driven in that direction, which raises ideas about causes, forces and impacts (Bateson, 1972). Narrative approaches attend more to the Batesonian emphasis on negative explanation and restraints. Negative explanation proposes that events occur in certain ways 'instead of' in other ways: 'We consider what alternative possibilities could conceivably have occurred and then ask why many of these alternatives were not followed, so that a particular event was one of those few that would, in fact, occur' (Bateson 1972: 399).

Any event, behaviour, belief or discourse may be thought of as 'restraint' in that when they are selected and attended to, others may not be noticed. The emphasis in thinking is no longer on 'because of' ideas (even though the 'cause' was 'circular') but rather 'instead of' ideas. One of the client's narratives may become the one that acts as a restraint, especially when there is a problem-saturated story. This narrative informs the client's thinking and its informing ideas restrain him from noticing alternatives. The perspective of 'restraints' rather than 'causes' is fundamental to an understanding of recent developments in the theoretical underpinnings of counselling.

Implications for practice

The objective of counselling is shifted when problems are seen as 'restraints'. Previously, the client or the client's family may have been viewed as the problem or the problem may even have been seen as serving a function. From the narrative perspective neither the person nor their relationships is viewed as the problem. 'Rather the problem becomes the problem, and the person's relationship with the problem becomes the problem' (White and Epston, 1990: 40). The objective of counselling becomes revealing stories about their relationships. The history of the problem is viewed as a story of restraint rather than of cause and effect. The counselling interview is conducted with a curiosity which seeks to investigate what has restrained the person from participating in alternative possibilities. The narrative of influence must be considered to be the overarching constraint or to contain the ideas that restrain. Problems are viewed as separate from the person, that is, existing in their ideas, beliefs (discourses) or the behaviours, but not the person. Thinking 'instead of' rather than 'because of' appears to have the effect of empowering people. The impression is never given to the client that the problem is ever as a consequence of personal inadequacies, incompetencies or imperfections. It is no longer sufficient simply to try to change their behaviour without first hearing the narratives clients use to make sense of their life. The counsellor will address these restraints and provide a context that will enable each client to see a world of alternative possibilities and expanding options rather than limitations and constraints. The counselling process can be conceived of as a journey of liberation from oppressive constraints to new possibilities.

The narrative metaphor introduces processes such as deconstructing, reconstructing and restorying. The counsellor puts these into practice by helping the client to generate an alternative story. There is no one or 'right' way of doing this. Pioneering work in the thinking and practice of the narrative metaphor has been carried out by Michael White (1989) and David Epston (1989), and readers should consult these references to gain further insight into the practice of the narrative metaphor. Michael

White, who is significantly influenced by Foucault's ideas of power and the subjugation of persons by systems of political thought, addressed the restraints by 'externalizing' the problem (White, 1989). This approach is one that encourages clients to objectify and at times to personify the problems that they experience as oppressive. The problem then becomes a separate entity and therefore external to the person or the relationship that has ascribed the problem. The process of 'externalizing' the problem can be understood as a way of loosening the restraints by separating people from them.

There is a significant difference between internalizing and externalizing discourses about the problem. Internalizing discourses locate the problem or the 'cause' of the problem in the persons' families. Externalizing discourses locate the problem in meaning systems which influence persons or families. This creates a completely different context for change.

Collaboration

Collaboration is a hallmark of the current approaches within a narrative metaphor to counselling. The counsellor is no longer considered as the 'expert'; the counsellor's experience and knowledge (called theory and expertise) is no longer privileged over the validity of the client's experience and knowledge, especially of the problem. This is a further step in the direction of reducing the power differential in therapy – to accept clients as collaborators and as full participants in the process of counselling and the development of an alternative story. Recent developments reflect an approach where the counsellor has given up all ideas of instructing people and has stopped trying to take on an expert position. The counsellor and client co-construct an alternative story to the 'problem-full' one initially told by the client or family. The 'new' story is a possibility-filled one generated and co-authored in equal partnership by counsellor and client.

Strongly associated with the idea of a collaborative partnership between counsellor and client is the idea of openness. Counsellors are encouraged to situate their ideas and questions in their own experience and to be available to answer any questions their clients may have about their thinking (White and Epston, 1990). In current practice, counsellors are trying to let clients hear what they are saying about them, as when reflecting teams discuss their ideas in front of the family or client. This is in contrast to the earlier practice of a team discussion behind the one-way mirror with team 'messages' then 'sent' to the clients via the therapist.

With the significant degree of change in the relative power of counsellor and client, there is a transformation in the counselling process which has become less rigidly structured and managed. Thus, an anthropological, research-type approach has infiltrated and influenced the format of the traditional counselling interview. The style of the interviewing tends to be more ethnographic in nature. According to Mischler (1986: 8), 'in the mainstream tradition [of interviewing] the idea of discourse is suppressed. Questions and answers for example are regarded as analogues of stimuli and responses rather than as forms of speech'. While he is referring to a research interview, Mischler's ideas may equally well be applied to the counsellor–client interview. Clients (interviewees) may be regarded as informants or competent observers while counsellors (interviewers) are regarded as reporters or investigators who also build up 'archives' of knowledge about the nature of the problem, from the information given by the interviewees. Recent developments are characterized by counsellors yielding control to clients of the flow and content of the interview, entering into a collaborative relationship and attending to what and how clients may learn from their efforts to respond meaningfully to questions within the context of their own worlds of experience.

Research evidence about effectiveness

Although the systems approach in counselling psychology has its origins in the study of schizophrenic disorder in families, there has been surprisingly little empirical research into the effectiveness of therapy. This may, in part, be due to the fact that this research has proved unproductive, and also because many of the pioneers in the field did not have a background in applied psychology. An extensive review of the literature failed to yield a list of outcome studies in this field. Historically, there has been a dichotomy between therapists and researchers in the systems approach. Therapists have repeatedly asserted the primacy of 'ideas', 'values', 'the relativity of observations' and 'process' in their clinical practice, thereby dismissing some of the criteria and conditions which to date have been thought to permit meaningful comparisons in research. Methodological difficulties pervade the research domain: there are rarely suitably matched controls (particularly families); approaches to and methods for psychotherapeutic interventions are not standardized; it is difficult to keep sources of variance to a minimum and there are a limited number of measures of family system interaction and functioning (Wynne, 1988). Furthermore, outcome or change in families can only be measured by surveying each individual family member. This raises questions as to whether outcome should be oriented towards an individual or the corporate family unit. Systemic research is always likely to be hindered by problems relating to technical specificity, replicability, generalizability and ethics, as well as differing views about clinical and statistical significance of results.

After more than three decades, it is incorrect to suggest that research into systemic therapy is in its infancy. On the contrary: there are several well-established international journals in this field, including *Family Process, Journal of Family Therapy, Journal of Marital and Family Therapy, Family Systems and Health* and *Journal of Systemic Therapy*. Qualitative research methods and theoretical discussions dominate the literature in this field and regrettably it seems unlikely that outcome research will feature predominantly in years to come.

Critique and conclusions

The systems approach in counselling psychology is relatively new in comparison to some other approaches. Recent developments in the field will be most clearly viewed and assessed at a distance and by the next generation of practitioners. The future of the systems approach belongs to practitioners who work towards an integration of different approaches within the systems paradigm, rather than those who seek to develop 'brand name' approaches (Broderick and Schrader, 1991).

There are three levels at which the systems approach can be criticized. The first concerns the adequacy of the metaphor, the second concerns the assumptions implicit in the family systems approach that the family is the essential unit of social life, and the third concerns the lack of a clear statement of mechanisms of cognitive and behavioural change.

The problem of the metaphor is simply stated. At the level of generality at which the concept is applied to counselling, the systems metaphor lacks predictive or prescriptive power but when systems theory is articulated into coherent models that possess predictive and prescriptive power, such as negative feedback systems, they do not map onto counselling. Cybernetic models have five major drawbacks as models of human social systems. The first is that the connections between components do not vary, the second is that the properties of the elements are fixed for the life of the system, the third is that the elements have to be qualitatively different from each other, the fourth is that there are limited connections between components and the fifth is that they tend towards a single stable state. A much better metaphor for the social system, and the individual's place within it, is the 'neural' network (Levine, 1991), which is a system comprising large numbers of highly interconnected, similar elements in similar ways. Neural networks learn adaptations to their environments, they are capable of occupying a range of stable states, and they can change over time. Consideration of the neural network model also focuses us on the properties of the individual elements (a metaphor of the individual person) since the properties of networks are highly sensitive to the characteristics of their elements.

While it is self-evident that people form parts of social systems, it seems artificial to focus on the family and the immediate social circle of the individual as the source of problems. Problems may manifest themselves as problems in these relationships but there is no reason to presuppose that is their source. Counselling that focuses on immediate relationships may fail because the relationships that are dysfunctional may be many steps removed from the counsellor and it is not clear how systemic counselling approaches seek to deal with them. For example, a client may be depressed and express concern about a problem at work and the counsellor may explore the nature of the client's social relationships within that environment. However, the locus of the problem may lie outside those immediate relationships, in the management structure, for example. Since the client may be unaware of these interactions it is not clear how systemic therapy would bring them into frame.

The final point is that systemic counselling models contain no explicit account of how emotional, cognitive or behavioural change takes place. There is no appeal to psychological processes operating within the individual. Given the complexity of the psychological processes involved in representing the environment and individuals within it, it is, a priori, unlikely that they are going to be particularly flexible. A complete account of effective counselling must include a description of these representational processes and the processes that lead to change.

There has been a large-scale swing away from using the cybernetic/ biological machine-type metaphor for conceptualizing about counselling to the more narrative-type metaphors where ideas of interest are those of narrative, semantics and linguistics. Essentially informing ideas of these metaphors are that they are non-objectivist and at the same time socially and politically sensitive. Narrative theory hits at the heart of pathological history therapies and stands in direct opposition to all deficit models. Gender issues, empirical verification of therapy, and legal and ethical issues are likely to become dominant areas of research and interest in practice in the systems paradigm in counselling psychology in the next decade.

References

Andolfi, M., Angelo, C., Menghi, P. and Nicolo-Corgliano, A.M. (1983) *Behind the Family Mask: Therapeutic Change in Rigid Family Systems*. New York: Brunner and Mazel.

Bateson, G. (1972) *Steps to an Ecology of Mind*. New York: Ballantine.

Bateson, G., Jackson, D.D., Hayley, J. and Weakland, J. (1956) 'Toward a theory of schizophrenia', *Behavioural Science*, 1: 251.

Bor, R., Miller, R. and Goldman, E. (1992) *Theory and Practice of HIV Counselling: a Systemic Approach*. London: Cassell.

Broderick, C.B. and Schrader, S.S. (1991) 'The history of professional marriage and family therapy', in A.S. Gurman and D.P. Kniskern (eds), *Handbook of Family Therapy*, vol. II. New York: Brunner and Mazel.

Bruner, J. (1986) *Actual Minds, Possible Worlds*. Cambridge, MA: Harvard University Press.

Carter, B. and McGoldrick, M. (1989) 'Overview: the changing family life cycle – a framework for family therapy', in B. Carter and M. McGoldrick (eds), *The Changing Family Life Cycle: a Framework for Family Therapy*, 2nd edn. Boston, MA: Allyn and Bacon.

Didion, J. (1979) *The White Album*. New York: Simon and Shuster.

Epston, D. (1989) *Collected Papers*. Adelaide, South Australia: Dulwich Centre Publications.

Gergen, K.J. (1991) *The Saturated Self*. New York: Basic Books.

Hoffman, L. (1993) *Exchanging Voices: a Collaborative Approach to Family Therapy*. London: Karnac.

Jones, E. (1993) *Family Systems Therapy*. Chichester: Wiley.

Keeney, B. (1983) *Aesthetics of Change*. New York: Guilford.

Levine, D.S. (1991) *An Introduction to Neural and Cognitive Modelling*. Hillsdale, NJ: Lawrence Erlbaum.

Liddle, H.A. (1983) 'Diagnosis and assessment in family therapy: a comparative analysis of six schools of thought', in J.C. Hansen and B.P. Keeney (eds), *Diagnosis and Assessment in Family Therapy*. Rockville, MD: Aspen.

McGoldrick, M. and Gerson, R. (1989) 'Genograms and the family life cycle', in B. Carter and M. McGoldrick (eds), *The Changing Family Life Cycle: a Framework for Family Therapy*, 2nd edn. Boston, MA: Allyn and Bacon.

Mischler, E.G. (1986) *Research Interviewing*. Cambridge, MA: Harvard University Press.

Penn, P. (1982) 'Circular questioning', *Family Process*, 21: 267–80.

Penn, P. (1985) 'Feed-forward: future questions, future maps', *Family Process*, 24, 299–310.

Rabinow, P. (1984) *The Foucault Reader*. New York: Pantheon.

Raimy, V. (ed.) (1950) *Training in Clinical Psychology*. New York: Prentice Hall.

Selvini-Palazzoli, M., Boscolo, L., Cecchin, G. and Prata, G. (1980a) 'The problem of the referring person', *Journal of Marital and Family Therapy*, 6: 3–9.

Selvini-Palazzoli, M., Boscolo, L., Cecchin, G. and Prata, G. (1980b) 'Hypothesizing–Circularity–Neutrality: three guidelines for the conductor of the session', *Family Process*, 19: 3–12.

Tomm, K. (1984) 'One perspective on the Milan systemic approach: part II. Description of session format, interviewing style and interventions', *Journal of Marital and Family Therapy*, 10: 253–71.

White, M. (1989) *Selected Papers*. Adelaide, South Australia: Dulwich Centre Publications.

White, M. and Epston, D. (1990) *Narrative Means to Therapeutic Ends*. New York: Norton.

Wynne, L. (ed.) (1988) *The State of the Art in Family Therapy Research*. New York: Family Process Press.

12

The Eclectic and Integrative Paradigm: Between the Scylla of Confluence and the Charybdis of Confusion

Petrūska Clarkson

A confluence is defined as 'a flowing together, the junction or union of two or more streams' (Onions, 1973: 397). Confusion is defined as 'discomfiture, embarrassment, perplexity, the action, mixture in which the distinction of the elements is lost' (Onions, 1973: 397). The notion of an integrative approach to counselling psychology may be threatening to some counselling psychologists and comforting to others. However, it is happening both within and between psychological schools. Whatever one's opinion, it is a growing tendency in the consciousness of thinkers and practitioners in counselling psychology on at least three continents and it shows no signs of going away. Dryden and Norcross (1990) summarized North American surveys of psychologists which showed that more psychologists are primarily identifying with eclectic or integrative practices than any one single orientation. According to Karasu, there is 'a variety of cooperative efforts to combine and integrate different therapeutic approaches drawn from the rich armamentarium of treatments available today [which] marks out entry into the latest stage of psychotherapeutic development – rapprochement, a needed and welcome change after years of unbridled expansion and divisiveness in the field' (1986: 324). The international Society for the Exploration of Psychotherapy Integration (SEPI) held its first annual conference in 1985. The British Institute for Integrative Psychotherapy was formed in 1987. A major international conference on integrative psychotherapy in 1990

This chapter is an integration of material drawn from: Clarkson, P. (1995) *The Therapeutic Relationship*. London: Whurr; Clarkson, P. and Shaw, P. (1995) 'Human relationships at work in organisations', in P. Clarkson (ed.), *Change in Organisations*. London: Whurr. pp. 43–55; Clarkson, P. (1992) 'Systemic integrative psychotherapy training', in W. Dryden (ed.), *Integrative and Eclectic Therapy*. Milton Keynes: Open University Press. pp. 269–95; Clarkson, P. (1989) 'Metanoia: a process of transformation', *Transactional Analysis Journal*, 19(4): 224–34.

brought together integrative counselling psychology practitioners from all over the world. There are now two international journals on integrative and/or eclectic psychotherapy – the *International Journal of Eclectic Psychotherapy* and the *Journal of Psychotherapy Integration*.

In my opinion this reflects an increasing openness to communication, cross-fertilization and divergent creativity. Simultaneously, it may reflect a decreasing allegiance (in some areas) to orthodoxy, unilateral perspectives and certainty regarding 'the truth' of any one particular approach to human behaviour. How it is defined, used, discussed and taught of course will give rise to as many debates, disputes and attempts at boundary demarcations as any of the other older, more singular approaches.

There are growing mentions of integration or eclectic intentions in psychology with positive connotations in recent psychotherapy, clinical psychology and counselling psychology literature in recent years. In Conduit (1987), for example, Davanloo is described as a 'powerful therapist who uses analytic history-taking, the catharsis of the new therapies, and the challenge of structural family therapy' (1987: 335). The Summer 1989 issue of the *British Journal of Psychotherapy* included a paper, 'On the integration of cognitive-behaviour theory with psychoanalysis' (Fonagy, 1989), and in the Spring issue there is another, 'The limits of cognitive-behaviour therapy: can it be integrated with psychodynamic therapy' (Douglas, 1989). Hinshelwood commented on 'the hopeful atmosphere of integration in psychotherapy' (1989: 473). A definition of psychotherapy which has been used in some informal discussions among members of the United Kingdom Council for Psychotherapy is 'the systematic use of a *relationship* between therapist and patient – as opposed to pharmacological or social methods – to produce changes in cognition, feelings and behaviour' (Holmes and Lindley, 1989: 3). In another editorial, Hinshelwood (1990) suggested that Clarkson's (1990) paper on the multiplicity of psychotherapeutic relationships as an integrative principle 'offers a way of circumventing the inherent contradictions and incompatibilities that exist between different psychotherapies: instead of incompatibilities we have different priorities and emphasis. And this leaves a way open for the beginnings of a possible integration of psychotherapies' (Hinshelwood, 1990: 119).

The integration of therapies, however, is not new. An analysis of a particular psychology will invariably unearth some borrowed form, theory, concept or technique from another psychotherapy or related discipline. Freud, for example, originally integrated Breuer's technique of discussing emotional problems of patients under hypnosis, to bring about catharsis within his developing psychoanalytic theory. Even within the humanistic psychotherapies, which evolved independently in the tradition of the psychodramatic work of Moreno, substantial integration (with or without acknowledgement) can be found. The notion of self-realization for example is anticipated in Aristotle (see *The Metaphysics Books* [1971]).

There is no one definition of integrative psychotherapy. As Norcross (1986: 8) noted: 'to refer to *the* eclectic approach to therapy is to fall prey to a therapeutic "uniformity myth"' (Dryden, 1984; Kiesler, 1966). There appear to be well over two dozen different types of eclecticism or integrative counselling psychology referred to in the psychological literature. Furthermore, many clinicians who describe themselves as eclectic or integrative select their own particular combination of approaches, or develop their own unique forms of integration. There are many integrative therapies in the same way as there are many family therapies or indeed many different psychoanalyses.

However, there is an endeavour and a project which is about *integrating* – more a verb and a process, than a product or an end result. Indeed, it is likely that any good, competent and growing counselling psychologist is always integrating themselves whether between or within 'schools', their professional and life experiences or between themselves and the learning they forge in the relationship with their clients. But even then integrating can become a new orthodoxy.

Which particular theories, concepts or techniques a clinician chooses to integrate can only be done on an individual and personal basis if there is to be a true integration and if it is done continuously. People and their problems come before any theories or techniques. The latter exist solely to serve the former, and any useful integration will always honour this position. As Jung wrote, 'That is why I say to any beginner: learn your theories as well as you can but put them aside when you touch the miracle of the living soul. Not theories but your own creative individuality alone must decide' (1928: 361).

The recent decade or so has seen great change in the landscape of counselling, counselling psychology, psychotherapy and psychoanalysis, see Clarkson (1995a). On the one hand there has been an increased preoccupation with professionalization, accountability, theoretical sophistication and research interest. And yet on the other hand there has at the least been growth in terms of a willingness to listen and learn from other approaches and other orientations. According to Norcross and Goldfried (1992: 7), eight interacting, mutually reinforcing factors have fostered the development of integration in the past decades:

1 Proliferation of therapies.
2 Inadequacy of single theories.
3 External socio-economic contingencies.
4 Ascendancy of short-term, problem-focused treatments.
5 Opportunities to observe and experiment with various treatments.

6 Paucity of differential effectiveness among therapies.
7 Recognition that therapeutic commonalities contribute heavily to outcome variance.
8 Development of a professional network for integration.

All these factors can be said to have given impetus to the search for an integrative paradigm or a framework for integrating aspects of other approaches where these can be found to be compatible or useful within any one specialized approach.

It is impossible to proceed without briefly dealing with the issue of differences and similarities between eclecticism and integrative psychology. Yager (1977) defined enlightened eclecticism as an attempt to approach each clinical situation from multiple theoretical perspectives, selecting those which are in closest accord with an individual patient's needs. Norcross and Grencavage (1990) summarize the consensual distinctions between eclecticism and integration in Table 12.1.

Eclecticism	Integration
Technical	Theoretical
Divergent (differences)	Convergent (commonalities)
Choosing from many	Combining many
Applying what is	Creating something new
Collection	Blend
Selection	Synthesis
Applying the parts	Unifying the parts
Atheoretical but empirical	More theoretical than empirical
Sum of parts	More than sum of parts
Realistic	Idealistic

Table 12.1 *Eclecticism versus integration*

The table summarizes quite precisely the differences between the eclectic and integrative paradigm. Lazarus most recently is particularly associated with what can be termed technical eclecticism. This means:

a multimodal assessment that evalautes a client's behaviours, affective reactions, sensations, images, cognitions, interpersonal relationships, and biological processes, typically reveals a matrix of discrete and interrelated problems – both intrapersonal and contextual – that facilitates clinical attention to a wide array of salient issues (1995: 35).

For Lazarus the questions are: '*What* treatment, by *whom*, is most effective for *this* individual, with *those* specific problems, and under *which* set of circumstances? It is impossible to embrace this dictum and yet remain within the boundaries of any delimited school of thought' (1995: 38).

As is clear from Lazarus's work (1995), he considers the integration of theoretical viewpoints irreconcilable. He does not consider that theoretical integration is possible.

The rest of the chapter will more specifically address an integration model which emphasizes the combination of commonalities across theoretical orientations resulting in a blend or synthesis of approaches to counselling psychology. The five-relationship model is the one I developed first and which indeed has been found to be useful in providing a matrix within which values, paradigms, understandings and techniques can be integrated in a coherent and systematic form for different clients or multiplicities embraced.

The underlying theory of personality and motivation

The theoretical development of counselling psychology reflected in practice can be conceptualized in terms of the three major streams of thought which originated around the beginning of this century: those emanating from Freud which led to the **psychoanalytic tradition** and its developments; the **behaviourist tradition** which can be traced back to the work of Pavlov (1928) and the **existential/humanistic tradition** of therapy which can be seen to emanate from the spirit and practice of Moreno, the psychodramatist and pioneering group psychotherapist (Greenberg, 1975). A necessarily abbreviated summary here suggests that the psychoanalytic tradition emphasizes the unconscious, drive theory (particularly *Thanatos* and *Eros*), transference and the repetition compulsion, ego psychology, object relations and more recently self-theory. The behaviourist (or now cognitive-behavioural) tradition emphasizes the principles of learning reflexes and operant conditioning, models of reinforcement and scientific accountability, modelling, links between cognition and behaviour, and between emotion and cognition, as well as cognitive structures, schemas and scripts. The humanistic/existential tradition can be characterized by a focus on existence, choice, autonomy, responsibility, anxiety, death, despair, freedom, values, potential for change, the desire for growth or self-actualization, social involvement and future orientation.

Maslow attached the term 'third force' to this latter grouping (1968). It can also be associated with a third force or drive in human behaviour – *Physis*. This has been defined as a generalized creative 'force of Nature, which eternally strives to make things grow and to make growing things more perfect' (Berne, 1968). The pre-Socratics conceived of *Physis* as the healing factor in illness, the energetic motive for *evolution* and *creativity* in the individual and collective psyche (Guerriere, 1980). *Physis* antedates

Eros and *Thanatos*. It is conceived as more biological since it represents the evolutionary impulse inherent in every cell. It is also viewed as more spiritual since it implies that it is in the nature of the person and the planet to evolve creatively.

These three primary traditions in counselling psychology have already been covered in the previous chapters specifically devoted to these particular paradigms. Suffice it here to say that these three twentieth-century primary parent views of human beings (with the attendant value orientations and theories of each) are often seen as in contradiction or opposition to each other. The more the angle of the lens viewing human behaviour is narrowed, the more persuasive such differences can become. Alternatively, if one looks at them through a wide-angle philosophical lens, these three philosophical traditions could be seen as mutually complementary and enriching. A view of the person then emerges which arguably includes the person as a **learner** (behaviourism), the person as a **reactor** (psychoanalysis), and the person as **creator** (humanistic/ existential position). This is an integrative position based on inclusion, not exclusion. In practice this means that no one approach is believed to contain an exclusive claim to the 'truth', but that between these different views, a more complete and fully rounded appreciation of the human being can be construed. This is the case of the integrative and eclectic paradigm.

Integration can then be conceived of as open and creative communication between these apparently conflicting and contradictory explanations of human beings (and how they think, feel, behave, grow and develop) and the coherently selective inclusion of useful and workable aspects of each (rather than the indiscriminate and total exclusion of one camp by another). Theories are understood as stories or metaphors used to make sense of ourselves, others and the world not representing facts or truth in and of themselves.

Thus, though each of the above may have a story of human beings that differentiates one from the other, there are various themes or sub-plots that (like in all good stories) recur within each. There are naturally some common principles such as the recognition of human problems and life as process and development. Further, sometimes even the apparent oppositions can often be shown to be due to category confusion, not genuine contradiction (Ryle, 1973). Perhaps psychological integration, even where apparent conflicts exist, becomes increasingly possible as we take some of the understandings from modern physics into a post-Newtonian psychology. Creativity (which is most needed in the work of healing) often emerges when apparently contradictory positions can be tolerated (Rothenberg, 1979). After all, even elementary particles 'seem to be waves on Mondays, Wednesdays and Fridays, and particles on Tuesdays,

Thursdays and Saturdays' (Sir William Bragg quoted in Koestler, 1972). Practitioners can perhaps grow scientifically minded enough to tolerate or even welcome similar conditions in our field.

It is anticipated that in the turbulent and troubled psychological waters of the end of this century communication may become more important than certainty, effectiveness more important than elegance for its own sake and intellectual and moral questioning of basic assumptions more important than adherence to a single *via integrata* (one true way of integration). The suggestion here is that we become more systemic and metaphorically pull back the telescope that is solely directed at the behavioural planet (for example) and allow a wider-angled lens to include the other planets, the humanistic and the psychoanalytic, in order to explore how they relate as a galaxy or **system** as a whole. This inclusivity necessitates a responsibility that is no longer to do with what is right or what is wrong, what is the truth and what is not the truth, but a responsibility to be able to explore why, when and how we select the theoretical constructs or the operational procedures that we do. Psychological counselling, like astronomy, is also a science. Therefore as such it needs to be teachable to others. Its practitioners need to be able to explore their thinking and their interventions in terms of what is important for a particular client at a particular moment, in particular circumstances, with a particular clinician.

Of course much precision may be lost in taking a wide-angle view on the human condition. This macroscopic view needs to be complemented with attention to specific and smaller details. Naturally, what the microscope improves in terms of precision and minute observation, it loses in large-scale perspective. Different instruments (telescopes or microscopes) are also, of course, suitable for different purposes. Obviously, for reasons of space, the discussion here has to be indicative rather than exhaustive, invoking the reader's existing knowledge, imaginative powers and collegial cooperation.

The nature of the relationship between counselling psychologist and individual client

More and more research studies (Bergin and Lambert, 1978; Luborsky et al., 1983; O'Malley et al., 1983) demonstrate that it is the relationship between the client and therapist, more than any other factor, which determines the effectiveness of psychological therapy. That is, success in psychological counselling can best be predicted by the properties of the client, therapist and their particular relationship (Norcross and Goldfried, 1992). Yet few books actually deal directly with the therapeutic relationship *per se*. Those that do often tend to focus on the transference–countertransference relationship to the exclusion of others.

A growing body of research pays attention to the match between client and psychologist, considering the influence of such factors as compatibility in terms of background, class, education and values (Garfield, 1992). For Goldfried (1980) the relationship is the cornerstone of all counselling psychology. Furthermore, an impressive body of research shows that one of the most overriding and influential factors in the outcome of psychological therapy is the relationship between therapist and client (Frank, 1979; Hynan, 1981).

The relationship is consistently being shown in research investigations as more significant than theoretical orientation. Therefore, it makes sense to investigate this factor, which appears to be of such overarching importance in statistical comparison of outcome studies, subjective reports and clinical evaluation approaches. 'We are born of relationship, nurtured in relationship, and educated in relationship. We represent every biological and social relationship of our forebears, as we interact and exist in a consensual domain called "society"' (Cottone, 1988: 363).

It is for this reason that the client (or patient) in the integrative paradigm is thought of as always in relationship, whether this be conceived of in object relations terms or in subject relations terms, as in existential approaches to psychotherapy (Clarkson, 1991).

One way of conceptualizing or imagining the healthy therapeutic relationship is to conceive of it as recapitulating the early familial maladaptions and in many perspectives it is construed as providing the arena for understanding, reparation or healing. Fundamentally, if a counselling psychologist can establish a relationship with someone who has lost the capacity for relationship (such as a schizophrenic individual), he or she has been retrieved in their relatedness with others. Thus they can begin to rejoin the human family. The Jungian Samuels states that: 'the psychology of the soul turns out to be about people in relationship' (1985: 21).

If indeed the therapeutic relationship is one of the most, if not the most important factor in successful counselling psychology, using the relationship would be a primary avenue for integration. The integrative paradigm thus uses the five major kinds of therapeutic relationship which have been emphasized by the major approaches to psychology.

The **working alliance** is the part of the client–psychologist relationship that enables the client and psychologist to work together even when the client experiences strong desires to the contrary. This relationship has accrued particular attention from cognitive-behavioural practitioners. The **transference–countertransference relationship** (of which psychoanalysis has been the major exponent) is the experience of unconscious wishes and fears transferred into the therapeutic partnership.

The **reparative/developmentally needed relationship** is the intentional provision by the counselling psychologist of a corrective, reparative, or replenishing relationship or action where the original parenting was deficient, abusive or over-protective. The **person-to-person relationship** is the real relationship or core relationship – the opposite of objective relationship. The experiments and expertise in this area have been developed primarily by the existentialist and humanistic psychotherapeutic approaches. The **transpersonal relationship** is the timeless facet of the therapeutic relationship, which is impossible to describe, but refers to the spiritual dimension of the healing relationship. Archetypal and classical Jungians, as well as the psychotherapies which refer to themselves as transpersonal such as psychosynthesis, have particularly addressed this dimension. It is important to remember these are not necessarily *stages* but *states* in therapy, often subtly overlapping, in and between which a client construes his or her unique experiences. All such individual experiences are of course within a collective and cultural context where race, gender, sexual choices, physical and intellectual ability, class and other considerations of history, geography and religion affect, infect and interpenetrate any attempt at relationship.

Considerations during assessment

Since therapy is so centrally determined by the quality of the relationship between client and counselling psychologist and the relationship is the common factor between them, tools are usually welcome which improve our 'self-as-instrument' and enable us to match more accurately the kinds of therapeutic relationship we can offer to what our clients may need from us. It is possible to utilize the discussion of the five kinds of therapeutic relationship to draw from the different preoccupations of the three modalities outlined above. In this way they can be used to sharpen clinical perception and planning at the initial interview, to improve assessment and assist with anticipating the likely effective therapy designs for patients with different issues or different structures. Counselling psychologists will need experience, training and supervision in different approaches to clients needing attention to their unique and special individual needs. Development of an adequate, comprehensive yet flexible range of practical techniques, which are at the same time grounded upon a thorough and profound grasp of the theoretical and philosophical assumptions underlying different approaches, is necessary.

Few questions need to be asked in the initial interview to establish a prognostic relationship profile which acts as an assessment guide. It is more a matter of listening with an awareness of the importance of an individual's ability to form and maintain different kinds of relationship. This includes an awesome respect for the way in which our past relationships have formed, deformed or transformed us. Clinicians listen for the history, the shape, the pattern, the time cycles or event punctuations of a person's relationships, their learning from these events and their existential manifestations in the person's life. By learning how to listen accurately and acutely to a person's relationship forms at the first interview or even first contact, the clinician can improve his/her intuition (by making and testing hypotheses and predictions), make contracts which are more workable and effective and formulate treatment designs based on greater clinical acumen and vision.

I have organized this next section in terms of the five, different therapeutic relationships. Some clients will obviously need their treatment/therapy conceptualized and operationalized more within one or two of these relationship vectors or all of them – depending on circumstances, needs, hurts and aspirations. The following section unpacks the correlation between differently needed relationships. This must be related to what the client's presenting need or problem may be.

Capacity to establish a working alliance

Listen for evidence of the existence and maintenance of previous working relationships and their outcomes, including the conclusions drawn by the client about the nature of accepting help and taking responsibility for his or her share in the work. For example, a woman complains of having gone to doctor after doctor who could not help her with a recurrent infection, or a patient gratefully remarks that a teacher showed them how to use a library. A trainee disappointedly recounts how a previous psychologist 'never picked up that I was lying to him', while another client tells the detailed story of how another psychologist had disappointed her by misunderstanding a communication and how she lost her trust in him as a result – but told the psychologist about it and subsequently saw that 'failure' as one of the most significant turning points in her story. Listen also for stories and examples from a person's working life. For example, did he or she work as a child or adolescent? Manage their own pocket money? Did they ever experience work as a source of important satisfaction? Is there any inkling of maintaining collegial relationships or respect, even with colleagues or managers the person did not like? What is the pattern for how working relationships end? One business man reported how one partnership after another was terminated in acrimony when he felt 'cheated'.

Clients who have been sent by their partners ('My wife says she'll leave me unless I get counselling'), who are psychotic (suffering from delusions or hallucinations), or whose functioning is impaired (for example through drug use or organic disorder) are not in a position to establish a working alliance or adult partnership in the healing process. Often, very basic issues of trust and responsibility may need to be worked through before the working alliance is firmly established. One of many ways of dealing with this is to make small contracts and have the client only agree with those he or she can sincerely keep, for example 'I will not kill myself before next Thursday when I see you again'. In order to establish a workable working alliance or contract, the person's reality testing will need to be both active and decontaminated. The diminishment or elimination of confusion will therefore probably be the primary focus of therapeutic activity.

The nature and shape of the transferential relationship

During the initial interview (often during the first three minutes of contact) patients will give the psychologist more or less overt cues as to the kind of transferential relationship they are used to creating or receiving, and the process of subtle hypnotic induction or projective identification commences. A client who comes into the consulting room shambling hesitantly and 'smelling of fear' has already at some subliminal and very primitive (rhinencephalic) levels communicated to the intuitive clinician the nature of their early important relationships with others. There are, of course, exceptions to this, such as people who come from basically happy and safe childhood homes, but who have been hurt, frightened and abused by political oppression or torture. Usually, however, the nature of our clients' earliest dyadic symbiotic relationships enter the therapeutic space powerfully, if often out of awareness, as it were seeking for completion of the unspoken interpersonal transaction (the externalization of the internalized self–other object relationship).

This unconscious striving for echoes of the necessary other is transferred from past relationships into present and potential ones with all the force of Freud's notion of the repetition compulsion and all the drama of Berne's notion of script. Every interpersonal stimulus will carry with it the implicit expectation of the desired, as well as feared, response based on the client's past experience and their unconscious hopes and anxieties for the future. Every response from the psychologist could move the client further towards self-understanding and clarity, or perpetuate the confusion between present and past potentials and self- and other-responsibility.

In addition to the cues and expectations intuited, sensed and observed from the client towards the practitioner, the client's **transferential history** is usually quite accessible and understandable from the stories they tell and the nature of their current relationships. For example,

'I married a much older man, but he ended up, just like my dad, a financially bankrupt alcoholic little boy who needs me so much I could not bear the guilt of leaving him' or, from someone who later shows many features of narcissistic disturbance: 'I am very successful in my field and therefore did considerable research about the experience and credentials of clinicians before I made this appointment with you.' The dramatis personae of the script may involve the receptionist ('I didn't want to bother you but . . .'), absent others ('My sister says that counselling has really helped her marriage') or impersonal forces such as the Church ('I know that my faith holds that abortions are wrong . . .').

It is usually possible to sense if the primary dynamic is going to be two-handed, three-handed or played to an audience: 'At university I participated in a research project which was published as . . .'); 'I imagine that you must get so bored with people telling you their life stories' on the one hand, to 'Is that all? I would have expected you to ask me more about . . .'. For clients whose primary problems are conflict-oriented, it is unlikely that a successful therapy can be brought to a conclusion without transference interpretations. This work often involves avoiding many of the invitations to repeat the original familial pattern on the one hand and the refusal to provide a fundamentally unbelievable idealized and therefore ultimately unproductive wish-fulfilment fantasy.

Clients who need primarily a transferential therapeutic relationship are more likely to be histrionic or neurotic personalities who are suffering from overparenting rather than from an absence of or blatantly sadistic parenting. Of course some clients may present with a transferential need in the first place which covers or defends the personality against the bleakness of a neglected or abused early child ego state.

Assessing a prospective client's need for a developmentally needed therapeutic relationship

It is important to remember, as has been pointed out elsewhere, that these different therapeutic relationships have been differentiated here for clarity and ease of theoretical discussion. In practice they naturally overlap. As indicated earlier, a practitioner who enters a transference relationship is of course also providing a developmentally needed or (in a developmental sense) necessary facility.

For some clients, however, a therapy primarily characterized by a transferential relationship may be contraindicated. In many cases, for example with schizophrenics and some kinds of narcissistic personality disorders, it may be more important to provide the patient with the corrective experiences which they lacked as children. The nature of their primary disturbance is more likely to be neglect, deprivation or abuse and

269

the general or primary direction of treatment will therefore be to replenish the developmental deficit through parenting, reparenting or even self-reparenting procedures.

The nature of the deficits or abuses may be more or less intuitively obvious at first interview, but it is none the less very important to attempt to differentiate patients who need a developmentally replenishing or reparative experience from patients who may need more of the psychologist's rational analytic engagement (as in the previously discussed cases where the transference relationship may be indicated in the first instance). Most clinicians have come across patients who had ignorantly or in desperation engaged in years of long-term, transference-based psychoanalysis only to sink deeper and deeper into depression as no human contact reached them, or who became more and more schizoid and bereft of humanity as they continued to be habituated to avoidance of eye contact and the absence of human warmth from lying on the couch. Of course the fact that this is not the case in all forms and practices of psychoanalysis is well attested to by the many variations and exceptions documented by analysts to the original idea of neutral non-engagement with the patient (as advocated and abrogated by Freud).

Assessing suitability and ability to form a person-to-person relationship in counselling psychology

Listen for the presence of person-to-person relationships or moments in the initial stories or life descriptions of a new client. Do they spontaneously report empathy for someone in authority: 'The boss was a bit tired that day, so I didn't take the rebuke too seriously' or a friendship which sounds equal: 'I have this friend who is different from all the others and sometimes we just sit together looking at the sunset without talking'? A person may say 'I noticed the flowers in your garden as I was coming up the road . . .' and it feels like a straight observation. This may have to do with sensing whether the client has found or rediscovered a 'true self' versus a false self available for contact. In other words, does an impasse already exist, or is the person still completely and fully identified with a false or constructed adapted self (Masterson, 1985; Miller, 1983; Winnicott, 1958).

Establishing a client's past or future potential for a transpersonal or transcendent relationship

This is usually indicated by the presence, absence or promise in a person's history, presentation or hopes of the need for significance outside the personal ego-based self. This search for meaning may be indicated by a religious, spiritual, political or existential quest for meaning and purpose or the hunger for such a quest. Through this avenue which embodies the spirit of *Physis* there is a connection with a sense of a cosmic or whole self in the Jungian sense. James (1974) conceptualizes this third self as emerging from the 'betweenness of people' in real contact. In this way of course it resembles what Buber (1970) referred to as the I–Thou contact which can happen in the real meeting between people and which reaches out beyond them to the sublime or transcendent, however the individual may phrase or understand it. Frankl (1973) also identified the neuroses which he attributed to a lack of meaning as noogenic neuroses. Maslow (1968) identified that one of the characteristics of the healthy personality is such an awareness and appreciation for sources of wonder or awe outside of the personal self. The presence or intention to meditate in a client is a valuable clue to their psychological recovery as much as is the willingness to be open to poetry or music, whether secular or sacred.

Problems in this area are due, on the one hand, to alienation, denial or estrangement from meaning or a core soul connection with principles of order or harmony (in Eastern or Western mystical traditions) or philosophical or aesthetic conceptualizations of meaning. On the other hand, clinicians often come across people who embraced such traditions or definitions too early, too much under pressure from parents, schools, church, evangelizing disciplines or charismatic gurus or as an avoidance of dealing with psychological pain and distress. Sometimes spiritual beliefs or political devotions are used to anaesthetize painful or disturbing psychological realities, and can act as a balm for people in distress as a result of their early experiences or current traumas.

The minister's daughter who forgives her rapist from the pulpit the day after the assault may be acting in true and good faith. To be compassionate towards herself she needs to include some time to digest the experience as a physical and psychological human being before sublimation. The forgiveness and compassion which follows the experience and acceptance of protest and outrage may be also true and perhaps longer lasting.

What does change mean and how is it brought about . . . what psychological theory of learning is being employed?

According to the Oxford Dictionary (Onions, 1973), change means: the act or fact of changing; substitution or succession of one thing in place of another; substitution of other conditions; variety; alteration in the state or quality of anything; variation; mutation. Change is of course not exclusive to psychological counselling or psychotherapy. Indeed people have changed since the beginning of time due to many factors. My research has shown that at least education, love, crisis and religious or political conversion can have as great an effect on a person's life as can counselling psychology. (Whether for good or for ill is another discussion.)

The polarities of change can be discussed as those of being between a sudden rapid and complete **reversal** kind of change and a gradual, slower and more partial **developmental** kind of change. This is the model which is well represented in Rogerian or client-centred counselling as discussed in Chapter 6 in this book. Change, whether in life, through extraneous factors or through psychological interventions, can thus be conceived of as either **revolutionary** or **evolutionary** – accomplished through 'cure' or through 'growth'.

Although, of course, they overlap, each of these two models of learning has particular implications for theory, ideology and practice. In my opinion frequent false disputes and insoluble dilemmas arise when practitioners falsely oppose these two points of view, rather than integrate or include them both in their paradigms of personal change – whatever the idioms they may choose to use in their stead. Given the limitations of space, I shall here focus on change of a fundamental nature.

Metanoia is derived from the Greek verb *metanoeo* which means (1) to perceive afterwards or too late, (2) to change one's mind or opinion, and (3) to turn around. The classical Greek translation also suggests 'to change one's mind on reflection' (Liddell, 1963: 439). This term is elsewhere defined as 'a change of the inner man' and a 'turning about' (Burchfield, 1976: 911). It also means a fundamental change of mind, a fundamental transformation of mind or character. In therapy I think it best refers to the **restructuring of personality**.

Such revolutionary changes may appear to occur suddenly or over a period of time. Usually people will report some turning point in their experience after which they no longer felt it possible to return to their previous way of being. These transformations often involve a paradigm shift or second-order change (Watzlawick et al., 1974), which can happen on any level. However, it usually involves physical, mental, emotional, social and sometimes spiritual reorganization. Such turning points in life and in counselling psychology are often revolutionary, but may equally be the result of evolutionary processes. What appears to be a sudden and dramatic shift may be the result of long preparation and incubation. As a successful actor once put it, 'It took me twelve years of preparation to be an overnight success'. On the other hand, sometimes the change within the person is indeed suddenly precipitated and appears to be totally discontinuous with a person's past history.

In this survey of biographical accounts, clinical cases and anecdotal material, several features of the change process have emerged with regularity, features that seem to be common to two or more of the categories discussed above. The following features have been identified and abstracted: intensity, despair, surrender, void (Bridges, 1980), the importance of relationship, community validation, a sense of mission and the appearance of archetypal images of transformation in dreams and in art. While these overlap and influence each other, they are separated here for purposes of discussion and further development.

Intensity

Intensity of emotional experience frequently correlates positively with life-changing events of experiences or metanoia. 'A high level of arousal of any emotion increases susceptibility to changes in consciousness' (Conway and Clarkson, 1987: 18). Counselling psychology (and its variants) also makes deliberate and intentional use of increases of emotional and/or physical intensity by heightening the transference through frequent sessions per week (psychoanalysis), breathing techniques which bring people in touch with their primal pain (rebirthing or bioenergetics), use of the techniques to bring the past vividly alive in the here-and-now (Polster and Polster, 1974), and heightening procedures (McNeel, 1976).

Despair

Despair is a frequent feature which precedes a life-transforming change. Like many alcoholics who become members of Alcoholics Anonymous, Jimmy Boyle, a hardened criminal, had to hit his own kind of rock-bottom before he changed. 'I knew that the screws in the Special Unit had this fear in their minds that Larry [another prisoner] and I would react violently to the sentences if they were very long. They didn't realise that once you have reached a certain depth you can go no lower' (Boyle, 1977: 235).

Surrender of previous frame of reference

The individual's frame of reference provides him or her with 'an overall perceptual, conceptual, affective and action set, which is used to define the self, other people, and the world, both structurally and dynamically' (Schiff et al., 1975: 51). A change in the individual's frame of reference, schema or script seems to accompany most major life changes, whether through therapy or some other event.

273

Community or group validation

In many experiences of change, the wider community – family, friends, employers and culture – also assumes an important role. For Jimmy Boyle in prison the acceptance and validation by his new community became the bridge to the new man. 'If . . . someone needed support due to some problem, then everyone would reach out and touch him, and by that I mean help him over the bad patch. Either way the group meeting was a very powerful force' (Boyle, 1977: 245).

A sense of mission/sharing

A frequent consequence of deep and profound experiences of personal change is that people want to share their experience with others. This is the phase of relearning. Clients who make major life changes in therapy or in AA groups, for example, often suggest a similar route to their friends or acquaintances.

> It was now that I was tasting a short spell on the outside that I realised just how committed I was to proving that people in hopeless situations like myself, who are serving very long sentences, can act responsibly and through their own experience, give something back into society. (Boyle, 1977: 257)

Archetypal images of transformation

There are several psychological moments in the turning-about-point (as discussed before). There are also correspondingly different images which point to them as collective representations through fairy tales or myths and Biblical stories. Certain archetypes occur with great frequency in the clinical experience of psychotherapists from many theoretical persuasions. These images may emerge through dreams, artwork, guided fantasies or through synchronistic experiences. There are a variety of such archetypal transformational images, for example the phoenix – a well-known symbol of death and rebirth by fire (Jung, 1964).

Family, group and organizational applications

Organizational applications

As we have seen, one of the first needs of the human being is for relationship. We know that without it a baby cannot survive, and without it adults cannot thrive (Provence and Lipton, 1962). It is to organizational life as water is to a fish. Ever since the Hawthorne experiments of the

Relationship	Contribution to the organization	Human motivation	Some signs of dysfunction
Unfinished (transference)	Grit in the oyster	Completion Resolution	Fixed, disruptive patterns of relationship
Working alliance	Achieving organizational tasks	Doing Competence Productivity	Task-dominated culture Sterile, driven work climate
Developmental	Developing organization's human resources	Growth Learning	Neediness Burn-out Over- or under-protection of staff
Personal	Developing the organization as a working community with a healthy culture	Intimacy Friendship Community	Uncontactful conflict and competition Fake bonhomie Loss of task focus
Transpersonal	Developing wider organization mission and purpose	Being Meaning Connection	Meaninglessness Anomie Ennui Disregard of ethics

Table 12.2   *An assessment framework for relationships at work*

1930s (Roethlisberger and Dickson, 1939), organization theorists and practitioners have recognized that organizations are social systems in which the relationships between people play a vital role.

To help clarify the roles of counselling and consulting skills and services within an organization the five-relationship model has been found helpful for consultancy, training and supervision. It is hypothesized that all human beings need all of these relationships in varying degrees and at different stages in their lives, and that the human need for these relationships is, after physiological survival, the primary motivation of the person. As these are continuing *adult* needs, we believe that a healthy organization is probably one that supports people in developing all five kinds of relationship within its overall fabric.

These ideas also provide another basis for understanding human motivation in organizational life. The **unfinished relationship** carries the human need for healing from the conflicts and hurts of the past. The **working alliance** satisfies our need for doing and for competence. The **developmental relationship** carries our deficits and our need for growth. The **personal relationship** carries our self needs, our need for recognition as unique individuals, while the **transpersonal relationship** carries our need for being, meaning and connection.

Table 12.2 summarizes the five relationships in terms of their contribution to the organization, the ways in which they may be dysfunctional, and the human motivation needs that each can satisfy.

Implications for counselling and consulting skills and services

Psychologists in organizations need to develop the ability to recognize the five different kinds of relationship, to distinguish them from one another, and to decide on the appropriateness of each one in a given situation. In meeting such training needs, an organization needs to judge when to use internal resources or to engage external help. I would suggest that working with the unfinished relationship often requires skills and experience less likely to be found in many organizations, although I believe it is very important that internal trainers, facilitators and consultants appreciate the nature of this relationship, the skills needed to work with it and the extent of their own competence. In my experience, the importance of this aspect of working relationships needs to be much better appreciated in organizations. For example, the current emphasis on creating empowerment in organizations through greater involvement and shared responsibility for decisions and actions at all levels is sometimes bedevilled by problems, which have at their root people's unresolved difficulties with issues of dependence, self-responsibility and personal change.

Group therapy applications

Using the five relationships (as is self-explanatory from Table 12.3) can form another matrix wherein practitioners from different trainings and different persuasions can integrate their personal preferences, their theories and also their clinical practice. Table 12.3 shows how it is possible to think about the major theoretical and applied contributions to group counselling and psychotherapy which can be conceptualized within a matrix formed from the five-relationship model. It indicates how the five relationship modalities relate to different theorists or disciplinary fields of knowledge and considers how typical intervention may be related to the significance and type of stages if one were to assume that developmental models are appropriate and/or useful in group psychotherapy. Detailed explorations of those are available elsewhere, for example see Clarkson (1995b) and Clarkson (1996).

Family therapy applications

The application of the model to the wide range of practices which are subsumed under the heading of family therapy is similar to that for group therapy.

Relationship type	Examples of theorists	Focus on individual/group	Typical interventions	Importance and type of developmental stages
Working alliance relationship	Bion et al.	Therapy of the group	Interpretation of basic assumptions in terms of the work or task of the group in relation to the leader	Developmental stages
Transference–counter-transference relationship	Foulkes et al.	Psychotherapy through the group	Interpretation of interactional matrix interpersonal relationships	Clarification of group imago
Developmentally needed or reparative relationship	Humanistic and integrative psychotherapists as well as: group therapy derived from Winnicott, Ferenczi, Miller & Fromm-Reichman	Individual in group	The provision or facilitation of experiences to provide the developmentally needed or reparative deficit	Independent of developmental stage of group
Person-to-person relationship	Existential Gestalt Yalom Moreno	Psychotherapy in the group	Encounter	Corresponding to that of Stern's approach to child development
Transpersonal relationship	Neo-Group Dynamics from Chaos & Complexity Theory Quantum Physics Jung	Therapy of the group and the individual and the wider whole	Facilitation of turbulence and differentiation of complexity, post-modernist or constructionist notions of 'decentred self'	'Timelessness' Relativity of time, different times, different subjectivities, different worlds.

Table 12.3   *The five relationships*

Research evidence about effectiveness

In discussing the nature of the relationship between counselling psychologist and client above, I have already summarized some of the research evidence relating to the effectiveness of an integrative approach. In a recent American survey investigating five major theoretical orientations (psychoanalytic, behavioural, humanist-existential, eclectic and cognitive), results suggested considerable transtheoretical convergence on the importance of novel exploratory activity and self-system development in psychotherapy (Mahoney et al., 1989: 251).

As the focus on the relationship is common across psychotherapeutic/analytic self-psychology and to some extent interpersonal dynamics psychotherapy, the psychologist has become more involved as a participant in the relationship and is more likely to show empathy in the therapy similar to that of Rogerian client-centred psychotherapy (Rogers, 1986), as Stolorow (1976) and Kahn (1985) have shown in regard to Kohut's work (1977). Cognitive behaviour therapists like Arnkoff (1982), Goldfried and Davison (1976) and Linehan (1988) are paying attention to the interpersonal relationship elements of behaviour therapy. Family therapists like Pinsoff (1983) have referred to the necessity to join or create rapport with the most powerful subsystem within a family if not with the whole family system.

There have been repeated encouragements and vociferous positions on why this would be bad, or impossible to find a common language for counselling psychology. I agree with Goldfried (1987) that it would be too costly of connotation, tradition and precision to sacrifice individual language systems for a uniform psychological language. I support Messer's (1987) plea that we should be multilingual. However, the development of a common language like Esperanto can have very fine advantages provided the original languages are preserved with their corresponding literature, history and refined articulation of nuances within the tongue. The development and use of a common language for common purposes may be a useful addition to our ability to communicate however.

> At a 1986 NIMH workshop on research in psychotherapy integration, it was pointed out that the language of psychotherapy may be used in four different ways: (1) to facilitate communication within a given orientation; (2) to retrieve basic research findings; (3) to dialogue across orientations; and (4) to conduct comparative psychotherapy process research. (Goldfried, 1987: 201)

So any one theory can be viewed as a singular way of looking at the field, and even though one may be temporarily deeply impressed and persuaded by one approach, there are always many other ways of doing psychology. There are a substantial number of clinicians, theoreticians and observer commentators who think that commonalities between approaches out-weigh theoretical differences between the schools (Bergin, 1971; Frank, 1979; Landman and Dawes, 1982; Luborsky et al., 1975). This is particularly true for more experienced clinicians, who tend to resemble each other more than less experienced practitioners resemble their seniors within the particular school (Fiedler, 1950).

This attitude ensures that as soon as convergence occurs, divergence is encouraged; and as soon as divergence occurs, convergence is encouraged. The natural need to integrate is necessarily followed by an organismic need to disintegrate, and destructing in human cycles needs to be followed by restructuring, since integration is not seen as a *product*, but the accomplishment of skilfulness and competency in a process which often spirals if it does not actually move circularly in a rhythmic, cyclic pulsation.

'The problem is: how does such a mixture work, how does it effect the patient if contrasting styles and ideas lie side by side?' (Hinshelwood, 1989: 473). In a discussion document, *The Future of Psychological Therapies in the NHS*, Kosviner (1989) focuses on clinical psychologists but could equally be addressing counselling psychologists and the emerging profession of counselling psychology:

> Those who see themselves as integrative therapists need standards of specialist expertise to be maintained within the profession, just as much as those developing specialist interest in one model. Without such standards, our credibility as integrators may be rightly questioned on the grounds that we are not sufficiently familiar with that which we are trying to integrate (1989: 38).

Finally, in the words of Norcross and Thomas (1988: 80)

> While we believe sophisticated integration has experienced, and will continue to experience, meaningful progress in our lifetimes, the greater legacy of this movement for counselling psychology may lie in the future. In particular it calls for the integration of practice and research. This legacy, for us, entails the promotion of open inquiry, intellectual relativism, and informed pluralism. As with the clinical enterprise itself, the seeds we sow now may produce enticing flowers in a few years, but may not bear the sustaining fruit for many years to come.

References

Aristotle ([1971]) *The Metaphysics Books I–IX*, (ed. G.P. Goold, trans. H. Tredennick). Cambridge, MA: Harvard University Press; London: Heinemann.

Arnkoff, D.B. (1982) 'Common and specific factors in cognitive therapy', in

M.J. Lambert (ed.), *A Guide to Psychotherapy and Patient Relationships.* Homewood, IL: Dorsey Press. pp. 85–125.

Bergin, A.E. (1971) 'The evaluation of therapeutic outcomes', in A.E. Bergin and S.L. Garfield (eds), *Handbook of Psychotherapy and Behavior Change.* New York: Wiley, pp. 217–20.

Bergin, A.E. and Lambert, M.J. (1978) 'The evaluation of therapeutic outcomes', in A.E. Bergin and S.L. Garfield (eds), *Handbook of Psychotherapy and Behavior Change,* 2nd edn. New York: Wiley. pp. 139–89.

Berne, E. (1968) *A Layman's Guide to Psychiatry and Psychoanalysis.* New York: Simon and Schuster (first published 1947).

Boyle, J. (1977) *A Sense of Freedom.* London: Pan Books.

Bridges, W. (1980) *Transitions.* Reading, MA: Addison-Wesley.

Buber, (1970) *I and Thou* (trans. W. Kaufmann). Edinburgh: T. and T. Clark (first published 1923).

Burchfield, R.W. (ed.) (1976) *A Supplement to the Oxford English Dictionary,* vols 1–4. Oxford: Oxford University Press.

Clarkson, P. (1990) 'A multiplicity of psychotherapeutic relationships', *British Journal of Psychotherapy,* 7: 148–63.

Clarkson, P. (1991) 'Individuality and commonality in Gestalt', *British Gestalt Journal,* 1: 28–37.

Clarkson, P. (1995a) 'Counselling Psychology in Britain – the next decade', *Counseling Psychology Quarterly,* 8(3): 197–204.

Clarkson, P. (1995b) *The Therapeutic Relationship.* London: Whurr,

Clarkson, P. (1996) *Researching the Therapeutic Relationship,* submitted for publication.

Conduit, E. (1987) 'Davanloo in Britain', *Changes,* 5(2): 333–7.

Conway, A. and Clarkson, P. (1987) 'Everyday hypnotic inductions', *Transactional Analysis Journal,* 17(2): 17–23.

Cottone, R.R. (1988) 'Epistemological and ontological issues in counselling: implications of social systems theory', *Counseling Psychology Quarterly,* 1(4): 357–65.

Douglas, A. (1989) 'The limits of cognitive-behaviour therapy: can it be integrated with psychodynamic therapy', *British Journal of Psychotherapy,* 5(3): 390–401.

Dryden, W. (1984) 'Issues in the eclectic practice of individual therapy', in W. Dryden (ed.), *Individual Therapy in Britain.* London: Harper and Row. pp. 341–63.

Dryden, W. and Norcross, J.C. (eds) (1990) *Eclecticism and Integration in Counselling and Psychotherapy.* Loughton, Essex: Gale Centre.

Fiedler, F.E.A. (1950) 'A comparison of therapeutic relationships in psycho-analytic, nondirective and Adlerian therapy', *Journal of Consulting Psychology,* 14: 436–45.

Fonagy, P. (1989) 'On the integration of cognitive-behaviour theory with psychoanalysis', *British Journal of Psychotherapy,* 5: 557–63.

Frank, J.D. (1979) 'The present status of outcome studies', *Journal of Consulting and Clinical Psychology,* 47: 310–16.

Frankl, V. (1973) *Man's Search for Meaning: an Introduction to Logotherapy*. London: Hodder and Stoughton (first published 1959).

Garfield, S.L. (1992) 'Eclectic psychotherapy: a common factors approach', in J.C. Norcross and M.R. Goldfried (eds), *Handbook of Psychotherapy Integration*. New York: Basic Books. pp. 169–201.

Goldfried, M.R. (1980) 'Toward the delineation of the therapeutic change principle', *American Psychologist*, 35: 991–9.

Goldfried, M.R. (1987) 'A common language for the psychotherapies: commentary', *Journal of Integrative and Eclectic Psychotherapy*, 6: 200–4.

Goldfried, M.R. and Davison, G.C. (1976) *Clinical Behaviour Therapy*. New York: Holt, Rinehart and Winston.

Greenberg, I.A. (ed.) (1975) *Psychodrama: Theory and Therapy*. London: Souvenir Press.

Guerriere, D. (1980) 'Physis, Sophia, Psyche', in J. Sallis and K. Maly (eds), *Heraclitean Fragments: a Companion Volume to the Heidegger/Fink Seminar on Heraclitus*. Alabama, CA: University of Alabama Press. pp. 87–134.

Hinshelwood, R.D. (1989) 'Editorial', *British Journal of Psychotherapy*, 5: 473.

Hinshelwood, R.D. (1990) 'Editorial', *British Journal of Psychotherapy*, 7: 119–20.

Holmes, J. and Lindley, R. (1989) *The Values of Psychotherapy*. Oxford: Oxford University Press.

Hynan, M.T. (1981) 'On the advantages of assuming that the techniques of psychotherapy are ineffective', *Psychotherapy: Theory, Research and Practice*, 18: 11–13.

James, M. (1974) 'Self-reparenting: theory and process', *Transactional Analysis Journal*, 4(3): 32–9.

Jung, C.G. (1928) 'Analytical psychology and education', in *Contributions to Analytical Psychology* (trans. H.G. and C.F. Baynes). London: Trench Trubner.

Jung, C.G. (1964) *Man and his Symbols*. London: Aldus Books.

Kahn, E. (1985) 'Heinz Kohut and Carl Rogers: a timely comparison', *American Psychologist* 40: 893–904.

Karasu, T.B. (1986) 'The psychotherapies: benefits and limitations', *American Journal of Psychotherapy*, XL (3): 324–42.

Kiesler, D.J. (1966) 'Some myths of psychotherapy research and the search for a paradigm', *Psychological Bulletin*, 65: 110–36.

Koestler, A. (1972) *The Roots of Coincidence*. London: Hutchinson.

Kohut, H. (1977) *The Restoration of the Self*. New York: International Universities Press.

Kosviner, A. (1989) 'The future of psychological therapies in the NHS', *Clinical Psychology Forum*, 23: 38–9.

Landman, J.T. and Dawes, R.M. (1982) 'Psychotherapy outcome: Smith and Glass' conclusions stand up under scrutiny', *American Psychologist*, 37: 504–16.

Lazarus, A.A. (1995) 'Different types of eclecticism and integration: let's be aware of the dangers', *Journal of Psychotherapy Integration*, 5(1): 27–39.

Liddell, H.G. (1963) *A Lexicon Abridged from Liddell and Scott's Greek–English Lexicon*. Oxford: Oxford University Press.

Linehan, M.M. (1988) 'Perspectives on the interpersonal relationship in behavior therapy', *Journal of Integrative and Eclectic Psychotherapy*, 7(3): 278–90.

Luborsky, L., Crits-Cristoph, R., Alexander, L., Margolis, M. and Cohen, M. (1983) 'Two helping alliance methods of predicting outcomes of psychotherapy', *Journal of Nervous and Mental Disease*, 17(1): 480–91.

Luborsky, L., Singer, B. and Luborsky, L. (1975) 'Comparative studies of psychotherapies: is it true that "Everybody has won and all must have prizes"?', *Archives of General Psychiatry*, 32: 995–1008.

McNeel, J.R. (1976) 'The parent interview', *Transactional Analysis Journal*, 6(1): 61–8.

Mahoney, M.J., Norcross, J.C., Prochaska, J.O. and Missar, C.D. (1989) 'Psychological development and optimal psychotherapy: converging perspectives among clinical psychologists', *Journal of Integrative and Eclectic Psychotherapy*, 8: 251–63.

Maslow, A. (1968) *Toward a Psychology of Being*, 2nd edn. New York: Van Nostrand.

Masterson, J.F. (1985) *The Real Self*. New York: Brunner/Mazel.

Messer, S.B. (1987) 'Can the Tower of Babel be completed? A critique of the common language proposal', *Journal of Integrative and Eclectic Psychotherapy*, 6: 195–9.

Miller, A. (1983) *The Drama of the Gifted Child and the Search for the True Self* (trans. R. Ward). London: Faber and Faber (first published 1979).

Norcross, J.C. (ed.) (1986) *Handbook of Eclectic Psychotherapy*. New York: Brunner/Mazel.

Norcross, J.C. and Goldfried, M.R. (1992) *Handbook of Psychotherapy Integration*. New York: Basic Books.

Norcross, J.C. and Grencavage, L.M. (1990) 'Eclecticism and integration in counselling and psychotherapy: major themes and obstacles', in W. Dryden and J.C. Norcross (eds), *Eclecticism and Integration in Counselling and Psychotherapy*. Loughton, Essex: Gale Centre. pp. 1–33.

Norcross, J.C. and Thomas, B.L. (1988) 'What's stopping us now? Obstacles to psychotherapy integration', *Journal of Integrative and Eclectic Psychotherapy*, 7(1): 74–80.

O'Malley, S.S., Suh, C.S. and Strupp, H.H. (1983) 'The Vanderbilt psychotherapy process scale: a report on the scale development and a process outcome study', *Journal of Consulting and Clinical Psychology*, 51: 581–6.

Onions, C.T. (ed.) (1973) *The Shorter Oxford English Dictionary*. Oxford: Oxford University Press.

Pavlov, I.P. (1928) *Lectures on Conditioned Reflexes* (trans. W.H. Ganff). New York: International Publishers.

Pinsoff, W.M. (1983) 'Integrative problem-centered therapy: towards the synthesis of family and individual psychotherapies', *Journal of Marital and Family Therapy*, 9: 19–35.

Polster, E. and Polster, M. (1974) *Gestalt Therapy Integrated: Contours of Theory and Practice*. New York: Vintage (first published 1973).

Provence, S. and Lipton, R.C. (1962) *Infants in Institutions*. New York: International Universities Press.

Roethlisberger, F.J. and Dickson, W.J. (1939) *Management and the Worker*. Harvard, MA: Harvard University Press.

Rogers, C. (1986) *Client-Centered Therapy*. London: Constable.

Rothenberg, A. (1979) *The Emerging Goddess*. Chicago: University of Chicago Press.

Ryle, G. (1973) *Dilemmas: The Tarner Lectures 1953*. Cambridge: Cambridge University Press.

Samuels, A. (1985) *Jung and the Post-Jungians*. London: Routledge and Kegan Paul.

Schiff, J.L., Schiff, A.W., Mellor, K., Schiff, E., Schiff, S., Richman, D., Fishman, J., Wolz, L., Fishman, C. and Momb, D. (1975) *Cathexis Reader: Transactional Analysis and Treatment of Psychosis*. New York: Harper and Row.

Stolorow, R.D. (1976) 'Psychoanalytic reflections on client-centered therapy in the light of modern conceptions of narcissism', *Psychotherapy: Theory, Research and Practice*, 13: 26–9.

Yager, J. (1977) 'Psychiatric eclecticism: a cognitive view', *American Journal of Psychiatry*, 134: 736–41.

Watzlawick, P., Weakland, J.H. and Fisch, R. (1974) *Change*. New York: W.W. Norton.

Winnicott, D. (1958) *Collected Papers: Through Paediatrics to Psycho-analysis*. London: Tavistock.

Part Four

Psychological Interventions: Developmental Issues

13

Narratives of Theory and Practice: the Psychology of Life-Span Development

Léonie Sugarman

Counselling and life-span developmental psychology bear a figure–ground relationship to each other. If counselling processes and skills, widely defined, are the figure, then life-span developmental psychology is part of the ground. Counselling psychology can, likewise, be seen as part of this ground. Both are capable of providing what Egan calls a working knowledge – that is, a theoretical and research knowledge translated into 'the kind of applied understandings that enable helpers to work with clients' (1990: 17). Thus, the study and understanding of life-span development can justifiably be seen as a task for counselling as well as developmental psychologists. Not all developmental psychology can readily be construed in this way, but the present chapter emphasizes theories, research and concepts which are compatible with the intellectual orientations of counselling psychology, and which helpers can use in the midst of their practice to assist in the understanding of their clients and in the management of their counselling.

At the level of research methodology there is also much compatibility between life-span development and counselling psychology. Both share an affinity with qualitative, 'new-paradigm' research. Methodologically, research in life-span developmental psychology frequently repudiates theoretically derived hypothesis testing in favour of 'more basic descriptive work, including a more systematic use of autobiography, storytelling and conversation, diaries, literature, clinical case histories, historical fiction, and the like, with a new emphasis upon the person's construction and reconstruction of the "life story," rather than what might be considered a more objective account of what happened' (Datan et al., 1987: 154).

Life-span development and change

The notion of life-span development was gathered fairly late under the umbrella of psychology. It was not until 1980 that it received the accolade of a paper devoted to it in the *Annual Review of Psychology*. Here life-span developmental psychology was defined as being 'concerned with the description, explanation, and modification (optimization) of developmental processes in the human life course from conception to death' (Baltes et al., 1980: 66). The emphasis on developmental processes and their optimization denote the compatibility between life-span and counselling psychology.

Of course, many accounts of the human life course were already in existence prior to the 1980 *Annual Review* paper. From literature, one of the most often cited is Jaques's 'All the world's a stage' speech from *As You Like It*. Here, we have, among other things, the infant, 'mewling and puking in its nurse's arms'; the lover, 'sighing like a furnace' and the soldier 'jealous in honour, sudden and quick in quarrel'. This speech enshrines one view of life-span development adopted by psychologists – namely, the 'natural' unfolding of stages assumed, either explicitly or implicitly, to be invariant, universal and cumulative.

An alternative view of the life course, also advocated by some psychologists and sociologists, is expressed, less poetically, in the children's rhyme about Solomon Grundy: 'Born on Monday; Christened on Tuesday; Married on Wednesday', and so on and so forth. Again we have the inexorable passage of time, in this instance punctuated less by internally triggered drives and aspirations and more by external life events. The rhyme lists a series of 'normal' – in both the statistical sense and the sense of being appropriate – events which Solomon Grundy might be expected to experience. By implication we see Solomon Grundy as a metaphor for Everyman and, indeed, Everywoman. However, today we might be less able to describe the 'normal' or 'natural' course of human life with such confident brevity. We cannot assume the ordering or, indeed, the occurrence, of such events to be either invariant or universal.

Why does development appear ordered?

Research in life-span developmental psychology has consistently addressed the question of the extent to which the shape and/or content of the human life course is ordered and predictable. Such order as is found tends to be conceptualized as a series of phases or stages which, in turn, are seen to be either the outcome of the maturational unfolding of the individual's potential, or, alternatively, as the outcome of societal conditions, norms and expectations. The first perspective is illustrated by Erikson's (1980) theory of eight developmental crises stretching from infancy to old age. It borrows from embryology the epigenetic principle that 'anything that grows has a ground plan, and out of this ground plan the parts arise, each part having its time of special ascendency, until all forms have arisen to form a functioning whole' (1980: 53). Jung, likewise, depicts each phase of the life course as having its own characteristics, potentialities and limitations: 'we cannot live the afternoon of life according to the program of life's morning, for what in the morning was true will at evening be a lie. Whoever carries into the afternoon the law of the morning . . . must pay with damage to his soul' (1972: 396).

The alternative viewpoint argues that, rather than being assumed to be the result of individual maturation, stages are a reflection of individuals' fulfilling of society's age-related roles and expectations (Kohli and Meyer, 1986). This approach, exemplified by the work of Neugarten (1977), whilst recognizing that some regularities of the life cycle do arise from within, focuses attention on how the life course is defined, constituted and changed by external occurrences. It examines how we use common markers to anticipate what form our life course will, and should, take. Many of these events correlate with age, and together they comprise an age-grade system – 'a prescriptive timetable for the ordering of life events' (Neugarten, 1977: 45).

Aspects of this timetable may be institutionalized, as when upper and/or lower age limits are set for such activities as school attendance, marriage, voting, or retirement. However, most aspects of a society's age-grade system are consensual rather than formal, comprising a general acceptance that there is a 'right' and a 'wrong' age for such activities as getting married, finishing our education or throwing a tantrum in public. Such social norms can be and are challenged – arguably many elements of the UK's age-grade system are less rigid than in the past. However, most people feel some degree of pressure to conform to prevailing age-graded conventions and may be worried about deviating from the norm. We operate in relation to a 'social clock' (Schlossberg et al., 1979) which enables us to state whether we are 'early', 'on time' or 'late' for a wide range of significant life events. Deviations from age norms tend to attract both negative self-assessments and criticism from others.

Despite adopting one perspective or the other, most researchers would accept that these two viewpoints represent differences of emphasis rather than mutually exclusive alternatives. To the extent societal norms are a response to inborn developmental patterns, then stages may be the outcome of the interaction between the individual and the environment. In other words, ordered change across the life course may reflect internal changes, external forces or a combination of the two.

There is a third perspective which de-emphasizes those changes which are age-related, and focuses instead on less predictable changes that might occur at almost any point in the life course. In its extreme form, this perspective leads to a view of the life course as fundamentally chaotic (Cohler, 1982), with any apparent order being spurious – something imposed on disparate experiences in order to make sense of them.

289

Thus, life-span developmental psychologists distinguish between three main categories of major change across the life course: universal age-graded changes; age-graded changes shared by a particular culture and/or generation; and changes that are not associated with any particular age or life stage. These are termed, respectively, normative age-related changes, normative history-graded changes, and non-normative changes (Baltes et al., 1980).

Continuity and the life course

Much of both life-span developmental psychology and counselling psychology is concerned with change. This acknowledges our awareness than we change – physically, cognitively, emotionally, socially – throughout life. Yet, we also know that we do not become totally different people. There is continuity as well as change in life-span development. Thus, in the true story of Martin Guerre (Davies, 1985), the idea that his wife did not realize it was an impostor who returned from war and assumed Guerre's identity is greeted with incredulity. Instead it is assumed that she must, for whatever reason, have colluded with this deception. On a more mundane level, we are surprised and often disconcerted when people act 'out of character'.

Explanations of continuity in life-span development mirror to a large extent explanations of change. First, there are biological, or genetic explanations of continuity. These involve the recognition that a range of characteristics – physical, cognitive and temperamental – are at least partially influenced by heredity. However, an individual's behaviour will always be the outcome of interaction between inborn inheritance and environmental forces (Loehlin, 1989; Plomin, 1989). Furthermore, inherited characteristics and tendencies show varying degrees of modifiability, and exploring the range and limits of such potential variability has been identified as a key task for life-span developmental psychology (Baltes, 1987).

The second explanation of continuity in life-span development emphasizes it as the outcome of continuity in the individual's physical, interpersonal, social and cultural environment. This perspective underlies many attempts to overcome disadvantage and discrimination by intervention through nutritional, educational and social opportunity programmes – attempting, in other words, to break the cycle of deprivation.

Environmental continuity may also be the outcome of our own actions. Thus, we gravitate towards school subjects and occupations we think we will find attractive and think we will succeed in. Such choices reflect a combination of our inborn characteristics (Holland, 1973), our values

(Gottfredson, 1981) and our opportunities (Roberts and Parsell, 1992) – with theorists varying in the importance attached to these different factors. In general, we tend, when we can, to choose those environments where we think we will fit in and be successful (Scarr, 1992).

A third approach to continuity across the life course is analogous to the perspective on change that sees the life course as inherently lacking in order. This approach concentrates on the subjective meaning of experiences rather than their objective properties, and is concerned with the ways in which we give meaning to our experiences by filtering them through internal models of who we are and what the world is like (Epstein, 1991). This person-centred approach to an individual's sense of continuity is likely to be of greater significance to counselling psychologists than indicators of continuity as indicated by, for example, stability of personality traits such as introversion–extraversion.

In fact, despite the preceding discussion, it is somewhat misleading to talk of the distinction between change and continuity. What we are really talking about is different types of change. Continuity is not synonymous with stagnation or lack of change. What it refers to is change which is gradual, incremental and quantitative rather than change which is discontinuous, time-bounded and qualitative. The life course contains both, and the concept of narrative construction is capable of encompassing how individuals maintain a sense of coherence – a sense of being the same person they have always been – despite the gradual, incremental changes associated with ageing, and despite major life disruptions.

Narrative and the life course

A narrative, or story, offers a way of making sense of our experiences by ordering them temporally according to a theme – a process known as emplotment (Ricoeur, 1984). If events are described randomly they are likely to make little sense, and so a requirement of even the simplest coherent narrative is that it has, like a life, a beginning, a middle and an end. From each set of life experiences more than one story could be told, and accounts of the life course reflect decisions made concerning which events are sufficiently significant to include, what themes best provide a coherent plot, and the degree and type of closure given to the story (Murray, 1986). These decisions reflect the theoretical and ideological perspectives of the biographer.

Narratives are replete with images as well as events (Howard, 1991) and, indeed, Ricoeur (1984) defines a narrative as an 'extended metaphor'. This term could also be used to describe the accounts offered by many life course researchers. Thus, Jung (1972) uses the image of the daily path of the sun – rising in the morning, reaching its zenith at midday and setting in the evening. Levinson (1986; Levinson et al., 1978), in similar vein, describes the phases of life as seasons. The metaphor of the journey is another recurring image. Thus, Ford and Lerner describe human development as 'a continuous and somewhat unpredictable journey throughout life, sailing from seas that have become familiar into oceans as yet uncharted toward destinations to be imagined, defined, and redefined as the voyage proceeds, with occasional, often unpredictable, transformations of one's vessel and sailing skills and the oceans upon which one sails resulting from unforeseen circumstances' (1992: 47). Ford and Lerner emphasize the open-ended and unpredictable elements in the life course, whereas Levinson et al. and Jung focuses more on the principle that there is a time and place for particular experiences and tasks.

The function of narratives

Narratives serve to help us discover and know who we are. Indeed, McAdams (1985: 57) defines identity as 'a life story which individuals begin construing, consciously or unconsciously in late adolescence'. Events in the narrative are evaluated against an endpoint to which the story, implicitly or explicitly, is directed (Gergen, 1988). Those events that contribute towards the attainment of a valued endpoint are positively evaluated; those that lead away from it are evaluated negatively. Thus, accounts of individual's lives may be evaluated as success stories or as failures. 'Good' stories display coherence and consistency, and comprise plots acceptable within a particular society. 'Bad' stories are ill-formed and/or deviate from definitions of success acceptable within a particular society. In this way narratives help define our cultural and social as well as our individual identity. Mair sees stories as enveloping and constituting us: 'We live in and through stories. . . . They hold us together and keep us apart. We inhabit the great stories of our culture. We live through stories. We are lived by the stories of our race and place' (1988: 127).

Thus, narratives give guidance and directionality to our lives. The fairy stories we hear as children not only keep us entertained, but are also instrumental in teaching us about the mores of our society (Bettelheim, 1976). Through these and other stories within our culture we learn about likely future events and experiences, and find role models concerning how to cope. In this way we extend our grip on the world (Viney and Bousefield, 1991). Stories which mirror our own lives have the power to console by reassuring us that our experiences are normal – both in the sense of being understandable and in the sense of being shared by others

(Taylor et al., 1993). The *Cautionary Tales* of Hilaire Belloc comprise dire warnings about the dangers of not following the rules. Rewritings of traditional tales, such as Roald Dahl's *Revolting Rhymes*, can serve to challenge cultural stereotypes.

When our own experience is reflected in the valued stories of our culture we feel validated. When our experience does not fit a culturally acceptable narrative form we may feel alienated and disenchanted. At the level of the individual McLeod (1996a) suggests that the depowering effect of silencing or enforced silence may be a central theme in counselling from a narrative perspective. By the same token, it follows that telling our stories can empower us. If our stories are heard within a community we 'may be better able to contribute to constructing how that community sees itself and its problems' (Viney and Bousefield, 1991).

Life course researchers, counselling psychologists and counsellors both construct and are constructed by the 'good' and 'bad' stories of their society. Such constructions relate to the question of what we, implicitly or explicitly, mean by the term development, and how we distinguish it from mere change.

What is development?

If we were to say that change and development were synonymous, then we would have no basis for arguing that one life course was preferable to, or 'more developed' than, any other, and, therefore, no justification as helpers for intervening in an individual's life course in order to facilitate change.

The concept of development centres on some notion of improvement. Changes in amount and/or in quality are evaluated against an explicit or implicit opinion as to what constitutes the 'preferable', the 'good' or the 'ideal'. Kaplan (1983) defined development as movement in the direction of perfection. Since it is a matter of opinion as to what constitutes perfection it is inevitable that definitions of development rest upon value judgements.

In Western societies definitions of development have a distinctly individualistic flavour – incorporating such things as being able to exercise increasing control over one's life, being self-reliant, fulfilling personal potential and accepting responsibility for one's actions. This perspective emphasizes the individual's control over his or her life course, leading to such definitions of development as it being the approximation towards self-constructed ends (Freeman, 1984). All these characteristics can be seen as facets of self-empowerment (Hopson and Scally, 1980) and bear a striking resemblance to the goals of counselling as outlined by the British

Association for Counselling's definition of the overall aim of counselling as being 'to provide an opportunity for the client to work towards living in a more satisfying and resourceful way' (British Association for Counselling, 1993: 2). Whilst descriptions of, for example, the mature (Allport, 1964), the self-actualized (Maslow, 1970), or the fully functioning (Rogers, 1967) person – all of which could be considered as candidates for a definition of development – do incorporate a sense of community and social concern, this is not to the extent that individuality is suppressed and subordinated to family and other social demands, as can be the case in Eastern cultures.

Erikson's (1980) concept of ego integrity captures the tenor of concepts of development implicit in much counselling psychology. Erikson sees ego integrity as the culmination and, to use his term, the ripe fruit, of all earlier development. Its main characteristic is acceptance: acceptance of one's self and one's life, and freedom from excessive regret that it has not been different; acceptance that one's life is one's own responsibility; acceptance of and respect for the validity of world-views different from one's own; acceptance of the smallness of one's place in the world, combined with a recognition of the reality of one's own contribution.

Prevalent in many accounts of the ultimate goal of development is the recognition that it refers to an ideal, not an attainable reality. 'The good life,' writes Rogers, 'is a *process*, not a state of being. It is a direction, not a destination' (1967: 186). Ford and Lerner's metaphor of life-span development as a journey is relevant here. As in literature, many of our most compelling narratives are journeys.

The life-span perspective

By now it should be clear that life-span developmental psychology does not comprise a single theory. Baltes (1987) suggests that it is best thought of as a family of theoretical propositions which provide a framework for encompassing a range of more narrowly focused descriptions, explanations and modifications, and act as a set of orienting principles for practitioners. He identified seven theoretical propositions as summing up the life-span perspective. They serve to draw together and summarize the threads of the discussion so far.

1 *Development is a life-long process* Life-span developmental psychology proposes that throughout the life course there is the potential for both continuous growth, which is gradual, incremental, cumulative and quantitative, and discontinuous development which is rapid, innovative, substantial and qualitative. This contrasts with the common assumption

within developmental psychology that childhood is the main period of growth and development – a period of 'becoming'; with adulthood seen as a stable plateau – a period of 'being' rather than becoming; and with old age again a period of change, but this time characterized by decline and loss – almost a period of 'ceasing to be'.

2 *Development is multidimensional and multidirectional* Life-span developmental psychology adopts a total life-space (Super, 1980), as well as a total life-span perspective. It is recognized that different elements of the person – intellectual, social, career, family, for example – may follow developmental trajectories which are at least partially independent. Furthermore, even within any one domain the concept of development need not be bound by a single criterion of growth or progress.

Clients often come to counselling to explore conflicts between different developmental trajectories – for example between the roles of worker and home-maker, of spouse and parent, or of child and parent. Counselling services are frequently organized around particular life stages or themes, but by adopting a life-span perspective counsellors and counselling psychologists can adopt a more holistic view of the person.

3 *Development involves loss as well as gain* Life-span psychologists typically view development as a joint expression of growth (gain) and decline (loss). Thus, decision-making inevitably involves the closing off (loss) of some options, and moving forward inevitably involves severing links with the past. By the same token, losses may result in developmental gains – for example in the form of new opportunities or the development of new coping skills. The underlying assumption is that any developmental progression displays both new adaptive capacity and loss of previously existing capacity. Gould speaks of the danger inherent in pursuing personal growth through transformation: 'As we push the boundary to gain internal freedom, we automatically destroy pieces of the illusion of absolute safety' (1980: 64).

4 *Development shows plasticity* Plasticity denotes the potential for a particular developmental path within a particular individual to be modified by life conditions and experiences. It refers to the potential for within-individual rather than between-individual variability. The degree of plasticity will vary across different strands of development, some (for example, career development) showing greater plasticity than others (for example, motor development).

The developmental preoccupations of childhood are more likely to show greater correlation with age and less plasticity than those of adulthood. Perceptual, motor and cognitive development during the first months or years of life do follow a relatively fixed order and timetable. This is reinforced, at least within any one society, by the regularities in child-rearing practices and education which the children experience. Whilst still affected by social conventions and practices, adulthood in general is less bound by such ordered and timed processes. It is to be expected, therefore, that there is a wider range of developmental possibilities for adults. The limiting of options for some people in old age through perceptual, motor and cognitive decline may reduce the plasticity of the developmental possibilities of this era.

5 *Development is historically and culturally embedded* Social and cultural environments change over time, both in terms of specific events such as wars or economic recession, which will be experienced by some generations but not by others; and in terms of such things as technological developments or changing social trends. Particular lifestyles will be condoned and others will be criticized as deviations from the pattern that a life course 'should' (according to the values of a particular society or social group) take. Whereas cultural differences serve to highlight the inappropriateness of transferring concepts of development from one social group to another, historical differences serve to make the past an uncertain and unreliable guide to the future.

Changing trends may involve qualitative as well as quantitative changes. Datan charts the progression: 'the exceptional becomes the scarce, the scarce becomes the infrequent, the infrequent becomes the acceptable, and finally, the acceptable becomes the norm' (1983: 41). A changed definition of 'normal' development is thus achieved. Married women's participation in the work force has passed through this sequence of stages during the present century.

6 *Development as the outcome of individual–environment transactions* Traditionally psychologists have identified the locus of development as within either the individual or the environment (Pervin and Lewis, 1978). Thus, in the former instance, maturationalists emphasize the part played by 'nature', notably innate, maturational and hereditary factors. Likewise, humanistic psychologists see development as the emergence of an inner self or essence. The environment is seen as inhibiting or facilitating, but not as causing development. Development occurs through the activity of the organism itself.

By contrast, learning theory and sociological perspectives focus attention on the role of environmental factors in causing development. The individual is seen as inherently passive and at rest, being prodded into action by external stimuli which are, thereby, the cause of development.

Life-span developmental psychology tends to direct thinking away from these two alternatives and towards a superordinate, interactive model (Reese, 1976) which renders obsolete the nature–nurture debate. Both an absolute organismic perspective and an absolute mechanistic perspective are rejected in favour of an interactive, contextual or systems view of an active organism as part of an active environment (Dowd, 1990). For counselling psychologists the implication of this is the need to look to the outer as well as the inner worlds inhabited by both client and counsellor.

7 *Development is a multidisciplinary concept* The broad and encompassing perspective adopted by life-span developmental psychologists facilitates acceptance that a purely psychological view can offer but a partial representation of the life course of individuals. Psychological development needs to be seen as the outcome of a range of different influence systems, each with associated disciplines of study. This can be illustrated by conceptualizing the environment as a hierarchical nest of systems in which the individual is embedded (Bronfenbrenner, 1977), and which can each influence individual development to a varying degree, and with varying degrees of directness (Kohli and Meyer, 1986). From anthropology we can learn about cultural influences (such as language, social mores, folk tales), and from sociology we can learn about the impact of societal institutions (government, health services, education, etc.). It is at the individual level that psychology makes its major contribution. Here we can learn about processes within the individual, and about interactions between individuals and the different personal settings in which they live, and also the interactions between different settings. At the sub-individual level we can look at the development of various biological or chemical processes, for example. Together these different influence systems provide the biological, personal, social and cultural milieu in which the individual develops. Baltes (1987) issues a plea for efforts at integrating the knowledge derived from different disciplinary perspectives – again the theme, so emblematic of the life-span perspective, of 'both/and' rather than 'either/or'.

Accounts of the life course

Given the context-bound flexibility of life-span development, it is not to be expected that accounts of the life course are universal, invariant or definitive. General descriptive concepts are more likely to have greater utility and durability than detailed accounts of specific life events. One useful portmanteau concept is Levinson et al.'s (1978) notion of the life course as an evolving life structure. A second useful concept is that of the developmental task, a concept advanced by Havighurst since the 1940s

(Chickering and Havighurst, 1981) and utilized by several researchers, including Levinson, since.

1 *An evolving life structure*   The notion of the life structure is a pivotal concept in Levinson et al.'s work. It is defined as the underlying pattern or design of a person's life at a given time. It comprises not only the characteristics of the person, but also the person's relationships with the socio-cultural world – people, things, places, institutions and cultures. The life structure exists on the boundary between the person and the environment, a link between them, being part of both and yet partially separate from them.

The life structure is not static, but evolves through an alternating series of structure-building and structure-changing (transitional) periods. Transitional periods are times of reappraisal and decision-making, times 'to explore possibilities for change in the self and the world, and to move toward commitment to the crucial choices that form the basis for a new life structure' (Levinson, 1986: 7). They are often experienced as periods of upheaval, both frightening and exciting. It is likely that more clients present for counselling during structure-changing phases than during the less chaotic structure-building phases. Whilst the latter are not devoid of change, they are primarily periods of consolidation, during which we form a new structure around the key choices we have made and pursue our values and goals within it. Even the best crafted life structures will, however, become outmoded within five to ten years. Another structure-changing phase, itself lasting about five years, is heralded when the existing life structure can no longer accommodate changes in ourselves and our relations with the world. Counsellors can use this notion of the evolving life structure to emplot the life stories they construct with clients.

2 *Developmental tasks*   Levinson describes the issues addressed during each structure-building and structure-changing phase as developmental tasks: tasks arising at or around a particular point in the life cycle, whose successful resolution facilitates 'healthy and successful growth in our society' (Chickering and Havighurst, 1981: 25). Such tasks arise from a combination of physical maturation, cultural pressures and individual aspirations. These origins mirror the three sources of order across the life course: maturational processes, social and environmental forces, and individual creativity. When physical maturation is the prime source of a developmental task – as, for example, with learning to walk – it may be possible to identify universal norms; but to the extent that social and cultural factors are implicated it is likely that tasks will be specific to a certain social group, culture and/or historical era. For example, choice of

occupation depends on such things as the structure of the labour market, the opportunities available locally, and the nature of the relationship between education and the world of work, as well as individual inclinations and aptitudes.

Detailed accounts of the life course of specific individuals or groups of individuals represent stories told from a particular disciplinary, cultural and historical perspective. However, it has long been suggested by literary scholars that there are only a limited number of story forms, for example: comedy, romance, tragedy, and satire (or irony) (Frye, 1957). Murray (1986) identified in the work of three life course researchers (Gould, 1978; Levinson et al., 1978; Sheehy, 1974) the narrative structures of, respectively, satire, tragedy and romance. Frye (1957) elates his four narrative structures, albeit not without criticism (Gergen, 1988), to the seasons of the year. There are echoes here of Jung's description of the life course.

However, not even those stories displaying a similar narrative structure are identical. Thus, McAdams (1985) paraphrases Kluckhohn, Murray and Schneider (1953) by describing every story as (a) like all other stories, (b) like some other stories, and (c) like no other stories. He identifies in the life stories of a sample of American adults evidence of one or more of the story forms found in Elsbree's (1982) taxonomy of what he terms generic plots. Evidence of these plots can, likewise, be found in researchers' accounts of the life course, and it is at this level, rather than in terms of specific, concrete details that greatest generalizability and consistency across groups and cohorts is to be found. Elsbree (1982) identifies five generic plots: establishing or consecrating a home; engaging in a contest; taking a journey; enduring suffering; and pursuing consummation.

1 *Establishing or consecrating a home* In the first of Elsbree's generic plots the basic image is that of building a home. General and specific evidence of this theme can be found throughout accounts of the life course. Creating a stable life structure, putting down roots, making commitments and establishing a more organized life are all recurrent themes in Levinson's (1986) model of adult development, albeit that these tasks must often be worked on in the context of other, contradictory demands. Similarly, age-related norms and expectations concerning such events as taking on a mortgage or having children (Neugarten, 1977) are also evidence of this theme.

Elsbree's first generic plot is not only revealed in the literal act of home-building. Thus, whilst Erikson's (1980) task of generativity – establishing and guiding the next generation – is usually expressed through parenthood, it may also be expressed through other forms of creativity and altruistic concern. In general terms, the plot of establishing or consecrating a home is concerned with sustaining human community and creating order out of chaos.

2 Engaging in a contest   Elsbree's second generic plot is reflected in the image of engaging in a contest, or fighting a battle. Thus, Sheehy (1974) describes the task of the mid-life period as being the achievement through battle of victory over the inner custodian – a 'nasty tyrant' within the self which commands that we meet the demands made of us by others, notably our parents.

Erikson's (1980) depiction of life-span development as a sequence of 'battles' or crises is illustrative of this theme on a grander scale. Erikson's theory describes an individual developing through adaptation to a series of societal demands. Each new demand provokes an emotional crisis, the successful resolution of which leads to the development of a new 'virtue' or 'vital strength'. Four crises are associated with childhood: Basic trust *v.* Basic mistrust; Autonomy *v.* Shame and doubt; Initiative *v.* Guilt; and Industry *v.* Inferiority. The crisis of Identity *v.* Role confusion is characteristic of adolescence, and a further three crises are confronted during adulthood: Intimacy *v.* Isolation; Generativity *v.* Stagnation; and Ego integrity *v.* Despair and disgust. The new virtues which, ideally, arise from each task are, respectively, those of hope, will, purpose, competence, fidelity, love, care, and wisdom.

In similar vein, Levinson et al. (1978) see all stages of development being characterized by conflicting tasks. For example, in the phase of Entering the Adult World, young adults need both to keep options open in order to explore possibilities and to make choices and commitments in order to create a stable life structure. Levinson et al. found evidence that, whilst work on one of these two tasks may predominate, the other is never totally absent.

3 Taking a journey   The image of the life course as a journey, Elsbree's third generic plot, is illustrated in the already quoted work of Ford and Lerner (1992). It recurs throughout Levinson et al.'s description of adult development as the evolution of a person's life structure through alternating structure-building and structure-changing (transitional) phases. They talk, for example, of the Early Adult Transition as 'a preliminary *step* into the adult world' (1978: 56, emphasis added), and all major transitional phases as *bridges*, or *boundary zones*, between two *states* of greater stability. Unresolved problems are described as '*baggage* from the past' (p. 322). The image of journey permeates our thinking about the life course. Do we 'know where we are going'? It is 'better to travel hopefully than to arrive'? It is one of the most pervasive images of life.

4 *Enduring suffering* It is a *sine qua non* of accounts of the life course that at least some degree of suffering, the fourth of Elsbree's plots, ensues as the fidelity of our life choices is tested and we face mounting pressure to change. Transitions inevitably involve breaking links with a past to which we are attached by affectional bonds and which, by definition, resist severance (Parkes, 1971). Similarly, the structure-changing periods in Levinson et al.'s model are described as periods of upheaval, both exciting and frightening, during which individuals must, among other things, confront and come to terms with their own limitations, flaws and mistakes.

5 *Pursuing consummation* Elsbree's final generic plot, that of pursuing consummation, is enshrined in many definitions of development proffered by life-span researchers. Thus Buhler (Buhler and Massarik, 1968), describes an 'effective' person as one who leads a goal-directed life, striving for self-fulfilment and self-actualization. Through this striving, basic needs can be transformed into life goals and, ideally, 'ultimate purposes'. Likewise, Levinson et al. identify as key developmental tasks of early adulthood the establishment of a Dream and the discovery of ways of living it out. This Dream 'has the quality of a vision, an imagined possibility that generates excitement and vitality' (1978: 91).

That many life stories fall short of full consummation is indicated in the emphasis within life-span and counselling psychology on the process rather than end state of development – one is a developing, not a developed person. Thus, Kaplan describes the concept of development as 'pertaining to a rarely, if ever, attained ideal' (1983: 188).

Several of Elsbree's generic plots may co-exist within the same story. A brief quote from Gould (1980) illustrates, in varying degrees, all of the above five plots. Gould describes personal growth as a search for security (illustrating the plot of maintaining a home), as a conflict (engaging in a contest), and a journey (to arrive somewhere new) in which we must endure suffering (through the disturbance of safety patterns) in order to pursue consummation (the license to be): 'As we expand our potential, we disturb the patterns within ourselves (our defensive system) and our relationship to those close to us. . . . That is why growth is a conflict – the disturbance of safety patterns; and that is why growth is more than learning and practicing new activities or changing by will power. It is a transformation of self in which we enlarge the license to be, only after going through mythical dangers in order to arrive at a new secure place that in turn will be left when the feelings of stagnation and claustrophobia initiate another cycle' (1980: 58). For Gould the thrust of adult development is towards a realization and acceptance of ourselves as creators of our own lives, and away from the assumption that the rules and standards of our childhood determine our destiny. Thus, whilst Levinson et al. talk of the evolving life structure, Gould talks of 'the evolution of adult consciousness as we release ourself from the constraints and ties of childhood consciousness' (1978: 15). He envisages this occurring as we sequentially correct the false assumptions we have lived by up until then, and which have restricted and restrained us unnecessarily.

Implications for practice

As life-span researchers seek to document, explain and enhance development over the life course they become involved in recording, co-constructing and interpreting the stories individuals create and use to describe and understand their lives. This is not too bad a definition of a counsellor either.

Indeed, Spence (1982) describes as the central mission of therapist and client the construction of the client's life story. In similar vein, McLeod (1996b) explores how counsellors 'work with narrative', and White and Epston (1990) talk of narrative means to therapeutic ends. Egan (1994) describes the first step of the first stage of counselling as helping clients tell their story. If the life story the client tells is problematic in some fundamental way then serious story repair, or rebiographing, may be indicated (Howard, 1991). Viney (1989), working from a personal construct perspective, describes psychotherapy as shared reconstruction. Rational-emotive therapy can be seen as an invitation to clients to create rational rather than irrational stories around their experience (Dryden, 1990). Life-review therapy (Lewis and Butler, 1974) is explicitly concerned with helping clients restructure their past into a positive and integrated story – a process that has much in common with Erikson's final developmental task: that of developing a sense of integrity.

Accounts of life-span development represent overarching meta-narratives against which a client's life can be referenced. A life-span perspective can also suggest developmental problems or issues that may occur during the life course (Rodgers, 1984). These can be thought of as some of the specific stories that form a part of the client's overall life story or narrative. The present discussions indicate that the following may be significant: lack of an articulated developmental goal; a disease rather than a developmental perspective on life events; a reluctance to let go of the past or present; inadequate management of earlier developmental tasks; deficient change management skills; and self-defeating life stories.

1 *Lack of an articulated developmental goal* Without a purpose or end state in relation to which events and experiences can be organized and

evaluated, no coherent personal narrative can be formed or maintained. Since this, in turn, 'leads to feelings of fragmentation and disintegration' (Cohler, 1982: 205), and since definitions of development are value-based statements, it suggests an important values clarification role for counsellors and counselling psychologists. Accounts of life-span development reflect culturally agreed definitions of development and development goals, and can provide a backcloth against which this work can be conducted.

2 *A disease rather than a developmental perspective on life events*   Despite the evidence that change and upheaval are features of the whole life course, we may, at least implicitly, expect adulthood to be a smooth rather than a bumpy ride. From this stance, disruptive life events are seen as undesirable deviations from, to use a colloquial expression, the straight and narrow. If they cannot be avoided, then they are treated almost as diseases, with interventions seeking to minimize their impact and bring the individual 'back on course' as quickly as possible (Danish et al., 1980). By way of contrast, a developmental orientation sees both positive and negative life events as an inevitable part of life, and views them as potential growth points.

3 *Reluctance to let go of the past, or present*   If a current way of life is rewarding and satisfying or, at the very least, providing the security of a familiar routine, then the temptation to resist internal and external pressures to change can be considerable. This is exacerbated when combined with the, probably implicit, erroneous assumption that it should not be necessary to change once adulthood is reached. Appreciation of the rhythms and patterns of life-span development enables counsellors to be involved in helping clients, first, to become aware of the age-graded expectations of their society, and, secondly, to create their own individualized goals in relation to this (Rodgers, 1984). This does not imply conforming to all social expectations and age-norms, but rather that adherence to and deviation from them should be undertaken consciously, with consideration being given to the likely impact of so doing. The life events and developmental tasks that comprise a society's age-grade system operate as 'a kind of culturally specific guidance system' (Reinert, 1980: 17), and clients can be helped to choose whether to challenge or comply with its dictates.

4 *Inadequate management of earlier developmental tasks*   To the extent it is accepted that development is cumulative, then present problems may result, at least in part, from inadequate or incomplete resolution of earlier developmental issues. Thus, Erikson (1980) suggests that the abandonment of self that is necessary to resolve successfully the crisis of Intimacy

v. Isolation is not possible until the crisis of Identity *v*. Role confusion has been addressed to the extent that the individual has a secure sense of who he or she is. Counsellors may need therefore to address issues emanating from outside clients' current life stage – both issues from earlier stages which may have been ignored or need reworking, and issues likely to arise in the future and which clients may wish to prepare for.

5 *Deficient change management skills*   If it is accepted that the life course is characterized by a regular need to initiate and/or respond to change, but that this is not necessarily recognized or accepted by clients, then it seems likely that many individuals will lack the skills needed to manage such changes. Transition management, goal-setting, action planning and implementation – with all their associated techniques of brainstorming, force-field analysis, prioritizing etc. – become potentially relevant issues for counsellors to address with clients.

6 *Self-defeating life stories*   Perhaps the most important and overarching benefit of adopting a life-span perspective is that it directs attention to the stories clients tell, and the way these stories are constructed, reviewed and reconstructed. 'As persons talk about their experiences, past events are reconstructed in a manner congruent with current understandings; the present is explained with reference to the reconstructed past; and both are used to generate expectations about the future' (Gergen, 1988: 108). This act of construing the narrative can be looked upon as a therapeutic exercise. The role of the counsellor is to facilitate this process, and work with the client to produce self-empowering rather than self-defeating or self-limiting stories (Viney, 1993).

In sum, the metaphor of the story can be used to describe the key theme of this chapter: life as the stories we create and live by; psychological disturbance as stories awry and incoherent; and counselling as exercises in story repair and reconstruction (Howard, 1991). Cultural differences can be understood in terms of differences in the preferred stories 'habitually entertained by ethnic, class, racial and cultural groups' (Howard, 1991: 187). An understanding of the rhythm and pattern of the life course can help counsellors and counselling psychologists become aware of how factors such as age, gender, educational level, occupation and culture influence the way individuals see the world (Thomas, 1990). The stories of many subgroups in society – women, ethnic minorities, the mentally ill, the elderly – are silenced or distorted. A task for both life-span psychology and counselling psychology is to encourage the powerless to tell their tales, both to confer a clear and constructive sense of identity on the teller, and to be instrumental in expanding a society's definition of acceptable narratives.

References

Allport, G.W. (1964) *Pattern and Growth in Personality*. New York: Holt, Rinehart and Winston.

Baltes, P.B. (1987) 'Theoretical propositions of life-span developmental psychology: on the dynamics between growth and decline', *Developmental Psychology*, 23: 611–26.

Baltes, P.B., Reese, H.W. and Lipsitt, L.P. (1980) 'Life-span developmental psychology', *Annual Review of Psychology*, 31: 65–110.

Bettelheim, B. (1976) *The Uses of Enchantment: the Meaning and Importance of Fairy Tales*. New York: Knopf.

British Association for Counselling (1993) *Code of Ethics and Practice for Counsellors*. Rugby, Warwickshire: BAC.

Bronfenbrenner, U. (1977) 'Toward an experimental ecology of human development', *American Psychologist*, 32: 513–31.

Buhler, C. and Massarik, F. (eds) (1968) *The Course of Human Life: a Study of Goals in the Humanistic Perspective*. New York: Springer.

Chickering, A.W. and Havighurst, R.J. (1981) 'The life cycle', in A.W. Chickering et al. (eds), *The Modern American College: Responding to the New Realities of Diverse Students and a Changing Society*. San Francisco, CA: Jossey Bass.

Cohler, B.J. (1982) 'Personal narrative and the life course', in P.B. Baltes and O.G. Brim (eds), *Life-Span Development and Behavior*, vol. 4. New York: Academic Press.

Danish, S.J., Smyer, M.A. and Nowak, C. (1980) 'Developmental intervention: enhancing life-event processes', in P.B. Baltes and O.G. Brim (eds), *Life-Span Development and Behavior*, vol. 3. New York: Academic Press.

Datan, N. (1983) 'Normative or not? Confessions of a fallen epistemologist', in E.J. Callahan and K.A. McKluskey (eds), *Life-Span Developmental Psychology: Non-normative Life Crises*. New York: Academic Press.

Datan, N., Rodeheaver, D. and Hughes, F. (1987) 'Adult development and aging', *Annual Review of Psychology*, 38: 153–80.

Davies, N.Z. (1985) *The Return of Martin Guerre*. Harmondsworth: Penguin.

Dowd, J.D. (1990) 'Ever since Durkheim: the socialization of human development', *Human Development*, 33, 138–59.

Dryden, W. (1990) *Rational-Emotive Counselling in Action*. London: Sage.

Egan, G.E. (1994) *The Skilled Helper*, 5th edn. Monterey, CA: Brooks/Cole.

Elsbree, L. (1982) *The Rituals of Life: Patterns in Narrative*. New York: Kennikat.

Epstein, S. (1991) 'Cognitive-experiential self theory: implications for developmental psychology', in M.R. Gunnar and L.A. Stroufe (eds), *Self Process and Development: the Minnesota Symposium on Child Development*, vol. 23. Hillsdale, NJ: Lawrence Erlbaum.

Erikson, E.H. (1980) *Identity and the Life Cycle: a Reissue*. New York: Norton.

Ford, D.H. and Lerner, R.M. (1992) *Developmental Systems Theory: an Integrative Approach*. London: Sage.

Freeman, M. (1984) 'History, narrative, and life-span developmental knowledge', *Human Development*, 27: 1–19.

Frye, N. (1957) *Anatomy of Criticism*. Princeton, NJ: Princeton University Press.

Gergen, M.M. (1988) 'Narrative structures in social explanation', in C. Antaki (ed.), *Analysing Everyday Explanation: a Casebook of Methods*. London: Sage.

Gottfredson, L.S. (1981) 'Circumscription and compromise: a developmental theory of occupational aspirations', *Journal of Counseling Psychology Monograph*, 28: 545–79.

Gould, R.L. (1978) *Transformations: Growth and Change in Adult Life*. New York: Simon and Schuster.

Gould, R.L. (1980) 'Transformational tasks in adulthood', in S.I. Greenspan and G.H. Pollock (eds), *The Course of Life: Psychoanalytic Contributions Toward Understanding Personality Development*, vol. III. *Adulthood and the Aging Process*. Washington, DC: National Institute of Mental Health.

Holland, J. (1973) *Making Vocational Choices*. Englewood Cliffs, NJ: Prentice Hall.

Hopson, B. and Scally, M. (1980) *Lifeskills Teaching*. London: McGraw-Hill.

Howard, G.S. (1991) 'Culture tales: a narrative approach to thinking, cross-cultural psychology, and psychotherapy', *American Psychologist*, 46: 187–97.

Jung, C.G. (1972) 'The transcendent function', in H. Read, M. Fordham, G. Adler and W. McGuire (eds), *The Structure and Dynamics of the Psyche*, 2nd edn. Volume 8 of *The Collected Works of C.G. Jung*. London: Routledge.

Kaplan, B. (1983) 'A trio of trials', in R.M. Lerner (ed.), *Developmental Psychology: Historical and Philosophical Perspectives*. Hillsdale, NJ: Lawrence Erlbaum.

Kluckhohn, C., Murray, H.A. and Schneider, D.M. (1953) *Personality in Nature, Society and Culture*. New York: Knopf.

Kohli, M. and Meyer, J.W. (eds) (1986) 'Social structure and social construction of life stages', *Human Development*, 29: 145–80.

Levinson, D.J. (1986) 'A conception of adult development', *American Psychologist*, 42: 3–13.

Levinson, D.J., Darrow, D.N., Klein, E.B., Levinson, M.H. and McKee, B. (1978) *The Seasons of a Man's Life*. New York: Knopf.

Lewis, M.I. and Butler, R.N. (1974) 'Life review therapy: putting memories to work in individual and group psychotherapy', *Geriatrics*, 29: 165–74.

Loehlin, J.C. (1989) 'Partitioning environmental and genetic contributions to behavioral development', *American Psychologist*, 44: 1285–92.

Mair, M. (1988) 'Psychology as storytelling', *International Journal of Personal Construct Psychology*, 1: 125–38.

Maslow, A.H. (1970) *Toward a Psychology of Being*, 2nd edn. New York: Van Nostrand Reinhold.

McAdams, D. (1985) *Power, Intimacy and the Life Cycle*. Homewood, IL: Dorsey.

McLeod, J. (1996a) 'The emerging narrative approach to counselling and psychotherapy', *British Journal of Guidance and Counselling*, 24: (forthcoming).

McLeod, J. (1996b) 'Working with narrative', in R. Bayne, I. Horton and J. Brimrose (eds), *New Directions in Counselling*. London: Routledge.

Murray, K. (1986) 'Literary pathfinding: the work of popular life constructors', in T.R. Sarbin (ed.), *Narrative Psychology: the Storied Nature of Human Conduct*. New York: Praeger.

Neugarten, B.L. (1977) 'Adaptation and the life cycle', in N.K. Schlossberg and A.D. Entine (eds), *Counseling Adults*. Monterey, CA: Brooks/Cole.

Parkes, C.M. (1971) 'Psycho-social transitions: a field for study', *Social Science and Medicine*, 5: 101–15.

Pervin, L.A. and Lewis, M. (1978) 'Overview of the internal–external issue', in L.A. Pervin and M. Lewis (eds), *Perspectives in Interactional Psychology*. New York: Plenum.

Plomin, R. (1989) 'Environment and genes', *American Psychologist*, 44: 105–11.

Reese, H.W. (1976) 'Conceptions of the active organism', *Human Development*, 19: 108–19.

Reinert, G. (1980) 'Educational psychology in the context of the human life span', in P.B. Baltes and O.G. Brim (eds), *Life-Span Development and Behavior*, vol. 3. New York: Academic Press.

Ricoeur, P. (1984) *Time and Narrative*, vol. 1. Chicago, IL: University of Chicago Press.

Roberts, K. and Parsell, G. (1992) 'Entering the labour market in Britain: the survival of traditional opportunity structures', *Sociological Review*, 40: 726–53.

Rodgers, R.F. (1984) 'Theories of adult development: research status and counseling implications', in S.D. Brown and R.W. Lent (eds), *Handbook of Counseling Psychology*. Chichester: Wiley.

Rogers, C.R. (1967) *On Becoming a Person*. London: Constable.

Scarr, S. (1992) 'Developmental theories for the 1990s: development and individual differences', *Child Development*, 63: 1–19.

Schlossberg, N.K., Troll, L.E. and Leibowitz, Z. (1977) *Perspectives on Counseling Adults: Issues and Skills*. Monterey, CA: Brooks/Cole.

Sheehy, G. (1974) *Passages: Predictable Crises of Adult Life*. New York: Dutton.

Spence, D.P. (1982) *Narrative Truth and Historical Truth: Meaning and Interpretation in Psychoanalysis*. New York: Norton.

Super, D.E. (1980) 'A life-span, life-space approach to career development', *Journal of Vocational Behavior*, 16: 282–98.

Taylor, S.E., Aspinwall, L.G., Giuliano, T.A., Dakof, G.A. and Reardon, K.K. (1993) 'Storytelling and coping with stressful life events', *Journal of Applied Social Psychology*, 23: 703–33.

Thomas, R.M. (1990) *Counseling and Life-Span Development*. Newbury Park, CA: Sage.

Viney, L.L. (1989) 'Psychotherapy as shared reconstruction', *International Journal of Personal Construct Psychology*, 3: 423–42.

Viney, L.L. (1993) *Life Stories: Personal Construct Therapy with the Elderly*. Chichester: Wiley.

Viney, L.L. and Bousefield, L. (1991) 'Narrative analysis: a technique for psychosocial research in AIDS', *Social Science and Medicine*, 32: 756–65.

White, M. and Epston, D. (1990) *Narrative Means to Therapeutic Ends*. New York: Dutton.

14

Psychological Counselling of Children and Young People

Jim Downey

A typical referral to the counselling psychologist working with children can be used to illustrate some of the central issues in this field of work.

> A mother has sought referral of her three children for psychological counselling. In the first session she explains each child's behaviour has changed, becoming challenging or worrying since she and their father separated some months ago. From her description, each child is behaving quite differently and independent of each other. None of the children has asked to be referred and one of them has actually said she does not wish to see anyone. The mother's request, however, is that you will help the children to talk through their upset and help them accept the separation and imminent divorce of their parents.

In psychological terms the family has suffered a 'loss event', probably traumatic and unexpected for the children if not the mother. We could safely predict all family members will also be struggling with the increased stress of sudden change, the loss of familiar patterns and routines and possibly continuing conflict between the parents.

Depending on each child's developmental status and their position in the family, it is possible each will have a different experience and understanding of the separation of their parents, the present circumstances etc. The mother's request raises the following issues.

1   **What is the most effective focus for intervention?** Do you immediately take the children on as clients and pursue the therapeutic goals outlined by the parent or do you investigate the possibility of increasing the mother's understanding of her children's adjustment reactions and needs and offer some practical advice on 'good' post-divorce parental arrangements.

2   **Is there evidence to support the selection of particular therapeutic approaches?** If you do see the children and assess them to be in need of specialist help, what treatment approaches are

likely to be most effective in facilitating positive change? This decision requires knowledge of the research into treatment efficacy.

3 **What are the implications for therapy of developmental status differences between children?** The three children are of different ages and psychological capacities. How could this affect the choice of approach?

Other issues arise too, such as being clear about who is the client; about children having the right to refuse therapy; and about the need to establish with everyone the limits to confidentiality in child work. However, the first three questions are repeatedly posed by child work and before any individual therapy can begin the counselling psychologist must make decisions in relation to each. These questions will be examined and developed across the chapter through reference to the scientific and developmental literature.

Plan of the chapter

The chapter falls into three broad sections, the first relating to issues concerned with identifying the most effective focus for intervention, a second section which looks at the scientific support for particular forms of therapy and a final section which reviews developmental changes of childhood and the implication of such changes for choice of therapy.

Before proceeding to the first section, however, there are a number of introductory points to be made followed by a brief consideration of the differences between children and adults in therapy.

Introductory remarks

Children and young people, up to the age of 18 years, represent 20–25 per cent of the total UK population.

Various epidemiological studies (see Cox and Rutter, 1985 for review) indicate that between 5 and 15 per cent of all children exhibit emotional or behavioural disturbance which affects their everyday life. Less pervasive difficulties such as isolated fears, sleeping difficulties, etc. are at still higher levels of prevalence. Within this broad sub-population of troubled children relatively few would attract a formal psychiatric diagnosis. Nevertheless, they will be frequently referred for help and usually, on assessment, deemed to require psychological input of one kind or another. It is this broad and ill-defined group of children to which the counselling child psychologist must provide a service.

The potential scope suggested by the title to this chapter more readily invites a book than a chapter and to offer any introductory account that might be of use to the counselling psychologist seeing children from this massively varied child population, allows only a few key areas to be covered. The range of psychological treatment approaches available to the counselling psychologist responding to difficulties of childhood is highly diverse. However, if the approaches are categorized according to their principal treatment focus they may be summarized as falling into four main categories. **Community approaches** (e.g. school, neighbourhood), **family approaches**, **group approaches** and **individual approaches**. This chapter has been asked to concentrate on therapeutic approaches offered to *individual* children, approaches which have also received support and validation from scientific studies. Unfortunately this still does not leave room for any detailed account of therapeutic approaches, neither can any attempt be made to describe the treatment of particular childhood presentations. The central supra-theoretical theme which will be addressed is that of developmental change and its relevance to the understanding of childhood difficulties and the selection of therapeutic approaches and methods. The developmental perspective is paramount for effective and sensitive work with children and their families. It not only incorporates a body of knowledge concerning changes in the cognitive and social capacity of children but also offers a way of conceptualizing the responses of children to their experiences. This provides a framework for assessment and intervention activities irrespective of age, gender, experience or difficulty. In addition it should assist in the making of clinical decisions in respect of the level and focus of therapeutic effort.

Finally, it is important to say that this chapter is primarily written for and about children who are receiving a 'good-enough' caring experience but whose developmental progress is at some level of risk, for example, poor negotiation of a stage or task of family or social development. More severely damaged children, whose care experience has been seriously inadequate or abusive, require a more specialized account than the one which can be given here.

The child in therapy

A consideration of some of the essential differences between child and adult work will be beneficial to the counselling psychologist faced with the questions raised above.

The counselling psychologist new to child work needs to be aware of two common errors which occur when adult therapists meet child clients. First there is a tendency to assume childhood distress and dysfunction is the same in its origin and experience as it is for adults (adultomorphic tendency). Secondly, there is a temptation to assume all children are psychologically alike and can therefore be treated in the same way (developmental uniformity myth). Once identified, it is tempting to believe the possibility of committing these errors has been removed. However, the ability to avoid these misperceptions is not based on good intent but on good developmental understanding.

Therapeutic work with adults is based on a range of assumptions, differently described and emphasized depending on clinical model and approach but at or near their centre is a proposition which holds that personal autonomy and choice is possible at the level of individual action.

The validity of this proposition, notwithstanding the challenges and caveats from moral, political and philosophical schools, depends upon the presence of an easily overlooked cognitive capacity: the capacity to render one's own behaviour, thoughts and feelings the subject of personal examination. A related but even more sophisticated cognitive capacity is further assumed in adult work, the capacity to 'step outside' one's own intimate social context in order that relationships, shared beliefs and meanings can also be examined. Much of adult therapy is directed towards a point where the client can exercise these 'capacities' to their personal psychological benefit, for example, through making new personal choices based on increased insight, awareness or understanding of their position.

For the counselling psychologist working with children it is vital that they recognize the capacity for self-reflection is a developmental acquisition born of biological maturation, social experience and cognitive development. Nor are the capacities suddenly present, but like all developmental capacities they emerge over extended time, becoming more robust, reliable and universally available to the child as use and experience establishes them.

Attention to a particular child's developmental capacity for self-reflection must therefore be an early consideration in any direct work undertaken. Clearly the robust presence, early emergence or absence of a self-reflective capacity has serious and practical implications for the way therapy is conducted and for the therapeutic interventions considered appropriate and accessible for a given child.

A second and related issue of crucial relevance to direct child work is the need to recognize, and where possible work with the child's primary social context, usually the family. Unlike adults, children are usually in no position, socially or psychologically, to 'leave' their family. The family is the social system which guides, controls and informs the child's development. It is from within the family that the child develops an idea of their own personal value, abilities and aspirations. Even as the child matures, personally and socially, and encounters extra-familial 'ideas', they are processed through their family's ideological 'filter'. In a very real sense the ideas and suggestions of the counselling psychologist may only have as much 'influence' as the child's family can tolerate or allow. It is vital therefore that the counselling psychologist develops an awareness of and stays respectful to the child's family values, beliefs and practices.

Lastly, a number of more general points can be made about the child in therapy which may render its practice different from typical adult therapy. It is relatively rare for children of any age to refer themselves for therapy. They are invariably referred by others. This difference in referral raises questions about the child's motivation for therapeutic work and their acceptance or understanding of therapeutic goals. The child must therefore find therapy intrinsically interesting if he or she is to be engaged. The use of play activities is one means of engaging the child's interest. They also provide an often essential non-verbal means of communication for the child whose verbal facility and comfort with extensive conversational exchange will be more restricted than an adult client's.

In summary then, the child may be an unwilling, unsuspecting or unmotivated client whose commitment and interest in therapeutic work may be very low. In therapy sessions they will require verbal and non-verbal communication options. The goals and methods of therapy must be commensurate with the child's developmental competence and ability. Finally, the child is so dependent on and psychologically captive to his or her family and wider context that it is only in exceptionally rare circumstances that the child can be 'treated' in isolation.

The focus of intervention

Individual psychotherapeutic work with children has a long history and whatever the actual therapeutic approach, the shared basic assumption is that through direct contact with the child the therapist can provide a corrective experience (catharsis, insight, reconditioning behaviour, re-structuring cognitions, etc.) which will lessen or remove the child's difficulties. However, questions about the effectiveness or wisdom of seeing children in isolation were increasingly raised during the 1960s, 1970s and 1980s (see Gelfand et al., 1982). There is evidence now that the vast majority of child therapists, practising in the USA or UK, routinely see a need to involve the child's parents at some level in the treatment process (Koocher and Pedulla, 1977).

An applied appreciation of child development is critical to the under-standing of child problems, the choice of therapeutic method and the evaluation of change. Children's needs and sensitivities vary with age, gender and experience, as does their vulnerability to different types of difficulty. The clinical and social significance of specific behaviours also changes with development and age. However, it is wholly inadequate to consider the child in isolation from the context in which their development and behaviour is occurring. Although the course of both normal and dysfunctional development is still poorly understood, it is clear that child behaviour and development is directly and indirectly influenced according to complex contextual relationships. Many studies have confirmed there is a very strong association between the psychological well-being of children and the characteristics of their family and wider context (Fauber et al., 1990). A plausible hypothesis is that most contextual variables ultimately have their impact on children through some disturbance in family process, and more specifically, in disrupted parenting practices.

The 'Goodness of Fit' model proposed by Chess and Thomas (1984) makes connections between child and context and provides the therapist with a practical framework for conceptualizing a child's presented difficulty. The central proposition of the model holds that high levels of consonance between the child and his or her environment potentiates optimal positive development. Where the demands and expectations of the environment consistently exceed the child's capacities, motivations and behavioural style, the potential for maladaptive patterns of functioning and distortions in development is present. The primary objectives of human behaviour are conceived by the model as relating to social competence and task mastery goals where, in interactive fashion, progress towards one type of goal influences the child's progress towards the other. Changes in environmental demand on the child which are marginally ahead of current functioning will produce stress in the child–environment relationship which can be resolved through an extension of personal skills. Such mastery experiences are perceived as positive in nature and contribute to a positive sense of self. Repeated failure experiences can lead to chronic stress which the child will seek relief from but through strategies of impulse and avoidance rather than mastery. The result is likely to be reduced social competence and a weakening of self-esteem.

The Goodness of Fit formulation helps structure a strategy of intervention that includes an assessment of the child's motivations, abilities and temperament, their behaviour patterns and their consequences, plus the expectations, demands and limitations of the environment. In all cultures children encounter points of transition which have been set by custom, belief and native awareness of when children are ready to meet a new demand. For instance, in Great Britain school entry is determined by many factors unrelated to child development, but at 3 years plus it is also timed to coincide with the child's increasing ability to tolerate extended separation from primary and intimate carers. The success with which individual children meet the challenge varies enormously, dependent as it is on the child's temperament, early preparatory experiences, school and family response to the child's adjustment behaviour, and so on. The outcome is that most children master the challenge and become more competent, independent and confident about themselves. Unfortunately some considerable few experience enormous difficulties in making the adjustment and their future social development can be placed in jeopardy.

Not all challenges arise out of societal or familial traditions. For instance, although divorce is an increasingly common experience for children, it is a non-normative event and as such is not timed to coincide with the child's ability to cope with the impact. It is clear from the research (e.g. Hetherington, 1989) that children in different developmental phases are likely to respond in ways which can be understood in terms of their developmental capacities, individual temperamental style and personal experiences. The research further indicates that the child's adjustment to the divorce event can be greatly influenced, for good or bad, by their parents' actions, availability and sensitivity to the child's need before and after the parental separation. Similar patterns of interactional change have been noted at other transition points in family life, for example bereavement, and found to be predictive of child adjustment.

The Family Life Cycle model (Carter and McGoldrick, 1989) attempts to describe the normative and non-normative transitions of family life. As with any developmental model, it suggests different families will negotiate different transitions more or less adaptively in terms of present and future functioning. The model requires the clinician to consider the child's presenting difficulty against the family's own developmental stage and current tasks. In a family where marital breakdown has occurred, for instance, the developmental tasks of individual children may be compromised or completely undermined by the changes in marital and parental functioning. The effects may be relatively short-lived or become persisting maladaptive patterns, for example a child assuming the role of parental confidant may have difficulties pursuing social independence goals. It can be seen that the utility of the Goodness of Fit framework and Family Life Cycle model are restricted only by the counselling psychologist's ability to move from a knowledge of the general to an ideographic appraisal of the particular child and his or her context.

The point to be emphasized is that in all child work cases the psychologist must pay serious heed to contextual variables. Any adequate formulation of childhood difficulties must acknowledge and include the dynamic and reciprocal relationships between children and their environment. Assessing for the presence of maladaptive family or parent–child 'interactions' is an important step in assessing the child's presented problem. Where such patterns are found to be present then a fundamental goal of any intervention must be to promote a change in the dysfunctional patterns. However, the counselling psychologist must still decide whether this is best achieved via work with an individual child, the parent(s), the parent and child, or the family. The final decision will depend on more than simply where the formulation indicates change is required. Another critical factor which must be taken into account is the expectation of therapy held by various family members. For instance, Houts et al. (1985) suggest that in some cases individual child therapy may be the only therapeutic option available if the parents are unwilling or unable to define the difficulty as a family, or even a parent–child problem. (See Street et al., 1991, for another way of responding to this dilemma.) Whether individual child work is decided by formulatory design or familial expectation, the therapeutic approach selected should ideally have a proven efficacy and be compatible with the child's developmental abilities and individual temperamental style.

The effectiveness of child therapies

A vast array of psychological therapies are reported in the child therapy literature but many are poorly described and most have not been seriously or scientifically evaluated. Notwithstanding the problems of definition (what constitutes psychotherapy) and measurement (what constitutes effectiveness) advances toward the identification of effective treatments have been particularly slow because of the complexity of child work. Issues of developmental change, individual variation, problem co-morbidity, the diversity of parent and family arrangements as well as the wide contextual variation in which child behaviour and development is located all contribute to the field's complexity. Furthermore, current research methodology is unable fully to identify and encompass the multi-level and multi-componented nature of interventions. This reduces the clinical validity of most studies, making it impossible to assert with any confidence that changes in the child's functioning are attributable to the individual work done with him or her. Moreover, research into treatment effectiveness has to date been predominantly concerned with the question of which treatments are demonstrably superior to other treatments.

Despite the overriding research interest in outcome and treatment superiority there is little that can be said for certain in either area. The research is typically found to evidence one or more of the following methodological flaws:

- Use of small, unspecified samples.
- Absence of control groups.
- Use of global outcome measures only.

- Failure to monitor the integrity of treatment.
- The absence of meaningful follow-up.

Nevertheless, until fairly recently there seemed to be a growing case from meta-analytic reviews (e.g. Weisz et al., 1987) to support the assertion that behavioural approaches are superior to more psychotherapeutic (emphasis on relationship and process of therapy) approaches across age levels, treated problems and levels of therapist experience. However, yet more recent meta-analytic studies (e.g. Barnnett et al., 1991) have challenged the validity of such a claim for superiority. In essence the case is made that behavioural approaches, developed as they are from the empirical scientific model, produce studies that usually satisfy methodological requirements better than psychotherapeutic studies. Barnnett et al. (1991) argue that the comparisons then made between behavioural and psychotherapeutic studies are invalid since their differing methodological rigour makes then non-comparable. Shirk and Russell (1992) add their support to this view, saying the comparison of treatment approaches is premature and on a number of criteria biased in favour of behavioural studies.

Behavioural and cognitive approaches

There is more empirical research evaluating the effectiveness of behavioural methods in child work than any other clinical approach. (As an approach, it lends itself more readily to empirical evaluation.) However, the majority of studies are not of direct individual work with children but of triadic work. That is to say, the therapist works essentially with the parent who receives advice on how changes in their own behaviour will lead to desired changes in the child's behaviour. Thus the parent–child dyad is the unit of analysis, the parental input is changed through education and coaching and the child may never be directly engaged by the therapist (e.g. Herbert and Iwaniec, 1981). Nevertheless there are also many well-controlled single-case studies in the behavioural literature which demonstrate the effectiveness of this clinical approach in direct work with individual children.

The clearest examples of effectiveness are usually found in clinical cases where anxieties and fears are the symptom to be addressed. Behavioural methods of *in vivo* exposure, modelling and various self-control strategies are all shown to be helpful (Ollendick and King, 1991). Other commonly treated problems with which behavioural methods are shown to be effective are anger management, social and interpersonal skills training. In spite of the generally supportive evidence it is important to note that the clinical literature plainly acknowledges the unpredictability of the effectiveness of behavioural interventions at an individual level.

Cognitive-behavioural therapy (CBT) emphasizes learning processes and the centrality of the individual's cognitive style in the remediation of psychological distress. Interventions are designed to change detrimental, maladaptive cognitions and cognitive styles that children may be developing. The approach offers the child active strategies and alternative cognitions which introduce more adaptive and individually beneficial styles.

Single-case and group comparison studies indicate CBT is effective in the treatment of a number of common childhood problems. For instance, impulsivity is addressed through the teaching of self-instructional talk and problem-solving skills. Anxious children are assisted through a combination of treatment strategies including systematic desensitization and relaxation training, modelling and the development of more helpful cognitions, e.g. cognitive restructuring where misperceptions and negative evaluative biases are challenged and replaced by more positive cognitions and images. As in adult therapy, however, it is with depressed children (usually adolescents) that CBT has been most frequently examined and found to be effective. A typical treatment might incorporate cognitive restructuring of maladaptive cognitions, the development of a coping template through the teaching of various self-control skills (self-monitoring, self-consequation, self-evaluation) and social skills training. Kendall (1993) provides a thorough review of the approach and its proven utility.

Of all the therapeutic approaches used directly with children it would appear the cognitive-behavioural is now the best supported by studies of treatment effectiveness. However, even here doubts have been recently raised over whether CBT's effectiveness does actually rest upon changes in faulty cognitions. Powell and Oei (1991) reviewed 63 clinical studies which applied a CBT approach and found only a small minority attempted to document the changes in cognitions that were assumed to have occurred. Most preferred to measure behavioural change and not one of the 63 studies could claim changes in cognition were causally responsible for the positive outcomes.

Psychotherapeutic approaches

Many therapeutic activities attract the title 'child psychotherapy' by which is usually implied, at minimum, that the child–therapist relationship is the primary 'instrument' for promoting change in feelings and behaviour of the child. However, variation in practice or emphasis appears then to revolve around at least three dimensions: the degree to which treatment is directive or non-directive, interpretative or supportive, and conducted principally through verbal discourse or indirect communication.

Whatever its form, clinical evidence for the usefulness of child psychotherapy is most abundant at the level of descriptive clinical case report. Very few rigorous empirical studies of psychotherapeutic approaches have actually been conducted and their scientific legitimacy has, surprisingly, yet to be established. A relatively untypical recent clinical study (Moran et al., 1991) may mark the way for future research in this area. Rather than simply describing session material, clinical impressions etc., as is the usual case, this study examined the impact of individual psychoanalysis on the treatment outcome of children being medically treated for poor diabetic control. The study reports the children receiving individual psychoanalysis fared significantly better than children who were treated in a routine medical manner. However, the study, whilst commendable for attempting to meet scientific criteria, also illustrates the frequent methodological shortcoming of clinical evaluations of psychotherapy. The absence of a true control group, psychological interventions at various levels, that is child, parental and nursing staff, inadequate description of psychological treatments etc., all reduce the power of the study such that it cannot claim to have shown the effectiveness of psychoanalysis.

A point worth making, despite the paucity of convincing research, is that a very large proportion of child therapists will openly acknowledge that psychotherapeutic methods and concepts influence their formulation of a case and their broad therapeutic approach (such as establishment of a good relationship with the child, the awareness of unconscious motivation, an interest in the process of therapy) if not their specific interventive inputs.

Therapy effectiveness: summary

The meagre conclusions which have been drawn from the meta-analysis of treatment effectiveness studies (e.g. Weisz et al., 1987), are that:

- Psychotherapy in any form is better than no-treatment for a large number of childhood problems, including anxiety, aggression, social withdrawal etc.
- Differences in treatment effectiveness tend to favour behavioural over non-behavioural approaches. (With the caveat that non-behavioural approaches may have suffered an unjust comparison in such meta-analyses.)

In addition, it would seem that with short-term therapy contacts (the vast majority of child therapeutic work), superior gains are likelier to be achieved where:

- specific techniques for change are used;
- treatment goals are explicit and defined;
- intervention focus is on overt behaviour;
- therapeutic focus is on the present rather than on the past.

Therapist characteristics

Even less can be said about the therapist characteristics associated with good therapy. Kolvin et al. (1981), in one of the few studies to examine this area in any detail, reported therapists rated as extrovert, assertive and open were more likely to be associated with positive treatment outcome. More traditional therapist characteristics such as empathy, warmth and genuineness were not. It would seem unwise therefore to assume that what holds for adult therapy, in terms of therapist characteristics and non-specific core conditions, will also hold for child therapy. However, many agree that effective therapy is more likely where:

- The therapist has received formal training in therapy and the psychological formulation of contextual and developmental factors.
- The therapist has flexible interpersonal relationship skills; capable of being active, directive and controlling when required and of being non-directive, supportive and passive when appropriate.
- The therapist engenders a positive expectation of therapy in the child.

Child characteristics

What every clinical research study reveals and every clinician knows is that no single therapeutic approach is effective for every child; individual differences in responsiveness are always found. Clearly many factors may contribute to this phenomenon, including the nature and characteristics of the problem, contextual variables, and individual characteristics of the child, such as gender, age and ability.

At present relatively little solid research evidence exists, though meta-analytic evaluation of therapeutic effectiveness studies suggests the child's developmental ability and the nature of the child's difficulty are likely to be related to treatment efficacy. For instance, Blagg (1992), in a review of psychodynamic and behavioural approaches to school refusal, reports that the treatment outcome is consistently good for children between 7 and 10 years irrespective of the treatment approach. However, for older children (11–16 years) the outcome is far less predictable, tending to be less successful and more dependent upon the type of treatment used.

Concluding remarks

The counselling psychologist is left with a mass of research evidence which does not provide clear evidence of treatment superiority (only of the broad effectiveness of most approaches); nor the therapist characteristics which are necessary for psychological change. Nevertheless, the responsible counselling psychologist must in his or her therapeutic practice attempt to maximize the value of what is known. In the field of child work this means combining knowledge about child development, knowledge of research findings in specific areas, e.g. divorce, bereavement etc., and knowledge about effective treatments.

Differences in developmental capacity

In this final section the broad phases of childhood will be reviewed in light of their dominant developmental characteristics. It will then be possible to consider what implication a child's developmental capacities have for the choice of therapeutic method. The counselling psychologist must be able to contemplate a child's behaviour and presentation in terms of that child's developmental resources and competencies. Developmental psychology has greatly extended our understanding of the cognitive and social changes of childhood but the counselling psychologist must remain aware that each child's developmental profile is unique and that normative data can only be used as a point of comparison for any given child. In particular it must be appreciated that a child's environment and experiences may accelerate or delay a particular child's ability or behaviour in any given area. For example, if the three children in our earlier divorce scenario had already experienced a previous parental divorce, their understanding of its significance and their vocabulary for describing the event would probably be more 'sophisticated' than a sibship of similar ages who were experiencing divorce for the first time. Furthermore, and a vital point for the clinician to keep in mind is that although the developmental changes to be outlined are usually associated with particular phases and age periods of childhood, it would be a serious error to believe this must be so. Individual children will reveal erratic levels of developmental functioning, sometimes ahead and sometimes behind what might be expected from other aspects of their behaviour. Most reliable of all is that under conditions of high personal stress there will be a tendency for the child to function at social and cognitive levels lower than would otherwise be the case.

It was proposed earlier that two central requirements of adult therapies are the capacity to self-reflect and the capacity to 'step-out' of one's immediate context and to imagine alternative possible arrangements. These socio-cognitive developmental capacities cannot be assumed to be available to children in therapy or, where they are in evidence, that they are as robust or as complete as they are for mature adults. It is primarily with these capacities in mind that the broad phases of childhood development will be reviewed.

Infancy and early childhood

In the early years the developing child needs the experience of a primary attachment relationship(s) which, when adequate, provides the child with:

- a sense of safety (security, stability, predictability);
- a sense of being positively valued;
- a sense of personal competence.

The scope for relationship variation in meeting these developmental requirements is vast and very many patterns of relationship are found. Nevertheless, serious deviations and inadequacies do occur and will pose a significant threat to the child's positive developmental progress. Chronic, adverse experiences, rather than brief trauma, are most assuredly predictive of poor developmental outcome and where such chronic patterns exist, every effort must be made to assist family and parent to achieve change which improves the general context and specifically the quality of relationship between child and parents.

In those cases where the child must be removed from family at a very young age there is, in the research evidence available, much room for optimism (see Schaffer, 1990, for a review). The young child's capacity for entering new attachment relationships is relatively malleable and even very damaged children late into their childhood can be greatly assisted by being offered alternative caring relationships.

In terms of self-awareness and self-knowledge, the very young child cannot yet look at what he or she knows but 'knows' more than they can articulate (Flavell, 1985). They 'know' what is familiar in their routinized social and physical 'world' and they know how to 'be' in various situations and in their intimate relationships. If any major and significant part of their world or relationships should change, they are likely to evidence negative affective arousal and lowered behaviour control for a period afterwards. The reasons for parental or professional concern about such distress are usually linked to its behavioural form, its intensity, its duration or its inexplicability.

321

Early school years (4–7 years)

The emergence, intensification or redefinition of behaviour patterns may mark any transition and lead to a referral for psychological therapy. The 4–7-year-old experiences a rapid increase in extrafamilial contacts on entry to school. The transition coincides with the child's cultural preparation and developmental readiness for increased social independence, extended separations from family, entry into new relationships and the capacity to adapt to new rules and roles. Its successful negotiation depends upon the child's progress towards a central developmental task of this age period, effective and acceptable levels of self-monitoring and self-control. At this age, and almost regardless of causal factors, the child will indicate through his (or her) actions, more than their words, that they are experiencing a severe challenge to personal developmental resources. Typically the concerned referrer will describe a pattern of behavioural excess or deficit usually accompanied by an increase in emotionality. The child who shows an increase in restlessness, non-compliance and angry, aggressive outbursts may well be responding to the same factors as the child who shows a pattern of self-absorption, social withdrawal and tearfulness. The former, typically, will be a boy and the latter a girl.

In general terms children in this phase of development have severe limitations in reporting on their own thoughts or in considering the future. The child tends to live in a very immediate world, dominated by the physical rather than the psychological. The child holds an essentially uninspected view of themselves and their world, what they 'know' are the labels and expressed values of their environment. For instance, at this age a child's description of self is likely to show 'normative distortions of reality' and a permeable distinction between reality and fantasy. In other words the child has absorbed what is valued and desirable in their culture and attributes positive characteristics to him/herself and rejects or denies negative attributes. The child's concept of self is itself fairly limited and typically includes broad and absolute estimates of primarily two areas: general competence (e.g. clever, athletic) and social acceptability (e.g. well-behaved, liked by others). Social comparisons of self are possible at this age but of apparently low relevance, children usually being more concerned with how *they* did, how their performance is judged, etc. (Ruble, 1987). They are now aware of their own identity characteristics, such as age, gender and race and in this period of development will show a tendency to associate with children they perceive to be similar to themselves – the fact of difference will not usually trouble them at this age unless it totally isolates or attracts repeated negative experience.

At an interpersonal level the child is likely to present an egocentric perspective, showing little appreciation of others' feelings, even less appreciation of others' intent and an evaluation of events in terms of the consequences for themselves. Their reports of interpersonal conflicts will usually omit their own contribution and reflect their developmentally limited ability to escape the direct experience of events through adopting a third-person perspective. It would be unfair to say this tendency is peculiar to young children but beyond this period of development more sanguine and balanced accounts of the interpersonal are potentially available with support and prompting. For the young child denial and dissociation are the likeliest response to persistent requests for more balanced, possibly self-incriminating interactive accounts.

Alongside this egocentric bias the child will also reveal a tendency to perceive events and others in concrete and absolute terms. A global re-categorization of people, rather than an expanding definition to incorporate variations, can however occur if the child is faced with severely discrepant information, e.g. A 'good Daddy' who makes a 'good Mummy' cry may, in the child's thinking, indicate that Mummy is now 'bad', resulting in a change in the child's behaviour towards her.

The limited capacity to reconcile incongruent information can extend to the child's account of emotional experience. Thus conflicting feelings are denied and the possible multiple sources of feelings unrecognized. In respect of feelings the younger child perceives emotional experience to be an aspect of external, tangible things and events. The possibility of control is not related to the self since feelings originate outside not inside. As children in this phase become slightly more sophisticated, feelings may be perceived as having an internal physical location, e.g. tummy, heart and the idea of influencing feelings though personal action begins to appear (Ruble, 1987). In the face of significant emotional distress, young children's limited skill repertoire means they have one major response option, to return to the parent or other attachment figure. Chronic problems may develop if the parent is unable to respond in a sensitive and supportive manner, e.g. by offering protection, reassurance and by acting to alter the problem or by helping the child develop more effective coping strategies.

In the face of repeated or chronic negative experience the inadequately supported child at this age will primarily experience feelings of anxiety. Their evaluation of personal distress will tend to concentrate on external, physical sources but their ability to make cause-and-effect links between feelings and events is limited unless they are contiguous in space and time. In reporting on the impact of events the child is likely to describe fairly concrete examples of how they have been affected. For instance in the separated parent scenario given earlier, a child of this age might describe his (or her) father's absence simply in terms of the lost or new activities, e.g. 'I don't go swimming now'; 'He gives me presents when I see him.'

In many situations children may, in struggling to make some sense of their distress, identify a physical location for the 'badness' which has caused the upset. Thus they may arrive at absolute, global evaluations of self, parent or even possessions as being the 'bad' thing.

Late middle childhood (8–12 years)

There is on first inspection an absence of normative transitions during the 8–12 years age range. However, it may be more accurate to regard this developmental period as one of steadily increasing social refinement. In school and at home the child is expected to behave more responsibly and independently as well as demonstrate areas of talent and interest. In responding to these expectations the child may be described by the parent as more secretive or less communicative but this appears to reflect the child's difficulty in distinguishing what adults do still want to know and their increasing appreciation of the fact that to share information with adults is to risk a decrease in 'control'. The central developmental 'tasks' of this period relate to the child's increasing use of strategies for self-control, social competence and the emergence of an elaborated self-concept (Maccoby, 1984).

Children referred at this age continue to present as did the younger child, that is, displaying behavioural excess or deficit, but the child in this developmental phase is likely to have conscious thoughts and ideas about their own situation. In therapy they are likely to be defensive and guarded about revealing their thoughts and the need to respect the child's concern and desire to remain in 'control' may lie at the heart of any therapy undertaken.

In this period the child becomes capable of unprompted self-reflection and makes use of logic and reason but in a fairly concrete and literal manner. Rules are rules and behaviour and people may be measured quite severely against them. The child becomes more aware of self and other and enters a period of social comparison in which self, family and people are compared with others and with rules of conduct. A principal concern of the child at this time is with fairness and justice, particularly in respect of treatment towards and outcomes for themselves. A strong egocentric bias persists but the child is now more consistently conscious of the needs and interests of others.

The child's self-concept becomes more elaborated, combining positive and negative aspects of self in a more global, integrated self-evaluation. Now the child is able – and therefore unlike the younger child – to speak of their various qualities, assets and perceived self-worth, rather than merely demonstrating them in their behaviour (Harter, 1985). The child is also capable of recognizing the variable qualities of others and can make conditional appraisals of self and other. Reflectivity, a relatively stable self-concept and social comparison, also means the child is more aware and sensitive to the appraisal of others. More subtle feelings of shame and pride are possible and can be intensified, cognitively, over time.

In peer relationships the child is more likely to demonstrate co-operation, reciprocity and impulse control for the sake of social relations. Relationships with adults continue to be based on an expectation that the adult will satisfy needs but the child is also more consciously motivated to be perceived in positive terms by the adult.

Emotional awareness has usually advanced to a point where the child appreciates his or her behaviour and thoughts can influence emotional experience, e.g. 'I think of happy things when I feel sad.' The child is also able to understand that events can create various and contradictory feelings. Nevertheless, despite the appearance of more subtle emotions, their ability to describe emotional experience remains limited.

In the face of personal difficulties children in this group are often placed in a serious quandary. Their ability to make evaluative judgements means they can, and often have ascribed blame to someone or something for their distress. In the domain of intimate relations, however, the child is capable of displaying strong egocentric distortions characteristic of a less sophisticated cognitive level than their general level of reasoning. The tendency in the face of repeated negative experience is for the child to seek assistance via indirect communication, but often with an already established view of his or her situation. In comparison with the younger child therefore, this child is less receptive to adult explanation and reassurance unless it is consistent with the child's own view. The child's social-cognitive perspective often results in another being held to blame, but again in intimate, valued relationships the child may blame him- or herself for any difficulty. The child's approach to life remains very much action-based but cognitions, ideas and beliefs are more potent than previously. Thoughts can sustain negative feelings for longer and lead to more pervasive disturbance than in the younger age group. Particularly susceptible to conscious feelings of self-blame, shame and guilt are the children with a tendency towards social withdrawal, and therefore more often girls. Boys are more likely to present with disruptive behaviour and a pervasive, anxious discomfort and possibly little conscious awareness of other feelings.

Adolescence

The normative transitions of this phase concern the social and physical changes of adolescence which are associated with a change in the way the young person views him- or herself and how the environment responds to them. The changes are many and require relatively rapid psychological and social adjustments from the young person. A central task in this phase of development is the need to draw some evaluative line around the self, to begin to define oneself in unique identity terms.

This developmental challenge is mediated by the young person's cognitive capacity for higher-order abstractions. In particular the adolescent is, for the first time in childhood, capable of locating him- or herself, as object, in an objectified personal history (past, present, future) and in an objectified interpersonal context. It would be a mistake to assume, however, that this is the cognitive level at which adolescents or indeed adults, operate for daily social interactions. Various studies (Lapsley, 1990) indicate that in interpersonal situations most of us operate at a fairly concrete level of analysis but draw on wider personal experience to reach judgements. Nevertheless, the late adolescent and adult can, through solitary personal introspection or through therapy, potentially achieve an abstract and distanced perspective on every type of experience.

Generally this cognitive capability will be exercised unevenly across personal experience and least consistently in areas of personal difficulty. The emergence of a more global awareness is associated with an increased preoccupation with the self in the present and a sensitized self-awareness and concern with how others perceive them (Lapsley, 1990). When their own self-concept is felt to be discrepant with the views of valued others or even with their own idealized self the young person may be thrown into profound distress. The nature and quality of interpersonal experiences therefore play a major role in the young person's self-evaluation and emotional stability. Cognitive 'independence' does not, however, 'free' the adolescent from their family or social context. Many studies (Hoffman and Weiss, 1987) demonstrate too clearly the correlation between family functioning and adolescent adjustment for this to be true. However, the presence of a metacognitive capacity does open up the possibility of adult-like, insight-oriented therapies whether cognitive-behavioural or psychotherapeutic.

The young person is able to evaluate feelings as a subjective experience and as part of a broader context involving internal and external events. Unlike earlier phases of childhood, the adolescent is now capable of regulating and modifying emotional experience, of concealing their affective state and of maintaining well-regulated autonomous functioning in the face of emotional arousal. However, in the immediate context of interpersonal difficulty and strong emotional arousal, capacities for cognitively distancing and controlling emotion and behaviour may be overwhelmed.

When difficulties arise for the young person their broader repertoire of coping strategies and metacognitive skills means they are more able to show persistence in seeking to solve personal discomfort. Problem-solving strategies may be more consciously identified and examined for adequacy. The feelings and actions of others may form a larger part of the evaluation of any action options. The ability to contemplate option possibilities is accompanied by an ability to sustain mood states without overt distress. (Contrast this with younger children in whom agitated distress is more likely but mood states less persistent.)

Adolescents are often highly resistant to adult interest or concern for their behaviour or distress. Their relationship with adults generally, and particularly when in personal distress, can be highly ambivalent. Adults are now perceived more realistically and as such are less convincing or trustworthy to this age group. The adolescent, in reaching for independence and individuation, may find him- or herself stranded between dependent childhood and independent adulthood. Not surprisingly their behaviour can shift dramatically between the two. The therapist who would engage the adolescent, probably more than for any other childhood period, needs to be honest in the public self they bring to therapy because the adolescent is more aware and sensitive to personal concealment and duplicity. It is often this struggle with flawed human reality which brings them into distress or conflict and anxious to achieve a level of separation and psychological independence.

Common psychological defences found in this developmental phase are again denial and more sophisticated rationalizations for conduct, beliefs, etc.

Implications of developmental abilities for choice of therapeutic method

In reviewing the changing socio–cognitive capacities of children it becomes clearer than therapeutic methods and approaches make different levels of demand on these developmental abilities. At this point therefore it is possible to reconsider the major therapeutic approaches and the degree of consonance they achieve with particular developmental phases of childhood.

The very young child does not have the capacity to enter any therapeutic approach which depends upon self-reflection and evaluation. Even more importantly, young children do not yet have the developmental capacities to learn about the 'world' or 'themselves' via verbal and cognitive processes. The child at this age learns primarily through repeated, active, experiential processes occurring in the context of secure, constantly available and guiding attachment relationships.

Only the psychoanalytic model of child therapy routinely structures therapy in such an intensive, extended and relationship-based manner. In most cases, however, it will be clear that any therapeutic assistance which may be offered will be most effective at the level of the child's carers. The commonest forms of intervention at this age are therefore indirect and likely to include elements of developmental counselling (explaining the behaviour) and (behavioural) advice on parental management of the difficulty, in a therapeutic relationship which supports and affirms parental competence.

Behavioural methods

The relationship created in typical therapeutic activity may be characterized as highly structured, problem-focused and prescriptive. The approach does not require insight into motives, awareness of feelings or thoughts nor even an understanding of the intervention rationale. However, in direct individual work it does depend on the child being motivated to trust/obey/please the therapist, being behaviourally self-aware and having developed a basic level of self-control. Under these conditions and via processes of modelling, skill rehearsal, active systematic desensitization and training in relaxation skills, children as young as 4 years of age may be engaged. Children of any age thereafter may also be assisted through entirely behavioural techniques though their increasing cognitive sophistication and increasing need for reasons for action means they may be more open to and assisted by cognitive-behavioural methods.

Cognitive-behavioural methods

The cognitive-behavioural approach makes gradually increasing demands upon the child client as the sophistication of the technique is raised. At the simpler level techniques belonging to self-control strategies such as self-instructional talking, self-reinforcement, cognitive management of anxiety, still require that the child is developmentally capable of cognitive and behavioural self-monitoring; of reporting on thoughts and feelings, of linking the two (intuitively or via rational processes) and assigning them an internal origin. An indication of a child who may be capable of these levels of developmental operation would be found where social comparisons are being routinely made and psychological processes are cited prominently in accounts of experience. As described earlier, these features of development begin to appear in late middle childhood.

Higher-level techniques of CBT – such as interpersonal problem-solving approaches – may also be within the developmental reach of the 8–12-year-old child since these children can usually offer a simple account of the 'other's' perspective. However, in interpersonal situations of high arousal the ability to maintain this wider perspective is very quickly reduced. Realistic, action-based approaches in which role play and rehearsal are prominent would be necessary for children at the lower end of the 8–12 age range to benefit from such techniques. With the introduction of cognitive restructuring techniques, based on the evaluation and testing of cognitions, the identification of underlying assumptions etc., the level of developmental functioning required is raised yet further. The child now needs to be capable of taking a third-person perspective in respect of themselves, their circumstances and their psychological experiences. In addition this last strategy would appear to involve the capacity to deal cognitively with multiple possibilities, multiple emotions and indirect causal links. These capacities are unlikely to be evident before pre-adolescence and are more likely to be reliably available to the young person of late adolescent years. With all age groups the cognitive behavioural therapist needs to be aware that in the area of interpersonal difficulties the problems may be rooted in emotional obstacles to the application of social-cognitive skills and not necessarily to a deficit or distortion in cognitions.

Psychotherapeutic methods

Although there are many variations, common elements of the child psychotherapies are the ideas of change occurring through experience of the therapeutic relationship itself, through the use of corrective, emotional experiences, through interpretation and the development of increased personal insight and awareness.

At ages younger than 7 years – and even older where the development of an 'internal model' of relationship has been seriously impaired – the child is unlikely to gain significantly from infrequent, brief contacts with a therapist. Relationship-based therapies with this age group therefore need to consider arranging – at least initially – a number of sessions per week if the child is to develop an enduring and transportable sense of the relationship. For children beyond this age and who are capable of actively sustaining ideas of relationship and experience through thought, the frequency of contact can probably be reduced. Obviously developmental capacity is not the only factor here. The level of disturbance and the nature of the child's on-going experience are critical factors in deciding on the intensity of contact.

A primary concern with psychotherapeutic methods based on interpretation, insight and self-reflection is that they may frequently exceed a young child's cognitive-developmental capacity. In particular methods which relate present behaviour or emotional experiences to distant causes, internal, personal origin and unconscious motives are likely to be beyond the cognitive developmental capacities of most children younger than late middle childhood. High demands for self-reflection and interpretive comment may outstrip the child's emergent capabilities and actually increase the likelihood of an external and concrete egocentric perspective being elicited. For instance, Shirk (1988) conducted an analysis of 'interpretations' offered to children in insight-oriented child therapy. He found that the causal structure implicit in many interpretations was far more complex than the causal reasoning capacities of most children up to pre-adolescence. Furthermore, in the consideration of intimate relations children of middle childhood through to adolescence and beyond may persistently demonstrate areas of egocentric distortion characteristic of less sophisticated levels. Psychodynamic phenomena, such as denial, dissociation etc., therefore could equally be interpreted as signs that cognitive capacities have been exceeded by the therapeutic methods employed.

An important caveat to the foregoing is that many psychotherapeutic approaches and techniques offer the child experiences which may have their primary impact via emotional, right-hemispherical or unconscious processes. Experiences evoked via play therapy, metaphor and analogy could therefore be seen as bypassing the restrictions of conscious, logical cognitive developmental capacities. The research and developmental literature on the processes by which such approaches may have their therapeutic effect is entirely undeveloped. Nevertheless, even these indirect therapeutic activities must remain mindful of the child's tendencies to resist and reinterpret experiences in a developmentally consistent fashion.

Conclusion

The processes of child therapy are embedded in and constrained by the child's developmental ability to participate. Whatever the clinical approach adopted certain elements will remain common across therapeutic encounters. For instance, all child therapies require and depend upon the transmission and reception of meaning between participants. Similarly all therapies require and depend upon the establishment of a **relationship** with the child which will support and sustain therapeutic activity. All major therapeutic approaches (behavioural, cognitive, psychotherapeutic) in child work rely to some degree upon the child's ability to engage in **self-reflection** – to reflect upon their own actions, feelings and thoughts when distant from the actual experiences being discussed. Yet others (cognitive and psychotherapeutic) may go further and expect the child to develop, through therapy, an increased **insight** into their own motivational structures. Without labouring the point it is clear all of these therapeutic objectives and their associated methods are crucially influenced by the child's cognitive-developmental capacities. This is not to ignore or underestimate the influence each child's unique personal history has upon their experience and understanding of the 'world'. Rather it is an appeal for both facets to be considered in arriving at an understanding of any individual child's behaviour and communication.

In broad terms it seems wise to anticipate that, in comparison to adults, children will be:

- More likely to be restricted to *the present*, in their view of themselves and their situation. The representation of the past may not be possible and is less likely to be seen as relevant to present conditions.
- As likely to exhibit their difficulties behaviourally as symbolically.
- Less able or inclined to be self-reflective (until adolescence) and more oriented to action-based, experiential learning.

Furthermore, it must be borne in mind that child difficulties with the process or tasks of therapy need not always be attributed to the absence or fragility of cognitive sophistication. Therapy may, as an activity, be of such length, interpersonal intensity and novelty that an excessive load is placed upon specific cognitive functions, such as memory, attention, concentration, leading to distractibility, withdrawal or emotional abreaction.

As yet the empirical evidence does not exist which can allow a therapist confidently to select specific treatments for specific children. This chapter has attempted to underline the importance of context and developmental ability in making therapeutic choices. Of all client groups children are possibly the least defended against the well-intentioned decisions and actions of therapists. The responsible counselling psychologist undertaking direct work with children must therefore show a respect for the lack of secure evidence and act with appropriate caution and sensitivity. The steps to be taken, it has been suggested in this chapter, are that the counselling psychologist should first evaluate the most advantageous focus for intervention, secondly examine the scientific support for the approach to be used (and, if available, the research data relating to the difficulty in question), and thirdly consider the child's developmental presentation and its meaning for the therapeutic methods to be used. Finally, however, the course of therapy must be determined more by the actual responses of the child in therapy than by theoretical frameworks or nomothetic research findings.

References

Barnnett, R., Docherty, J. and Frommelt, G. (1991) 'A review of child psychotherapy research since 1963', *Journal of the American Academy of Child and Adolescent Psychiatry*, 30: 1–14.

Blagg, N. (1992) 'School phobia', in D. Lane and A. Miller (eds), *Child and Adolescent Therapy: a Handbook*. Milton Keynes: Open University Press.

Carter, B. and McGoldrick, M. (1989) *The Changing Family Life Cycle: a Framework for Family Therapy*, 2nd edn. Boston, MA: Allyn and Bacon.

Chess, S. and Thomas, A. (1984) *Origins and Evolution of Behavior Disorders: From Infancy to Adult Life*. New York: Brunner/Mazel.

Cox, A. and Rutter, M. (1985) 'Diagnostic appraisal and interviewing', in M. Rutter and L. Hersov (eds), *Child and Adolescent Psychiatry*. Oxford: Blackwell.

Fauber, R., Forehand, R., Thomas, A.M. and Wierson, M. (1990) 'A mediational model of the impact of marital conflict on adolescent adjustment in intact and divorced families: the role of disrupted parenting', *Child Development*, 61: 1112–23.

Flavell, J. (1985) *Cognitive Development*, 2nd edn. Englewood Cliffs, NJ: Prentice Hall.

Gelfand, D.M., Jenson, W.R. and Drew, C.J. (1982) *Understanding Child Behaviour Disorders*. New York: Holt, Rinehart and Winston.

Harter, S. (1985) *Processes Underlying the Construct, Maintenance and Enhancement of the Self*, vol. 3. Hillsdale, NJ: Lawrence Erlbaum.

Herbert, M. and Iwaniec, D. (1981) 'Behavioural psychotherapy in natural homesettings: an empirical study applied to conduct disorders and incontinent children', *Behavioural Psychotherapy*, 9: 55–76.

Hetherington, E. (1989) 'Coping with family transitions: winners, losers and survivors', *Child Development*, 60: 1–14.

Hoffman, J. and Weiss, B. (1987) 'Family dynamics and the presenting problems of college students', *Journal of Counseling Psychology*, 34: 157–63.

Houts, A.C., Shutty, M.S. and Emery, R.E. (1985) 'The impact of children on adults', in B. Lahey and A. Kazdin (eds), *Advances in Clinical Child Psychology*, vol. 8. New York: Plenum Press.

Kendall, P. (1993) 'Cognitive behavioural therapies with youth: guiding theory, current status and emerging developments', *Journal of Consulting and Clinical Psychology*, 61(2): 235–47.

Kolvin, I., Garside, R., Nichol, A., Macmillan, A., Wolstenholme, F. and Leitch, I. (1981) *Help Starts Here: the Maladjusted Child in Ordinary School*. London: Tavistock.

Koocher, G.P. and Pedulla, B.M. (1977) 'Current practices in child psychotherapy', *Professional Psychology*, 8: 275–87.

Lapsley, D. (1990) 'The adolescent egocentrism theory and the "new look" at the imaginary audience and personal fable', in R. Lerner, A. Petersen and J. Brooks-Gunn (eds), *The Encyclopedia of Adolescence*. New York: Garland.

Maccoby, E. (1984) 'Middle childhood in the context of the family', in

W. Collins (ed.), *Development during Middle Childhood: the Years from 6 to 12.* Washington, DC: National Academic Press.

Moran, G., Fonagy, P., Kurtz, A., Bolton, A. and Brook, C. (1991) 'A controlled study of the psychoanalytic treatment of brittle diabetes', *Journal of the American Academy of Child and Adolescent Psychiatry.* 30: 926–35.

Ollendick, T. and King, N. (1991) 'Fears and phobias of childhood', in M. Herbert (ed.), *Clinical Child Psychology: Social Learning, Development and Behaviours.* Chichester: Wiley.

Powell, M. and Oei, T. (1991) 'Cognitive processes underlying the behavioural change in cognitive behaviour therapy with childhood disorders: a review of experimental evidence', *Behaviour Psychotherapy*, 19: 247–65.

Ruble, D. (1987) 'The acquisition of self-knowledge: a self-socialization perspective', in N. Eisenberg (ed.), *Contemporary Topics in Developmental Psychology.* New York: Wiley.

Schaffer, H. (1990) *Making Decisions about Children.* Oxford: Blackwell.

Shirk, S. (1988) *Cognitive Development and Child Psychotherapy.* New York: Plenum Press.

Shirk, S. and Russell, R. (1992) 'A re-evaluation of estimates of child therapy effectiveness', *Journal of the American Academy of Child and Adolescent Psychiatry*, 31: 703–9.

Street, E.C., Downey, J. and Brazier, A. (1991) 'The development of therapeutic consultations in child-focused family work', *Journal of Family Therapy*, 13(3): 311–33.

Weisz, J., Weiss, B., Alicke, M. and Knotz, M. (1987) 'Effectiveness of psychotherapy with children and adolescents: a meta-analysis for clinicians', *Journal of Consulting and Clinical Psychology*, 55: 542–9.

333

15

Psychological Counselling with Young Adults

Cassie Cooper

How, why is the so-called rite of passage from adolescence to young adulthood so often marked by such unhappiness and misery for all concerned? What sense of futility, anger and deep depression seems to take hold of young men and women as they approach the threshold of their adult life? Why is society so clumsy and inhibited in coping with this age group, when, after all, every one of us has gone through some of these traumas and can certainly remember our own feelings of resentment and frustration?

We know and understand that it is a period of passionate self-absorption, often active when consideration for the feelings of others has a low priority in the struggle to develop an identity.

We also know that this striving towards adulthood highlights a number of uncomfortable truths about our society. This age group brings into sharp focus the fact that parents are growing old, that the society they espouse will be supplanted and overtaken by a new generation. These are sexually developed young men and women who are about to overtake their parents in forming relationships that will eventually supplant and replace their families.

They are a 'difficult' group, seeming at this later stage of development finally to relinquish all those years of parenting and schooling. Too late now it seems to press on them any forms of parental influence.

The counsellor who endeavours to work with the problems of the young adult (as a form of applied psychology) tries to provide reality-determined issues and concepts whilst considering how best he or she can make use of disciplined methods to understand the problems of this age group which may not be as unverifiable as we assume.

In a certain sense we should think of every young man and woman as a budding psychologist. The normal processes of maturation enable each and every one of us to develop a particular view of life and to operate strategies for predicting and responding to life events however traumatic they may be. We learn as we go which major physical and intellectual developments are taking place.

Psychological problems for the young adult (defined as the period from age 18 to 25 years) are generally concerned with personal difficulties which occur in relation to family and friends, the young adult's perception of the world and around attitudes to the self. These problems – as they are manifested – can be characterized by feelings of anxiety or tension, dissatisfaction with their own behaviour, excessive worries about minor problems, a sense of failure to meet desired goals in life, and inability to function in the wider world.

There are times when clients themselves are unaware that they have a problem, but significant others may be adversely affected by their behaviour and have cause to complain about the situation, often having to watch their loved ones lose hope, become self-destructive, unhappy and resort to delinquent behaviour.

Young men and women in this age group may well be unemployed, divorced, in debt, facing discrimination by race, economic stringency, sexual, moral or religious demands, medical disability, bereavement and loss. In looking at these problems we need to know if they stem from the life script formed by an earlier age. Do we acknowledge that changes cannot evolve in a smooth untroubled process of transition and that painful and destructive dysfunctions and shifts are inevitable? Do so-called changes in our clients really reflect growth and understanding or are they an attempt by troubled young men and women to gain approval from parents, teachers, friends and counsellors?

For many years the field of psychology treated the topic of personality development in early adulthood and its ensuing problems with benign neglect. Most psychologists concluded that once the storms of adolescence had abated, the young adult was able to make the transition to adulthood. He or she having completed their schooling either went on to higher education, became a member of the workforce, left home, got married and 'settled down'. Nothing more would be heard from them until they approached the periods characterized by media catch-phrases – 'thirty-something', 'mid-life crisis', 'forty-year itch' and the ensuing generation gap which widens until the inevitability of old age and death. We now know that things are not so straightforward, that young adults do not enter a period of tranquillity, sameness and predictability.

Most of the accepted theories about independence are psychoanalytic in origin. They postulate that a successful transition from adolescence to young adulthood demands a rejection of parental definitions of identity. That rejection means that at this time the young man or woman is torn between the longing to be regressive and loyal to past childhood association and facilitations, and the vague promises held out of adult autonomy. Acceptance of this view poses the idea that you now are what you were once, only more so. Whatever has occurred later in your life is just merely an elaboration or distillation of your early childhood experiences.

Taking this view, the outer trappings of leaving home matter less than a person's inner psychological state. It seems to be an act of independence to leave home, sometimes banging the door in fury and frustration, but this is not always to gain psychological autonomy. To leave home and call one's parents twice a week, depending on the family for advice and for money, can be far less autonomous than those who choose to remain at home, living with parents but financially able to support themselves and feeling able to come and go as they please.

In this chapter we will examine the theoretical perspectives which provide highly contrasting solutions to the problems listed below.

1   The stormy and peaceful transitions in the **individuation** processes.
2   Problems of **separation** – the development of independence ego-strength.
3   Failure to establish a work pattern either in education or employment. Ideas of **success and failure**.
4   Inability to develop the **capacity to involve and develop intimate relationships** with members of the opposite sex and/or members of the same sex.

The individuation process

> It is a paradoxical proposition that if you have been happily and securely attached to your family and to your parents it is easier to establish your own identity and to leave home without things going wrong than if you are anxious about them or at war with them. (Bowlby, 1979)

Young adulthood is not necessarily a stormy period for everyone. Most young people manage the transition from home to the wider world without difficulty. The Central Policy Review Research Team in its 1992 survey showed that 80 per cent of 24-year-olds had left home, most of them having married or were living with 'partners'. During these six crucial years four-fifths of the young adult population had left home.

However, another figure from the same survey is set against these findings in that one-third of the marriages contracted under the age of 20 resulted in divorce within the next 15 years and one-fifth of the marriages contracted between 20 and 24 ended in divorce. Marriage and/or partnership, when used as a way in which to leave home, appeared to be successful only as a stepping stone.

There is considerable evidence, however, that in both a physical and psychological sense leaving home is becoming more difficult for the young. Since 1989 the proportion of young people between the ages of 20 and 29 living at home has increased by 25 per cent. One reason is clearly due to economic factors. Many young people who may want to establish their own home and family are finding it much harder to do so. Another reason is that marriage has to be postponed. Marriage was seen to be the ceremonial point of no return in the separation process from the parental home but the average age of marriage has risen from 22.8 for men and 20.3 for women (in 1950) to 27.4 for men and 25.1 for women (in 1989). Early formation theories echo the psychoanalytic theme of the need to 'break away' from childhood identities – the idea of leaving home, whether it be by one means or another, lies in the challenge it poses to assumptions of what is meant by dependency and the omnipotence of parents; it is pushing oneself to a form of liberation from them through study, work or marriage, and finally assuming a parental role oneself.

Dependency is a prime characteristic of human nature, but as we grow older the need to prove ourselves as independent becomes a priority. Independence is widely accepted as part of our Western culture and philosophy and is highly valued in our current society. It is associated with powerful words and images such as strength, individualism and leadership.

The notion of dependence is, in contrast, devalued and often associated with helplessness, indecision, weakness and childish behaviour. Dependence and independence are seen as opposite poles, delicately poised, which can tip in either direction but the desirable weighting is seen to lie in the area of independence, the golden goal of achievement and growth. Although psychoanalytic theories stress the importance of an early period of dependence of the child on his or her parents, it has never been seen as a positive goal. Dependence is viewed as a 'means to', a process which can lead to emotional security or ultimately to achievement of independence.

Psychologists see part of their role as facilitating their clients to become more independent, but can we say that any of us is ever truly independent or that independence is necessarily such a good thing? George Kelly (1955) argued that adults, like children, are dependent too but that they extend their dependencies discriminatingly to more people, more things and more institutions. He went on to suggest that the attitude taken by 'helping professionals' should not be one of labelling their clients as dependent or independent but one where 'we throw emphasis upon variations in their dispersion' and see it as a salient aspect of personal growth.

According to Eric Erikson's (1981) influential theories of psychological development, the young adult is struggling to attain and perhaps more importantly to retain a sense of ego identity, a sense of self that is free and distinct from the experiences of childhood and adolescence. This task, says

Erikson, is accomplished during a 'psychosocial moratorium' when the young person is free to experiment with new possibilities – for example in careers or ideologies – without having to make a firm commitment to any as yet.

Mary, a first-year student reading for a degree in graphic design, was referred for counselling after she had taken an overdose of paracetamol. Her suicide attempt followed a futile attempt to write an essay in Complementary Studies which was entitled 'A Search for Meaning'. She had written:

> I write this as an autobiography incorporating my thoughts and feelings of this day. Yesterday my mind was filled with different problems and needs than I have today. Even tomorrow, if there is one, I may write an entirely different autobiography because of new experiences. Today I am caught up in a swirl of religious torments. I also question my choice of a career. What am I doing here? And, as always, I seek self-knowledge but feel that this is harmful to me. Thus I cannot stress too much that I am *creature of only today* and as such my thoughts, my activities are undergoing change. My life does not focus on a single clearly defined point. Instead, I perceive conflicting images of me, this is a form of weakness.

Mary was unable to complete the essay. My client's confusion about her religious identification stemmed from the powerful pressures she felt were exerted upon her by other students to rebel against her background (her parents were orthodox Jews), and to reject aspects of personal behaviour which she knew were of vital concern to her parents.

She was unable to accept the evolution of herself as a person capable of self-control. Hatred of herself was one of the symptoms of this conflict. In the counselling process she was able to understand that confusion about religious identity was but one aspect of her uncertainty as to who she was. She was determined to continue with her intensive search for self-knowledge in all aspects of her life and later brought for me to read the concluding paragraphs of her now completed essay.

> At the outset of this essay I mentioned religion. I have thought about myself as a spiritual person a good deal. Just recently I have begun to feel that I am making progress in understanding my religious leanings and spiritual needs. I have always had a strong religious sense yet I cannot quite understand whether to be spiritual or religious means that I have to believe in God.
>
> What is me on this particular day is a search for self-knowledge. My personality, my career, my faith, my ability to decide my spiritual being, all represent facets of the *me*. I have made great progress in discovering who I am but I must continue striving. Here I am a composite of eighteen and a half years of learning and experience. I am confused yet eager to plunge forth again.

This client was able to take hold of the simple dictum that if a person feels they can allow themselves to touch upon their true self – they may – in therapeutic terms – be described as having some form of understanding of why they choose to stay alive. Conversely, if you are able to reach some form of understanding, it may be possible to be your own true self and in this lies the core component of individual power.

Finding an identity is a critical preliminary step to success in the stages of development which follow – especially those which are concerned with forming intimate friendships and sexual relationships. Obviously leaving home can support the successful resolution of creating a separate identity since it removes a young person from the direct control of parents, but the young person has to distinguish here between physically leaving home and doing so symbolically. If home is symbolic of primary childhood identifications and influences and leaving is identified with questioning parental values and influences, then a symbolic leaving can be essential to attaining an adult identity – but if such a symbolic leaving becomes difficult, then it matters little if the young person is able to leave in actuality.

Individuation is a bottleneck through which each person has to squeeze individually, but which, in most families, presents a potential crisis for all. It is a process that cannot be hurried – not simply an event, but a process which continues in a rather indefinite way and which everyone has to face sooner or later.

Young people are clearly perplexed by the separation process and there are few guidelines. Is there a right time for this or that? A right age to leave, or are there only specific individual cases? Do our current cultural perspectives offer any means of assuring a smooth transition into adulthood – with no clear social norms? Who is to tell a parent that they are clinging too long to their sons and daughters or, erring in the opposite direction, pushing them out of the door too soon?

> It is not often appreciated just how important this transition is when young people break down at the very point when they should be taking off. By breakdown, I do not only mean mental breakdown, although that is included (75% of newly diagnosed schizophrenics are aged between 17 and 25) (Curran, Partridge and Storey, 1980). I also mean academic failure, drug abuse, overdoses, criminal activities, unwanted pregnancies and all the other problems that are so frequently associated with this age group. (Kraemer, 1982)

Separation

The defiant way to leave home is, of course, to run away, but while an abrupt exit is perplexing for all concerned, the inner dynamics of a gradual separation can be equally paradoxical. At the time of separation when the young man or woman is striving for autonomy there are conflicting thoughts about abandoning the home base. It is comforting to believe that there is a home base to return to in time of need. Here is the difficulty. In order to separate, it is necessary to acquire a psychological detachment from parents; the simultaneous wish for distinctiveness and approval. If you are 'different' from your parents then you may feel separate from them but if parents feel different from their sons and daughters it could represent the loss of their love and support.

There is also the symptom of what could be termed 'paralysing apathy'. Jay Haley (1990) traces many of these problems to the need to preserve the family by sacrificing one's own growth. The young student's failure for example often serves to keep parents from confronting issues in their marriage that might otherwise have led to a divorce. If children are unable to separate, able to keep their parents intensely involved with their own problems, then parents may neglect their own difficulties. Young men and women are prepared to pay a high price – their own emotional growth – for the sake of so-called stability in their family life.

We understand these realignments of needs and wants as readjustments made necessary by increased anxieties and called forth by these acute life crises within the family. To label such reactions as 'pathological' or bad helps neither to understand the problems. To help chart a purposeful course of action towards them, their inner psycho-logic, their rationale must be understood.

This unfinished business of childhood provides the basis for adult development.

> As children we are fundamentally helpless in the face of both danger and inner passions of lust, rage and greed. We depend wholly on our parents to control both of these threats and we analyze a series of false assumptions, illusions, that allow us to believe that we are perfectly safe. Maintaining these beliefs has the benefit of preserving our sense of security but it also has a cost. We are confined by the rules that bound us as children. We cannot get free of these confining inhibitions without facing the illusory nature of some of our most fundamental beliefs and without giving up the security they provide. But when we do get free we come to see reality more clearly and thus stop the unexpected shocks that must repeatedly occur when our illusions collide with life. And . . . we also gain from this process real freedom to be our own persons, in touch with our inner needs and passions, living vital and meaningful lives. (McCrae and Costa, 1990)

Thus for the counselling psychologist, the work must be at this developmental level to shed major false assumptions in order to achieve further levels of adult maturity. According to Gould, for ages 16–22 the developmental task is 'leaving our parents' world' and the major false assumption to be renounced is 'I'll always belong to my parents and believe in their world' (Gould, 1978). Young people want to be separate, they want their autonomy but they are afraid that if they express their true feelings they will no longer be loved. They are not yet able to take hold of the idea that being 'different' can make you unlovable. Disagreements with friends and parents are experienced as a kind of betrayal. The pressure in this age group is to be like everyone else.

Those young people who are unable to break away from the myth that 'I'll always be with my parents, they will always be there for me, I believe they know what is best for me' are sentenced to play out in their lives their parents' restricted attitudes and lifestyles. Religious observance, sexual attitudes, political allegiances: when these unconscious controls reach a crescendo, how often do we hear the heartfelt cry, 'I wish they were dead'? The stronger the fear of not being able to sever the umbilical cord, the greater the intensity of anger before leaving.

A frequent scenario of this painful period is the abrupt and bitter exit from the family. Some of those who have to stay at home do so in a state of constant warfare, usually with the mother. Those who do leave home – for whatever reason – keep up a running battle, a hostile dependent entanglement between offspring and mother. In many cases they fail in the key tasks of young adulthood. Even when living alone they neither form meaningful relationships outside the family nor embark on a career other than that of 'a problem'.

Alan, at the age of 25, worked as a nurse at a local hospital and elected to do a basic counselling course as a preparation for his eventual upgrading to Registered Mental Nurse. He said he felt powerless, burnt-out and empty. Alan said:

> I thought I had discovered a vocation and a purpose in life after the terrible time I had with my family after I came out as a homosexual. For years I went with my parents to Church and prayed to God who alone would have the power to turn me into a woman. I never felt comfortable as a man. Then I became cut off from religion and did not feel I could believe in a God who would make me feel such a nothing. Spiritual feelings do not work anymore. Religion has blown itself apart. Now I get the odd guilty twinge at Christmas and when going to a cinema on a Sunday my behaviour is too outrageous for God. I am living with a Catholic. All my family could ever say about me was that I was 'terribly good with people'. So I became a nurse and comforted myself and them with this good image. A patient once said I was 'a beacon sailing round the darker places in the ward'. It made me happy for about ten minutes. This is what my mother wants of me. To be a nice person, to look after the sick, to become straight, bring home a nice wife, have a hair cut, and to believe in her version of God.
>
> My reaction is to behave outrageously. I want to embarrass my mother. I can't even do that now. All the power has been knocked out of me.

> Everyone tells me that I have the ability to make people feel good about themselves, but if only I could make myself feel good.

Alan wanted to equate his vocation as a nurse with his need to suffer. He wanted to model himself on his father who was very religious but he was always uneasy about the relationship with his parents. 'Religion got in the way. They never did love each other and didn't love each other when they first married.' He therefore questioned whether he had a right to have been born. He felt deprived of affection and was convinced that he was not wanted, especially so when they realized that he was a homosexual, an outcast from their family. As a young man he regarded the world as a hostile place and this belief was strengthened by his own impotent image of himself.

The need to feel validated persisted and to fulfil this need he undertook unconventional projects which reflected his confusion. He sought to help others who appeared more confused than he was and as spiritually devoid of strength. This proved unsuccessful and his actions brought nothing but pain to himself and proved of questionable value to others. He ended a recent session by saying, 'I am disgusted with myself because I have done nothing good'. He immediately corrected this unfavourable evaluation: 'Probably I am wrong because I know generally I am good at my work. Psychologically, however, I am a real mess.'

Success and failure

Donald Super (1990) offers some of the most respected theories of life-stage development, particularly in the areas of work and higher education. He focuses on changes in the concept of self and how these affect inevitably the choice of education and career. Super delivers a theory of occupational development, and in relation to the age group 15–25 identifies this as the first stage, one of 'exploration and trial'.

But the world is changing at least as fast as Alvin Tofler predicted, and these changes bring with them dismaying consequences. The relative stability of the get rich 1980s has been replaced with a real unease. Nothing seems to be safe or predictable and the employment scene is one of the most dramatic demonstrations of this. Most young men and women of today feel less in control of their destinies – optimism is low and depression is high. Society responds by avoidance, we are not able to confront the realities of the dissonance between how we educate young men and women in preparation for the world of work that they will enter.

For the past 20 years psychologists have concerned themselves with the emotional and social well-being of their clients. It was possible to do this because we lived in a period of economic growth and expansion and most young people had little anxiety about jobs. Time was spent on deciding which jobs would be the most fulfilling.

But times have changed. School leavers and graduates worry about finding work and now 16.4% of the male and 10.2% of the female workforce between the ages of 18 and 25 remain unemployed (Central Statistical Office, 1994). This age group appears to be the hardest hit of all unemployed groups. To be unemployed at the beginning of an adult work life is to head towards the term 'unemployable' – the vicious process of no experience/no work and so on. We belong to a society which is conditioned to believe that work is fundamental to our well-being. Most people want and need to work. In a situation where we all know that work is not obtainable and the signs are that it may become scarcer still, by definition we have a large-scale mental health problem to face.

Those in this age group who may have elected for further and higher education question the usefulness of an education system founded on the assumption that work will follow learning. Seductive recruiting by educational institutions often results in students making unrealistic or passive choices of courses and careers with all the predictable sequels which follow. 'Drop outs' are the disenchanted or pessimistic students, rather than inadequate ones – their mood is often related to their ultimate chances of getting the kind of jobs they have been led (by parents, teachers and the media) to believe they need and deserve.

Sobering studies of unemployment in this and other age groups highlight particular psychological problems. The appalling suicide rate of 'redundant' senior executives, family disturbances when the breadwinner is out of work, these are the problems with which the counselling psychologist is engaged. The case history of a young chronically un-employed person reads like a description of clinical depression. The initial failure to find work and so-called 'success' leads to renewed efforts which result in frustration and futility with life. Turned inwards, these thoughts become a sense of personal failure leading to apathy, immobilization and depression – feelings which are not addressed by Social Security hand-outs and Jobcentre schemes. Families are distraught. Parents often blame their son or daughter for not getting a job – some blame themselves. Successful parents can be cynical and judgemental, others feel anxious and helpless. Some parents feel it keenly as a family disgrace. Young people resort to drugs and delinquency as a panacea for their enforced inactivity. Young women get pregnant to have something productive to do. Ninety-six conceptions in every 1000 are in this age group with the subsequent number of abortions increasing dramatically from 55% in 1971 to 68.5% in 1993.

343

Finding a focus or not finding a focus can stir the family tremendously. The so-called success of one's children is the weakest link in the chain of family life and is therefore most likely to be destroyed if there is a problem. Perhaps the difficulties hinge on the fact that parents themselves have not emotionally been able to separate and when confronted by their children, who in turn have chosen to become parents themselves, are finding that they are in two stages of life at the same time. There are other potential sources of tension at this time for the young adult. This is particularly so when for one reason or another they are likely to become more successful than their parents were or are at this stage of life. This is not only a matter of academic success but it could also be a happier marriage and a more financially rewarding career. Their parents may very well seem to be both proud and supportive, but often young men and women are unable to grasp the opportunities before them feeling in some way disloyal, betraying their parents, if they go ahead and take hold of their good fortune. Faced with this situation parents become stressed and cannot understand why it is that their son or daughter is 'determined to spoil his or her chances in life with bad and sometimes mad behaviour' (Kraemer, 1982).

John Peel, writing in the *Radio Times* (1994) highlighted this problem when he wrote:

> As our William occasionally reminds me, he has already better qualifications than his dad's hard-won 4 'O' levels. William is not much impressed by my argument that I have spent many years before the mast, adrift and storm tossed on the sea of life and this gives me the authority to tell him to carry his plate back to the kitchen and be quick about it. Being William he came close to getting straight B's but when he took his GCSE, his record was blunted somewhat by a couple of straight C's. Being William an A would have caused him as much embarrassment as a D. I would check this with him but he is of course still in bed exhausted with the strain of having spent the summer watching videos. William is, as is pointed out to me whenever, in exasperation and with blood spurting from the top of my head, I shriek 'why doesn't that boy ever do anything?' waiting for his A-level results.

Researchers David Levi, Helm Sterlin and Robert Sagard at the National Institute for Mental Health, New York (1980), reported on the rather grim clinical profiles of 30 families who came for counselling because of a troubled young adult. In nearly all the cases their problems were linked to a crisis in the lives of their middle-aged fathers where the father was exhibiting deep doubts and uncertainties about the meaning of his own life. Open options in both love and work which their offspring appeared to have, seemed to lead these fathers to regret the choices they had made in their own lives. Fathers who do not have a strong sense of self-worth feel threatened by moves in the family towards independence. They respond either with criticism or a total disengagement.

Anita, a British-born daughter of Asian immigrants, was referred for counselling by her GP, who became concerned when she asked him for anti-depressants. She has just resigned her job as a social work assistant, a job she obviously enjoyed. This was our first interview. Her mother had accompanied her to the doctor.

I am Anita and you have heard what my mother has to say about me and about our family dilemma. Here's what I want to say. My view is totally different from that of my mother. Yes I would agree with her definition of myself as a survivor. I need to be a survivor in this household.

I have a father who I hardly see. He's so far away I wonder if I have ever had a relationship with him. Is he a father, does he know what being a father means? To me it seems that the most important thing to him is money and his pride. He has all these expectations of me but gives little thought to what I actually want. There is simply no room for re-negotiation.

That's all I can actually say about my father because I know so little about him as a person. He has never sat down and said what his childhood was like. He has never talked about his childhood back home. He's probably told my mother that he's had a hard life because she's always making excuses for him. If I question him in any way I'm told that I should show him more respect, what is there to respect, to hang on to if I don't know him?

Sometimes I feel that my only relationship to him is that he is my mother's husband. My friend Emma has such a wonderful relationship with her father. As far as mom goes it is different but in a way it isn't. It's hard to explain but I'll try. I know more about my mother, about her childhood and how she was brought up. She had a really hard life and I suppose I should count myself lucky, in fact I feel really guilty sometimes when she tells me about the childhood she had – or didn't have. It makes me feel angry at them and at her. She seemed to accept it all and didn't make any demands – she gave in. What I can't understand is having experienced all that herself – no love from her mother, just setting her up for her duties as a wife, and she just went along with it like she had no life of her own. But I know that she wasn't happy yet she wants me to be the same. This is where I get confused. You see I'm living in this country and to some degree I have been given freedom to develop in my own way and then demands are made upon me. I feel that I am getting mixed messages. Does she want me to be myself or does she want me to be like her? I want to show her affection and to give her love but somehow I feel she rejects it because she wasn't able to express these feelings with her own mother.

I care about her so much and it irritates me so much that she can be so weak. I know her so well but she knows so little about me. I wonder how I can make her understand. Can I just say, 'Mom, sit down, let's talk, let's cry, let's laugh together' but I just can't seem to do it. I feel unable to say words.

Is it me or is it her? I wonder if she actually wants to know and I fear that she may not really care what happens to me. That kind of rejection I could not live with. I need her, I need somebody to love me. I could just please her and sit at home and learn to cook and learn to be a good housewife, but then I have myself to deal with. How could I live that way when I know another way of being? She never knew that, so maybe it wasn't so hard for her. My other alternative is to reject all this. Just leave, but I don't want to do that; the cost is too great to be cut off from my family and odd as it may seem I do like the culture. I do believe in my religion although I don't practise it and I want my children to have the benefit of it but there has to be a balance. The question is where do I find it? How do I achieve it and where do I start?

I see my mother looking at me, she doesn't know how to deal with the situation. Obviously I am unhappy, I feel depressed and hopeless. It has been suggested that I should go to our doctor as I don't look well. In our family there is no recognition of depression. In my mother's eyes I have a wonderful life compared with her. Why would I feel depressed? What reason do I have for this blackness and bleakness of thought? Maybe I should just do what my mother does. Take anti-depressants and become mindless maybe I'll forget who I am. Maybe they'll even take some notice of me. How can they say they are only happy when I'm happy and everything they are doing is for their children? When I make it quite clear that I'm not happy. By the way. What I fail to understand is that they don't want to go along with what will make me happy and therefore them happy. I want to continue studying, I want to be someone and I'm quite willing to negotiate. I'll study somewhere near home if they want. You know I don't even object to the idea of arranged marriages. I object to forced marriages. As long as I had some say and I felt that my feelings were being taken into consideration, that I was valued and loved and not just a guest in the house, I would do as they wish and that would in return make me happy. Surely what I'm asking for is not wrong. Sometimes I just feel like going up to them and shaking them and shouting do you hear me? Help me!

Anita's confused mixture of loyalty and guilt forced her to seek a form of reparation for the difficulties between her mother and her father. Splits in the family reinforced her own fear of becoming a success. Success meant that she became different from the other members of the family and this could be seen to be an abandonment of her relationship with them. Her fight for individuation and autonomy was regarded with suspicion and fear by her mother and incompatible with the so-called ideals of 'femininity'. She was betraying her cultural and religious background by aiming to be like her non-Asian peer group.

Making her feel 'different' and suggesting that her behaviour would contaminate other members of the family served to draw attention from the conflict between her parents. Lawrence Wrightsman (1994) has cited the term 'cultural camouflage' to describe the universal tendency of Asian family members to avoid responsibility for their feelings, action and destiny by attributing their differences either to their own cultural and religious background or to the influence of Western ideas.

> In the traditional Asian context women are identified more transactionally than individually as daughters to their parents, wives to their husbands, daughter-in-law to their parents-in-law and in their most valued role as mother of sons . . . traditionally a daughter is less valued than a son as she has no significant ritual role to fulfil within her natal family . . . post partum depression is almost exclusively associated with the birth of female children in India. (Guzder and Krishna, 1993)

According to recently published figures the suicide rate for young Asian women is two to three times the national average.

In this age group, suicide is a highly sensitive, controversial and stigmatizing issue, whether carried out, attempted or merely considered (as in all three clients cited in this chapter). The problem of suicide is enigmatic in many ways. Contrary to a still common belief, it is not dependent on a specific illness or mental state and it cuts across all diagnostic categories.

The problem is even more complex in this age group because suicidal behaviour at this stage cannot be separated from the unique and challenging developmental processes of early adulthood and their tight connections with family dynamics and social context. Furthermore, research data on suicide attempts may vary widely depending on how this information is obtained – from hospital outpatient departments or psychiatric hospitals and clinics.

The number of young men and women who commit suicide has risen by more than a quarter since 1979. In 1992 there were 4,362 male suicides – a 27 per cent increase over the previous 12 years. The male increase was most marked in the 15–44 age group (Central Statistical Office, 1994). The report offers no explanation for this increase but the Samaritans have suggested that men have a reluctance to discuss their feelings with those who might help them. Young people contemplating suicide do not always go to their GP or a counsellor. Of those under 35, only one-fifth sought help in that time.

It is perhaps a sign of the times that young people when they feel troubled or alarmed by feelings precipitated by stress put off consulting a doctor because they do not see themselves as ill or for fear of being diagnosed as a psychiatric case which carries a stigma and could damage their future career. When they do seek help it is often after an 'attempt' at suicide.

On the whole counselling psychologists have not been well prepared for the subject. Many, even psychiatrists, share with laymen simple misconceptions about suicide. In fact we may feel so uneasy with the matter that we choose to deny, ignore or avoid confrontation with it.

The violence and apparent irrationality of suicidal behaviours contribute to many of the observed individual or institutional defensive attitudes. Also the lack of specificity and poor predictive value of risk factors may be discouraging in clinical practice.

The same is true of the so-called warning clues – such as failure in academic performance or obtaining a job, or falling in or out of love. But suicide attempts are highly meaningful and are often dedicated symptoms of intense suffering. These acts appear to be critical responses to a usually long-standing series of unresolved overt or covert difficulties. One can only identify the pre-suicidal syndrome as a narrowing of personal capabilities and dynamic activities, the inhibition of aggression towards others and a turning of those feelings inwards resulting in fantasies of death.

It is at this time that the young adult becomes more aware of death and destruction, owning to 'bad/evil' feelings, including the power to hurt and destroy others and themselves,

> . . . becoming more aware of the many ways in which other persons, even loved ones, have acted destructively towards them. What is worse, the realization comes that they may have done irrevocably hurtful things to parents, lovers, friends, rivals . . . but there is a positive aspect to this recognition of the capacity to be destructive. By recognizing one's power to tear down things, you can begin to realize how truly powerful one can be in creating new and useful forms of life . . . powerful forces of destructiveness and of creativity co-exist in the human soul and can be integrated in many ways though never entirely. (Levinson, 1980)

The capacity to involve and develop intimate relationships

Although emphasis in this chapter has been given to the context in which I work – the application of psychodynamic theory to counselling psychology – it should be noted that there are well in excess of 250 theories of counselling and therapy. Small wonder then that there is not a consensus on which theory in the context of working with the young adult stands out as more appropriate or more significant than any other.

There are those among us who argue for the all-persuasive importance of **social structures** to counselling and psychotherapy whilst others, particularly in the field of family therapy, maintain that the **systems** approach is of equal importance. There are also those counselling psychologists who place an emphasis on consideration of **single variables** that may particularly affect this group – namely consideration of race and gender.

The influence of these perspectives for counselling practice are well defined by Jenny Bimrose, writing on counselling and social context (1993). She urges counsellors to become more familiar with the different dimensions of this debate so that they can identify the perspective from which they are currently operating or perhaps what their intended focus could be for the future. She illustrates this point by correlating the concept of social context in counselling to the actual practical skills required in each of three perspectives.

Individualistic   using the traditional theoretical perspectives of psychology plus core skills of empathy, acceptance and understanding, etc.

Integrationist   Counsellors offering skills to their clients which can be used to change systems, i.e. working with special groups. This method is effective when used in conjunction with individual counselling.

Structuralist   Concerning oneself with single contextual variables such as race or gender which pose a particular challenge to the counsellor.

A complex array of therapies, techniques, methodologies and arguments face the individual practitioner. If there is little agreement on any of these the one thing that we do know is that there are significant numbers of young people in this age group who experience symptoms that cause distress to themselves, their families and their friends and which percolate throughout the tiers of society in general.

Perhaps the most important stage encountered in the developmental tasks of the young adult is that of establishing a workable and acceptable system of values and relationships and this is by no means the prerogative of the most articulate and highly educated young people in our society. Most of the young men and women who seek help from counselling show a genuine – if confused – concern with moral issues, with questions of social justice, violence and discrimination. Many of them have few illusions about the discrepancies between their own pretensions and performances. They are often acutely conscious of living up to their own ideals and of the extent to which they may fell short of what they might expect from themselves. Many of the moral principles they supported as schoolchildren or were struggling at one time to realize, were very close to those adumbrated by traditional social or religious codes which, as they grew older, demanded new reasons for adhering to them and new sanctions to validate them. What is quite clear, however, is that the main touchstone for their assessment of their own and other people's moral standards lies in the quality of personal relationships and that this means more to each one than some of the traditional sanctions of morality. It could be that the bewilderment, uncertainty and experimentation on

349

moral issues that they present are signs that with time and luck may provide a future morality characterized less by constraint, punishment and inhibition and more by autonomy, sympathy, altruism and love.

During the past ten years young people indicated a considerable concern, often at unconscious levels, with the threat of atomic warfare. 'Why bother?' they would ask. But there is a real distinction between today's generation and that which preceded it. The focus of this concern in the 1990s has shifted to the possible pollution and degradation of 'space-ship Earth'. The awful predicament is the same – the means to eliminate life is in the hands of man- and woman-kind.

Of course, all periods involve change, but it is unquestionable that in this past decade we have experienced a culture of exceptionally rapid and complicated social change where society has manifested deep conflicts in its values and uncertainties in its attitudes to even the most fundamental aspects of human relationships. We still are in the midst of agonized and protracted debates on such issues as abortion law reform, euthanasia, the teaching of contraception, the effect of HIV and AIDS on world populations, the problems of the Third World, etc. to recognize the symptoms. The basis of family life is itself subjected to re-appraisal and criticism, and knowledge of the physical bases of bi-sexuality and androgyny is blurring what previously seemed to be clear-cut sexual distinctions.

Young adulthood has its own special characteristics and its special contribution to psychological life and development rests on the premise that this is a period during which the young adult's mental picture of him- or herself, begun in adolescence, will have firmed up, and when a specific and fixed sexual identity will be established.

This is the time during which the person will seek to find answers through relationships, through various social and sexual experiences and responses. These hinge on previous conditionings as to what is acceptable to his or her conscience and ideals and what it is that must at all costs to their future psychological well-being be rejected or denied.

The entry into young adulthood is marked by compromise. Compromise between what we think we might want and what our conscience allows us to live with. Earlier ways of feeling male or female are put under a new kind of stress. Previous experiences in childhood and adolescence of finding pleasure and feeling cared for are put under pressure because of the presence of a sexually mature and developed body.

It appears that society has tried to avoid a basic clarification. We are all seemingly aware of the differences between a male and female and generally we can agree about the concepts of masculinity and femininity, but we have made the mistake of assuming that a man possesses masculinity whilst a woman exhibits femininity. We now know that if many people in life appear to conform to these expectations, they may well have been trained to do so. Gender schema theory is one attempt to explain how this thing has happened.

> Gender schema processing is considered a readiness on the part of children to encode and organise information according to how culture defines sex roles. For example, a child may observe that boys are usually described as 'strong or brave' whereas girls are more usually described as 'nice or sweet'. Cultural stereotypes, therefore, become self-fulfilling prophecies because the child learns not only that the sexes differ but more importantly that certain attributes are associated more with one sex than the other. The extreme degree to which our society classified behaviour and objects into masculine versus feminine only intensifies the development of a gender scheme. (Bascow, 1992)

The weighting placed on expressing only one side of our sexual make-up costs us dearly. The young adult is challenged to face up to this deficiency. In regarding himself as 'masculine' the young man has to conceptualize himself as being tough, an achiever, powerful and potent as opposed to the feminine 'feeling' orientation.

The notion of androgyny has accumulated a share of controversy since it was introduced into the psychological literature in the 1960s. We are continually learning more about what it means to be androgynous. Basically this word is just a convenient way of defining those persons who are able to show a *combination* of high scores on both masculinity and femininity scales. Men who score high on the masculinity scale may well be classified as having higher self-esteem, higher achievement needs, to be dominant and aggressive. Femininity scales are related to different kinds of behaviour – the ability to show empathy, social skills, sensitivity to other people's feelings. The androgynous person – by definition – has both sets of skills and this combination has shown itself to be most advantageous in the forming of long-standing relationships. In one set of studies male and female subjects representing various combinations of masculinity and femininity scores met each other in a waiting room. The results may contradict some common assumptions. The lowest level of interaction and reported enjoyment was found amongst the pairs sex typed as high in masculinity and femininity. In contrast when *both* persons were androgynous, levels of interaction and mutual enjoyment were high (Ickes and Barnes, 1987/8).

Men and women have been socialized to behave in sexist ways and they have difficulty in developing and integrating new roles that are compatible with non-sexist behaviour. Sex role strain (a major presenting problem) is the result of the rigid gender roles which restrict people's abilities to actualize their human potential.

Women are more likely to experience role conflict. They have limitations placed on them because of the pervasive ideas linked to the feminine sex role in our society – polarized between the page three 'Bimbo', the mother of children or the high-powered executive complete with briefcase.

Young men in our society face another kind of sexual conflict. Being a 'man' creates oppressive effects. Masculine mystique still implies that femininity is inferior to masculinity as a gender orientation.

Rigid gender roles can lead – in some young men– to what has been labelled as 'fear of femininity' (O'Neill, 1981). This is defined as a strong concern that one is seen to possess feminine values, attitudes and behaviours and that this has a negative effect – that they will be seen as weak, submissive and dependent. This can be identified in the restriction to express one's own feelings or the right to be seen to be tender and vulnerable. It can be seen in the current wave of homophobia – fears of being homosexual and having prejudicial beliefs of stereotypes about what it means to be gay.

We can see this illustrated in the current obsession with achievement and success, with the preoccupation with work and status – establishing either accomplishment or delinquent behaviour as a means of substantiating and exhibiting one's value (O'Neill, 1981).

Conclusions

The intention in this chapter has been to show that the result or the outcome of earlier development and of its distortions becomes fixed only by the end of the period designated as young adulthood. There will have been in the past many times when breakdown was allowed to pass without too much notice or concern with the result that at this time the young man or woman will be faced with severe distortions of their lives at best and often with mental illness at worst.

However, with the concept of breakdown of a process, before the results are fixed about a sexual identity, a sense of self or meaning, there is a possibility at this time of reversibility. In working with our clients we are made aware of the fact that many of them need not have reached the point of despair or illness at which they are and that the difference in their lives could well have been made earlier if they had been taken seriously and if their feelings had not been dismissed as a passing phase.

Depression and other forms of mental suffering are not, therefore, only a problem of individuals but also of groups and societies. There is no question that suffering involves biology or that we see individual variations and thresholds for becoming depressed, or that sadly some depressions are genetically loaded. However, what this chapter has tried to articulate is that the problems of the young adult are associated with roles and relationships, with self-organization and self-value. This leads the counselling psychologist to recognize human needs and the problems of creating environments that are not psychologically toxic.

Erikson's (1981) three adult identity phases – finding intimate relationships in early adulthood, establishing social links with different generations in middle adulthood and engaging in a retrospective life review process in late adulthood – were reflected in a study by Kamptner (1989) which concerned the material possessions most valued and treasured in these age groups. The young adults studied referred to the social ties that their cars, jewellery, music equipment, photographs and general memorabilia symbolized and the pleasure they provided. This study highlighted the changes that occur with age in the referent of treasured possessions, from those connected with 'mother' in early life to self in middle childhood and later to others in adulthood. He noted that the younger person's concern with functional items – status-orientated and reinforced by peer group fads and fashions – was gradually substituted for more personal items until in the 25–30 age group it was replaced by those items which indicated an increasing concern with social networks and social history as represented in these objects.

We are bombarded with pictures of people who are better, brighter, more wealthy, more beautiful. We are fed myths of the happy family (despite divorce rates of 40 per cent). Old people get beaten up in their homes, young people lose their jobs, roam the streets and are socially marginalized. Young adults are the casualties of our society, treated as subordinates and cannot be assessed as agents of value since there are so many competitors for that role.

Our consumer society gives them things too easily, things which are attractive and valuable only if earned by their own efforts. 'When they hop in and out of bed young people begin to despise sex as such' (Winnicott, 1969). The obsession with style, with brand awareness, does mean something. It is the defence mechanism of young people who feel powerless. You may have no say over whether you can get a job but you have incredible choices in how you can look, what you would like to have – choices which the advertisers and the manufacturers can offer you. Consumer choice has come to mean a great deal to this generation. It offers a way of escape and a means of self-expression.

How have we got into the state when there are so many people who feel depressed and ashamed of themselves? We have a social fabric that is orientated to social success – if we have failed it is because we no longer act as humans and have forgotten our human needs for love, respect and compassion (Lorenz, 1952). This is in consequence to early life histories of affectionless parenting, economic stress, past and present abuse and the rendering of young people into objects of glorification.

No government will take on board that unemployment will be a major factor in suicide for some, a major source of despair for others – the modern dictum is to keep on swallowing the tablets.

References

Bascow, S.A. (1992) *Gender Stereotypes and Roles*. New York, Pacific Grove, CA: Brooks/Cole.

Bimrose, J. (1993) 'Counselling and social context', *Counselling and Psychology for Health Professionals*, 35: 149–65.

Bowlby, J. (1979) 'Self-reliance and conditions that promote it', in *The Making and Breaking of Affectional Bonds*. London: Tavistock.

Central Policy Review Staff and Central Statistical Office (1992) *People and Their Families*. London: HMSO.

Central Statistical Office (1994) *Social Trends*. London: HMSO.

Erikson, E.H. (1981) *Identity and the Life Cycle: A Reissue*. New York: Norton.

Gould, R.L. (1978) *Transformations, Growth and Change in Adult Life*. New York: Simon and Schuster.

Guzder, J. and Krishna, M. (1993) 'Sita Shakti', in *Cultural Paradigms for Indian Women* (British Psychological Society, Psychotherapy Newsletter No. 13). pp. 30–67.

Haley, J. (1990) *Leaving Home*. New York: McGraw-Hill.

Ickes, W. and Barnes, R.D. (1987/8) 'The role of sex and self-monitoring in unstructured dyadic interactions', *Journal of Personality and Social Psychology*, 35: 315–30.

Kamptner, N.L. (1989) 'Personal possessions and their meanings in childhood, adolescence and old age', in S. Spacapan and S. Oskamp (eds), *The Social Psychology of Aging*. London: Sage. pp. 165–96.

Kelly, G.A. (1955) *The Psychology of Personal Constructs*. New York: Norton.

Kraemer, S. (1982) 'Leaving home', *Journal of Adolescence*, 5: 51–62.

Levi, D., Sterlin, H. and Sagard, R. (1980) *Report of the National Institute for Mental Health*. New York: NIMH.

Levinson, D.J. (1980) 'Towards a conception of the adult life course', in N.J. Smelser and E.H. Erikson (eds) *Themes of Work and Love in Adulthood*. Cambridge, MA: Harvard University Press. pp. 265–90.

Lorenz, K. (1952) *King Solomon's Ring*. London: Methuen.

McCrae, R.R. and Costa, P.T. Jr (1990) *Personality in Adulthood*. New York: Guilford.

O'Neill, J.M. (1981) 'Patterns of gender role, conflict and strain. Sexism and fear of femininity in men's lives', *Personnel and Guidance Journal*, 60: 203–10.

Peel, J. (1994) 'A family album', *Radio Times*, 20/26 August.

Super, D.E. (1990) 'A life-span, life-space approach to career development', in D. Brown, I. Brookes and Associates (eds), *Career Choice and Development*. San Francisco: Jossey Bass. pp. 197–261.

Winnicott, D.W. (1969) *The Maturational Processes and the Facilitating Environment*. London: The Hogarth Press.

Wrightsman, L.S. (1994) *Adult Personality Development*. London: Sage.

16

Psychological Counselling in Mid-Life Issues

Paul Brown and Anne Abel Smith

> Middle age is often said to represent a time of personal crisis, or, at the least, to be a troubling transition between the prime of life and the decline of old age, as the individual measures his or her goals, accomplishments, and commitments in terms of 'time left' in life. The popular image of midlife upheaval depicts last-ditch efforts to recapture youth and last-change efforts to start a new life. However . . . in midlife continuities of love, relationships, family commitments, work involvements, and personality patterns often seem more salient than any changes that occur. (Berger, 1994: 559)

In preparing the chapter which follows we have discovered a paucity of literature describing counselling practice on mid-life issues. We have also noted a tendency for the descriptive and (limited) experimental literature to confuse the crisis and developmental perspectives of mid-life to which Berger refers in the opening quotation. Our approach, therefore, has been to start from a description of what characterizes mid-life; to specify the issues that arise; and to address those issues and some implications for practice.

It cannot be stressed too strongly, however, that the counselling psychologist needs to maintain an open ear to the particularity of any one person's experience; and to resist the temptation to force that experience into what might be inappropriate patterns deriving from a still-emerging understanding of the mid-life process.

What characterizes mid-life?

Unlike the major life events of birth, marriage and death, there are no absolutes about mid-life. That people find themselves (in all senses of the word 'find') in mid-life is perhaps its most particular characteristic.

Shakespeare described seven ages of man (*As You Like It*, II. vii), from the 'puking infant' to an old age of being 'sans eyes, sans teeth, sans everything'. Levinson (1978) is the person in recent psychological history who especially created structure around the concept of there being an adult life cycle of psychological events and who set out to anatomize its structure. In doing so he notes the five life stages delineated by the

Spanish philosopher José Ortega y Gasset (1978: 28), and describes the eight ego states posited by Erikson (p. 29) in his theory of the life cycle.

Erikson's first four stages cover early and middle childhood. The fifth, Identity *v.* Identity confusion, occupies adolescence and the move into early adult life. The sixth stage, Intimacy *v.* Isolation, arises in the twenties. Generativity *v.* Stagnation occurs about 40, and Integrity *v.* Despair at about 60.

Levinson (1978) described four phases of the human life cycle, of which the first includes childhood and adolescence. The three adult stages have some correspondence to Erikson's five adult stages. Levinson's four stages each last roughly 25 years and overlap, 'so that a new one is getting under way as the previous one is being terminated' (1978: 18). The sequence was derived from biographical research which started on 40 men in the age range 35–45 at the beginning of the study in 1969, but which later expanded to cover the entire developmental sequence of the adult years.

Levinson's stages are the effective starting point for the growth of interest in mid-life process that followed the publication of his 1978 work, stimulated by an earlier presentation of many of its central themes by Sheehy in 1974. Levinson's life stages are:

1 Childhood and adolescence: age 0–22
2 Early adulthood: age 17–45
3 Middle adulthood: age 40–65
4 Late adulthood: age 60 onwards

Levinson describes each of these periods as an 'era' – a 'time of life' in the broadest sense.

> Although important changes go on within it, each era has its own distinctive and unifying qualities, which have to do with the character of living. . . . An era is . . . not a stage in biological development, in personality development or in career development. It is much broader and more inclusive than a developmental stage or period. . . . The eras are analogous to the acts of a play, the major divisions of a novel, or the gross segments into which a biographer divides the life of his subject. (1978: 18–19).

Levinson also goes on to observe further that:

> The move from one era to the next is neither simple nor brief. It requires a basic change in the fabric of one's life, and this takes more than a day, a month or even a year. The transition between eras consistently takes four or five years – not less than three and rarely more than six. . . . A developmental transition creates a boundary zone in which a man terminates the outgoing era and initiates the incoming one. (p. 19)

In this context the mid-life transition for men occupies roughly the years from 40 to 45. It serves to terminate early adulthood and to initiate middle adulthood. The post-Levinson literature tends to confuse the shorter transitional periods which mark the entrances and exits to a phase with the longer processes in-between the transitional stages, so that the terms 'mid-life process' and 'mid-life crisis' have become almost synonymous – as if the only events of the mid-life period were crisis-driven.

In his pioneering work Levinson chose avowedly to concentrate on the adult life process of men and not to include that of women. He did not want to make the assumption that the two genders develop in either identical or totally different ways, and took the view that later empirical work would clarify what the similarities and dissimilarities across the genders might be. The same would also be true for adults of varying race, class, sexual orientation and functional abilities. We make further reference to this below.

Levinson's very precise definition of the mid-life transitional period as covering five years (40–45) is not one that has been maintained in the mid-life literature that has developed since 1978. Jaques (1965, 1990) puts the critical age of transition at around 35. Hunter and Sundel ascribe (though we believe quite wrongly) to Levinson the time span from '40 to 60 with five years before and after as transition or entrance–exit periods' (1989: 11) for the mid-life period. Sheehy quotes research which shows that 'working class men describe themselves as middle-aged at forty and old by sixty. Business executives and professionals, by contrast, do not see themselves as reaching middle age till fifty, and old age means seventy to them' (1974: 305).

Although there is scant reference to it in the literature, it might be reasonable to assume that, in the absence of precise biological features, the individual perception of what constitutes 'mid-life' would bear some relation to expected life expectancy. Individuals typically count their years with some precision, and can easily calculate the mid-point of their expectations. In Western culture, with a life expectancy that is not short of 80 years for both men and women, setting the mid-life point at somewhere between 35 and 40 would have a happy logic to it. On such a basis it might be expected that in countries with much shorter survival spans the mid-life period would be perceived as arriving earlier, and/or be briefer, and/or be more intensely experienced. There is very little cross-cultural work that explores these commonsensical assumptions. Based on a psychoanalytic formulation about mid-life being to do with relinquishing infantile omnipotence, Takenori (1980) argues that the mid-life transition stage happens later in Japanese men and women than in Americans. Within the same sort of psychoanalytically derived theorizing, denial of the possibility of death or defensive assumption of immortality might well cause any one individual's perceptions about what constitutes the mid-life phase to vary.

A practical question for counselling practice which arises from the rather fluid state of definition about what constitutes the boundaries of the mid-life process is whether there are characteristics which distinguish the period of middle life (generally set not younger than 35, and not lasting beyond 65) from the transitional periods (generally agreed to be about five years) which mark the entry to and exit from the mid-life period. As this is not a question which is systematically tackled in the literature, the consequence is that a distinction between the phenomena of mid-life and the transitional periods at entry and exit are not clearly maintained. It might be assumed, *a priori*, that there would be different types of phenomena arising during the shorter transitional periods than during the longer period in between the transitional states. If such a distinction could be maintained, then 'mid-life' and its transitional states might, for any one individual, be defined phenomenologically rather than chronologically – a process which is increasingly adopted with respect to the biology of ageing.

Levinson is quite clear that mid-life process needs to be described not from a biological, psychological or social perspective alone (to which one might also add a spiritual dimension), but from an understanding of how these main themes might interact and bring their varied influences to bear summatively. To illuminate what is happening for any one individual, however, it is necessary to find a starting point of description. To do this Levinson (1978: 24ff.) takes three particular vantage points as offering differing perspectives. These are: (1) changes in biological and psychological functioning; (2) the sequence of generations; and (3) the evolution of careers and enterprises. He indicates that the focus should be on different but interweaving elements in observing the landscape of the individual's life.

It is perhaps important to remember that Levinson's work is not derived from a primary interest in disorder, dis-ease or distress. His research was aimed at the description of life processes that might be the common lot of man. It is from the work of Jaques (1965) that the particular exploration of a concept of mid-life crisis comes. Levinson's work put a larger framework around Jaques's more narrowly defined interest in the early death of creative individuals. It is an uncritical merging of Jaques's specific interest and Levinson's larger body of thought that has confused the mid-life literature.

For practical purposes, it seems to us useful to limit the concept of mid-life process to the years between 40 and 55, with transitional stages happening five years either side of those years. The complete mid-life stage is therefore contained within the period 35–60, whilst recognizing that the exit period (55–60) is as much to do with entering late adulthood as completing the mid-life period. Brim (1976), in an early formulation of theories of the male mid-life crisis, was clear that data do not indicate that mid-life stages form an invariant progression of events but that stages are characterized as transitions from one relatively steady state to another.

What are the mid-life issues?

The foundation of Levinson's theory of adult life phases is that within each individual life there is structure; that life structure evolves through a sequence of alternating periods in which a relatively stable, structure-**building** period is followed by a transitional, structure-**changing** period.

> The major developmental tasks of a structure-building period are to make crucial choices, to create a structure around them, to enrich the structure and pursue one's goals within it. These periods ordinarily last six to eight years. In a transitional period the major tasks are to re-appraise the existing structure, explore new possibilities in self and world, and work towards new choices that provide a basis for new structures. . . . The transitional periods generally last four or five years. (1978: 318)

The struggles that occur within transitional periods (the structure-changing time) can sometimes be seen especially vividly in marriages where there is a marked difference in chronological age. In such a marriage the younger person may not be at all ready to grapple with the transitional needs of the older person, especially if these needs prove particularly disruptive. Such was the case in the following set of circumstances:

> Melanie, an English woman of 47, was married to Bill, an American journalist of 64. They had lived in England for five years but returned regularly to the States where Bill felt more at home in his New York habitat than in London; and where their two daughters, aged 15 and 12, felt their real home to be; and where Melanie had enjoyed her expatriate status.
>
> They had come to England because of Bill's work. None of them had really wanted to, and the appointment he had taken up was proving to be the twilight of his career rather than its apogee. Three years ago he started an affair with a woman 30 years his junior, and Melanie had discovered it a year later. Bill had given up the affair, not without difficulty, over the subsequent nine months. Melanie had recently started training as a counsellor.

360

> She came to talk about the adjustments she was trying to make in her life – a continuing marriage to a man she saw as flawed; the wish to maintain stability for her daughters through their adolescence; her increasing insights into what human behaviour is all about; feeling unattractive; having no base in which she felt secure; worrying about the prospect of Bill becoming 70 ('old') when she would still be active middle-fifties. None of her life seemed to be in sync.

The sorts of experiences described above are often quite difficult to fit within what is at best poorly developed and at worst often highly speculative theory. For O'Connor, whose focus is more to do with crisis than general description, the issues that develop around 35 are an ever-increasing awareness of the ageing process itself. 'Men become aware of their increasing baldness, their flabby and deteriorating physique and the major discrepancy between the mirror reflection . . . and their memory of the much younger, virile athlete' (1981: 37).

This sounds to us a rather over-generalized and simplistic view of jogger-man. Hunter and Sundel see a more complex process. They are keen to demythologize the crisis-ridden image of the mid-life period.

> Conflicting images about midlife abound. We hear that it is the peak period of life. People at this stage are seen as wise and powerful – in charge of themselves and others. They have 'a sense of competence, self-confidence, and purpose'. On the other hand, a typical assumption is that 'life after 40' starts a downhill slide in energy, attractiveness, occupational performance, and happiness at home. Men are often depicted as 'bored with their jobs, their wives, their lives'. It is supposed that they find true happiness by leaving spouses and having facelifts – 'designed to reinvigorate them after their apparent midlife crisis'.
>
> Midlife men, then, are thought to be anxious, conflicted, and going through a crisis. The women are menopausal, fretful, and depressed. The culprit of the negative psychological reactions is seen to be signs of ageing or losing youth (e.g., menopause, hair loss, slowing of reaction time, the fortieth or fiftieth birthday). The strongest cues that affect how old one feels are most likely changes in health and appearance.
>
> The idea that the central theme of midlife is crisis often appears in the popular press and media. It also appears in the scientific literature, but the crisis image is only one model used to conceptualize development at midlife. A competing model is based on a transition image. There is a debate in the social sciences regarding which model best describes and explains the developmental changes that occur during midlife. The crisis model assumes that normative developmental changes, including a crisis at midlife, occur within the individual at certain ages. The alternative conceptualization, or transition model, rejects the notion that a midlife crisis or any other crisis is a normative developmental event. Still, in the popular press, media and some of

the scientific literature, the crisis model appears to dominate. (1989: 13; in-text references omitted)

While Levinson (1978) observed that in his exploratory research 80 per cent of the men studied described major turmoil during the mid-life period, Cooper (1977, quoted in Chiriboga, 1989), using a Midlife Crisis Scale, reported only 2 per cent of 300 respondents having feelings that suggested any kind of crisis; and this low figure has been replicated in the range 2–5 per cent in a variety of other studies since. This very considerable discrepancy may tell us as much about the sensitivities of different methods of inquiry as about the incidence of mid-life crisis, however. Moreover, the normal struggles of everyday life should not necessarily be assigned to a mid-life crisis category. Consider whether the following circumstances would constitute evidence of a mid-life crisis or not.

> At the age of 43, Steven had built up a very successful business in the financial services industry and two years later had sold out. From a Jewish working-class background he now found himself the possessor of a not insubstantial fortune.
>
> Five years previously, which had been make-or-break time for his company and his ambitions to sell out, his wife had had an affair with her dentist, and left despite his own wish to repair their marriage. Six months before he sold his company, a whirlwind romance with an Israeli lawyer aged 41 had resulted in a pregnancy, followed by marriage and the arrival of twins. For nearly two years he had tried to become a man of leisure, settle into life with his new family, and work out what to do next. Diana, his wife, had stopped work upon the arrival of the twins, had whatever domestic help she needed, and was also beginning to feel restless about the lack of professional stimulation.
>
> They came for counselling together, wanting to think through how they might merge their lives more deliberately than the headlong romance, marriage and arrival of family had allowed.
>
> To start with, it seemed useful to ask how, even though married, they might go about courting each other. Over the next year each of them discovered more about the other than they had previously known. They seriously considered but abandoned the idea of spending a couple of years wandering the world as a way of cementing their relationship in shared experiences they would both like to have. The detailed exploration of how they might go about such a trip and where it might lead them had sufficed. They abandoned it without regret. Diana took up a research degree in law. Steven started investing in small company start-ups, seeing if he could create with and for others

what he had created for himself. The twins started going to nursery school. Life went on.

We ourselves would not consider the above circumstances to be primarily those of a mid-life crisis. It is of course true that we had no knowledge of what was driving Steven's first wife's shift into the relationship which caused the breakdown of his marriage; nor did we have any knowledge about what was driving her dentist-lover, or even his age. Steven's circumstances were driven more by market forces – an offer to buy his company, in which his part was that he did not reject the offer. Steven and Diana between them put a great deal of effort into structure-building. That, however, is a task of much of life.

Within the overall framework of the individual life structure, Levinson sees the mid-life transition phase as having an initial focus on reappraising the past. The question, 'what have I done with my life?' begins to intrude as the illusions of early adult life give way to externally appraised reality. As the mid-life transition proceeds, a shift takes place from past to future.

Change may take place in either the *external* or *internal* aspects of life. The more dramatic external changes include divorce, remarriage, major shifts in occupation and lifestyle, marked decline in level of functioning, notable progress in creative output or in upward social mobility.

For men who make few apparent external changes in this period, close observation will generally detect important though less obvious internal changes. Social outlook, personal values and the beginnings of a sense of creating a legacy appear. If the primary task of mid-life transition is to re-evaluate and probably modify the life structure of the thirties, then the test of the transition that has been made is the satisfactoriness of the life structure which emerges from it.

In the key transition periods, the developmental process of what Jung called 'individuation' occurs. His theory of mid-life individuation is not systematically described in any single work, but it has continuous emphasis in his understanding of the development of a person's relationship to himself (or herself) and the external world. Whilst Erikson gave primary emphasis to Generativity *v.* Stagnation as a stage of ego development in the middle years, and Jaques saw the central theme at mid-life as coming to terms with one's own mortality, Jung's complex concept of the process of individuation focuses, at mid-life, in a renewed effort at establishing an independent identity.

The four tasks of Jung's mid-life individuation (as summarized by Levinson, 1978: 197), are to find one's own position in the polarities of youth/age; destructiveness/creativity; masculinity/femininity; and attachment/separateness. Hunter and Sundel (1989) impose a more global,

363

psychologically defined, non-polar macro-structure upon the mid-life process and see there being five areas which merit consideration – physical status; shifts in cognitive structures; mental health and personality development; the social context of marriage and family; and personal development linked to social responsibility.

From our own perspective of practice and the existing literature, we ourselves consider that the following list of topics is one from which mid-life process, transitional phases and any attendant crises may usefully be viewed.

1   Existing relationships (including extra-marital), marriage and family matters, including children, parents, and previous marital and dependent relationships.
2   Health; functional abilities; sexuality (functional as well as orientation) and gender.
3   Personal and economic security in the context of current socio-economic climate.
4   Career and work.
5   Race and class.
6   Spiritual convictions.
7   The development of wisdom.

We have included matters in the above which are of significance to women as well as to men. Although most writers find it easier to focus on mid-life in men rather than in women, O'Connor (1981) quite rightly observes that the male in crisis does, in most instances, act out his crisis in the male–female context.

What is perhaps especially apparent in the differences between men and women in the mid-life process is that while the man begins to be concerned with his inner world, the woman begins to be more concerned with the external world. For women who have had their roles generally defined within a nurturing/caring model, the sense of discontent that a lack of apparent overt achievement brings in those Western societies which undervalue domestic and mothering skills is a major determinant of the woman's perception of her mid-life position. Women who have spent their twenties in pursuit of a career, and are faced in their thirties with the biological imperatives of a limited time horizon in which they might have children, and who try to juggle their potential for having children with career options whilst, in many cases, feeling quite disillusioned about male-based striving models, clearly have as complex a set of processes to try to integrate as the convoluted structure of this sentence suggests. Gilbert and Davidson (1989) are especially lucid on the mid-life issues which face dual-career families.

Addressing the issues and some implications for practice

While the list of issues above may usefully form the basis of factual inquiry, the counselling practitioner needs to bear in mind at the same time those wide-ranging fundamental psychological themes which may appear with varying kinds of impact at any phase of life – attachment, loss, separation, hope and the various manifestations of fear, anger, hostility and love in particular.

From a practical point of view, it may be helpful to carry in one's mind a two-dimensional model in which any of the life events listed in 1–7 above can be tested against the fundamental psychological themes that resonate throughout human experience. It is into this context that the ideas of Erikson and Jung can be combined with the actual events of day-to-day life, thereby integrating the life event, biographical approach of Levinson with the thematic process considerations of ego-psychology. This is the particular province of psychological counselling in the mid-life period. Brewi and Brennan (1992: abstract) describe the amorphous particularity of the mid-life process in the following terms:

> Dying and rising in midlife (whether in the crisis, the transition or midlife itself) is filled with peril, because in delusion everything held dear in life's first half may be overthrown. Midlife is a time of increased consciousness. At midlife the opposites, the shadow, and other archetypes that reveal themselves are encountered, discerned, befriended, and integrated. Accepting the ambiguity that characterizes this stage of life and letting it happen without jumping quickly to decisions is an essential first step.

In the case illustration below, themes about attachment and fear of loss resonate and echo within and between the two psyches that have engaged in this particular marriage:

> Martha telephoned wanting an appointment for her husband. 'I'm fed up with his pestering me about sex,' she said.
>
> Philip came, not entirely unwillingly, asking to be told whether his interest in sex was abnormal. He wanted Martha to dress in shorter skirts, wear more exotic underwear, and if she didn't want to look like a tart all the time, then try at least once or twice a month for him. He couldn't understand why Martha withheld her sexual favours from him when she had on three occasions had brief affairs during their marriage, though on each occasion in response to affairs which he claimed to have had though subsequently denied.
>
> It seemed sensible to meet Martha. She kept the next appointment by herself – a woman in her late thirties, dressed in a waif-like, Laura

Ashley-derived style, furious at Philip's demands upon her, but with a seductive sexuality very evidently in place.

With such a set of issues, the counselling psychologist has to choose a point of entry. Metaphor is invariably helpful in such circumstances.

At the third session, together, we talked about what had been learnt in their individual sessions about childhood patterns. The metaphor we used was that marriage choices rely upon the unconscious software of early life and family experience. Only in marriage is there an attempt to plug the software systems together. It is surprising what the matches that feel like mis-matches can be.

Martha had been the younger daughter in a family where her father verbally abused a cowed and frightened mother to an extortionate degree; had occasionally brought one of his many extra-marital girlfriends back to the marital home; and took great pleasure in displaying a small but powerful physique at the local tennis club in summer and the swimming baths in winter. Martha had decided by the age of 10 that she would never let any man treat her the way her mother was treated. In using her as a confidante for her own misery as well as stories of father's sexual behaviour, mother had unwittingly sexualized Martha from a small child onwards.

Philip had come from a family where there were no physical contacts of any kind between any members of the family that he could recall. His interest in matters sexual had developed covertly through forbidden reading of *Playboy* as a teenager.

He had seen marriage as the place where his fantasies could be realized. When they were not, his mild and gentle demeanour switched into vicious verbal abuse of a kind with which Martha was all too familiar.

Martha and Philip had previously sought interpretive psychodynamic help, and had attended regularly for more than a year without benefit. They said they wanted help in how to be, not how to understand. The software model created an opportunity both to understand and to try modifications of the program. That was an approach with which they managed to engage.

As is apparent from the above, the complexity of understanding the mid-life process for counselling or therapeutic reasons should not be under-estimated. It is crucial for the practitioner to be very aware of and open to the interactive effects of life events as they appear in real-life settings as well as the concurrent and modifying impact of underlying psychological themes. It may also be of especial importance – as in all counselling work – that the practitioner is especially sensitive to his/her own current mid-life state. Jones (1990) has described the impact that a series of personal crises, including the suicide of a colleague and his own divorce, had upon his clinical work, and vice versa.

The starting point for a practitioner concentrating on mid-life matters is to be able to delineate accurately and sympathetically the events of the life of the person seeking help; to inform the facts with a sensitive appreciation of underlying process; and in so doing enable those discoveries to be made by the client which will help establish the new perspectives and which will in turn contribute to managing the mid-life phase.

There is wide agreement in the literature that mid-life is a period for re-evaluating relationships of all kinds, but that does not necessarily mean catastrophic change. Indeed, there is increasing evidence that mid-life is more readily seen as a period of great satisfaction and achievement than a crisis-ridden state (Blieszner, 1988).

Schmidt (1984) questions whether mid-life crisis should be considered as a disease or a lifestyle issue, and concludes in favour of the latter. She sees both 'dropping out' and 'self-fulfilment' as a type of regression or inability to tolerate conflict situations. Individual psychology strategies, such as examination of lifestyle and redefinition of goals, appear to be particularly well suited as strategies for coping with mid-life crisis.

One of the major life re-evaluations is that of the possibility of divorce. Rollins (1989) presents evidence to show that, in the USA, divorce is much less likely to occur at mid-life than earlier in life. As mid-life coincides with what are regarded as the high stress periods for families, and there is also research evidence to suggest that marital satisfaction is lower in mid-life than at earlier or later stages, mid-life marriage appears to contain paradoxical processes which are not easily explained. Iwanir and Ayal (1991) describe a technique for provoking change within a mid-life marriage by the implementation of trial separation and divorce, raising at the same time concerns about whether therapists should maintain neutrality or take a stand concerning marriage in general and the relationship at hand in particular. Maltas (1992) presents two case examples illustrating the impact of mid-life turmoil on marriage, and adopts a model which supposes that a marriage can only fully become a marriage after illusions are lost, the possibility of separation is faced, and the individuals each choose to stay.

The influence of children upon the progress of the mid-life era has received a certain amount of attention. Prosen et al. (1981) discuss the interaction of the adolescent's lifestyle with the ongoing life cycle experiences of his/her parents. Successful intervention involves describing and discussing the maladaptive attempts of both the mid-life parent(s) and the adolescent(s) to solve their individual problems as well as showing them the way in which they are likely to have negatively reinforced and yet paradoxically mimicked the other's behaviours. La-Sorsa and Fodor (1990) explore especially the mother–daughter dyad at ages 13–19 and 35–55 respectively, when both are likely to be engaged in self-definition mediated by competition and rebellion. Returning to the theme of marital satisfaction, but this time involving adolescents too, Koski and Steinberg (1990) observed that the gender of the adolescent had no specific effect upon a mother's marital satisfaction; but that high marital satisfaction had a beneficial effect upon parental satisfaction and the management of mid-life crisis.

With an increasing tilt towards an aged population in Western societies, a new mid-life stressor is being identified as 'the sandwich generation'. Chiriboga (1989) and Zal (1992) describe the increasingly complex demands of middle age when the family roles of parent, spouse, child and preferred caregiver have to be managed within one individual spanning three generations simultaneously. Women in particular may find themselves squeezed between competing obligations to their own parents, children, spouses and their own plans for the more active years of the second half of life.

Given the popular view that mid-life is characterized by crisis, epidemiological studies have attempted to determine whether there is support for such a concept from the point of view of health patterns. Ciernia (1985) notes that three of the most commonly referenced problems in mid-life men are alcoholism, divorce and suicide. His conclusions about divorce support those of Rollins (1989); suggest that suicide rates generally decline in the middle years; and that alcohol consumption decreases with age rather than increases. This is not the picture of a turbulent period with adjustment disorders predominating.

This is not to say, however, that there are not clear and observable physiological changes which manifest themselves in both women and men during the middle years. There are; and they are well described by Weg (1989). It is the awareness and perception of these changes, modified by the predominating psychological processes within the individual, which make them of particular interest in the mid-life stages.

Gender and sexuality have, however, attracted a good deal of attention in the mid-life phase. Although research in mid-life developmental psychology has an overwhelmingly male bias, and largely middle-class at that, the clinical work on human sexuality of Masters and Johnson (1970) and Kaplan (1974) has clarified many aspects of mid-life sexuality in women as well as men that would not otherwise have become apparent. Despite the gradual physiological changes that occur in both men and women over the middle years, they both have the capacity to remain sexually active well into older adult life. Indeed there is substantial evidence that women's enjoyment of sexual activity increases significantly throughout the late thirties and into the forties, creating a sexual confidence and spontaneous interest which is sometimes a cause of anxiety to male partners. Rubin (1982) found in a survey of 160 mid-life women that the picture was one of generally improving sexuality. Though more time might be required to establish effective vaginal lubrication and orgasmic response, this simply parallels the processes in the male which require more time and stimulation to establish effective erectile responsivity.

Weg offers the overall view that the life course for women (in America) has undergone significant changes in the last 10–15 years, and especially for the middle-aged female.

> There is greater participation in the work force, a growing number of societally acceptable social roles, and a changing attitude towards the integration of family and work force activities. The middle-aged woman has grown less naive, dependent and fearful. The woman who has the option of moving away from isolation in the home and who aspires to opportunity, privilege and power in the social arena, will continue to reach for intimacy, pleasure and autonomy in the sexual realm. The middle years can become a time for renewal, regeneration and discovery. (1989: 36)

The cessation of ovulation and menstruation that leads to the menopause in women is without immediate physical parallel in men. Whilst there are clear physiological changes associated with it there are a surprising number of operational definitions as to what the menopause actually is, and these often include words such a **premenopause, perimenopause** and **postmenopause** that have none other than descriptive value. Dan and Bernhard (1989) consider that the menopause is a socially constructed concept, and that how it is used depends upon the purposes of the person using the term. It typically occurs in the same age range of 35–55 that characterizes the mid-life phase; has different modal distributions in different cultures; and is viewed very differently from culture to culture and within a culture. Dan and Bernhard report a study which found that 'nurses viewed menopause more negatively than did their menopausal clients. The nurses perceived menopausal women as moody, disinterested in sex, and the victims of "hot flashes". In contrast, the menopausal women reported that they felt freer, more in control of their lives, and enjoyed better communication (including sexual) than they had prior to the menopause' (1989: 53).

Individual lives take place in the context of a macro-economic climate. McIlroy (1984) describes a series of changes in the USA, beginning with the 1950s, in which, she observes, Americans lived an ethic of self-sacrifice and denial. In the 1960s this was replaced with an ethic of self-fulfilment – what has been called the 'me now' generation. She predicted that the 1980s would be a period of people trying to balance life's sacred/expressive aspects and instrumental aspects, making a shift away from self towards connectedness in the world. To the extent that environmental issues have become a major concern in the ten years since her paper, there may be some justification for her view. The societal shifts she sees as likely to be mirrored in mid-life issues come from people being especially concerned with physical changes, mortality, the recognition of limitations, career re-assessment, and concern about power and responsibility. Glad (1989) characterized Reagan's shift to the political right when he became Governor and then President as serving his own needs for social re-adjustment when his professional life as an actor and union activist had bottomed out, successfully turning his anger about his own blocked career on to different targets in pursuit of visible success again.

Individual lives also take place within the context of the individual's pre-existing personality. Haan (1989) has given this particular attention. In a longitudinal study over 50 years, measuring 73 variables at seven different points in time on the same group of people, it was observed that mid-life was a time when three of the seven dimensions to which the 73 variables were reduced registered their highest point. These three dimensions were assertive, cognitively committed and outgoing. All dropped in later adulthood. Women especially showed these changes in comparison with their earlier years. Men became only more outgoing over the same period.

Haan concluded the following from this longitudinal study.

1   At mid-life, participants were functioning more comfortably than at any time before, which contradicts the popular sense that mid-life is necessarily a time of crisis.

2   There is a good deal of shift and change in personality across the years, with a high degree of instability (from a predictive point of view) across the transitional period from adolescence to adulthood.

3   In adult years three attributes of personality – assertiveness, outgoing-ness and dependability – were age-*in*sensitive. Three other variables – self-confidence, warmth and cognitive commitment – were age-sensitive, but the sexes differ in the timing of their reactivity. For men these changes occur from early to middle adulthood, especially with regard to self-confidence and warmth. For women, gains occurred from middle to late adulthood across all three aspects. The results suggest that some personality characteristics may be relatively stable throughout life whilst other aspects are more fluid at middle age. If this is the case, then it would not be appropriate to think of mid-life

as being a unitary structure. It also lends support to the idea that mid-life is a particular period of re-assessment and adjustment.

4   Three dimensions that seemed to represent vigour, self-certainty and efficient problem-solving peaked at mid-life and then began to drop, although not always to a significant degree.

These results are, of course, for groups of people and represent trends rather than expectancies for any one individual. In counselling practice they should therefore be taken as guides rather than fixed expectations. What they do especially point towards, however, is the possibility that current life circumstances may be of especial importance in creating personality shifts in mid-life; and that such events should be given as much consideration as any psychodynamic formations that might underlie specific counselling practice.

Careers have been a major focus of the mid-life literature too. As Chiriboga (1989: 136) observes, the world of work exerts a compelling demand upon the time of working men and women. 'For women, the middle years are often enhanced by career entry and re-entry, with women reporting gains in both self-esteem and satisfaction. For men, on the other hand, the second half of the mid-life period may be fraught with increasing anxiety and frustration as the rewards begin to diminish from what had been a primary source of life satisfaction.'

Willis (1989) lays especial emphasis on the threat of professional obsolescence during this period – obsolescence reflecting the failure of individuals to continue learning as new knowledge and techniques become available. In computer-dependent occupations, the speed of change may be very rapid indeed. The term **professional half-life** has been coined to describe the time it takes for 50 per cent of one's professional knowledge to become invalid or obsolete. For computer scientists, the half-life is only two to three years; among engineers, it is five to six years. Thus middle-aged professionals have to develop mechanisms for continuously keeping themselves updated, with learning becoming a life process rather than an initial investment.

Jaques's seminal study on 'Death and the mid-life crisis' (1965) is perhaps especially responsible for the popular sense that there is a sudden and acute perception of an impending ending which overtakes individuals in their late thirties. This is to over-generalize his observations on the biographical processes of exceptionally creative individuals whose actual or creative lives ended in their late thirties, Mozart being an especially vivid example. Ciernia (1985) tested the hypothesis that a male mid-life crisis does exist and that a male's confrontation with his own mortality is significantly related to the mid-life crisis by asking 227 businessmen in the age range 35–60 years to complete a death concern scale. The results were linked to perception and severity of mid-life crisis. The results strongly supported the proposition that death concern is related to such crises. Morgan et al. (1985) argue that organizations have a special responsibility to take note of mid-life processes, not only out of concern for the individuals who may be in significant processes of re-evaluation but also because the middle-aged may become an especially useful mentoring resource to the organization as a whole if growth at this period is constructively facilitated. They characterized individuals in four categories – miserables, marginals, movers and motivators. It was the last named group who remain a valuable organizational asset. Proposals for effective organizational management on mid-life process include the providing of more autonomy and independence by implementing alternative work schedules, job sharing and flexible time; establishing consciousness-raising groups; the provision of professional counselling and sabbatical leave arrangements.

So far as race and class are concerned, the mid-life literature is very sparse. Mid-life matters seem to most researchers to involve only white middle-class men and occasionally women; and usually of professional and white-collar rather than blue-collar occupations. Humphrey and Palmer (1990/1) investigated the effects of race, gender and marital status on the timing of 3,187 suicides in North Carolina across the three adult life stages. Compared to older suicide victims, mid-life victims are more apt to be female and married. Compared to older victims, mid-life victims are more likely to be Caucasian and married. Taking suicide as indicative of disturbance, there was no evidence that mid-life was a time of exceptional stress when compared with the other two groups. Markson and Gognalons (1991) compared data from Switzerland, France and America in trying to establish whether there were common mid-life behaviours and feelings cross-culturally. They concluded that the concept of mid-life can be isolated from specific cultural and historical factors between cultures, but note also that there are substantial differences between different class groups *within* cultures.

Spiritual convictions have received scant attention other than within a broad, humanistic framework concerning personal growth and self-actualization as goal-directed activities within the mid-life era. Conn (1986) observes that, from a Jungian perspective, mid-life might be assumed to be the pre-eminent time for religious conversion.

Perhaps it is under the general influence of Jungian theory and thought that the middle years have come to be seen as quintessentially the period of personal growth. In *The Middle Passage*, Hollis (1993) sets the central mid-life question as being, 'Who am I apart from my history and the roles I have played?' Mid-life is seen from a Jungian perspective as an occasion for redefining and reorienting the personality, a necessary rite of passage between the extended adolescence of the first adulthood and our inevitable appointment with old age and mortality. Hollis sets out to show how the middle passage may be traversed consciously, rendering the second half of life immeasurably richer and offering the possibility of attaining some modicum of wisdom.

Final observations for counselling practice

As indicated earlier, any particular individual engaged in a mid-life process needs to be considered from an intensely individual perspective, bearing in mind that the experience for that individual is much more likely to be unique than normative. In the concluding chapter of *Midlife Myths: Issues, Findings and Practice Implications* (a key text upon which we are delighted to acknowledge that we have relied extensively in the preparation of this chapter), the editors Hunter and Sundel observe that the major gap in practitioner knowledge has been related to lack of systematic research. Counsellors and others have either used broadly based developmental theories from Freud, Jung or Erikson, while behaviour therapists have tended to eschew adult life developmental theory altogether.

Hunter and Sundel (1989: 274) observe that ten key questions to which there were some research-based answers available were addressed within their book. The questions were:

1 Can sexual pleasure by maintained by men and women during mid-life?
2 Does menopause cause emotional disturbance in women?
3 Are individuals in mid-life less mature in the way they think?
4 Does intelligence decline during mid-life?
5 Does the individual at mid-life experience crisis?
6 Does the individual's personality become dull and inflexible during mid-life?
7 Does marital satisfaction decline and does divorce peak at mid-life?
8 Do the stresses of a dual-career marriage outweigh the benefits during mid-life?
9 Are middle-aged individuals isolated and alienated from their families?
10 Is there personal development beyond self-absorption at mid-life?

We have alluded to some of the conclusions arising from these questions in our text above, and would recommend detailed reading of the original text for further understanding. It might be appropriate to offer in some detail, however, the overall conclusions drawn by Hunter and Sundel.

In the first place, the generalizability of group research findings to individuals seeking counselling always needs careful consideration regarding the specific applicability of any one finding. Moreover, from a UK vantage point, the mid-life research literature such as it is comes almost entirely from American white middle-class male subjects. Its applicability to different ethnic, socio-economic and racial groups is very questionable, and its immediate applicability to women very questionable indeed.

In the same way that one man might feel that occupational redundancy in mid-life creates enormous scope for his future and is a challenge that he embraces, whilst another feels suicidal at the loss and intensely fearful for his future, so the range of reactions that a practitioner might see occurring in mid-life are likely to be very considerable indeed. Some women have very little adverse experience during the menopause, whilst others feel it is a defining trauma of their middle years. Wide differences in reaction to life events seem to be especially characteristic of the mid-life period in both men and women.

The gender bias in such research as there is has tended to create an emphasis on crisis and produce an exaggerated, negative image of mid-life in general. The evidence thus far tends to suggest that mid-life is a period which favours women in that they experience more positive personality changes than men; show greater variability in life patterns; are more comfortable and articulate in expressing their feelings; and derive greater benefits than men from dual-career possibilities.

The main thesis of Hunter and Sundel's volume is that mid-life is a period of many more positives than negatives. Despite the fact that research has developed only slowly over the past two decades, there is an increasing sense that a broadly based developmental perspective across the adult life span is beginning to emerge.

Our own view for the development of practice is that, at this stage of knowledge, it seems sensible for a counsellor to create an understanding that comes both from the biographical description of life events (and their influences one upon another over time) and a perspective from dynamic or ego psychology. This integrated approach will, we believe, best help clients to develop an understanding of what significance attaches to the circumstances of their lives.

References

Berger, Kathleen, S. (1994) *The Developing Person Throughout the Life Span*. New York: Worth Publishers.

Blieszner, Rosemary (1988) 'Individual development and intimate relationships in middle and late adulthood', in R.E. Milardo (ed.), *Families and Social Networks*. Newbury Park, CA: Sage. pp. 147–67.

Brewi, Janice and Brennan, Anne (1992) 'Midlife and the spirituality of the child', *Quadrant*, 25: 59–71.

Brim, Orville G. (1976) 'Theories of the male mid-life crisis', *Counseling Psychologist*, 6: 2–9.

Chiriboga, D.A. (1989) 'Mental health at the midpoint: crisis, challenge or relief?', in S. Hunter and M. Sundel (eds), *Midlife Myths*. Newbury Park, CA: Sage. pp. 116–44.

Ciernia, J.R. (1985) 'Death concerns and businessmen's mid-life crisis', *Psychological Reports*, 56: 83–7.

Conn, W.E. (1986) 'Adult conversions', *Pastoral Psychology*, 34: 225–36.

Dan, Alice J. and Bernhard, Linda A. (1989) 'Menopause and other health issues for midlife women', in S. Hunter and M. Sundel (eds), *Midlife Myths*. Newbury Park, CA: Sage. pp. 51–62.

Gilbert, Lucia A. and Davidson, S. (1989) 'Dual career families at midlife', in S. Hunter and M. Sundel (eds), *Midlife Myths*. Newbury Park, CA: Sage. pp. 195–209.

Glad, B. (1989) 'Reagan's midlife crisis and the turn to the right', *Political Psychology* 10(4): 593–624.

Haan, N. (1989) 'Personality at midlife', in S. Hunter and M. Sundel (eds), *Midlife Myths*. Newbury Park, CA: Sage. pp. 145–56.

Hollis, James (1993) *The Middle Passage: From Misery to Meaning in Life*. Toronto, ON: Inner City Books.

Humphrey, J.A. and Palmer, S. (1990/1) 'The effects of race, gender and marital status on suicides among young adults, middle-aged adults, and older adults', *Omega Journal of Death and Dying*, 22: 277–85.

Hunter, S. and Sundel, M. (eds) (1989) *Midlife Myths: Issues, Findings and Practice Implications*. Newbury Park, CA: Sage.

Iwanir, S. and Ayal, Haviva (1991) 'Midlife divorce initiation: from crisis to developmental transition', *Contemporary Family Therapy*, 13: 609–23.

Jaques, E. (1965) 'Death and the mid-life crisis', *International Journal of Psychoanalysis*, 46: 502–14.

Jaques, E. (1990) *Creativity and Work*. Madison, CT: International Universities Press.

Jones, S.E. (1990) 'The working psychologist in personal crisis', Annual Convention of the American Psychological Association, Boston, MA.

Kaplan, Helen Singer (1974) *The New Sex Therapy*. London: Baillière Tindall.

Koski, Kelly J. and Steinberg, Laurence (1990) 'Parenting satisfaction of mothers during midlife', *Journal of Youth and Adolescence*, 19: 465–74.

la-Sorsa, Valerie A. and Fodor, Iris G. (1990) 'Adolescent daughter/midlife mother dyad: a new look at separation and self-definition'. Special Issue: *Women at Midlife and Beyond. Psychology of Women Quarterly*, 14: 593–606.

Levinson, D.J. (1978) *The Seasons of a Man's Life*. New York: Ballantine.

McIlroy, Joan H. (1984) 'Midlife in the 1980s: philosophy, economy and psychology', *Personnel and Guidance Journal*, 62(10): 623–8.

Maltas, C. (1992) 'Trouble in paradise: marital crises of midlife', *Psychiatry*, 55: 122–31.

375

Markson, Elizabeth W. and Gognalons, Nicolet M. (1991) 'Midlife: crisis of nodal point? Some cross-cultural views', in Beth B. Hess and Elizabeth W. Markson (eds), *Growing Old in America*. New Brunswick, NJ: Transaction Publishers.

Masters, W.H. and Johnson, Virginia (1970) *Human Sexual Inadequacy*. London: J.A. Churchill.

Morgan, P.I., Patton, J. and Baker, H.K. (1985) 'The organization's role in managing midlife crisis', *Training and Development Journal*, 39: 56–9.

O'Connor, P. (1981) *Understanding the Mid-Life Crisis*. Sydney: Macmillan.

Prosen, Harry, Toews, John, and Martin, Robert (1981) 'Parental midlife crisis and adolescent rebellion', *Adolescent Psychiatry*, 9: 170–9.

Rollins, B.C. (1989) 'Marital quality at midlife', in S. Hunter and M. Sundel (eds), *Midlife Myths*. Newbury Park, CA: Sage. pp. 184–94.

Rubin, L. (1982) 'Sex and sexuality: women at midlife', in M. Kirkpatricks (ed.), *Women's Sexual Experiences – Exploration of the Dark Continent*. New York: Plenum. pp. 61–82.

Schmidt, Julianna (1984) 'Is "midlife crisis" a disease?' *Zeitschrift für Individualpsychologie*', 9: 101–4.

Sheehy, Gail (1974) *Passages – Predictable Crises of Adult Life*. New York: Dutton.

Takenori, Y. (1980) 'Author's reply to comments', *Hiroshima Forum for Psychology*, 7: 85–6.

Weg, Ruth, B. (1989) 'Sexuality/sensuality in the middle years', in S. Hunter and M. Sundel (eds), *Midlife Myths*. Newbury Park, CA: Sage. pp. 31–50.

Willis, Sherry, L. (1989) 'Adult intelligence', in S. Hunter and M. Sundel (eds), *Midlife Myths*. Newbury Park, CA: Sage. pp. 97–111.

Zal, H.M. (1992) *The Sandwich Generation: Caught Between Growing Children and Aging Parents*. New York: Plenum Press.

17

Psychological Counselling with Older Adults
Charles Twining

The challenge of ageing

Counselling older adults presents at least two major challenges to counselling psychology: the growth in the numbers and proportion of older people in Western society and the inevitability of ageing for us all.

Changing demography

The growth in the numbers of older people is by now fairly well known. There are now more older people in the world than there have ever been. The proportion of pensioners in Britain is higher than ever before: the number of people over the age of 85 in the UK will have increased by more than 60 per cent over the 20-year period from 1981 to 2001. Changes in fertility, mortality and migration are producing a variety of demographic effects around the world (Grisby, 1991).

The reasons for these changes in the UK are threefold. First there has been a sensational fall in infant mortality. Life expectancy at birth has risen steadily during this century. A baby boy born at the turn of the century had a life expectancy of about 46 years. A baby boy born in 1981 could expect on average to live till 70 years of age. This is the result of better sewers, better nutrition and medical advances, almost certainly in that order.

Secondly, there is the larger number of babies born in the early decades of this century. This has been described as people having Victorian-sized families with Edwardian life expectancy. Many of today's 85-year-olds grew up with several brothers and sisters. An 86-year-old woman whom I visited recently told me that she was one of ten children. Compared with the previous, Victorian, generation, more Edwardian babies survived childhood and thus are today's older people.

Thirdly, there is some evidence to indicate that perhaps we may be living a little longer; our life span may be changing. It is usually reckoned that the maximum normal human life span is about 115 years, but even in old age more of us are living longer. In February 1995 Mme Jeanne Calment celebrated her 120th birthday in France. She is the oldest living

377

person whose age can be confirmed. Perhaps the 'theoretical maximum' ought to be at least 125 years. There are certainly more centenarians now than ever before. However the effect of increased life span is nothing like as pronounced as birth rates and infant mortality in determining the number of very elderly people.

Changing attitudes

The challenge to ourselves is to address our own attitudes to ageing. The pensions industry knows very well how difficult it is to get young people to plan for retirement. Counselling older people means facing our own future, the inevitability of ageing and the risks of disability and dependency.

If one must reluctantly adopt some of the terminology of the market-place in caring, older people are certainly therefore a growth market. This should mean that older people are increasingly the recipients of all types of help, including counselling. In fact probably we know next to nothing about the extent to which counselling services as they presently exist address the needs of older people. What evidence we do have, for example the development of counselling psychology in primary care, rather suggests that older clients remain the exception rather than the rule. There has been progress in developing psychological therapies for older people but this tends to have been in specialist areas rather than as the norm in generic services. There are, however, examples of coun-selling directed at a very wide age range (Griffiths, 1994).

The reasons for this are no doubt numerous, but at least one of them relates to one of the key issues in the study of ageing, cohort differ-ences. The proper study of ageing as it is experienced by individuals is at its heart a longitudinal business. In fact this is exactly the right approach for counselling psychology which aims to facilitate individual growth and development. We are interested in how individuals change over time.

In childhood such study is lengthy but not impossible to achieve: a complete study to young adulthood can be done within a working life for example. But if we want to study ageing, the timescale is that much more. We probably need to recruit subjects well before they are 40 and we will want to follow them up until they are at least 75 or 80 years old.

Of course we can do things more quickly by comparing current age groups, for example those who are in their forties with those in their eighties. Unfortunately, this tells us a lot about age differences and not much about age changes. I was born in 1950, my friend May was born in 1910. The differences resulting from our different experiences are at least as great as differences due to ageing.

These age differences are certainly one of the most interesting features of helping older people: they have really wonderful stories to tell. However, these age differences must not trick us into thinking that how older people are now is how we will be then. Psychologically speaking age differences tend to be much bigger than age changes. If you want to know how you will be when you are 80 (and you stand a very good chance of getting to that age) take a good look at yourself now; but at your emotions, not in the mirror. The outward physical changes of ageing are far more marked than those affecting the persona.

The other side of the cohort effect coin is selective survival. Those who live into advanced old age tend to be rather different from those who die younger. Thus if you look at a random sample of people who are, let us say, 85, they are not the same as a random sample of those who were 45 forty years ago. Over a large group there are significant predictors of longevity such as socio-economic group, occupation, level of education and even IQ. Again, it makes it difficult to generalize from age comparisons to ageing changes. At an individual level, which is where counselling psychology begins, this fortunately does not make much difference. It is individual life experience which matters most. It is, however, something that matters if you are trying to make sense of ageing research and applying it to the concerns of individuals.

This chapter will focus on what are some of the most relevant findings from ageing research regarding memory, cognition, affect and personality. A reasonable grasp of these is essential both to challenge one's own stereotypes of ageing and to be alert to inappropriate expectations among older people themselves. Ageing is not a condition separate from our own experience. It is certainly not an illness. In fact it is a process we all share and which we aspire to assimilate. Counselling older people is not about 'us' helping 'them', trying to use our skills to help someone to develop to be more like us, or at least some form of 'normal' adjustment. Quite apart from anything else the client may have at least twice as much relevant experience of the ageing process as the counsellor. It is hardly appropriate to cast the novice as the expert. Rather it is about trying to help clients assimilate the realities of ageing. This may in some cases be best done by facilitating peer counselling (France, 1989).

Helping clients to test reality means having some idea what that reality might be. As the client is the more experienced at a personal level there is little point in looking to your own experience. What we know from the formal study of ageing can, however, help in understanding what is and is not part of the universal ageing process. This may mean we can help people to tackle problems which they, and others, might have wrongly put down to 'growing old'. You need to have some idea what you can expect 'at your age'. We must also consider how this knowledge can be

379

translated into principles for counselling older people. What are the common tasks to be accomplished and what can be done to help?

Many of the precipitants of distress, for example bereavement, health problems, family discord etc. can happen at any age. Their special features are dealt with in other chapters. The focus here is on the special features of ageing.

Finally, we shall consider some of the professional issues, including a recognition of our own ageing and mortality and how counselling psychology fits in with the way health and social care are given to older people.

Understanding normal ageing

What counselling psychology may bring to the helping process includes knowledge of the scientific study of ageing as it affects people in general. This body of knowledge and its theoretical basis may help put the client's experience in the context of a broader picture. It may help both parties make sense of what is happening. However, just as the counsellor tries to help the client understand their experience and make sense of it, so the counsellor will be learning more about the realities of ageing at an individual level.

The theoretical challenges of the study of ageing are reflected at the level of individual experience. There are many myths about ageing and often they are believed strongly by older people themselves. It is helpful in understanding ageing therefore if we test our own views against reality. For example, we may usefully distinguish between the changes which happen universally, which we may see as primary ageing, and those which may result from extrinsic factors which are therefore secondary ageing.

The distinction is perhaps easiest to see at a biological level. We know that many organs of the body, including the brain, do not regenerate during adult life. Thus there is a fairly constant decline in functions such as lung capacity and liver function quite closely related to age. Other changes such as those happening to skin, for example, depend a great deal on extrinsic factors in the environment. In the case of skin the most important of these is exposure to sunlight. Thus one of the most 'typical' signs of ageing, wrinkles on your face, is actually largely dependent on how much you are out in the sun. Thus older people in sunny Mediterranean countries may appear older than we think they are based on a northern European view.

The changes in the brain include some which do seem to be almost universal with age. The capacity and speed of processing of information declines very much like lung and liver function. Even quite simple measures such as choice reaction time or abilities on divided-attention tasks can demonstrate at least slight but steady decline in everybody. This looks very much like primary psychological ageing. Other skills, such as problem-solving, seem to depend rather more on influences such as education and usage. Thus there may be changes in psychological function which are very common at the time of retirement but which are secondary to this important social and economic change.

For both biological (Fairweather, 1991) and psychological (Bromley, 1990) changes, we must be careful to keep in perspective the magnitude as well as the direction of change. Thus in normal ageing the changes in choice reaction time are there but they are very slight. They do not even become noticeable in everyday life until we are probably at least over 70 or 75. It takes the determination and deviousness of the experimental psychologist to show them in earlier years.

The magnitude of such normal changes is generally very much smaller than that caused by diseases common in later life such as heart disease. It begins to look increasingly that even some of the 'universal' changes of cognitive function are really associated with sub-clinical disease.

Certainly the cognitive changes of normal ageing are several orders of magnitude less than those experienced by those suffering from a progressive dementia. However, because the early symptoms are in the same direction as normal ageing it is very easy to put the changes down to 'just growing old'. This has been a charge frequently levelled at doctors, especially general practitioners. However, it is often also the case that older people themselves expect too much decline in function as they age.

This problem of stereotypes may be further compounded by the increasing variability which comes with ageing. This variability is seen both between individuals and between skills (Holland and Rabbitt, 1991). As far as individuals are concerned most studies of ageing which have addressed this issue find that the average performance and individual differences are related to age: in statistical terms, the mean changes and the standard deviation increases.

This means that any stereotype of a 'typical' older person is more likely to be wrong: knowing someone's age does not enable you to predict much else about them. This increased variability reflects an apparent injustice in ageing: those who have the better function to start with seem to keep that function more than those who start from a lower level. He that hath not, from him shall be taken.

The psychological changes found with normal ageing may conveniently be considered in the categories of cognition and personality. Obviously these are not for any individual separate from the biological and social changes. However, it is important to try to separate the psychological effects in a systematic way. This allows us to help the client test the reality of what may be very powerful assumptions concerning growing older.

Memory

The usual answer to the question 'which mental functions change with age?' is 'memory'. It appears commonly believed that memory declines as we age and this is often the reason for failing to recognize serious brain disorder.

In this case common sense is correct, memory does decline, but very much less than most people think. The changes are seen both in immediate memory (our ability to store and retrieve information for a few seconds) and in longer-term memory (anything longer than this). In terms of immediate memory, the normal limit for reliable performance in young adults is about seven items give or take two. We have no great problems using rehearsal to remember six-figure telephone numbers for short periods but we need to 'chunk' the information into separate bits for long-distance calls. The telephone companies have been researching this for years and present numbers so that we can remember them more easily. Those who advertise on radio also know how important it is to use numbers which are not 'random': it makes them very much easier to remember.

By the time we are seventy years old there will be some decline but it is only slight. Typically we might now be only able reliably to recall seven or eight numbers rather than eight or nine. It still has very little effect on most of our day-to-day activity.

Similarly, there is a slight decline in longer-term memory. Unfortunately one of the few positive stereotypes of ageing, that older people are actually better than younger people at very remote memory ('What was it like when . . .?') turns out to be false. Very remote memory is not quite as accurate as when we are young, but of course we can remember much further back because we were there.

The way we store and retrieve memories makes a difference. The easiest way to test memory is by recall: give someone a set of information and ask them to reproduce it some time later. Ageing effects are certainly noticeable here. However, we all know that it is easier to recognize something than it is to recall it. Testing memory using recognition shows less ageing effect.

Older people also tend to use less efficient learning strategies. We can show that how deeply we think about information, how we process it, effects our later recall. If we just tell subjects to 'learn' something, older people tend not to do as well as if we give them an efficient strategy. Younger subjects tend to do as well being told to 'learn this' as they do if we tell them an effective strategy.

As a general principle, it seems that the more complex the memory task, the bigger the age effect. One simple example is the comparison between immediate memory span for digits forwards and back. Having the extra burden of repeating the digits backwards gives more ageing effects. The implication of this for clinical practice is that making something easier to remember helps everybody, but especially older people.

Probably the most reliable finding from the psychology of ageing is the decrease in our ability to process information rapidly. Certainly it is one of the most obvious changes experienced by older people themselves. Even something as simple as sorting playing cards can be shown to have clear ageing effects: older people take longer. We also find, like memory, that task difficulty makes the ageing effects more pronounced. Thus having to sort cards into many different categories shows up ageing more than, say, just sorting into two.

Similar results are found in the processing of words. Normal sentences are well remembered by both young and old, random strings of words are more difficult and show a significant age effect. Increased speed of information presentation adds further to the ageing effect.

The effects of task speed and complexity are analogous to those seen in relation to individual differences in intelligence. It has been argued that it may even be possible to use intelligence differences as a model for studying ageing effects. However, there is an obvious danger in equating ageing with becoming less intelligent. There is no excuse for treating all older people as if they are slightly stupid.

In fact, the range of changes seen in intellectual ability illustrates rather well the complexities of ageing. There is no simple answer to the question 'Does ageing affect intelligence?' 'Yes' and 'No' are both correct. If we look at the evidence for changes in primary intellectual functions we find that there is both change and continuity. Nearly everybody shows change in at least one area of primary mental ability. For the great majority of people, however, most primary mental abilities are stable over several years in later life.

Just to make things more complex, the extent of decline may be related to initial level – the more you have the longer you keep it. Certainly there are several examples of cognitive function showing increasing individual differences with age. One way of summarizing all of this is that, looked at from the outside, over a whole group of older people, there are many reasons to conclude that ageing has real effects.

Looked at from the inside, from the perspective of the individual who is ageing, continuity is much more obvious than change.

Personality

The general principle of continuity is particularly in evidence in the area of personality. There are relatively few good studies of personality and ageing, not least because the measures are often less reliable than those of intellectual function. Self-report tends to be a less robust measure than observations of performance.

In addition personality measures are more subject to cohort and cultural changes, which can make the same measure mean different things at different times. Concepts like stress and anxiety have actually come into common use only in the lifetime of today's older people. The meanings of words can change in subtle but important ways and the willingness to describe emotions alters responses significantly. If the change is great then we will probably avoid making silly comparisons. For example one measure of extraversion developed some years ago asked the question 'Can you let yourself go at a gay party?'

Other changes will be less obvious but we should not be surprised to find that cohort effects tend to be much bigger than ageing effects. There are some ageing effects, however, which seem to be reliable. These include a tendency towards increased emotionality and a decrease in extraversion.

It is worth noting here that the way personality dimensions are labelled can have quite powerful effects on our interpretation. Using alternative labels we could just as well say that ageing is associated with increased introversion or self-sufficiency and increased neuroticism.

The fact that personality is inferred from patterns of behaviour also means that we must be alert to the way other factors change behaviour. Older people are much more likely than younger people to suffer from some form of limiting physical or social condition. If you do not go out and meet people so often now you are 85 it is much more likely to be because you are arthritic, bereaved or poor rather than because you have become more introverted.

Likewise, if we consider changes in sexual behaviour, these depend on health and social factors much more than primary age changes. Indeed the evidence suggests that there are additive effects such that a decrease in sexual behaviour accelerates the physical changes which we tend to see as in some way more 'primary'. There is no reason to assume that older people are freed from potential problems associated with sexual behaviour (Linsk, 1994).

The implications for counselling older people

The many findings in relation to normal ageing have some very real implications for counselling psychology. They can conveniently be summarized into three factors. The first of these is the importance of **variability**. The foundations of counselling psychology are very much concerned with the importance of individual differences and in helping people to their individual solutions. Older people are simply more different one from another than younger people. It means that having any stereotype of a 'typical' older person, good or bad, is simply more likely to be wrong.

Variability is also found in the effects of normal ageing on different skills. Some skills, particularly those involving processing lots of information quickly, show more decline than those which rely more on acquired knowledge. Looked at from an individual perspective, we are each likely to find some skills which decline with age but nearly all of us will keep some skills intact.

The second key feature is **continuity**: people do not change rapidly or radically as a result of normal ageing. Thus, for example, although there are some reliable changes in personality, the most noticeable thing is that people stay the same. If an older person, or especially his or her family, says that personality has changed it should ring alarm bells that something other than normal ageing is going on.

The third key factor is **cohort differences**. When a counsellor is trying to relate to the older client it is very likely that there will be very significant age differences. It may be one reason why it has been found that older clients would tend to prefer older counsellors (Kunkel and Williams, 1991). You need to work harder at empathy.

Principles of counselling older adults

Just as with any other client, the aim in counselling older people is to help the client achieve an increase in his or her well-being. Perhaps because so many of the effects of ageing are seen as negative, decline in function for example, quite a lot of work has gone into looking at the morale or life satisfaction of older people. Just for once the news is good: most older people are happy, and indeed many rate the present as the best time of their life.

Life satisfaction

Not surprisingly, the things which make a difference to life satisfaction for older people are the things which are important to us all, including health, wealth and personal relationships. Of course these are all often threatened in later life. Health is more likely to be compromised by long-term problems such as joint disorders or cardiovascular disease. Older people consume by far the biggest portion per head of health resources and many serious illnesses increase in prevalence and incidence with age. In some cases this has even meant that they are perceived as being 'due to' old age. The obvious example has been 'senile dementia'. Technically this simply means a loss of intellectual function happening in late life but the very word 'senile' has become a pejorative term, indeed an insult.

Ageing versus illness

Just because a disease is more common at a particular age does not mean that it is due to age. Measles is most common in children, but we know it is not caused by being a child. One of the biggest shifts in professional and public opinion has been to identify the dementias of late life as separate and specific illnesses. Most people seem now to have heard of Alzheimer's disease, the commonest type of dementia. It is no co-incidence that this is happening just as we begin to make progress in treatments to alleviate this condition.

The really important thing from a counselling psychology viewpoint is that such a change of view stops people dismissing illness as just due to age. This has not just been a problem for professionals, older people themselves often fail to seek help because they assume that nothing can be done. Studies have shown that diseases in older people can present to doctors later than in younger people and with signs rather than symptoms. In part this is because aches and pains are often put down to an inevitable consequence of growing older. One memorable example is the lady who wrote to the *South Wales Echo* problem page a few years ago worried about getting exhausted walking to the bus stop. She was frightened that she would become housebound and dependent on her family. She wrote, 'I expect you will say it's just my age.' She was 60 years old. The advice was 'Go and see your doctor.' Thus one principle of counselling psychology with older people is that we must be aware of and challenge ageist assumptions, not least among older people themselves.

Successful ageing

Conversely, we also need to recognize denial of ageing. Reichard's study of older men is now really rather out of date in that it looked only at men and makes all sorts of assumptions about patterns of work and retirement. However, the types or styles of adjustment described are still useful pointers to individual adjustment in later life (Reichard et al., 1962).

There were two groups which appeared to contain individuals who were broadly 'happy': those who continued to be active and those who were termed the 'rocking chair' type who were content to be more passive and let the world rush by. Those who were not so happy included those who rushed around terrified to slow down to confront ageing, and those who gave up and reflected bitterly on the past, either blaming others for not giving them opportunities or themselves for their failures. All of these are either frightened of dying or see death as a merciful release from their present distress.

One important point is that you cannot predict adjustment from level of activity. Reichard looked primarily at engagement in social roles; Coleman (1986) has reached similar conclusions with regard to reminiscence. Reminiscence has often been thought of as a typical behaviour of older people. They like to think and talk about the remote past and doing so is 'normal for their age' and associated with better adjustment.

Studies suggest, however, that some reminiscence is common at all ages. Obviously it is likely to be more varied and striking in older people since they have so much more experience to draw upon, but it is not particularly characteristic of old age. It is neither necessarily a good nor a bad thing. Some people are quite happy to reminisce and it makes them feel good, others find such reflection more of a painful rumination which makes them feel bad. Those who do not reminisce include those who are quite happy with here and now and see no need to dwell on the past and those who are unhappy and avoid thinking back because it is painful.

Thus Erikson's notion of a final life stage where people must look back over their life (Erikson, 1982) and make sense of it all in order to approach their death with equanimity is probably only half the story. Certainly those who are able to do so are those who feel content with themselves and the ways things are. However, those who do not thus review things are not necessarily unhappy. We must beware of insisting that everybody conforms to some standard notion of successful adjustment of ageing. In this respect it is rather like adjustment following bereavement. There is a typical pattern of grieving and resolution but not everybody who gets over a bereavement will do so in the same way.

Grief and loss

Of course bereavement is one of the commonest challenges to adjustment in later life. It seems sometimes to be assumed that it represents less of a challenge for older people because it is more timely, perhaps even that older people get more practice at losing those close to them. There may be some effect of loss being more expected but some losses are untimely at any age, for example the loss of a child is devastating even when you are 85 and your child was 60. Those losing adult children are especially vulnerable to complicated grief.

Moreover, all the evidence points to a cumulative effect of bereavement and other losses combining with personal resources to determine how well older people adjust to change. In her studies of older people and depression, Murphy (1982) compared those referred to a psychiatric outpatient clinic with a random sample of older people living at home. It seemed that the more life events and chronic difficulties experienced by the older person, the greater was the risk that she or he was suffering from a major depressive episode. This relationship was particularly strong in those who had not been referred to specialist help. This is consistent with a tendency not to recognize major depression as requiring help if it happens in the context of multiple losses. It can all too easily be assumed that the older person is so distressed as a 'normal' consequence of what has happened to them.

In fact there is plenty of evidence to indicate that depression, and other affective disturbance is not normal in later life. The prevalence and incidence for functional psychiatric disorders are remarkably unrelated to age, very different from organic disorders, the dementias. What does seem to be different from the findings in younger people is the effect of long-term health problems (Evans et al., 1991). These are a risk factor for depression in older people whereas in younger adults no such relationship is obvious.

Social support is certainly very important in mediating the effects of loss and life events. In Murphy's sample even having just one confidant with whom you could talk reduced the risk of depression. There are obvious implications for the provision of counselling here. It suggests that there may be some people who are at special risk of psychological disturbance and it should be possible to alleviate or even prevent problems. This is certainly what has been concluded from the work on bereavement counselling (Parkes, 1992). The evidence is that simply offering everybody who is bereaved counselling is not cost-effective. Some simple risk factors (for example, living alone, unexpected loss) enable us to target help so that it is effective.

Positive ageing

Of course, not all the experiences of later life are negative. Many older people rate the present as the best part of their life. Typically the reasons given for this include more leisure time, being able to spend more time with one's family and lack of work pressures. In fact the determinants of life satisfaction in later life are pretty much as we would expect: as mentioned earlier, health, wealth and family come out top of most lists. Some changes, such as becoming a grandparent, are often seen as positive, although difficulties in such relationships, for example following parental divorce, can also be sources of distress.

Family relationships

Because families are so important there has been a growing interest in the application of family or 'systems' approaches to helping older people with psychological problems (Sukosky, 1994). Many difficulties certainly happen in a family context and may indeed by brought to light because of family changes. Helping the relationships in the family to change may often be the best way of helping the older person.

Retirement itself may bring about changes in the family relationships, including the way in which domestic roles are apportioned. In today's cohort of older people there have often always been traditional divisions between female roles of being a housewife and male roles as breadwinner. Some couples find it very strange being together for so much of the time once the husband has retired. Most people actually make a very good adjustment to retirement but a minority, perhaps 10 per cent, find it less than satisfactory (Braithwaite and Gibson, 1987). Changes in role can also be the result of illness, especially when that illness results in long-term disability. How readily you adjust to caring for someone else depends on how much role change this involves for you both.

If the person is very dependent, one way of coping may be to perceive one's role as being similar to something you have experienced before and have some competence in. Thus older carers themselves may describe looking after a very dependent partner as being like looking after a child. Shakespeare's views on ageing are not very good as expectations of normal ageing but well on target for disability. Such coping strategies do work quite well most of the time, although they can make it difficult to foster autonomy and certainly can conflict with other roles such as being a sexual partner.

Most carers of older people are women and most are themselves older and the older carer, most often a spouse, tends to experience less strain than the younger, typically daughter, carer (Jones and Vetter, 1984). Having someone to look after you is almost certainly the best way of ensuring that you live at home when you are old and disabled. It works best if you can find someone you can be really close to for about 40 or 50 years before you need looking after. Love and marriage still make an apparently unbeatable foundation for community care.

That foundation is, however, tested most severely by the onslaught of dementia. Progressive loss of memory and intellect has been described as the unravelling of personality. Certainly it can be one of the most stressful of disabilities and have the most serious implications for carers. The prevalence rates for dementia double for every five years over the age of 65, so that whilst it only affects perhaps 1 or 2 per cent of young pensioners, it affects perhaps 30 per cent of those over the age of 85 (Henderson, 1987). If you are very old then, if you have a carer, he or she is likely also to be elderly. It will often be that older carer who can benefit from counselling psychology.

The aim of such counselling may be to help that carer make sense of conflicting emotions of love and anger, guilt and exhaustion. The reality of such care can indeed be the '36-hour day', where one day merges into another with no sign of relief. Difficult behaviour such as aggression, wandering or incontinence causes particular strain (Gilleard, 1984). Not only is there the real burden of practical care and constant vigilance, but the person for whom you are caring may not even recognize who you are. Informal care, like any behaviour, is greatly sustained by rewards of which recognition and thanks are much more powerful than money. Where such appreciation is lacking what is surprising is not that caring can break down but how rarely this happens.

Carers of all sorts can gain much from supporting one another. It seems often to be assumed that 'social support' is something which you receive from others. In fact for many people it comes just as much from the sense of being able to offer someone else help and support: feeling you have a valued contribution to make. In this context a situation such as a carer support group may be of more use than simply seeing a counsellor on an individual basis. The best role for the counsellor may be to support people in coming together, although this may require much individual help, for example in accepting the reality of a progressive dementia or a limited recovery from stroke.

Spiritual needs

Religious belief is often thought of as being more important to older people. Certainly there are age differences in formal religious worship but there is very little to suggest that people in general are now less inclined to believe in a God. Conventional psychological theories have tended to see religious belief as a problem or even a symptom related to inadequacy. Certainly seeing religious belief and behaviour as 'superstitious' does not emphasize the possible benefits to believers.

Despite everything, it remains the case that most people in nearly all countries believe in God or some sort of universal spirit. In a recent review, data collated by Koenig (1993) show that in only one country, Japan, does the percentage of people believing in God fall below 50 per cent. In fact the majority of countries record figures in excess of 70 per cent. The research data available suggest that 'devout religiousness enhances health and well-being and helps to protect against anxiety and depression, especially in later life' (Koenig et al., 1988).

It is important therefore that the possibility of receiving spiritual support and counselling is available, especially for older people. In those countries where age differences have been studied, belief in God is more common in older people. In many ways the approach necessary for the spiritual support of older people is very close to the principles of counselling psychology as a whole. It must be non-judgemental and facilitative. It is not appropriate for the counsellor to try to persuade the client to accept the counsellor's beliefs. It may well be necessary to suggest that spiritual help is required, however, and access to the necessary support should be available (Magee, 1993).

Life review and reminiscence can raise all sorts of issues which impinge on religious faith. It may be seen as very important to get things right with God as one approaches mortality. Whether you believe in an afterlife can radically affect how you cope with grief and loss. Counselling may need to give way to the confessional.

Professional issues

This interface between spiritual support and counselling older people touches on some of the important professional issues which must face anyone counselling older people. Mainly these centre around exactly that – the people whom you are counselling are older than you are.

In many ways this is a great benefit: if counselling psychology is helping people to tap into their own resources and experience there is that much more to draw upon. It is not so good however if the counsellor sees him- or herself, or is seen by the client, as being the 'expert'. To be in that role in relation to a client could really be seen as counter-therapeutic. I know less about myself than you do who are younger; I am not doing very well.

Why talk to me? Why talk to anybody? The very first problem to be overcome may be to establish why it could be appropriate for an older person to seek counselling in the first place. It is not clear whether any tendency for older people to be less likely to receive counselling is ageism on the part of the referrers, the counsellors or older people themselves. It has certainly often been said that older people are less inclined to psychological therapies, usually thought of as a cohort effect. Such therapies simply did not exist in their current form many years ago. One obvious example of changing approaches to psychological therapies is the difference between the response to 'shell shock' in the 1914–1918 war and post-traumatic stress disorder in the 1990s.

A tendency towards somatization of affective symptoms together with co-existing physical pathology can make it difficult to engage some older people in psychological help. They may have a long experience of the alleviation of distress through medical treatment, especially drugs. Suggesting a psychological approach may be taken to infer that their problems are 'all in the mind' or worse still that they are making them up. If the client can be persuaded that such approaches are complementary rather than competitive then it is possible to proceed.

As with counselling in general, many of the professional issues concern the importance of being aware of one's own attitudes, needs and responses in the counselling psychology framework. However there are some issues which are particularly relevant to counselling older people. These include dealing with frailty and mortality, parental role reversal and cohort differences. There are also practical issues such as the length and number of sessions and dealing with sensory impairment. There are good reasons why counselling older people should be explicitly addressed in training (Crose, 1991, 1992; Duffy, 1992; Myers et al., 1991; Thomas and Martin, 1992).

The reality of ageing

Ageing is not a 'problem', it is an essential part of human experience. Whereas we may seek to avoid many of life's problems, we cannot escape ageing. Ageing is simply part of the life cycle and ageing successfully involves adjustment and assimilation not avoidance. The experience of continuity rather than change is the hallmark of the individual experience of ageing: you do not see yourself at 75 and healthy as really very different from how you were 50 years previously. One of the challenges for the counsellor may be to try to capture and share that sense of continuity.

This is more difficult when you have only met someone after they have aged significantly. People who have known you for a long time can see you as 'the person you were plus ageing, illness or other experience', others tend to see the ageing first. Listening to personal history is probably the best way around this. Older people tend to be even more diverse than younger people and have a great richness of personal experience to share. Whilst we must be mindful that there may be experiences which older people do not wish to remember, there is always more than enough to draw on. From the counsellor's point of view this is one of the most rewarding features of working with older people: it really can be living history. It is often one of the most important processes in establishing rapport. Knowing that someone is interested in you and the life you have led is in itself therapeutic.

Of course this not the same as living in or dwelling on the past. It is not very helpful simply to spend time thinking about how good things were and how they have changed. The past is a context against which we are helping that person to make sense of the present. It often reveals considerable strengths which have been overshadowed by more recent events, especially stresses. Reflecting upon how one coped with problems in the past may help people to understand how they are thinking, acting and feeling now. Because continuity rather than change is dominant in normal ageing, understanding one's past is very relevant.

In order to be non-judgemental it is important to have confronted one's own ageing and mortality. Generally speaking older people are not frightened of death, although they may well be frightened about dying. The latter is especially so if they have had experience of someone suffering a lengthy or painful death. That experience may itself have been very many years ago and reflect the palliative limitations of that time. It can all too easily be assumed that similar limitations apply today. Whilst it is wrong to suggest that we now have all the answers, we have made a little therapeutic progress at least in the past 50 years.

One practical effect of an acceptance of death is that older people may be more likely to say that they think they would be better off dead if they are facing serious ill-health or disability. The counsellor needs to tread carefully to distinguish between philosophical reflections on ageing and serious depressive illness. Some statistics at least suggest that older people are more likely to commit suicide. Certainly they are less likely to use para-suicide. Thus talk of wanting to die must be taken seriously but is not necessarily a sign of depressive disorder. It is often the reason for referral for therapy.

The counsellor must also be prepared for the death of a client. An operational definition of ageing is 'the phenomena associated with increasing age-specific mortality'. Older people are more likely to die than younger people. It therefore follows inevitably that sometimes a client who may have appeared quite healthy at the previous appointment, dies unexpectedly. Certainly for those training as therapists this may be a difficult experience. In fact dying after a short or sudden illness might be seen as the ideal outcome of successful ageing. It is not, however, something we tend to contemplate actively just as most adults have not made a will. Supervision and support are most important here.

In thinking about one's own mortality we may do well also to have addressed our own spiritual needs, at least to the point where we can ensure that clients are able to discuss their own beliefs if they so wish. The right counsellor may often be a priest or other spiritual adviser.

Working in teams

Older people are more likely to be coping with more than one problem at once. It is therefore likely that they will need more than one sort of help at once. The model of exclusive treatment: 'You refer the client to me, I do my expert activity, I discharge them back to you', is therefore much less likely to be appropriate. Working in teams involves acknowledging both shared roles and special skills. It means keeping up to date, for example, with the progress of the client's medical care so that he or she can address what may be a changing reality. Obviously good communication is vital. This needs to start by understanding what others providing care are looking for (Crose and Kixmiller, 1994).

In many respects the family may be seen as the client, other important members of the team trying to help. The family may have quite different goals and there are times when family therapy rather than simple counselling are appropriate. It can be a very important area for enhancing the client's control over his or her life.

Often the client's other problems will include physical frailty and sensory difficulties. These may impose some limitations on session length and environment. Specific communication difficulties may be helped by using the right aids (making sure you keep a spare set of hearing aid batteries, sit with your face well lit, avoid group sessions, etc.). However these are required not because the client is older but because they are impaired. An older client with no such problem is likely to have more stamina than the counsellor.

Just as with other aspects of health and social care, the goals of counselling psychology should be agreed with the client as a result of a discussion of individual needs. The way the client sees the problem can be very different from those who have suggested help. One example might be the distinction between isolation, an objective count of the number of social interactions in a given period, and loneliness, the subjective experience of lack of social contact. Very low rates of social contact which the client perceives as important and meaningful may be quite sufficient to meet that person's needs.

This individual approach should also be carried through to the measurement of outcome: this is by no means always as easy to define for older clients as it is for younger people. However this is no reason to avoid the issue. We can expect that there will be increasing use of suitable measures of psychological well-being, though these will need to be validated on this population if they are to be of any real use.

There are now many examples of counselling work with older people. They cover all types of problems including depression (Dhooper et al., 1993), stroke (Evans et al., 1994), work with carers (Hern and Weis, 1991) and groupwork (Waters, 1990). The richness of experience and individuality of older people mean that counselling them is perhaps one of the most rewarding experiences for counsellors and, hereby perhaps, for clients. If we can adopt the right degree of humility, hone our listening skills and cope with complexity, both counsellor and client can learn much that can help us achieve one of life's great goals: a happy old age.

References

Braithwaite, V.A. and Gibson, D.M. (1987) 'Adjustment to retirement: What we know and what we need to know, *Ageing and Society*, 7: 1–18.

Bromley, D.B. (1990) *Behavioural Gerontology: Central Issues in the Psychology of Ageing*. Chichester: Wiley.

Coleman, P.G. (1986) *Ageing and Reminiscence Processes: Social and Clinical Implications*. Chichester: Wiley.

Crose, R. (1991) 'What's special about counselling older women?', *Canadian Journal of Counselling*, 25(4): Special Issue, pp. 617–23.

Crose, R. (1992) 'Gerontology is only aging, it's not dead yet', *Counseling Psychologist*, 20(2): 330–5.

Crose, R. and Kixmiller, J.S. (1994) 'Counseling psychologists as nursing home consultants: What do administrators want?', *Counseling Psychologist*, 22(1): 104–14.

deVries, B. and Petty, B.J. (1992) 'Peer counseling training: analysis of personal growth for older adults', *Educational Gerontology*, 18(4): 381–93.

Dhooper, S.S., Green, S.M., Huff, M.B. and Austin-Murphy, J. (1993) 'Efficacy of a group approach to reducing depression in nursing home elderly residents', *Journal of Gerontological Social Work*, 20(34): 87–100.

Duffy, M. (1992) 'Challenges in geriatric psychotherapy', Special Issue 'The Process of Aging and Working with Older Adults', *Individual Psychology: Journal of Adlerian Theory, Research and Practice*, 48(4): 432–40.

Erikson, E.H. (1982) *The Life Cycle Completed*. New York: Norton.

Evans, M.E., Copeland, J.R.M. and Dewey, M.E. (1991) 'Depression in the elderly: effects of physical illness and selected social factors', *International Journal of Geriatric Psychiatry* 6: 787–95.

Evans, R.L., Connis, R.T., Bishop, D.S., Hendricks, R.D. et al. (1994) 'Stroke: a family dilemma', Special Issue 'Disability and Rehabilitation in Older Persons', *Disability and Rehabilitation: an International Multidisciplinary Journal*, 16(3): 110–18.

Fairweather, D.S. (1991) 'Aging as a biological phenomenon', *Reviews in Clinical Gerontology*, 1: 3–16.

France, M.H. (1989) 'Residents as helpers: peer counselling in a long term care facility', *Canadian Journal of Counselling*, 23(1): 113–19.

Fry, P.S. (1992) 'Major social theories of aging and their implications for counseling concepts and practice: a critical review', *Counseling Psychologist*, 20(2): 246–329.

Gilleard, C.J. (1984) *Living with Dementia: Community Care of the Elderly Mentally Infirm.* London: Croom Helm.

Gorey, K.M. and Cryns, A.G. (1991) 'Group work as interventive modality with the older depressed client: a meta-analytic review', *Journal of Gerontological Social Work*, 16(12): 137–57.

Griffiths, P. (1994) 'The development of the first rehabilitation counselling course in Europe', *International Journal for the Advancement of Counselling*, 17(1): 71–5.

Grisby, J.S. (1991) 'Paths for future population ageing', *The Gerontologist*, 31(2): 195–203.

Henderson, A.S. (1987) 'Alzheimer's disease: Epidemiology', in B. Pitt (ed.), *Dementia.* Edinburgh: Churchill Livingstone.

Hern, B.G. and Weis, D.M. (1991) 'A group counseling experience with the very old', Special Issue 'Group Work with the Aging and their Caregivers', *Journal for Specialists in Group Work*, 16(3): 143–51.

Holland, C.A. and Rabbitt, P. (1991) 'The course and causes of cognitive change with advancing age', *Reviews in Clinical Gerontology*, 1: 81–96.

Jones, D.A. and Vetter, N.J. (1994) 'A survey of those who care for the elderly at home: their problems and their needs', *Social Science and Medicine*, 19: 511–14.

Koenig, H.G., Kvale, J.N. and Ferrel, C. (1988) 'Religion and well-being in later life', *The Gerontologist*, 28(1): 18–28.

Kunkel, M.A. and Williams, C. (1991) 'Age and expectations about counseling: two methodological perspectives', *Journal of Counseling and Development*, 70(2): 314–20.

Linsk, N.L. (1994) 'HIV and the elderly', Special Issue 'HIV/AIDS', *Family in Society*, 76(6): 362–72.

Magee, J.J. (1993) 'Using religious paradox to facilitate life review groups with shamedriven older adults', *Pastoral Psychology*, 41(3): 159–68.

Morgan, J.P. (1994) 'Bereavement in older adults', *Journal of Mental Health Counseling*, 16(3): 318–26.

Murphy, E. (1982) 'The social origins of depression in old age', *British Journal of Psychiatry*, 141: 135–42.

Myers, J.E., Loesch, L.D. and Sweeney, T.J. (1991) 'Trends in gerontological counselor preparation', *Counselor Education and Supervision*, 30(3): 194–204.

Parkes, C.M. (1992) 'Bereavement and mental health in the elderly', *Reviews in Clinical Gerontology*, 2: 45–51.

Reichard, S., Livson, F. and Petersen, P.G. (1962) *Aging and Personality.* New York: Wiley.

Sukosky, D.G. (1994) 'Life review in family psychotherapy', *Journal of Family Psychotherapy*, 5(2): 21–39.

Thomas, M.C. and Martin, V. (1992) 'Training counselors to facilitate the transitions of aging through group work', Special Section 'Training in Gerontological Counseling', *Counselor Education and Supervision*, 32(1): 51–60.

Thompson, J.D. and Scott, N.A. (1991) 'Counseling service features: elders' preferences and utilization', *Clinical Gerontologist*, 11(1): 39–46.

Waters, E.B. (1990) 'The life review: strategies for working with individuals and groups', Special Issue 'Techniques for Counseling Older Persons', *Journal of Mental Health Counseling*, 12(3): 270–8.

Part Five

Themes and Contexts

18

Counselling Psychology in the Context of Health and Illness

Roslyn Corney

In the twentieth century, health care has changed dramatically with the rapid growth in knowledge in the medical sciences as well as the development of sophisticated diagnostic and treatment facilities. There has also been a change in priorities in health care due to rising living standards, better sanitation and nutrition. Infectious diseases have been reduced to be replaced by an increase in chronic and degenerative problems. The leading causes of death today include heart disease, cancer and stroke. This change in morbidity has led to an increase in long-term treatments with the emphasis on control rather than cure. In addition, there has also been an increasing emphasis on preventive medicine. Both preventive medicine and the management of chronic illness need the active participation and involvement of the patient. Attention also needs to be paid to social and psychological factors as well as physical problems. Thus the importance of psychological processes in the experience of health and illness has become increasingly recognized and acknowledged.

Psychologists have been very much involved in researching this inter-play between mind and body. The emergence of the discipline of Health Psychology occurred in the mid-1970s and has developed considerably since then. This chapter will consider the role of psychology in health and illness and link this with the role of counselling psychologists within both primary and secondary care settings.

Health promotion and disease prevention

A number of behavioural risk factors have been isolated which pose a threat to health, including smoking, diet, lack of exercise and drug taking. It has been estimated that a quarter of all deaths from cancer could be avoided by modifying individuals' smoking habits and that reducing the weight of middle-aged men by 10 per cent could reduce coronary heart disease by one-fifth (Kannel and Eaker, 1986).

The aim of health promotion is to enable people to increase their control over and improve their health. This includes the use of positive health behaviours such as eating a balanced diet and exercising regularly, the use of preventive health behaviour such as breast examination, and the avoidance of behaviours that are deleterious to health such as smoking and the excessive use of alcohol. Health education programmes have a number of aims: to provide information relating to health and to change both attitudes and health-related behaviour in ways which are conducive to health.

A number of theoretical models have been put forward to explain health-related behaviour. Fishbein and colleagues put forward the theory of reasoned action and this was revised later as the theory of planned behaviour (Ajzen and Madden, 1986). These theories take into account that behaviour is guided by intentions and that these are influenced by our attitudes towards that behaviour as well as subjective norms about the appropriateness of it (which are influenced by what significant others think and do). The revised model also includes another variable, the individual's perceived control over the target behaviour.

Becker's model of health beliefs is also influential (1974). It suggests that actions are dependent on the perceived threat of a health problem and an evaluation of the pros and cons of taking action. Perceived threat is a function of the individual's perception of the seriousness of the health problem as well as his or her beliefs on their perceived susceptibility to it. Perceived threat is also influenced by the degree of prior knowledge or personal contact with the problem. Cues to action include symptoms, media campaigns or an invitation to attend a clinic. In weighing up the pros and cons of taking a preventive action, people consider the benefits as well as the problems or difficulties with taking such action. Thus if an individual believes that they are personally susceptible to the condition in question, that the resulting illness will be serious and that preventive action is not too difficult or 'costly', they will be more likely to take up preventive behaviours. However, individuals do not always act rationally and research does show that many people are unrealistically optimistic about their future health, a specific example of the wider psychological phenomenon of self-serving bias.

Preventive medicine

In primary prevention, activities are aimed at preventing incidence of disease or disorder (for example, reducing smoking campaigns). In secondary prevention, activities are aimed at the early detection of disease or disorder (for example, breast cancer screening) in order to reduce its duration or severity. In tertiary programmes, activities are aimed at reducing the disability or handicaps which result from the disease or disorder (for example, adjustment programmes).

Recent studies on primary prevention have indicated that more success can be achieved by concentrating on high-risk populations, that is those who are identified as being particularly vulnerable to the disease, rather than concentrating on population-wide health campaigns. For example, population-wide AIDS campaigns were found to have only a limited effect at changing people's health behaviour. However, AIDS education and prevention campaigns which target specific gay communities have resulted in a number of major modifications of personal health-related behaviour (Stall et al., 1988). For messages to be effective they must have personal relevance, be presented by individuals with whom the group concerned can identify and be delivered at a community level.

Individual or group counselling can be an important adjunct to medical interventions at all three levels of preventive medicine. However, it is more likely that counsellors will be involved in working more intensively with people drawn from high-risk populations. It is for this reason that counselling psychologists are less likely to be involved in primary prevention programmes (except in the area of mental health) than in secondary and tertiary prevention programmes. Counselling may involve working with groups or individuals, using a variety of techniques including behavioural methods, offering support, discussing issues as well as more non-directive counselling. However, at all three levels, an understanding of relevant social and psychological theory and research is essential as altering unhealthy behaviours is often difficult to achieve.

The role of the counselling psychologist with physical illness

Mechanic in 1966 estimated that 95 per cent of all medical and surgical patients could profit from psychotherapy or behavioural medicine interventions. The role of the counsellor in medical settings is normally twofold: first to counsel patients and their relatives either individually or in groups and secondly to work with the health professionals and staff involved.

Many hospital departments such as those of obstetrics, gynaecology and oncology have a counsellor as part of their team, although in many cases, the 'counsellor' has few or no qualifications in counselling (Fallowfield and Roberts, 1992). The counsellor ideally is on hand to see patients at times of crisis (when an illness is diagnosed for example) as well as seeing patients on an ongoing basis.

When individuals become ill, their concerns, preoccupations and worries have been shown to change dramatically, focusing around the illness and the effect it may have on their daily activities, their work and their family life. The most common reactions of patients to illness are distress and anxiety. Overall estimates suggest that between 30 and 60 per cent of general hospital patients suffer significant levels of psychological distress at the time of hospitalization and during the first year afterwards (Nichols, 1984).

Distress is also common among relatives which in turn affects the patient. In a study conducted by Mayou and colleagues on patients suffering from coronary heart disease, 80 per cent of patients and half of their spouses revealed mild or moderate distress while in hospital and approximately half of the patients and spouses still felt distressed two months later (cited in Nichols, 1984).

Recognizing the patient's feelings and concerns is important in medical terms as the presence of psychological distress has been found to have a negative effect on recovery from illness. In a large-scale survey, Querido studied 1,630 patients admitted to a hospital in Amsterdam. Six months after discharge, 70 per cent of patients who were classified as distressed whilst in hospital were in an unsatisfactory condition medically in comparison with only 30 per cent of those classified as non-distressed. While 1,128 of the 1,630 patients had been given a favourable medical prognosis, only 660 had lived up to this expectation. The majority of those who failed to improve had been classified as distressed while in hospital (cited in Nichols, 1984). These findings plus those of others indicate the need for professionals working with the ill to acknowledge and respond to their distress.

Distress at all phases of an illness can usually be reduced by providing information about the illness and treatment. It is often the period of uncertainty, of not knowing, which patients state as the most difficult period to bear.

Ley, in his review of the literature, suggests that there is no evidence of increased anxiety or depression when patients are told of their diagnosis (1988). Even studies of cancer patients suggest that the majority of patients would prefer to be informed although there is still some debate whether all patients should be told. Surveys indicate that most patients wish to know as much as possible about their illness, its causes, treatments and outcome. Reviews of studies on a range of surgical patients show generally positive results of giving adequate information and preparation before surgery. Preparation has been shown to affect postoperative pain and symptoms, time taken to recover as well as anxiety levels.

However, providing information is not always straightforward. It often needs to be given in a sensitive manner after exploring what the individual already understands, wants to hear and can cope with at that particular time (Maguire, 1991). Medical staff do not always have the time available or the skills, and the role of the counselling psychologist could be valuable in this regard, either in undertaking the role themselves or in educating and advising others.

Other studies have also indicated that emotional distress can be reduced by actively involving the patient in treatment and in decisions regarding treatment. The patient regards himself as being actively involved in treating or fighting the illness and exercising choice rather than feeling passive and helpless. Patients who need to make a decision over treatment may find it helpful to discuss the alternatives with a counsellor. This is becoming more common with the increasing recognition of the importance of allowing the patient choice of treatment. This choice (often called informed choice) must be taken after the patient has been given all relevant information about options. This may often need the involvement of a counsellor to make sure that the information given has been both assimilated and the implications understood.

Developing the skills of other health professionals

Giving information and support to patients and relatives is one of the most important tasks performed by any health professional. Done well it can improve compliance and recovery and may save lives. The counsellor may therefore consider that one of his or her tasks is to increase the staff's awareness of distress in patients and their relatives as well as an understanding of the different ways in which this distress may be manifested. They may also see themselves as having a role in encouraging and developing the communication skills of all staff involved in the care of patients.

Although a number of studies have amply demonstrated the importance of good communication skills, it has only been relatively recently that attention has been paid to developing interviewing and communication skills in medical education. It is perhaps assumed that these skills will come with practice and by observing the interactions of experienced doctors and health professionals. Yet dissatisfaction with medical communication is one of the most common of patients' complaints. It is also a major factor why some patients choose other forms of help and treatment, such as alternative medicine, with its focus on actively involving the patient in treatment and encouraging the patient to talk freely about their problems.

While most encounters are initiated by patients, the purpose of the meeting may be very different for the patient than the health professional. A doctor who attends to the patient's concerns, worries and own theories about the illness is more likely to find out what is wrong (Tuckett et al., 1986). Patients bring to the consultation their own ideas, and health professionals who discover these theories and discuss them fully with the patient will be aided in both making a diagnosis and in treatment. Failure to discuss these theories has been shown to leave the patient confused and in conflict which in turn has been shown to affect compliance with treatment and satisfaction with the consultation.

Patient non-compliance with treatment regimes is thought to be widespread. It has been estimated that one-third of all patients do not cooperate with short-term treatments and half or more do not cooperate with long-term treatments. While non-compliance results in a wastage of scarce health resources, it may also result in the recurrence of symptoms, illness and even death.

However, the counsellor must also be aware that the avoidance of emotional issues by staff may be a self-protective mechanism (as it can be in patients). It has often been said that the only way that health professionals, in particular doctors, can bear the burden of clinical responsibility and remain objective while making decisions is by distancing themselves from any of the distressing consequences (Nichols, 1984). Indeed, studies have found that medical students became less interested in their patients as people over time. Senior students were less likely than junior students to question patients on psychological or social dimensions. Students therefore become more doctor-centred as they progress through medical school. Thus the emotional needs of the health professionals themselves must also be considered and counsellors should always be aware of the importance of offering emotional support to their medical colleagues.

While workers in other caring professions, such as counselling and social work, have supervision sessions built into their work, few health professionals have these opportunities. There may be no forum where they can be given support and help to disentangle their own feelings, avoidances, prejudices and emotional responses. Counselling psychologists may be able to supply this type of support and supervision.

Counsellors may also suggest ways in which a more patient-centred approach is adopted. A 'patient-centred' health professional learns to seek out the 'real' problem by attending to a variety of verbal and non-verbal cues presented by the patient rather than attend to the presenting problem which may not be their most major problem (Byrne and Long, 1976). Thus many of the communication skills needed by health professionals are similar to those used by counselling psychologists in their daily work with clients. Studies have consistently demonstrated that patients prefer doctors who show sensitivity, warmth and concern to those who appear detached and unconcerned (DiMatteo, 1985). Thus discussions on particular patients or joint consultations can be important ways of developing the skills and confidence of all staff members, including those of the counsellor.

Mental health problems and somatic illness

The previous sections in this chapter have concentrated on the role of psychology with physical illness and on the emotional feelings aroused by such illness. However, much of medical care and resources in this country and in the United States are taken up by patients presenting either with mental distress or with symptoms of ill-health where nothing organically wrong can be found.

It has been estimated that 60 per cent of visits to physicians in the United States are by patients who have nothing physically wrong with them (Follette and Cummings, 1967, cited in Cummings, 1990) and Shapiro, in 1971, estimated that the number of stress-related visits to physicians ranged from 50 to 80 per cent of all consultations. People vary considerably in their help-seeking behaviour; some individuals will attend their doctor for minor ailments of recent origin while others delay even for serious problems. Attending a GP's surgery is likely to be influenced by a number of factors, including symptoms experienced, recognition of the problem and knowledge about the condition, presence or absence of psychosocial problems and social support, willingness to divulge personal information, accessibility to health care facilities (both in time available, cost and travelling distance) and relevant health beliefs including perception of the effectiveness of medical care (Corney, 1990).

Epidemiological studies, in Great Britain and the United States, suggest that the rate of mental distress in the population is in the range of 10–15 per cent at any point in time (Goldberg and Huxley, 1992). Most of this distress takes the form of anxiety and/or depression. In the United Kingdom, the main point of medical contact for people with mental distress is not the psychiatric services or community psychiatric teams but the general practitioner (GP). National Morbidity Statistics also show the amount of time spent by GPs on patients presenting these problems: mental distress ranks as the third most common cause of consultation in primary care (9 per cent), following those related to the respiratory system (15 per cent) and those related to the cardiovascular system (11 per cent).

Depression and anxiety and psychosocial problems are commonly interlinked. The role of 'life events' and stressful situations has been investigated and discussed in a number of studies while growing interest has been shown in the effect on distress of the presence or absence of supportive relationships (Goldberg and Huxley, 1992). A higher degree of social impairment is found in depressed patients than in the 'normal' population. While some of these social and relationship problems occur before the individual becomes distressed and may be linked with onset, the feelings of distress themselves are likely to put extra strains on personal relationships as well as affect work performance and other social activities.

Although some individuals will be distressed for only a short period and may not need professional help to bring about this change, many others have chronic difficulties. Mann and his colleagues (1981) conducted a follow-up study in two general practices in the Midlands of 100 patients selected by their general practitioner as suffering from 'non-psychotic illness'. At one year, only 52 per cent of the cohort had recovered. Their findings suggest that a quarter of the hundred people became chronically distressed and a further half seem to have a remitting course. This chronic subgroup has also been recognized in the United States.

This chronic subgroup are most likely to have long-term relationship or social problems. In two GP studies, the patient's social circumstances were found to be the strongest predictors of outcome. Social supports may also play a key role in determining outcome, those with poor relationships improving less often. For example, a study of depressed women in general practice indicated that those women with marital problems were less likely to have improved at one year than those with no or other types of social problems (Corney, 1987).

These studies reinforce the argument that treatment should not just be aimed at reducing the clinical symptoms alone by the use of medication. Many patients are unhappy about taking psychotropic drugs and there is also a proportion of patients who do not respond to these drugs. Even when drugs are effective, counselling can address any social and psychological problems occurring.

Another factor in favour of early psychological and social intervention is the relationship found between distress and physical health. Distress, especially chronic distress, can bring about a variety of physical symptoms and illnesses. In one study, newly widowed men were found to be 40 per cent more likely to die in the year following the death of their spouse than a control group of men matched for age and occupation. They died from a number of causes, but heart disease was the most common (Rees and Lutkins, 1967). There is evidence that depressed immune function is linked with lack of social support of chronic stress and in his book *The Social Causes of Illness* Totman reviews the evidence linking disruptive life events to a multitude of conditions from leukaemia to the common cold (Totman, 1979).

In the light of the above evidence, it is not surprising that the employment of counsellors by general practitioners is one of the major growth areas in counselling at the present time. This is not only due to the increasing recognition of the importance of counselling and psychotherapy in medical care but also because recent legislative changes make it easier for GPs to employ counsellors. Since the New GP Contract which came into force in 1990, the range of staff eligible for reimbursement through the ancillary staff scheme has been extended so that staff with a wider range of skills and training qualify (including counsellors). Some Family Health Service Authorities have been willing to fund counsellors working in general practice using this scheme (this is the same scheme that funds practice nurses). Other GPs used money available for health promotion by getting counsellors to organize their sessions into clinics (often called stress clinics), although this source of money has now been curtailed. However, the advent of GP fundholding means that fundholders can pay for counselling sessions out of their budget.

Why do we need counselling skills in general practice? How great is the need for trained counselling psychologists? As has been already indicated, up to one-third of patients consulting their GPs have psychological symptoms or psychosomatic complaints. Many of these have been brought out by some personal crisis such as a bereavement, marital stresses, or the discovery of a serious or chronic illness. In addition, the GP is the professional most likely to be contacted for help with these problems rather than any others and he or she may be the only professional contacted. Often patients seek the help and advice of their GP with the hope that the doctor, 'the expert', will be able to prescribe a solution. Others just want the opportunity to talk through their problems with someone they know and trust.

In most cases, the GP's ability to offer support or sympathy may be adequate or all that is needed. However, because of pressures of time, the GP is unable to offer much more than a brief chat and sometimes a prescription. In previous years, the only outside help available was referral to a psychiatrist or a clinical psychologist (usually with a long waiting list). In many cases, referral to a psychiatrist would not be appropriate as it is not the symptoms that need 'treatment' so much as the patient's personal and social situation. In addition, a psychiatric referral carries the stigma of being seen as mentally ill and medicalizes what are essentially common life problems.

The value of counselling attachments to general practice is that the patients who need this sort of help can be referred on without too much delay. Studies of counsellor attachments to general practice have found that they facilitate referral and feedback between the counsellor and the GP if communications are good. Thus counselling may be offered and accepted by clients at an earlier stage of their problems (Corney and Jenkins, 1992).

With GP attachments, clients can see a counsellor in a familiar environment with no or little stigma attached. The fact that the doctor has suggested counselling may overcome the client's fear or initial scepticism of the value of counselling. Take-up of appointments for counselling in general practice is also higher than that at a marriage guidance clinic or in a psychiatric outpatient clinic. One of the problems of referring patients to psychiatrists is that many patients fail to turn up for the first appointment (Illman, 1983, cited by Corney, 1992).

One major advantage to attachments is that counsellors and health professionals can start to work in close conjunction. If good working relationships are developed between the counselling psychologist and the health professionals based in primary care, mutual learning and development of skills can occur. The supportive role of the counsellor may be particularly important in this context, as primary care staff are not protected in the same way as those in hospital settings. They have to offer an open door to all their registered patients (only a very small minority will be turned away) while hospital staff have waiting lists and can also discharge patients when they feel appropriate. In a survey of general practitioners working with marriage guidance counsellors (Corney, 1986), respondents felt that the counsellors' main task was counselling referred clients, but a third of the doctors mentioned that the counsellor also provided support to practice members.

GPs who work with counsellors appear to value their work with patients and appreciate the opportunity to share and discuss their own feelings about patients and their relationships with them (McLeod, 1992, cited in Corney and Jenkins, 1992). Employing a counsellor in the practice team seems to heighten team members' awareness of their own reactions to patients and encourages them to improve their own counselling skills. Time needs to be invested by the counsellor in supporting and developing the skills of practice members who are interested in taking on a role in this area. McLeod points out that a counsellor who builds up a good relationship with a practice and who finds time for case discussion provides a new and useful resource in primary care. Very few team members have the luxury of time to reflect on their practice and yet offering such time could enable primary health care team members to function more effectively and feel more supported.

Although counsellors may see their role as enabling other staff to take on some of the emotional and psychological problems of their patients, it is also important that medical staff are aware that problems (and harm) can ensue when untrained staff attempt to counsel disturbed clients who need more experienced help. It can be dangerous when unsupported staff are left dealing with complex and difficult emotional problems on their own. A counsellor working closely with the team can advise staff on their management of patients as well as when to refer on.

Although studies of counsellor attachments (Corney and Jenkins, 1992) indicate that the majority of their referrals are patients with psychosocial problems of all kinds, there still may be an important role for the counselling psychologist in primary care in terms of patients whose major problem is that of a physical illness. Helping clients manage their chronic illness, discussing options for treatment or being involved in health promotion are all important areas which can be developed by counselling psychologists.

Other roles of the counselling psychologist in primary care

It may be of value for a counsellor placed in a health setting not only to deal with individual cases but to consider how the service could be changed to meet more effectively the psychological needs of the patients in that setting. The counselling psychologist may wish to appraise what overall strategies could be adopted to improve the ways in which the team or practice manages these psychological problems.

One way is to encourage the development of good practice protocols. This can include guidance on the identification/psychosocial management of distress in certain groups of 'at risk' patients, for example, the bereaved, postnatal women or those recently diagnosed with a chronic physical illness. Guidelines could also be developed on the giving of information on various illnesses and treatments to help reduce patients' anxiety and fear.

Protocols could also be written and developed on which patients should be referred on for more experienced counselling help (and at what point). The counsellor could also make sure that information is made available on agencies such as self-help groups or befrienders who could help the client. Arranging for these groups to give talks to the team or practice on their work may facilitate a number of developments.

Effectiveness of counselling

Before we can argue for the substantial increase in the employment of counselling psychologists within the National Health Service, we have to show that their involvement will bring about an improved outcome in patients or clients or that it reduces medical costs (or both).

Investigating effectiveness is a complex issue. We need to find out who can benefit most from counselling as well as what level of skills in the counsellor is necessary for benefit to occur. It is likely that these two issues are interlinked; some patients may benefit from less skilled help while others may need a counsellor with much training and experience and may be harmed by someone without this.

There is also the issue of the type of therapy given. At the present time, most research suggests that it is not the methodology that is important but the qualities of the counsellor; counsellors who offer warmth, genuineness and empathy have been shown to be consistently effective.

Subjective accounts

Subjective accounts suggest that the attachments of counsellors work well, with much consumer, counsellor and GP satisfaction. One study conducted in 1980 by the Waydenfelds (cited by Corney, 1992) found that 44 out of the 47 clients who completed a client questionnaire indicated that help was received. Another study by Anderson and Hasler (1979, cited in Corney, 1992) sent questionnaires to the first 80 patients referred to the counsellor. Fifty-five patients returned them (69 per cent). Of this group, 47 agreed that counselling should be available in general practice, 43 would use the counselling service again and 46 would recommend it to their relatives or friends.

Subjective accounts are valuable, but need to be treated with caution. It may be very difficult to criticize a service, especially when arranged by the general practice upon which one relies. It is also possible that similar favourable reports would be obtained if clients were given the same amount of time by an untrained, warm and caring befriender or by a self-help group which could also offer practical assistance on a longer-term basis.

Utilization of medical services

Other studies have considered whether counselling has had any effect on the utilization of medical services (Corney, 1992). The results have been used as a measure of outcome (for example, if the client visits the doctor less or stops taking psychotropic drugs he is assumed to be well or better). Many studies have shown a reduction in visits made to the doctor after cessation of counselling in contrast with a period before. A similar number of studies have found a reduction in the number of psychotropic and other drugs prescribed. Other studies have indicated that there was a reduction in referrals to psychiatrists after a counselling attachment had been instigated.

However, the reduction in medical utilization rates has also been used to argue a case for the cost-effectiveness of counselling. Consideration needs to be given, however, to whether we should try to argue the case for attaching counsellors in general practice only in terms of cost-effectiveness. A successful attachment of a counsellor may result in more time being spent in discussing cases with other members of the primary care team. It may also result in the primary care professionals spending more time in their consultations with patients as they start to adopt a more caring patient-centred approach. While this change in approach may have far-reaching consequences in terms of comprehensive care and patient satisfaction, the effects may be extremely difficult to trace and cost.

Studies in the United States indicate that the use of psychotherapy and behavioural medicine services can be cost-effective as they reduce medical utilization and this is why some health insurance companies have added psychotherapy to the list of services covered by their schemes (Cummings, 1990). The Hawaii Medicaid Project (Cummings et al., 1993) found that targeted focused psychological treatment produced a dramatic and significant reduction in the subsequent medical needs and medical resource consumption of a group of patients. This six-year study included patients with heart disease, hypertension, diabetes and even substance abuse. At the present time, a similar clinical trial is planned for the UK, although it may be more difficult to show a reduction in the use of resources as health expenditure per patient is generally much lower in this country than in the United States.

Clinical trials undertaken

In medicine, clinical trials are normally undertaken in order to evaluate whether a treatment works or not. In clinical trials, the progress of one group of patients who receive the treatment is compared with the progress of patients who do not. However, clinical trials into the effectiveness of counselling are extremely difficult to undertake and most studies that have attempted to evaluate counselling are flawed in some way, some more than others (Corney, 1992).

This chapter does not include all the clinical trials of therapy undertaken in general practice. It includes some of the trials undertaken on psychologists as well as those on counsellors. A number of studies are also in progress.

The first clinical trial conducted was carried out by Ashurst and colleagues. In this study, 726 patients aged between 16 and 65 from a health centre and a group practice were randomly assigned to counselling or to routine GP treatment (Ashurst and Ward, 1983, cited in Corney, 1992). Patients were referred to the study if they had consulted their GP for a neurotic disorder. High proportions had been prescribed psychotropic drugs. The two counsellors generally favoured a non-directive approach, made use of progressive relaxation, supportive counselling, interpretative psychotherapy, transactional analysis, behavioural techniques, Gestalt and dream work.

While a high proportion of the patients valued the help they had received, no striking differences in outcome (measured one year later) between groups were elicited, although it was felt by the authors that some individuals benefited considerably. One of the problems with this pioneering study was the question of client motivation. Not all the patients recruited into the study specifically wanted counselling help and this is likely to have reduced the effects of treatment.

Another study was carried out in Sydney, Australia, and it compared the outcome of three groups to which patients had been randomly assigned (Brodaty and Andrews, 1983, cited in Corney, 1992). Patients were again aged between 18 and 65 and had had persistent psychological symptoms for at least 6 months. In one group, 18 patients received 8 weekly half-hour sessions of brief problem-orientated dynamic psychotherapy from a trained psychotherapist. Another group of 18 individuals received 8 weekly half-hour appointments with their family doctor (who had no specific training). The third group of 20 patients received no additional therapy. No differences were found between the three treatment groups in outcome scores measuring symptom severity, social dysfunction, physical disability or medication.

In a third study, Boot and colleagues (1994) found that the group of patients referred to a counsellor had improved much more than those receiving GP treatment as usual and this difference was statistically significant. Those referred to the counsellor also felt more satisfied with the service and fewer were taking psychotropic drugs or were referred elsewhere. However, outcome (using the screening questionnaire, the General Health Questionnaire) was measured only six weeks after initial referral to the study and there were problems with the randomization procedure and the number of patients who dropped out of the study.

Studies in primary care of the effectiveness of psychologists have also shown that high proportions of patients felt that they were helped. They also have shown reduced psychotropic drug prescriptions and fewer consultations, although these effects may not be long-lasting (Corney, 1992).

As with counselling, however, the evidence of more sophisticated studies with control groups is more conflicting, with many studies only showing short-term effects. In a study conducted by Robson, France and Bland, assessments were made initially and 14, 22, 34 and 52 weeks later. Patients referred to a psychologist improved more quickly on scales measuring psychosocial changes, they made fewer visits to the doctor and received fewer psychotropic drug prescriptions. At one year, however, there were no major differences between groups in outcome because of the continued improvement of the control patients. The reduction in the number of visits to the doctor was more pronounced in the interpersonal and habit disorder subgroups and less noticeable for depressed and anxious patients. The authors estimated, however, that 28 per cent of the clinical psychologists' salaries could be found from drug economies alone (Robson et al., cited in Corney, 1992).

The studies carried out by Teasdale and co-authors (1984, cited in Corney, 1992) show similar results, with patients receiving treatment improving more quickly but with few differences at later follow-up assessments due to continued improvement of the controls. Earll and Kincey found no differences between groups at 7 months in the majority of ratings used, including GP consultation rates (1982). However, patients receiving psychological treatment had reduced psychotropic drug prescriptions during the treatment period and were very satisfied with the treatment received.

Another study investigated cognitive therapy as given by a trained social worker. In this crossover trial, depressed patients were allocated to individual cognitive therapy, group cognitive therapy or a waiting-list control group. Those who had cognitive therapy from a social worker did significantly better at three months than those on the waiting list. There were no significant differences between patients treated with group or individual cognitive therapy. Unfortunately, no longer-term assessment was possible because the study was a crossover trial (Ross and Scott, 1985, cited in Corney, 1992).

One study conducted on patients with major depression compared antidepressant medication prescribed by a psychiatrist, cognitive behaviour therapy (as given by a clinical psychologist), counselling and case work (given by a social worker) and routine care by a general practitioner (Scott and Freeman, 1992). They found that all treatment groups had improved at 16 weeks and that the clinical advantages of all the specialist treatments were small. However, the psychological treatments, especially social work counselling, were positively evaluated by patients. The main problem with this study was that only 121 patients were included, which perhaps is too small a number for statistically significant differences to be found in such a complex trial.

A group of researchers conducted a meta-analysis of 11 British studies of specialist mental health treatment in general practice (Balestrieri et al., 1988, cited in Corney, 1992). In each study the outcome of treatment by a specialist mental health professional located in general practice was compared with the outcome of the usual treatment by general practitioners. The main finding was that treatment by mental health professionals was about 10 per cent more successful than that usually given by general practitioners. Counselling, behaviour therapy and general psychiatry proved to be similar in their overall effect. The influence of counselling seemed to be greatest on social functioning, whereas behaviour therapy seemed mainly to reduce contacts with the psychiatric services.

While the majority of clients and professionals believe that they have been helped, the majority of clinical trials on counsellors and psychologists have not shown a major effect of treatment, especially in the long term. This lack of difference may be due to the fact that high proportions of patients will improve, regardless of treatment received, and that it is the group of clients who will not improve without help that need to be identified. More studies are needed, particularly those which measure long-term effects.

Why counselling psychology?

What does the counselling psychologist have to offer in this context in addition to the counsellor or the clinical psychologist? While the clinical psychologist is a specialist in mental illness, it will be apparent from the chapter that the vast majority of people seen in medical settings who could benefit from psychological help would not necessarily be classified in this manner. The distress exhibited by the majority of patients in primary and secondary care is a 'normal' reaction to either physical illness or some other problem in their lives. Counselling is an important skill with this group and although a clinical psychologist will use counselling in their work, the counselling psychologist's training is specifically focused around the development of this skill.

The counselling psychologist, with her or his prior training in psychology, will in most cases have a wider knowledge base than that of a counsellor without such training. Counselling psychologists also bring an understanding of a wide range of psychological theory and research and this may be valuable in their work in preventive medicine, consultancy, developing protocols and training others. Psychologists have also developed an impressive number of targeted, brief interventions. They have innovated brief, intermitted therapy which is relevant throughout the life cycle and is both focused and problem-solving. Psychologists have also learnt the importance of testing and evaluating their work and have gained experience in a range of methodologies in order to do this. This makes them most suitable for work within medical settings which constantly needs evaluation and reflection. There is such a large demand for psychological services that priorities must be made and this is best done by considering what brings about the most benefit to patients. Detailed evaluations are therefore crucial.

As the recognition of the role of psychological factors in health and illness is increasing, individuals with both a counselling and psychology background will have a major role in developing services to meet the need of clients in both primary and secondary care settings.

References

Ajzen, I. and Madden, T. (1986) 'Prediction of goal-directed behaviour: attitudes, intentions, and perceived behavioural control', *Journal of Experimental Social Psychology*, 22: 453–74.

Becker, M. (1974) 'The health belief model and personal health behaviour', *Health Education Monograph*, 2: 324–508.

Boot, D., Gillies, P., Fenelon, J., Reubin, R., Wilkins, M. and Gray, P. (1994) 'Evaluation of the short term impact of counselling in general practice', *Patient Education and Counselling*, 24: 79–89.

Byrne, P. and Long, B. (1976) *Doctors Talking to Patients*. London: HMSO.

Corney, R. (1986) 'Marriage guidance counselling in general practice', *Journal of the Royal College of General Practitioners*, 36: 424–6.

Corney, R. (1987) 'Marital problems and treatment outcome in depressed women', *British Journal of Psychiatry*, 151: 652–9.

Corney, R. (1990) 'Sex differences in general practice: attendance and helpseeking for minor illness', *Journal of Psychosomatic Research*, 34(5): 525–34.

Corney, R. (1992) 'Studies of the effectiveness of counselling in general practice', in R. Corney and R. Jenkins (eds), *Counselling in General Practice*. London: Routledge.

Corney, R. and Jenkins, R. (1992) *Counselling in General Practice*. London: Routledge.

Cummings, N. (1990) 'Arguments for the financial efficacy of psychological services in health care settings', in J. Sweet (ed.), *Handbook of Clinical Psychology in Medical Settings*. New York: Plenum.

Cummings, N., Dorken, H., Pallak, M. and Henke, C. (1993) *Medicaid, Managed Behavioural Health and Implications for Public Policy*. A report of the HCFA-Hawaii Medicaid Project and Other Readings. Health Care Utilization and Cost Series, vol. 2. Foundation for Behavioral Health, San Francisco, USA.

DiMatteo, M. (1985) 'Physician–patient communication: promoting a positive health care setting', in J. Rosen and L. Solomon (eds), *Prevention in Health Psychology*. Hanovern, NH: University Press of New England.

Earll, L. and Kincey, J. (1982) 'Clinical psychology in general practice', *Journal of the Royal College of General Practitioners*, 32: 32–7.

Fallowfield, L. and Roberts, R. (1992) Cancer counselling in the United Kingdom', *Psychological Health*, 6: 107–17.

Goldberg, D. and Huxley, P. (1992) *Common Mental Disorders*. London: Routledge.

Kannel, W. and Eaker, E. (1986) 'Psychosocial and other features of coronary heart disease: insights from the Framingham Study', *American Heart Journal*, 112: 1066–73.

Ley, P. (1988) *Communicating with Patients*. London: Croom Helm.

Maguire, P. (1991) 'Managing difficult communication tasks', in R. Corney (ed.), *Developing Communication and Counselling Skills in Medicine*. London: Routledge.

Mann, A., Jenkins, R. and Belsey, E. (1981) 'The outcome of neurotic illness in general practice', *Psychological Medicine*, 11: 535–50.

Mechanic, D. (1966) 'Response factors in illness: the study of illness behaviour', *Social Psychiatry*, 1: 106–15.

Nichols, K. (1984) *Psychological Care in Physical Illness*. London: Croom Helm.

Rees, W. and Lutkins, S. (1967) 'Mortality and bereavement', *British Medical Journal*, 4: 13–16.

Scott, A. and Freeman, C. (1992) 'Edinburgh primary care depression study: treatment outcome, patient satisfaction, and cost after 16 weeks', *British Medical Journal*, 304: 883–7.

Shapiro, A. (1971) 'Placebo effects in medicine, psychotherapy and psychoanalysis', in S. Garfield and A. Bergin (eds), *Handbook of Psychotherapy and Behavioral Change: an Empirical Analysis*. New York: Wiley.

Stall, R., Coates, T. and Hoff, C. (1988) 'Behavioural risk reduction for HIV infection among gay and bisexual men', *American Psychologist*, 43: 878–85.

Totman, R. (1979) *The Social Causes of Illness*. London: Souvenir Press.

Tuckett, D., Boulton, M., Olson, C. and Williams, A. (1986) *Meetings Between Experts: an Approach to Sharing Ideas in Medical Consultations*. London: Tavistock.

19

Counselling Psychology and Naturally Occurring Systems (Families and Couples)

Eddy Street

This chapter presents its material in three sections. First the historical and theoretical developments of counselling psychology with families and couples are outlined and some problems of definition are identified. In the second section the theoretical aspects of the interactional/systemic approach are discussed, including a brief overview of the principal models informing counselling practice. The final section focuses on the theoretical and empirical evaluation of the field and this highlights some particular themes from the research that are informative of practice.

Historical overview

In outlining the contributory set of ideas and practices that lead to the formation of any therapeutic endeavour it is difficult to provide a completely coherent account because such endeavours are typically the product of both disparate and linked developments, involving as they do the activities of single-minded pioneers. Broderick and Schrader (1981) have attempted to provide a historical account of working with families and couples and it is possible to identify two particular strands and themes within this history. First there are those practice strands linked to psychodynamic notions. Thus early social workers were the first to work directly with couples and families and as their practice developed so did the influence of the ideas from the social psychiatry school. Similarly early marriage counsellors took up these ideas in contrast to the moral and religious values that initially informed their work with spouses. The early family and couples (essentially marital) counsellors therefore evolved from the psychoanalytic tradition and tended to be linked to the psychiatric profession. Amongst the USA pioneers were Bell, Ackerman and Bowen, while in Britain the representative was Skynner.

The second thematic strand is that which links the development of family work with research activities. In the USA a number of projects addressed themselves to processes in families in which a member was suffering from schizophrenia, all emphasizing different ways in which the

419

family works to deny individual experience and the formation of a separate identity. A major contribution of these researchers was their conception of psychiatric illness as a developmental process within a distorted familial environment and hence they took the focus away from the medical model and intrapsychic concepts. In terms of the quality of research, however, this work tended to fail both in design and in its ability to identify actual patterns of communication that were unique to families with a schizophrenic member. Nevertheless, it was particularly Bateson and his group (Bateson, 1973) who developed the application of General Systems Theory (GST) to this field and it has been this that has had such an organizing impact in later therapeutic and theoretical developments.

On the basis that there is an attempt to modify the interactions between components of natural systems, it is a common feature of this field to consider couple/marital therapy as a sub-division of family therapy. Wilson and James (1991) have commented on the problems that this can sometimes cause in the research and theoretical arena as it is not clear whether 'family' and 'marital/couple' are being used synonymously or whether they are being referred to as separate and distinct entities. This is also confused by the clear difference between 'marital' relationships involving heterosexual partners who have subscribed to the institution of marriage and 'couple' relationships which include homosexual and heterosexual partners who consider themselves as being in relation. At the counselling practice level the additional complicating element is that not all counselling psychologists see themselves as family *and* couples counsellors but as one or the other. Schroder (1991) has made some attempts to address this issue in practical terms but with regard to the general counselling psychology of this area it does remain somewhat ambiguous whether there are one or two fields. This chapter will present the integrated view, with limitation of space unfortunately precluding continual reference to the arguments that originate from the separate fields view. Neither is it possible to offer an extended discussion of the arguments for and against each position. One of the central tasks that counselling psychology faces in this area is to reconcile these two views: hopefully this chapter will help set some of the parameters that need to be taken into account in this task.

Theoretical considerations

Individuals and interacting systems

The 'systems' view evolved to account for the social interactive nature of the individual. Thus the characteristics of naturally occurring systems are seen as applying directly to the functioning of interacting individuals and are outlined in an earlier chapter. However, as the counselling of families and couples involves individual action as well as the action of the system itself, it is important to begin the discussion of the psychology of the counselling context with a consideration of the self in the interacting system.

The self in the system The interactional view is distinguished by its attention to processes over time. This is in contrast to those perspectives that have generally sought to identify the fixed traits of a 'normal' individual living in a 'normal' family informed by psychological models of self that operate in terms of metaphors for individual action, for example, the individual as machine, the individual as scientist, etc. The interactional focus of interest is on the pattern of connections between individuals that are seen as being complementary or interdependent with respect to some outcome, placing the self within the sphere of social discourse. Individual characteristics are therefore considered as the behaviour illustrating the connection rather than something located within the individual. Hence individuals are described as demonstrating certain behaviour rather than them being labelled as a particular type of person. Therefore to say that a person is 'the possessive type' does not capture the sense of all the interactions around him or her at a particular time, it is more accurate to report that when certain interactions occur the person displays behaviour that may be called 'possessive'. Human action and activity in this framework is therefore seen as embedded within the connections, the communication, between people, for to be involved in a communicating system is at the core of human identity as identity evolves socially. Hence it is within the discussion of the social nature of identity that the process of counselling occurs.

Understanding self and relationship How then does the 'self' operate in a couple relationship or a family? The psychological notion of a person requires that an individual displays self-awareness and also has the capacity to say what he/she is doing. In human beings the ability to represent oneself to oneself makes it possible for the individual to learn about the connection between bodily states of emotion and the different contextual experiences of identity. This ability of self-reflection and self-representation allows the individual to express his or her own emotions to another and it also permits us to appreciate the intentionality of another through empathy. This is necessary, as a condition for having the concept of oneself as a person is that other people should also recognize one as being a person. For this to happen a group of people must be able to know that each one of them has an idea as to what he/she is doing and is

421

able to communicate that idea to others. As so much of our personal, private view of ourselves evolves out of our communication within our close relationships, interactions within these relationships play the crucial role in the view we have of who we are.

Individual and relationship awareness In order to be able to maintain communication within relationships individuals need to formulate action ahead of events; they need to create strategies and tactics prior to being involved in situations that are complex and which contain 'information inputs' from a variety of sources. To plan in this way a reflexive withdrawal from on-going events is needed. The individual can then focus on her or his plans for future action. However, momentarily this removes the individual from the consciousness of the moment where the on-going activities of others will have important influences on the interactions occurring. This 'time out' allows the person to work out what he or she is going to do but the period results in the loss of awareness of how the system is operating. A consequence of planning in this way is that the individual relates action to something that is antici-pated rather than to the process of the moment. The degree to which any individual indulges in an excessively focused view of his or her own particular conception of events in the system will determine the extent to which that person is removed from appreciating his or her position within the functioning system. Within families and couples this happens continually as individuals focus on 'this is what I need', or 'this is what others do to me', rather than considering the process of interaction for the family as a whole or the couple as an entity. Couples and families therefore have the ability to be aware of the social interactive nature of themselves but this awareness requires the individual to subsume his or her identity within that of the system and unfortunately this does not occur at times when problems arise. As Bateson (1973) notes, even though humans are embedded in biological, ecological and social systems, there is a twist in the psychology of the individual person whereby consciousness is almost of necessity blinded to the systemic nature of human beings. Even though we are an element of interacting systems, we somehow forget it.

Because every behaviour is at one and the same time an expression of the person and a communication to others (Watzlawick et al., 1974), there is a strong tendency to experience our communications solely as expressions of the self. We emphasize the 'What I do' to the neglect of 'This is my contribution to what We do'. In order for a couple or family to operate successfully there therefore needs to be a negotiation involving each person's 'contribution'. It is by this process that an agreed 'meaning' of the social context for all evolves. As these meanings are constructed then perceptions, opinions, expressions and actions of the 'self' are also changed. Gergen (1991) has discussed the manner in which self-definition realigns over time as social circumstances change. A person's experience of self is so much a social phenomenon, so much a responsive process, that we cannot imagine it to hold constant as families and couples change and develop.

The self and development in a relationship context Initially change occurs in families and couples as the outcome of simple developmental pressures. Terkelsen (1980) poses a three-level model of such changes. At the basic level are those relatively short behavioural sequences that characterize day-to-day functions. Some elements of such sequences may change depending on daily conditions. At the next level is 'first-order change' where individuals alter their own behaviour to accommodate their developing mastery of their situation. The uppermost layer involves 'second-order change', being the system's adaptation to individual changes that results in an alteration of meaning within the system, new meaning then generating new behavioural sequences. Obviously one form of change feeds into the next in a circular fashion illustrating Hoffman's (1993) assertion that development is not a continuous process but one characterized by transformations, second-order changes and the sudden appearance of functional patterns that simply did not exist before. Development of 'self' and the behaviour that indicates it cannot therefore necessarily be conceived as a process that follows rigid patterning. Gergen (1982) has criticized standard developmental theories that assume a universal standard by which individuals can measure their functioning. He argues that the whole idea of the 'normal' lifespan trajectory is very problematic. The timing and nature of developmental shifts cannot be predicted. A predetermined and optimal path for development cannot be specified. The self can therefore be considered to change through an individual life. Hence counsellors cannot construct their practice on the view that a divergence from the optimal path for individuals, couples, or families is a failure representing poor adjustment, for indeed there is no optimal path. In this respect counsellors should be aware that it is possible for even the greatest trauma to be overcome developmentally as the resilience and unpredictability of human beings are enormous.

Models of functioning

Given the social nature of human beings, the scientific needs of a good theory of relationship functioning can readily be linked with the needs of the counselling situation. A good theory should therefore first offer an adequate means of discussing motivation in the relationship context given that the system is perceived as being more than a collection of individuals. This will be related to the way individual, couple and family needs are negotiated. Secondly, the theory should offer a means of constructing a notion of psychological reality for everyone in the family. The question 'Whose reality?' is a central one that runs through the family/marital counselling task. Therefore there is a need to understand the way each individual's experience and perception is merged in with a set of common meanings held by the family. Thirdly, the theory should find a way of addressing themes that arise from personal, family and socio-cultural value systems, particularly the issues of gender role, racial questions, autonomy and expression of feeling. This obviously includes those values that are brought to the counselling situation by the counselling psychologist and his or her personal and professional system.

In addition to those points listed above, another foundation for any model of therapeutic activity will be the view held of the notion of the 'normal'. Offer and Sabshin (1974) have synthesized the theoretical and clinical concepts of mental health into four major perspectives on normality:

- **Normality as health,** from a medico-psychiatric model being based on the criterion of absence of pathology.
- **Normality as average**, an approach common in sociological and behavioural studies, uses the statistical norm, or average, to identify typical patterns and traits.
- **Normality as utopia**, an approach embodied in psychoanalytic and humanistic theories, conceives of normality as ideal or optimal functioning, or as 'self-actualization' of potential.
- **Normality as process**, attends to developmental processes throughout the life cycle in the context of interactional systems. This perspective based on GST is considered by Offer and Sabshin to be the most fruitful in that it allows for consideration of unique coping styles and multiple routes for adaptation.

Within the field of family and couple counselling models are now generally ascribing to the view of normality as process. The most obvious common denominator to these models is the concept that families and relationships are patterned and thus repeat time and again the same class of interaction. However, there tends to be a difference in emphasis, with some models focusing on general functioning and others commenting on this via their outline of therapeutic and counselling principles. Some general theories have developed from studies based on self-report, whereas others have arisen from observational methodologies. All these models are discussed by Walsh (1993) and all are constructed on a dimensional basis of varying number with the types of issues being problem-solving, communication and expressiveness, roles allocation, affective responsiveness and involvement (including cohesion), conflict management and behavioural control, whether the family is inwardly orientated or outwardly focused, and the degree of adaptability to change. It is readily apparent that all these models are discussing the same processes with different terminology and much of the difference may just be due to methodological approaches and even semantics. Work in this area is relatively recent and it is noticeable that the dialogue between these researchers is only now beginning, hence the search for communality is only in its infancy. It is beyond the scope of this chapter fully to discuss the evaluation of these particular theories of family functioning.

Those models that focus on the activities of counselling psychology also work on the concept that families and relationships are patterned and thus repeat the same interaction, a corollary to this concept being the idea that symptoms are related to or part of some of the interaction patterns. Any attempt to theorize at this level has the problem of providing a means of describing the moment-to-moment interaction that occurs. To describe a pattern in its entirety for any given system is impossible because it requires the ability to observe and define a highly complex and continuous stream of behavioural sequences that are connected and persist over time. Despite this difficulty, Breunlin and Schwartz (1986) propose a model that examines the relationships of sequences with the entire pattern of an interpersonal system that is based on time frames. They identify four classes of sequences:

1   From seconds to hours
2   A day to a week
3   Several weeks to a year
4   Time that spans at least one generation

Some sequences are recursive in that in their repetition an element of themselves guarantees the repetition. Some sequences are non-recursive in that they involve sequences of behaviours that do not repeat over time. Within a given generation life-cycle events such as births and marriages are non-recursive in that they do not repeat. However, on taking a frame longer than a generation there may be a recursive element as families repeat similar patterns. As these sequences are interlocking at any one time a small interactive sequence may reflect the past, the present and the expectations of the future. Any problem is embedded in one or more interactional sequences.

The meaning ascribed to any sequence by those involved in it will come to play an important function in how that interaction progresses. Meaning is central to the interaction process in that it constructs the psychological parameters that enable individuals to coordinate their action, manage their relationship and hence deal with any problem that emerges. In a manner that builds on the time frame sequences, Cronen and Pearce (1985) link the different levels of meaning available, suggesting five which, as with the time frames, are interlocking. So that the reader appreciates the circularity of short to long and long to short, these levels of meaning are in the opposite order to time frames.

5   **Family myth** – includes general conceptions of how society, personal and family relationships work. This operates over generations.
4   **Life script** – a person's conception of self in interaction. This changes during a lifetime.
3   **Relationship** – the conception of how and on what terms two or more persons engage in interaction. This involves both long and immediate elements of interaction.
2   **Episode** – a short pattern of reciprocated interaction, being equivalent to the seconds-to-hours time frame.
1   **Speech act** – the verbal or non-verbal messages that come from one person. This is the individual element of interaction and only makes sense in terms of the analysis of that interaction.

Families and couples are faced with the task of organizing these different levels of interactive time and meaning so that it forms a wholeness for themselves. In doing this they have to deal with three essential tasks of social interaction that define who they perceive themselves to be. They need to establish who is involved in their interactions and in what way. They need to experience a sense of control and influence over what happens to themselves. They also need to share the affective elements of those other tasks with other individuals. The construction of an overarching view of these tasks has been elaborated by the Family FIRO Model as outlined by Doherty and his colleagues (Doherty and Colangelo, 1984). This model holds that the themes of inclusion, control and intimacy predominate in human relatedness, determining the framework for understanding the types of interactions that occur within a family. Having outlined those models that provide an overview of interactive processes their framework allows us to note the relationship between the different theoretical formulations of family and couple counselling. Hence, different models of systemic intervention, be they focused on family and/or marital interaction, approach the time frame and thematic dimensions differentially depending on their theoretical orientation. This is due to inclusion themes being more obvious in the shorter time frames, control themes occurring more readily in the medium-length sequences, whereas the longer sequences are clearly linked to intimacy issues. Thus Minuchin's structural therapy (Minuchin, 1974) emphasizes boundary, role patterns and connectedness within families in

	Themes of family life		
Time frame			
Sequences	*Inclusion*	*Control*	*Intimacy*
1 Short (hours)	Structural	|	
		|	
2 Medium (up to a week)	|	Behavioural	
		Brief	
3 Medium (up to a year)		Strategic	
		Milan	|
		|	Symbolic
			Experiential
4 Long (over one generation)		|	Contextual
			Psychodynamic
			Transgenerational
			|

Figure 19.1 *Schools of family therapy and counselling*

which short in-session interactions are addressed. Those models that emphasize control themes, such as strategic approaches (Haley, 1976), the earlier Milan approaches (Palazzoli et al., 1978), brief models (Watzlawick et al., 1974) and behavioural approaches (Jacobson and Margolin, 1979; Crowe and Ridley, 1990) emphasize intermediate time frames. In these approaches counselling psychology consists of changing the role system for mutual regulation either by overt steps (for example, teaching new behavioural strategies or eliciting new problem-solving behaviour) or covert therapeutic moves (paradoxical prescriptions). Counselling psychologists with a focus on intimacy tend to be transgenerational in their consideration of time; psychodynamic formulations (Daniell, 1985), the Family Systems Theory of Bowen (Bowen, 1978), Whitaker's Symbolic Experiential Model (Whitaker and Keith, 1981) and the Contextual Therapy of Boszormenyi-Nagy (Boszormenyi-Nagy and Krasner, 1986) are approaches within this category, providing as they do goals for optimal individual and family functioning which involves dyadic intimacy outside of normative role patterns. Street (1994) has presented a means of examining the relation between the various schools of family and couple work utilizing the time frames and thematic issues as organizing principles, and this is displayed in Figure 19.1.

A tradition that has not conformed to dealing with couples and families in terms of time frames has been the person-centred (Rogerian) approach (Gaylin, 1993). This approach has now been taken up by authors from within a systemic framework (see Street, 1994). This approach deals directly within the meaning framework as generated by the family or couple. In this sense therefore it is family- or couple-centred. Aspects of this approach are discussed later in this chapter.

Evaluating theory and practice

There are three broad questions in the evaluation of family and couple counselling that need to be addressed by the counselling psychologist:

1   Is the model/theory used to describe human action adequate? This is a theoretical evaluation and specifically this questions the usefulness of General Systems Theory as an overarching and organizing theory within this area.
2   How can change in the counselling context be maximized? This is a question of practicalities and is typically asked in an empirical manner and hence is an empirical evaluation.
3   Which skills are identified as being necessary for effective practice?

Each question will be examined in turn.

The adequacy of overarching theory – General Systems Theory

Theoretically the systemic approach has been applied at two levels by counselling psychologists. First, at a general level it has been used as a guide to psychological inquiry in the broad sense. Secondly, it has made a contribution to the development of theories of counselling action and therefore as such it is a guide to therapeutic action. Therefore any evaluation of systems theory needs to ask the following two questions.

Is the theory a useful guide to psychological inquiry?   There is no doubt that General Systems Theory has created a new medium for thinking about particular phenomena, but the relationship between its abstract theoretical constructs and empirical facts remains tenuous, especially in the study of human social phenomena (Vetere and Gale, 1987). Indeed, it might be more appropriate to describe this theory as a conceptual framework which spans a wide range of disciplines and links up with less general models; hence one encounters a wide range of other models, for example, psychodynamic, cognitive-behavioural, easily being incorporated into explanations based on GST. Unfortunately, as a theory it lacks adequate methods of analysis that spring from its formulations. Consequently when engaged in scientific inquiry it is difficult to establish and apply systems principles. This is particularly so in the investigation of family interactions where a major problem has been inadequate operationalization of concepts so that data may be collected in a meaningful way. Researchers into the psychology of personal relationships including families require a theory that comprehensively presents concepts which generate testable predictions not only in terms of general behaviour but also with regard to behaviour specific to the counselling situation. Vetere and Gale (1987) list the requirements of such a theory. It should:

1 Describe and explain family and couple structure, dynamics, process and change.
2 Describe invariant interpersonal structures and emotional dynamics within families and couples, particularly concerning the transmission of distress onto individuals.
3 Account for family relationships as the interface between the individual and culture, that is to say, how does the family mediate between external environmental events and individual development, thus acting as a filter through which the child interprets the world?
4 Describe the process of individuation and differentiation of the family members.
5 Predict health and pathology within the family, that is, provide a source of hypotheses about family function and what causes dysfunction.
6 Prescribe therapeutic strategies for dealing with dysfunction.
7 Account for the seemingly antithetical functions of stability and change, particularly when viewed within the family's developmental cycle.

Clearly GST has not met these requirements and scientifically the family systems approach has not generated enough empirical research suitable for an evaluation of its methodological sophistication. At present therefore there are still not enough examples of links made between abstract formulations of GST and the reality of everyday interaction. GST is therefore not adequate as a general theory but it does provide a framework for describing complex time-related interactional behaviour for which traditional sociological and psychological theories are not conceptually or methodologically suited.

Is GST helpful as a guide to therapeutic action?   The concept of a system as applied to a family or couple relationship carries with it the implication of a set of rules that lead to the organization of structure. In the early development of the field the application of this concept focused on dysfunctional processes presumed to be implicated in the ongoing maintenance of individual symptoms, if not in their origins. The family or couple were considered to be unaware of their own rules and their dysfunctional structure. Under these conditions, as Hoffman (1993) has pointed out, the counsellor becomes cast as a person who analyses the system, determining those rules in operation and then moves that system to a position where a more helpful set of rules and structure apply. The counselling psychologist hence has enormous power as he or she by definition is in charge of the process. As a consequence a client–counsellor distance is inbuilt and the language used to discuss therapeutic processes become adversarial. This is linked to a general difficulty of Batesonian descriptions of systems in that it does not include a language to account for experiential events. The focus on the system of the family and couple also leads to the neglect of external social issues that never-theless affect it; hence for the early systemic therapists issues of race, class and gender were nearly invisible. These formulations developed in this manner because of the separation of the observer from the observed, which as Hoffman (1993) has indicated reflects the dominant masculine value system of Western science. These criticisms have led Hoffman to identify six characteristics of therapeutic practice that are needed to overcome these difficulties.

1 An 'observing system' stance and the inclusion of the therapist's own context.
2 A collaborative rather than a hierarchical structure.
3 Goals that emphasize setting a context for change, not specifying a change.
4 Ways to guard against too much instrumentality.
5 A 'circular' assessment of the problem.
6 A non-pejorative, non-judgemental view.

These problems with the systems approach indicate the fundamental difficulty central to all theorizing about human change and behaviour in that any approach that attempts to deal with how individuals function contextually must at one and the same time be interactional, whilst addressing the issues of human subjectivity, with the subjectivity being that of both the clients and the counsellor.

Taking into account all these criticisms of the GST framework, Hoffman (1993) has argued that the field would be better served by adopting an approach such as social constructionism. It is suggested by some that this 'post-Milan' approach represents a new and different model of change. In terms of the more practical issues of counselling it is now being noted by several authors that the field is moving to a style which finds many echoes in the person-centred approach to counselling. There is a sense therefore that the systems approach to family and couple counselling in its development is shifting towards a way of working that it initially saw as being in contradistinction to itself. It is now picking up on those skills and counselling psychology attitudes allied to the person-centred approach which for some time were allowed to be neglected. The perspective that focused on limitations, deficits and pathology is being overtaken by a paradigm long familiar in the counselling literature that is competency-based and health-orientated, and which recognizes and amplifies strengths and resources. Therefore, as Walsh (1993) notes, there is a clear shift in working with naturally occurring systems from a deficit model informing therapy and counselling to one that emphasizes resources, moving the counsellor from the analysis of what went wrong to being involved in the search for what can be done to enhance family functioning.

Maximizing change in counselling – empirically evaluating effectiveness

The study of interaction raises questions about the nature of science and methodology, for 'systemic thinking' forms the characteristics of 'new' science. This model of scientific enquiry has critiqued the basis on which 'old' science attempts to know and understand the world. The 'old' view holds that cause and effect can be understood, it being possible to make observations which are objective and independent with those observations being understood as outlining the 'truth'. The critique of the traditional approach has given rise to the question as to the nature of research inquiry into counselling for couples and families. The two principal themes raised by this criticism have been those of objectivity and causality. A systems view challenges the traditional cause-and-effect model, with circular causality implying no distinction between 'independent' ('cause') and 'dependent' ('effect') variables. Thinking systemically does not merely require the investigation of a larger unit of analysis but also the investigation of how the elements that make up the unit are connected and patterned. This view of science holds that knowledge is not something 'out there' nor is it something we process in our heads, it is rather something people do together. It is also argued that the researcher is not able to be objective and the measures, methods and constructs he or she uses are nothing other than the researcher's way of 'punctuating' phenomena. This then is a different paradigm for constructing the science of counselling psychology and once again moves towards the social constructionist position (Gergen, 1982). Notwithstanding these major differences between 'old' and 'new' science in a general and specific sense,

431

the new approaches should incorporate and be incorporated by the more traditional scientific endeavours. Gurman (1983) illustrates this by the numerous ways traditional psychotherapeutic research designs implicitly involve systemic concepts of context, connectedness and interdependence. For example:

1 The study of the interactive effects of patient, therapist, treatment and setting variables.
2 The use of multidimensional change measures.
3 The use of multiple vantage points for assessing change; this involves considering, for example, change in the individuals, change in couple behaviour, change in family interaction, etc.
4 The use of repeated measures to assess both level and patterns of change over time.

Thus it is not appropriate to discard the 'old' simply because the 'new' has appeared, particularly as the new epistemology has not effectively translated its approach into practical research projects. In this respect, however, it should be noted that the more recent development of audit methods within medical and allied activities involve an approach that is essentially systemic.

So what does scientific endeavour tell us about the progress in this field? First, as Kuehl et al. (1990) have pointed out, research into family and couples treatments in common with mainstream psychotherapy research has studiously ignored the experiences of users. Almost everything which gets written and discussed about counselling psychology therefore reflects counselling psychologists' experiences not users' experiences. Bearing in mind this caveat, in the last major research review on marital and family therapy Gurman and his colleagues (Gurman et al., 1986) state that it has now been 'established convincingly that in general, the practice of family and marital therapy leads to positive outcomes'. This has been largely based on Gurman and Kniskern's (1978) meta-analysis of outcome data when they concluded that beneficial outcomes occur in about two-thirds of cases, this being based on improvement rates from 36 studies. Markus et al. (1990) completed a similar analysis on 19 studies, concluding that the average client receiving family counselling is better off than 76 per cent of clients in the various control groups. The follow-up results suggest that the effect of family work increases during the first year following termination, and that it stays large until 18 months after contact. After more than 18 months the effect may decrease, though clearly the long-term effectiveness needs to be studied with more extended follow-up periods. Eisler (1990) has cautioned against the use of meta-analysis for providing definitive answers about family work but it would appear in general that there is some consistency of findings utilizing this methodology. Gurman and his colleagues (Gurman et al., 1986) have gone on to argue that what is important is the demonstration of effectiveness of particular approaches with particular client groups. Their initial overview of this notes the general lack of research and demonstrates that there really are only two approaches – the behavioural and the psychoeducational, which can claim strong support from outcome research studies. There is some support for the Milan approach, though the evidence is somewhat patchy.

The results of other reviews suggest that working with families may prove successful when combined with other approaches. Langes et al. (1993) concluded that family approaches have relevant contributions with schizophrenia, mood disorders, childhood conduct disorders, addiction to drugs and eating disorders, the most successful outcomes often being derived from treatment programmes where there was the combining of techniques from different treatment modalities. The impact on anxiety disorders and alcohol addiction are less clear. Again, in another review, Lam (1991) considered psychoeducational family interventions in schizophrenia and concluded that the most encouraging findings involved a mix of the educational and problem-solving (behavioural) approaches. It may well be that the integration of different theoretical frameworks and the development of a more eclectic approach to the delivery of counselling services will yield long-term benefits.

In taking an overview of the field with regard to the empirical investigations, Gurman et al. (1986) identify what they consider to be the general conclusions.

- The developmental level of the identified patient (for example, child/adolescent/adult) does not affect treatment outcomes significantly.
- Positive results typically occur in treatments of short duration, that is 1–20 sessions.
- Family therapy is probably as effective as, and possibly more effective than many commonly offered (usually individual) treatments for problems attributed to family conflict.
- There is no empirical support for the superiority of co-therapy compared with marital or family counselling conducted by a single therapist.
- When both spouses are involved in counselling conjointly in the face of marital problems, there is a greater chance of positive outcome than when only one spouse is seen.

In the discussion of outcome several issues can be looked at in more detail as they point to important features that have a clear influence on the overall effectiveness of family and marital counselling.

Counselling drop-out As with other areas of this field, the study of this phenomenon is lacking. Biskhoff and Sprenkle (1993) have provided a review of the issues encountered in this area, with Garfield (1986) having presented a comprehensive overview of the empirical work. In general this review reports the most consistent finding as being that drop-outs are higher for clients in the lower range of socio-economic status. In comparing the relative drop-out rates for individual as opposed to family work, Dare et al. (1990) reported that females with anorexia nervosa were less likely to drop out of family therapy if they were younger than 18, and less likely to drop out of individual therapy if they were older than 18. Another client variable having some bearing on continuing attendance is the client's referral source, with the consistent finding that those who are self-referred or who are referred by individual professionals are more likely to keep attending than those referred by an institution. In a manner similar to other findings, the sex-roles of family members have an important bearing on the drop-out phenomenon; LeFave (1980) reported that families attending the initial interview without the father were significantly more likely to drop out than those families attending with the father. It is quite probable that clients will drop out when they consider that their expectations are not being met but unfortunately this is one of those central issues that has not been addressed empirically. Therapist characteristics that influence drop-out were investigated by Shields et al. (1991), who found that in common with previous results, therapist executive activities involving structuring the interview and joining with all family members were associated with 'completer' cases.

Interventions have been reported of ways of increasing attendance; Szapocznik et al. (1988) undertook to contact families before the first session and, if necessary, to visit them at home in order to overcome the initial problems of attending. They found that not only was attendance improved in the first instance but there were lower rates of drop-out for those who encountered the active recruitment programme. A similar approach was reported by Pimpernell and Treacher (1990), who with probation (i.e. institutional referred) clients used an informational video tape to overcome resistance to attend.

Deterioration as a result of counselling Deterioration of individuals and relationships sometimes does occur within the counselling process. Gurman and Kniskern (1978) have reviewed the conceptual issues relevant to a definition of worsening in marital counselling and present some methodological guidelines for the assessment of deterioration within systems. In their meta-analysis of 36 outcome studies in which deterioration rates were reported they concluded that approximately 5–10 per cent of individual clients or marital or family relationships worsen as the result of marital/family counselling, a figure that is consistent with the frequencies of worsening reported for other modalities of counselling psychology and psychotherapy. A common finding is that deterioration is higher for marital problems when dealt with by individual and group work than marital counselling itself. The authors argue that the unimpressive improvement rate of individual-marital counselling and its high deterioration rate does little to support the continued practice of this modality of treatment for marital difficulties.

Counsellor characteristics   Gurman and his colleagues (Gurman et al., 1986) concluded that there was good evidence that particular counsellor characteristics appear to 'sponsor' effectiveness. Thus a reasonable mastery of technical skills may be sufficient for preventing worsening or for maintaining pre-treatment functioning but more refined relationship skills seem necessary to yield genuinely positive outcomes. In other words, a style of providing little structure in early treatment sessions and confronting highly affective material may be reliably associated with observed deterioration compared to a style of stimulating interaction and giving support. The role of client expectations is important in this respect. Crane et al. (1986) found that the counsellor's ability to present counselling as consistent and congruent with client expectations is a good predictor of client perception of outcome. However, there do appear to be gender differences in client perceptions and preferences. Brannen and Collard (1982) found that men were less satisfied than women with a non-directive 'ventilative' style of marital counselling, expressing a preference for structured advice giving or goal setting. Bennun (1989) found that the treatment outcome of a variety of family problems related to the fathers' rating of the therapists being competent, active and guiding the session directly. Kuehl et al. (1990) also found that clients who viewed their counselling psychologist as personable, caring and competent were more likely to be satisfied with their therapeutic experience. However, from the dissatisfied client's perspective, in this study counsellors were seen as resistant when, for a theoretical reason, they continued to propose a problem/solution relationship the client would not accept. These results suggest counselling psychologists should proceed with caution when trying to convince a client of the utility or rightness of an approach the client does not accept for, as Wilson and James (1991) note, client satisfaction would seem to be significantly determined by their own expectations of what should take place, expectations which can be discrepant with those of counselling psychologists.

Investigations into the process of counselling   Unfortunately process research has not been substantial in terms of informing the inquiry of overall effectiveness in family and marital counselling. This work was initially reviewed by Pinsof (1981), who concluded that the primary access strategy used by researchers was that of direct observation, with there being more emphasis on counsellor behaviour than on that of the client. As Pinsof notes, this work continues to be exploratory, with no coherent body of findings emerging. It is apparent that in the sounder methodological studies the contents of the scale are derived from research concerns, that is, features that the researcher believes can be measured validly. Although a claim is often made with these scales that they are cast in terms closely resembling clinical theories, the match is often not that clear, with the result being that this research is constructing a view of the counselling process that is empirically led rather than one that is led by the conceptualizations of the clinical theories. Certainly there is a need for the principal theoretical formulations to express their ideas in ways that are open to empirical investigation. This requires that micro-theories of counsellor behaviour be developed, as ultimately the counselling psychologist has to address the means of encouraging change within any context. Greenberg (1991) has argued that the approach to psychotherapy research typified by most of the work reviewed by Gurman and his colleagues is in fact defensive in that it merely attempts to justify the existence of the therapeutic approach rather than attempting to discover how it works and what leads to change. If this could be done then one could go on to specify the necessary skills to produce change. Greenberg presents a process-analytic approach to psychotherapy research that stresses the importance of meaning and the testing out of that meaning. Greenberg suggests that what is required is a study of the similarities of performance and experience of individuals involved in similar therapeutic situations so that common features and processes can be isolated. His fundamental assumption is that in specified therapy and counselling contexts, behaviour and experience are lawfully explainable and valid specific models or micro-theory can be developed to help explain change processes. Clearly, in our designated field of couple and family work we do not seem to have begun to elucidate possible explainable laws and, as Pinsoff (1981) has remarked, the field has not as yet developed a comprehensive view of the moment-by-moment process of counselling. It is in this area that the development of qualitative methods of research is necessary as these methods hold the potential for exploring meanings, perceptions and other subjectivities in and about human relationships and the counselling process with them (see Moon et al., 1990). In our field we have not as yet outlined the basic foundation skills necessary for systems change and this does indicate that as counselling psychologists we need to be developing a comprehensive skills analysis of this field.

Skills analysis

When it comes to discussing skills, theories of family therapy and counselling psychology have tended to be expressed in terms at a high level of generality, hence they do not provide operational definitions of skills which could aid the construction of notions of counsellor performance that would be available to study. Unfortunately, there is a general lack of refined models for analysing skills so that they can then be reconstructed through the training process. The traditional categorization system of these skills is based on perceptual, conceptual and executive skills. Developing on this tripartite division, Tomm and Wright (1979) have operationalized a number of skills which are based on the process element of counselling and therapy sessions defined within terms of engagement, problem identification, change facilitation and termination. Such means of identifying skills unfortunately fail to place the skills within an appropriate theoretical framework. Street (1994) has presented a structure for considering the skills of working with families and couples that rests on attitudes basic to the counselling process. Thus the attitudes of respect, enquiry and action orientation are seen as being hierarchically ordered. Hence the counselling psychologist needs to begin by demonstrating respect before understanding is possible, which comes through enquiry; once an appropriate understanding is achieved this then allows interventions to be activated. With this framework it then becomes possible to consider particular counsellor skills as outlined by other authors. This approach moves the consideration of skills out of an overemphasis on the cognitive and behavioural aspects of action by counselling psychologists and introduces the counselling psychologist's internal frame of reference.

The identification of any set of skills has to be linked to how they play a part in constructive family systems change. We also need to specify the conditions necessary to initiate that change and sufficient to inaugurate the process. This is obviously related to the question Carl Rogers set himself about the necessary and sufficient conditions to bring about change (Rogers, 1957). His answer to his own question became a benchmark in the development of counselling practice and clearly in the field of family and couple counselling an outline of the necessary and sufficient conditions for constructive systems change is required. Street (1994) has attempted this by adding the relational-interactive elements to Rogers's construction. Essentially this involves the counsellor being confident that each individual in the system is being allowed a voice so that he or she can experience empathic understanding of each individual's awareness of his or her own experience. This needs to occur at the same time that the counsellor experiences an understanding of the interactive processes of the system. The communication of this understanding is also at the levels of individual and system in that the counsellor communicates his/her understanding of each individual's experience to them singly and as a group and also communicates his/her understanding of the interaction of the system. In order to be able to meet these conditions another is added that addresses the difference between counselling one person and more than one person at the same time, this condition involves 'setting' the counselling context so that each individual is heard and responded to. As with Rogers's formulation for individual work, the concept being advanced here is that the essential conditions of change exist in a single configuration. Even though counsellors may use them differentially, an implication is that the techniques of various schools are unimportant except to the extent that they serve as channels for fulfilling the conditions. Each counsellor needs to develop a model of practice for him- or herself as a means by which these conditions can be maximized. This approach of specifying a framework for skills development not only offers the individual practitioner a means of achieving a modus operandi but it also serves the purpose of directing research activity.

Conclusion

There can be little doubt that the theorizing about family and marital counselling has undergone many changes since the field began to organize and define itself. From a position of standing in contradistinction to many of the traditional models of counselling practice aspects of many of those models have become incorporated in the general framework. It is clear, however, that as psychological enquiry moves away from the study of the 'human animal' and begins a more rigorous appraisal of 'ourselves' and the human condition, that family and marital counselling is undergoing a fundamental shift of paradigm. Counselling psychology has a central role to play in this process, not so much in the answers and solutions it proposes but essentially in the psychological nature of the questions it poses. There are no conclusions for this chapter save that it is continuously necessary to pose such questions in order to enhance the process of assisting individuals, couples and families in distress.

References

Bateson, G. (1973) *Steps to an Ecology of Mind*. St Albans: Paladin.
Bennun, I. (1989) 'Perceptions of the therapist in family therapy', *Journal of Family Therapy*, 11: 243–56.

Biskhoff, R.J. and Sprenkle, D.H. (1993) 'Dropping out of marriage and family therapy: a critical review of research', *Family Process*, 32: 353–75.

Boszormenyi-Nagy, I. and Krasner, B.R. (1986) *Between Give and Take: a Clinical Guide to Contextual Therapy*. New York: Brunner/Mazel.

Bowen, M. (1978) *Family Therapy in Clinical Practice*. New York: Jason Aronson.

Brannen, J. and Collard, J. (1982) *Marriages in Trouble*. London: Routledge.

Breunlin, D.C. and Schwartz, R.C. (1986) 'Sequences: toward a common denominator of family therapy', *Family Process*, 25: 67–87.

Broderick, C.B. and Schrader, S.S. (1981) 'The history of professional marriage and family therapy', in A.S. Gurman and D.P. Kniskern (eds), *Handbook of Family Therapy*. New York: Brunner/Mazel.

Crane, D.R., Griffin, W. and Hill, R.D. (1986) 'Influence of therapist skills on client perceptions of marriage and family therapy outcome: implications for supervision', *Journal of Marital and Family Therapy*, 12: 91–6.

Cronen, V.E. and Pearce, W.B. (1985) 'Towards an explanation of how the Milan method works: an invitation to a systemic epistemology and the evolution of family systems', in D. Campbell and R. Draper (eds), *Applications of Systemic Family Therapy: the Milan Approach*. London: Grune and Stratton.

Crowe, M. and Ridley, J. (1990) *Therapy with Couples: a Behavioural Systems Approach to Marital and Sexual Problems*. Oxford: Blackwell.

Daniell, D. (1985) 'Marital therapy. The psychodynamic approach', in W. Dryden (ed.), *Marital Therapy in Britain*. London: Harper and Row.

Dare, C., Eisler, I., Russell, G.F.M. and Szmukler, G.I. (1990) 'The clinical and theoretical impact of a controlled trial of family therapy in anorexia nervosa', *Journal of Marital and Family Therapy*, 16: 39–57.

Doherty, W.J. and Colangelo, N. (1984) 'The Family FIRO Model: a modest proposal for organizing family treatment', *Journal of Marital and Family Therapy*, 10: 19–29.

Eisler, I. (1990) 'Meta-analysis: Magic Wand or exploratory tool? Comment on Markus et al.', *Journal of Family Therapy*, 12: 223–8.

Garfield, S.L. (1986) 'Research on client variables in psychotherapy', in S.L. Garfield and A.E. Bergin (eds), *Handbook of Psychotherapy and Behavior Change*, 3rd edn. New York: Wiley.

Gaylin, N.L. (1993) 'Person-centred family therapy', in D. Brazier (ed.), *Beyond Carl Rogers*. London: Constable.

Gergen, K. (1982) *Toward Transformation in Social Knowledge*. New York: Springer Verlag.

Gergen, K. (1991) *The Saturated Self*. New York: Basic Books.

Greenberg, L.S. (1991) 'Research on the process of change', *Psychotherapy Research*, 1: 3–16.

Gurman, A.S. (1983) 'Family therapy research and the new epistemology', *Journal of Marital and Family Therapy*, 9: 227–34.

Gurman, A.S. and Kniskern, D. (1978) 'Research on marital and family therapy: progress, perspective and prospect', in S. Garfield and A. Bergin (eds), *Handbook of Psychotherapy and Behavior Change*, 2nd edn. New York: Wiley.

Gurman, A.S. and Kniskern, D.P. (1981) 'Family therapy outcome research:

knowns and unknowns', in A.S. Gurman and D.P. Kniskern (eds), *Handbook of Family Therapy*. New York: Brunner/Mazel.

Gurman, A.S., Kniskern, D. and Pinsof, W. (1986) 'Research on the process and outcome of marital and family therapy', in S. Garfield and A. Bergin (eds), *Handbook of Psychotherapy and Behavior Change*, 3rd edn. New York: Wiley.

Haley, J. (1976) *Problem Solving Therapy*. New York: Harper and Row.

Hoffman, L. (1993) *Exchanging Voices*. London: Karnac.

Jacobson, N.S. and Margolin, G. (1979) *Marital Therapy*. New York: Brunner/ Mazel.

Kuehl, B. Newfield, N. and Joanning, H. (1990) 'A client-based description of family therapy', *Journal of Family Psychology*, 3: 310–21.

Lam, D.H. (1991) 'Psychological family intervention in schizophrenia: a review of empirical studies', *Psychological Medicine*, 21: 423–41.

Langes, A., Schaap, C. and van Widenfelt, B. (1993) 'Family therapy and psychopathology: developments in research and approaches to treatments', *Journal of Family Therapy*, 15: 113–46.

LeFave, M.K. (1980) 'Correlates of engagement on family therapy', *Journal of Marital and Family Therapy*, 6: 75–81.

Markus, E., Lange, A. and Pettigrew, T.F. (1990) 'Effectiveness of family therapy: a meta-analysis', *Journal of Family Therapy*, 12: 205–21.

Minuchin, S. (1974) *Families and Family Therapy*. London: Tavistock.

Moon, S., Dillon, B. and Sprenkle, D. (1990) 'Family therapy and qualitative research', *Journal of Marital and Family Therapy*, 16: 357–73.

Offer, D. and Sabshin, M. (1974) *Normality: Theoretical and Clinical Concepts of Mental Health*, 2nd edn. New York: Basic Books.

Palazzoli, M.S., Cecchin, G., Prata, G. and Boscolo, L. (1978) *Paradox and Counterparadox*. New York: Jason Aronson.

Pimpernell, P. and Treacher, A. (1990) 'Using a videotape to overcome client reluctance to engage in family therapy – some preliminary findings from a probation setting', *Journal of Family Therapy*, 12: 59–72.

Pinsoff, W.M. (1981) 'Family therapy process research', in A.S. Gurman and D.P. Kniskern (eds), *Handbook of Family Therapy*. New York: Brunner/Mazel.

Rogers, C. (1951) *Client-Centered Therapy*. Boston, MA: Houghton Mifflin.

Rogers, C. (1957) 'The necessary and sufficient conditions for therapeutic personality change', *Journal of Consulting Psychology*, 21: 95–103.

Schroder, T. (1991) 'Approaches to couple therapy', in D. Hooper and W. Dryden. (eds), *Couple Therapy: a Handbook*. Milton Keynes: Open University Press.

Shields, C.G., Sprenkle, D.H. and Constantine, J.A. (1991) 'Anatomy of an initial interview. The importance of joining and structuring skills', *American Journal of Family Therapy*, 19: 3–18.

Street, E. (1994) *Counselling for Family Problems*. London: Sage.

Szapocznik, J., Perez-Vidal, A., Brickman, A.L., Foote, F.H., Santisteban, D., Hervis, O. and Kurtines, W.H. (1988) 'Engaging adolescent drug abusers and their families in treatment: a strategic structural systems approach', *Journal of Consulting and Clinical Psychology*, 56: 552–7.

Terkelsen, K.G. (1980) 'Toward a theory of the family life cycle', in E. Carter and M. McGoldrick (eds), *The Family Life Cycle*. New York: Gardner Press.

Tomm, K. and Wright, L.M. (1979) 'Family therapy skills', *Family Process*, 18: 227–50.

Vetere, A. and Gale, A. (1987) *Ecological Studies of Family Life*. Chichester: Wiley.

Walsh, F. (1993) *Normal Family Processes*, 2nd edn. New York: Guilford Press.

Watzlawick, P., Weakland, J. and Fisch, R. (1974) *Change: Principles of Problem Formation and Problem Resolution*. New York: Norton.

Whitaker, C.A. and Keith, D.U. (1981) 'Symbolic-experiential family therapy', in A.S. Gurman and D.P. Kniskern (eds), *Handbook of Family Therapy*. New York: Brunner/Mazel.

Wilson, K. and James, J. (1991) 'Research in therapy with couples: an overview', in D. Hooper and W. Dryden (eds), *Couple Therapy: a Handbook*. Milton Keynes: Open University Press.

20

Counselling Psychology in Groups
Maria Gilbert and Diana Shmukler

Theoretical framework

Our central theoretical approach can best be described as an integrative one, both on the level of theory and on the level of interventions into a system such as is created in a constructed group. In this chapter we will integrate three major arenas in which change can be effected; an intra-psychic or internal arena, which reflects the person's internal dialogue; an interpersonal or transactional arena, which occurs between people in dyads or triads in a group, often in the form of psychological games; and finally, the systemic or group arena where the issues of culture, race, class and sex will emerge. At this level the group may be viewed as a microcosm of the world at large, in that universal themes will arise in the life of the group.

Such themes invariably include the exploration of intimacy, concepts of equality and the recognition of individual difference, the acknowledgement of the darker sides of human nature and achieving a balance between caring for self and caring for others. In our integrative framework we attend to the interface between the subjective internal process, the interactional social process and the unconscious processes that occur as whole-group phenomena. As the life of the group unfolds this process will inevitably reflect many of the norms and tacit assumptions of the prevailing culture or sub-culture in which the group is located. For example, the issues of racial discrimination or class prejudice which are embedded in the British way of life will surface in the form of fixed frames of reference that influence group members' behaviour to others outside of their conscious awareness. The presence of a group of people enables such rigid beliefs to be challenged and examined, and the premises clearly explored in terms of their origin and their impact.

In terms of an integrated approach to intervention, we acknowledge the importance of interventions that address the cognitive, affective and behavioural domains of functioning in members of the group who wish to effect change in their lives. In a survey of the mechanisms of group psychotherapy, Corsini and Rosenberg (1955) examined three hundred articles in the literature of group psychotherapy to locate the expressions used by members in relation to their effect on the dynamics in groups. They finally reduced their categories to three common factors: 'an intellectual one, consisting of universalization, intellectualization, and spectator therapy; an emotional one, consisting of acceptance, altruism, and transference; and an actional factor, consisting of reality testing, interaction and ventilation' (1955: 150). This finding supports experience in the field of counselling psychology. For change to be durable and persistent over time, it appears that interventions need to address the cognitive, affective and behavioural domains. We believe that a wide range of interventions, which may include confrontation, explanation, the use of metaphor, techniques aimed at emotional release such as Gestalt experiments with polarities, as well as interpretation, will be effective in addressing the three categories outlined by Corsini and Rosenberg. Counselling psychology bases its practice in research and promotes a 'research attitude' in its approach to group work.

In summary, we see the task of a group facilitator as assisting group members to effect change cognitively, affectively and behaviourally at the intrapsychic, interpersonal and systemic levels. Each group member addresses the three crucial existential questions:

- Who am I? (**Intrapsychic**)
- Who are all those others? (**Interpersonal**)
- What am I doing in the world? (**Systemic or contextual**)

In a well-functioning counselling group, members have the opportunity to change and update their schemata and rigid categories for processing reality. They can build more effective and rewarding relationships with others and may also address issues of the meaning and relevance of their lives in the larger socio-political context in which they share common concerns with members of the human race. A constructed group experience is geared at its most effective to provide for its members a change in their frame of reference so that they can approach the problems and challenges in their lives in a radically different way. This shift in perspective is generally accompanied by an increased awareness of the range of options available to the person in any given context. A counselling group provides a unique opportunity for affective education, for learning about effective communication and for acquiring the skills required for maintaining rewarding relationships.

The nature and purpose of a constructed group

A constructed group provides a laboratory for experimentation and a safe context for learning new skills which can then be transferred into the person's everyday life. It is both experimental and real in the sense that people's real thoughts, feelings and behaviours in relation to themselves and other people are explored in a context that is structured along very specific parameters for this purpose. A group is carefully constructed with boundaries around time, place and membership. It is conducted in a place that is protected from intrusion and provides a safe space for the members.

People with a common need are brought together and the opportunity is created for them to experience their reactions in relation to other people and to raise their awareness of the impact of this experience on their view of themselves. This situation allows them to understand and learn about being in relationship and how relating to others influences getting their needs met. The question being addressed is: How can I get what I want in the world and at the same time get on with other people? New members of a group often feel they have been talking too much or taking up too much time until they understand the norm of participation in the group.

The central psychological focus of the learning in a constructed group is for the participants to understand how their internal worlds intersect with the external world. What is implied here is an understanding of how the internal world colours their functioning and experience, particularly with other people, and how this may affect issues concerning work and intimate relationships.

The constructed group provides a bridge between the safety of a therapeutic environment and the client's daily context. In this sense, the constructed group functions as a transitional space or a 'play' space (Winnicott, 1971) where clients can experiment with new ways of expressing themselves. The process of group interaction varies from people stating their thoughts, to exploring their fantasies and expressing their needs and feelings to each other with a view to understanding the effect both on themselves and on other people.

Each participant brings into the group their own personal history and their cultural heritage, thus creating a climate or group culture that is reflective of the diversity of all its members. It is therefore inevitable that issues of race, culture, class, sexual identity and group affiliation will emerge and become part of the group content and process (the 'group business'). In this sense each group is unique in its particular constellation and climate, yet on the other hand common themes emerge across groups that appear to reflect shared human concerns. Both the uniqueness and the universality contribute to the learning potential of a group as these reflect the nature of our psychological make-up and the world in which we live.

In line with our integrative approach to group work, we include certain concepts from the general body of psychological theory. These

444

concepts are both consistent with our general approach and have important relevance for group work. Winnicott's (1971) notion of transitional space is one of these. He describes a transitional area as one which is created in an intermediate space between inner and our shared outer reality. When the notion is used to describe a therapeutic space, it denotes a protected area in which the participants (therapist and client/s) share the intimate and internal as well as external aspects of experience. Clients are supported and encouraged to express their internal processes such as thoughts, fantasies and ideas in a safe place. The safety ensures that they will not be criticized, judged or evaluated on the basis of their inner lives. Thus the opportunity is created for a freeing of repressed material that is outside of awareness.

Winnicott believed that therapy occurs in the overlap of the two transitional areas, that of the therapist and the client. Where the client does not have the capacity to move between his or her inner experience and the external reality, this becomes the therapeutic task. If the therapist does not have this capacity well developed, then such a therapist, according to Winnicott, is not really suitable for the work. In our description of the tasks of the leader in a counselling psychology group, we assume that group leaders have the capacity to create a safe bounded space such that a transitional area is provided for participants. All the qualities that are concomitant with imagination, humour and creativity are linked to this ability. The capacity for metaphor and symbolization and the ability to describe inner experience and feelings, and share memories and fantasies are also included.

From a different perspective, the group can be thought of as a transition between the world and people's psychological reality. In this way it is a secure place in which to experiment and 'play with' new ways of being. Some approaches to counselling actively encourage role playing and rehearsal and this aspect is also included in our model as a strategy where relevant and helpful. The overarching idea of the group as being a transitional space allows for us to consider it as a place for play and experimentation. Holding the boundaries firm is crucial to the creation of this safe place. Early in the life of a group, members will test the boundaries; for example, by coming late or escalating an emotional process close to the end of the group to see how the leader maintains the time boundary. On a metaphorical level, a group quickly comes to represent a family for many members. Unconsciously other people in a group are assigned family roles such as siblings, parents or partners. 'You remind me of . . .'. Therefore it seems to us that thinking of a counselling group in these terms allows us to describe and include the psychological aspects which are central to growth and healing. It is a notion which enables us to emphasize those aspects which are important for a therapeutic endeavour such as safety, boundaries, confidentiality and protected space.

Summing up this section on our perspective of the psychological environment created in groups, we can do no better than quote Pine in describing factors central to therapeutic change, who writes: 'People will develop if there is a reasonable stability to their environment so that they can develop a reasonable trust in it; if the environment enriches, makes demands and spurs them on, so much the better' (1985: 132).

Assessment process

As a general principle we favour heterogeneous groups for counselling, since these are more likely to resemble in some way the groups we interact with and belong to 'in the world out there', such as family groupings, work contexts or our friendship circles. Such a group offers more scope for the kinds of projections that people carry from the past that may be affecting their current reality testing. Where a safe place is created, the transferential phenomena will occur and allow these metaphors to operate. A heterogeneous group is likely to elicit in members a wide range of transferential phenomena related not only to the early caregivers, but also to siblings, people in authority positions and to peer experiences in the school playground and the classroom. This offers the opportunity for the exploration of a multiplicity of reactions that may not always emerge in the individual counselling relationship.

However, there are certain areas in which a homogeneous group may be of particular benefit to a person since it offers the unique opportunity of being with a group constructed around a particular theme, experience or human characteristic, e.g. groups for victims of sexual abuse and rape; AIDS groups; debriefing groups for people who have jointly experienced a disaster; groups for parents, for adolescents, for men or for women. Where people have shared a common experience, talking with others in a similar dilemma may add to the situation a sense of 'normalizing the experience' so that individuals can accept what has happened to them without guilt, self-punishment and ceaseless remorse. By 'normalizing' in this context we mean the understanding that a person's reaction, for example to an assault or disaster, represents a normal response to an abnormal situation reflecting the organism's adaptive response to extreme stress. It does not constitute anything shameful or a personal failure, as many victims tend to frame it. A homogeneous group offers a unique opportunity for such sharing and contributes the factors of 'universality, altruism and imparting information' (Yalom, 1970) that are particularly important for people who are currently experiencing themselves as

446

excluded, 'odd and different' or isolated by a devastating experience or trauma. Great relief is experienced by people when they see that their experience is shared and understood by others. Most victims of violence or abuse, because of the shame associated with what has happened, believe that their internal reactions are unique because of 'something wrong with me'. A possible intervention at such a point would be: 'There was something wrong, but it's not you who are wrong.'

Counselling groups have been conducted in a wide variety of contexts with client populations ranging from patients in psychiatric settings to the inmates of gaols, with students, the aged, many different special interest groups too innumerable to mention and clients in outpatient settings who wish to improve their social and job-related skills. Assessment involves in part a consideration of the suitability of a particular person for group treatment, but this choice will be mediated by the level of expertise of the proposed group leader and the context in which the group is to be situated.

In a study of casualties resulting from encounter groups Yalom and Lieberman (1971) concluded that certain types of group leaders tended to have a higher casualty rate in their groups. Type A leaders described as 'Aggressive Stimulators' were reported by participants as having some of the more severe casualties resulting from 'attack by leader'. Participants in groups conducted by more impersonal and *laissez-faire* leaders tended to suffer a type of casualty where 'attack by the group' was responsible for the mode of injury. Rejection played a role in most of the casualties (Yalom and Lieberman, 1971). These findings suggest that the qualities of the leader are at least as important as those of the group participant in the assessment process. It would appear that group leaders who display acceptance and warmth and who set firm boundaries in a group are most suitable for this type of work. It is also important that confrontation is carefully considered and balanced with support in a holding environment so that group members do not feel under attack by the leader. If a leader is too easy-going or distant and uninvolved, the opposite problem may result and the group may attack or scapegoat a particular individual without the leader's effective intervention to prevent this destructive process. This again underlines the importance of protection and safety for effective work in counselling groups.

Group members do, however, need to be able to withstand frustration and tolerate moderate levels of anxiety without regressing or acting out in ways destructive to the group. We have found that people with severe disorders of the self, particularly where acting-out is a strong feature and where an adult-to-adult agreement about the purpose of being in the group cannot be mutually made and maintained, will not benefit from being in a counselling group. A capacity to maintain adult ego-state

447

functioning in the service of adequate reality-testing (Berne, 1966) and the ability to be observers of their own process and that of others is a minimal requirement for group attendance.

However, within these limits people with poor ego functioning may indeed benefit from the structure, the natural atmosphere and the clear boundaries of a constructed group. The setting of clear goals by each group member is a source of security and gives structure to the situation. Glatzer points out that 'the reassuring presence of other group members decreases dependence on the therapist and reduces initial anxiety about passive submission to an omnipotent figure which, in turn, makes the analyst seem more human and less frightening' (1978: 307). In this connection Aaron Stein suggested that combined group and individual therapy might be suitable for 'narcissistic and borderline patients with defective ego boundaries who are unable to withstand minimal tensions' (1981: 335) and need the support of a close dyadic relationship to work through their issues. In our experience, such clients are often best seen in individual counselling for a period of time before moving to a group. Except for this provision and in the case of people who are actively psychotic, we consider that most people can benefit from group treatment that is conducted by a competent group leader if they are motivated and come willingly to the group. Enforced attendance is not likely to yield productive outcomes, since people are more likely to resist any intervention if compelled to attend. In such a case, nothing productive will be achieved unless an effective working alliance can be negotiated with group members. A further contraindication would be the situation where a member was in a deep and early transference with the group leader. Such a participant may not be able emotionally to share the leader's attention and feel excluded at every transaction not directed to him or her.

We consider that an individual assessment interview is essential before entry into a group. The dynamics that would cause us not to recommend group counselling would be a rigid projection of blame, a tendency towards rapid regression in a therapeutic situation, acting out of a suicidal or violent nature and an incapacity to reflect upon one's own process and the impact of one's behaviour on others.

The nature and facilitation of change in a counselling psychology group

For the purposes of clarity we will consider separately each of the three levels of change described in the first section above. We recognize that such divisions are artificial, as any interaction in a group could be considered from all these perspectives simultaneously. Most approaches to group therapy focus on one only, rather than all of them.

Intrapsychic change

The intrapsychic level describes the internal process and is the most fundamental level of personality change. Most in-depth and long-term approaches to psychotherapy and counselling aim for intrapsychic change. From this perspective, it is assumed that once change has occurred in the intrapsychic process, people will effect the external changes that make their lives easier. Furthermore, these changes are long-lasting and usually irreversible. The major disadvantage of this approach is its time-consuming and lengthy nature.

From a group counselling point of view, the model would be that of individual work in the group or the so-called 'hot seat' approach. By this we mean that the individual therapy is conducted by the facilitator in the group while the rest of the group members observe and participate through identification. The group also forms a backdrop or a chorus to the work, often lending psychic energy to the process. Often members will spontaneously confirm that a person working on an issue not only evokes or reminds them of their situation but they will spontaneously say: 'You were working for me there too', or 'You did that work on my behalf as well'.

In our model we see this as one form of process in a group. There will be occasions when it will be not only appropriate, but also exceedingly useful, to focus on the individual in the group. The intrapsychic work conducted in this format is instructive and interesting to the other members. Work at this level often expedites other members' understanding of their own internal processes by vicarious identification, as well as providing a window into another's inner experience.

Many techniques for doing intrapsychic work in a group context arise from the humanistic approaches to counselling and therapy, in particular Gestalt therapy, interactional therapy and transactional analysis. These approaches have in common an emphasis on the current manifestation of dysfunction in the here-and-now behaviours in the group. The therapist engages with what is immediately presented by the group members, seeing this as a reflection of characteristic patterns of presenting self.

We will describe in some detail an approach central to intrapsychic as well as interpersonal change. Its usefulness and power is contained in the way it integrates cognition, affect and behaviour. The technique developed by Erskine and Zalcman (1979) focuses on cognitive, affective and behavioural aspects of the change process. By looking at the repetitive, non-productive patterns that occur, therapists are able to gain immediate access to people's internal processes. The theory which underpins this technique is that unmet needs, usually dating to early childhood experience, lead to the construction of a faulty belief system in order to contain and understand the deprivation and/or trauma.

The belief system (or core interpersonal schema) centres around beliefs about the self, others and the quality of life or larger context of experience. These beliefs are connected to a set of dysfunctional behaviours which often reinforce the beliefs. Memories of related and similar experiences, fantasies and dreams are used to support the central belief structure and reinforce its circularity. Connected to this cognitive-behavioural system are repressed feelings and needs which were not acceptable in the original scenario/relationships. This interrelated system is formulated in terms of the 'script decisions'. These script decisions determine how the person frames, colours and understands many experiences in his or her life, based on early conclusions about reality.

The way that change is effected is through intervening in this circular system. This could involve addressing the faulty cognitions, looking at the unproductive behaviours or surfacing and identifying the unmet needs. Although working with the script system could be considered a cognitive-behavioural approach to change (as in cognitive-analytic therapy), when the early unmet needs are touched, often deep affective working through results in a cathartic release and a reversal of the script process. The goal of this approach to therapy is to help the individual achieve more constructive ways of solving problems and relating to others in the here-and-now rather than reverting to old patterns developed under stress.

For example, the participant describes how she comes into the group and begins to feel more and more isolated. On tracking her feeling, it emerges that she was often left alone and anxious at night and then might lie awake hearing adults arguing or fighting. The situation in the group triggered her feeling of confusion and pain about what was going on. An inquiry into how that affected her internal process reveals her belief that she is 'helpless, not good enough and stupid', and that others and the world are not 'safe'. Consequently she withdraws and feels isolated. The group counsellor works with the belief system to convey the message that she is 'little' at the time rather than stupid, and adults need to get help if they cannot manage their emotional lives.

In groups a phenomenon often occurs where one person's circular belief system interlocks with that of another, leading to the kind of misunderstanding and confused communication so characteristic of relationship problems. Behaviour on the part of one person triggers the belief system of the other such that the second person then behaves in such a way that reinforces their own and the other's worst expectations. One person believes, 'They're out to get me', another that 'Others have to be watched in case they make a mistake'; both sets of beliefs are clearly based on their early feelings and experiences. Rapidly these interlocking beliefs will lead to projections and acting out on both sides which then needs to be addressed in the here-and-now reality of the group experience. This leads us naturally on to the second level of change.

Interpersonal change

The interpersonal aspects are those that are dealt with most powerfully and effectively in constructed systems. It is here that a space is created that allows for the replay of habitual patterns of communication between individuals in the group. Group participants will project onto each other features of significant figures in their present or past context. The conscious and unconscious aspects, overt and covert transactions are revealed for observation and analysis by the facilitator and other group members. Feedback from the group allows for an understanding and explication of particular patterns of interacting. Further, the impact of this behaviour on others can be explored in a safe and non-threatening environment. Rehearsal, suggestions and insights into ways of handling conflict and other problems result from this process in the group.

One of Eric Berne's great clinical contributions was his description of the psychological games that people play (Berne, 1964). Unfortunately, the pop psychological aspect of the book *Games People Play* often obscures its profundity and the elegant description of interpersonal dynamics. The analysis of games in a group forms a powerful and central focus. Individual insight gained in this process frees the 'players' of the games to engage in a productive interaction. It can also lead to deep emotional insights, in that Berne contends that game-playing could be seen as part of the psychological defence system. Analysing games then, often flows into intrapsychic working through of underlying unresolved conflicts. Psychologically unsophisticated group members readily get into a simple 'Yes but . . .' game. One player puts a problem to the group and other members propose solutions, all of which are 'Yes butted', supported with 'good' reasons. On analysis it becomes clear that the psychological game, in confirming 'No one can help me', is a much more powerful motivation than finding a solution to the problem.

On the positive side, a constructed group offers a safe space for experimenting with new interactional choices and can lead to the improvement of relationship skills. As people check their personal reality against the perceptions of others, their assumptions about their impact may be challenged. The opportunity for honest and courageous feedback from peers in the group committed to a common goal of growth is for many people the most valuable aspect of their group membership.

Systemic/communal aspects

The third level or systemic aspect of groups can be classified as counselling of the group as a whole, in that the group rather than the individual is the focus of attention and analysis. A constructed system takes on a life of its own that is larger than the individuals that form it. People become invested in the survival of the group, and work towards group maintenance and cohesion. All members bring to the group their experiences of previous systems of which they have been a member; in particular, the formative experiences in the family of origin and at school are brought into and played out in the group. These take the form of psychological roles that people adopt and which influence their projections on others.

On the other hand, psychological roles are also assigned to people by the rest of the group on the basis of their representing a particular class, cultural group or race. Consequently, such a person's interaction with other group members is circumscribed by such a label. It is as though this person is performing a particular function in the system that fits the image that members hold of society and its components. This provides the counselling psychologist with rich material for intervening in the group process.

Another way in which psychological roles operate is represented by the individual, who may express anger in a particular manner. Clearly this anger is part of the individual's range of responses to the immediate situation; at the same time, however, if he or she is expressing anger on behalf of the group, the other members are relieved of experiencing and expressing possibly uncomfortable feelings of their own.

An interpretation such as 'The men are remarkably silent in the group today' can evoke for some members the experience in the constructed system of the men who were absent physically or emotionally in their own families. As the stuck points in the system are addressed and understood, individuals begin to understand how they assume roles and positions in their own lives. Although they are in a constructed system, by its very nature it allows for the re-creation of the other systems they have experienced, or live in at present. Once roles and positions are brought into awareness, people have a choice about whether they wish to continue to assume or adopt them.

In addition to the unconscious assumptions and processes, analysis of group themes and tasks brings about other important arenas for change. The normalization of problems (Yalom, 1970) is central to acceptance and health. Equally powerful is the instillation of hope; seeing that others can and do change gives great encouragement to group members that change is possible.

Learning to balance one's own needs with the needs of others is another useful and powerful process that occurs in a group. Taking up time in the group, being sure to be heard and at the same time not dominating the conversation are aspects of this process. Group forces monitor and control these aspects. Our experience confirms Bion's (1959) belief that there are powerful forces for healing in a group. In the long run a group will confront reality aspects, curing its members of neurosis by challenging projections and fantasies.

We see as a central task the creation of an environment in which each member can own their own tendencies towards destructiveness and pathology with courage and honesty. It is only through this process that individuals can understand the impact they make and the effect of their projections on others.

The group leader's role and the tasks of the leader in the counselling psychology group

The leader has a dual role: to create a holding environment that provides safety for clients, whilst at the same time using available opportunities to facilitate change in maladaptive and non-problem-solving strategies of client interaction. The group needs to provide enough safety for clients to feel supported in reflecting upon and changing patterns of behaviour and interaction that form part of their long-standing defence systems; yet not become so 'cosy' that members begin to use the group as a haven or alternative to forming external support systems of their own in the wider environment. Maintaining this balance between support and confrontation is the primary task of an effective group facilitator. Facilitating a constructed group involves creating a learning environment for people to confront non-functional patterns and experiment with new options in relationships with others. Group members provide for one another an 'experimental' group situation which closely resembles the groups in their daily lives, yet has the unique dimension that interactions can be halted, 'put on hold', so that they can be analysed, explored and understood to provide new learning for the future outside of the group. This focus on evaluating effective outcomes for group members is central to what we refer to as the 'research mind-set' in counselling psychology.

It is not unusual for members of a constructed group to utter a sentiment like: 'Nowhere else in my life is it possible for me to put my interactions on hold and discuss what lies beneath and behind them – and to get really honest feedback from others that I know I can trust because they have my welfare at heart.' We consider that such a statement reflects the working alliance that exists between the group members and between them and the facilitator. Even when resentment or anger is expressed, if the working alliance is in place, then group members can interact with the understanding that goodwill prevails. If such a working alliance is not in place, members will feel unsafe and there is a chance that the group will disintegrate.

The group leader provides a model for dealing with affect in a direct and non-punitive manner and will accept the anger/dissatisfaction of group members when that is aimed against the leader. Above all, the group leader needs to be able to withstand provocation without retaliation so that non-productive interaction patterns can emerge in the group and provide material for discussion and change. The group leader needs to emerge intact from this process as a model that negative affect can be tolerated and dealt with in creative ways. For this reason, amongst others, it is vital that the group leader is well supported in a supervisory context. One of the chief challenges for the group leader is the task of setting limits and maintaining boundaries so that the structure and life of the group is safeguarded and can provide the 'holding environment' essential for the successful attainment of goals.

Another of the leader's tasks is to move the group forward to deal with its primary business of providing a protected space for exploration and change. The leader will usually keep the group focused on interactions in the group and between its members, the 'here-and-now' process that is currently occurring in the group. This focus is based on the assumption that people will play out their fixed and rigid defensive patterns of behaviour in the group with the other members and so provide 'live material' for the group facilitator's attention and that of group members. The group context also offers a unique place and opportunity to select new interactional options and try these out for size, judging from the response received from other group members how these are likely to be received in the outside world. The group leader needs to be alert to the ongoing process in the group, to the 'games' that people play, to the group themes that emerge, and to tendencies to project and scapegoat as a means of avoiding the anxiety associated with change. Group members may be less aware initially of the repetitive patterns that lead them to similar unsatisfactory outcomes as in the past; the group leader's task is to highlight such patterns and support people in the process of learning to achieve more satisfactory outcomes in their lives and relationships.

In summary, the counselling psychologist as group leader provides a context in which affective education can take place, where rigid interpersonal schemata can be changed and where new behaviours can be tried out and chosen as alternatives to inflexible, unproductive modes of operation. The leader's tasks fall into two broad categories: containment, support, facilitation; and confrontation, challenge, interpretation. We do not wish to leave this section without mentioning the importance of humour as a tool for creative change. Laughter and fun can be as powerful in the process of growth and change as the solemn realizations that also form part of the overall canvas.

A group leader's role is demanding of energy and inner resources. We consider it vital that group leaders have regular supervision sessions in which to explore their own responses in the group, deal with counter-transference as it arises and get assistance with interventions and techniques. Berne (1966: 252–3) drew up a series of questions to guide group therapists' interventions. These are so clear and to the point that we quote them here:

1 What am I trying to cure the patient of today?
2 Has he [or she] said or done anything which could form the basis for a therapeutic hypothesis?
3 What is the psychological hypothesis about his personality?
4 How can I best validate it?
5 How will he respond transactionally to what I say?
6 To which of his ego states should I be talking?
7 Which of his ego states will be most likely to hear me?
8 Which form of intervention is indicated?
9 How will it affect the other patients?
10 What are the other possibilities, and how will I deal with each of them?
11 Is this manifestation I am concerned with pathological?

'If it is not pathological, the whole project is dropped right there, since strictly speaking, the operation would then be irrelevant and would waste valuable time' (Berne, 1966: 253).

We are not suggesting that the group leader will be able to take the time out before each intervention to go through this list! However, we have found these questions extremely useful as a supervisory tool to assist the group leader to assess interventions that were made in previous sessions and hence to move on to effective and creative planning for future sessions. We also consider that these questions support the development of a 'research mind-set' which focuses on relevant and effective outcomes for the work of counselling psychologists.

It is important for group leaders to have an awareness of the type of leadership stance that they adopt and the possible impact on participants. Research suggests that the most effective leaders will be flexible and able to adjust their style to suit the needs and characteristics of the individuals in the group. In a group that contains a number of vulnerable people with a fragile sense of self, the group leader would be more supportive and carefully modulate confrontations, while at the same time providing a safe structure. As in individual counselling, so also in group counselling the question 'What type of counselling, by whom and for what treatment group, etc.' remains largely unanswered by the current state of the research. The most helpful study remains that of Yalom, in which he identified by means of a factor analysis four basic leadership functions: emotional stimulation and confrontation; caring and offering support; providing a cognitive framework for understanding experience; and setting limits and maintaining boundaries (1970: 501).

Research evidence about effectiveness and outcomes in groups

The importance of outcome research to counselling and therapy is being increasingly stressed with the focus on measurable outcomes and results. Research results in group treatment are closely linked with the common factors research in individual therapy. A survey of group researches by Bergin and Garfield (1994) over a period of 50 years describes two major conclusions: (1) that group treatment has been more effective than no-treatment; and in some circumstances more effective than other psychological treatments; and (2) that there are certain positive identifiable common factors that are associated with positive outcomes.

Much of the earlier research into group outcomes was done with Encounter groups and T-groups with college students as subjects. For example Lieberman, Yalom and Miles (1973) reported that participants valued the experience in encounter groups in that 78 per cent confirmed that they found them constructive. Even after a 6-month follow-up, one third of the participants had undergone moderate or considerable positive change. In their view, their study suggested enough resemblance between encounter groups and counselling/therapy groups to conclude that similar rules of learning apply. This tentative conclusion is not shared by others in the field, who suggest the importance of distinguishing carefully between growth groups and therapy groups, since both the aims and the needs of participants may vary greatly. In a survey of group psychotherapy outcome research Parloff and Dies concentrated on research conducted with clinical categories of clients. They maintained that differences in factors such as motivation, goals and degree of demoralization 'make generalizations from studies of treatment of non-clinical groups to patient groups very suspect' (1977: 283). Their survey suggests that, for clinical groups, group therapy augments other treatment approaches, but may be limited as a sole approach to treatment. For the counselling psychologist it becomes important to evaluate such research results and use them as a guide to selecting suitable participants for group work.

Parloff and Dies presented an interesting question for subsequent researchers: 'What kinds of changes are produced by what kinds of interventions provided by what kinds of therapists with what kinds of patients/problems under what kinds of conditions? Such complex questions regarding the effectiveness of group psychotherapy need to be addressed collaboratively by both empirically and clinically-oriented professionals' (1977: 316). This challenge is relevant to future research relating to group work in counselling psychology.

Yalom's seminal research, based on careful observation in groups, remains the most useful to date in addressing the challenge issued by Parloff and Dies. Yalom's curative factors have been consistently recognized in group practice and research as crucial for effective change. He identified eleven primary factors: instillation of hope; universality; imparting of information; altruism; the corrective recapitulation of the primary family group; development of socializing techniques; imitative behaviour; interpersonal learning; group cohesiveness; catharsis; and existential factors. A particular leadership style or a particular orientation to group counselling would be likely to stress some of these factors over others, but effective groups combine most of these in differing degrees. However, research has not yet managed to isolate the specific effects of particular variables: it is in this realm that group outcome research is still inconclusive, often yielding contradictory results or reporting on studies which by their very nature cannot be replicated. On the other hand, some of these curative factors consistently emerge as being more crucial than others. Cohesion, interpersonal learning, catharsis and self-understanding have been identified in various researches as the most central and valued by the participants.

We can do no better at this point that to quote the conclusions reached by Bednar and Kaul:

> We suggest that the underlying problem in the area of definitional adequacy is not a lack of effort by most well-trained group researchers. Rather it is a lack of descriptive data based on truly astute observations about group events that add order, detail and information about the central events in group treatments. (1994: 638)

We wish to give our support to the importance of detailed observation of group events and processes with a view to identifying the 'change moments' in groups and those specific factors and leadership behaviours that contribute to successful outcomes for individual members. It is in this endeavour that we believe counselling psychologists, with their background in research, have a vital and important contribution to make.

Conclusions and recommendations

In line with the outcome research on groups, we have no doubt that groups are an effective modality for change; overall the results show that participants gain along a number of different dimensions. A well-run group is an efficient and economical way of addressing and dealing with a variety of complex psychological issues and processes. In spite of a mass of research material, we still do not know precisely what specific factors in groups lead to the effective results that group leaders frequently report. We do know that a flexible but firm leadership style that provides both support and challenge is valued by participants. In our opinion, groups encompass cognitive, affective and behavioural opportunities that are central to psychological growth and change. This is supported by our clinical experience and some of the research findings.

As a general recommendation, we join the plea for more detailed and careful research of group phenomena as these relate to outcomes for individual members. We believe that the combined wisdom emerging from clinical experience and the careful and objective approach of research could enhance both our conceptual understanding and our practice of group counselling, thereby strengthening an already powerful approach to addressing psychological distress.

References

Bednar, R.L. and Kaul, T.J. (1994) 'Experiential group research: can the cannon fire?', in A.E. Bergin and S.L. Garfield (eds), *Handbook of Psychotherapy and Behavior Change*, 4th edn. New York: Wiley. pp. 631–3.

Bergin, A.E. and Garfield, S.L. (eds) (1994) *Handbook of Psychotherapy and Behavior Change*, 4th edn. New York: Wiley.

Berne, E. (1964) *Games People Play*. New York: Grove Press.

Berne, E. (1966) *Principles of Group Treatment*. New York: Grove Press.

Bion, W.R. (1959) *Experiences in Groups and Other Papers*. New York: Basic Books.

Corsini, R.J. and Rosenberg, B. (1955) 'Mechanisms of group psychotherapy', *Journal of Abnormal and Social Psychology*, 15: 406–11. Also published as 'Mechanisms of group psychotherapy: processes and dynamics' in K.R. MacKenzie (ed.), *Classics in Group Psychotherapy* (1992). New York: Guilford Press. pp. 144–53.

Erskine, R.G. and Zalcman, M.J. (1979) 'The racket system', *Transactional Analysis Journal*, 9(1): 51–9.

Glatzer, H.T. (1978) 'The working alliance in analytic group psychotherapy', *Journal of Group Psychotherapy*, 28: 147–61. Also published in K.R. MacKenzie (ed.), *Classics in Group Psychotherapy* (1992). New York: Guilford Press. pp. 305–16.

Lieberman, M.A., Yalom, I.D. and Miles, M.B. (1973) *Encounter Groups: First Facts.* New York: Basic Books.

Parloff, M.B. and Dies, R.R. (1977) 'Group psychotherapy outcome research', *International Journal of Group Psychotherapy,* 27: 281–319.

Pine, F. (1985) *Developmental Theory and Clinical Process.* New Haven, CT: Yale University Press.

Stein, A. (1981) 'Indications for concurrent (combined and conjoint) individual and group psychotherapy', in L.R. Wolberg and M.L. Aronson (eds), *Group and Family Therapy.* New York: Brunner/Mazel.

Winnicott, D.W. (1971) *Playing and Reality.* Harmondsworth: Penguin.

Yalom, I.D. (1970) *The Theory and Practice of Group Psychotherapy.* New York: Basic Books.

Yalom, I.D. and Lieberman, M.A. (1971) 'A study of encounter group casualties', *Archive of General Psychiatry,* 25: 16–30.

21

Career Development Work with Individuals

Jennifer M. Kidd

Careers work encompasses a range of tasks and activities. The term 'guidance' has come to be used as an umbrella term to describe the various potential elements; these include group work, information-giving, teaching, self-help activities and assessment, as well as individual career counselling. Within most of these, of course, basic counselling skills will be essential. This chapter has several objectives: some require a generic perspective on careers work, while others can only be addressed by examining specific activities.

The first objective is to introduce the reader to the field by outlining the kinds of services available to those needing help with career issues and by introducing some of the theoretical perspectives which have informed practice. Here, it will be necessary to take a broad view of career development work which encompasses a range of activities as well as individual career counselling. As we move on to examine the ways in which various theories and conceptual frameworks can inform practice it will be more appropriate to restrict our attention to one-to-one counselling, although many of the issues discussed will also be relevant to those who work with groups, or whose role is primarily one of providing information or basic assessment. In the final section of the chapter, which deals with research evaluating the effectiveness of careers work, we return to a broader perspective, so as to do justice to the breadth of the literature.

The range of issues presented in careers work is extremely broad. Examples of some of the concerns which clients bring to the practitioner include:

- I want a job where I don't have to bring work home. Perhaps I should change direction completely.
- I've just been made redundant. What opportunities are there for someone in their fifties?
- I've just left university with an arts degree. What does this qualify me for?
- I would like to work for myself, but it's a big step leaving the security of a monthly salary and a pension scheme.
- I've just left school and my mum wants me to start applying for jobs.

- I've spent 15 years bringing up a family. How can I build up the confidence to return to work?
- I'm not happy in my job. Should I change my employer or should I contemplate a complete career change?
- My employer is making more and more demands on me. How can I be more assertive, and tell her how *I* see things?
- I've been out of work now for three years and I don't even get job interviews any more. Perhaps I should resign myself to retirement.

What these examples show is that clients can be of any age and in any stage in their careers. Moreover, it is clear that they may need help with decisions about jobs, with managing their work responsibilities in relation to other aspects of their lives, with interpersonal issues, or with finding information about career opportunities. Also, many of these presenting problems may mask deeper emotional issues which will not become apparent until later. The matters discussed in this chapter should be relevant to counselling psychologists working in a range of settings who may be presented with any of these issues.

Provision

Although a wide range of public and private sector agencies provide career guidance services, the type of service offered varies considerably – from one short interview to two or three days' in-depth assessment and counselling. At the time of writing, guidance is available to adults from Training and Enterprise Councils and Local Enterprise Companies through the 'Gateways to Learning' programme and the 'Skill Choice' initiatives. Also, many local Careers Services see adults. In some areas Educational Guidance Services for Adults also exist to provide help with choices concerning education and training. All secondary-school and further education students have access to the Careers Service and students in higher education are able to use the careers advisory services run by these institutions. Youth training and employment training schemes also provide career guidance for trainees, often as a means of assessing their suitability for certain types of training. Partly in response to the need for employees to become more flexible and self-reliant in their career development, many large organizations now offer individuals support in their career planning. Individual career counselling is offered by some organizations, but other initiatives are more common, for example, career planning workshops and mentoring schemes. For those able and willing to pay, there is an increasing number of independent services offering individual career counselling. The work of the major providers in the mid-1990s is outlined below.

The Careers Service

The Careers Service is required to offer career guidance to those in full-time education at any institution outside the higher education sector, to part-time students in work-related further education and to young people under 21 who have left education up to two years previously. Many Services also offer help to other adults. Until recently the Service was administered by Local Education Authorities, with inspection and guidance from the Department of Employment. In the early 1990s, however, a system of competitive tendering was introduced, and control of the Service now varies in different regions. In most areas, the Service is run by various forms of partnership between Local Education Authorities and Training and Enterprise Councils. In others, however, private or voluntary-sector agencies, or in some cases Services from other areas, have been awarded contracts to run the Service. The professional qualification for careers advisers, as career officers are now called, is the Diploma in Careers Guidance and individual interviewing is a significant part of their work load. Time constraints are severe, however, particularly with regard to school-based work, and it is not always possible to offer school leavers more than one or two 40-minute interviews.

Training and Enterprise Councils and Local Enterprise Companies (TECs and LECs)

Almost all TECs are now involved in the 'Gateway to Learning' programme, which is part-funded by the Employment Department. The programme takes a different form in each TEC, but most offer free guidance vouchers to specific target groups which are redeemable for guidance sessions at recognized agencies. Guidance is also available from TECs and LECs for some employees through the 'Skill Choice' initiative, though in this case individuals or their employers are required to meet part of the overall cost of the service. Within both these programmes, many TECs offer two or more levels of guidance: an initial diagnostic session; longer in-depth career counselling; and psychometric testing or help with preparing CVs. Funding for these initiatives is short-term, however, and it is unclear what form this kind of provision will take in the future.

Careers services in higher education

Students in higher education and recent graduates are able to use the careers advisory services in their institutions. The service normally includes individual interviews for those who want them, but there has recently been some movement towards self-help activities, particularly with the introduction of computer-aided guidance systems, such as PROSPECT, which help students assess their interests, values and skills, retrieve information on educational and occupational opportunities, and learn decision-making skills. Careers advisers in higher education have a wide range of employment and training backgrounds and this is likely to affect the approach they take to individual interviewing, particularly the amount of emphasis given to advice and information as opposed to counselling.

Career planning within organizations

Organizations are increasingly providing support for career development to their employees. Although some of these initiatives are rooted in the organization's own needs for developing their staff (for example, development centres and fast-track schemes), others are more employee-focused, with the aim of helping individuals with their career planning. Examples of the latter type of activity are career-planning workshops, developmental appraisals and individual career counselling. These services are more likely to be offered to professional, technical and managerial staff, but a few recent initiatives have targeted 'shop-floor' employees. Vauxhall Motors, for example, under the 'Gateway to Learning' scheme, currently offer individual counselling to all employees at their Luton plant to help them identify strengths and areas for potential development. It is rare, however, for employees to have access to professionally trained career counsellors, unless they are undergoing outplacement.

Independent career counselling services

Perhaps because of limited provision by employers and public sector providers, many adults seeking career counselling turn to fee-charging services. Many of these are staffed by psychologists or professionally trained career counsellors, though since there is no legislation controlling their operation there is no guarantee that counsellors have any relevant training or experience. The best agencies offer psychometric testing and feedback, a series of counselling sessions, access to careers information, coaching in job hunting and CV writing, and interview practice.

Outplacement

Outplacement agencies offer help to employees facing redundancy. A comprehensive service will involve activities similar to those offered by independent career counselling services, though often with more emphasis on emotional support to cope with the trauma of redundancy. Few services employ staff with any significant amount of training in counselling, however. Clients are usually companies, rather than individuals, and outplacement is often offered to employees as part of an overall redundancy package to senior staff. Where lower-level staff are offered a service, it may be rather different from the one-to-one programmes offered to executives: it is more likely to be group-based and there will be less in-depth psychometric assessment. An important part of the service, generally, however, is likely to be job-search: many services base their marketing on how quickly their 'candidates' become re-employed.

Conceptual frameworks

We turn now to examine some theoretical perspectives relevant to careers work. Over the past 50 years or so, the primary goals of careers guidance have shifted, in line with changing views about individual career development and about careers themselves. At the beginning of the century simple 'matching' models provided the conceptual base for the 'scientific guidance' provided by the Juvenile Employment Bureaux of the 1920s and 1930s where assessments of abilities and interests, sometimes using psychometric test results, led to occupational recommendations. It was not until the 1960s that these approaches began to be augmented and to some extent replaced in Britain by models derived from developmental theories of careers. In this section, we summarize some of the most influential career theories and examine their impact on career guidance and counselling practice.

Person–environment fit theories

Perhaps the earliest 'theory' of occupational choice was that of Parsons (1909) who, in the United States, established one of the first vocational guidance agencies. The model which guided his work consisted of three propositions:

- People are different from each other.
- So are jobs.
- It should be possible, by a study of both, to achieve a match between person and job.

From that time, thinking about occupational choice was increasingly dominated by the need to generate verifiable data about individuals and jobs. Psychometric tests of aptitudes and interest were developed to support this task. Parsons's model may seem simplistic, but his matching approach has been accepted and elaborated upon by later writers. In

Britain, for example, Rodger's Seven-Point Plan (Rodger, 1952) was until recently a commonly used framework for diagnosis, assessment and recommendation, particularly amongst careers advisers. This is simply a list of questions to deal with in the interview, organized under seven headings. The headings are as follows:

1 Physical make-up.
2 Attainments.
3 General intelligence.
4 Special aptitudes.
5 Interests.
6 Disposition.
7 Circumstances.

One of the most widely researched and influential person–environment fit theories of occupational choice is that of John Holland (1973). He proposed that individuals seek occupational environments which are congruent with their interests (or preferences for particular work activities). The theory states that:

- People and occupational environments can be categorized into six interest types: realistic, investigative, artistic, social, enterprising and conventional.
- Occupational choice is the result of attempts to achieve congruence between interests and environment.
- Congruence results in job satisfaction and stability.

Although Holland's main proposition, that individuals make occupational choices that are congruent with their interests, has generally been supported by research (see, for example, Spokane, 1985), recent work casts some doubt on his assertion that congruence results in satisfaction (Tranberg et al., 1993). Some jobs, not surprisingly, are intrinsically more satisfying than others!

Holland's model provides one theoretical rationale for a diagnostic approach to careers work. A core activity for the career counsellor is the assessment of occupational interests and the identification of occupations which match the client's interest profile. Some of the instruments which might be used are outlined later in this chapter. The theory can be criticized, however, for its predominantly static approach to occupational choice. Holland also fails to consider social and economic factors as determinants of choice, and we know very little about what happens to employees in 'incongruent' occupations over time. One might ask whether interests and occupations become more congruent as the individual becomes socialized into an organization, and how organizations might facilitate this process.

Developmental theories

Other writers have taken a developmental view of careers, paying attention to the processes leading up to the initial choice of job and to later developmental tasks.

Donald Super is perhaps the most well-known proponent of this type of theory, with his proposition that career development proceeds through stages as the individual seeks to implement the self-concept in an occupation. His original stage theory (Super, 1957), portrayed career development as proceeding through five stages: growth, exploration, establishment, maintenance and decline. A more recent formulation (Super et al., 1988) incorporates four stages, and within each, three sub-stages:

- exploration
    crystallization
    specification
    implementation
- establishment
    stabilizing
    consolidating
    advancing
- maintenance
    holding
    updating
    innovating
- disengagement
    deceleration
    retirement planning
    retirement living

This model also has a revised view of the relationship between age and stage, which was previously fairly fixed. Individuals are acknowledged to 'recycle' – those experiencing mid-career change, for example, would be expected to demonstrate some of the concerns of early working life.

Super has also provided us with a framework for viewing careers within the context of the individual's total 'life space' and the various roles within it. His life-span, life-space model (Super, 1980) uses the image of a rainbow with bands that represent the different roles a person assumes during the course of his or her life. Initially, the life space contains only one role, that of the child, but during adulthood many people experience seven or eight roles, as when a person is employed in an occupation, studying part-time, being a parent, being a spouse, maintaining a home, supporting ageing parents and pursuing hobbies. Obviously other roles can be identified too, and not all roles apply to all individuals. Also, the sequencing of roles may vary.

Portraying roles in this way illustrates how the number and nature of activities that we may have to assume in adulthood may be difficult to integrate. On the other hand, roles may enrich each other, as when studying part-time (learner role) enhances performance and satisfaction at work (worker role).

Super's work has stimulated a vast amount of research into the exploration stage of development, particularly into the role of self-concepts in the entry into work. Much less research effort has been directed to issues within later stages, however. This may be because the processes set out as being characteristic of the later stages are discussed in a very general descriptive way. There is little attempt at explanation and it is difficult to formulate testable hypotheses beyond general statements. The model also fails to address the question of what happens to individuals once they become participants in organizations.

The impact of Super's work and other developmental models (see, for example, Ginzberg et al., 1951) on the practice of careers guidance was profound, though. They suggested an educational approach to careers work, which emphasized helping the individual become more aware of self and the world of work and using this knowledge in career decision-making. The overarching aim of careers guidance became one of helping individuals make decisions for themselves, rather than persuading them to accept expert recommendations. These models also provided a powerful rationale for the introduction of careers education in schools, and their implications for individual career counselling were no less radical. Simple matching approaches and techniques were questioned, and practitioners were encouraged to use client-centred counselling skills in individual and group work.

In essence, then, the earliest models of guidance emphasized **content**, in the form of **gathering information** about the client's abilities, interests and circumstances, and of **giving information** about options. These models have been supplemented by approaches which attend much more to the **process** of career counselling and the **relationship** between the practitioner and the client, and to helping clients develop the skills and knowledge to engage in autonomous decision-making.

Opportunity structure theory

In Britain, the most robust challenge to psychological theories of career development, whether person–environment fit or developmental, came from Ken Roberts, a sociologist. He castigated psychologists for not taking account situational variables such as social class and labour market opportunities, and argued that for many, choice is a myth, since occupational entry is determined largely by the system of social stratification

(Roberts, 1968). Roberts's 'opportunity structure' theory operates largely at the societal level of analysis, so it has little to say directly about career interventions at the level of the individual. What it does do, however, is go some way towards defining the structural constraints within which career guidance takes place. If we accept the influence of social and opportunity structures on occupational entry, one obvious role for guidance is to attempt to lubricate the mechanisms through which individuals become 'allocated' to jobs. On the other hand, however, guidance could help individuals explore and question the impact of these structural forces. The materials produced by the Schools Council Careers Education and Guidance Project in the 1970s had precisely these latter aims.

Career management theories

At the risk of overgeneralizing, it is probably true to say that, historically, British writers have paid more attention to the impact of economic and social factors on career development, particularly initial occupational choices, than their American counterparts. A more interactive perspective on careers has recently begun to emerge on both sides of the Atlantic, however. In the past few years, at least, this has been prompted by the need to take account of employees' insecurity and uncertainty in the face of organizational 'downsizing' and delayering, and the increase in part-time and fixed-term contracts of employment.

In Britain, Herriot and Pemberton (in press), for example, have built on the American work of Argyris (1960) and Rousseau (1990) to propose a model which defines organizational careers as 'sequences of renegotiations of psychological contracts', based on perceived matches between what each party wants and what the other has to offer. Two kinds of contract result from these negotiations: transactional, where there is simply an instrumental exchange between the parties (for example, performance in exchange for compensation); and relational, where mutual commitment is implied (such as loyalty in exchange for security). The strong emotional reactions experienced by individuals when their relationship with their employer breaks down (for example, where the employee is made redundant or where a promised promotion fails to materialize) are, it is argued, often a consequence of the breaking of a relational contract.

The work of Nicholson and West (1988) is another example of the move towards a more dynamic view of the relationship between individuals and organizations. They portray careers as sequences of 'work-role transitions' where individuals experience recurring states of adjustment to change and preparation for new roles, either within the same organization or after a change of employer.

468

The main strength of both these models is that they attempt to explain careers as ongoing events and experiences which take place in an organizational context where change is a continuous feature. Although they are essentially models of organizational careers and they have relatively little to say about the self-employed, and, indeed, about those in semi- and unskilled work, their central message is that career development is much more than sequences of occupational decisions; it involves ongoing interactions and negotiations with the social environment. The implication for individuals, then, is that in order to have a base for negotiation with employers, they need to be clear about their work identities and values (that is, how they view work in the context of other aspects of their life, and what they want from it). Furthermore, negotiation skills are important in career management, and individuals need to recognize their negotiating power.

Debates about the future of work lead to similar conclusions about the range of career planning and career management skills that will be required. The scenario of labour market opportunities consisting largely of short-term contracts, part-time work and 'portfolio' careers may be overstated, but the moves already apparent towards greater numerical and functional flexibility will demand that individuals will need to be clear about their development needs, more knowledgeable about the labour market generally, and be prepared to develop the meta-skills of continuously monitoring self and situation (Kidd and Killeen, 1992). Emotionally, individuals will need the capacity to cope with uncertainty and insecurity, with the likelihood of frequent job moves, and also, of course, with the prospect of periods of unemployment. Those coping well will view the future optimistically, may positively welcome changes of job and employer and the challenge of working with new people, and will have the confidence to challenge exploitative practices in the workplace. This affective component has largely been overlooked in career development theory, though London (1983) has suggested the term 'career resilience' to describe the maintenance or persistence aspect of career development.

This leads to a threefold model of career development, incorporating decision-making skills, career management skills and what might be called, after London, 'career resilience' (though the term is used here more broadly). The main features of each of the three components are set out in Figure 21.1.

It follows, then, that career development work with individuals will need to attend to all these components. It also needs to be recognized, however, that many presenting problems will be ramifications of broader personal and emotional issues, as was suggested at the beginning of this chapter.

Career decision-making (Specific knowledge and skills)	Career management (Identity clarification and meta-skills)	Career resilience (Attitudes and emotions)
Relating self- and opportunity-awareness	Ongoing assessment of values and goals Monitoring and exploring self and situation Negotiating	Confidence Hope Flexibility Self-esteem Self-reliance

Figure 21.1 *Components of career development*

As we saw earlier, within most sectors, the range of activities encompassed in career development work has become increasingly broad, covering group work and self-help activities as well as individual counselling. It seems likely that these developments will continue, as computer-aided careers guidance systems and career resource centres become more sophisticated and practitioners and clients see the value of workshop-type activities, both in employing organizations and elsewhere. However, whilst these types of intervention are well suited to provide opportunities for basic self-assessment activities and for information-seeking, they are unlikely to be able to provide adequate support for the angry client facing redundancy, or for someone trying to build the confidence to re-enter the labour market after a period at home, bringing up a family. One-to-one work is likely to continue to form the basis of provision for many clients, possibly combined with other activities, and many will also benefit from in-depth psychometric assessment, where individual feedback and interpretation are crucial. The next section of this chapter, therefore, will focus on the individual career counselling process.

The career counselling process

The challenge for counselling psychologists involved in careers work is to be able to work effectively with both career and wider personal issues, attending to the cognitive and affective aspects of both. This task also presents a challenge for career counselling theory. In contrast to career development theory, which attempts to describe and explain development,

Stages	Key tasks
1 Building the relationship	Establishing the working alliance
2 Enabling clients' self-understanding	Assessment
3 Exploring new perspectives	Information-giving
4 Forming strategies and plans	Challenging
	Reviewing progress
	Goal-setting

Table 21.1   *Some key tasks within each stage of career counselling*

theories of career counselling aim to prescribe how counsellors might intervene in career development.

As we have seen, new perspectives on careers and on career counselling have emerged over time to meet the needs of individuals in dealing with the tasks of career development. Significantly, though, the role of these new theories has generally been to **supplement** the range of theories available to practitioners, rather than **replace** any of them. Currently, then, there exists a rich and diverse set of models and conceptual frameworks for the counselling psychologist to work with. Few career counsellors take a 'single-school' approach – in a recent study of careers officers, careers advisers in higher education and educational guidance workers, less than 21 per cent reported that they used one model of interviewing (Kidd et al., 1993). For many then, an 'eclectic' approach will prevail, and practitioners may need to be helped to appreciate how elements from a range of theoretical perspectives can contribute to effective practice. In this section some of the theories and perspectives that have potential in helping us understand the flow of sessions with the client will be outlined.

The career counselling process is characterized as comprising four stages: building the relationship; enabling clients' self-understanding; exploring new perspectives; and forming strategies and plans. This is, of course, an over-simple model of the process – in many cases sessions will move back and forth between these stages – but it will serve to illustrate some of the key activities. Within these stages, the aim is to identify the main tasks for client and counsellor and illustrate how certain theoretical perspectives contribute to a fuller understanding of each. Space constraints preclude a comprehensive discussion of the nature of each stage and relevant counsellor skills. For this, the reader is referred to one of the key texts on career counselling. Walsh and Osipow's (1990) text, for example, discusses tasks and skills in relation to a range of theoretical orientations, while Nathan and Hill's (1992) book is more practice-based.

The stages and associated main tasks are set out in Table 21.1.

Stage 1   Building the relationship

The image of the career counselling psychologist as 'expert', offering advice and recommendations on suitable careers, is an enduring one. Moreover, many clients expect the counselling sessions to revolve around information about jobs or courses and are disappointed when they do not receive this. It is important, therefore, to help clients understand that career counselling is a collaborative venture, and that they need to be an active participant in the process at every stage.

As Nathan and Hill (1992) have pointed out, it is possible to begin to encourage clients to have realistic expectations of the counselling process even before the two parties meet. Written information about the goals of counselling and how these might be achieved helps to minimize misunderstandings, as can a telephone conversation. Agreeing a client–counsellor contract is crucial in the first session, however. At a basic level, issues of confidentiality and the number, length and frequency of meetings will need to be discussed, but the nature of the counselling process itself will also need to be covered, including the responsibilities of the counsellor and the client, the techniques that might be used, and the limits of the relationship.

A considerable body of literature confirms the importance of the 'working alliance' to the success of any helping relationship. Among the first to use this term was Bordin (1979), who saw the working alliance as arising out of the transference relationship that the client develops with the counsellor in psychoanalysis, but he also emphasized its importance in other helping settings, including teaching and group work. According to Bordin, the three dimensions of the working alliance are the clarity and strength of the personal **bonds** between the client and the counsellor, and the extent of agreement about first the **goals** of the helping process, and secondly the **tasks** to be carried out.

Egan (1994) also discusses the importance of establishing a contract with the client at the start of the relationship, which may need to be renegotiated several times during the course of the process. This may seem fairly straightforward, but research with careers officers suggests that many were confused about what the contract should consist of and were concerned that the contract could come to dominate the interview, particularly where it was relatively short (Kidd et al., 1993).

Considering the client's cultural origin may be particularly important here. Clients from cultures that emphasize respect for authority may find it difficult to accept that the responsibility for decision-making is their own and not the counselling psychologist's. Furthermore, those from cultures where family and group responsibilities take precedence over individual needs may be unused and reluctant to engage in self-reflection and assessment. This will need to be recognized by the counselling psychologist both early on and throughout the counselling process.

Confusion about the working alliance may arise from within the counselling psychologist as well as from the client. Career counsellors who work mainly with young clients facing initial career decisions, perhaps using a predominantly person–environment fit orientation, may feel uncomfortable faced with a middle-aged man who has just been made redundant. The consequence may be that they fail to explore the issue of how much support they can offer the client in coming to terms with his situation, and may want to move too quickly into assessment and information-giving activities.

Stage 2 Enabling clients' self-understanding

During the second stage of the helping process the main task is to help clients deepen their understanding and their insight into their situation. A core activity is likely to be some form of assessment of career-relevant attributes, such as interests, aptitudes and values. Much of the value of assessment at this stage is that it helps clients become familiar with conceptual frameworks to organize their knowledge of self and situation, and simple self-assessment tools, as well as knowledge gained through the interview itself, frequently produce insights which are just as illuminating as those gained by psychometric instruments.

Counselling psychologists working within a person–environment fit orientation emphasize the diagnostic value of tests and inventories. In contrast, those using developmental and person-centred approaches often see test results mainly as a stimulus to discussion. Commonly used occupational interests measures include the Strong-Campbell Interests Inventory and the SHL Advanced Occupational Interests Inventory. Several self-help devices are also available (see, for example, the interests questionnaire in *Build Your Own Rainbow*, Hopson and Scally, 1989). Instruments to assess work values, or the satisfactions sought from work, include Pryor's Work Aspect Preference Scale and Super's Work Values Inventory, and most self-help books include check-lists of values. Of particular relevance to work with adults are measures based on Schein's concept of career anchors (see, for example, Shein, 1990). Examples of standardized tests for the assessment of aptitudes are the Differential Aptitudes Test and the Morrisby Differential Test Battery. A comprehensive review of instruments that might be used in career assessment is given in Bartram et al. (1990).

It should be noted that many test publishers restrict the supply of their tests to psychologists, those with level A and B testing qualifications from the British Psychological Society or those who have attended the publisher's own course on the use of a particular test.

A less structured way of helping clients assess abilities and skills is to employ a technique known as 'systematic reflection on experience'. This is particularly useful for helping individuals identify 'transferable skills' from previous experiences in work and in other settings, such as leisure activities. Clients are asked to reflect on a particular experience, which may be a previous job or some other activity, and the counsellor helps them to:

- **Review the experience** – by describing how they carried out the activity and the satisfactions sought and achieved from it.
- **Conclude from the experience** – by describing what they feel they learned about their skills and abilities from the activity.
- **Plan next steps** – by identifying other situations in which that learning may be appropriate, and describing how they might generalize that learning to these situations.

It may be helpful to provide a framework for categorizing the skills that emerge. One way of doing this would be to classify them under four headings:

- **Data** – the skills used to organize and evaluate facts or data.
- **Ideas** – the skills used in creatively using words, concepts, figures and music.
- **People** – the skills used in working with other people, helping, teaching, serving, motivating, or persuading.
- **Things** – the skills used in making, repairing or servicing things.

Systematic reflection on experience is an approach which may be particularly helpful in working with people who are unemployed or have been out of the labour market for some time, or who have few formal qualifications. Because it enables clients to focus on what has been learned from 'informal learning' and on strengths rather than weaknesses, it can be a powerful tool in promoting self-confidence and self-esteem.

Other assessment techniques during this stage of the counselling process are informed by rather different models of careers. As we saw earlier, developmental theories of careers pay more attention to continuous, life-long processes of career development. They also view career decision-making and career management within the context of other life roles. A developmental approach to assessment therefore needs to encourage clients to take a holistic view of career issues, helping them explore the relative importance of work in their lives and potential conflicts between life roles.

Super's rainbow diagram, or some variation of it, may be helpful in increasing clients' awareness of roles. Also, some feelings and ideas may be hard to verbalize and graphic devices like the rainbow may be helpful for clients who find it easier to express themselves in diagrams rather than words. There are numerous other examples of these sorts of tools, of course, including life-lines and force-field analysis (Hopson and Scally, 1989).

With female clients, particularly, it may be important to encourage the client to assess the ways in which perceptions of sex roles may have affected aspirations. Several suggestions for conducting a 'sex-role analysis' are offered by Brooks and Forrest (1994): these include structured questioning within the interview, and sentence completion and card-sort exercises to increase awareness of sex-role expectations.

Stage 3   Exploring new perspectives

At the third stage a key task is to help clients develop new perspectives on their problems. The counselling psychologist's active contribution at this point is crucial, especially in challenging the client in various ways and helping him or her 'reality test' their expectations and aspirations. Egan (1994) defines challenging as 'an invitation to examine internal or external behaviour that seems to be self-defeating, harmful to others, or both, and to change the behaviour if it is found to be so'. So clients may be challenged, for example, to confront inconsistent beliefs about themselves, question strategically unsound plans, and recognize mismatches of job ideas with local opportunities. Writers who view challenging as central to the career counselling process include Krumboltz (1981) who emphasizes the role of social learning in career development, and those who have applied rational-emotive therapy to career counselling (see, for example, Dryden, 1979).

Krumboltz's social learning framework highlights the importance of behavioural counselling skills such as reinforcement and modelling. Of particular relevance to this stage, however, are the cognitive strategies which the counselling psychologist may employ to challenge erroneous beliefs. Some of Mitchell and Krumboltz's (1990) guidelines for assessing and changing 'faulty' beliefs are as follows:

- Identify the assumptions and presuppositions behind the expressed belief.
- Examine inconsistencies between words and actions.
- Confront what seem to be simplistic answers.
- Challenge attempts to build illogical arguments.
- Attempt to assess the validity of strongly held beliefs.

It goes without saying that an insensitive use of these kinds of strategies and techniques will be unhelpful or even damaging. Challenging is unlikely to be appropriate early in the career counselling process and it should only be attempted once a trusting relationship has been established.

Labour market information may also be needed at this stage. Most clients will need information about occupational and educational options as well as trends within the labour market generally. A vast amount of career-related information is available, through directories such as the American Directory of Occupational Titles and within computer databases, such as MICRODOORS and the ECCTIS. Most of the careers material, however, is concerned with the characteristics of occupations, such as work activities, skills needed, levels of entry, and types of education and training needed. In contrast, information about organizational environments, in terms of size, structure, culture and human resource strategies is much less readily available. While counselling psychologists working with clients on problems relating to occupational choices are well served with respect to information resources, therefore, those helping individuals with predominantly mid-life career management concerns, such as negotiating career systems and pathways within their organization or contemplating an organizational career move within the same occupational field have very few information resources to refer to. As our earlier discussion of labour market changes and changes in concepts of career showed, clients will increasingly need knowledge of organizations' human resource systems and cultures: for example, the extent to which they operate an internal or external labour market, how much support for employee development is offered, how much emphasis is placed on team as opposed to individual performance, and, crucially, their overall business strategy and plans for the future. Much of this kind of information will be outside the public domain, but some services, outplacement agencies in particular, meet some of these needs through their networks with employers.

Within facilitative, client-centred models of career counselling, where a central goal is to encourage clients to seek out information for themselves, the most appropriate role for the counsellor is that of the supportive 'general practitioner' (Nathan and Hill, 1992). A knowledge of how to access information and where to refer clients who need specialist information is more in line with the values of counselling than specific information-giving within the interview. Indeed, as Nathan and Hill point out, when the career counselling session is used as a vehicle for feeding the client information, this may confuse the counselling contract and lead the client into a passive role. The counselling psychologist will also need to help clients relate occupational information to their self-assessments, evaluate it, and deal with their emotional reactions to it. Challenging will be an important skill here.

Stage 4   Forming strategies and plans

It should be clear that client responsibility lies at the heart of the counselling model proposed here. This means that 'action' will be an integral part of the process at all stages as well as in the final phases. Action does not necessarily imply changes in behaviour: the term is used to denote internal changes in thoughts and feelings, as well as observable actions. A client, may, for example, have made progress towards clarifying whether self-employment would really suit her; have become more confident about the transferable skills he possesses; or be nearer to a decision about a career after graduation.

Towards the end of the counselling process particularly, time will need to be set aside for reviewing progress. Nathan and Hill (1992) suggest that such a review will serve a number of purposes, for example:

- It prepares the client for the end of the relationship.
- It helps the client to see career counselling in perspective.
- Highlighting progress made will strengthen the client's confidence and resolve.
- It emphasizes the client's continuing responsibility for her or his own development.

In doing this, it may be helpful to review the contract made at the beginning of counselling, and recall the agreed objectives.

A central activity in preparing for the end of the counselling relationship will be helping clients set goals and decide on the steps they need to take to achieve them. The literature on goal-setting is helpful here (see, for example, Locke and Latham, 1984). To be achievable, goals need to be:

- Clear, specific and expressed in behavioural terms.
- Measurable.
- Realistic.
- Owned by the individual.
- In line with the client's values.
- Realistically scheduled.

The process of goal-setting should clearly specify the targets to be reached. A client who, for example, wishes to explore further the possibility of self-employment might decide that the first task is to approach acquaintances who work for themselves to explore advantages and disadvantages. This goal might be measurable in terms of the number of people talked to and the range of lifestyle aspects of self-employment explored.

Goals should be achievable, but not too easy, and within the client's control. A client who sets himself the task of writing six job applications a week may be realistic about what he can achieve in this time, but if part of the goal is to be offered two interviews as a result, failing to achieve this could be damaging to his motivation and self-esteem.

According to Locke and Latham, participation in goal-setting and ownership of goals leads to increased performance and feelings of competence. This seems to be because there is an increased likelihood of the individual acting to achieve the goals. Participation will also increase the possibility that goals will be congruent with clients' value systems.

Setting a realistic time plan for the achievement of goals seems to be important for successful accomplishment. This may involve identifying sub-goals which lead individuals to the main goal by making incremental demands on them.

Written action plans are increasingly used to express clients' goals and means of achieving them. This is especially so in the Careers Service, as government funding has begun to depend on numbers of action plans completed. When used simply as evidence that an interview has taken place action plans can be unhelpful and inappropriate, particularly when pre-structured plans are used. However, plans geared to the specific needs of the client are a useful way of clarifying the client's commitment to certain activities, and the act of writing the plan can be a powerful impetus to action.

Evaluation of the effectiveness of careers work

In this final section, we move on to consider the question of the effectiveness of career development work, broadly defined. Early evaluation studies were concerned with the effectiveness of career guidance offered in the form of occupational recommendations made to young people by juvenile employment officers. Career outcomes were used as criteria: evaluators assessed whether clients who accepted the recommendations made showed greater job satisfaction and success and less occupational mobility than those who did not (see, for example, Burt et al., 1926). Few studies employed control groups to test the hypothesis that those exposed to guidance benefited in comparison to those who were not.

As Clarke (1981) has pointed out, however, there are considerable methodological problems with these kinds of studies. These include questionable validity and reliability of many of the outcome measures and doubts about their appropriateness. (Job mobility, for example, was viewed as unsatisfactory and indicative of a lack of adjustment to work.) Furthermore, there was no way of knowing whether the occupational recommendations made arose from the guidance intervention – they may simply have reflected the pre-existing intentions of the young person.

With moves towards a more developmental approach, evaluators, particularly those in the United States, began to attend to assessing the 'learning outcomes' of career guidance and counselling. Learning outcomes can be defined as the 'skills, knowledge and attitudes which facilitate rational occupational and educational decision-making and the effective implementation of occupational and educational decisions' (Kidd and Killeen, 1992). They include awareness of one's own abilities and interests, knowledge of opportunities and options, decision-making skills, transition skills and general attitudes to decision-making.

Figure 21.2 summarizes these outcomes diagrammatically, elaborating Law and Watts's (1977) fourfold 'DOTS' classification of guidance outcomes: decision learning, opportunity awareness, transition learning and self-awareness.

Much of the evidence for these kinds of learning outcomes comes from American studies using controlled trials with pre/post designs. Self-report instruments, such as the Career Factors Inventory (Chartrand et al., 1990) and My Vocational Situation (Holland et al., 1980) are commonly used to assess outcomes, but tests of career knowledge and skills, for example those within so-called 'career maturity' instruments such as the Career Development Inventory (Super et al., 1981) and the Career Maturity Inventory (Crites, 1978) are also available. (A comprehensive review of more than 60 learning outcome instruments is contained in Killeen et al., 1994.)

So how effective is careers work in these terms? The clearest evidence for effectiveness comes from meta-analyses, which pool the findings of large numbers of published studies. In the most rigorous meta-analysis carried out to date, Oliver and Spokane (1988) analysed the findings of 58 controlled trials, showing that the average subject improved 29 percentile points after guidance. The interventions covered a wide range of activities including careers education courses with group work and self-help materials, work experience programmes and individual career counselling, though detailed information on the nature and duration of the intervention was not always given.

This gives a fair indication of the positive benefits of guidance, but we also need to look at individual studies to assess the types of outcomes produced by different types of interventions. A recent review of 46 individual studies (Killeen and Kidd, 1991) showed that there is evidence for most types of guidance interventions in relation to most categories of

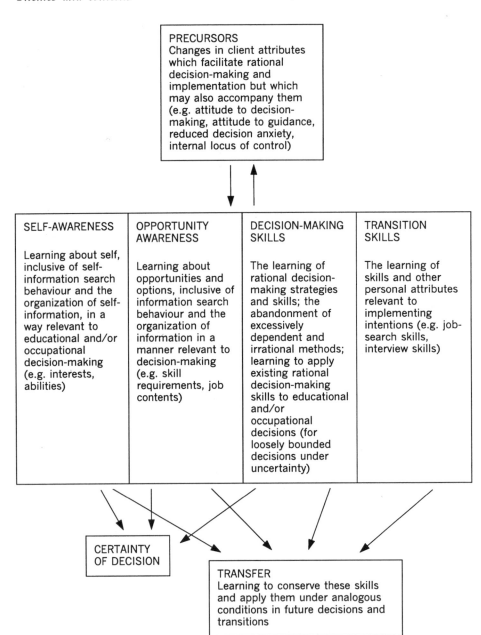

Figure 21.2 *Learning outcomes and closely associated outcomes of guidance (from Killeen and Kidd, 1991)*

outcomes. Comparing different types of interventions, individual career counselling produced the greatest effect per hour of treatment; it was four times as effective as group work, but twice as costly (Oliver and Spokane, 1988). The evidence also suggests, not surprisingly, that some types of intervention are more helpful to some individuals than others. Kivlighan et al. (1981), for example, showed that 'task-orientated' clients responded more favourably to individual counselling based on problem-solving techniques, while 'people-centred' clients responded better to group counselling.

If all types of intervention are beneficial to some degree, how and why do the effects occur? Holland et al. (1981), examining the interventions employed in hundreds of studies varying widely in sophistication, concluded that four essential ingredients were required for success. These were:

- The acquisition of cognitive frameworks for understanding self, opportunities, and their relationship.
- Information about self and the world of work, using these frameworks.
- Cognitive rehearsal of aspirations.
- Social support or reinforcement.

It seems to be reasonably clear, then, that career guidance and counselling enhances career-related knowledge and attitudes, at least in the short term. British evidence is scarce, however, as are studies of adult clients. There is also a need for longitudinal research which links immediate learning outcomes with ultimate career or economic outcomes, such as job satisfaction and performance, duration of unemployment and participation in education and training (Killeen et al., 1992).

A further drawback with the evaluation research carried out so far is that, in contrast to career decision-making, very little attention has been given to assessing the career management or career resilience components of career development, such as exploratory behaviour, negotiating skills and a sense of confidence in the future. Among the scant evidence available is an evaluation of a career development programme for women (Kingdon and Bimline, 1987) which produced increases in self-esteem and growth motivation and a study by Noe et al. (1990) which indicated that encouraging subordinates to set career goals resulted in greater career commitment and an increased ability to adapt to changing circumstances.

For the future, then, research will need to address a broader range of outcomes than hitherto. Of equal importance, though, is a rigorous examination of the variety of activities practitioners engage in within the realm of careers work. As we have seen, career guidance is a multi-faceted process, and research needs to attend to the relative impact of different approaches and techniques, and the merits of taking an eclectic as opposed to a 'single-school' approach.

Concluding comments

One of the aims of this chapter has been to set the practice of careers work within a theoretical context. Given the diversity of settings in which career guidance and counselling takes place, the range of issues it has to address, and the variety of interventions which may be used, it is clear that our understanding of the processes involved can be enhanced by applying paradigms and perspectives from several disciplines within the social sciences. Even in this brief review, we have seen how differentialist psychology, developmental psychology and functionalist sociology all contribute in their various ways to a more complete understanding of careers, and, furthermore, how a range of perspectives on counselling can inform the career counselling process. Had space permitted, it would have been possible to have discussed and debated contributions from other areas of psychology, such as group dynamics, and, indeed, the relevance of other social science disciplines, for example economics and anthropology. We need multiple perspectives on career development, on the social and organizational environments within which careers are experienced, and on career counselling practice, but the danger, of course, is that the resulting overall body of knowledge becomes too fragmented and unwieldy for practitioners to work with. The challenge for counselling psychologists working with career issues is to draw on these various perspectives to build a coherent psychological framework for practice and for further research, while remaining open to new ideas from a range of disciplines within the social sciences.

References

Argyris, C. (1960) *Understanding Organizational Behavior*. Homewood, IL: Dorsey Press.

Bartram, D., Lindley, P.A. and Foster, J. (1990) *Review of Psychometric Tests for Assessment in Vocational Training*. Hull: Newland Park Associates, University of Hull/BPS.

Bordin, E.S. (1979) 'The generalizability of the psychoanalytic concept of the working alliance', *Psychotherapy, Research and Practice*, 16: 252–60.

Brooks, L. and Forrest, L. (1994) 'Feminism and career counselling', in Walsh, W.B. and Osipow, S.H. (eds), *Career Counseling for Women*. Hillsdale, NJ: Lawrence Erlbaum.

Burt, C., Gaw, F., Ramsey, L., Smith, M. and Spielman, W. (1926) *A Study in*

Vocational Guidance. MRC Industrial Fatigue Research Board Report No. 33. London: HMSO.

Chartrand, J.M., Robbins, S.B., Morrill, W.H. and Boggs, K. (1990) 'Development and validation of the career factors inventory', *Journal of Counseling Psychology*, 37: 191–201.

Clarke, L. (1981) *The Practice of Vocational Guidance: a Critical Review of Research in the United Kingdom*. London: HMSO.

Crites, J.O. (1978) *Career Maturity Inventory: Theory and Research Handbook*. Monterey, CA: CTB/McGraw-Hill.

Dryden, W. (1979) 'Rational-emotive therapy and its contribution to careers counselling', *British Journal of Guidance and Counselling*, 7: 181–7.

Egan, G. (1994) *The Skilled Helper*, 5th edn. Pacific Grove, CA: Brooks/Cole.

Ginzberg, E., Ginsburg, S.W., Axelrad, S. and Herma, J.L. (1951) *Occupational Choice: and Approach to a General Theory*. New York: Columbia University Press.

Herriot, P. and Pemberton, C. (in press) 'Contracting careers', *Human Relations*.

Holland, J.L. (1973) *Making Vocational Choices: a Theory of Careers*. Englewood Cliffs, NJ: Prentice Hall.

Holland, J.L., Daiger, D.C. and Power, P.G. (1980) *My Vocational Situation*. Palo Alto, CA: Consulting Psychologists Press.

Holland, J.L., Magoon, T.M. and Spokane, A.R. (1981) 'Counseling psychology: career interventions, research and theory', *Annual Review of Psychology*, 32: 279–305.

Hopson, B. and Scally, M. (1989) *Build Your Own Rainbow: a Handbook for Career and Life Management*. Leeds: Lifeskills Associates.

Kidd, J.M. and Killeen, J. (1992) 'Are the effects of careers guidance worth having? Changes in practice and outcomes', *Journal of Occupational and Organizational Psychology*, 65: 219–34.

Kidd, J.M., Killeen, J., Jarvis, J. and Offer, M. (1993) *Working Models of Careers Guidance: the Interview*. Report to the Employment Department. Birkbeck College, University of London.

Killeen, J. and Kidd, J.M. (1991) *Learning Outcomes of Guidance: a Review of Recent Research*. London: Department of Employment Research Paper No. 85.

Killeen, J., White, M. and Watts, A.G. (1992) *The Economic Value of Careers Guidance*. London: Policy Studies Institute.

Killeen, J., Kidd, J.M., Hawthorn, R., Sampson, J. and White, M. (1994) *A Review of Measures of the Learning Outcomes of Guidance*. Cambridge: NICEC.

Kingdon, M.A. and Bimline, C.A. (1987) 'Evaluating the effectiveness of career development training for women', *Career Development Quarterly*, 35: 220–7.

Kivlighan, D.M., Hageseth, J.A., Tipton, R.M. and McGovern, T.V. (1981) 'Effects of matching treatment, approaches and personality types in group vocational counseling', *Journal of Counseling Psychology*, 28: 315–20.

Krumboltz, J.D. (1981) 'A social learning theory of career selection', in D.H. Montross and C.J. Shinkman (eds) *Career Development in the 1980s*. Springfield, IL: Charles C. Thomas.

Law, B. and Watts, A.G. (1977) *School, Careers and Community*. London: Church Information Office.

Locke, E.A. and Latham, G.P. (1984) *Goal Setting: a Motivational Technique that Works!* Englewood Cliffs, NJ: Prentice Hall.

London, M. (1983) 'Toward a theory of career motivation', *Academy of Management Review*, 8: 620–30.

Mitchell, L.K. and Krumboltz, J.D. (1990) 'Social learning approach to career decision making: Krumboltz's theory', in D. Brown and L. Brooks (eds), *Career Choice and Development: Applying Contemporary Theories to Practice*. San Francisco, CA: Jossey Bass.

Nathan, R. and Hill, L. (1992) *Career Counselling*. London: Sage.

Nicholson, N. and West, M. (1988) *Managerial Job Change: Men and Women in Transition*. Cambridge: Cambridge University Press.

Noe, R.A., Noe, A.W. and Bachhuber, J.A. (1990) 'Correlates of career motivation', *Journal of Vocational Behavior*, 37: 340–56.

Oliver, L. and Spokane, A.R. (1988) 'Career counselling outcome: what contributes to client gain?', *Journal of Counseling Psychology*, 35: 447–62.

Parsons, F. (1909) *Choosing a Vocation*. Boston, MA: Houghton Mifflin.

Roberts, K. (1968) 'The entry into employment: an approach towards a general theory', *Sociological Review*, 16: 165–84.

Rodger, A. (1952) *The Seven-Point Plan*. London: NIIP.

Rousseau, D.M. (1990) 'New hire perceptions of their own and their employer's obligations: a study of psychological contracts', *Journal of Organizational Behavior*, 11: 389–400.

Schein, E.H. (1990) *Careers Anchors: Discovering your Real Values*. San Diego, CA: Pfeiffer.

Spokane, A.R. (1985) 'A review of research on person–environment congruence in Holland's theory of careers', *Journal of Vocational Behavior*, 31: 37–44.

Super, D.E. (1957) *The Psychology of Careers*. New York: Harper.

Super, D.E. (1980) 'A life-span, life-space approach to career development', *Journal of Vocational Behavior*, 16: 282–98.

Super, D.E., Thompson, A.S., Lindeman, R.H., Jordaan, J.P. and Myers, R.A. (1981) *Career Development Inventory*. Palo Alto, CA: Consulting Psychologists Press.

Super, D.E., Thompson, A.S., Lindeman, R.H., Myers, R.A. and Jordaan, J.P. (1988) *Adult Career Concerns Inventory*. Palo Alto, CA: Consulting Psychologists Press.

Tranberg, M., Slane, S. and Ekeberg, S.E. (1993) 'The relationship between interest congruence and satisfaction: a meta-analysis', *Journal of Vocational Behavior*, 42: 253–64.

Walsh, W.B. and Osipow, S.H. (eds) (1990) *Career Counseling*. Hillsdale, NJ: Lawrence Erlbaum.

22

Counselling Psychology in the Workplace

Vanja Orlans

The practice of psychological counselling in the work setting is a relatively new area of professional endeavour, especially perhaps within the United Kingdom. At the same time, it has developed quite rapidly and continues to grow in popularity with both counsellors and organizations. The British Association for Counselling has a well-established professional section concerned with counselling at work, Employee Assistance Programmes are being more widely marketed, and managers are becoming more knowledgeable about, and acceptant of, psychological counselling as a potentially useful resource to both individuals and the organization as a whole. A very recent development in the field has been the establishment of a Division of Counselling Psychology within the British Psychological Society – the culmination of many years of activity within that professional association, and an official recognition of a growing field of important theory and practice. The application of the theory and practice of counselling psychology to the work setting is a field which is still in its infancy, however, in terms of a coherent body of knowledge, practice and accreditation. My hope is that the ideas which I set out in this chapter may usefully contribute in particular to the further development of 'a legitimate body of psychological knowledge', a 'professional field of psychological activity' (British Psychological Society, 1994), and most importantly, to the links between concepts and their application in practice.

'Counselling' and 'Counselling Psychology'

First, a few words about the distinction between 'counselling' and 'counselling psychology'. My use of the term 'counselling' in the context of this chapter denotes a set of intervention practices which are employed to facilitate the development of individuals and groups towards a greater awareness and ability to manage life's problems and challenges, and to make more effective life choices. Regardless of the particular theoretical orientation, we are concerned here with a set of clinical skills on the part of the 'counsellor', which are then applied within a particular kind of helping relationship. 'Counselling psychology', however, is a field which extends beyond a consideration of the helping relationship *per se*. In this case, the 'counselling' component is based on a broader psychological ground – the counselling psychologist is, first, a 'psychologist', and secondly, a 'counsellor'. There is thus a difference in 'frame' between the two kinds of professionals, although there may also be a great deal of overlap in terms of the applied work of both practitioners.

Counselling psychology as a field of practice is a very young profession in the UK – it has only recently been designated officially by the British Psychological Society as a field of practice in its own right. Notwithstanding this fact, those of us who are both applied psychologists and practising counsellors have, for some time, been busy with many issues which go beyond the usual boundaries of 'counselling', thus contributing in a variety of ways to the development of 'counselling psychology' in the UK. At the same time, there are many trained counsellors who are not psychologists by profession, who have also been working more recently within the work setting, contributing both their ideas and their clinical skills. This chapter encompasses both sets of activities. The broad framework presented reflects my own training and experience as a counselling psychologist. At the same time I would like to address readers who might have trained primarily as counsellors, and offer them some ideas which might be both stimulating and useful in their work. In relation to the use of different terms, the reader should note that I use the term 'counselling' to refer to a set of *practices* – particular interventions within a broader systems perspective.

A typical professional counsellor training programme will allocate the bulk of its time to teaching participants the perspectives and skills which they must learn in order to operate competently as counsellors in clinical practice. The training will, in addition, often adopt a particular frame of reference, that is, person-centred, transactional analysis, Gestalt, etc. Generally speaking, there is little time allocated to comparisons across different approaches – at least in any depth – and there is relatively little input on the effectiveness of counselling as a whole and its application to different domains. This is meant to be a statement of fact, not a criticism – there would not be time, even on a relatively comprehensive programme, to cover all of these aspects. It is my view, however, that these aspects form a central part of counselling psychology – a field which is more broadly defined within the discipline of psychology as a whole, and which therefore needs to incorporate both the clinical aspects of practice, as well as a more wide-ranging, and potentially critical, perspective which would aim to cover many different theoretical approaches.

This emphasis on the closer association between 'theory' and 'practice' is a challenge in general within the field of psychology which has traditionally tended to separate these dimensions on the basis that researchers are supposed to develop the theories, while practitioners are supposed to 'act'. The result in many branches of psychology has been the promotion of an artificial dualism which not only affects the resulting quality of developed theory, but also suggests a somewhat fragmented approach to human action (see Shipley and Orlans, 1988, for further discussion of this point in relation to stress research). In the fields of both counselling and counselling psychology the theory/practice issue is one which is currently becoming more important and which is likely to remain so in a climate where counsellor competence is being more closely scrutinized and controlled, and where the development of training standards and professional recognition are being so widely debated and developed. These circumstances present a particular challenge to counselling psychologists who, by definition, encompass aspects of both involved practice and analysis 'from a perspective'.

Counselling psychology in context

While the application of the clinical practice of psychological counselling to the work context could well be seen as a natural progression of an already established field of practice, there are qualitative differences in the two settings of 'the clinic' and 'the organization' which are important to illuminate and understand. Although it is helpful to draw on a systems perspective when working clinically, there are a number of specific conditions which are especially pertinent to the work setting. In the clinical setting, for example, the counselling psychologist is dealing directly with the client in the sense of being able to make a *relatively* straightforward contact as to what the relationship and work might be about. In relation to the organizational setting, however, the practitioner's first-level contract is with the employing institution, and within this he or she will need to define the possibilities and limits of the counselling relationship itself. It is clear that the latter situation, which is often also fraught with wider conflicts and political dynamics, demands a particular kind of systems level of awareness on the part of the counselling psychologist, as well as, potentially, a greater level of self-support.

It is not just the change of *domain*, however, which is important here. What we are dealing with is the very nature of the way in which the counselling activity is viewed *theoretically speaking*. We can either view this practice, in general, as separate from its context, or we can adopt a perspective which views this or any other activity as inseparable from the setting in which it takes place. This theme has long been debated within the field of psychology in general – see, for example, the debates surrounding Stanley Milgram's original experiments on obedience (Milgram, 1974) – and has been relevant also in discussions of methodology where a rather fragmented traditional model of 'science' has been set against notions of 'perspective' as demonstrated by Einstein's Theory of Relativity. In viewing the practice of psychological counselling in a way which incorporates the setting in which it takes place, we adopt a more holistic or 'meta' perspective to this activity – one which is potentially less fragmented, and more creative, than artificially limiting any analysis simply to the clinical domain. We move from a more individually based perspective, to one which is systems-orientated, and where any analysis or diagnostic activity must take account of a larger data field. The adoption of a broader contextual approach to psychological counselling allows us to develop an interactive, process-orientated theoretical underpinning to our work – a meta-perspective which can be truly generalizable in a way which lower levels of analysis cannot.

Approaches to 'context'

It is interesting to consider these ideas in relation to particular theoretical approaches in the fields of counselling and counselling psychology. Approaches which traditionally have included 'context' or 'system' as an explicit part of their theoretical framework will be closer to the thinking outlined in this chapter than those approaches which are more individually focused. Contrast, for example, the Gestalt approach (see Clarkson, 1989), with its emphasis on field theory (Lewin, 1952), with more cognitive approaches such as that developed by Kelly (1955) (see also Bannister and Fransella, 1971, regarding the application of personal construct theory). It is interesting to note also that certain theoretical schools appear to be moving more towards a position which increasingly views individuals as inseparable from their environment. For example, Brazier (1993) illustrates the ways in which the person-centred approach is currently highlighting the relevance of contextual factors (see especially the chapter by Ned Gaylin in that volume).

These developments may also be affected by the general trend towards integration in the fields of both psychological counselling and psychotherapy (see, for example, Norcross and Arkowitz, 1992). We could argue, however, that counselling psychologists trained in a more context-orientated discipline are likely to have developed a set of skills which can more readily be applied within the organizational domain. Notwithstanding differences in understanding or skill which arise from differences in the theories which underpin training, there is still, in my view, a need for a perspective at the meta-level which can provide an organizing framework for a number of different approaches, and which can also delineate a number of generalizable principles with sound philosophical and methodological underpinnings.

We can consider the idea of 'context' from two perspectives – one more theoretical and philosophical, the other more practical. First, as outlined above, there is the extent to which the relevance of context is an explicit part of the theoretical underpinning to particular training programmes – or implicit in such training when viewed from a meta-perspective – and the extent to which graduates of different programmes will have different kinds of awareness. An additional way of approaching the issue of context, however, is to consider the positioning of a counselling activity within a particular organization. For instance, a psychological counselling scheme might be organized in a form which renders it separate from the rest of the organization, or it might be designed in a way which integrates this activity with broader aspects of organizational functioning. Whatever the structural aspects of a particular scheme, the organization will nevertheless be present as 'the ground' to that scheme – whether it be explicit or tacit. A more explicitly linked scheme can potentially be more effective in the organization as a whole, since it highlights the importance of 'systemic thinking', and may enable the counselling psychologist to distinguish more readily between 'pathological individual conditions' and 'environmentally induced reactions'. Bott (1988), in relation to family therapy work, refers to the distinction made in systems thinking between 'first order change' within the system, and 'second order change' *of* the system, and demonstrates the implications of such thinking for diagnosis.

A contextual model of counselling

A model of an organizational counselling scheme is outlined in Figure 22.1 below. In that model, 'the organization' is the explicit starting point for psychological counselling activities – a 'key client' in the system as a whole. Counselling interventions occur within this system, but are a part of a process which cycles back to the organizational level. For example, the organization might experience some sense of strain, turbulence, or distress within a part of it which would become the 'figure' for discussion about relevant intervention strategies. One possible strategy which might be identified could be the implementation of some form of counselling facility. Thinking 'organizationally', we would expect this intervention to have an impact on both the individual client, and on the organization as a whole, especially when considered over time. The next task then would be to explore strategies which would link the individual back to the organization. This might take the form of monitoring take-up rates, collating broadly defined 'presenting problems' in a way which did not affect the confidentiality contract in the counselling setting, or monitoring group profiles of work-related issues (again, paying careful attention to

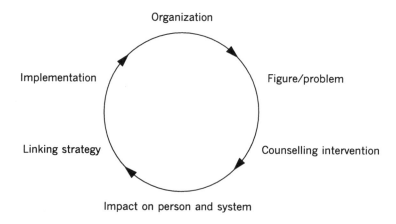

Figure 22.1   *A model of organizational counselling*

confidentiality concerns). This could lead to organizational-level interventions which would become part of a broader management strategy.

We consequently develop a cycle which moves through the individual
level of work and support, returning to the organizational starting point.
The process as a whole mirrors a learning cycle not dissimilar to that
which takes place at the level of the journey between counselling
psychologist and client. When clients come for counselling they are often
struggling with fragmentation in their 'systemic' lives. In the course of the
counselling process, these difficulties are explored in the consulting room
where a safe environment for experimentation and change is initially
established. If the process as a whole is successful, clients will then take
their new insights and abilities back into their wider systems where
further adaptations and learnings continue. The result for the client – and
sometimes for aspects of the system – is a greater sense of movement or
'flow' through different parts of that individual's world.

It is clear that the model above represents an ideal. Not all organizations
are willing to commit to a more wide-ranging process of this kind,
possibly because of lack of funds and relevant human resources, or because
such a process could be viewed as more threatening and more likely to
throw up additional issues such as confusions about individual/organiz-
ational responsibility, resource allocation conflicts, etc. which would then
require further discussion and working through. The approach does,
however, serve to highlight the centrality of the organization in the
process, as well as ensuring that the counselling component retains an
explicit link with the system as a whole. Where psychological counselling
activities are organized in a more fragmented way – that is, where there
are no explicit links made between the counselling process and the

organization – it is still possible to make the wider process explicit by examining the counselling facility in question from the perspective of the above model. This can be a useful learning exercise, serving to highlight implicit contracts and expectations, and can be a starting point for creative discussion in the evaluation of particular psychological counselling schemes.

These points are raised here primarily to emphasize the importance of including context as part of our analyses in developing an understanding of work-based counselling activities, and in highlighting the fact that the link with the organization is there, even if the choice is to leave this link unexplored, unacknowledged, or at the tacit level of awareness. In the following section I provide an overview of different types of psychological counselling programmes which may be implemented within the work setting, pointing out the ways in which each relates to the model outlined above.

Strategies and programmes in work-based counselling

Psychological counselling facilities within the work setting can range from the micro to the macro. At the micro end of the spectrum we find a facility which some people might not include in an overview of counselling at work. I refer here to 'counselling' which is offered in the work setting by professionals such as company medical officers, occupational health nurses and welfare officers. In companies which have an established occupational health facility, for example, it is often the occupational health nurse who is likely to be approached quite frequently for psychological counselling and support – under the guise, maybe, of a range of minor physical ailments.

The stigma of emotionality

In exploring this process within the organizational setting, we are reminded that there is still considerable stigma in the world at large about 'emotional problems' and 'counselling'. This can be especially so within competitive work settings – described sometimes as 'jungle cultures' with the emphasis on the survival of the fittest – where employees who experience themselves as not measuring up to the 'fitness standard' feel very reluctant – indeed sometimes frightened – to own up to emotional distress. An easier and safer option is to see a 'medical person' in the organizational setting, or take time off work with a medical certificate based on a physical complaint. In the extreme case, an employee might continue without taking time off until a major health problem (for example, a heart attack) offers a means of escape. My own experience with organizations suggests that individuals are more 'protective' about their emotional problems than we might sometimes assume, and are often reluctant to take up an offer of psychological counselling, at least until they are convinced of the confidential nature of such a scheme, or until it becomes an established facility within the setting concerned.

The problem of stigma in relation to emotional distress can help us to understand why a non-counselling professional (in terms of the absence of specific training) can end up in a counselling role within the work setting. In a survey carried out some years ago focusing primarily on large organizations (Orlans and Shipley, 1983) we found that occupational health nurses did play a counselling role in a number of the organizations surveyed, even though none had had any form of professional counselling training. We also found that welfare officers played a significant counselling role, being well placed to deal with a variety of life problems be they financial, legal, marital or personal. Psychologically, their role is that of 'someone to talk to' as well as being providers of useful advice. One problem with the welfare function, however, is the term 'welfare' itself. It has connotations of charity, sounds rather out of date and perhaps somewhat patronizing, and, more importantly, the function has relatively low status in many organizations. All of these reasons contribute to usage of the facility by staff at lower levels in the hierarchy.

Also at the micro end of the spectrum, but with a more explicit emphasis on psychological counselling *per se*, is a facility where an employee who is identified as experiencing an emotional problem – which might or might not be deemed to be 'work-related' – is referred to a counselling psychologist outside the organization for one or more sessions, depending on what a particular organization is willing to support financially. The counselling psychologist concerned might be working independently in private practice, or might be part of a network of psychological counsellors who undertake such work. The growth in popularity of counselling among organizational managers has led to the development of specialized firms who market such resources to companies. Typically, professionals (sometimes throughout the UK) are invited to join a special register of organizational counsellors. Clients are referred to these professionals via the mediating company who also pay the fees to the counsellors.

Levels of analysis

With reference to the organizational counselling model outlined earlier, psychological counselling schemes at the micro end of the spectrum tend, more often than not, to focus on the individual level of analysis and problem management, with the organizational dimensions being left as an unacknowledged part of the 'ground'. This can be understandable given the logistics in many of these schemes: counsellors are unfamiliar with the organization concerned; there are no mechanisms for contact between counsellor and organization; the definition of 'the problem' is individual in focus. While an individual-level problem analysis and management might in many ways be appropriate and necessary, I would like to draw attention to what I have termed 'the band-aid phenomenon' – that is, where an employee is offered no more than a band-aid to cover a 'hurt' without any attention being paid to causative or preventative factors in the wider work setting. This is not to decry the usefulness of 'band-aids' in helping a particular individual deal with a life problem. One study by Firth and Shapiro (1986), for example, highlights the effectiveness of brief psychotherapy for the alleviation of job-related distress. They also suggest that it is more productive to identify and offer help to those individuals who are recognized as currently distressed, rather than offering more general programmes to all workers – a strategy which would require an organizational frame of reference.

We do, in my view, need to approach individually orientated strategies with a critical perspective, for to offer such a solution as a way of not addressing wider concerns raises ethical dimensions in the counselling work which I believe need to be acknowledged and discussed. We need to bear in mind the fact that individuals who come for psychological counselling may be carrying the problems of a wider context with them. An example of this is the well-known work by Brown and Harris (1978) on depression in women, where they highlighted the enormous importance of social factors in the origin of depressive symptoms. Other postmodernist writers such as Gergen and Kaye (1992) approach the issue in a slightly different way, drawing attention to the implicit field in the therapeutic relationship itself. In highlighting the therapist's 'narrative' as an abstract formulation, artificially divorced from particular cultural or historical circumstances, they make the point that: 'None of the modernist narratives deal with the specific conditions of living in ghetto poverty, with a brother who has AIDS, with a child who has Down's Syndrome, with a boss who is sexually abusive, and so on' (1992: 172).

Although the efficacy of psychological counselling has been widely researched from a clinical perspective, there are not many studies which are concerned to evaluate the effectiveness of these interventions in the context of the organizational setting. In this setting the different aspects of the context, the short-term nature of treatment, and the most effective approach for the work setting are all relevant factors for analysis. Barkham and Shapiro (1990) review a number of different interventions for dealing with job-related distress, and present some of the findings from a pilot study implementing brief psychotherapeutic models. Their results demonstrate the effectiveness of short-term psychological counselling interventions for presenting problems, both in terms of improvement in client functioning, and in terms also of cost-effectiveness to the organization. Cooper et al. (1990) outline a programme of short-term psychological counselling which has recently been implemented in the Post Office, and present evaluation data on the effectiveness of this scheme. Results from an initial sample of 78 questionnaires, and the analysis of 155 sickness absence records, indicate significant improvements in mental well-being and a reduction of days lost at work.

Broad-based strategies in organizations

At the macro end of the spectrum with regard to organizational counselling facilities we have the Employee Assistance programme (EAP). Such programmes are widespread within the USA and Canada. They are assumed to meet the needs of both employers and employees, as well an enhancing the image of the company as a whole. These programmes emanate from the USA and have their origins in schemes which were concerned with specific problem areas, notably alcohol abuse, and where resources which already existed in the community could be harnessed for organizational needs. As these programmes developed within companies there was an expansion into more 'broad-brush' schemes which provided resources for a range of problems (emotional, financial, legal, etc.) potentially confronting employees and their families. The early programmes which focused solely on alcohol abuse were more overtly coercive than the many broad-brush programmes which exist today, although the attitudes tended to vary somewhat with organizations who had greater safety concerns at the workplace being more adamant about insisting that employees with difficulties take part in the scheme. The growth of EAPs in North America coincided with the general rise of the humanistic movement in the 1960s.

Employee Assistance Programmes are clearly designed to provide a mixture of advice and psychological counselling to employees with problems. Initial contact with the EAP counsellor is partly to offer first-level exploratory psychological counselling in order that the client can more clearly define 'the problem'. The next step is then to ascertain the extent to which the client might benefit from on-going psychological support, the extent to which specific information (e.g. legal, financial) is required, and the extent to which the client might gain more from specialist help (e.g. problems of substance abuse or AIDS). Tittmar (1988) proposes a distinction between the 'Employee Assistance Programme' and the 'Employee Counselling Programme', highlighting the difference between those programmes which are more specifically focused (for example, on alcohol problems), and those which are concerned to provide more generalized psychological counselling. While there is indeed a variation in the way in which individual schemes operate, my usage of the term 'EAP' here is designed to refer to both types of programmes. Counselling psychologists can play an important role in many different kinds of programmes, in terms either of their involvement in the actual psychological counselling process, or in relation to the management of the intervention process as a whole as suggested by the model of organizational counselling outlined earlier (cf. also discussion on skills and training below).

Employee Assistance Programmes are resourced in different ways depending on the size of the company, and the financial and other resources that are available. One type of programme utilizes trained professional psychological counsellors who are employed full-time in the organization concerned. These professionals provide first-line help to individuals and their families, and are often available to employees 24 hours a day. The emphasis is initially on short-term counselling; employees who need further help over time, or who need access to more specialist advice and support, are referred on to the relevant professionals. The terms on which a person is referred on – that is to say, whether they are supported financially by the company, and to what degree – is a matter for individual company policy. It is important to remember that broad-brush EAPs deal with a range of problems – financial, legal, substance abuse, emotional issues, HIV, family matters – and referral on will be to a professional in the designated problem area. The way in which an EAP is used by company employees will depend on whether there is any element of coercion (occasionally the case with substance abuse), and whether the company is successful in convincing employees that the service is independent and confidential.

A different type of Employee Assistance Programme which we came across in the survey referred to above was one which did not utilize professionally trained counsellors, but which selected employees from the work environment, and trained them in counselling skills. These employees were 'advertised' to their peers who were encouraged to 'talk through' difficulties which they might be experiencing in the work setting. Peer counsellors in this scheme were supervised by personnel professionals who also assisted in referring on clients where problems were greater than could effectively by handled by the peer counselling approach.

Companies that are too small to set up their own EAP, but which want a similar service, can turn to an external resource rather than employing their own counselling psychologists. There are now organizations who market externally organized Employee Assistance Programmes, providing counsellors for a range of employee problems. Counsellors involved in such schemes are generally paid by the external EAP provider. Whether or not the 'referral to an outside counsellor' actually constitutes an Employee Assistance Programme is a matter for debate. Much will depend on the extent to which the external provider emphasizes integration of the scheme as far a possible with other company functions.

The issue of effectiveness

With the growth of Employee Assistance Programmes came the desire to prove their effectiveness. Organizations of course wanted to show that their programmes were both effective in solving employee problems, as well as being cost-effective. This made evaluation of such programmes difficult, with companies often being reluctant to use independent researchers. The literature on evaluation tends to distinguish between EAPs (with the focus on alcohol abuse), and broader programmes concerned more generally with stress management and reduction. One author (Murphy, 1988) suggests that EAPs can be viewed as stress reduction strategies to the extent that emotional stress is viewed as a causative factor in alcohol abuse, problem drinking is itself a cause of stress, and/or EAPs have a function in reducing the stress of supervisors whose job it is to deal with alcohol problems at work. At the same time, Murphy prefers to consider the evaluation of EAPs separately from stress management techniques and training. The same author also highlights a third category of employee assistance which he refers to as 'stressor reduction strategies'. He points out that this category is not at all common within the organizational setting, since organizations prefer to target the employee rather than situational factors!

Evaluation studies tend to focus on a range of techniques rather than on psychological counselling *per se*. In a review of the evaluation of stress management techniques in the work setting, Murphy (1984) highlights the problem of non-specific effects. Outcomes may, for example, relate more to the enthusiasm of the worker in taking part in a programme rather than to a specific technique of strategy. He points out that 'significant decreases in physiological measures observed in control groups may be a function of taking time out of the workday and sitting in a comfortable chair for 40 minutes or more' (1984: 8). In another study, by Bruning and Frew (1985), the researchers compared the effects of management skills training (including time management, conflict management and goal-setting) with meditation, physical exercise and combinations of these. While all techniques brought about reduction in pulse rate and systolic blood pressure, the largest reductions were observed for management skills training! Such studies underpin the importance of looking beyond the individual level of analysis and problem management to strategies which are more broadly preventative and which have the potential for producing a greater generalizable effect, both perhaps for the individual and for the company as a whole.

How an EAP programme actually works in practice will depend on the extent to which the scheme is a fully integrated part of the organizational structure as a whole, the availability of suitably trained professionals who can handle the role of counselling psychologist in that setting and the extent to which senior management is committed to the implementation of primary prevention strategies within the company concerned. Most EAPs and stress management activities within organizations, however, are more concerned with the secondary and tertiary stages of prevention (that is, the detection of early problems and the subsequent alleviation of this distress), than with the longer-term reduction in relevant risk factors within the organization as a whole. This may relate partly to a concern about costs, partly to the limitations of counsellors' skills in dealing with the complexities of organizational dynamics, and partly to a fear on the part of senior management that a commitment to primary prevention might open Pandora's Box. There is also a general cultural dimension at work here: in the survey referred to earlier (Orlans and Shipley, 1983), we found that the majority of organizations in our sample promoted the dictum 'if you can't take the heat, get out of the kitchen'. The cultural emphasis on success and achievement against all odds, and ignoring of the human costs, is one that is likely to resist 'pampering' its organizational employees.

Counselling values in the work setting

Even a cursory look at the literature on counselling highlights the potential for discrepancies between many values promoted in that context, and those to be found in most organizational settings. Carl Rogers (e.g. 1951, 1959), who has been one of the most influential theorists in the field of counselling, emphasizes three 'core conditions' which he regards as both necessary and sufficient for client change and development to occur. These core conditions, which are created by a combination of both skill and attitude on the part of the counsellor, are empathic understanding, respect for the client in the deepest sense, and congruence or genuineness. While there are variations among different schools of counselling as to whether certain conditions are regarded as sufficient in themselves for change, most approaches highlight the importance of empathic attunement in the counsellor–client relationship, as well as respect for the client's world-view and recognition of a client's capacity, and ultimate right, to choose his or her own destiny as far as possible.

Two worlds considered

The British Association for Counselling (1993) states that the overall aim of the counselling process is 'to provide an opportunity for the client to work towards living in a more satisfying and resourceful way', and that the counsellor's role in this process is 'to facilitate the client's work in ways which respect the client's values, personal resources and capacity for self-determination'. In the course of the counselling relationship, judgements are often suspended or bracketed, difference and idiosyncrasy are embraced and even celebrated, and the subjective experiences of the person are accepted and utilized in the course of this learning process which takes place over time.

If we turn now to the organizational domain, we find a world where judgement and decision-making are valued and actively developed among organizational members; where the emphasis is largely on objective experience and the pursuit of objective facts; where rational choice takes priority over feeling states; and where the system demands conformity to a set of rules and procedures, and exercises relevant controls within a hierarchical system to ensure that these are adhered to. I do not mean to suggest that these factors are not present to varying degrees in the counselling relationship – behavioural approaches to psychological counselling, for example, have as their keystone an objective, cause-and-effect model; cognitive approaches also would emphasize the importance of rational thinking, goal-setting and decision-making. At the same time, we know from the research literature that a crucial factor which underpins client change is the quality of the relationship between counsellor and client – whatever the counsellor's therapeutic orientation (see, for example, *inter alia*, review studies by Bergin and Solomon, 1970; Truax and Mitchell, 1971; Rogers, 1975). Organizations, however, do not tend to see themselves as being in business to form relationships – their task is to produce the 'widgets', or sell a service, with financial return being the key indicator of 'success'. 'Morale' and 'relationships' are important to the extent that they support this process – they are not ends in themselves. While more person-orientated organizations do in fact exist, we can also see how the changing legislative environment both in the UK, in Europe and in the USA, could be seen to have provided a coercive framework for some of these developments.

I am aware that the comments above might be taken as generalizations which run the risk of polarizing the two worlds of 'psychological coun-selling' and 'work'. At the same time, they do highlight some important differences between the two worlds – differences which need to be addressed if the two domains are to be brought together – not in the idealistic sense which pervaded the 1960s, but rather in the more pluralistic, communication-orientated mode of the 1980s and 1990s. Failure to take up this challenge at the planning and implementation stage of an organizational counselling programme can lead to conflicts re-surfacing in a range of disguises at a later stage. It can also result in the wasting of valuable resources including time, money, creativity and commitment on the part of counsellors, clients and managers, and increases the risk that any counselling facility introduced will proceed on the margins of organizational functioning – a version of the 'band-aid' activity referred to earlier.

Introducing a psychological counselling scheme into the work setting can also throw up contradictions within the system which have con-tinuously been present under the surface, but which have not been openly acknowledged. I am thinking predominantly of the tension in most organizational settings between 'helping' and 'controlling' employees. There is very often confusion on this issue, as well as a fear that to discuss the matter openly is likely to promote a greater 'us and them' awareness, open Pandora's Box, or possibly even encourage trade union involvement and the prospect of additional negotiating factors being placed on the table. For these reasons, there is a tendency to steer clear of this debate.

At the same time, much could be achieved by more open collaboration between different professionals. Many counselling psychologists have trained, and often move, in a world characterized to a considerable extent by cooperation and support, whereas the emphasis in the typical organiz-ational culture is on competition and 'winning'. The counsellor's role is also generally more reactive than that of the manager. Yet another difference is that counsellors tend to think and work in a qualitative way, whereas managers tend to think more quantitatively. It can be helpful if both parties can understand and explore these differences in ways that enable them to feel challenged rather than threatened. Both managers and psychological counsellors in any particular organizational setting are likely to gain substantially from an exploration of their own assumptions, values and goals, and to identify ways in which they might engage with each other as 'reflective practitioners' (Schoen, 1983). Positive outcomes could include: a greater understanding on the part of both counsellors and managers of important issues in the other person's world; better communication as a support to an on-going programme; a psychological counselling service which does not operate on the margins of organizational functioning; the integration of counselling activities with other organizational support functions; and a potentially wider usage of the service.

Knowledge base and skills of counsellors

Basic professional training programmes for counsellors can only be expected to produce a broad standard of competency for a range of 'clinical' settings. They are not designed – and the time frame does not allow – for training which would equip students with skills and insights for specialist settings. We must also remember that the fields of counselling and counselling psychology have only relatively recently become organized professions with professional accrediting bodies. In the UK the British Association for Counselling oversees general counselling practice, and it is only very recently that the British Psychological Society has introduced a separate Division of Counselling Psychology and the category of Chartered Counselling Psychologist. These developments have not as yet extended to the field of employee counselling, in terms at least of specialist recognized training and related accreditation. One international body, the Employee Assistance Professionals' Association (EAPS) does, however, address issues of counsellor development in this area, and administers a code of ethics for EAP practitioners. I would argue that there is now a case in the context of the UK to develop a more structured provision of specialist training for counsellors who wish to practise in the work setting. Such training could build on a basic counselling qualification, emphasizing the application and further development of skills already developed within the clinical domain. This post-qualification programme would be wide-ranging in itself, and would, in my view, need to include a range of topics.

Post-qualification areas of competence

Counsellors or counselling psychologists who had not had a background in organizational work would first need to become acquainted with the principles and dynamics of organizational behaviour. There is, in any case, a trend towards the closer association between clinical psychology, counselling and organizational behaviour, which may partly be due to the general cultural move away from the 'fragmentation' of diverse fields of practice, and partly to the recognition that several specialist perspectives may usefully be applied to certain 'problem' areas (Cooper, 1986). Training in this sphere would include a review of some fundamental theoretical ideas of the kind referred to earlier in my discussion of 'context'. Also included here would be an illumination of the 'meta-theoretical perspective' and its application to the counselling setting. Legislative dimensions concerned with health and safety of employees within the UK setting as well as in Europe and the USA might also usefully be reviewed.

A second broad area to be covered in an advanced training would be the many different types of counselling programme which could be implemented within the work setting, from the smaller, 'one part-time counsellor' type to the larger-scale Employee Assistance Programmes outlined earlier. Also relevant, however, is some understanding and practice in specialist areas which are likely to be more broadly utilized within the work context. For example, career counselling has, for a number of years, been widely conducted within the work setting, and is often linked to appraisal schemes. More recently, we have seen a considerable increase in the provision of redundancy counselling and outplacement schemes.

Of relevance also is the importance of distinguishing between 'counselling' and the use of 'counselling skills' as the latter have gained in popularity in the context of management training activities – often with insufficient exploration as to how these activities might differ in practice. Additional subjects which could fruitfully be covered in such a post-qualification programme would include an examination of the concept of 'organizational health', a review of Equal Opportunities legislation and policy, a consideration of research and evaluation issues together with a review of psychometric material which is often used in work settings, and an exploration of ethics, boundaries and responsibilities in employee counselling. While there might not be space in the programme to cover all of these subjects in great detail, it would at least serve to give counsellors a working knowledge of a range of issues relevant to organizational life.

Such training would partly cover 'subject areas' but would also equip professionals to deal more effectively with some of the dynamics in the job of employee counsellor. Counsellors might also develop confidence and a set of assertion skills which would enable them to interact more effectively with managers about work-related concerns. This would provide additional support (especially for an internally based counsellor) for dealing with some of the challenges of a role which is not independent of the organization, and where both individuals and the organization as a whole are 'key clients'. The latter kind of challenge might be more familiar to counsellors who work extensively with families, although even here the contracting issue is not quite the same. Those professionals are likely, however, to be more aware of the systems dimensions of presenting difficulties and the different ways in which problems manifest in such systems.

501

In the organizational setting also we find problems of power and politics very much in the foreground. Professionals who work in such settings need to be particularly aware of ways in which they can collude with strategies and dynamics that may not be in the best interest of individual clients or the system as a whole. A related issue is concerned with the question 'Who owns the problem?' – that is, deciding to what extent a presenting difficulty may be located within the individual client, and to what extent it should be located at another level in the organization. Tackling such issues effectively requires a high level of knowledge, skill and self-support on the part of the counsellor concerned. In addition to the points made above, a post-qualification programme for organizational counsellors would also need to include the provision of supervised practice and assessment, and opportunities for counsellors to share and discuss their work in a supportive environment. This would allow space for discussion of such questions as 'Who is my client?', 'Who owns the problem?', and 'What are the ethical implications of my work?'.

A review

In this chapter I have attempted to cover what I consider to be the key issues which need to be reviewed and explored in relation to the implementation of psychological counselling programmes in the work setting – whether these be implemented by 'counsellors' or by 'counselling psychologists'. Theoretical aspects of the field were highlighted at the start – partly because of the importance, in my view, of re-thinking some of our theoretical approaches in the fields of both counselling and counselling psychology, but partly also because, as Kurt Lewin has pointed out, 'there is nothing so practical as a good theory'. My reviews of counselling programmes for the workplace develop out of this theoretical perspective though with a more practical focus. Throughout I have attempted to emphasize the importance of developing a broader perspective – one which emphasizes many different elements in a total 'field' which is at once both demanding and challenging. The challenge is posed for professional counsellors who wish to extend their skills and insights into the organizational realm, for managers and decision-makers who wish to introduce some form of counselling into the work setting, and for counselling psychologists who are interested in developing a process-orientated, multi-level perspective to systems work. We need sounder underpinnings to our work in this field and I hope that my own insights and ideas – which have evolved in the course of my research and practice – have made some contribution to what is likely to be an on-going debate in a developing area.

References

Bannister, D. and Fransella, F. (1971) *Inquiring Man: the Theory of Personal Constructs*. Harmondsworth: Penguin.

Barkham, M. and Shapiro, D.A. (1990) 'Brief psychotherapeutic interventions for job-related distress: a pilot study of prescriptive and exploratory therapy', *Counselling Psychology Quarterly*, 3(2): 133–47.

Bergin, A. and Solomon, S. (1970) 'Personality and performance correlates of empathic understanding in psychotherapy', in J. Hart and T. Tomlinson (eds), *New Directions in Client-Centered Therapy*. Boston, MA: Houghton Mifflin.

Bott, D. (1988) 'The relevance of systemic thinking to student counselling', *Counselling Psychology Quarterly*, 1(4): 367–75.

Brazier, D. (ed.) (1993) *Beyond Carl Rogers*. London: Constable.

British Association for Counselling (1993) *Code of Ethics and Practice for Counsellors*. Rugby: BAC.

British Psychological Society (1994) *Division of Counselling Psychology: Rules*. Leicester: BPS.

Brown, G.W. and Harris, T. (1978) *Social Origins of Depression: a Study of Psychiatric Disorder in Women*. London: Tavistock.

Bruning, N.S. and Frew, D.R. (1985) 'The impact of various stress management training strategies: a longitudinal experiment', in R.B. Robinson and J.A. Pearce, (eds), *Academy of Management Proceedings*. San Diego, CA: Academy of Management.

Clarkson, P. (1989) *Gestalt Counselling in Action*. London: Sage.

Cooper, C.L. (1986) 'Job distress: recent research and the emerging role of the clinical occupational psychologist', *Bulletin of the British Psychological Society*, 39 (September): 325–31.

Cooper, C.L., Sadri, G., Allison, T. and Reynolds, P. (1990) 'Stress counselling in the Post Office', *Counselling Psychology Quarterly*, 3(1): 3–11.

Firth, J. and Shapiro, D.A. (1986) 'An evaluation of psychotherapy for job-related distress, *Journal of Occupational Psychology*, 59: 111–19.

Gaylin, N.L. (1993) 'Person-centred family therapy', in D. Brazier (ed.), *Beyond Carl Rogers*. London: Constable.

Gergen, K.J. and Kaye, J. (1992) 'Beyond narrative in the negotiation of therapeutic meaning', in S. McNamee and K.J. Gergen (eds), *Therapy as Social Construction*. London: Sage.

Kelly, G. (1955) *The Psychology of Personal Constructs*', Vols 1 and 2. New York: W.W. Norton.

Lewin, K. (1952) *Field Theory in Social Science: Selected Theoretical Papers*. London: Tavistock.

Milgram, S. (1974) *Obedience to Authority: an Experimental View*. New York: Harper and Row.

Murphy, L.R. (1984) 'Occupational stress management: a review and appraisal', *Journal of Occupational Psychology*, 57: 1–15.

Murphy, L.R. (1988) 'Workplace interventions for stress reduction and prevention', in C.L. Cooper and R. Payne (eds), *Causes, Coping and Consequences of Stress at Work*. Chichester: Wiley.

Norcross, J.C. and Arkowitz, H. (1992) 'The evolution and current status of psychotherapy integration', in W. Dryden (ed.), *Integrative and Eclectic Therapy: a Handbook*. Buckingham: Open University Press.

Orlans, V. and Shipley, P. (1983) *A Survey of Stress Management and Prevention Facilities in a Sample of UK Organizations*. A Report for the Stress Research and Control Centre, Birkbeck College, University of London.

Rogers, C.R. (1951) *Client-centered Therapy: Its Current Practice, Implications, and Theory*. Boston, MA: Houghton Mifflin.

Rogers, C.R. (1959) 'A theory of therapy, personality, and interpersonal relationships, as developed in the client-centered framework', in S. Koch (ed.), *Psychology: a Study of Science*. New York: McGraw-Hill. pp. 184–256.

Rogers, C. (1975) 'Empathic: an unappreciated way of being', *Counseling Psychologist*, 5(2): 2–10.

Schoen, D.A. (1983) *The Reflective Practitioner: How Professionals Think in Action*. London: Temple Smith.

Shipley, P. and Orlans, V. (1988) 'Stress research: an interventionist perspective', in J.R. Hurrell, L.R. Sauter and C.L. Cooper (eds), *Occupational Stress: Issues and Developments in Research*. London: Taylor and Francis. pp. 110–22.

Tittmar, H.G. (1988) 'Counselling for problem drinking: employee assistance programs versus employee counselling programs (a commentary)', *Counselling Psychology Quarterly*, 1(2 and 3): 221–8.

Truax, C. and Mitchell, K. (1971) 'Research on certain therapist interpersonal skills in relation to process and outcome', in A. Bergin and S. Garfield (eds), *Handbook of Psychotherapy*. New York: Wiley.

23

Enhancing Learning Skills

Peter Ross

This chapter focuses primarily on the enhancement of learning skills at university. It will be helpful to make some distinctions clear at this point, so that the reader will be sensitive to the meaning of terms from the literature, and so that the layout of this chapter will be seen as logical.

We are all used to the idea that a person may have good social skills but be socially inept. Anxiety often destroys the way the skills are deployed so the person cannot achieve a smooth social passage. Similarly, a person may have good learning skills, such as revision technique, but not use them in some or all situations due to inhibiting emotional factors. The literature often refers to the integration of skill and emotion as 'learning competence', but the context will make the broad or narrow use of 'skill' quite clear.

Neither emotional confidence or skills nor their integration happen suddenly. They are built layer by layer on previous experience. For this reason, it is necessary, in this chapter, to look at the process of the breakdown of learning competence as well as the process of maintenance and enhancement of existing competencies. The nature of the learning experience at secondary school level and the processes of transition, therefore, are of relevance.

Some of the research mentioned is from literature explicitly labelled 'counselling psychology'. Some of it is from educational psychology, the sociology of education, and the politics of education. It is all of relevance and subsumed here under 'counselling psychology'. This has been done because whatever the label of origin, the insights generated are a helpful background against which to do that most integrative of all activities, counsel people. It is done, too, because the research emerges from concern to understand the context of a problem and not see it as a pathology to be cured in isolation from everything else; and because the emotional implications of the research mean that, very often, the qualities of a counselling relationship are needed to facilitate client progress. For all these reasons, considerable space will be devoted to the development and implementation of self-concept in an educational context and, of course, to how this self-concept supports or undermines achievement.

The chapter therefore begins by looking at how gender is related to achievement. Then different kinds of knowledge acquisition and transfer are explored. This is followed by an examination of some facets of the experience of transition and, in particular, how personality, social class, homesickness and culture shock may defeat performance.

As the topic of test anxiety occupies considerable space in the literature as well as being the preoccupation of many a student, this follows. Then the special problems related to graduate student life are considered.

Although methods of counselling and other ideas to enhance learning competence may be found implied throughout the chapter, a section follows to give coherence to this. Finally, evidence of effectiveness is discussed, and conclusions drawn.

What is achievement?

A close-focus snapshot of achievement in higher education in Britain, followed by a wide-focus snapshot, provide some interesting contrasts. These contrasts will, in turn, provide a useful starting point for our exploration.

In the 1993 historical tripos at Cambridge, 15.9 per cent of the men gained firsts in part one as against 2.2 per cent of the women. In part two, 21.4 per cent of the men gained firsts as against 7.4 per cent of the women. The situation at Oxford is not very different. Why? Is one group just more skilled than another? Or are they implementing equally skilled but different selves? A look at the Universities' Statistical Record (USR) for the past decade or so is as revealing. Between 1979 and 1989 the number of pass degrees reduced from 16.8 per cent to 11.3 per cent. The number of first class degrees increased just a little but the number of second class degrees increased from 60.7 per cent to 71.4 per cent. Among the second class degrees, a '2.1' is now much more common that a '2.2', the latter having been the expectation and achievement of most students for generations. Is this a real improvement in achievement, even an improvement in teaching and learning skills, or could it be that UK universities are repositioning themselves in the market place of national and international competition?

The record of a decade or so shows that women gained fewer first class honours than men, even in traditionally 'female' subjects like English, Psychology and Nursing. Similarly, men also disproportionately under-achieve. About 9 per cent of men achieve thirds compared with only about 4 per cent of women. In fact, if we add the upper-second class degrees to firsts, we discover women do better than men in 34 of 50 subjects. We also discover, from the USR, that many universities now have more female undergraduates than male ones, and the USR statistics collected faithfully each year by University Careers Advisers tell us that women are less likely to be unemployed than men, six months after leaving university.

Why then are so many people concerned with female 'under-achievement' in the face of the facts? Does it suggest we think men can choose, and take, responsibility for themselves, but women cannot? Does it suggest we think women need better skills and confidence in taking the slightly more risky line in an examination script that (usually male) examiners value so highly? Or do women really have more sensible priorities and balance academic and personal lives better (as evidenced by the employment figures) but men cannot reconcile academic values with outside ones? Nowadays, firsts are valued almost exclusively as the entry threshold for research. Even here, there seems little connection between this and success.

Employers can often be heard to wonder out loud if a graduate with a first will get bored too easily. Employers make no secret of valuing confident personal skills derived of involvement in student organizations – the ability to work in a team, to organize, to negotiate, to delegate and so on. The employment evidence suggests women have got the balance about right.

Human beings are, without exception, addicted to being special. So, if the majority of women have chosen to be special in such a way, it may well say something about female roles in society. These roles vary of necessity in a dynamic way with the roles of men. Let us assume that the majority of men have also chosen to be special by their posture in society. That is to say, perhaps both men and women expect men to be more risk-taking (and, therefore, of necessity, do both 'better' and 'worse') than women. If this is so, we can expect that the underlying different self-concept may be implemented differently as learning skills are enhanced too. We do not yet understand why gender groups make the sequences of choices we observe. Thus sensitized, we can proceed to the literature.

Gender and identity

Most researchers have taken the view that the facts show women achieving less than men. Although the view already taken here records reservations about that, there is no doubt whatsoever that gender differences exist. It is helpful at the outset to note that the differences do not appear to exist in the results of mature students (Rogers, 1989), so the focus of inquiry must be on how the young differ academically.

Kelly (1988) did a meta-analysis of huge numbers of studies, world-wide, and reaffirmed that, as many had suspected, more interaction occurs between male students and teachers than between female students and teachers. Kelly was particularly concerned to note the 'invisible' nature of the problem. Although observers see it, classroom participants seldom see it. Billington (1993), in a subtle study of sixth form colleges in North West England, explored sex differences in student estimations of female and male student–teacher interaction in mixed-sex English and mathematics classes. He discovered that female students seemed to see female student–teacher interaction more clearly than they did male student–teacher interaction. Male students saw male student–teacher interaction more clearly than female student–teacher interaction. While helping to illuminate the previous study, it is not at all clear why students of this age should see members of their own sex more clearly. It may relate to the overwhelming importance of peer group pressure at this time.

At any rate, there was no direct evidence of a bias to males. Mifsud (1993) also found that, in secondary schools, boys did not get more praise, nor more criticism, nor have more teacher contact, nor initiate more interaction, nor get more questions, nor have more response opportunities. The evidence from the literature is, in fact, contradictory.

However, the vast bulk of the literature is clear about a number of factors of relevance. Among these are: that self-concept formation arises from interactions with significant others; that parental acceptance is fundamental to positive self-concept; that this role is largely taken over by teachers and peers as students enter school; that the formation of academic self-concept during middle childhood has a profound effect upon general self-concept and confidence. Almost 40 years ago, one of the founding fathers of identity studies argued for the latter (Erikson, 1959) and, recently, research confirmed it yet again (Leondari, 1993). So it is clear that the accumulated experiences of learning in childhood have an important impact on the effective underpinnings of general confidence in adults.

Researchers are largely agreed that female identity is embedded in relationships (especially a woman with her mother) in contrast to the way a boy has had to break away from relationships (especially with mother) to become a man. This difference in sensitivity to the influence of others is reflected in some of the research. Boggiano and Katz (1991) wondered why some students strive harder in the face of failure and others become resigned and helpless. They discovered that students with a tendency to extrinsic orientation fared best on slowly graded tasks, worked best to please the teacher and were very dependent on feedback. Intrinsically motivated students (i.e. 'the confident') took risks the others did not.

It may, therefore, be seen that self-esteem and confidence, with important different emphasis in meaning, may be critical to enhancing learning skills and achievement. Griffiths (1993) points out that self-esteem has largely been seen as a function of achievement – a very male formulation. She notes that from William James's formulation of 1892, 'self-esteem is the ratio of success to pretension' (ideal self), to Carl Rogers's more recent suggestion that unconditional positive regard and empathy builds self-esteem so people can set their own goals, achievement has been the theme. Indeed, high self-esteem as a function of experiences of being respected and valued is often assumed to lead to risk-taking and, therefore, achievement. By contrast, Griffiths points out that, for women, being embedded in the context of relationships may be of fundamental importance to self-esteem, that in some sense such embeddedness is an achievement. She points out that every self-concept exists in the midst of a process of constructing a narrative about ourselves. Being invited to belong, or being excluded from, or constrained by a group and their activities may be crucial to this. These 'belongingnesses' increase in number and complexity with maturity. Acceptance comes from family, community, class, colour, sex, creed, etc. and not achievement. Authenticity comes from avowing one's history and gradually transforming it, which may not be compatible with either total belonging (a 'first'?) or total unbelonging (a 'third'?). Family members are lovable to each other, regardless of achievement.

Thus it now becomes possible to appreciate the power of the Davies and Harré (1989) argument in trying to discover the meaning of the Oxford gender disparities. They suggest that one factor may be the very knowledge that scripts are randomly numbered and marked blind that prevents clear articulation of ideas – ideas which might be better presented in knowledge of relation of script to other. They suggest the agonistic rather than collaborative style of teaching may be a problem for women, and this would include science taught in a 'positivist–logicist' framework rather than in a fluid developmental one. Murphy (1982) found evidence to support this. He discovered that girls tend to do worse in examinations when multiple-choice questions are used than when concern for a contextual understanding can be shown. Although this research is far from conclusive, there are implications here for both university induction programmes and for counselling the academically unconfident.

Surface, Deep and Strategic learning skills

Basic tactics

Student productivity is most widely thought of (Fraser et al., 1987) as being a function of:

- **Aptitude**: ability, motivation and developmental stage.
- **Teaching**: the equipment and facilities as well as the quality and quantity of tutoring.
- **Environment**: support from home, from friendship networks, and from peers.

The thing which brings all this together is the student herself or, more accurately, the extent to which she takes charge of her own learning. The first task of any adviser is to encourage active learning rather than passive learning. It is very important to realize that, at this point, tension becomes part of the dynamic. Just as politicians pay lip service to the importance of democracy but frequently have a vested interest in preventing the voters knowing about what is really going on, so teachers may sometimes have a vested interest in student learning not being too active and therefore have an investment in not being too explicit with feedback and test results. Teachers value a certain amount of compliance in their students. Nevertheless, the pro-active student (to use the current jargon) is the assumption behind a very useful learning model proposed by Entwistle (1992) which labels learning skills as Surface, Deep and Strategic.

Entwistle suggests that a **Surface** level of involvement treats the work as an imposition, that the intention is to complete the task with minimum work, minimum reflection and minimum integration. This results, perhaps, in a failure to distinguish principles from examples. A **Deep** approach on the other hand involves active interaction with the material. The intention is really to understand fundamental principles. Evidence is weighed up in detail, logic is examined, and the student relates the material to the detail of previous knowledge and current experience. A **Strategic** approach involves determining marking schemes and criteria, the use of previous examination papers in revision and even gearing effort and attention to the perceived preferences of the teacher regardless of the student's own preferences.

No doubt most students vary their approach. As an undergraduate, I recall getting essay and assignment lists at the beginning of each term. I would carefully mark the list to show my tutor that I had either no interest in the topic and would do only the minimum to pass the course requirements while expecting no more effort from the marker than a tick, or that I intended to put huge effort in and would appreciate comments written all over the work by the marker and detailed discussion subsequently. This approach increased job satisfaction all around, but came unstuck when, much to the amusement of my tutor, I would rather diffidently announce that I had discovered an interest in a topic following some initial reading and that, therefore, all bets were off!

With increased competition for entry to university, there is a tendency among some teachers to encourage a strategic approach to learning to obtain university entry. There is evidence that the habit then creates problems in the transition period of the freshman year. Encouraging student flexibility of approach must be beneficial. This is an important life skill, for when in paid employment in years to come, time constraints will force priority-making just as it does at undergraduate level.

To make decisions on appropriate active approaches to work, students must be knowledgeable about possible approaches, and about themselves. It is at this point that the most subtle teaching and tutoring skills come into play. I recall a young history teacher despairing at getting an essay from me on the topic of medieval monasteries. He mentioned the problem to my tutor, who knowing of my interest in sailing, handed me a small book which had a chapter on the 'monastic' life of the lighthouse keeper. He had the essay within days.

Every university is littered with tactical study skill 'how to do it' books. Indeed, Study Advisers may run workshops on topics such as 'How to write essays'. In this short chapter, it is not intended to deal in detail with these matters, however valuable, as the material is widely available elsewhere. Instead, empowering students with 'Deep' knowledge about more subtle forms of knowledge acquisition will be suggested, based on recent research.

Knowledge about knowledge structures

A good deal of recent research in cognitive psychology has been devoted to discovering how background knowledge of a domain influences the formation of, and learning of, concepts. It has long been known that people usually perform better when they have knowledge. But why? As an undergraduate, I recall being an experimental subject for learning tasks. These were usually very difficult, being devoid of any obvious meaning, but this was important to try to make explicit any structural properties under test. By contrast, real-world learning is meaning-rich. As such, it can aid concept learning by telling students what the relevant features are likely to be, so simplifying and speeding learning through reducing student hypotheses-making. Knowledge helps students discover the rules which link otherwise disparate features, and may help memory storage. To take a simple example, anyone who has attended a lecture on fish imagery in Shakespeare can never again watch or read a play in quite the same way! Murphy and Allopenna (1994) have shown that, not only can knowledge check and support learning, but aid it. Like anything else, knowledge has both benefits and costs in learning. In pointing out the knowledge structures of their subject matter, including the uncertain fuzzy edge boundaries of what might be known, and how it might be known, rather than what is known for sure, faster learning results. But the cost is that, if so-called knowledge is less than correct, it can slow down learning. In fact, the fastest learning appears to occur if the structure of the knowledge is consistent with the structure of the input. Researchers are in an ideal position to make explicit to their students all the possible ways of looking at the phenomena under scrutiny, so giving them practice at manipulation of knowledge boundaries before the boundaries freeze and just 'the facts' remain, for all practical purposes. Researchers are also in an ideal position to sensitize students to what can be missed, and has been catastrophically missed in the past, by those who know a great deal about a field.

Unsupervised learning

But what if there is no teacher to suggest categories, themes, frames, scripts, boundary rules, or network methods? And if there is no teacher to give us feedback that we have 'got it right'? In fact, a great deal of home study and study in a library is like this. By analogy, every researcher has the problem of inventing descriptions and criteria for trial classifications against which to contrast their material with what is 'known' already. As Clapper and Bower (1994) point out, some pattern or signal has to be distinguished against the background 'noise' to provide a starting point for a category. As they note, the kinds of language we adopt are crucial. For example, one can say 'Individual stimuli are collections of features. Each feature is a specific value of a generic attribute. Values are discrete (big step boundaries like square versus circle) or continuous (shades).' Different languages will provide different 'glasses' to look through, though natural categories are often fuzzy.

A good, but simple, example is provided by my recent effort to learn the Beaufort Scale of Wind Force. Many universities now teach sailing theory, though in my own case a Royal Yachting Association tutor who knew everything about sailing but little about teaching, simply said 'You must know that!' An item looks like this: 'Force 8 (Gale) – Moderately high waves, breaking crests, foam streaks. Deep reefed mains. Storm jib. Wind speed 34–40 knots.' There are ten similar items. The learning problem is that these things emerged 'naturalistically' over generations of experience at sea, and the only apparent logic is Force 1 to 10, which is not difficult to remember. Any attempt to learn them horizontally as a list (as written above) seems doomed. What about vertically? The wind speeds read 1–3, 4–6, 7–10, 11–16, 17–21, 22–27, etc. Again, no logic. But wait! 4, 7, 11, rhyme. At last, a possible 'category' emerges! It has some utility, but not enough to predict the other numbers directly by one rule. In fact, a linked change of two rules gives the other numbers easily enough, and so on. Good teachers do not leave students to invent boundaries but the necessity to do so here neatly illustrates the naturalistic problem of finding predictive feature correlations.

Clapper and Bower (1994) point out that logic would suggest that a person would scan the entire set of stimuli in order to compute an optimal classification scheme for the entire set. In fact, what we actually do is opportunistically create new categories and 'learn' incrementally in such situations. The important point here is that knowing the possible approaches to structuring knowledge in our own subject areas empowers us to learn. Without that knowledge, we struggle, and remain passive dependants on 'correct' boundaries of knowledge provided by others. We need teachers to teach us how recipes are made as well as teach us a specific recipe and enjoyment of that specific product.

Confidence, creativity and accuracy

It has been known for a long time that, in general, people's levels of confidence are far too high for tasks which offer even moderate levels of difficulty. An often-quoted assumption is that this is because alternatives to the hypotheses in question are simply neglected. We have an over-optimistic 'positive set'. This remains a serious problem for all subject areas at university level where self-taught student time far outweighs being formally taught. Koepler (1994), however, has discovered that this happens if students are asked to evolve an hypothesis provided for them, but not if they are asked to generate one. In the latter case they, of necessity, have to produce a series of hypotheses and choose the one most likely to be 'true'. Their confidence in it is commendably less, and a lot more likely to be an accurate judgement of its value.

Utilizing expert knowledge

Up to this point, our concern has been with enhancing learning skills for original learning of topics, through making students aware of the rules governing knowledge of various kinds. But what happens when we try to utilize knowledge already gained? Consider, for example, a recent task of mine. It fell to me to try to teach Masters degree students how to assess counselling clients where their symptoms could have been a function of various kinds of psychological depression or a virus. The decision reached, and the confidence in it, would have fundamental implications for treatment strategy. An important first step was to ensure the student knew that decision processes under pressure (with clients stacked up to be seen) were often different from decision processes where the nature of the demand (to assess) was known in advance, where the kind of assessment was known and enabled prior experiences of the problem type to be reflected upon, and where decisions may well have to be justified (to a GP, or insurance company, or coroner's court in the event of suicide) rather than be routinely noted. We then needed to look at the way cues from both the presenting situation and our own emotional reactions triggered different 'expert knowledge' processing routines as we 'called up' selected past experiences as templates. Although it is not possible to go further into detail here, the important point is that all this needed discussion before any actual content knowledge was involved. Once again, knowledge about knowledge processes is vital. Whittlesea et al. (1994) may be helpful on this issue.

Much of what has been suggested here has been aimed at ensuring students feel empowered by their experience of the accuracy of their judgement and, hence, predictions. Once predictions turn out to be false, or inaccurate, confidence is undermined and a feeling of helplessness is not far away. This, in turn, given enough accumulation of experience and intensification of emotion, forms one possible building block for depression.

One of the earliest casualties of this scenario is, of course, concentration. It is these emotionally charged factors in the breakdown of learning skills to which we can turn in the section after next.

The mentally and emotionally stuck

It is evident by now that the author advocates the optimum use of a student's capacity to teach himself. Years of experience in counselling students who have become so emotionally and mentally stuck that they are in danger of dropping out of university, have convinced me that students all too easily develop an all too passive attitude to learning as they are fed by their teachers each day. The most important thing here is an active and, therefore, positive attitude. What does this mean? What I see before me is (i) fear — fear of failure, fear of having to justify — and (ii) low energy - whether despair, helplessness or depression. The first priority is, therefore, to galvanize the student into energetic action. 'This is not a rehearsal for life' I might say. 'It's real life. This moment will never come again. Let's not waste it. Let's make sure you are getting from it the things you most want.'

Most students, who up to now have thought only about how to deliver what their teachers want, are intrigued. Having caught real attention, my intention is to lure them back to their natural integrated state as stimulus-seeking animals rather than their current 'distanced from own feelings' state. 'What do I want?' they ask. Thus, forced to engage in the normal dynamic of observer of self/self rather than that of a child pleasing her parent they invariably work towards 'to have fun', 'to enjoy myself', 'to feel fulfilled', 'to feel I'm getting somewhere', etc. Whatever the reply, what it amounts to is 'to feel study is relevant to getting me to my objectives and to feel it doing so'. Thus the hardest part of the work has been done: to reframe the situation. Now 'my objectives' are at the fore. If necessary, the student could, no doubt, be encouraged to jump up and down at home chanting 'me, me, me, and sod everyone else' to reduce fear, increase assertion and motivation, etc. but it has never been necessary in my experience. The student's experience of an accepting, valuing, empathic relationship seems to be quite sufficient!

This is not a 'how to do it' book but, instead, one on the underlying psychology. The previous paragraph is written, however, to bridge the gap between reality and the research. Reality is the counsellor, the study adviser, the tutor or the teacher saying to the student (who will shortly be encouraged to say it to himself): 'Now, imagine that book you don't understand is an essay written for you, the teacher, by your student. You're not very impressed by it. It's not well written. Now, be the teacher and write down the questions you need to ask to see if the student really understands the material.' Thus, creativity is harnessed because fear is abolished. Variations on this theme may be to get the student to teach you, the much more junior student, and so on, but the dynamic described is the central principle.

The research supports this 'active student as self teacher' view, not only for the 'stuck' but for routine purposes also. Wankowski (1991) shows how this may be elaborated, albeit from a somewhat differing base. 'What was your student's objective in this part of the essay?' we can ask. 'What strategy and facts are marshalled in the argument?' 'Is the argument logical?' and so on. As Wankowski notes, Wlodkowski (1985) is a resource book of the greatest value.

Those who use person-centred or cognitive approaches will find the end of the second paragraph above rings bells with them, while those who take a personal construct approach will be at ease with the 'explorer' theme. In each case, the relevant research is applicable.

The breakdown of learning competence in transitions

Introduction – a personal vignette

About six weeks after entry to university, I was beginning to doubt my wisdom in thinking I could get a degree. I had received good marks for essays, classes were fine, I enjoyed lectures, but my hours in the library were less rewarding. I often despaired at my inability to master material quickly, and there was so much of it. If it was this difficult now, what of the much more difficult future? I went to see my tutor. 'Should I leave?' I asked. There was a long silence as we sipped coffee. 'I had exactly the same problems as a new student,' he said, looking me directly in the eye. 'Now, as an eminent professor, I still frequently feel the same way.' Again, a long pause. 'Only, now, I have the confidence to know that it's just that the material is badly written.' A surge of relief went through me as we chatted on. It was only much later that I realized three things had been achieved by this highly skilled man. I had been made to feel I shared an 'insider's' secret which conferred a sense of belonging on me, I had received my first lesson on how to cope with the inevitable feelings of failure and incompetence which accompany academic life, and I felt my emotional bond with the man grow a little due to the very personal encounter. In short, I left his room a much more confident student, motivation restored and much enhanced. Motivation is the most important thing of all, for it can compensate for the lack of many skills.

School to university

Wankowski (1991) points to crucial emotional factors in student disenchantment. At school, the relationship between student and teacher is a mutually satisfying one. The teachers get their emotional and economic pay-off through pupil success in examinations, it fulfils them. The students enjoy the 'intimacy' and 'specialness' of the attention given by the teachers. In short, mutual emotional satisfaction results. University teachers get their primary emotional pay-off from mutuality with other researchers in their field throughout the world. Their status in their academic department rests largely on their publications, and increasingly on how much research money they can attract. Teaching and tutoring are often distractions, along with administration, from this emotionally rewarding activity. Students are encouraged to become independent learners, giving themselves self-critical feedback until finally they are sufficiently independent to use teachers as 'consultants'. Quite naturally, students coming straight from the sixth form emotional hothouse, have expectations of rapid academic success at university. Confidence dissipates rapidly when they discover how 'ordinary' they are in their new environment, and even more so with the experience of difficulties. They have to take responsibility for asking for support, whereas in the past it has simply been there. Away from family and friends, not yet having consolidated new relationships with peers, many find the pace of academic work too much, and spiral out of control all too rapidly. An easily formed empathic relationship with a tutor or counsellor can be magic in such cases.

Personality and success

It has long been known that there is little correlation between 'A' level results and degree success. Wankowski, however, discovered that if one applies the Eysenck Personality Inventory to successful entrants, there is a good correlation for those labelled stable introvert (phlegmatic), as opposed to the unstable introverts and the extroverts.

The vulnerable student, therefore, tends to be impulsive, is thrown by the need for rapid adjustment to the new environment, needs emotional support, feedback and stimulation in large quantities but is reluctant to ask for it, especially from authority. His work patterns rapidly become haphazard, and tenacity and resilience quickly dissipate. He is often 'sent' for counselling, too late, as opposed to seeking help himself.

The successful student tends to be relatively independent already, have the confidence to not let pressure and inconsistencies bother him. He enjoys the idiosyncrasies of staff rather than is thrown by them. He does not fear authority. He makes friends easily. He enjoys long hours alone in the library, and is not addicted to constant social stimulation. Meeting a problem, he discusses it early with others rather than letting it become a crisis. Being rewarding to be with, staff and other students tend to give him more attention than he perhaps should have. He becomes even more resilient, and independent.

Although these factors are particularly important in the transition from school to university, they are also of importance throughout under-graduate life for a sizeable number of students. Therefore, the dissemi-nation of those facts among teachers, lecturers, potential students and students, could reduce the problem. Independence is a learned skill like any other. Although personality factors are involved, workshops run by many counselling services on 'Developing Personal Confidence', 'Asser-tion' and the like can help greatly.

Social class

Macfarlane (1993) points out that social class is an important factor in transition and achievement. The lack of knowledge and, therefore, confidence, which comes from being the first person from a family to enter higher education, has always been recognized as a potential problem. Even at 18, many working-class children have less facility in language than the middle class. Social skills, vital to rapid adjustment, may differ markedly, as very different social models have been available in the family. Values and interests may differ from the norms of the new environment, and create conflict where support should be, even where social skills are good. The University of Reading has a Land Management department which attracts many students from land-owning families. Quite by accident, a hall of residence corridor had been populated by these students and a lone student from a very poor background found herself among them. Unable to find common values, interests and activities 'with anyone' she felt so alienated 'from the university' she almost left at the end of the first week. She was rescued by a rapid change of hall and a few counselling sessions to rebuild her shattered emotions.

Homesickness

Homesickness has attracted much speculation over the centuries. When Napoleon's armies roamed Europe it was thought that perhaps it was due to changes of atmospheric pressure – farmers coming down from the hills to fight, whales beaching themselves on arising from the depths, and so on. The remedy tried was being spun around in a higher tower. Nowadays, homesickness continues to debilitate. Fisher (1989) found that about 60 per cent of first-year university students reported symptoms. The experience of Reading University is similar, but less than 1 per cent of that 60 per cent require serious counselling time. Each year, perhaps a dozen or so rapidly return home, some eschewing all help, some unable even to cope with intensive care. Attempts are made to skill new students in dealing with the problem by sending them written information in advance. Many university counselling services assist with welcome pro- grammes and encourage students to resist the temptation to get stuck into academic work immediately. Instead, putting time into making friends and joining clubs, societies and sports teams can be much more important in preventing drop-out.

Culture shock

The culture shock experienced by international students can often be severe (Furnham and Bochner, 1986). Much of the distress is expressed somatically, so that initial presentation is often to a physician with subsequent referral for counselling. Once again, advice is offered to prospective students encouraging them to take advantage of any possible trips away from home within their own country, or to nearby countries, before embarking on a journey half way around the world. Many British universities refuse to accept students where a condition of the grant is that it must be repaid in case of academic failure, so reducing stress. In these ways and others, prevention can be attempted.

The counselling psychology of homesickness and of culture shock overlaps a good deal. Bowlby (1969, 1973, 1980) has described in detail the effects of, and processes involved in, separation from, and loss of, people and familiar places. The many theories of bereavement, involving high levels of shock, panic, anxiety, disbelief, reminiscing and pre-occupation with home and lost family (see Fisher, 1989) are very relevant here too. However, the student has chosen to deprive herself of the valued home, unlike the situation in bereavement when the death of a loved one is imposed. The evidence shows that students sent by their governments to study overseas 'for their country' as opposed to having actively chosen to do so largely for their own benefit, have more emotional problems, especially in transition. For the same reasons, students who have suddenly been given a visa or scarce currency against all expectation and previous refusal, and who arrive without a period of psychological preparation, usually show more distress than others. The most important theoretical background, however, is the literature on 'learned helplessness' and 'hopelessness in depression' (see especially Seligman and Seligman, 1975, but also the central theory of Fisher, 1989). This 'learned helplessness' approach is crucial, not only because it provides counsellors with strategies, but because the ideas appeal intuitively to students on induction programmes and can therefore be used to empower them with the skills of prevention. It is easy to give students examples of how, in coming from one culture (including a British sub-culture) to another, predictions of how others will react when we do something familiar to us are quite simply confounded. One can describe the sense of frustration and then mounting anger which accompanies further attempts to influence and change which are, in turn, confounded. Finally, one can describe the mounting sense of helplessness and finally hopelessness which follows and undermines our whole sense of identity. Most students can readily work out simple strategies which flow from this. First, make it a priority to continue to play rugby here if you did at home, or any other activity, so you experience a continuity of the 'rules' being the same! Secondly, spend significant time in the early weeks with students from your own country. Their behaviour will fulfil your expectations and give you some balance against all the unfulfilled ones. Thirdly, make sure you discuss frequently with both your fellow nationals and a friendly home resident, the 'strange' experiences you have so you can assign meaning to them within the model and regain your sense of powerfulness.

There is too little space available to elaborate further, but the general drift is clear – knowledge empowers, not only by providing meaning and a feeling of control but by suggesting action and skills which can be employed to enhance this.

Test anxiety and stress

Tests of many different kinds form part of the everyday experiences of all students in higher education. Enhancing their skills to take these tests is, therefore, important. These skills are skills associated with the tests themselves and skills associated with reducing the anxiety preceding and/ or accompanying the tests. British universities have a long tradition of placing great emphasis on the final examinations, which can account for all of the marks, or a proportion of them. The remainder may be allocated for course work, a dissertation, field trip reports, etc. Sometimes marks from the previous year are taken into account. The increasing development of modular degrees may take the edge off much of this, but at the moment 'finals' still account for a great deal of anxiety and for this reason will be the focus here.

It will readily be apparent that if a student can learn the skills of coping with one form of anxiety or stress, it will facilitate later coping; and should the counsellor or tutor succeed in teaching these skills, much saving of later resources may accrue too.

Those who teach the skills of taking tests discover the need to focus on two facets of the experience in particular. The first is to explain the psychology of long-term and short-term memory and translate this into possible actions. Depending on subject, this may have implications for revision techniques; for example, reducing down data on to small cards which contain triggers for memory systems. This compressed data is discharged on paper and 'unpacked' immediately the examination begins (and sometimes before one has even read the paper!).

The second facet is to explain about preferences for risk-taking, and help each student find a stance with which they are comfortable. The literature on cognitive dissonance can assist the counsellor here. This might mean very deep study of only a small number of areas on the assumption that one will answer any question on them which comes up and that these areas will come up, or selective study, or a wide-spectrum approach. Each has important implications for time and strategy in revision. It is important to check that students have these kinds of psychologically based skills as well as the more mundane, such as time management, before proceeding, as considerable confidence can thereby be gained.

It is, of course, essential to deal with the immediacy of anxiety or stress symptoms, when presented, before anything else. A student who is hyperventilating will not have the concentration to benefit from any helper's wisdom. One who attributes physical symptoms to impending death and feeds her panic with such thoughts needs the situation explained and reframed in preparation for more demanding involvement in self-help skills. For this purpose, simple physical explanations provided in a handout can be invaluable. Paying attention to the symptoms and assigning negative meanings to them is always a far greater problem than the symptoms themselves.

Clark (1994) makes clear that, in a person-centred approach, the focus is not skills-based, but on getting the client to trust herself, to put down roots in her own values rather than be controlled by those of others. In gaining awareness through the relationship with the counsellor she not only learns to shift the focus of evaluation from the 'other, outside' to the 'self, inside' but to self-appreciation too.

Psychodynamic approaches depend, as always, on a combination of insight and exploitation of the power of transference. As one is attempting to work fast, humour is helpful in taking the sting out of deep insights when the relationship is still very fragile.

The most common approach to test anxiety is, however, the cognitive-behavioural one in its many forms. This teaches the student quite directly how to choose and use skills of thinking and feeling influence. Whatever the actual brand within this broad spectrum of work, research shows again and again (and whether the application is in depression, anxiety or anything else) that presentation of a credible rationale is a key component. Given that this rationale and the action plan and homework which spring from it will be very different from the current thinking of the client, the second key component is to ensure the client is able to experience the counsellor's acceptance, and even pleasure, in the relationship if humour can be generated. Complete acceptance of the person must be distinguished from pointing out thinking and feeling choices, and their consequences. When this kind of therapy goes wrong, it most often is a function of insufficient attention paid to this aspect of the relationship. Humour can so easily be injected, even at the start: 'Well, I am so relieved to hear you suffer all these distressing symptoms! Given what you say to yourself, there would be something really serious wrong with you if you did not!'

Abrams and Ellis (1994) give an exceptionally clear account of rational emotive behaviour therapy (REBT) procedures, but few who use other cognitive-behavioural approaches would find much to quibble with. Clark (1990) provides what is probably the best general account of cognitive-behavioural procedures in practice.

A great deal of research shows that complex cognitive processes become automatic with only a little repetition. Were it not to do so, so much of our attention would be absorbed in processing the trivia of everyday life that we would be much disabled. Just as a person who has always worn glasses is unable to see the world a different way, so we are all in difficulties being aware of our basic assumptions. It is the job of the counsellor to make explicit the assumptions of the client, so the client can be invited to examine them, and their consequences. Must, should, ought, have to, and similar action words all bear examination together with words and phrases which incorporate judgements, such as: stupid, foolish, can't stand it, failure, and so on. Each is very gently unpacked. The client is made aware of how constant repetition creates problems of feeling and shown how to begin to change the situation. Students, being mostly both young and bright, react very well to this kind of approach.

Graduate student learning skills

There is little research on the subject of enhancing the skills specific to graduate students. Wright (1992) surveyed what little there is.

The basic problem is uncertainty with regard to what a PhD is and, therefore, what skills are required to reach that objective. By tradition, it has been thought of as a distinct contribution to original knowledge. But it is also seen as training, learning and knowledge generation of many different kinds. In recent years, efforts have been made to run courses in research methods for such students or to precede the PhD with a Masters degree doing the same. Many of those who write books on study skills have advocated this, seeing one-to-one teaching as too time-consuming. But the reality is that surveys show most graduate students have little interest in research skills in general but every interest in the specialized skills they themselves will need.

Within the experimental 'hard' sciences, the PhD is often a small but detailed addition to knowledge gained by joining a research team already under way. The student has a topic selected for him, and little interpretation is ultimately needed. Within the arts, reinterpretation of known facts is often the centrepiece of the work. The topic has been chosen by the student and an extensive 'broad canvas' context is needed in the write-up. Paradigms are at different states of development in different fields and impose different skills. For example, a student of physics will usually work in a team. A student of fine art will work largely alone. The student who switches fields presents a particular problem. For example, a student of biochemistry who has never had to write an essay begins a PhD in, say, food science flavour research and discovers he cannot write properly. After much consternation in the academic department concerned, he is sent for counselling and is discovered to be dyslexic!

The above facts have given rise to the notion of the importance of having a Profile of Research Skills necessary for doing a PhD in any particular area. One can then test incoming students and work with them to correct defects. Such a profile might look like this:

- Independence as a learner
  The capacity to think for oneself, initiate exploration
  Willingness to consult without being dependent
- Intellectual skills
  Convergent and divergent thinking flexibility
  Knowledge of problem-solving routines for the subject
- Relationship skills
  Social skills; team-building; diplomatic skills
- Confidence
  Capacity to sell ideas and research; able to present findings to grant sponsors
  Capacity to think positively when meeting inevitable setbacks
- Common sense
  Able to manage equipment pragmatically and fix it; manual dexterity
  Use technicians and support staff in a positive way
- Organizational skills
  Capacity to plan, organize, meet deadlines, use library facilities, etc
- Motivation
  Critically important not to be doing a PhD just because the money is available and the graduate couldn't get a job or think of anything else to do!

As may be seen, some of these factors are for consideration at selection, some can be taught. Whether the political realities of life would allow a half-empty chemistry department, desperate for students and particularly those who come with grants, to turn someone down for lack of such skills, is doubtful, but at least provision could be made for special support, thereby reducing the possibility of failure. Much research needs to be done on this.

Methods of enhancing learning competence

Although this book is not a 'how to do it' type book, throughout the chapters suggestions have been made for helping strategies. Although the mundane 'how to write an essay' type skill has been ignored, the more complex knowledge structures in Deep and Strategic learning skills have been mentioned. Helping students through their developing an active approach has been emphasized throughout while personal vignettes have displayed the important impact of emotionally charged 'belongingness', etc. Some attempt has also been made, for example in the section on test anxiety and stress, to make clear that a number of therapeutic orientations, such as person-centred, psychodynamic and cognitive-behavioural, can all be successfully employed. In the section on the mentally and emotionally struck, yet another approach, that of role reversal, has been suggested as having much to commend it.

It cannot be emphasized enough that the key to enhancing learning competence is the power of a counselling relationship. The counsellor or tutor, in being accepting, patient, focused and empathic, models for the student the constructive relationship the student could have with him- or herself, thereby freeing up the blockage. This is why role reversal strategies and 'as if' strategies work. They reframe the relationship, and with it dissolve the inhibiting emotional underpinnings of the original relationship.

Creativity is crucial. So, for example, a dyslexic student, only too aware that a disability with short-term memory is undermining confidence, can be focused emotionally on the success of being a good musician. This emotion then generalizes to enhance all confidence and an additional try at further verbal techniques. Another example of a common problem is loss of motivation which so often stems from a sense of powerlessness to shape and influence events. The anxiety resulting from this perception further reduces concentration, so exacerbating the problem. With the help of tutor or counsellor, any sense of map, structure, stepwise sequence, lever or even timetable with discrete steps, can help to produce a perception of the possibility of success and hence renewed motivation. In each case, empowerment is the goal, as has so often been the theme here.

Evidence of effectiveness

Do any of these ideas and methods actually work? The everyday experience of counsellors, study advisers and their student clients suggests that they do. To go the extra step of proving that is another matter. Indeed, it is only by proving and disproving methods in comparative terms that the field will improve. The author knows of no reliable and methodologically valid research which shows such methods to be effective beyond any reasonable doubt.

There is, however, much evidence of effectiveness from practitioners evaluating their own work. Mostly in these studies, the student clients have been asked to evaluate the work. Wankowski (1991) and Frederick et al. (1981) are good examples of these and both studies report very positive outcomes. The outcomes are in line with similar yearly (but unpublished) survey results at the University of Reading Learning Resources Centre.

Other measures, such as lower drop-out rate, lower examination failure rate etc., are difficult to isolate as a function of a study adviser's intervention as opposed to the many other factors which influence outcome. The costs of such research are so large and the problems of depriving equally deserving comparison groups of help so great that no methodologically reliable work has yet appeared.

Conclusions

The initial sections of this chapter on gender and achievement throw into sharp relief the fact that different groups may choose different outcomes, of equal value to them if not to commentators. Enhancing learning skills is about enhancing choice in achievement, not telling people what opportunity costs are acceptable to them, and what balances they should see as acceptable in enhancing their identity. Students need to be empowered through knowledge of the learning processes as well as of content, and an approach using Surface, Deep and Strategic learning skills has been surveyed here. Many of the enhancement ideas suggested here have focused on various aspects of process.

It has only been possible to cover briefly the breakdown of learning competence in the transition from school to university, in homesickness, and in cultural adjustment, as well as the implications of personality and social class factors. What these aspects reveal, however, is the complex way skill and emotion interact to produce confident flexible behaviour, or its opposite, and the necessity for a counselling relationship to unscramble the problem within a time scale which makes continuation on academic courses possible.

Various methods of enhancing learning skills have been mentioned throughout the text, though reliable evidence of effectiveness is hard to find. Further research is clearly very necessary if the field is to develop.

References

Abrams, M. and Ellis, A. (1994) 'Rational emotive behaviour therapy in the treatment of stress', *British Journal of Guidance and Counselling*, 22(1): 39–49.

Billington, J. (1993) 'Sex differences in student estimations of female and male student–teacher interaction', *Research in Education*, 50: 17–26.

Boggiano, A.K. and Katz, P. (1991) 'Maladaptive achievement patterns in students: the role of teachers' controlling strategies', *Journal of Social Issues*, 47(4): 35–51.

525

Bowlby, J. (1969, 1973, 1980) *Attachment and Loss* (vols 1, 2 and 3). New York: Basic Books.

Clapper, J.P. and Bower, G.H. (1994) 'Category invention in unsupervised learning', *Journal of Experimental Psychology: Learning, Memory and Cognition*, 20(2): 443–60.

Clark, D.M. (1990) 'Anxiety states', in K. Hawton, P.M. Salkovskis, J. Kirk and D.M. Clark (eds), *Cognitive Behaviour Therapy for Psychiatric Problems – A Practical Guide*. Oxford: Oxford University Press. ch. 7.

Clark, P. (1994) 'A person-centred approach to stress management', *British Journal of Guidance and Counselling*, 22(1): 27–37.

Davies, B. and Harré, R. (1989) 'Explaining the Oxbridge figures', *Oxford Review of Education*, 15(3): 221–5.

Entwhistle, N.J. (1992) 'How students learn and how they fail', in J. Radford (ed.), *Talent, Teaching and Achievement*. London: Sigma Forlag/Jessica Kingsley.

Erikson, E.H. (1959) 'Identity and the life cycle', *Psychological Issues*, 1: 18–164.

Fisher, S. (1989) *Homesickness, Cognition and Health*. Hove: Lawrence Erlbaum.

Fraser, B.J., Walberg, H.J., Welch, W.W. and Hattie, J.A. (1987) 'Syntheses of educational productivity research', *International Journal of Educational Research*, 11: 145–252.

Frederick, J., Hancock, L., James, B., Bowden, J. and MacMillan, C. (1981) *Learning Skills: a Review of Needs and Services to University Students*. Parkville: Centre for the Study of Higher Education, University of Melbourne.

Furnham, A. and Bochner, S. (1986) *Culture Shock*. London: Methuen.

Griffiths, M. (1993) 'Self identity and self esteem: achieving equality in education', *Oxford Review of Education*, 19: 3.

Kelly, A. (1988) 'Gender differences in teacher–pupil interaction: a meta-analytic review', *Research in Education*, 39: 1–23.

Koepler, D.J. (1994) 'Hypothesis generation and confidence in judgement', *Journal of Experimental Psychology: Learning, Memory and Cognition*, 20(2): 461–9.

Leondari, A. (1993) 'Comparability of self concept among normal achievers, low achievers and children with learning difficulties', *Education Studies*, 19(3): 357–71.

Macfarlane, B. (1993) 'The results of recession: students and university degree performance during the 1980s', *Research in Education*, 49: 1–10.

Mifsud, C. (1993) 'Gender differentials in the classroom', *Research in Education*, 49: 11–22.

Murphy, G.L. and Allopenna, P.D. (1994) 'The locus of knowledge effects in concept learning', *Journal of Experimental Psychology: Learning, Memory and Cognition*, 20(4): 904–19.

Murphy, R. (1982) 'Sex differences in objective test performance', *British Journal of Educational Psychology*, 52: 213–19.

Rogers, J. (1989) *Adult Learning*, 3rd edn. Milton Keynes: Open University Press.

Seligman, M. and Seligman, P. (1975) *Helplessness*. San Francisco: Freeman.

Wankowski J. (1991) 'Disenchantment, a syndrome of discontinuity of learning competence' and 'Increasing students' power for self teaching', in K. Raaheim, J. Wankowski and J. Radford (eds), *Helping Students to Learn*. Milton Keynes: The Society for Research into Higher Education and Open University Press. chs 7 and 11.

Whittlesea, B.W., Brooks, L.R. and Westcott, C. (1994) 'After the learning is over: factors controlling the selective application of general and particular knowledge', *Journal of Experimental Psychology: Learning, Memory and Cognition*, 20(2): 259–74.

Wlodkowski, R.J. (1985) *Enhancing Adult Motivation to Learn: a Guide to Improving Instruction and Increasing Learner Achievement*. San Francisco: Jossey-Bass.

Wright, J. (1992) 'Selection, supervision and the academic management of research leading to the degree of PhD'. University of Nottingham (unpublished PhD thesis).

24

Developing Stress Management Programmes

Stephen Palmer

Since the turn of the century the field of stress and its subsequent management has been widely researched. Yet there is still no clear consensus by researchers as to what are the most effective interventions for a given situation in spite of the energetic and flourishing activity of practitioners. This particularly applies to the field of occupational stress management where many promises are made that interventions will reduce occupational stress even though much of the existing research may not take into account the multifaceted nature of stress and therefore be methodologically flawed (see Reynolds and Briner, 1994).

This chapter will focus more on the major issues and problem areas involved in stress, stress management and the development of stress management programmes rather than concentrating on how to set up a programme. It includes sections on the physiology of stress and the main theories of stress.

Physiology of stress

Assuming an individual perceives a situation as threatening, two physiological systems are activated. The first involves the autonomic nervous system (ANS), which is responsible for controlling the heart, lungs, stomach, blood vessels and glands. The ANS consists of two sub-systems: the sympathetic (SNS) and the parasympathetic (PNS) nervous systems. Messages are conveyed along neurones from the cerebral cortex and the limbic system to the hypothalamus. (The limbic system is associated with the emotions of anger and fear which correspond to the well-known 'fight' or 'flight' stress response.) The anterior hypothalamus triggers the sympathetic arousal of the ANS. The main sympathetic neurotransmitter is called noradrenaline which is released at nerve endings. The adrenal gland is located on top of both kidneys and is involved with the production of a number of stress hormones. The SNS is directly connected via a nerve to the adrenal medulla, the central part of the adrenal gland, which produces noradrenaline and adrenaline. Depending upon the relative levels of these two catecholamines, which are released into the blood supply, the body is prepared to either fight or flee. Generally noradrenaline is associated with anger and the fight response, whilst adrenaline is associated with fear and the flight response. In contrast to the SNS which prepares the body for action, the PNS aids relaxation and conserves energy. The PNS sends its messages by a neurotransmitter called acetylcholine which is stored at nerve endings.

The second system is known as the endocrine or pituitary–adrenal cortex system. In this system the hypothalamus instructs the pituitary to release adrenocorticotrophic hormone (ACTH) into the blood which then activates the outer part of the adrenal gland, the adrenal cortex. The adrenal cortex synthesizes cortisol which aids fat and glucose mobilization, reduces the inflammatory response and lowers allergic reactions. Individuals who generally feel depressed and believe that they have a loss or lack of control over events experience increased levels of cortisol and this reduces the effectiveness of the immune system leading to increased susceptibility of individuals to suffer from minor colds to more life-threatening diseases (see Gregson and Looker, 1994). This is seen in individuals who have suffered from long-term stress. The adrenal cortex releases aldosterone which increases blood volume and thereby increases blood pressure. The pituitary also releases thyroid stimulating hormone which stimulates the thyroid gland to secret thyroxin. Thyroxin is responsible for increasing the metabolic rate and raises blood sugar levels. If the individual perceives that the threatening situation has passed then the PNS restores the person to a state of equilibrium. If the person has suffered from a severe trauma this is less likely to occur immediately after the threat is over. Some research suggests that individuals prone to distress have reduced PNS activity which unfortunately heightens the response of their ANS. This could account for the difficulty in treating clients with Generalized Anxiety Disorder.

The literature of stress-related disorders and diseases is prolific. However, it is important for the counselling psychologist to ensure that the disorders are directly attributed to stress-response over-activation and are not due to organic causes such as tumours, etc. Some of the psychological symptoms of stress include anxiety, anger, depression, intrusive thoughts/ images, obsessions and reduced self-esteem. The behavioural responses to stress include aggression, substance abuse, avoidance, checking rituals, insomnia, talking fast and withdrawing from relationships. The physio-logical symptoms of stress include allergies, angina, asthma, backache, cancer, coronary heart disease, diabetes, diarrhoea, high blood pressure, migraines, muscle tension, palpitations and ulcers. This list is not com-prehensive and many more psychological, behavioural and physiological responses and symptoms of stress have been found or claimed in the literature, leading to a simple theory of cause and effect for the lay person and sometimes the practitioner too!

History and theories of stress

In this section we will focus on the various ways in which stress has been conceptualized, taking a historical perspective. It is worth noting that before a stress management programme is developed, the practitioner needs to decide which approach best fits the individual or organization as this may shape the type of intervention undertaken.

The word 'stress' was originally derived from 'stringere', a Latin word used three centuries ago to describe hardships. Subsequently it denoted strain or effort. At the turn of this century the relationship between illness and 'busy' individuals was observed. In 1908, Yerkes and Dodson concluded from their research that up to a certain optimum point, performance improved as pressure or stress increased. However, beyond this optimum point, performance was reduced. Later Walter Cannon in 1935 developed the concept of homeostasis which basically reasserted the earlier views of Claude Bernard from the previous century who suggested that regardless of external changes an individual's internal systems should ideally remain unaltered. This could almost be likened to a modern central heating system which is thermostatically controlled.

The basic theories of stress can be summarized under three headings: stimulus, response and interactive variables, which will now be examined.

The **stimulus** variable or engineering approach conceptualizes stress as a noxious stimulus or demand that is externally imposed upon an individual which can lead to ill health. In this model stress can also be caused by too much or too little external stimulation.

The **response** variable or physiological approach is based on Selye's (1956) triphasic model involving the initial alarm reaction (sympathetic-adrenal medullary activation), the stage of resistance (adrenal-cortical activation) and the stage of exhaustion (final reactivation of the sympathetic-adrenal medullary system). This response process is known as the **general adaptation syndrome**, where an individual will eventually suffer from physiological 'diseases of adaptation' to stress caused by aversive or noxious external stimuli if the last stage of exhaustion is reached. However, the model does not take into account that some noxious external stimuli (such as heat) do not necessarily trigger the stress response.

Both the stimulus variable and response model are based on the stimulus–response paradigm (SR) and disregard the importance of cognitions and perceptions which may exacerbate, moderate or inhibit the activation of the stress response in any given situation. In applying the SR paradigm, much research has been undertaken into the possible effect of specific life events upon individuals. A number of life event scales (e.g. Holmes and Rahe, 1967) have been developed which were based on averaging procedures which totally ignored the personal meaning of life events for each individual and subsequently only weakly predict stress-related illness episodes. It is recommended that the **interaction** between the external and internal worlds of the individual needs to be included in any practice-based theory of stress.

The interactive variable or psychological approach to stress attempts to overcome the deficiencies of the earlier models. There have been a number of proposed psychological theories: the interactional and the transactional. The interactional theories centre on the fit between the person and their environment (e.g. Bowers, 1973). Others focused on the interactive nature of job demands and decision latitude (Karasek, 1981), but later studies have indicated that there is only weak evidence to support real interactions between specific demands leading to disease. If anything, research discovered that the additive nature of different demands increased ill health.

Generally, transactional theories of stress focus on the cognitive and affective aspects of an individual's interactions with their environment and the coping styles they may adopt or lack. One of the most well-known theories is that of Lazarus and Folkman (1984), who defined stress as resulting from an imbalance between demands and resources. They assert that a person evaluates a particular incident, demand or on-going situation. This initial evaluation, known as primary appraisal, involves a continuous monitoring of the environment and analysis of whether a problem exists. If a problem is recognized then the stress response may be activated and unpleasant feelings and emotions may be experienced. The next stage, secondary appraisal, follows when the person evaluates his or her resources and options. Unlike the earlier models of stress, the important issue is whether the person recognizes that a problem exists. Once recognized, if the demands are greater than the resources only then does stress occur. If the resources are greater than the demands then the person may view the situation as a challenge and not a stress scenario. If the person is too inexperienced to recognize that a particular problem exists then this would not be considered as a stress scenario. This is an important distinction as, ironically, it is the subjective and not the objective assessment of any scenario that may trigger the stress response.

Cox (1978) developed a five-stage transactional model of occupational stress which was later developed into a general multimodal-transactional theory of stress to help counsellors and counselling psychologists apply stress theory to stress counselling practice (in Palmer and Dryden, 1995)

531

and thereby enabling the appropriate selection of psychotherapeutic, psychoeducational, emotion- and skills-focused interventions. According to Palmer and Dryden, in stressful situations attempts are usually made by individuals to deal and cope with the problem by making a combination of behavioural, affective, sensory, imaginal, cognitive, interpersonal and physiological changes. If the problem remains, however, eventually the person's health may be negatively affected.

One aspect of stress research that can lead to misunderstandings is that in the literature the concepts of 'stress' and 'strain' are often confused. In physics stress is externally imposed upon a substance and the strain is the substance's reaction to the stress. This can be equated to the loss of a job being a stressor and the psychophysiological reaction being the strain.

The next section will focus on a number of issues that need to be considered when developing stress management programmes for individuals, families or organizations.

General issues

Coping

Although coping is a fundamental part of the equation in interactional and transactional models of stress, it is an area that has been under-researched and not well understood. It has three main properties.

1   It is a process involving what the person thinks and how the person behaves in a stressful situation.
2   It is context-dependent as it is affected by the specific situation or initial appraisal of it, and then by any resources the individual has to deal with the situation.
3   Coping as a process is 'independent of outcome', that is, it does not depend upon whether it does or does not lead to a successful result.

Coping can be divided into emotion-focused and task-focused strategies which include rationalizing/re-appraisal of the problem, de-awfulizing a problem, seeking social support, denial, information-seeking, delaying action by using distraction/relaxation, developing better skills and competency to deal with the specific problem, and symptom management. In addition, coping has been described as a problem-solving strategy which starts with 'recognition and diagnosis (analysis) followed by actions and evaluation through to re-analysis' (Cox, 1993: 21; see this reference for an overview of this subject). However, this cycle of action may actually exacerbate a stress scenario if an unhelpful approach is chosen. Helpful or adaptive behaviour is considered as developmental, whereas unhelpful or maladaptive behaviour is defensive in nature and includes problem denial, procrastination and substance abuse. Research indicates that if individuals on balance use more maladaptive coping strategies in contrast to adaptive ones, then they increase their chances of suffering from negative health outcomes.

Social support

One major coping strategy that can reduce stress or help reframe stressful situations is appropriate social support. A spouse, a member of the family, a work colleague or friend may provide a stressed individual with somebody who appears to care and listen. This helper may enable the individual to use problem-solving skills or reframe the importance of specific events. Research has shown that compatible spouses help the partner cope with stress-related problems. In another study unemployed workers who were able to obtain social support from the community, family and friends had significantly fewer symptoms of stress than those who had less support. In addition, those who had less support also had a higher serum cholesterol level and suffered more depression (Gore, 1978). Caplan (1967) suggests that the family reflects its members' values and behaviours and thereby offers support and 'reality testing'. A family's belief system helps an individual to interpret and understand the way the world works. Family members may offer 'guidance, mediation, opinions and often, practical assistance such as baby-sitting, repair work or financial aid' (Cooper et al., 1988: 72). It can also provide a rest place and support when a member suffers disappointment or failure. However, a family that does not offer support or is itself a stressor, may leave its members more susceptible to stress. In the workplace, co-workers can act as a surrogate family providing support, constructive feedback and friendship which helps buffer the individual from stress. One study (Margolis et al., 1974) with 1,400 subjects found that the lack of support systems and non-participation were significant predictors of work-related stress and strain. In work and non-work situations social support that helps an individual to assess and resolve a problem is preferable to colluding support that prevents a person from accurately appraising the stress scenario.

Locus of control

This concept was developed by J.B. Rotter (1966) in the 1960s and focuses on the amount of control individuals believe they have over situations. Individuals with an external locus of control believe that they have limited or no influence over events whilst internals believe that they do have influence. This construct can be viewed as a continuum and not bipolar. Perceptions of control increase the ability to deal with frustrating situations and thereby reduce anxiety and stress, whereas little or no perceived control can increase anxiety and depression, and negatively affect psychological health. Paradoxically, when individuals with an internal locus of control perceive that they are unable to influence the outcome of a stress problem, their level of anxiety is inclined to rise higher than a person who has an external locus of control. There is a possibility that when given a choice 'internals' choose occupations where they can exert control over their work environment thereby reducing stress.

The coping construct could be viewed as individuals attempting to exercise control over their stressful environment and perhaps the control construct is the most relevant issue and not coping. Therefore stress management programmes that help individuals to believe they have control over situations or control over their responses to different situations, whether realistic or otherwise, may ameliorate the effects of stress.

Type A behaviour

In the late 1950s two cardiologists, Meyer Friedman and Ray Rosenman (1959), asserted that specific overt behaviours were associated with increases in blood cholesterol, blood clotting time, incidence of arcus senilis and clinical coronary artery disease. They developed methods of assessment and later labelled the particular behaviour pattern Type A for descriptive purposes. The specific overt behaviours included a chronic sense of time urgency, impatience, polyphasic activity, explosive speech patterns, aggressiveness, free-floating hostility, extremely competitive, high-achieving and very strongly committed and involved in work. One of the mainstays of Type A assessment is the structured interview (SI) (Rosenman, 1978) method, although self-report instruments such as the Bortner Rating Scale (BRS), Framingham Type A Scale (FTAS) and the Jenkins Activity Survey (JAS) are often used as they are less time-consuming and easy to apply. However, the validity of the JAS self-report instrument has been questioned as its classificatory agreement with the SI is low and the JAS has sometimes led to negative outcomes in studies.

Studies such as the Western Collaborative Group Study found that Type A individuals are twice as likely to experience coronary heart disease than non-Type A individuals (known as Type B). Studies that have not used the JAS as a measure tend to support this conclusion in population studies.

Interestingly, Ragland and Brand (1988) reported a greater risk of mortality with Type B individuals who had survived a CHD incident than with a similar group of Type A individuals. This may indicate that Type A individuals who died at their first CHD incident may differ from Type A survivors and perhaps the latter deal with the CHD incident in a more adaptive manner than Type B individuals.

Type A behaviour has been described as a coping pattern, a learnt style of behaviour, and as a personality trait by various researchers. Glass (1977) asserts that Type A behaviour is due to a strong desire to control events which can lead to exhaustion in challenging situations where there is a lack of control or ambiguity. Glass believes that the Type A individual is more likely than the Type B individual to feel helpless in these situations. Price (1982) suggests that the Type A behaviour and hostility is due to low self-esteem which is moderated by constant achievement. There is some evidence for both theories which would suggest that cognitive or rational emotive behavioural therapy designed to dispute irrational beliefs about control and/or self-esteem may be beneficial. More recent research has found that 'anger-in' and 'potential for hostility' were the two main predictors of atherosclerosis (Dembroski et al., 1985). Individuals with both problems increased their chances of developing atherosclerosis. This research indicates that the most relevant issue that needs to be focused on in cardiac counselling or preventative stress management training may be these areas and not other so-called indicators of Type A behaviour such as impatience.

Fortunately, research shows that the three main CHD risk factors, that is, Type A behaviour, hypertension and serum cholesterol, can be reduced by using stress management techniques (see Bennett and Carroll, 1990). Some of the methods successfully used to reduce Type A behaviour have included relaxation, cognitive restructuring, graded behavioural assignments, anger management training, anxiety management, cognitive-behavioural therapy, rational emotive behaviour therapy, meditation, assertiveness training, stress inoculation, problem-solving, general coping abilities training, visuo-motor behaviour rehearsal and weight training. The simplest intervention involving the daily self-monitoring of blood pressure has also resulted in a decrease in blood pressure. It is unclear how this intervention works. In one study behaviour therapy had better results than psychoanalytic therapy and control groups at a 6-month follow-up. A few studies have found an increase in cholesterol levels after psychotherapy or stress management interventions which has been difficult to understand. However, generally one stress management intervention may lower the three risk factors for CHD. It is worth noting that there are some differences in outcome between the research studies undertaken in Europe and those of North America. Perhaps the self-report instruments are not valid for the different cultures, and counselling psychologists may need to take these issues into consideration when developing programmes.

The 'hardy personality'

One of the problems with the Type A construct is that it does not adequately explain why some individuals do not suffer from stress-related illness even though they are in stressful situations or occupations. Suzanne Kobasa (1979) developed the 'hardy personality' theory to account for this inconsistency. She suggested that 'hardy individuals' shared three major beliefs, summarized below:

Commitment: belief in oneself and what one is doing, including involvement in many life situations such as work, family, relationships and social institutions and thereby maintaining a balance.

Control: belief in oneself having influence over the course of events. Also seeking explanations for why something is happening with a focus on one's own responsibility.

Challenge: belief that change is the normative mode of living.

Hardy individuals would tend to perceive difficult situations as challenges and not as stressful by using cognitive coping skills to keep stressors in perspective. Unpleasant events would be interpreted as new opportunities instead of threatening situations. This may explain why some Type A individuals do not suffer from ill health or cardiovascular disease as they also have beliefs similar to those of hardy individuals. Due to hardy individuals being committed to many life situations they are more likely to be able to obtain social support which is an additional buffer against stressors. The hardy individual theory goes a stage further than Rotter's locus of control theory as it includes additional constructs. The belief that change is the normative mode of living would help hardy individuals to cope with the change that is now occurring in industry with downsizing and redundancies.

Other factors

There are a range of other different factors that counselling psychologists need to consider when developing stress management programmes: age, ethnicity, cultural background and sex. An individual's biological age may influence how the stress response is activated and whether the individual perceives a particular situation as stressful. At different stages in life an individual may have different goals and objectives which can be thwarted by life events. For example, a job redundancy at 25 years may be seen in a different light from a redundancy at 55 years by the same person especially if there are financial and familial responsibilities at a particular age. A young manager may respond to a stressful situation by feeling slightly anxious and with a minute rise in blood pressure. The same manager in a similar situation 20 years later may suffer from panic attacks and angina due to long-term stress, smoking and poor diet. If an individual's self-esteem has been heavily dependent on work-related achievement, on retirement the person can develop reduced self-esteem leading to depression or psychosomatic symptoms of depression. Preventative programmes can focus on these issues depending upon the age of the individuals.

Minority groups in work and social settings can experience both overt and covert racial prejudice which may lead to heightened levels of stress. Racist attitudes and behaviour can exacerbate a low self-esteem that minority group members may have due to their social setting and previous life experiences. They may also have a reduced social support network which can act as a buffer against stress. Cooper et al. (1988: 68–9) suggest that 'when someone from a minority group moves into a supervisory or management job held previously only by whites, no successful role models or mentors will be available to offer support'. American studies have consistently shown that black employees have less job satisfaction than whites, although this may reflect the type of work black employees are given and their relative socio-economic status. Often the belief systems and behaviours of members from cultural sub-groups may be in conflict with those from the predominant cultures. Unfortunately, the Eurocentric bias in counselling approaches and the fact that most counselling psychologists and trainers are white, educated, middle class, possibly possessing different values and communication styles, could lead to inadvertent cultural oppression by the imposition of Western values on their ethnic minority clients (see Alladin, 1993). This raises issues for counselling psychologists developing stress management programmes for minority groups or mixed groups in counselling, clinical, family or industrial settings.

Life expectancy of men is lower than women by about eight years. This could be due to a number of factors including Type A behaviour, alcohol intake and smoking as well as genetic and hormonal reasons. With the changing role of women in society and, in particular, the dual-career couple, women may experience additional stressors. Although the so-called 'New Man' may exist, surveys have indicated that behaviourally he is more likely to be an 'Ambivalent New Man'. Therefore women may have a career and a home to maintain. This may lead to role conflict and role overload. In Western society female white-collar employees in dual-career families suffer more stress than female blue-collar workers. This could be due to female blue-collar employees being in work longer and consequently having had more time to adapt (Cooper et al., 1988).

Some of the main issues relating to stress and its management have now been covered. The next section focuses on the stress management programmes for the individual, the family and for organizations, still with reference to the available research.

Stress management programmes for the individual

When developing stress management programmes for the individual the counselling psychologist will be influenced by the needs of the client who may require stress counselling/management for a current problem or preventative stress management to help cope with daily hassles and general stress reduction, or a combination of both. If the individual is stressed by a current problem then interventions based on cognitive-behavioural and problem-solving methods are generally effective. Although relaxation and distraction techniques may have some benefit for symptom management they may not necessarily help the individual to reappraise or resolve the problem or stress scenario. If the problem will resolve itself over the course of time then non-directive counselling may appear to be just as effective as more prescriptive or focused approaches. In fact Blowers et al. (1987) reported modest improvements with both non-directive counselling and anxiety management training in the treatment of generalized anxiety. However, further research is required to discover whether non-directive counselling helps individuals manage or resolve future problems. Surviving a difficult life event may in itself lead to an increase in self-efficacy which will help the person adaptively appraise and thereby manage similar events in the future.

In counselling, a thorough assessment of the problem and the client's symptoms may guide the counsellor towards the appropriate interventions to use. Palmer and Dryden (1995) have found using the multimodal assessment procedures developed by Lazarus helpful. This involves close examination of the seven modalities that Lazarus believes comprise the entire range of personality: Behaviour, Affect, Sensation, Imagery, Cognition, Interpersonal, Drugs/biology. A questionnaire can be used to assist this process (Lazarus and Lazarus, 1991). By assessing each modality, it may become apparent that an individual, for example, avoids doing certain useful behaviours, feels anxious, has physical tension, catastrophic imagery, irrational thoughts, passive–aggressive behaviour, and is taking medication for headaches. Once the assessment of each modality is finished a series of research-based techniques and interventions could be discussed and the rationale explained to the client and the most useful interventions applied. Technique selection may depend upon which modality the client may be more sensitive to. Therefore, in the previous example, if a client's catastrophic imagery appears to trigger high levels of anxiety then coping imagery may become the desired intervention. Furthermore, individuals suffering from specific stressors such as financial problems do not necessarily find the interpersonal and emotional strategies as helpful as those individuals with relationship difficulties. These factors need to be considered when developing stress management programmes.

Taking into account the stress research and interactional theories of stress there could be a variety of objectives in an intervention, for example:

- to solve the problem;
- to alter the way the client responds;
- to help the client reappraise the stressor;
- to help the client change the nature of the stressor.

These may need a range of skills, techniques or interventions to help the individual to manage stress. Consequently, the counselling psychologist also needs to be competent in these skills. As research does not indicate whether stress management programmes are any less effective when applied in group settings as opposed to one-to-one sessions, counselling psychologists working in under-resourced organizations may need seriously to consider running groups. This requires additional skills, such as facilitation, etc.

Effectiveness of interventions

The important ethical issue for the counselling psychologist is to design an intervention that is based on research and has face validity with the client. For example, there is limited research that points to psychodynamic interventions helping individuals to overcome situation-specific phobias and panic attacks, whereas there is much more published research showing the benefits of using cognitive-behavioural techniques. There is an interesting paradox in the field of psychotherapy and stress management, that however compelling the published research is for a particular approach, different forms of psychotherapy generally 'appear' to have similar outcomes (Shapiro and Shapiro, 1982). This 'equivalence paradox' is still being researched to find the specific mechanisms that lead to change during psychotherapy and stress management training (Reynolds et al., 1993). When exploratory therapy (psychodynamic and interpersonal) and prescriptive therapy (multimodal cognitive-behavioural) were compared the clients gained personal insight during exploratory therapy and problem definition/solution after prescriptive therapy. The overall outcomes may appear to have been equivalent but not necessarily at either the skills or personal insight levels. Long-term follow-ups would have provided useful information to ascertain which approach actually helped the individual to deal effectively with future stress scenarios.

If the client wants to receive preventive stress management training then a psychoeducational approach could be applied. Some examples are stress inoculation training, cognitive-behavioural skills training, rational emotive behaviour training, multimodal skills training, assertion training, Type A modification, relaxation training, lifestyle management and physical outlets. From the initial assessment, skills deficits such as cognitive skills or relaxation skills may become apparent and these could be the focus of the intervention. These methods have also been used successfully in group stress management training. What is not so clear from the published research is which is the best approach or technique to use for a particular individual. Furthermore, most research has been undertaken with subjects suffering from clinical disorders such as generalized anxiety. What is needed is more research with non-clinical populations and evidence that preventive stress management programmes actually help such individuals manage future stress scenarios.

Considering that the research indicates that a wide range of interventions may help reduce stress and the risk factors involved in coronary heart disease, the most important aspect of a stress management programme may be to help clients increase their subjective belief of control over a particular stressful situation or their psychophysiological response to it. This may help to explain why even placebo interventions such as 'bogus' subconscious retraining (White et al., 1992) can help to reduce stress and anxiety if a convincing rationale is provided. This study found that didactic psychoeducational cognitive, behavioural, or cognitive-behavioural 'stress control' training for large groups had enhanced post-therapy improvements whilst even the placebo group maintained progress compared to the waiting list. In this study the cognitive and the behavioural training groups were slightly more effective than the cognitive-behavioural group. White has suggested that more training may have been required to teach both cognitive and behavioural techniques to the subjects. This could possibly account for the cognitive-behavioural group being less effective. In a different study, Butler et al. (1991) found cognitive-behavioural therapy superior to behaviour therapy. Powell (1987) found that clients rated 'the experience of being in a group and meeting people with similar problems' and 'information about anxiety and stress' higher than learning any active coping skills. This may indicate that counselling psychologists running stress management programmes should see their role as facilitators, educators and organizers of self-help services rather than just individual therapists.

Stress management programmes for the family

Stress and strain in families or households is common. This poses a problem for the counselling psychologist in that sometimes family-orientated interventions may be more effective than individual counselling for a member of a family. Stress in families and households has been measured by a variety of indices including 'expressed emotion' (Vaughn and Leff, 1976). Family-based interventions have usually focused on the enhancement of constructive communication thereby reducing 'high expressed emotion', that is discussions in preference to rows. However, when the underlying causes of conflicts were mainly due to a family member suffering from severe physical or mental disorders, improved communication alone did not always reduce stress. This led to the inclusion of additional problem-solving strategies into the approach (see Falloon et al., 1993).

Falloon et al. (1993: 11) listed the problems most likely to benefit from behavioural family therapy strategies: children's conduct disorders, learning disabilities and autism, adolescent behavioural disturbance, marital and family conflict, sexual dysfunction, drug and alcohol misuse, family violence and child abuse, premarital counselling, divorce mediation, eating disorders, suicide prevention, residential care, criminal offending problems, depression, bipolar disorders, schizophrenia, anxiety disorders, relapse prevention, chronic physical health problems, dementias, prevention of stress-related disorders in high-risk groups. The main steps of a time-limited family-based stress management intervention as described by Falloon et al. (1993: 223) are:

- assessment of current ways of dealing with stress, and current personal goals;
- education about specific disorders;
- enhancing communication about problems and goals;
- enhancing problem-solving as a household group;
- specific strategies for dealing with difficult problems.

A thorough assessment will help the design of the stress management programme whereby the individual and group needs and skills deficits are ascertained. The emphasis on communication skills training is to ensure that group members learn how to communicate and listen actively to each other. This is essential if the household or family members are going to use a six-step group problem-solving approach to deal with any problems or stress scenarios as they arise. The six steps are as follows.

- Identify the problem (or goal).
- List all possible solutions.

- Highlight probable consequences.
- Agree on the 'best' strategy.
- Plan and implement.
- Review results.

One of the long-term goals is to train the family to be able to cope with stressful problems without the constant aid of a counsellor. The problem-solving approach has also been used in couples counselling, adolescent conflict, and dementias. Controlled studies demonstrate the effectiveness of the problem-solving approach in a variety of different settings (see Falloon, 1991). The challenge for the counselling psychologist is to make an accurate assessment, teach the necessary skills and encourage the participants to use their skills to resolve a crisis in the most efficient way. The stress management intervention is considered effective if it is able to avert the impact of a stressful event within seven days of its occurrence (Falloon et al., 1993).

What would be useful are more studies comparing different family-based interventions, for example, problem-solving approach versus relaxation training, and the indications and contraindications of interventions based on research outcomes.

Stress management programmes for organizations

In the United Kingdom, it has been estimated that 360 million working days are lost every year through sickness (Sigman, 1992). This apparently costs industry £8 billion per annum and, according to the Health and Safety Executive, at least 50 per cent of the lost days are stress-related. If these statistics are to be believed then stress has become one of the major causes of absenteeism in the workplace. Is it any wonder that the 'stress industry' has become big business for stress researchers and practitioners all keen to help employers reduce stress and increase profits. This section will focus on the main causes of organizational stress, stress management interventions undertaken in industry and whether, in fact, the increasing practitioner activity is underpinned by flawed research. If counselling psychologists wish to offer clients (organizational or individual) effective stress management programmes it is important that they understand the key issues involved.

Figure 24.1 illustrates diagrammatically the organizational stress process and highlights the relationship between stress factors, the individual and the symptoms. According to Cooper and Marshall (1976), there are a number of common stress factors which include those intrinsic to the job, relationships at work, role in the organization, career development,

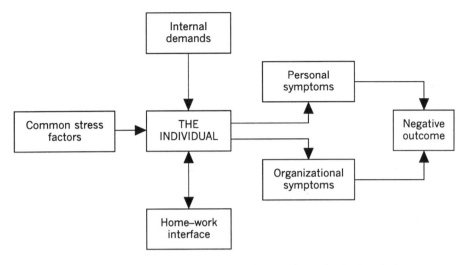

Figure 24.1   *The relationship between stress factors, the individual and the symptoms (Palmer, 1993: 7)*

organizational structure and climate. In addition, the individual may place internal demands upon him- or herself which may exacerbate a seemingly innocuous event into a stressful situation. The home–work interface may also be a cause of stress.

According to the research, the organizational indicators or symptoms of stress include: high staff turnover, high absenteeism, increased health care claims, increased industrial accidents, industrial relations difficulties, lowered efficiency, low morale, poor quality control, poor job perform-ance, staff burnout and suicide. However, these symptoms need to be seen in a wider socio-economic context as during world-wide recession employees may be reluctant to change jobs or take time off work for illness, especially if such action would put their income in jeopardy. The symptoms of stress that the individual may suffer from include hyper-tension, anxiety, depression and alcohol abuse to serious conditions such as coronary heart disease.

To understand occupational stress it is useful to look at the common factors, home–work interface and the internal demands.

Factors intrinsic to the job

The more common environmental workplace stressors include air pollution, dust/fibres, heat, humidity, lighting, noise, noxious chemicals/ nicotine, sick building syndrome, static electricity, uncomfortable chairs/ work stations, and visual display unit glare. These stressors may come under the remit of health and safety regulations, and unlike other workplace stressors employers can be obligated to rectify these problems. Studies have found other factors intrinsic to the job, including boring repetitive tasks, dangerous work, deadlines, excessive travel, isolated working conditions, long hours, shift work, work underload/overload, and the work too difficult for the individual. Sloane and Cooper (1986) found that some occupations are more stressful than others, for example, acting, advertising, dentistry and the police service are more stressful than accountancy, geology, insurance, nature conservancy and horticulture.

Relationships at work

Interpersonal relationship difficulties can be a major cause of stress in the workplace. Problems can arise for a variety of reasons, which can include office politics, competition, Type A behaviour and hostile individuals. Recent studies have highlighted bullying as another pressure. Quick and Quick (1984) believe that group/peer pressures, leadership style, abrasive personalities, social incongruence and social density are also stressors.

Role in the organization

There are a number of different role demands that can contribute to stress: ambiguity, conflict, definition, expectations, incompatibility, overload, underload and sign. The long-term effects can be very detrimental to the individual's health; for example, research indicates that employees who supervise others are more likely to suffer from coronary heart disease compared to those who are responsible for machinery. Often employees are unaware of the source of their role stress and therefore are unable to change or manage it.

Career development

Career development can cause stress at different stages of an employee's progress or lack of progress through a company. Promotion prospects can become increasingly difficult to achieve as an employee moves higher up in an organization, and in addition, older employees may need to retrain to be able to use new technology. This can lead to stress in some individuals. Older employees tend to share a number of fears: demotion, obsolescence, redundancy, job security and forced early retirement. In some 'high-tech' industries, computing software for example, the income earned at the bottom of the career ladder can sometimes be the same or higher than those in management.

Organizational structure and climate

Some organizations have a structure and climate that may restrict the autonomy of employees whereby they do not believe that they have much control or influence over their workload. They may find the work unchallenging and boring and this can contribute to job dissatisfaction, resentment, apathy and reduced self-esteem. Ageism, racism and/or sexism can also be prevalent in some organizations, with management not taking a proactive approach to deal with these issues. Some organizations are reluctant to involve staff over redundancies thereby increasing uncertainty and lack of control. In addition, downsizing has brought an increase in the use of technology and reduced staffing levels with those remaining doing more work.

Internal demands

If it is assumed that the transactional theories offer the most useful models for the practitioner to conceptualize the stress process then an important factor in the equation is the internal demands employees place upon themselves (and others) in any given situation. This may help to create stress in a situation unnecessarily. A good example of this is a person, who has strong perfectionist beliefs, not being able to achieve a work deadline. This may seem like a 'catastrophe' for this individual, whereas another person with different beliefs may not become stressed. Taking this one step further, Abrams and Ellis (1994: 40) adopt a radical cognitive view and assert that 'stress does not exist in itself. Stress is like good and evil: it exists only in its perceptions and reactions [sic] of the beholder (or the stressee)'.

A number of the key beliefs that seem to exacerbate work-related stress, and which are regularly raised by participants attending multimodal stress management workshops were itemized by Palmer (1993). Adapted, they are as follows.

I/others must perform well at all times.
I/others must always reach deadlines.
The organization and others must treat me fairly at all times.
I should get what I want otherwise I can't stand it.
Significant others must appreciate my work otherwise I am worthless.
I must be in control of the situation otherwise it would be awful and I couldn't stand it.

Models of occupational stress that overlook the importance of internal demands in creating stress scenarios do not aid the practitioner in the development of stress management programmes.

Home–work interface

If employees are suffering from stress due to problems at home, in some cases this can reduce their performance and effectiveness at work due to, for example, a lack of concentration. Conversely, if employees are suffering from occupational stress then this may affect their homelife as they literally take their worries home and become, for example, irritable with the family. Sometimes a negative stress cycle can be created whereby a problem in one domain can cause stress in the other domain which subsequently adds stress to the original domain. This compounds the individual's initial problem. Figure 24.2 illustrates this negative stress cycle.

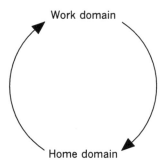

Figure 24.2   *The negative stress cycle*

When assessing the type of problems employees brought to occupational stress counsellors in the Post Office, Cooper and Cartwright (1994) found that 24 per cent were about relationship problems 'with the majority focusing on marital difficulties' (1994: 70). As predicted, counselling substantially reduced absenteeism amongst those employees who received it. Some research has found that women are more prone than men to bring their 'work stress' home and this may be due to incompatible demands (Swedish Work Environment Fund, 1989: 13).

Managing workplace stress

The individual and organizational methods for either managing or reducing workplace stress have focused on interventions at three different levels (see Quick and Quick, 1984):

Primary prevention (stressor-directed).
Secondary prevention (response-directed).
Tertiary prevention (symptom-directed).

We will briefly look at individual-focused interventions. At the primary prevention level the employee can attempt to manage his or her personal perceptions of stressors by changing their internal demands, reducing Type A behaviour, re-appraising situations more realistically, disputing cognitive distortions, etc. The employee can manage the personal work environment by using time management, assertion and communication skills, overload/underload avoidance, social support, task variation, etc., and manage their lifestyle by appropriate leisure time use, maintaining a balance, suitable diet, etc.

At the secondary prevention level, the employee can attempt to alter the ways in which he or she responds to stressors by using relaxation methods such as meditation, Benson relaxation response, progressive relaxation, hypnosis, biofeedback, etc. Physical outlets such as muscle strength and endurance training, yoga, aerobic exercise, jogging, walking, sports, etc. can also be employed. Emotional outlets such as talking and writing about their stressors can be beneficial.

Finally, at the tertiary prevention level the main aim is to help the employee once he or she is suffering from the symptoms of stress by attending symptom-specific programmes (for example, anxiety management), individual or group psychotherapy, or by receiving medical care. This would include staff with post-traumatic stress disorder.

Organization-focused interventions at the primary level attempt to remove or reduce the employee's exposure to the stressor (or hazard). If this is not possible then the impact of the stressor upon the employee is reduced. This can include focusing on work design and ergonomics. Elkin and Rosch (1990) suggest a range of strategies at the organizational level to reduce stress: redesign the task and work environment; establish flexible work schedules; encourage participative management; promote employee involvement in career development; analyse work roles and establish goals; provide social support and feedback; build cohesive teams; establish fair employment policies; share the rewards. At the secondary level, methods are used to improve the ability of the organization to recognize and subsequently deal with stress-related problems as they arise (see Cox et al., 1990). This can involve the use of regular stress audits (Cooper and Cartwright, 1994) and psychometric tests such as the Occupational Stress Indicator. This is a proactive approach as opposed to the more usual reactive approach. Tertiary interventions focus on helping employees deal with and recover from work-related problems and include stress counselling and employee assistance.

Effectiveness of organizational interventions

Occupational stress is a compelling and powerful notion. This power is embedded in the belief that occupational stress is a causal factor in the development and maintenance of ill-health. Although the notion of the stress concept has been repeatedly criticized and the evidence to support the relationship between stress and ill-health is conflicting and inconclusive, even the mere suspicion that stress may cause ill-health has apparently been sufficient to raise concerns about individual well-being and its social, financial and commercial implications. (Reynolds and Briner, 1994: 75–6)

These authors' concern about organizational stress management programmes is based on reviewing the relevant literature and needs further examination. Essentially, the majority of workplace interventions are focused on the individual and are usually based on multimodal cognitive-behaviour therapy, theory and methods. In clinical settings these methods have been comprehensively evaluated on individuals with clinical disorders, for example depression and anxiety, and have been shown to be effective. In contrast, when these methods are applied to a non-clinical population not suffering from stress, there is less evidence to suggest that positive gains are achieved and maintained. In addition, most studies do not include a long-term follow-up to assess whether the interventions 'inoculate' the employees against future stress scenarios. However, there are notable exceptions (e.g. Kushnir and Malkinson, 1993). Some recent studies have confirmed the efficacy of worksite stress management in reducing anxiety, urinary catecholamines and blood pressure. One study by Bruning and Frew (1985) compared the effects of meditation, exercise and management skills training and a combination of these interventions on the galvanic skin response, blood pressure and pulse rate. Interestingly, the study indicated that management skills training consisting of conflict resolution, goal-setting and time management had the best effect on reducing blood pressure and pulse rate. Studies that have assessed organizational outcomes, such as work performance, job satisfaction and absenteeism rates, have found inconsistent results. This may reflect the type of intervention and/or the selection of the subjects. More convincingly, one study (Jones et al., 1988) found that workplace stress levels in a group of hospitals correlated with the frequency of malpractice claims. Hospitals in the group that implemented a stress management programme significantly reduced the number of claims.

Research has found that distressed employees who receive cognitive-behavioural stress counselling as part of a company programme do benefit (see Cooper and Cartwright, 1994). Even these studies can only be 'quasi-experimental' as there are many possible factors that could affect their validity. This criticism also applies to studies that appear to support the effectiveness of employee assistance programmes. Another major problem in the field of occupational stress research is that there is a dearth of well-designed evaluated studies which focus on the elimination or reduction of the sources of stress in the workplace. In addition, the majority of studies have targeted white-collar workers for the focus of interventions. So what research has been evaluated has not usually included all levels of workers. This could mislead practitioners who are drawing upon research to design programmes based on white-collar sub-groups and not blue-collar workers.

Organizational stress management interventions are inherently difficult to evaluate due to the many factors involved that could affect the outcome. In addition, organizations tend to resist organization-focused interventions, preferring employee-focused interventions such as stress management workshops or counselling. However, putting aside the lack of well-controlled studies, generally the published research does indicate that interventions do help to reduce stress. In conclusion, the field of organizational stress management needs more research to evaluate the methods used, and practitioners need to develop programmes based on careful examination of the literature and subsequent application of theory to practice.

Conclusion

Stress management programmes have been undertaken in a variety of settings. Where distressed individuals have received stress counselling or group training/therapy, there has generally been substantial improvement in their condition. When non-clinical populations have received stress management, there is less evidence for long-term benefits. However, this could reflect the limitations of the studies or the skills of the practitioners teaching the relevant components. In the 1960s Rotter found that an individual's locus of control often determined his or her response to different situations. Since then much time has been spent on studying Type A behaviour, social support and coping strategies. Yet, in the past three decades, stress research seems to have gone full circle, with evidence pointing to the core construct of control (actual or perceived) over a situation or control over the emotional response to a situation possibly being the main issue. This would suggest that interventions focusing on some element of control, whether insight- or skills-based, may help to reduce stress. Bearing in mind the 'equivalence paradox', more session-impact research is needed to guide the practitioner in choosing the appropriate intervention(s) for the individual, family or organization. During the next decade counselling psychologists will be in an ideal position to carry out further research and practice in this field of work.

References

Abrams, M. and Ellis, A. (1994) 'Rational emotive behaviour therapy in the treatment of stress', *British Journal of Guidance and Counselling*, 22(1): 39–50.

Alladin, W.J. (1993) 'Ethnic matching in counselling: how important is it to ethnically match clients and counsellors?', in W. Dryden (ed.), *Questions and Answers on Counselling in Action*. London: Sage.

Bennett, P. and Carroll, D. (1990) 'Stress management approaches to the prevention of coronary heart disease', *British Journal of Clinical Psychology*, 29: 1–12.

Blowers, C., Cobb, J. and Matthews, A.M. (1987) 'Generalized anxiety: a controlled treatment study', *Behaviour Research and Therapy*, 25: 493–502.

Bowers, K.S. (1973) 'Situationism in psychology: an analysis and critique', *Psychological Review*, 80: 307–35.

Bruning, N.S. and Frew, D.R. (1985) 'The impact of various stress management training strategies: a longitudinal experiment', in R.B. Robinson and J.A. Pearce (eds), *Academy of Management Proceedings*. San Diego, CA: Academy of Management.

Butler, G., Fennell, M., Robson, P. and Gelder, M. (1991) 'A comparison of behaviour therapy and cognitive-behaviour therapy in the treatment of Generalized Anxiety Disorder', *Journal of Consulting and Clinical Psychology*, 59: 167–75.

Cannon, W.B. (1935) 'Stresses and strains of homeostasis', *American Journal of Medical Science*, 189(1).

Caplan, G. (1967) 'The family as a support system', in G. Caplan and M. Killilea (eds), *Support System and Mutual Help: Multidisciplinary Explorations*. New York: Grune and Stratton.

Cooper, C.L. and Cartwright, S. (1994) 'Stress management interventions in the workplace: stress counselling and stress audits', *British Journal of Guidance and Counselling*, 22(1): 65–73.

Cooper, C.L. and Marshall, J. (1976) 'Occupational sources of stress: a review of the literature relating to coronary heart disease and mental ill health', *Journal of Occupational Psychology*, 49: 11–28.

Cooper, C.L., Cooper, R.D. and Eaker, L.H. (1988) *Living with Stress*. Harmondsworth: Penguin.

Cox, T. (1978) *Stress*. London: Macmillan.

Cox, T. (1993) *Stress Research and Stress Management: Putting Theory to Work*. London: Health and Safety Executive.

Cox, T., Leather, P. and Cox, S. (1990) 'Stress, health and organisations', *Occupational Health Review*, 23: 13–18.

Dembroski, T.M., MacDougall, J.M., Williams, R.B., Haney, T.L. and Blumenthal, J.A. (1985) 'Components of Type A, hostility, and anger-in: relationship to angiographic findings', *Psychosomatic Medicine*, 47: 219–33.

Elkin, A.J. and Rosch, P.J. (1990) 'Promoting mental health at work', *Occupational Medicine State of the Art Review*, 5: 739–54.

Falloon, R.H. (1991) 'Behavioral family therapy', in A.S. Gurman and D. Kniskern (eds), *Handbook of Family Therapy.* New York: Brunner/Mazel.

Falloon, R.H., Laporta, M., Fadden, G. and Graham-Hole, V. (1993) *Managing Stress in Families: Cognitive and Behavioural Strategies for Enhancing Coping Skills.* London: Routledge.

Friedman, M. and Rosenman, R.H. (1959) 'Association of a specific overt behavior pattern with increases in blood cholesterol, blood clotting time, incidence of arcus senilis and clinical coronary artery disease', *Journal of the American Medical Association,* 2169: 1286–96.

Glass, D.C. (1977) *Behavior Patterns, Stress and Coronary Disease.* Hillsdale, NJ: Lawrence Erlbaum.

Gore, S. (1978) 'The effects of social supports in moderating the health consequences of unemployment', *Journal of Health and Social Behaviour,* 19: 157–65.

Gregson, O. and Looker, T. (1994) 'The biological basis of stress management', *British Journal of Guidance and Counselling,* 22: 1.

Holmes, T.H. and Rahe, R.H. (1967) 'The social readjustment rating scale, *Journal of Psychosomatic Research,* 11: 213–18.

Jones, R.L., Barge, B.N., Steffy, B.D., Fay, L.M., Kunz, L.K. and Wuebker, L.J. (1988) 'Stress and medical malpractice: organisational risk assessment and intervention', *Journal of Applied Psychology,* 73: 727–35.

Karasek, R.A. (1981) 'Job socialisation and job strain: the implications of two psychosocial mechanisms for job design', in B. Gardell and G. Johansson (eds), *Working Life: a Social Science Contribution to Work Reform.* Chichester: Wiley.

Kobasa, S. (1979) 'Stressful life events, personality and health: an inquiry into hardiness', *Journal of Personality and Social Psychology,* 45: 1–13.

Kushnir, T. and Malkinson, R. (1993) 'A rational-emotive group intervention for preventing and coping with stress among safety officers', *Journal of Rational-Emotive and Cognitive Behavior Therapy,* 11(4): 195–206.

Lazarus, A.A. and Lazarus, C.N. (1991) *Multimodal Life History Inventory.* Champaign, IL: Research Press.

Lazarus, R.S. and Folkman, R. (1984) *Stress, Appraisal, and Coping.* New York: Springer.

Margolis, B.L., Kroes, W.H. and Quinn, R.P. (1974) 'Job stress: an unlisted occupational hazard', *Journal of Occupational Medicine,* 16(10): 654–61.

Palmer, S. (1993) 'Organisational stress; symptoms, causes and reduction', *Newsletter of the Society of Public Health.*

Palmer, S. and Dryden, W. (1995) *Counselling for Stress Problems.* London: Sage.

Powell, T.J. (1987) 'Anxiety management groups in clinical practice: a preliminary report', *Behavioural Psychotherapy,* 15: 181–7.

Price, V. (1982) *Type A Behavior Pattern: a Model for Research and Practice.* New York: Academic Press.

Quick, J.C. and Quick, J.D. (1984) *Organizational Stress and Preventive Management.* New York: McGraw-Hill.

Ragland, D.R. and Brand, R.J. (1988) 'Type A behavior and mortality from coronary heart disease', *New England Journal of Medicine,* 318: 65–9.

Reynolds, S., Taylor, E. and Shapiro, D.A. (1993) 'Session impact in stress management training', *Journal of Occupational and Organisational Psychology*, 66: 99–113.

Reynolds, S. and Briner, R.B. (1994) 'Stress management at work: with whom, for whom and to what ends?', *British Journal of Guidance and Counselling*, 22: 1.

Rosenman, R.H. (1978) 'The interview method of assessment of the coronary-prone behavior pattern', in T.M. Dembroski, S.G. Haynes and M. Feinleib (eds), *Coronary-Prone Behavior*. New York: Springer-Verlag.

Rotter, J.B. (1966) 'Generalized expectancies for internal versus external control of reinforcement', *Psychological Monographs*, 80: 1.

Selye, H. (1956) *Stress of Life*. New York: McGraw-Hill.

Shapiro, D.A. and Shapiro, D. (1982) 'Meta-analysis of comparative therapy outcome research: a replication and refinement', *Psychological Bulletin*, 92: 581–604.

Sigman, A. (1992) 'The state of corporate health care', *Personnel Management*, February, pp. 24–31.

Sloane, S.J. and Cooper, C.L. (1986) *Pilots under Stress*. London: Routledge and Kegan Paul.

Swedish Work Environment Fund and authors (1989) *Stress, Health, Job Satisfaction*. Stockholm: Swedish Work Environment Fund.

Vaughn, C.E. and Leff, J.P. (1976) 'The measurement of expressed emotion in families of psychiatric patients', *British Journal of Social and Clinical Psychology*, 15: 157–65.

White, J., Keenan, M. and Brookes, N. (1992) 'Stress control: a controlled comparative investigation of large group therapy for generalised anxiety disorder', *Behavioural Psychotherapy*, 20: 97–114.

Yerkes, R.M. and Dodson, J.D. (1908) 'The relation of strength of stimulus to rapidity of habit-formation', *Journal of Comparative Neurology and Psychology*, 18: 459–82.

Part Six

Social, Professional and Ethical Issues

25

Ethical Issues in Counselling Psychology

Carol Shillito-Clarke

Counselling psychology in Britain is a relatively new branch of psychology and one for which the development of clear ethical guidelines combining the requirements of good psychological and therapeutic practice is much needed. Psychologists are not renowned for unethical behaviour. Indeed, an informal survey of complaints made to the British Psychological Society's (BPS) ethics committee suggests that complaints about unethical behaviour have been made about less than 0.1 per cent of the membership over the past three years (BPS, personal communication). Unethical behaviour by counsellors and other therapists, although probably on a similar small scale, has been widely publicized in the popular press in the past few years. While there has been little published research into the ethics of counselling and psychotherapy to support such stories (Bond, 1993), it is important that counselling psychologists each take responsibility to set and maintain the highest standards of both professions.

The aim of this chapter is not to engage in abstract moral discourse or to give definitive answers to every ethical issue arising from the theory and practice of counselling psychology. Rather it is to draw attention to the kinds of ethical issues that arise and encourage counselling psychologists to ask questions of themselves, of their practice and their relationships with those with whom they work. As Lakin proposes, 'Whereas ethical dilemmas in the practice of psychotherapy are inevitable, unethical actions and behaviours are not' (Lakin, 1991: 11). An ethical dilemma exists whenever there are 'good, but contradictory ethical reasons to take conflicting and incompatible courses of action' (Kitchener, 1984: 43). Simple answers are not always available for ethical questions. Different people may argue for different answers. It is hoped that this chapter will encourage the recognition, discussion and investigation of ethical dilemmas in counselling psychology and help prevent unethical behaviour and action.

The chapter will first clarify what 'ethics' is about and its relationship to personal and socio-cultural values. The kinds of ethical dilemmas that may arise from different sources for the counselling psychologist are then explored. The chapter ends with a consideration of some of the ways in which practitioners may avoid major pitfalls and resolve lesser ethical problems.

What do we mean by 'ethics' in counselling psychology?

Ethics is a moral philosophy, or science of morality, which seeks to establish guidelines by which human character and action may be judged as good or bad, right or wrong. Moral philosophy dates back to Plato and Aristotle and the debate about the goal of human behaviour: happiness (hedonism) or reason (rationalism). Later, as exemplified in the writings of Thomas Aquinas, Christian values and the 'will of God' dominated the ethical standards of medieval western Europe. Since the Renaissance, utilitarianism, promoted by philosophers such as Bentham, Hobbes and Mill, has been set against deontological theories (the priority of duty over rights or happiness), such as those of Kant.

Utilitarians argue that the guiding principle for human behaviour should be whatever determines the greatest benefit (or happiness) for the greatest number of people. John Stuart Mill extended utilitarianism to describe an integrated system in which no rule can be considered in isolation but must be considered relative to other and perhaps more significant rules. The principle of autonomy (self-rule) is important here. 'For Mill, the ultimate criterion of what constitutes human well-being is whatever would be preferred by people whose choices were not constrained by ignorance and irrationality' (Holmes and Lindley, 1991: 62). Thus people may choose to sacrifice some pleasure in order to preserve or increase their autonomy. Deontological theorists, on the other hand, emphasize universal and absolute standards of 'right' and 'wrong'. There is a 'categorical imperative' for all people to uphold these standards irrespective of circumstance through the exercise of individual conscience.

In counselling psychology today, both these approaches may be observed, for example, in the use of deception in a paradoxical intervention. Utilitarians will claim that the end of symptom control justifies the means of achieving it. Deontologists will regard it as ethically wrong; the use of deception denying the individual the 'universal' right to informed choice and a trustworthy relationship.

A model for moral and ethical reasoning

A model of moral justification devised by Beauchamp and Childress (1989) is useful to describe the relationship between individual conscience, rules, principles and philosophical theories. Beauchamp and

Critical-evaluative level	Theories	
	Principles	Autonomy Beneficence Non-maleficence Justice Fidelity
	Rules	
Intuitive level	**Individual conscience**	

Figure 25.1   *Model of moral and ethical reasoning. (Based on Beauchamp and Childress, 1989, and Kitchener, 1984)*

Childress propose two levels of ethical reasoning (see Figure 25.1). The **intuitive level** represents the immediate response of the individual's moral conscience. This will be based on their moral upbringing and experience. While this is often a sound guide for ethical behaviour, it may not be sufficiently well articulated to cope with unusual or unforeseen circumstances. Under time pressure or pleading for special-case status, the intuitive level may not be a sound enough guide. The **critical-evaluative** level is used to illuminate, refine and guide moral reasoning (Kitchener, 1984).

The critical-evaluative level comprises three hierarchically related stages. The lowest stage is **rules**: specific laws and codes of conduct. **Principles,** or universally applicable values of equal merit, are above rules but below **theories** or philosophical ideas about the nature and meaning of human existence. The hierarchical structure of the critical-evaluative level is important for moral reasoning and problem-solving. It proposes that because the levels are inter-related, the solution to an ethical problem which is difficult at one level may be clearer at a higher and more abstract level. For example the legal right to abortion (rule) is covered by the moral principle of respect for autonomy and challenged by the principle of non-maleficence, both of which reflect different theoretical con-structions about the meaning and sanctity of life.

Beauchamp and Childress consider four moral principles to have *prima facie* validity. That is, the principle is binding unless, in a given situation, there is a more significant principle which overrides it. The principles are: respect for autonomy, beneficence, non-maleficence and justice. To these we can add the principle of fidelity which is considered to be of particular importance for psychologists by Kitchener (1984).

Autonomy is founded on two values: the freedom of the individual to make their own choices and the freedom to decide their own actions. Within counselling psychology, autonomy implies unconditional regard; the maximization of the client's informed choice and their right to choose their own destiny; the intrinsic worth of each person and the right to self-fulfilment. The concept of free choice and action is not unlimited; it is axiomatically bounded by respect for others' freedom and autonomy. For instance, the client's right to confidentiality in respect of their stated desire to harm another must be balanced against the rights of that other person to avoid being harmed. The concept of free choice also raises theoretical questions about the individual's ability to know, and distinguish between, their conscious and unconscious desires. The concepts of limited and intermittent competence to make decisions are important aspects of autonomy and will be discussed further in the section on informed consent.

Beneficence values caring for and working to promote the greatest good for others. Counselling psychologists, as members of a 'caring profession', have an obligation to benefit their clients through their interventions. This obligation may not comfortably accord with the therapeutic experience of 'things getting worse before they get better' as the client faces the difficulties he or she has hitherto tried to ignore. Competence on the part of the practitioner is obviously important here, together with respect for the client's autonomy in deciding what is beneficial.

Non-maleficence, the principle of 'do no harm', or 'do the least harm', values the responsible use of individual power and ability. For the counselling psychologist, this principle is probably more important than that of beneficence. The principle is important when facing the problem of encouraging the client to experience distress and discomfort whilst in therapy in order to effect change. It is also important in research, where the possible benefit of the many must be weighted against the possibly negative experience of a few. These issues will be explored later in the chapter.

Justice values fairness and the equal distribution of costs and benefits. In counselling psychology it is perhaps most salient in areas of provision of services. The arguments for and against the costs of private practice, short- or long-term therapy and access to training in counselling psychology are all relevant. It is also a key issue in research. How can the researcher compensate clients for their contribution?

Fidelity, or the value of trust in a relationship, is especially important for counselling psychologists and is implicated in the previous four principles (Kitchener, 1984). It is fundamental to the therapeutic relationship, the quality of which depends on trustworthy and unpretentious communication, clear boundaries and respect for the individual's autonomy. Good contracting, informed consent and confidentiality, are not only relevant to the therapeutic work of counselling psychologists but also to the domains of training, consultation and research.

Values

All ethical principles are underpinned by systems of values reflecting the nature of the person. Value systems are built up by the individual through cultural socialization processes and experience, mediated by history and environment. Many values are introjected or accepted without question in childhood. Where values are questioned and reflected upon they may be affirmed or rejected and new values substituted. However, as Cooper (1992) points out, the individual is also subject to primitive needs of which she or he may be unconscious but which may affect or conflict with the values expressed. This may be a source of intrapersonal ethical questions for the counselling psychologist.

In an increasingly pluralistic society, different people, even in one community, may hold value systems that differ widely. Neighbourliness may be perceived as nosiness; individuality may be construed as abdication of social responsibility. Counselling psychologists will differ from one another and from their clients on how they conceive and value psychological health and dysfunction. For example, interventions promoting rationality or spontaneity, emotional expression or impulse control, subjectivity or objectivity, will relate to the values inherent in preferred theoretical models. Therapy seeks desired outcomes and cannot be value-free. Therefore the value systems counselling psychologist and client bring to any encounter need to be recognized. The key issue thus becomes: who determines what is desirable? Can a 'cure' be achieved in six weeks or is it merely symptom relief, leaving the original disorder unrepaired? Do clients really know what is wrong with them and when they are 'better'?

Power and ethics

In counselling psychology, as in all branches of the 'caring' professions, the practitioner is in a position of power relative to the client. The client is psychologically vulnerable by virtue of having a problem or difficulty which he or she cannot resolve unaided. The client who wishes to be helped, must give the counselling psychologist personal information about him- or herself. Such knowledge, often about something which the client is afraid of or ashamed of, gives further power to the counselling psychologist. It is therefore important that he or she can trust the practitioner to use that knowledge to help or empower them and not be used against them. Hence the fundamental importance of the principle of fidelity in counselling psychology.

The practitioner also holds power by claiming experience, expertise and the right to be paid. Counselling psychologists whose philosophical origins are rooted in the humanistic tradition may wish to argue a position of equality with their clients. However, it must be remembered that the client may hold a very different perception, particularly at the beginning of the work and depending on the context of the referral. The label 'psychologist' itself carries numerous fearful connotations, and is often confused with those of 'psychiatrist' and 'psychoanalyst' by many lay people.

Whenever there are differences of values and beliefs and differences in perceived power, there is the opportunity for one person to abuse or exploit another. Codes of ethics and practice are therefore established by professional bodies to provide a regulatory framework for the protection of vulnerable clients. These operate at the rules level of ethical reasoning and may or may not be supported by legislation.

Codes of ethics

The codes of ethics of professional bodies such as the BPS, identify a minimum set of standards for ethical practice that is acceptable to the majority of members and to which all members of that Society must be accountable in their practice. Those whose practice is shown, on evidence, to fall below the standards set may be sanctioned by the Society although not necessarily by the law. Although such codes of ethics are required as part of the institution's charter they are not necessarily fixed for all time and may be renegotiated in the light of experience. While the code is primarily for the protection of clients, it may also serve to protect the counselling psychologist against possible manipulation or exploitation by a vengeful or disturbed client.

A code of ethical conduct can only be a broad framework and is unlikely to be able to account for some of the subtle ethical conflicts of interests. Szymanska and Palmer (1993) cite an unpublished case in which a therapist was threatened by a professional body with disciplinary action for bringing the profession into disrepute if she continued to support a charge of sexual abuse against another member.

The responsibility for resolving any ethical dilemma rests with the counselling psychologist and not with the client. 'Taking account of their obligations under the law, they shall hold the interest and welfare of those in receipt of their services to be paramount at all times and ensure that the interests of participants in research shall be safeguarded' (BPS, 1993: 1). Consideration must be given to ethical issues concerned with competence, and with individual values both at a conscious and unconscious level. The limits of, and boundaries around, the practitioner/client relationship; the different kinds of work such as therapy, consultancy or research, and the contexts in which counselling psychologists work, also need to be considered. Each of these areas of potential ethical conflict is dealt with in some detail in the following sections.

Ethical issues arising within the individual counselling psychologist

This first area has to do with dilemmas concerning the way any one of us may experience conflict between our needs as a human being and our professional role and status as a counselling psychologist.

Validation of self-image and esteem

Psychological theories of the nature and origins of the sense of self differ. However, many agree that there is a difference between the way each person perceives him- or herself and the way they believe they are perceived by others; the way they are and the way they 'ought' to be. Ethical dilemmas can arise when practitioners are confronted by a client or situation which is in opposition to their 'ideal' image.

For instance, a client with whom I am working starts expressing ideas and values that are significantly opposed to mine. Because I uphold the principle of autonomy I feel I should respect the client's different construction of the world. However, my experience is one of distaste and dislike of the client. I do not like myself for my feelings and my bias. In line with the principle of fidelity I believe I should be open about my feelings, but can I be sure that to do so will not cause my client some psychological harm? Perhaps I actually wish to cause the client some harm at some unconscious level. It may be that the problem of my feelings is a temporary phenomenon, an aspect of 'counter-transference' perhaps. Is it appropriate to share my feelings with the client and risk doing harm rather than good, or to keep them to myself and hope that my incongruence will not impair my work?

This may not seem to be a major dilemma and some theoretical models have clear guidelines for dealing with it. However, it is an example of a question that frequently troubles trainees and, in more subtle forms, more experienced practitioners.

The promotion of personal values and beliefs in the guise of counselling psychology violates the principles of autonomy and fidelity. Any discriminatory attitudes about race, gender, disability, class, religion, ability and opportunity should not be allowed to affect counselling practice. However, this assumes that the practitioner is fully aware of how he or she demonstrates such values and beliefs through language and non-verbal behaviour. Psychology has taught us much about the subtlety of communication through means such as embedded suggestion and the self-fulfilling prophecy. The obligation of all counselling psychologists should therefore be 'to make every effort to be aware of our own attitudes that could affect our intervention strategies' (Lakin, 1991: 82).

Competence

After unethical relationships, psychologists working beyond their competence is the second most frequent cause of complaint made to the BPS (private communication). The BPS emphasizes that it is the psychologist's duty to 'maintain and develop their professional competence, to recognize and work within its limits and to identify and ameliorate factors which restrict it' (BPS, 1993: 1). Each person is therefore responsible for recognizing the limitations of their knowledge and experience, for working to extend those limitations and for ensuring that others do not misrepresent them. Ethical dilemmas arise from the definitions of 'established competence' and 'appropriate preparation'. These in turn pose questions about the amount and kind of training in counselling psychology, and counselling specialisms, needed to claim 'competence' as a counselling psychologist.

Unexpected issues erupting after the initial counselling assessment have implications for the counselling relationship, particularly for inexperienced counsellors. A referral to a counselling psychologist with more specialized experience may accord with the principle of beneficence but may negatively affect the fidelity of the established relationship and the therapeutic benefits which have accrued from that relationship. A second difficulty may arise through wishing to respect the client's autonomy should they choose to stay with the less competent practitioner. In this instance the principle of non-maleficence may provide a valuable guideline.

From time to time, it is important for every counselling psychologist to review their personal and professional behaviour in relation to ethical standards. Questions need to be asked about possible changes in practice, particularly in regard to demands for greater efficiency and demonstrable success. It is also important to question how we evaluate our own work and professional standing relative to other practitioners against such criteria as numbers of clients being seen, length of waiting lists and number of client sessions. Finding clear answers is less important than asking the questions. In each case checking the autonomy of the client's perceived needs against one's own, and clarifying the fidelity of the working relationship is the ethical requirement.

Fitness to practise

Fitness to practise includes the psychological, emotional and physical states of the counselling psychologist. The BAC Code of Ethics and Practice for Counsellors stresses 'counsellors have a responsibility to themselves and their clients to maintain their own effectiveness, resilience and ability to help clients. They are expected to monitor their own personal functioning and to seek help and/or withdraw from counselling whether temporarily or permanently, when their personal resources are sufficiently depleted to require this' (BAC, 1993). This is an elaboration of the BPS requirement for personal conduct, and emphasizes the reciprocal nature of the practitioner/client relationship. Because the work of counsellors, and counselling psychologists, necessitates them becoming an intrinsic tool in the therapeutic process, any decline in their ability will affect the effectiveness of therapy. The client is put at risk of harm through the therapist's reduced ability to perceive and respond. They are being given a model that does not promote health and the practitioner is also failing to treat her or himself with due care and respect.

Self-awareness and knowledge play a part here as 'fitness' requires recognition of personal states and honesty in acknowledging inadequacy, albeit temporary. At times of personal chaos it can feel very important to try to maintain a semblance of order and control through work. When riddled with self-doubt and dislike, not confronting a client who apparently needs and values help can be very seductive. Even when struggling against a tide of general demands and commitments, or awash with flu, the demands of the mortgage and the credit card can be hard to ignore. The ethical dilemma here is between beneficence and non-maleficence: for a time, not actually doing good for the client whilst aiming to do no harm. Not abusing the relationship (fidelity) and respecting the client's right to autonomy to choose other help are also at stake. In such a position, even temporarily, it is an ethical requirement for the counselling psychologist to consult with his or her supervisor and find as much personal support outside of the work relationship as possible.

Personal safety

Counselling psychologists have an ethical responsibility to their clients as well as to themselves to safeguard their physical state. This includes being clear about the boundaries around personal availability and about behaviour towards oneself that is not acceptable from clients. It also includes having some training in assessment of the client's psychological state in order to avoid taking on a dangerous client or provoking some kind of attack. A client who makes a violent outburst may be seriously disturbed by what he or she has done. It is therefore important for counselling psychologists to be aware of their ethical and legal responsibilities to the client (Cohen, 1992). In Britain, resort to litigation is not as prevalent as in the United States, but there are many ways in which the counselling psychologist may incur legal liability and practitioners have an ethical responsibility to avoid illegal activities (Bond, 1993; Cohen, 1992). The BPS recommends all counselling psychologists to take out professional indemnity insurance, whether self-employed or covered by an employer's insurance.

Some of the issues considered in this section are not strictly 'ethical dilemmas', but an awareness of areas of personal concern and contradictions of this kind are important. Development of personal ethical systems provides a stronger base for avoiding being drawn into greater problems. A lack of awareness of the need to validate an ideal personal or professional image, or a disregard for the shadowy aspects of personality or personal limitation, increases vulnerability. The counselling psychologist risks falling or being coerced into some unethical behaviour to protect personal self-image or esteem. As Dryden suggests, 'therapists have to acknowledge that their needs are more often implicated in the therapeutic process than they might like to think' (Dryden, 1985: 182).

Ethical issues arising through the work of the counselling psychologist

Here I wish to address the ethical issues arising from the interaction of one person working with others; the primary relationships the counselling psychologist has with clients, supervisor, employers and colleagues and also the less obvious relationships with people in the client's world. Problems arise from discrepancies in interpersonal perception. These are compounded when there is some confusion about the different roles people have and the contingent boundaries between professional and personal interests.

Ethical issues arising from the counselling psychologist/client relationship

As has been mentioned above, the relationship between the counselling psychologist and the client is one in which there is an imbalance of perceived power. The client is in a vulnerable position and research suggests that the success of the work depends significantly on the quality of the relationship (Elton Wilson and Barkham, 1994), that is, the extent to which the client can trust the counselling psychologist. Ethical issues relating to the quality of the relationship concern the clarity of the contract, the management of the practice and the maintenance of appropriate relationship boundaries, particularly around confidentiality.

Respect for the client's autonomy

> Psychologists accord appropriate respect to the fundamental rights, dignity and worth of all people. They respect the rights of individuals to privacy, confidentiality, self-determination and autonomy, mindful that legal and other obligations may lead to inconsistency and conflict with the exercise of these rights. Psychologists are aware of cultural, individual and role differences, including those due to age, gender, race, ethnicity, national origin, religion, sexual orientation, disability, language and socio-economic status. Psychologists try to eliminate the effect on their work of biases based on these factors and they do not knowingly participate in or condone unfair discriminatory practice. (American Psychological Association, 1992)

The counselling psychologist's self-awareness has been discussed and is one of the main factors in developing anti-oppressive practice, that is, practice which addresses 'interconnections between issues of power within the therapeutic relationship and the cultural and socio-political contexts' (Strawbridge, 1994: 6). Ethical dilemmas arise when clients' beliefs, values, morals, needs and understanding of their situation are at odds with those of the counselling psychologist. Differences may be exacerbated if practitioners are not aware of and respectful towards both the clients' construction of their world and their dominant racial and cultural beliefs. This is particularly significant in the case of the Western theoretical emphasis on the self which undervalues the importance of self in relation to family, community and culture (d'Ardenne and Mahtani, 1989; Strawbridge, 1994).

In their book on transcultural counselling, d'Ardenne and Mahtani (1989) point out that factors such as the expectations of the relationship between the client and the therapist, the directiveness of approach and the nature of the goals of counselling may all vary with the cultural background of the client and the therapist. Their view is that there is a particular imbalance of power when a white therapist works with a client from a minority ethnic group, and that 'even when white counsellors are demonstrably ineffective with clients from other cultures, clients continue to believe in the counsellor's expertise . . . [and] come to blame themselves for failures within the relationship' (d'Ardenne and Mahtani, 1989: 75). It is therefore ethically important for the counselling psychologist to be alert to issues of power which may be present for the client and to be open to and respectful of the client's values. The question 'Am I really acting in my client's best interests?' and 'Would I work differently if the client was of a different race (or culture/gender)?' are crucial here.

Ethical issues of autonomy can develop from differing theoretical approaches to the client (Spinelli, 1994). The psychodynamic emphasis on interpretation of the transference relationship implies that the counselling psychologist may know more about what is going on for the client than the client does. To what extent is the client then really free to challenge or reject the interpretation? To what extent is a vulnerable client in a position to reject the concept of rational thought and choose 'irrational' behaviour? This may be a particular problem in a time-limited pro- gramme where 'success' is defined by outcome measures. The humanistic models place great emphasis on respecting the client's autonomy. However, do all clients necessarily want or know how to use the responsibility for defining their needs? Such questions may be easy to answer theoretically but the answers may be difficult to incorporate into practice. Ethics become important when the client challenges the perceived wisdom of the theory, or the 'authority' of the counselling psychologist, does not respond to treatment or precipitates an unexpected outcome. Respect for the client's autonomy is not always easy to uphold, particularly when it challenges that of the practitioner.

Contracting and informed consent Respect for the client's autonomy, together with the principle of fidelity, is reflected in the nature of the contract with the counselling psychologist. The client must be able to give 'valid consent' that they have 'adequately understood the nature of the investigation or intervention and its anticipated consequences' (BPS, 1993: 2). In order to give informed consent the client must be given a clear and explicit explanation of: the therapeutic process; the management of the sessions in terms of time and place and confidentiality; boundaries around the relationship with the practitioner; possible outcomes of the work; the responsibilities of the client in terms of attendance, termination and, where appropriate, payment, before work begins. Clients should also be aware that, under the Data Protection Act 1984, they have the right to know if information about themselves is stored on computer and to see their records. They also have the right to terminate their work at any time or request referral to another source of help.

A clear contract gives freedom of choice to the client and promotes the principles of fidelity and beneficence. Again, while this is clear in theory, the practice may be complicated by the emotional and psychological state of the client. Children, the elderly and those with learning difficulties require special consideration. The problem is to balance the client's right to free choice against their ability to understand the arguments for and against treatment. In such cases, it may be useful to include the concepts of limited and intermittent competence in decision-making (Kitchener, 1984). Limited competence usually refers to those such as children and retarded adults, who are not considered capable of making rational decisions. Intermittent competence refers to a fluctuating state of rationality, as in cases of Alzheimer's disease. In both cases, the individual's choice should be respected when possible and supported by responsible others.

Some counselling psychologists negotiate a working contract with the client, others prefer to set the same contract for all their clients. In cases where the contract is set by the counselling psychologist's employer, it is still the practitioner's responsibility to ensure that the contract is comprehensive. However explicit the contract is, the counselling psychologist may face ethical dilemmas deciding what personal information from case notes to share with the client, what boundaries to draw round availability of support outside the designated therapeutic meetings and whether to put pressure on a client to terminate or to continue working. The desire to have a client stay or go may also be subtly affected by organizational pressures such as outcome statistics and other indicators of effective management. *Therapists' Dilemmas* (Dryden, 1985) offers a number of examples of such professional difficulties.

A further source of ethical conflict around contracting occurs when unexpected change has to be accommodated. A classic situation is when a fee-paying client can no longer afford the fee. Counselling psychologists have to respect their own autonomy as well as that of the client and not do harm to themselves. Placing the client's need for help over the practitioner's need for an income may appear to be the charitable act and one of non-maleficence. However, in ethical terms it can deny the practitioner's autonomy and that of the client. It also alters the contract and thereby the principle of fidelity. In trying to evaluate the best answer, different contexts and theoretical perspectives must be taken into account. Above all, care must be taken against the charge of 'exploitation' which is unethical in every code of conduct.

Confidentiality One of the most difficult areas to negotiate ethically when working as a counselling psychologist is that of confidentiality. Trust, and the fidelity of the therapeutic relationship, often depends on the client knowing that her or his secrets are safe with the practitioner: that they are not the subject of gossip or otherwise made public. What, to whom and in what form information about the client should be transmitted is a matter for debate. Confidentiality and the law is a highly complex and thorny issue. Counselling psychologists are advised by the BPS to be aware of the specific legal and ethical context of their work and the general legal requirements concerning giving and withholding information and to seek professional support and guidance as necessary. All counselling psychologists are also advised to carry personal indemnity insurance, over and above any organizational provision.

Promising total confidentiality is unethical because it denies the practitioner's requirement for access to supervision, the contractual obligations to team colleagues or to an employer, intra-agency support systems for the client and some legal requirements. It does not ensure the principle of non-maleficence. If total confidentiality is an impossibility, the question is where to draw ethical boundaries that both protect the client and facilitate practice. The question may be complicated by either or both counselling psychologist and client having more than one role in respect to the other such as working for the same organization, or moving in the same social circles. The key issues here are informed consent, possible identification of the client, breaking confidentiality in the interests of others' safety and the time limits on confidentiality. In setting limits on confidentiality neither client nor counselling psychologist can know how ethically others may behave and how situations may change with time.

One of the most difficult ethical questions is whether to break a client's confidentiality under exceptional circumstances. The most obvious examples are the threat of suicide or physical/sexual abuse of a minor. The principle of non-maleficence towards self (suicide) or other (abuse) has to be weighed against the client's autonomy, the others' autonomy (abuse) and the fidelity of the relationship. Individual counselling psychologists may have clear moral answers to the dilemma. Codes seem to agree that breaching confidentiality is acceptable if the practitioner has tried, and failed, to get the client's consent and if there has been consultation with an experienced colleague.

In the event of the client's death, the BAC code specifies that: 'Agreements about confidentiality continue after the client's death unless there are over-riding legal or ethical considerations' (BAC, 1993). What is less clear, however, is what happens in the event of the counselling psychologist's death or prolonged, involuntary absence, perhaps due to a serious accident. In such cases, clients may need identification and notification of what has happened. They will invariably need some continuity of support that does not breach confidentiality. Such care may be difficult to organize without unauthorized access to case notes, particularly in the chaos around sudden death or disablement. This is also not a matter this is usually discussed in the initial contract. How practitioners choose to resolve such dilemmas will vary. What is more certain is the ethical responsibility to give thought to and make provision for such unexpected circumstances.

Sexual harassment   Sexual harassment is not only unethical, it is against the law as represented by the Race Relations Act (1976), the Sexual Discrimination Act (1975) and the Employment Protection (Consolidation) Act (1978). Different professional bodies and institutions may have differing definitions and policies on sexual harassment. The BPS, in a statement 'Sexual Harassment at Work and the Ethics of Dual Relationships' defines the problem as:

Any unwelcome verbal or sexual advances, requests for sexual favours or other verbal or physical conduct of a sexual nature when

either (a) the conduct interferes with another person's work or creates an intimidating, hostile or offensive working environment
or (b) submission to this conduct is made implicitly or explicitly a term or condition of a person's education or employment
or (c) submission or rejection of such conduct is used as a basis of decisions affecting a person's employment and/or educational prospects.

Sexual harassment can consist of a single intense or severe act or of multiple persistent or pervasive acts and it does not have to be explicitly sexual in nature. Any behaviour which ridicules, denigrates or abuses a person because of his or her gender may be deemed harassment. (BPS, 1993: 45)

Sexual harassment can occur irrespective of similarity or difference in gender and sexual orientation of the parties involved. Not all sexual harassment is easy to identify or prove. Unacceptable touching, sexual advances and bargaining, or use of sexist jokes and training material may be easy to point out. Other instances such as sexist or overly sexualized interpretations of case material (by counselling psychologist and supervisor), endearments and covert favouritism, or the way in which differences in sexual orientation are dealt with, may be more subtle. Where the perpetrator holds some position of authority over the recipient, reporting the experience may be much harder, particularly for women (BPS, 1993).

It is for reasons such as these that any action which is identified as sexual harassment by the recipient, must be taken seriously, even if the other person is unaware that their behaviour is causing offence. Obviously, where a person is unaware of how subtle forms of sexually related behaviour are received, opportunity to change that behaviour in the light of feedback should be allowed before the official complaints procedure is instituted. But accusations should never be dismissed.

In order to avoid behaving unethically, it is therefore incumbent on the counselling psychologist to develop their awareness of their own sexual values and attitudes; to be alert to others' interpretations and to be prepared to change behaviour in the light of informed feedback.

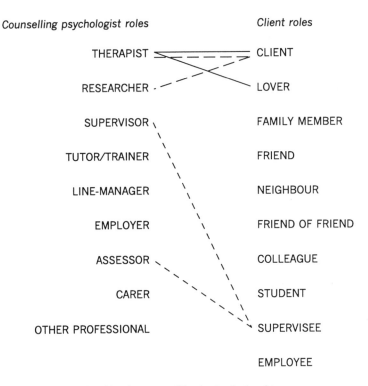

Figure 25.2 *Model for describing possible dual relationships*

Dual relationships Dual relationships arise when either the counselling psychologist or their client hold more than one role in respect of their relationship with the other person. Because counselling psychologists may be employed in more than one role, or may offer more than one service, they are often at risk of role conflict within a relationship. This is illustrated in Figure 25.2. If more than one line can be drawn between the roles of the counselling psychologist and those of the client, a dual relationship will result. For example: the client is also the counselling psychologist's lover (unbroken line); the counselling psychologist is conducting research on her/his client (broken line); or the counselling psychologist is asked to act as examiner to her/his clinical supervisee (dotted line).

Dual relationships that are of a personal loving and/or sexual nature and have arisen from the professional relationship between counselling psychologist and client, student or junior worker, are always unethical. In therapy the reasons include avoidance of exploitation of the imbalance of power between therapist and client, the ability of the client to give consent or be able to evaluate whether such intimacy will be ultimately beneficial, and the nature of the therapeutic relationship not being compromised.

Janice Russell's book *Out of Bounds* describes the results of her research into sexual exploitation in counselling and therapy. She concludes that some practitioners do abuse their position either deliberately or through 'ignorance, lack of skill or unawareness' and the results may be far reaching (Russell, 1993). Russell is adamant that exploitation is never the fault of the client. However it is not unknown for a client to believe, incorrectly, that they have been the subject of sexual interest and involvement with their therapist. In such cases, it is important to recognize that the therapist has a responsibility to be aware of the client's fantasy, to be very clear in maintaining boundaries that do not foster such fantasies and to take careful supervision.

In education, loving and sexual relationships between staff and students are also unethical. Glaser and Thorpe (1986) surveyed 500 female clinical psychology students in the United States. Seventeen per cent reported sexually intimate relationships with their 'educators'. While the reported rate of negative consequences was low, many trainees subsequently regretted allowing the relationship. Szymanska and Palmer (1993) regret the 'negligible' amount of research in Britain to date and plead for greater emphasis on ethical relationships in counsellor training.

One of the difficulties concerned with issues of sexuality and the client/counselling psychologist relationship is that some practitioners may be afraid of being accused of appearing to be sexually exploitative if they explore issues of sexuality and present sexual attraction. Yet without doing so, when appropriate, they may not be able to help their clients effectively. Spinelli (1994) further argues that acknowledging feelings of sexual attraction to the client may enable the practitioner to define clear boundaries and prevent or minimize the potential for abuse.

Not all dual relationships are sexually exploitative and unethical. Some may pre-date the professional relationship. For instance, the counselling psychologist whose partner becomes a student on the same course or who elects to work or do research with their partner. It is important to recognize the subtle and not always conscious forces that dual relationships may call into play not only between the partners but also with others such as colleagues and course participants. In every case, it is the counselling psychologist who must take responsibility for the relationship. Good supervision and further training may give confidence in handling difficult situations. Raising self-awareness of one's own sexual values, beliefs and relationships is also important.

Ethical issues arising out of other professional relationships

Counselling psychologists are involved in many professional relationships, other than those with therapy clients, that may raise issues of ethical consideration. Regular supervision or consultancy is a requirement for practitioners, who may in turn supervise other counselling psychologists. Many work as trainers, lecturers and researchers as well as advisers to other professionals. Those who manage or work with a team of colleagues will have ethical responsibilities to them as well. Issues such as anti-oppressive practice, clear contracting and confidentiality will apply as much to these relationships as to that with the client. In each case there may be other potential ethical dilemmas.

Supervision Counselling psychology is unlike any other branch of psychology in its requirement for all practitioners to be in regular consultative support from a suitably qualified professional supervisor. The supervisor may be put in a difficult ethical position by virtue of needing to support the practitioner, protect the client and maintain the standards of the profession. Ethical questions arising between counselling psychologist and supervisor centre on: the responsibilities held by each party and the autonomy of each person to define their boundaries; the levels of competency required to ensure non-maleficent practice; the boundaries of confidentiality and fidelity in the supervisory relationship; and lines of responsibility.

Education The counselling psychologist in the role of trainer, lecturer or adviser, takes the responsibility for course content, depth of treatment and, where appropriate, assessment. This may lead to tension between the standards deemed appropriate by the counselling psychologist and those deemed adequate by a cost-conscious employer. As in counselling, boundaries of confidentiality around students' personal material, disclosed in training groups, personal development work and supervision, must be observed. This can lead to ethical difficulties over who has ultimate responsibility for the student and their practice; for instance, when a student discloses to the personal development group leader some issue that could jeopardize their place on the course, or when a supervisor realizes that a student is being encouraged to ignore their advice by a tutor with a different theoretical orientation.

The use of client material to illustrate points of teaching and learning by both staff and students is a necessary part of counselling psychology education. But what happens to the boundaries around client confidentiality? It is essential to obtain a client's permission to use their case material for research purposes or for a major case study. What about anecdotes or examples used to illustrate an essay or lecture or book chapter? Should the client be made aware that they are working with a student or educator and that they may be the subject of an essay or lecture? This would respect their autonomous right to limit confidentiality but might jeopardize their trust in the practitioner, or cause them to doubt the competence of a trainee practitioner. Is it a question of non-maleficence (the client will never know and the material will be so disguised or abbreviated as to be anonymous) versus beneficence (the importance of training others to help)? These are ethical questions which are not easily resolved but which need to be addressed by all those offering training.

Management In addition to all the above, BPS makes it clear that counselling psychologists in managerial positions are responsible for ensuring that those for whom they are responsible are not required to work beyond their level of competence; that their qualifications, capabilities and views are not misrepresented; that they conduct themselves appropriately and that suitable sources of referral are available. Managers can thus find themselves having to mediate between the requirements, rights and interests of the organization and those of the employee. The creation and adoption of a policy document to cover issues of competing aims, requirements, rights – particularly around confidentiality – and provision of resources is advocated by Sugarman (1992). However, threats of financial accountability and redundancy have an insidious way of eating into policy documents and paring agreed standards to the minimum.

Colleagues As counselling psychologists, we have an ethical responsibility to report colleagues suspected of ethical misconduct. This may lead to ethical conflicts between concern over the colleague's behaviour, relationships with the colleague and with others with whom he or she works, and a perceived ethical 'duty'. It is one thing to complain about a colleague's behaviour and another to have to live with the consequences of that complaint. Where other colleagues may be involved, the risk may become one of ethical duty versus social rejection and even retaliation: a hard choice.

Society It is important to remember that as counselling psychologists we each have a social responsibility to society at large, and particularly the society in which we live and work (Woolfe, 1983). Questions of ethical behaviour therefore have implications beyond our immediate work situation, organization or professional body. The theories we use, the questions we ask, the practices we support or argue against, have far-reaching consequences. For instance: if my client suffers from 'stress', is that due to his inability to cope or because organizational requirements for productivity are unrealistically high? By working privately, am I contributing to a society that values a market economy and individual success over the provision of social care and mutual responsibility (Pilgrim 1991)? How do we balance individual autonomy against beneficence towards others?

573

Ethical issues in counselling psychology research

Just as counselling psychology is a relatively new field of psychological inquiry, research into counselling psychology is mostly recent and is raising new questions about ethical procedures. The BPS, in common with other psychological associations, has a number of clear and comprehensive guidelines for conducting research ethically. Other organizations supporting psychology research are referred to the BPS *Code of Conduct, Ethical Principles and Guidelines* as well as other authors cited in this chapter for a fuller treatment.

Meara and Schmidt (1991) consider that the main problem for research in counselling lies in the significantly different values, priorities and practices of research and counselling. Traditionally, research is public and relies on the classical scientific method which requires measurable, reliable and replicable outcomes generalizable to broad populations. Counselling is about confidentiality, and the uniqueness of the individual and often vulnerable *person*. While the need for research in counselling psychology is strongly supported, there is no consensus about how it should be conducted or to what end. Heppner et al. (1992) stress that the focus of scientific research should be to 'extend our knowledge bases with accurate, reliable and thus usable information' (1992: 82). They further temper this statement with the essential question, 'knowledge for what?', weighting the ethical principle of non-maleficence over that of possible beneficence. Others, such as Reason and Rowan (1981) and Mair (1989) have argued for research that goes beyond traditional 'scientific' ways of, and reasons for, acquiring knowledge. Stressing acknowledgement of the humanity of the 'subject' and the intersubjective nature of enquiry, the key ethical principles are autonomy and fidelity. It may be that ethical decision-making in research will require identification with one set of principles rather than another. For instance, to what extent is a research method congruent with this therapeutic orientation or the methodology compatible with that way of counselling? Central to ethical research in counselling psychology, therefore, are questions about the purpose of the research and the relationship between the client/research subject and the counselling psychologist particularly when he or she is in the dual role of therapist and researcher.

Design

Whatever the research paradigm, there are a number of ethical concerns to be considered. For instance, in common with much medical research, the use of a control group and randomized allocation of subjects may inadvertently compromise the principle of non-maleficence. One or other group could miss out on a beneficial experience. Either group could suffer harm through not receiving help or the 'help' being less appropriate than no intervention.

The researcher has the responsibility for identifying and eliminating or minimizing risks to the client (Heppner et al., 1992). These may include the risk of actual physical or mental harm, when working with clients who may be abusive of themselves or others. They may also include the risk of emotional distress such as embarrassment, stress, loss of self-esteem or personal dignity. Because such risks will depend largely on the individual's construction of the situation, they may vary enormously between people and over time. What, to the client, seemed a good idea at one time may be regarded very differently at another time. The benefits to the client who is the subject of the research and to future clients will also need to be taken into account. Whether clients can be recompensed in some way, with extra time or fee reductions for instance (the principle of justice), must also be considered. In every case of doubt, the researcher should ask if there is another design or procedure that could be used more ethically.

Informed consent

Many of the situations involved in the design and execution of research require that the clients are aware of, and informed about, the nature and purpose of the research and have given their agreement to participate. Beauchamp and Childress (1989) argue that, before informed consent can be given by a client, three conditions must be met. First, they must have as much relevant information about the research project as is possible. This may include what is required of them, the implications for the therapy process and possible outcomes for them personally as well as publicly. Secondly, the client must be able to choose freely to participate without jeopardizing the quality or quantity of their therapy or the relationship with the therapist (the principles of autonomy and fidelity). Thirdly, the researcher needs to be competent to assess the previous two conditions. This also requires that the researcher is self-aware enough to balance her or his personal and professional investment in the research project with the client's needs to make an autonomous decision. Pressure to get the client's agreement to participate and then not to withdraw before the end or withhold permission for the use of data may be quite subtle, particularly if a career or research grant is at stake.

Ethical use of data and publication

Client confidentiality is paramount in all research. Care to preserve anonymity needs to be taken, not only in the gathering of data but also in its storage. It may not always be possible to protect the client's identity or that of those of whom they speak. This is particularly important with audio and video tapes. The destruction of such data at the end of the project is critical for the protection of the client. However, if such data is destroyed there is no opportunity to check whether the researcher has misinterpreted or falsified the findings. The deliberate falsification or suppression of data that disconfirms the desired results is, of course, unethical.

Finding answers to ethical questions

As was suggested at the start of this chapter, there are very few easy answers to ethical questions because of the continual interaction between the individual's ethical beliefs and those of the community, society and culture in which she or he lives and works. What is important is that each of us accepts the responsibility for accountability in our work. This requires being able to make reasoned decisions based on evidence and being able to reflect on and review those decisions in the light of new information. Counselling psychologists may develop their abilities through training, self-awareness, supervision, continuing professional development and systematic investigation into the consequences of their ethical decisions.

Training

Ethical issues, rather like gender and multi-cultural issues, are often taught as separate modules on both counselling and psychology courses. I hope that this chapter has shown that ethical issues underpin every aspect of the counselling psychologist's professional and personal life. What is needed in every element of a training course, in addition to familiarization with appropriate codes of ethics and guidelines for good practice, is frequent questioning and reflection on the ethical implications of ideas and actions, both conscious and unconscious. Discussions with others provide an important recognition of the diversity of others' understanding and values. They also encourage challenge, articulation, elaboration and review of previously held values and beliefs.

Development of self-awareness

One of the hallmarks of counselling psychology is the emphasis on self-awareness. This is required as part of the counselling psychologist's basic training through personal psychological counselling and a range of opportunities to question their own values, beliefs, experience and level of personal development. Hopefully this will lead to greater openness in the discussion of ethical dilemmas and responsiveness to potential difficulties. We also need to foster a climate in which acknowledgement of, and involvement in the resolution of ethical dilemmas is regarded without prejudice.

Supervision and continuing professional development

Supervision is a requirement for all those who hold a practising licence in counselling psychology in Britain. As discussed earlier, the primary aim of supervision is the protection of the client and therefore protection of the counselling psychologist. It is important that the supervisor is appropriately qualified, aware of ethical issues and able to support the vulnerability of the supervisee.

Systematic investigation

Conducting a formal experiment into any form of ethical behaviour would itself be unethical. However, as Meara and Schmidt (1991) point out, there is little formal or informal systematic investigation into the consequences of ethical decisions made during work. More emphasis on the outcomes of ethical decisions may help clarify and define future similar decision-making. Published research could also encourage awareness and debate (Heppner et al., 1992; Szymanska and Palmer, 1993).

Working through ethical decisions and dilemmas

One of the most useful recent models for ethical problem-solving is that proposed by Tim Bond (1993). Below, I provide a development of this model for counselling psychologists, based on the 5Cs, which stand for: **Clarify, Consult, Consider, Choose, Check**.

1 **Clarify**
   Describe in writing as clearly as possible what is the issue at stake.
   Identify as far as possible what are the elements of the problem.
   If more than one person is involved, imagine how each might also describe it.
   Bring together all supporting evidence for and against.
2 **Consult**
   Read through the code of ethics for your professional body, and all

other available codes and guidelines. If you belong to more than one professional organization work to that code that gives you the tightest and most specific information.

If possibly relevant, check your legal position with a solicitor or the legal advice service offered by your insurance scheme.

Discuss thoroughly with your supervisor and any other experienced professional colleagues who may be able to give you a different and unbiased opinion. Be careful to maintain the necessary boundaries of confidentiality.

Keep notes of all these consultations.

3   **Consider courses of action**

Brainstorm all possible courses of action that may be available to you: leave nothing out and, if possible, ask a colleague to help.

Compare the ethical principles of beneficence (the best possible outcome), justice (the fairest outcome), respect for autonomy (particularly that of the client) and perhaps most importantly of all, non-maleficence (avoiding harm).

Consider the consequences, particularly in terms of justification to other clients, professionals, the press and personal conscience.

4   **Choose**

Select the best course of action and sleep on it.

Review once more before implementing action.

5   **Check the outcome**

Did it go as you expected? If not, what happened?

Would another situation have been better? How might you have predicted it?

What have you learned about yourself?

What experience have you gained which you can draw on in the future?

Conclusion

This chapter has identified the moral principles of autonomy, beneficence, non-maleficence, justice and fidelity that underlie the ethical decisions that must be taken by the counselling psychologist in their daily life and work. It has emphasized that different ethical interpretations are inevitable because of the different values held by clients and counselling psychologists alike – our different upbringings, cultures, experiences and understanding. Different theoretical approaches to counselling psychology also embody different values, which need to be taken into account. All such differences must be recognized and respected. The codes of ethics and practice of relevant professional bodies such as BPS offer sound guidelines but may not be able to account for the subtle nature of many ethical dilemmas.

It is suggested that in order to work through, if not pre-empt ethical difficulties, counselling psychologists should be trained and encouraged to develop their personal awareness of ethical issues and boundaries, both within themselves and between themselves and those with whom they work. Use of professional consultation, careful analysis and informed reflection are also important. Above all, it is urged that the profession should foster a climate in which ethics are regarded as an intrinsic part of the daily life and work of the practitioner, debate about ethical dilemmas is encouraged and more investigation and research is conducted into the process and outcome of their resolution.

References

American Psychological Association (1992) *Ethical Principles of Psychologists and Code of Conduct*. Washington, DC: APA Inc.

Beauchamp, T.L. and Childress, J.F. (1989) *Principles of Biomedical Ethics*, 3rd edn. New York: Oxford University Press.

Bond, T. (1993) *Standards and Ethics for Counselling in Action*. London: Sage.

British Association for Counselling (1993) *Code of Ethics and Practice for Counsellors*. Rugby: BAC.

British Psychological Society (1993) *Code of Conduct, Ethical Principles and Guidelines*. Leicester: BPS.

Cohen, K. (1992) 'Some legal issues in counselling and psychotherapy', *British Journal of Guidance and Counselling*, 20(1): 10.

Cooper, G.F. (1992) 'Ethical issues in counselling and psychotherapy: the background', *British Journal of Guidance and Counselling*, 20(1): 1.

d'Ardenne, P. and Mahtani, A. (1989) *Transcultural Counselling in Action*. London: Sage.

Dryden, W. (1985) *Therapists' Dilemmas*. London: Harper and Row.

Elton Wilson, J. and Barkham, M. (1994) 'A practitioner-scientist approach to psychotherapy process and outcome research', in P. Clarkson and M. Pokorny (eds), *A Handbook of Psychotherapy*. London: Routledge.

Glaser, R.D. and Thorpe, J.S. (1986) 'Unethical intimacy: a survey of sexual contact between psychology educators and women graduate students', *American Psychologist*, 41: 43–51.

Heppner, P.P., Kivlighan, D.M. and Wampold, B.E. (1992) *Research Design in Counselling*. Pacific Grove, CA: Brooks/Cole.

Holmes, J. and Lindley, R. (1991) *The Values of Psychotherapy*. Oxford: Oxford University Press.

Kitchener, K.S. (1984) 'Intuition, critical evaluation and ethical principles', *The Counselling Psychologist*, 21(3): 43–55.

Lakin, M. (1991) *Coping with Ethical Dilemmas in Psychotherapy*. New York: Pergamon Press.

Mair, M. (1989) *Between Psychology and Psychotherapy: a Poetics of Experience*. London: Routledge.

Meara, N.M. and Schmidt, L.D. (1991) 'The ethics of researching counselling/ therapy processes' in C.E. Watkins and L.J. Schneider (eds), *Research in Counselling*. Hillsdale, NJ: Lawrence Erlbaum.

Pilgrim, D. (1991) 'Psychotherapy and social blinkers', *The Psychologist*, 14(2): 56–60.

Reason, P. and Rowan, J. (1981) *Human Inquiry: a Sourcebook of New Paradigm Research*. Chichester: Wiley.

Russell, J. (1993) *Out of Bounds: Sexual Exploitation in Counselling and Therapy*. London: Sage.

Spinelli, E. (1994) *Demystifying Therapy*. London: Constable.

Strawbridge, S. (1994) 'Towards anti-oppressive practice in counselling psychology', *Counselling Psychology Review*, 9(1): 5.

Sugarman, L. (1992) 'Ethical issues in counselling at work', *British Journal of Guidance and Counselling*, 20(1): 64.

Szymanska, K. and Palmer, S. (1993) 'Therapist–client sexual contact', *Counselling Psychology Review*, 8(4): 22.

Woolfe, R. (1983) 'Counselling in a world of crisis: towards a sociology of counselling', *International Journal for the Advancement of Counselling*, 6: 167–76.

26

Training and Professional Development in the Context of Counselling Psychology

William Farrell

In the UK, systematic professional training in counselling psychology is a new phenomenon, but in a discipline that professes to be all about change and development throughout the life span, it feels as if the form and content of training and professional development should epitomize all that is best in the field. Furthermore, it feels as if a counselling psychologist should, with minimal difficulty, be able to provide a comprehensive and well-grounded outline of this. However, to write this chapter is in fact a daunting task and the discussion presented here represents instead a journey, a struggle, a cyclical process. Perhaps it will suffice to say that this reflects the nature of the issues that counselling psychologists face in work with their clients.

The aim of this chapter is to discuss training and professional development in counselling psychology. This involves consideration of:

1 Basic graduate training in the field.
2 The training of counselling psychologists to act as trainers and supervisors for various groups. These include counselling psychologists, other applied psychologists, non-psychologist psychotherapists and counsellors, and other professionals and volunteers.
3 Continuing post-qualification personal and professional development of counselling psychologists, both for direct service to clients and for work as trainers and supervisors.

Throughout this discussion run three important themes, which will be gathered and examined at the end. These are:

4 The role of supervision.
5 Relationships with other professional groups.
6 Employment opportunities for counselling psychologists.

Much of the discussion is limited to USA and UK contexts, because this is where most of the data is to hand.

The divisions of activity in counselling psychology into (1), (2) and (3) above imply a sequence similar to a stage model of life-span personal development, so an individual counselling psychologist might pass through all of these stages in turn. On the other hand, as with models of life-span personal development, others might miss out stages, stay far longer in one than in others, or pursue idiosyncratic and recurring pathways through the stages. Stage models of personal development are useful, in that they provide a structure. At the same time, they are problematic, in that they may seem to prescribe an oppressive uniformity. The benefits and limitations apply when such models are used to consider professional development.

Training and professional development: preliminary considerations

Sources

Before entering this discussion, it may be useful to consider on what this is based. Given the home of this discipline in psychology, it would be favourable to report that the views on training and professional development which are included are based on clear, prescriptive conclusions from well-constructed and executed research. However, as is evident from reviews and discussion of training in counselling psychology (Russell et al., 1984), in counselling psychology research (Fretz, 1986; Magoon and Holland, 1984), in consultation by counselling psychologists (Dustin and Blocher, 1984; Gallesich, 1985), in counselling (Dryden and Feltham, 1994), in psychotherapy integration (Andrews et al., 1992) and of the training of counselling trainers and supervisors (Clarkson and Gilbert, 1991), of the teaching and learning of psychotherapeutic skills (Matarazzo and Patterson, 1986), of the training and supervision of individual therapists (Aveline, 1990, 1992), and of supervision (Holloway, 1992), things are not so simple.

All of the texts referred to above are recommended for further study to understand in detail the reasons for this complexity. Space prohibits a full treatment here, but by way of a brief summary, the findings from research are limited. Early attempts to research the process of training were flawed conceptually and methodologically. In the case of the conceptual flaws, these included the fact that models of supervision, a central focus of research in this field, tended to be single-theory models, outgrowths of the particular counselling approach (such as psychodynamic, experiential/ humanistic or cognitive-behavioural) on which they were based. In terms of the methodological flaws, studies tended to focus on the easiest options, such as the process of micro-training of novice counsellors and therapists or analogue studies, to not include control groups, and to fail to consider all manner of factors such as trainee personality, nature of interaction with clients and interactions between dependent variables (Russell et al., 1984). Furthermore and crucially, few studies have linked the consequences of various forms of training to actual work with clients. However, it is encouraging that Holloway (1992) was able to report considerable progress since the review by Russell et al. (1984), both in the development of integrative models of supervision and of research based upon them, which addresses some of these criticisms.

The level of training

Another complex issue is the level to which 'basic graduate training' should progress. In the USA, there continue to be a large number of graduates from Master's level programmes in counselling psychology, who are effectively prevented from joining the profession by the decision of the American Psychological Association to restrict membership to those professional psychologists with Doctoral qualifications. There are also issues about exactly which Doctoral degree is appropriate. On the one hand, there are those who especially value the PhD, and the contribution of those holding this degree to the research literature. On the other hand, counselling psychologists were amongst the first professional psychologists to challenge the 'Boulder' model of the scientist-practitioner (named after the APA Conference held in 1949 at Boulder, Colorado, at which it was originated), to argue for the role of practitioner-scholar, and to promote the PsyD degree.

In the UK, patterns are changing at present, as most clinical psychology programmes have become three years' full-time duration, and a significant number now lead to the award of a doctoral degree (such as DPsych, DPsychol). The British Psychological Society Diploma in Clinical Psychology is about to be transformed into a Master's degree of the Open University. It seems highly possible that this qualification, together with the other Society qualifications (including the Diploma in Counselling Psychology), will become a Doctoral degree at a later date, not least because of the amount and type of student effort involved. It would therefore seem as if there is a clear trend towards the level of basic training in counselling psychology becoming a Doctoral degree.

The boundary for inclusion in the profession

At the same time, there is a distinctive and contrary principle widespread in the profession, displayed in the Vail recommendations (named after the APA Conference held in 1973 at Vail, Colorado) but repeated variously elsewhere. This is that the relative permeability of the boundary at the entry to the profession should be maintained. This is because of the respect of this discipline for equity in the regard of human experience; for the evidence on the effectiveness of differently trained, relatively less trained or untrained workers; and for the continuum of therapeutic skill from the leaders of the profession into the ordinary population. It is notable in the UK that the Special Group in Counselling Psychology of the BPS, which was founded in 1989 and became the Division of Counselling Psychology in 1994, was the first group in the Society to have a structure including members with both a non-professional, psychology graduate-level 'scientific' interest together with those with post-graduate professional training. This is a form which may well become the model for new groups within the Society, such as in health psychology. This replaces the pattern, for example, in British occupational psychology, where a scientific Section and a professional Division exist side by side.

The content of training

One issue on which there does, however, seem to be a wide-ranging agreement is the cardinal elements of basic graduate training. These include:

1   A theoretical basis for the understanding of problems of clients, their origins and context.
2   Potential means of intervention, and the systematic application of this knowledge.
3   Basic foundational skills.
4   The need for a certain level of personal development, to enable the fullest possible understanding of the position of clients, the least likelihood of 'blind spots' and other more active forms of unethical behaviour.
5   A series of carefully graded experiences, from skills practice with peers, through intensively supervised experiences at or near the training site (e.g. practicum), supervised experiences in 'real' field settings (internship or placement), to specialized requirements for licensing, lateral transfer from allied fields of applied psychology, and advanced practitioner status (residency).
6   Skills to enable the consumption and production of relevant research.
7   Skills to enable the practice of consultation, that is, enabling the work of others.
8   Skills to enable the practice of psycho-education.

Sometimes, the description of these elements and the process of their acquisition is based on survey techniques (e.g. Skovholt and Ronnestad, 1992). However, the inclusion of varying proportions of these cardinal elements may have more to do with tradition, external pressures from governments, political pressures from other professions such as psychiatry (Fretz and Simon, 1992), demands for quality assurance, limitations imposed by those who fund training, and increasingly in most contexts, market forces. Some clear indications and findings have emerged, but as with the practice of counselling psychology and the psychological therapies, these are sparse. As noted above, a particular point to be borne in mind with this discipline is the role of supervision. This has displaced training in a wider sense from the relevant chapter in the second of Brown and Lent's handbooks (Brown and Lent, 1984, 1992; Holloway, 1992) and will be considered separately below.

Graduate training

Defining the field

It is perhaps in the field of graduate training more than anywhere else that the central identity of counselling psychology as a discipline can be seen. Although the grandparents of the discipline could, and indeed have had to be, trained by and with professionals of differing backgrounds, it is through the construction of the main pathway leading into the profession that values, assumptions and indeed aspirations become explicit. The other main central plank of any discipline is the range of practice, and this is comprehensively addressed elsewhere in this volume, although it is perhaps worthwhile to remind oneself what the discipline aims to accomplish. Brown and Lent (1984, 1992) have retained in the second edition of their handbook their depiction of the field of counselling psychology in the USA as one,

> notable for its diversity and vigorous evolution. Influenced by diverse political and social forces as well as by developments from mainstream psychology, it has expanded from an initial concern with educational and vocational guidance to the remediation and prevention of personal, interpersonal, vocational and educational concerns. Further reflecting counseling psychology's growth is the great diversity in work settings, types of services performed, and theoretical orientations that characterise today's counseling psychologists. (1992: xi)

The specific origins of the discipline in the UK are different. There are not the roots in guidance and current practice in the vocational field, and an alternative emphasis is on the practice of counselling and psycho-therapy by psychologists. None the less, the diversity of concerns, settings and methods is the same, as is the consequent need for training and professional development to somehow attempt to match these demands.

585

However, it is only when there is a clear and unambiguous route of entry through training that any discipline can be said to lead to a profession, and this was illustrated in the UK when the British Psychological Society's approval of the Regulations for the Diploma in Counselling Psychology (1994c) led rapidly to the establishment of the Division of Counselling Psychology, even though it will be some years before any individual has travelled the entire route from approved undergraduate degree to fully qualified professional status. Elsewhere, the USA stands out as the country with the longest history of the discipline, with Canada, Australia and the UK having followed a long way behind, but in these countries too the training pathway (including this discipline's firm emphasis on this extending to the length of professional working life) is what has identified the discipline as distinct from others.

The case for difference

There are those in the representative bodies of professional psychology societies in various countries who would argue, given the nature of our world, with rapid and unpredictable change and the need for professions to match, that it would be better to reduce the distinctions between branches of applied psychology, and indeed between psychology and other disciplines which underpin the practice of helping and health care, and to aim instead for specialties within a generic discipline (British Psychological Society, 1991; Fretz and Simon, 1992). At the same time, others see this very context as a reason now more than ever to be firm about professional boundaries, lest complex professional tasks are reduced to a series of competencies that can be packaged, taught and sold, thereby destroying the potential for a strong and unique discipline to create new responses to as yet unknown future challenges (Elton Wilson, 1994).

A parallel to this apparent dilemma can be seen in the field of politics, where it makes sense for people to associate and interact on an increasingly global scale, whilst at the same time the world is beset by a growing number of ethnic conflicts about the most primitive of issues, as ethnic identity becomes more and more a crucial issue. As change results in the break-up of previously powerful vested interests, with a move of focus from training inputs to competence outputs, from completed time-serving to demonstrable competencies, so it becomes less possible to distinguish between mental health professionals from various backgrounds on the basis of what they can be seen to do. Indeed, 'umbrella' professions such as psychotherapy and counselling have emerged and are developing. Thus graduate training becomes a major differentiator between individuals who may, for a time at least, work closely alongside each other doing apparently similar work.

Differences from other branches of psychology

So what is different about training in counselling psychology? This begs the question of different *from what*? In a fascinating discussion in a parallel context, namely how to train researchers to do New Paradigm research, Rheinharz (1981) highlights the importance of starting with a thorough grounding in the Old Paradigm, not least in order to create an energy born of a mix of frustration and idealism. Counselling psychology is a kind of hybrid between two very different disciplines, and thus has two sources of such energy.

In relation to psychology, as noted above the difference is mainly from other applied specialisms, although it is also from the pure science aspects of the discipline. In most countries, traditional applied branches of psychology have included clinical psychology, educational or school psychology, and industrial/organizational (I/O) or occupational psychology. These specialisms themselves have been and are subject to development, challenge and change, but it is notable that these divisions are broadly about areas of application (to health care, education and the world of work), whereas counselling psychology has no such single area, with applications anywhere within the field of human life, across the continua of adjustment and development, through the range of associational groupings and throughout the life span, and aiming to address the full range of human diversity, including gender, race, ethnicity, class and sexual orientation. The central focus is instead on the use of the relationship between counselling psychologist and client (whether this is an individual, couple, family or stranger group, or an organization), and the use of that relationship to facilitate change. This depends on expertise, including understanding development and its vicissitudes, and the theory underlying a range of responses, but unlike other branches of applied psychology there is an essential focus on what Martin Buber termed the 'I–thou' (Clarkson and Gilbert, 1991) nature of the interaction.

Regarding difference from more scientific conceptions of psychology, a central aspect is the uniqueness of individuals and the importance of their phenomenological world articulated within a professional relationship, and a different view of what is needed to become and stay adept at working in this sphere. Certainly in the USA, one reason for the focus of research on training and supervision of neophyte therapists was that supervision was not seen originally as extending beyond qualification, whereas the issues of malpractice and licensing have changed this picture (Fretz and Simon, 1992). In the UK, an issue that the BPS Division of Counselling Psychology will need to address is the concept of a Chartered Psychologist as one able to continue in practice 'without supervision' (British Psychological Society, 1994a). This may reflect semantic confusion resulting from the various uses of the word supervision, but there is also an underlying question of the implied model of a professional psychologist as a technical expert.

Differences from counselling and psychotherapy

In relation to counselling and psychotherapy, differences would seem to be about rigour, complexity and flexibility. Charles-Edwards et al. (1990) noted an intrinsic conflict, in the British context at least, between the values of counselling and professionalism. However, this perspective may have changed: the 1994 British Association for Counselling (BAC) Annual Conference was focused on 'Counselling: an Emerging Profession'. Perhaps more significant is an apparent orthodoxy in counselling of the cardinal elements of training being theory, practice and personal development, with rare mentions of research. In the scheme for BAC Recognition of Training Courses in Counselling (British Association for Counselling, 1990), which should eventually determine a central component of the scheme for BAC Individual Accreditation of Counsellors as it becomes typical to have undertaken a Recognized Course, it is notable that courses making successful applications for Recognition are expected to present one clear theoretical model of counselling as part of their rationale, which should be reflected throughout the curriculum. Eclecticism or an integrative approach are not precluded, but if one of these is to be the theoretical orientation of a course, the meaning and implications of this decision are expected to be fully articulated and argued, and demonstrated throughout every aspect of how the course operates.

Again, within psychotherapy in the UK at least, the federal structure of the United Kingdom Council of Psychotherapists (UKCP) encourages training bodies to identify clearly with one orientation or another. Although 'Integrative' is part of the title of the second largest Section of UKCP, the other main identifier of this grouping is 'Humanistic': to be cynical, it is OK to be integrative, but your neighbours will thus inevitably be humanistic. In contrast, it is virtually implicit that counselling psychologists will be capable of integrative practice. Depending on the setting, this may require the demonstration of a personally integrated approach, with due acknowledgement of the range of accepted wisdom that can be based on theory, practice or research, or rather just the capacity to be proficient in two or more approaches. However, whatever the requirements, the acceptance and promotion of just one approach to the practice of counselling or indeed counselling psychology would not be acceptable, even if the practitioner had, for ethical reasons of competence given their disposition, one preferred mode of practice.

Regarding complexity and flexibility as applied to practice, it is notable that the number and range of clientele required to be treated in approved psychotherapy trainings is very limited. It may be that this reflects a time when these were intended to be specialist post-qualification trainings for practising mental health professionals, so that breadth and depth of practice wisdom could be assumed and did not need to be addressed directly on such courses, but as noted above, such courses are becoming, in themselves alone, professional trainings.

Summary: the core of basic graduate training in counselling psychology

So much for the neighbours: what of the discipline itself? Fretz and Simon (1992) note the contradiction between the exertions of counselling psychologists in the USA and the wealth of recommendations that they have produced at a series of national conferences, and the difficulty in getting those recommendations implemented. Traditions do exist, though, even if it may be hard fully to celebrate these in the form of training. In a seminal document in the UK, where the discipline has more of an opportunity to emerge almost from nowhere, it is notable that the British Psychological Society's Training Committee in Counselling Psychology (British Psychological Society, 1993) is keen to stress the importance of the core philosophy of courses seeking approval, but is equally keen that this should be distinctive and original, and indeed the major focus for the attention of approval teams.

Whatever the philosophy, it seems inevitable that the cardinal elements noted above should be included, namely theory (of development and its vicissitudes, of the context of difficulties, and of means of intervention), basic foundational skills, personal development, graded experiences of practice, research skills, consultation skills and psychoeducational skills.

Accepted good practice in training suggests strongly that these components should be taught in as integrated a way as is possible, so, for example, theory can be drawn out of experiential exercises and used to design skills with which to intervene.

Again, the problem of making research relevant is crucial in counselling psychology. This is actually no less the case in other branches of applied psychology or indeed in counselling and psychotherapy, but for a discipline that has systematic inquiry as a cornerstone, it cannot be overlooked in counselling psychology as it might elsewhere. A number of writers have grappled with this issue (Magoon and Holland, 1984; Fretz, 1986; Reason and Rowan, 1981), and come up with a range of solutions. One is that the core model of the professional should change from scientist-practitioner to that of practitioner-scholar, with the emphasis on the fundamental skill of the practitioner, including a reflexivity in practice on which inquiry can be based, rather than vice versa.

The inclusion of psychoeducational and consultation skills is also crucial to this profession, with its core emphasis on involvement across the life span with the whole range of ability and disturbance, including prevention and development. To encompass all of this within a basic training is clearly over-ambitious, but perhaps the key point is that a basic training is just that. Thus, to accomplish the mission of the profession, a well-rounded practitioner ideally needs (amongst a range of other things), therapeutic skills with individuals, couples, families, groups and communities. Taken alone, any one of these modalities requires a lengthy period of training: the standard pattern in the UK is becoming set at four years' part-time post-graduate study. What distinguishes the discipline of counselling psychology is a set of core values, which are translatable into practice, and what the basic training must do is transmit these values in such a way that they can be internalized into a basis for subsequent learning, much of which will need to be part of continuing professional development.

Trainer and supervisor training

Professional and conceptual issues

One issue that emerges from the literature on training in counselling psychology is the clear need for supervisors to be trained, and increasingly, for that training to reflect the integrative and scientific models of supervision that are slowly emerging. At present in the UK, supervisor training and recognition is almost a sole preserve of the field of counselling. As with BAC Accreditation of Counsellors, there is a requirement that the various parts of the submission for Recognition are congruent. These include an account of some of the applicant's supervision work (either audio or video taped or verbatim), the reactions of the supervisee to the supervision received, and an account of the applicant's philosophical and psychological understanding of supervision. The stipulations for supervision of counselling psychologists preparing for the BPS Diploma in Counselling Psychology are, as yet, minimal.

Clarkson and Gilbert (1991) have set out the most comprehensive view of the requirements for the training of supervisors and trainers, although this is in relation to their preparation for the training of counsellors. In the UK at least, the distinctiveness of the process, or of the candidates who wish to become trainers or supervisors, in the field of training of counselling psychologists has yet to be made explicit. The only exception to this is that those in the role of Co-ordinator of Training for the BPS Diploma in Counselling Psychology will normally be Chartered Counselling Psychologists, those in the role of Research Supervisor will normally be Chartered Psychologists, those in the roles of Supervisor of Client Work will have 'appropriate training and/or experience in supervision', and those in the role of Personal Counselling Psychologist (i.e. personal therapist) 'must hold qualifications and/or experience acceptable to the Board of Examiners', for example, UKCP Registered Psychotherapists, Chartered Counselling Psychologists, or BAC Accredited Counsellors (British Psychological Society, 1994b).

Clarkson and Gilbert have put forward a cyclical model of learning by trainee trainers, based on the work of Kolb et al. (1984) and Robinson (1974), involving phases of awareness, accommodation and assimilation, as trainee trainers move from unconscious incompetence to conscious incompetence, to conscious competence and finally to unconscious competence, before another cycle of learning begins. They also stress that the continual nature of this cyclical process is not for some mystical notion of perfection, but rather a natural expression of an evolutionary drive, so necessary in a discipline such as counselling, which continues to evolve and demands of its practitioners continued flexibility and willingness to keep developing. 'Being in touch with this evolutionary drive . . . enables trainers of trainers and supervisors to experience, model and inspire their charges in similar ways' (Clarkson and Gilbert, 1991). In terms of the complexity of the learning cycle or cycles in continuing professional education, these ideas on the process of supervisor and trainer training are simple, requiring the addition of 'double loops' (Schon, 1987), or even 'triple' and yet further loops (Burgoyne, 1992). These ideas are expanded below in relation to continuing professional development in the various spheres of counselling psychology.

The content of trainer and supervisor training

Clarkson and Gilbert (1991) do offer some very useful ideas on the content of trainer and supervisor training, and their list includes coverage of the following areas.

1 Knowledge of learning theory, integrated with the positive aspects of experience as learners.
2 Sound knowledge of the subject matter.
3 The nature and varieties of relationship.
4 The importance and use of individual learning styles.
5 Contracts and contracting.

6 Conceptual models.

7 Educational methods, means and media.

8 Intervention strategies and techniques.

9 Transference, counter-transference and parallel processes in supervision.

10 Selecting priorities and sequences.

11 Values and ethics.

12 Organizational or contextual factors; group dynamics, group development and group management – methods and goals.

13 Developmental stages of learning: timing and rhythm.

14 Evaluation of process and outcome.

15 Special preparation for examination or assessment procedures.

16 Self-care and modelling of personal and professional development.

17 The relationship between student and teacher or trainer and training group.

Clarkson and Gilbert expand on these headings. In relation to individual styles they note the schemata of Kolb et al. (1984), differentiating between accommodators, divergers, convergers and assimilators, depending on their relative position on the two axes of concrete experience to abstract conceptualization, and active experimentation to reflective observation. They also refer to Honey and Mumford's (1986) types of learning style preferences – Activist, Reflector, Theorist and Pragmatist. These and other schemata are useful ways of organizing what will be inevitable differences, and which may originate from factors including temperament, academic ability and all manner of cultural variables. The suggestion is that these differences are important practically, in terms of designing learning experiences and structures, but also philosophically, in terms of cherishing individuality and uniqueness. In addition, trainee trainers and supervisors need to be aware of their own strengths and to utilize these, but to try to develop as far as possible in complementary ways in order to extend their own range of competence. As elsewhere in the discipline, the need for integrative theoretical models is crucial.

Yet another of Clarkson and Gilbert's (1991) useful organizing ideas is that of bands of supervision, which they argue can also be extended to the training context. These are: Assessment and Treatment Planning – how to think about the situation; Strategies and Intervention Techniques – what can be done in the situation; Parallel Process – interferences or facilitation in the situation; Theory – explanations in the situation; Ethics and Professional Practice – values in the situation. They suggest that these notions provide a helpful tool for focusing attention and concentration in a particular session, and criteria for selection will include developmental levels of trainees, issues that trainees consistently avoid, as well as the priority given to critical issues (such as suicide) over any other material that has been presented.

Trainer and supervisor training: a summary

In summary, both of these roles (trainer and supervisor) require a degree of conscious competence that exceeds that required to be a competent practitioner: a firm grasp of authority; a well-formed appreciation of the dynamics of supervision or training, including particularly the triangular nature of supervision and group dynamics in training; and the commitment that Clarkson and Gilbert note to continuing growth and development for oneself. This last point, together with continuing professional development for practice, is examined in more detail below. Finally, thought still needs to be given to the *specific* preparation of trainers and supervisors of counselling psychologists that does not overlap with the preparation of trainers and supervisors of counsellors. Specific needs that stand out are for trainers and supervisors to be able to develop in their respective charges the skills of research, consultation and the design and evaluation of interventions.

Continuing professional development of counselling psychologists as practitioners, trainers and supervisors

Conceptual and professional issues

It should be clear from the above that there is a strong argument that, although the practice of counselling psychology, the supervision of counselling psychologists and the training of counselling psychologists have considerable overlaps, they are separate fields of professional activity requiring their own training and continuing professional development. Not all counselling psychologists will necessarily be suited to all of these roles, although many will combine two or even three in their professional practice. On the other hand, it very soon becomes obvious, in the consideration of any field of professional activity, that it is no longer possible – if indeed it ever was so – to look on basic graduate training as all the professional training one need ever do.

There is a growing literature in the field of continuing professional education (Burgoyne, 1992; Cervero, 1988; Houle, 1980), and a recognition that the task of facilitating continuing learning in the various professions is an area of activity that has integrity in its own right. Schon (1983, 1987) details some of the reasons for this phenomenon, including demoralization that the promise of professionalization has not been realized, and instead that there have been several disastrous outcomes. More pragmatically, Burgoyne (1992), writing in the field of management education, considers why facilitating learning rather than, or as well as, teaching or training a particular set of theories or techniques, is an attractive option. He relates this to the work of management, which may be to deal primarily with the 'unprogrammed' problems that are left when 'programmed' work is arranged to be done by technical specialisms. Additionally, he argues, managerial work may be continuously changing as a result of the change that it brings about itself to organizational forms and practices.

There would seem to be some strong parallels here to counselling psychology, particularly in the core activities of counselling, psycho-therapy and supervision, but also in work such as research and consultation. In management education, Burgoyne argues that it may be difficult or impossible to identify a stable core of theory and technique to teach, and although there tends to be a conventional core to programmes such as, in Burgoyne's case, the Master in Business Administration, which experience a high demand, these programmes come in for severe criticism for their relevance. In this context, teaching managers to learn, so that they can themselves cope with varying and unforeseen circumstances, becomes an attractive option. Burgoyne notes that change, diversity and uncertainty may also be true of other areas of professional practice, and make the same approach true in them also: this too would seem to be highly salient in counselling psychology. In some fields, the need for further training is driven partly by technical progress. This is partly so in human service professions, but more than this, it is necessary for practitioners to cultivate and retain a number of facilities, including what Schon has termed reflection-in-action (Schon, 1983, 1987). These ideas are based on a detailed study of a selection of professions (interestingly, one of which is psychotherapy supervision), but can arguably be extended to all kinds of professional activity. Therefore, although practice, supervision and training in counselling psychology need to be seen as different activities, they are all examples of the same kind of activity, and in this respect, the requirements of practitioners in these fields for continuing professional development have some elements that are shared.

The organization of continuing professional development

This raises a controversial issue. As noted above, one strongly expressed concern in counselling psychology has been that trainers should be counselling psychologists, and another has been, in the USA for example, that new professionals trained outside of the mainstream, by counsellor-educators or on EdD programmes, might be disadvantaged in some way.

In the UK, a major conservative notion that has endured into the Regulations for the BPS Diploma in Counselling Psychology (British Psychological Society, 1993) is that to gain approval for the purposes of equivalence of their training, courses will need to recruit only those students with the Graduate Basis for Registration as a Chartered Psychologist. Clarkson and Gilbert (1991) note that practitioners are likely to choose supervisors (and by implication trainers) who continue to practise. Indeed, this is an integral part of the BAC schemes for Recognition of Supervisors and Trainers, in that successful applicants should either be Accredited Counsellors or eligible for such accreditation.

Set against this viewpoint, some would argue that to exclude other professional groups from sharing some of the basic graduate education of counselling psychologists is a loss of a potential source of richness and diversity. Even some UK medical schools, an apparent bastion of conservatism, are teaching the whole range of health professionals together for large parts of their undergraduate curriculum. As argued above, continuing rather than pre-service professional education will have a central role in the professional development of counselling psychologists. This situation is shared with almost every other profession. It seems, therefore, that some of this continuing professional development should also take place alongside other professionals from related disciplines. A radical view would include professionals from apparently unrelated disciplines, such as philosophy and literature. It is arguable that the facilitators of this process of continuing professional development need to include professionals from the related disciplines, and from the new specialist field of continuing professional education (Cervero, 1988). These facilitators may not be counselling psychologists, counsellors, or psychologists, and the last group, professionals in continuing professional education, may not even be mental health professionals. Which view on this, or rather which balance of view, is correct is a question that counselling psychology as a profession will need to address with some urgency.

Some UK writers (Burgoyne, 1992; Presland, 1993) have described systematic ways that continuing professional development can be structured into organizational life rather than left to the whim of the individual, and this may become both subject to increasing challenge and yet of increased relevance given changing patterns of service delivery resulting from 'reforms' in public services. A series of reports in the USA have noted changes in the employment settings of counselling psychologists, with an overall trend away from higher education and towards private practice, which can include a range of patterns from single-handed independent practitioners to various forms of group practice. In the UK, there is no established pattern of organization for the delivery of counselling psychology services, so it may or may not be relevant to attempt to face the challenges faced by clinical and educational psychologist colleagues, with the consequent implications for continuing professional development.

For example, one change in the UK involves the move from a system where there was a nationally prescribed pattern of clinical psychology services. In the past, a district service would have had an establishment based upon central recommendations, and either had a budget for continuing professional development or been able to use the resources from unfilled posts for this purpose. In some cases, because of the training bottle-neck in clinical psychology and the difficulty of recruitment of clinical psychologists to unpopular geographical areas or specialisms, unfilled posts might have accounted for the bulk of the establishment of a district service. Thus, their value to a district manager represented a considerable and flexible resource which could be devoted to a range of options, including continuing professional development of those staff who were in post. Post-reform, the introduction of the notion of a 'purchaser/ provider split' means that now groups of staff need to bid to supply a service for a purchaser. Without a full staff it becomes impossible to bid for contracts and hence to acquire budgets from which to begin to attempt to meet needs for continuing professional development (CPD), and one net effect is to bring into question the need for disciplines such as counselling psychology in preference to other related mental health professionals, who may seem cheaper and less problematic to employ. This will be explored further below.

Kreiser and colleagues (1991) have proposed the notion of a 'professional family' for the CPD of mental health counsellors and this may be one model that merits further exploration.

The role of supervision, relationships with other professions and employment opportunities for counselling psychologists

These issues were raised at the beginning of this chapter as representing themes permeating the discipline.

The role of supervision

Regarding supervision, it should be clear that this is an activity that will carry on throughout the professional life of counselling psychologists, at least in terms of receiving supervision if not the offering of it to supervisees. Thus, it may be seen variously as the most important means of training for the profession, the most important means of quality control in practice, the most important means of continuing professional and personal development, and given postmodern views of the nature of research, one of the most important areas and means of systematic enquiry into the phenomenal world of clients and the operation of the discipline of counselling psychology. It is clearly an arena where considerable integration has taken place in the field of psychotherapy and counselling. It is an arena that raises issues for counselling psychology in relation to other professionals to be discussed below, but briefly, there is a case for counselling psychologists to claim leadership roles, which may involve supervisory responsibilities, in relation to other mental health professionals.

A particular issue that remains to be addressed is the supervision of counselling psychologists as opposed to counsellors or psychotherapists. Much of the literature on supervision (e.g. Holloway, 1992) involves the research study by counselling psychologists of the supervision of counselling, and implicitly, of counsellors. Texts on the theory and practice of supervision (e.g. Bernard and Goodyear, 1992) are frequently written by counselling psychologists, and based on the theoretical and research work of other counselling psychologists, but refer to the supervision of counsellors in general, including but far from exclusively those who happen to be counselling psychologists. Arguably, the practice of counselling psychology is broad-based, and includes the various areas of activity discussed in this chapter, as well as public policy, which has not yet been mentioned.

Although the need for career-long supervision has been particularly demonstrated in the area of the practice of counselling (by counselling psychologists and others), of scarcely less importance is the supervision of the practice of supervision, with all of its attendant complexity and need for reflective space and concerns about the protection of both clients of counsellors and counsellors/supervisees. Only latterly has the need for oversight in the practice of training become widely recognized: concern within UKCP to provide ethical protection for psychotherapy patients brought to light the vulnerability and frequently abusive experiences of psychotherapy trainees. BAC Codes of Ethics for trainers have moved towards the requirement for basic and continuing training in training for trainers, and the requirement for consultative support for practising trainers. If counselling psychology is to adopt such standards, and there is no reason to assume that it should and will not, and in addition, if it is to apply these to the specialized fields of consultation and research, a working counselling psychologist with a broad-based practice would need to have at least five relationships with supervisors (for their practice of counselling and psychotherapy, supervision, training, consultation and research), and possibly even more if a range of therapeutic modalities (including individual, couple, family and group work) is practised. It may be that there needs to emerge a specialist form of supervision by counselling psychologists, which, if not covering all of this range of activity, might be able to cover a great deal, and this will require the careful development of systematic training for this role. As with other areas highlighted in this chapter, there seems to have been very little thought or writing on this topic.

Relationships with other professions

This is an area that has a history in the USA (Fretz and Simon, 1992), but only a recent past in the UK. Many other professionals seem unaware of the existence of counselling psychology, and whilst in the USA this seems to lead to a perennial concern with identity, in the UK it seems to require a considerable public-relations exercise directed towards other psychologists, other professionals, and by no means least, the general public. Thus, many opportunities remain to be seized, or many battles to be fought. Professions with which the discipline has professional boundaries include: psychotherapists and counsellors; other applied psychologists (hitherto clinical, school or educational, and industrial/organizational or occupational, but increasingly health and sports psychologists); management consultants; professionals in training and development; medical practitioners, particularly psychiatrists, but also general practitioners; social workers; educationalists; nurses; and other therapeutic professions including art, drama, music and occupational therapy. Because of the broad scope of the discipline, the list can seem almost endless.

A major boundary issue in the USA involves the rivalry between psychiatry and psychology, and the competition for hospital privileges and reimbursement by insurance companies and similar bodies. Fretz and Simon (1992) report that one consequence of this is to reinforce conservative training curriculum and practice pressures from within mainstream psychology, as it seems crucial to those concerned that training receiving APA approval is standard and uniform in order to resist what are probably specious criticisms from psychiatry that psychology is a disparate and unreliable discipline. In the UK, third-party reimbursement has not to date been such a crucial issue. However, this seems to be changing as more counselling psychologists inevitably begin to work in independent practice. At the same time, bodies such as commercial employers are assuming responsibilities for employee welfare, and, together with new employers of counsellors such as fund-holding GP practices, for the training, supervision and continuing professional development of in-house counsellors.

The employment consequences of so-called reforms to the 'post-

Griffiths' National Health Service have been hinted at above in the consideration of collective continuing professional development. It seems clear that this could well create opportunities for counselling psychologists, and thus raise professional rivalries with other professions. Together with changes in the field of employment, which have been prompted partly by the introduction of the EC single market, there is a focus on competence together with a requirement for professionals to tender competitively to win the right to provide services. The positive side of this is that hegemonies can be more easily challenged, so, for example, psychiatric gate-keeping of therapeutic services has come to be seen by many as a needlessly costly and non-competent arrangement, and the tenancy of clinical management and leadership roles is more open to dispute than before. However, there are potential new boundary disputes for counselling psychologists, particularly with colleagues in clinical, educational and occupational psychology, and counselling. Interestingly, a form of organizational process, a mirror of the defence employed by some abused individuals to identify with the aggressor, can be seen, as psychology agencies dominated by clinical psychologists with little or no counselling expertise term themselves 'psychology and counselling agencies' and bid to take responsibility for the supervision of counsellors. This is similar to the way in which the Psychology of Women Section of the BPS used arguments that had been used (ultimately unsuccessfully) against them subsequently to join the (successful) opposition to the formation of a Section for the Psychology of Lesbianism.

It seems that apart from some areas of concern to some psycho-therapists, there are unlikely to be many contestants for the central mission of counselling psychology, with its distinctive emphasis across the life span and the range of human diversity. However, given the range of concerns of counselling psychologists, they are likely to find themselves much of the time in the professional backyards of many other professionals. Given the focus of counselling psychologists on the establishment, maintenance and repair of satisfying and productive relationships, this should surely present the profession with a challenge to make of this an opportunity rather than a destructive crisis, and one of the achievements of what Fretz (1993) has termed the 'third age' of counselling psychology may well be to make the most of this very opportunity.

Employment opportunities for counselling psychologists

As implied above, employment opportunities will clearly have to be fought for with professionals from other disciplines. A traditional base of the profession in the USA, and to a lesser extent in the UK, has been higher education, and this seems set to continue and expand. Particular examples include work in training, and in the full range of counselling service work. Successive surveys in the USA have noted an increasing trend for the destination of graduates from doctoral programmes to be various forms of independent practice, and this seems likely to be the case in the UK too. One change in the UK, particularly post-recession, is for various forms of combination by groups of psychologists in independent practice, effectively as psychology agencies, who are then in a position to bid for major contract work, and it seems that this will be a growth area for the employment of counselling psychologists. In the UK at least, two notable fields of employment that have burgeoned for fully understandable reasons are those of counselling in general practice/primary care, and workplace- or employment-related counselling, and whilst these are areas of growth that are shared with counsellors, with BAC having a Division of Counselling in Medical Settings and a Division of Counselling at Work, there may be distinctive roles for counselling psychologists. However, we would do well to seek to base these roles on sustainable premises, and avoid becoming the new hegemonists in relation to counselling colleagues.

An area that has previously been noted to have failed to fulfil its apparent growth potential is that of counselling (and now, by extension, counselling psychology) in school settings in the UK. This is not at all the case in countries such as the USA, Australia and New Zealand. This may reflect the battle that has raged in public education in the UK over means and ends. Here too, 'reforms' such as Local Management of Schools have devastated carefully developed psychological resources that do not thrive under such arrangements, and this has probably included the potential for novel counselling psychology resources (and employment opportunities). This must therefore remain a potential area for the future.

The same is true for the topic of Fretz's (1993) Presidential address to the Counseling Psychology Division of the APA: counselling psychology services for elders and their networks. Given an ageing population in many countries of the world and changing patterns of work and leisure, a role for the discipline needs to be developed in this part of the life span. Finally, ethnic conflict was used earlier as a parallel for professional rivalry, but although not all counselling psychologists could hope to emulate the pioneering and charismatically based work of Carl Rogers on world conflict resolution, a major concern for the future is the construction of positive means of dealing with ethnic and other aspects of the rich tapestry of human diversity. Fretz argues that the first two phases of the development of counselling psychology involved the relentless search for universals, and then attempts to patch up the tears in the fabric of human experience that resulted from the inappropriate application of those assumed universals to the range of difference that all humans embody. This leaves a humbling task for this third phase, so that difference can be seen as intrinsic and to be valued rather than a problem to be addressed after all the important decisions have been made.

Training and professional development: conclusion

I have attempted in this chapter to sketch out a path, or rather a network of pathways, that leads into and through the profession of counselling psychology. Some of this, particularly from the USA experience, is well trodden, but much of it remains to be developed in detail. In summary, this ground covers the basic training of around three years' full-time post-graduate duration, to roughly Doctoral level, and aims to produce people with the capacity to continue learning reflexively to be counsellors and psychotherapists, supervisors, trainers, researchers and consultants, and with a preparedness for a life-long experience of personal and professional development.

One of the central points that Aveline stresses in his work (Aveline, 1992), which represents his personal accumulation of practice wisdom, is the need for a **context**. In his case, this is a regional NHS psychotherapy service, but the point is still salient whatever the pattern of local service organization and delivery, and indeed, whatever the locality. Thus is may be important to stress and articulate the cardinal elements of a compre-hensive training in counselling psychology, which might well include the details of theoretical teaching and learning; skill learning and practice; practicum; internship and residency or their equivalents; personal therapy; and training and supervised practice in research, training, supervision and consultation. It may be that in pioneer settings for counselling psychology such as in the UK, it is important to start from what is available. In geographically remote areas, this might involve a dyadic trainer and apprentice relationship in which a number (but clearly not all) of the above elements take place. However, even here, this would need to be supplemented by other, complementary experiences. This could involve intensive workshop trainings (such as summer schools), which might focus on one component, such as skill learning and practice, or, rather like the block-weekend group-analytic training run by the London-based Institute for Group Analysis throughout the world (Pines, 1993), could themselves include the majority of the components of the training, with only ongoing practice and peer supervision taking place in between blocks.

All of this represents a move towards a context: experienced trainers have noted, when concern has been expressed about the fragmentary tendency of modular schemes, that student bodies have a tendency to gravitate together to oppose these tendencies. Indeed, the issue of peers as counsellors was extensively addressed by Varenhost (1984). Aveline's point is that the existence of a context, with enough intimacy for support, yet enough space for trainees (and indeed neophyte supervisors, trainers, researchers and consultants) to make mistakes with some impunity, and for all concerned to have the opportunity to learn, develop and adapt their work to local cultural values, may, as with the parallel importance of the relationship in therapy, result in a kind of training equivalence paradox. Thus, it may be that good things are notable in different trainings, but that good results ensue from seemingly very different patterns of combination of such elements. The attempt simply to determine the 'active ingredients' may, as with research into psychotherapy outcome, for the time being at least, prove frustrating.

References

Andrews, J.D.W., Norcross, J.C. and Halgin, R.P. (1992) 'Training in psychotherapy integration', in J.C. Norcross and M.R. Goldfried (eds), *Handbook of Psychotherapy Integration*. New York: Basic Books.

Aveline, M. (1990) 'Training and supervision of individual therapists', in W. Dryden (ed.), *Individual Therapy: a Handbook*. Milton Keynes: Open University Press (reprinted in Aveline, 1992).

Aveline, M. (1992) *From Medicine to Psychotherapy*. London: Whurr.

Bernard, J.M. and Goodyear, R.K. (1992) *Fundamentals of Clinical Supervision*. Boston, MA: Allyn and Bacon.

British Association for Counselling (1990) *The Recognition of Counsellor Training Courses*, 2nd edn. Rugby: BAC.

British Psychological Society (1991) *Report of the Task Force on Changing Trends in the Future of Professional Psychology*. Leicester: BPS.

British Psychological Society (1993) *Guidelines for the Assessment of Postgraduate Training Courses in Counselling Psychology*. MQB Training Committee in Counselling Psychology. Leicester: BPS.

British Psychological Society (1994a) *Register of Chartered Psychologists*. Leicester: BPS.

British Psychological Society (1994b) *Guidelines for Supervisors and Co-ordinators of Training for the Diploma in Counselling Psychology*. Leicester: BPS.

British Psychological Society (1994c) *Regulations and Syllabus for the Diploma in Counselling Psychology*. Leicester: BPS.

Brown, S.D. and Lent, R.W. (eds) (1984) *Handbook of Counseling Psychology*. New York: Wiley.

Brown, S.D. and Lent, R.W. (eds) (1992) *Handbook of Counseling Psychology*, 2nd edn. New York: Wiley.

Burgoyne, J.G. (1992) 'Frameworks for understanding individual and collective professional development', *Educational and Child Psychology*, 9(2): 42–54.

Cervero, R.M. (1988) *Effective Continuing Education for Professionals.* San Francisco, Jossey Bass.

Charles-Edwards, D., Dryden, W. and Woolfe, R. (1990) 'Professional issues in counselling', in W. Dryden, D. Charles-Edwards and R. Woolfe (eds), *Handbook of Counselling in Britain.* London: Tavistock/Routledge.

Clarkson, P. and Gilbert, M. (1991) 'The training of counsellor trainers and supervisors', in W. Dryden and B. Thorne (eds), *Training and Supervision for Counselling in Action.* London: Sage.

Dryden, W. and Feltham, C. (1994) *Developing Counsellor Training.* London: Sage.

Dustin, D. and Blocher, D.H. (1984) 'Theories and models of consultation', in S.D. Brown and R.W. Lent (eds), *Handbook of Counseling Psychology.* New York: Wiley.

Elton Wilson, J. (1994) 'Current trends in counselling psychology', *Counselling Psychology Review,* 9(4): 5–12.

Fretz, B.R. (1986) (ed.) 'Research training in counseling psychology', Special Issue, *The Counseling Psychologist* 14(1): 3–168.

Fretz, B.P. (1993) 'The Division 17 Presidential Address: Counseling psychology – a transformation for the third age', *The Counseling Psychologist,* 21(1): 154–70.

Fretz, B.R. and Simon, N.P. (1992) 'Professional issues in counseling psychology: continuity, change and challenge' in S.D. Brown and R.W. Lent (eds), *Handbook of Counseling Psychology,* 2nd edn. New York: Wiley.

Gallesich, J. (1985) 'Towards a meta-theory of consultation', *The Counseling Psychologist,* 13: 336–54.

Holloway, E.L. (1992) 'Supervision: a way of teaching and learning', in S.D. Brown and R.W. Lent (eds), *Handbook of Counseling Psychology,* 2nd edn. New York: Wiley.

Honey, P. and Mumford, A. (1986) *The Manual of Learning Styles,* 2nd edn. Maidenhead: Peter Honey.

Houle, C.A. (1980) *Continuing Learning in the Professions.* San Francisco: Jossey Bass.

Kolb, D.A., Rubin, I.M. and McIntyre, J.M. (eds) (1984) *Organisational Psychology,* 2nd edn. Englewood Cliffs, NJ: Prentice Hall.

Kreiser, J.S., Ham, M.A.D., Wiggers, T.T. and Feldstein, J.C. (1991) 'The professional "family": a model for mental health counselor development beyond graduate school', *Journal of Mental Health Counseling,* 13(2): 305–14.

Magoon, T.M. and Holland, J.L. (1984) 'Research training and supervision' in S.D. Brown and R.W. Lent (eds), *Handbook of Counseling Psychology.* New York: Wiley.

Matarazzo, R.G. and Patterson, D.R. (1986) 'Methods of teaching therapeutic skill', in S.L. Garfield and A.E. Bergin (eds), *A Handbook of Psychotherapy and Behavior Change,* 3rd edn. New York: Wiley.

Pines, M. (ed.) (1993) 'Papers on training and supervision', *Group Analysis,* 26(2): 131–82.

Presland, J. (1993) 'Planning for continuing professional development', *Educational Psychology in Practice*, 8(4): 225–33.

Reason, P. and Rowan, J. (eds) (1981) *Human Inquiry: a Sourcebook of New Paradigm Research*. Chichester: Wiley.

Rheinharz, S. (1981) 'The training of new paradigm researchers' in P. Reason and J. Rowan (eds), *Human Inquiry: a Sourcebook of New Paradigm Research*. Chichester: Wiley.

Robinson, W.L. (1974) 'Conscious competency – the mark of a competent instructor', *Personnel Journal*, 53: 538–9.

Russell, R.K., Crimmings, A.M. and Lent R.W. (1984) 'Counselor training and supervision: theory and research', in S.D. Brown and R.W. Lent (eds), *Handbook of Counseling Psychology*. New York: Wiley.

Schon, D.A. (1983) *The Reflective Practitioner – How Professionals Think in Action*. New York: Basic Books.

Schon, D.A. (1987) *Educating the Reflective Practitioner: Towards a New Design for Teaching and Learning in the Professions*. San Francisco: Jossey Bass.

Skovholt, T.M. and Ronnestad, M.H. (1992) 'Themes in therapist and counselor development', *Journal of Counseling and Development*, 70(4): 505–15.

Varenhost, B.B. (1984) 'Peer counseling: past promises, current status and future directions', in S.D. Brown and R.W. Lent (eds), *Handbook of Counseling Psychology*. New York: Wiley.

27

Counselling Psychology: a Sociological Perspective

Sheelagh Strawbridge and Ray Woolfe

This chapter differs from other chapters in this book in that it is primarily inspired by the discipline of sociology rather than psychology. Psychology thus ceases to be the tool through which counselling is examined and itself becomes the object of inquiry. This is congruent with the notion of the counselling psychologist as a reflective practitioner, a theme which is developed later in the chapter. The insights offered by sociology provide a tool through which the process of reflection can be facilitated.

We have entitled the chapter 'a sociological perspective' in order to acknowledge that sociology like psychology is a multifaceted discipline, which offers a variety of perspectives. For instance, much sociological research has focused on the subject of key divisions within society such as race, gender and social class. It is important for counselling psychology to be able to draw upon sociological insights relating to the social characteristics of clients and to develop a detailed knowledge about client populations. Do clients tend to be female rather than male and if so, why is this the case? Do clients tend to be white rather than black and if so, what are the reasons? Are clients predominantly middle class and why should this be so? Is brief therapy largely the province of under-privileged groups and how does the process of bringing together clients and counselling psychologists work? What is the age distribution of clients and what factors influence this?

The questions raised above seem, in the short term, unlikely to disappear and it takes little imagination to see that there are some key issues which demand attention. One concerns the lack of a widely available free counselling psychology service within the National Health Service and how the need to pay may exclude poorer sections of society. Another relates to the way in which counselling psychology is likely to be an enterprise largely by and for white people unless it can develop a transcultural perspective.

We have elected not to pursue the above questions, however, for three reasons. The first is that to do them any justice would require much more than one chapter. The second is that, at this stage in the development of counselling psychology, the statistical data needed are notable mainly for their absence, although more general material on mental health and illness is available (see Pilgrim and Rogers, 1993). The third and most important reason is that sociology provides powerful conceptual tools which allow the adoption of a more overarching and, therefore, more inclusive perspective.

The approach which we have adopted in this chapter derives from the efforts by sociologists to respond to a series of linked questions which have confronted them ever since the birth of the subject after the French Revolution. Indeed it could be argued that these questions provide the *raison d'etre* for the very existence of sociology. They concern the way in which societies on the one hand manage to cohere or maintain themselves and on the other hand manage to change. The classical literature of sociology, represented by the writings of Durkheim, Marx, and Weber, revolves around this debate. It provides us with a framework and tools with which to examine counselling psychology.

The framework places counselling psychology, and indeed psychology itself, within a wider social structure. The work of psychologists may be seen as assisting in either maintaining or challenging the fabric of this social structure. Seen in this manner, counselling psychology is not just a psychological activity but is also a cultural enterprise; hence the need for a sociological perspective (see Woolfe, 1983). The corollary of this position is the provocative one that psychology could be said to be upholding the status quo by helping to paper over societal cracks, thus assisting in the preservation of inequalities of race, social class and gender, etc. The chapter will consider this, drawing on the sociological study of ideology and of knowledge.

There is one final point we ask you to bear in mind as you read this chapter. Sociology provides a macro level of analysis. It seeks to illuminate the interface between the individual and society. When practice implications of the 'how to do it' variety are derived from its insights, these are often at a social policy level. For example, evidence about different types of family structures in contemporary Britain may be employed to advocate changes in social security regulations or evidence about the usage by black clients of psychological services may be used to amend the delivery of these services. There is a critical difference here with psychology. Psychology operates at a micro level. Practice implications of the 'how to do it' variety resulting from psychological inquiry are normally at the individual, pair or small group level.

While this book is not one of the 'how to do it' variety, it would be impossible and perhaps unwise for a volume of this kind not to address the general question of implications for practice. This chapter does engage in that kind of debate, but it does so, as befits a sociological perspective, at a macro level of analysis. In the first part, for example, there is discussion of how reframing the nature of the way in which helpers see disabled people can change the focus of work with them. Similarly it looks at how the way in which organizational structure and functioning is framed will influence interventions. So while the chapter does contain many implications for practice, they are at a different level from that which might be expected from other chapters, i.e. consideration of what the individual counselling psychologist does with the individual client.

In summary, this chapter explores the significance of the social and political context in which counselling psychology has developed and is being practised. It comprises two sections: the first considers the more general ways in which counselling psychology functions 'ideologically' in contributing to the reproduction of social conditions. In the second section, drawing on insights from the sociology of knowledge, there is a more specific focus on the relationship between counselling psychology and mainstream 'scientific' psychology (see also Strawbridge, 1992). This account incorporates a discussion of how the former challenges the established paradigm. This draws on the notion of 'postmodernism', which we define as a complex set of ideas that question the possibility of any single conception of reason or truth. Counselling psychology is seen as postmodern in offering a practice-led model of psychology which emphasizes the pragmatic and fragmentary nature of knowledge and of the centrality of values in professional decision-making. This is very much in line with the argument advanced in the first chapter of this book that the key defining characteristic of counselling psychology is its concern with the attitudes and values of practitioners.

Counselling psychology and the reproduction of social conditions

Counselling psychology and ideology

Imagine that as a psychologist you were asked to discuss the acquisition of knowledge which takes place through the education system. You might suggest that it is a series of activities which normally take place in classrooms. You might then continue to talk about the importance of an interaction between pupils and teachers enacted through the content of a series of formal bodies of knowledge. While this description is reasonably accurate, it contains only half the story. The education system is a key vehicle through which class and other social divisions in society such as those relating to gender and race are reproduced. Interpersonal interactions do not take place in a social vacuum. They are part of a wider process, to which they contribute, in which pupils are filtered, channelled, selected and routed into positions within society. The effect of this process is that society re-creates itself across generations.

A similar analysis can be applied to counselling psychology. This involves moving beyond perceiving the discipline entirely in terms of a therapeutic relationship between client and counselling psychologist and asking the question what function or roles does counselling psychology fulfil for the society of which it is part? This involves perceiving counselling psychology not just as the formal application of psychological knowledge to the practice of counselling, but locating it within the social, economic and political structure in which it takes place and of which it is part. This involves asking questions such as how counselling psychology relates to society and what part it plays in reproducing society.

The overarching concept which holds these ideas together is 'ideology'; what ideological functions does counselling psychology perform and how does it fulfil them? Rose (1989) has examined the history of psychology from such a perspective and has demonstrated the ways in which it performs an ideological function.

There is a tendency in everyday language to refer to belief systems with which we disagree as ideological, the term being used in a rather pejorative fashion. Conversely we tend to treat our own belief systems as though they are ideologically neutral. While we talk about ethics and ethical codes, we rarely stop to question the fundamental values under-lying counselling psychology. Concepts such as empathy, acceptance and congruence seem of such unchallangeable worth that their role within a wider social structure is taken for granted and rarely examined. The emphasis is on getting on with the job in the knowledge that the work which counselling psychologists are doing is intrinsically valuable and worthwhile. To refer to counselling psychology as an enterprise which fulfils an ideological function may at first sight, therefore, be surprising. However, if we deconstruct counselling psychology we find that, like all human enterprises, it is not neutral and that it upholds certain points of view rather than others. Chief among these is a belief in individual autonomy; the view that the individual is a free agent operating in an open-market situation.

Individualizing the problem

The belief in individual freedom has many consequences. The most important is to support a political position that the problems which people bring to counselling psychologists are largely of their own making and can thus be resolved on an individual basis. As actors in this system, counselling psychologists can be said to play an important role, the effect of which is to assist in maintaining the status quo. The process operates by directing attention away from the social and political causes of problems towards an emphasis upon individual and personal causation and responsibility. It thereby helps to consolidate the belief system that people are in control of their own destinies.

Consider redundancy, an area in which many counselling psychologists are engaged, as a case in point. The Keynesian view of unemployment which dominated British economic thought from the mid-1930s to the late 1970s emphasized its structural nature and accordingly the need for governments to invest in order to stimulate demand for goods and services. However, there was a major shift during the 1980s and first half of the 1990s. In this period, the argument of the New Right, that unemployment is not so much a macro economic and political issue as a phenomenon linked to personal attitudes towards and efforts to find work, achieved widespread legitimacy. Its effects are dramatically exemplified by the remark attributed to the sometime Conservative Secretary of State for Employment, Norman Tebbitt, that when his father was unemployed in the 1930s he didn't sit around but got on his bike and went off to search for work.

Seen in this fashion, failure to find work, particularly by young people, comes to be understood as a function of individual motivation (or lack of it) and as related to a deficiency in social and interpersonal skills. It can be argued that counselling psychologists potentially benefit from this formulation. The more that problems are perceived as individual and attitudinal rather than structural in origin, the more important becomes the role of the counselling psychologist. It is the counselling psychologist who is seen as having the training competencies necessary to help individuals to overcome the interpersonal, attitudinal and emotional blocks which are seen as holding them back. This leads to the expansion of psychoeducational programmes in fields such as interviewing skills and social and life skills. In these ways, the risk is that counselling psychologists are seen to collude with a process in which by a subtle shift of emphasis, the problem becomes defined in terms of changing deviant or under-socialized individuals rather than changing social structures.

Framed within this perspective, the counselling psychologist becomes a part of the problem rather than a part of the solution in so far as the effect of their work is to direct attention away from those cultural and structural features which generated the problem in the first place. This process has been described as one in which we 'anaesthetize' ourselves to the ideological function of helping activities (Strawbridge, 1994).

In addition, however, there is a wider impact on the practice of counselling psychologists. This is shifted away from its traditional person-centred, humanistic emphasis on individual fulfilment towards a more narrowly behavioural approach focusing on skills development. The cognitive-behavioural revolution in psychology during the 1980s has been matched in the field of counselling psychology by a continuing increase in skills-based, problem-solving and brief therapy models. In this period, arguably the most important written work on basic counselling training is that of Egan (1994). He has been a major influence upon a generation of trainers in counselling psychology. His work encapsulates the spirit of the enterprise economy, with its emphasis on the acquisition of skills as a precondition for changing one's life. Insight and awareness become relegated to secondary factors as change agents.

A parallel development has been a growing interest in short-term, brief therapy in which more directive, focused procedures are advocated. This is evidenced in methods such as cognitive-analytical therapy (Ryle, 1990) and solution-focused brief therapy (de Shazer, 1985). We do not in any way wish to deny the value of any of these approaches nor are we suggesting that they are inherently more or less valuable than the person-centred approach which tended to predominate during the 1960s and 1970s. Counselling psychology is nothing if not eclectic in its use of different models. What we are suggesting, however, is that the models which are preferred at any one time reflect the spirit of the age and the culture in which they exist. They are part of and at the same time help to form and reproduce that culture.

At this juncture, it may be important to pause for a moment, to take breath and to state in simple terms what is and what is not being suggested in this chapter. The ideas which are being advanced may perhaps seem controversial in a book of this kind and may at a personal level feel uncomfortable. A sense of proportion is, however, helpful and indeed essential. Individual professionals, as this chapter argues, work within a system. But that is not to say they are wholly determined by that system. Choice always exists for individuals in some form. Society constrains but even under the most authoritarian system it cannot wholly determine the nature of individual response. Individuals have choices, but within limits. Individuals, therefore, are neither wholly free nor wholly constrained and to paraphrase a famous statement made by Marx, 'human beings make history, albeit not in circumstances of their own choosing'. If this chapter is emphasizing the constraints it is doing so as a corrective to dominant psychological thought; its intention is not to deny that individuals make choices.

Having paused for reflection, we return to our basic position, which is that any belief that counselling psychology exists in some kind of cultural vacuum is a myth. However, it is important to understand the importance of myths. In particular they help to sustain group identity even though this may be at the cost of distorting the truth. We can take gender as an example. It is only since the 1960s that there has developed an explicit understanding of the ways in which traditional gender roles have been constructed within a patriarchal system. Feminist writers have been active in articulating some of the practical implications of this belief. They have suggested that one effect of helping activities such as counselling psychology is to sustain social systems of which a key one is the family, disregarding the possibility that such systems may be oppressive to some of their members, particularly married women. The question can be asked as to whose purposes are served in treating a woman say for depression in order that she can then go back to the system in which her depression was nurtured in the first place. The argument runs that she is not so much depressed as oppressed. Walker (1990: 108), in surveying the literature on marital satisfaction, suggests that 'marriage has a protective role for men, but a detrimental effect on women, in terms of their mental health'.

More generally, it has been widely argued that 'illnesses' such as depression are what Marshall (1988) describes as 'learned patterns of socially deviant behaviour of idiosyncratic thought that [result] from stress, powerlessness and isolation'. If so, it follows that preventive measures require some consideration of social change and a redistribution of power between groups. Smail puts this point more graphically when he says that 'The explanation of our conduct is not to be sought in a psychological analysis of individuals, but in a socio-economic, historical analysis of relations between people and of the ways these have shaped the world we have to live in' (1987: 70).

One response by psychologists to the demand for a more contextualized form of practice is to be found in systemic approaches and these have been particularly influential in the field of family therapy. Individual symptoms are seen as reflecting wider communication problems in the working of a system. However, while there is some recognition of system pathology, such approaches remain inherently conservative in that they fail to offer a critique of the contemporary family and thus would appear to uphold the unequal role of women and the sexual status quo (see for example Williams and Watson, 1988). These writers highlight the neglect of sexual inequality within family therapy.

Systems approaches direct our thinking back towards the structural-functional paradigm favoured by American sociologists such as Parsons, Merton and Shils in the post-war period (see for example Merton, 1957). In this model, the social world is seen as consisting of stable social systems, with clearly defined boundaries and interconnected parts. Any change in one part will generate compensatory changes in other parts. An analogy might be the human body. If one part of the system changes (for example, an organ becomes diseased), change takes place elsewhere which restores the system to its original state of balance and equilibrium.

Homeostasis is thus restored. In this world-view, it is difficult to see how radical structural change can take place as the emphasis is clearly on systemic stability.

Psychological reductionism

The individualization of problems can be understood as part of a wider process of what Pilgrim (1991), in the context of psychotherapy, refers to as psychological reductionism. He suggests that this can be of two sorts. The first is when social actions are reduced to individual motives. He offers the example of the trade union activist whose actions are explained in terms of 'authority problems' or when a fee-paying client's reluctance to pay is interpreted within the context of transference without reference to their financial circumstances and ability to pay. Pilgrim suggests that reductionism also operates at the organizational level. He argues that the discourse associated with the consultancy work of bodies such as the Tavistock Clinic and Institute for Human Relations reduces social policy decisions about mental health to psychological considerations of child care, particularly mothering. It also reduces class-derived industrial conflict to tensions within and between small groups.

This critique is not just applicable to psychodynamic approaches. The cognitive-behavioural paradigm is also subject to the same analysis. Concepts such as coping strategies and stress management are basic to the work of many counselling psychologists, yet their effect, particularly when applied in organizational contexts, is often to reinforce the belief that there is something lacking in individuals rather than that individual stress is a rational response to organizational pathology.

An interactionist model

The logic of this argument is that if counselling psychology is concerned with empowering people, it has to develop a concept of its own activity and method of working which is broader than the notion of skills development or even of the more humanistic notion of a helping relationship incorporating certain key core conditions such as empathy, acceptance and congruence. This involves a rather different way of looking at the world from that to which counselling psychologists have become accustomed. The desired model is interactive or contextual rather than reductionist.

An example from an organizational context of what may be required is provided by mentioning a classical study (Menzies, 1970) which seeks to explain social systems as defences against anxiety. Menzies argues that nursing rituals are essentially defences against the extreme emotional pain associated with working with sick, ill, distressed and dying people. However, Chapman (1983) argues that hospital rituals can be explained in a very different fashion as ways of conveying social messages. She suggests that Menzies's analysis divorces nurses' behaviour from the cultural norms and values which underlie hospital activities. She refers, as an example, to a case of the consultant who regularly humiliates the senior nurse on the ward round by asking her to do menial, domestic tasks. This act, she suggests, has nothing to do with alleviating anxiety but 'is a social ritual based on the undervaluing of female nurturing and caring roles and the overvaluing of male, instrumental and technical roles in the health service'. She concludes that nursing rituals are not so much defences against anxiety as a way in which power is exerted and the social order reinforced.

Counselling psychologists who operate in a consultative capacity, if they are able to operate within such a frame, have the potential to conduct an analysis which takes into account the social as well as the psychological implications of patterns of functioning within organizations. An example of such an approach by a counselling psychologist is to be found in the work of McLeod (1994), who examines the history of the National Marriage Guidance Council (Relate) as a case study to illustrate some of the basic organizational dilemmas and conflicts experienced in counselling agencies. Three areas of organizational dynamics are shown to have an influence upon work with clients: the social and cultural environment of the agency, organizational structure and ideology, and the life span of the organization.

Another example of how the application of an interactionist model can assist the counselling psychologist to make a more sophisticated assessment of a situation is to be found in the context of disability. Oliver (1978) explores how people who become disabled in adult life adjust to their disability. He argues that a conventional model of loss and grieving is almost inevitably applied, in which the person is expected to work sequentially through a number of stages. Oliver, however sets up an alternative model which he describes as 'symbolic interactionist'. He argues that researchers are predisposed to arrive at the conventional model for two reasons. First, as able-bodied people, they are conditioned to posit adjustment to disability as a problem. Few if any studies begin with the proposition that disability is not a problem despite the fact that, in his view, the evidence is that satisfactory adjustment is the norm rather than the exception. Secondly, because of the pervasive power of the model, disabled people have internalized a view of themselves which is consistent with the theory fed to researchers.

The alternative model begins by suggesting that while individuals may experience some of the feelings of loss, there is no basic process that must be worked through. Much depends on the meaning attached to the disability by significant others. The paraplegic in a spinal injury unit will, says Oliver, encounter doctors, nurses and psychologists who put forward a positive view of paraplegia which emphasizes such factors as personal independence, ability to work, compete in sport, etc. In contrast, family members may not receive such support and may internalize a much less positive view of disability, which emphasizes all the negative aspects such as the management of incontinence, the problem of sores, finance and immobility. The message they may receive is to buck-up and get on with it.

The meaning attached to the disability is negotiated for the newly disabled person through interaction with both of these groups, families and professionals. The basic point is that the perception of the grieving process as central results not as a direct consequence of the disability itself but emerges out of the variety of meanings from significant and generalized others with whom the disabled person interacts.

The message here is that individual emotional and psychological responses depend at least in part upon social interaction. This greatly influences self-concept and is consistent with the existential belief that our sense of self is derived from our experiences rather than being a cause of them. The myth of the disabled person as helpless and dependent derives from a society which can be described as disabling. Oliver goes on to suggest that similar myths have become attached to families with handicapped children, for example that shame and guilt are inevitable responses. The myth is reinforced by research which does not understand that the data received from respondents represent a meaning system formed through past interactions.

Counselling psychologists are not merely observers or just researchers in this process. On the contrary, they are players, often important players, in the construction of meaning systems. Normality in areas such as intelligence, behaviour and mental health is heavily influenced by psychologists. It follows from this that what counselling psychologists might regard as normal psychological processes may be much more relative than is usually assumed and are rooted in habituated, socially constructed ways of thinking about issues.

The purpose of these accounts of how an interactionist model can be applied to areas such as organizations and disability is not to disempower counselling psychologists by dismissing their work as part of an oppressive system. On the contrary, what this discussion indicates is that there is an enormous potential for empowerment if counselling psychologists are able to reflect in this fashion upon their activities as researchers and practitioners. This has implications for methods of working with clients: for example, encouraging women or gay/lesbian people to work together in groups so as to appreciate the commonality of their experience rather than their separation, uniqueness and differences which is the philosophy underlying one-to-one relationships. This strategy emphasizes the educative and consciousness-raising role of the counselling psychologist and sees him or her as more than a remedial therapist.

The process of coming to know another person through the negotiation of a shared understanding also has major implications for the manner in which counselling psychologists engage in research. What was once called qualitative research and is now in the USA referred to as 'human science' emphasizes the cooperative nature of the research venture in which two parties become partners in a shared attempt to construct a common meaning. In translating meaning into experience, however, people can only employ the meanings available to them and these meanings, as we have already suggested, often derive from a position of lack of awareness of oppression. Woolley (1993), talking about people like herself, who become deaf in adult life, says that 'as hearing able-bodied people we learned how to see disabled and deaf people as dependent and pretty useless members of society. As deafened people, we have carried this prejudice towards disabled people into our own deafness.' Pilgrim (1990) argues that in dealing with this issue researchers need to deconstruct clients' texts. This involves 'a tacking to and fro between account and context'. Through this process, the issues which are raised in research (and in therapy) can be understood as products of social categories like social class, race and disablement and not just as individualized products.

Empowerment

Much of what we have said so far in this chapter bears upon the concept of empowerment and it is valuable to articulate a number of possible meanings of the term. Counselling psychology is strongly rooted in the humanistic tradition of writers such as Rogers and Maslow. This emphasizes the potential of human beings to develop, given the right conditions. The person-centred practice which has emerged from Rogers's work elevates the relationship between counselling psychologist and client to a position of centrality so far as the former's well-being is concerned. Nor is this the only paradigm in which the relationship between counselling psychologist and client is seen as a crucial variable in helping. Indeed, the consistency with which the importance of this factor has been identified has operated as a significant force in the move towards integration of approaches. Howe (1993) reviews a range of research studies over a 60-year period on the question of what those on the receiving end of counselling say about the experience. His central finding is that the particular theory used by the counsellor is less important than the quality of the experience. The key themes that emerge in successful therapy are 'accept me, understand me, talk with me'. In other words, the emphasis is on the development of a working relationship. However, this leaves an issue about the way in which power is expressed in the relationship.

It is commonly argued, particularly within the humanistic tradition, that the therapeutic relationship is characterized by an equality between the two parties. Through the relationship the client becomes empowered. However, this position should not be accepted without discussion. It can be argued that there is something intrinsically unequal and hierarchical in a relationship in which one person has training and experience, while the other is in need of help, is vulnerable and likely to be unused to this type of relationship.

Issues such as these have been most systematically addressed by helpers working within a feminist framework. It has been suggested that inequality is reduced and the potential for empowerment increased if female clients have female counselling psychologists. As both will have experienced the oppressive nature of a patriarchal, sexist society, they will share a common knowledge base. By a similar criterion, black clients should be entitled to black counselling psychologists.

A more concrete example of what a more egalitarian relationship looks like is provided by Watson and Williams (1992), who identified a number of strategies which facilitated a relationship of equality between therapist and client in their work with women. These were: (a) attempting to clarify the process of their work to participants with whom they were involved; (b) making their own personal standpoint explicit; (c) encouraging participants to express their rights over, for example, the choice of a therapist; (d) encouraging participants to negotiate the aims and to evaluate the outcomes of therapy; and (e) emphasizing participants' strengths.

Conclusion

We have described how counselling psychology can be thought of as a component of a system that emphasizes individual freedom and choice and helps to reproduce that system. We have also introduced another ideological position, which argues that individuals are constrained and even determined. Gramsci (1971) expresses the latter in using the term 'cultural hegemony' to describe the way in which ruling groups dominate by controlling the world of ideas and not just through brute political or economic force. Individuals may believe that they are free, but the reality is rather different. Seen thus, the effect of counselling psychology is to facilitate spontaneous consent by reinforcing and legitimizing the views of powerful groups. This does not appear to be a model of empowerment for the client.

However, while acknowledging that such a position is overly deterministic, we have argued that it contains value in directing our attention towards a more interactionist model of the relationship between counselling psychologist and client. This focuses on the social context in which the work takes place and in doing so offers messages about the nature of practice and its potential for facilitating social as well as personal change.

Counselling psychology and the mainstream

Psychology as a discipline

Although counselling psychology developed as a branch of professional psychology, rooted in the clinical and research work of Carl Rogers, Abraham Maslow, Rollo May and others, historically the relationship between counselling and mainstream 'academic' psychology has not always been an easy one. One reason for this lies in the way psychology has developed as a discipline and the claims it has made about being 'scientific'. Counselling psychology has developed models of practice and inquiry which are at odds with the dominant view of science within the discipline. A branch of sociological inquiry which can help us to understand the tensions in this relationship and the basis on which counselling psychology makes its own claims to knowledge, is the sociology of knowledge.

The sociology of knowledge explores the socially and historically varied ways in which people think. Fundamental questions like 'What motivates peoples' actions?', 'How do we judge the quality of a work of art?', 'How is the physical world made up?', have been asked and answered differently in other societies and in our own in different historical periods. The sociology of knowledge seeks both to describe ways of thinking and to link them to key aspects of social life. For example, we may assume that the way we think about time is simply the result of technological progress, the development of accurate measuring devices coupled with the ability to synchronize local times. However, the historian Edward Thompson links this way of thinking about time, as standard and measured by clocks, to changing work patterns required by the factory system in industrial capitalism. Agricultural rhythms, related to daylight and seasonal changes, were inappropriate to the organization of work in factories and time-keeping by clocks became a central work discipline that required a major adjustment in thinking (Thompson, 1967).

Looking at modern science as a way of thinking, its development is now generally linked with the 'Enlightenment'. This was a new framework of ideas about nature, human beings and society originating in the mid-eighteenth century and centred in France. It marked the beginning of what has been described as the modern period or 'modernity' and was characterized by its challenge to the traditional European world-view dominated by Christianity and the Church's authority. It insisted on reason and rationality as the basis of knowledge and the model of scientific knowledge rooted in the 'scientific revolution' of the seventeenth century was promoted as the key to the expansion of all human knowledge. This belief in the power of science was coupled with equally strong beliefs in technological and social progress. Social progress would itself be enhanced by the scientific understanding of human beings and the workings of human societies.

The model of science central to Enlightenment thinking was grounded in the philosophy of positivist empiricism. It stressed that knowledge claims must be based on 'objectively observable' facts verifiable against sense experience. This was important, as it proposed a rational, empirically based method for creating knowledge free from religious dogma and moral values rooted in theology. The Enlightenment project was extremely successful and the model of scientific knowledge at its heart became the yardstick against which all claims to rational knowledge were judged.

Modern psychology had its origins in the second half of the nineteenth century as one of the disciplines aiming to apply scientific methods to the study of human beings. It assumed that there are discoverable laws that could constitute a body of knowledge allowing the prediction and control of human behaviour. Once discovered these laws could be applied to the treatment of criminality and mental illness, the assessment of abilities and aptitudes, the education of children, the organization of work and so on. There are a number of linked elements in this view of a scientific psychology which are challenged by counselling psychology. These are the emphasis on:

- value-free inquiry;
- the objective observation of behaviour;
- the detachment of the psychologist/observer;
- the measurability/quantifiability of data and the derivation of statistical laws;
- prediction and control; and
- the separation of 'pure' research from its applications in practice.

In contrast, drawing on an alternative model, counselling psychology emphasizes:

- the value basis of practice;
- subjective experience, feelings and meanings;
- the empathic engagement of the psychologist with the world of the client;
- the acceptance of the subjective world of the client as meaningful and valid in its own terms;
- the need to negotiate between perceptions and world-views without assuming an objectively discoverable 'truth';
- the qualitative description of experience;
- the development of insight and increased capacity for choice; and
- the primacy of practice in generating knowledge.

So long as the 'modern' model of natural science was seen as the only legitimate basis for psychological research, counselling psychology could hardly be acknowledged as genuine 'scientific' psychology. The acceptance of counselling psychology within the British Psychological Society leads us, therefore, to question what has changed. As psychology continues to define itself as a scientific discipline, we must presume that previously excluded, alternative models of knowledge and methods of inquiry may now be included within a changed or changing definition of science or scientific psychology.

Counselling psychology and scientific psychology

No one can question the power of science when we consider its enormous influence in our lives. It is, therefore, not surprising that the natural science model was pre-eminent in the development of modern psychology. Nevertheless, history is always complex and, from the earliest conceptions of social science and psychology, people have questioned the appropriateness of using the same methods to study both the natural and the human world. Such questions were asked by the 'humanistic' psychologists who constituted a self-defined tendency, in North American psychology, from around 1940. Carl Rogers and Abraham Maslow were key figures who, although seen as rebels, were highly regarded and elected to the presidency of the American Psychological Association in 1947 and 1968 respectively.

Humanistic psychology became the 'third force' in American psychology in the context of the civil rights movement and a general questioning of Western concepts of progress in the post-holocaust world. It gained momentum in the climate of protest against the worst excesses of technological society, the threat of nuclear war and the Vietnam war. Counselling first emerged amongst a number of democratizing practices in humanistic psychology and challenged both psychoanalytic and behavioural models of clinical practice. It foregrounded the quality of the therapeutic relationship rooted in core values and emphasized both the validity of the subjective experience and the capacity for self-determination of the person in the client role.

Whilst some claimed the ideas of humanistic psychology as utterly original and revolutionary, Rogers, Maslow and others were more aware of their philosophical and methodological roots in a distinctive European phenomenological tradition. Rogers linked his own work to this tradition (e.g., Rogers, 1964). Spinelli too notes the connections but suggests that humanistic psychology reflects a North American attitude emphasizing technique 'if it works, do it' and adopting an over-optimistic view of human nature and human freedom (1989: 159).

The phenomenological tradition dates back at least to the nineteenth century, by which time history, psychology, sociology, economics and social anthropology had emerged as rigorous empirical disciplines. Claims were made that their subject matter is crucially different from that of the natural sciences and requires differing methods of study. To distinguish this group of disciplines, John Stuart Mill coined the term 'moral sciences' which became *Geisteswissenschaften* in German and re-translated as 'human sciences'. Their distinctiveness was strongly argued by the German philosopher William Dilthey, who linked the notion of human science to a theory of understanding and influenced the development of research into human consciousness, subjective experience, meaning and culture.

Since the nineteenth century, the human science tradition has existed in Europe as an alternative with established methods grounded in phenomenological philosophy. It was less in evidence in Britain and America, where the natural science model, based in positivist philosophy, predominated in psychology and the social sciences at least until the 1960s.

In parallel with the growth of humanistic psychology in America, the phenomenological tradition was itself enjoying a period of revitalization in the climate of political and intellectual upheaval in Europe in the 1960s and it was posing a vigorous challenge to all over-deterministic conceptions of history, social structure, social processes and human behaviour. Marxists, confronting the realities of Stalinism, renewed their interest in the early, more humanist, writings of Marx and made a significant contribution to this challenge. Consciousness and human agency were re-discovered and the development of methods appropriate to the study of self-conscious, reflective and self-determining beings was enthusiastically undertaken. The range of rigorous, qualitative research methods we now have available owes much to this period.

This humanism of the early 1960s in turn became the subject of critiques which, among other things, re-asserted the role of social structures in shaping human identities and human history. Humanism was seen as over-emphasizing the responsibility of individual human beings for their own circumstances and life changes. These 'structuralist' critiques, nevertheless, shared with humanism a concern with meaning and consciousness as central in human life. They drew on developments in linguistics which define languages as symbolic systems that provide the structures of meaning which make thinking possible. Consciousness is thus seen as a fundamentally social property and human action as taking place in the context of socially structured meaning systems, something which, as we have seen, person-centred counselling can overlook.

From this time it has been more acceptable, in Britain and America, to engage in forms of psychological research and practice grounded in humanistic and phenomenological traditions as well as drawing on the insights of structural linguistics and structuralism more generally. Nevertheless, mainstream academic psychology has held firm to the natural science model and, in Britain in particular, it has been in the context of organizations committed to the development of counselling and psychotherapy, largely outside this mainstream, that counselling psychology has been nurtured. Its recognition by the professional body as a branch of psychology has been greatly facilitated, not only by the resurgence of questioning of the appropriateness of the natural science model for human science, but also by the more general questioning of the 'modern' model of science as a basis for our understanding of the natural world. Developments in the sociology of scientific knowledge have proposed new ways of seeing scientific practices and the whole project of the Enlightenment has been fundamentally challenged by postmodernism and poststructuralism.

Changing conceptions of science

The sociology of knowledge was initially conceived as the study of 'ideological' and 'common sense' thinking. It was not until the 1930s that Robert Merton drew attention to science as a social institution and the importance of the social contexts within which it develops. Because science is seen to be 'useful', it attracts economic and political support. Merton connected the growth of science in the seventeenth century to a combination of economic and military conditions and to the Puritan values which stressed diligent labour in a worldly calling as the way to express faith. He also explored the ways in which conditions in Nazi Germany inhibited scientific developments, for example, by its suppression of 'Jewish' science, including Einstein's theory of relativity. The impetus given to the development of psychological testing by the military need to screen recruits and the influence of drug companies in medical research are further examples of the significance of social and political influences on science.

These early sociological studies of science made a distinction between the technical and the social aspects of scientific knowledge. They concentrated on the social conditions under which scientific knowledge is produced and the socio-political influences on the development and use of science and technology. The manifest achievements of scientific thinking supported the belief that, no matter how much the amount and kind of research done was socially influenced, the knowledge produced was unaffected. Nature itself was seen as the reality against which scientific theories were 'objectively' tested.

More recent philosophical conceptions of the nature of scientific knowledge have weakened this view. It is now generally accepted that observations of the world are always made from a particular viewpoint and are theory-dependent. Karl Popper (1959 [1934]) argued, however, that scientific theories have a special status because they are rationally tested by systematic observations and experiments. Although they can never be conclusively proved, good theories resist every effort to falsify them, whilst making definite claims and predictions which indicate how they could be disproved.

Popper's 'falsificationist' view of science was widely accepted both as a description of what scientists actually do and as a model of good practice. It was certainly influential in the development of mainstream conceptions of scientific psychology. There are, however, serious objections to falsificationism, partly due to the complexity of theories and of their relationship to observations. (For an extended discussion of this see Lakatos and Musgrave, 1970.)

A very different and controversial view of science was proposed by Thomas Kuhn (1962). Far from seeing science as a highly rational activity, he argued that historical studies demonstrate its fundamentally social character and the importance of the communities in which scientists work. Each mature scientific community has a consensual culture with a shared 'paradigm', a whole way of thinking and working within an established framework of theories, ideas and methods. Young scientists are socialized into these cultures and must, if empirical work is to be done, learn to take the paradigm for granted in much the same way as we are socialized into the taken-for-granted frameworks of our everyday lives. Kuhn calls work within a paradigm 'normal science' and describes it as a kind of puzzle-solving activity which fleshes out the bare bones of the paradigm with detailed knowledge.

Research within 'normal science' inevitably produces observations and experimental results that conflict with the paradigm and eventually render it unstable. Professional scientists become insecure about the nature of their discipline and the crisis deepens when a rival paradigm makes its appearance. This will present a very different picture of the world. It will regard different kinds of questions as meaningful and will apply different research methods and standards. Scientists who convert to the new paradigm do so for reasons that are more social than rational. Younger ones, with their productive careers ahead of them, those with a peripheral status or contact with other fields and disciplines and those who occupy more than one role, such as practitioner-scientists in medicine, are more likely to convert and be involved in the process of innovation than more established colleagues. The generation and establishment of a new paradigm is termed a 'scientific revolution'.

So Kuhn holds that social forces affect the theoretical judgements of scientists as well as the conditions under which scientific knowledge is produced. His work paved the way for sociological studies of the practices of scientists, the process of research and the content of scientific knowledge. These are rather technical studies carried out by sociologists familiar with the scientific work being done. Moving beyond Kuhn, they provide detailed evidence of the social character of science (e.g., Knorr-Cetina and Mulkay, 1983). In recent years feminist critiques have raised further issues about the value framework of the 'modern' model of science and the more general concept of rationality on which it is based (e.g. Bleier, 1986; Harding, 1986). These critiques have also pointed out that differing conceptions of nature and knowledge are to be found if we look outside European, white, colonial and bourgeois culture.

Whilst differing theoretical perspectives and methodologies are encompassed by mainstream academic psychology, most have aimed to be scientific – defined in terms of the modern natural science model. We have already noted that in emphasizing the value basis and primacy of practice, the empathic engagement with subjective worlds, the capacity for insight and choice, and in questioning dominant conceptions of objectivity, counselling psychology has developed approaches to practice and enquiry at odds with this model. It is only now, as this view of science has been modified, that counselling psychology can establish its claim both as a branch of knowledge and a professional psychological practice.

Interestingly, counselling psychologists fit Kuhn's description of those scientists likely to convert to a new paradigm: having peripheral status within the discipline, being in contact with other fields and disciplines and often occupying more than one role. However, what we seem to be encountering is not so much a paradigm shift within a science but a broader questioning of the pre-eminence of the modern Western scientific conception of rationality. This questioning has been termed postmodern and postmodernism challenges the view that there can be any

623

defensible conception of a single unifying model of rationality. It has been suggested that this postmodernist 'play of multiple emergent knowledges vying for legitimacy' goes beyond Kuhnian frameworks (Lather, 1990: 92).

Postmodernism and counselling psychology

The modernization marked by the Enlightenment undermined the traditional authority of the Church, along with the values and ways of thinking it supported, and a perceived danger, built into the dynamism of the modern economy and culture, is the constant upheaval and undermining of values, truth and authority. This has been termed the 'legitimation crisis' of modern times. One of the imperatives of modernity has been to resist this by establishing a rational basis for truth, values and authority and we have noted the importance of science in providing a model of rationality which seemed adequate to this task. Modernist movements in the arts such as cubism, surrealism and Bauhaus architecture belong to the twentieth century and these were critical of modern life, rejecting bourgeois values and mass culture. Their critiques were, however, made in the name of social progress in order to build a better, more rationally ordered society, and, like modern science, 'modernism' could still be identified with the project of the Enlightenment.

The scientific model of rationality has, as we have seen, been seriously questioned. Modernism in the arts has also been subjected to critiques, often embedded in new styles and practices, that first attracted the term 'postmodernist'. This term now has a much wider significance, extending to a declaration of the death of the whole project of the Enlightenment or 'modernity'. Postmodernism is a complex and debatable set of ideas and practices to which we cannot here do justice. It can be linked to poststructuralism, which was first associated with a number of French thinkers including Michel Foucault and Gilles Deleuze, who became critical of the Marxist belief in the rationality of the historical process. They turned to Nietzsche for inspiration and eventually produced a general assault on all philosophical conceptions of reason and truth which were declared to be repressive. Like Max Weber, they argued that the world can never be grasped within a single unified theoretical system. Life is inherently multifarious and contradictory and all thinking and evaluation limited within perspectives. They maintained a similar view of the relation between language and consciousness to the structuralists, but rejected the conception of languages as large unified systems in favour of smaller systems or 'discourses' located in specific forms of social relationships.

A central concern of postmodernist/poststructuralist thinkers is the way grand theories and overarching systems of thought tend towards totalitarianism. When we think of Auschwitz, Stalinism and Khomeini it is easy to see their point and one positive influence has been in stressing and valuing human difference. The danger, however, lies in an extreme relativism of standards of truth and value in which anything goes and might means right. Jean-François Lyotard, himself an influential poststructuralist, like Foucault drew back in his later works from this tendency to equate truth with power. In 1979 he published two books (Lyotard, [1979] 1984; Lyotard and Thebaud, [1979] 1985). In the first he tries to develop a concept of justice which does not depend on universal rational principles and in the second he attempts to connect this to a broad characterization of the present age and its political possibilities. In this work he maintains a poststructuralist stance against overarching belief systems, stemming from the Enlightenment, which he calls the great 'meta-narratives' of the modern period. He seeks to identify the liberating potential in postmodernism, arguing that it is 'little narratives' that are the quintessential form of imaginative invention. Moreover, consensus is not the goal of dialogue but a stage within it. Justice is, however, neither outmoded as a value nor suspect. We must, therefore, arrive at an idea and practice of justice which is not linked to that of consensus. He says that the recognition of the varied forms of social life is the first step because it implies a renunciation of terror. The second step is a principle limiting any consensus. Social life is seen as governed by a multiplicity of 'little narratives' inherently open to challenge and cancellation. Postmodernism has the potential of liberating us from the terror consequent on the search for a totalizing grand narrative.

When we consider the approaches to practice and inquiry developed in counselling psychology we can find some strikingly postmodernist characteristics. Perhaps most significantly, in its respect for the subjective truths expressed in the 'little narratives' of our individual lives, its celebrating and valuing of difference and in its espoused intent to 'empower', it has the potential to contribute to challenging oppression.

Polkinghorne (1992) has drawn attention to the more general features of a postmodernist, practice-led, model of psychology. He argues that the psychology of practice emerged under the shadow of academic psychology and that, whilst the latter focused on the discovery of general laws of human behaviour, the former focused on pragmatic action in the service of mental health and personal development. Finding academic psychology's model of knowledge of limited relevance in responding to clients, the psychology of practice developed its own body of knowledge consisting of a 'fragmented collection of discordant theories and techniques', based on actual interactions between practitioners and clients.

Although rarely made explicit, underlying the generation of knowledge through practice is a particular model of knowledge or 'epistemology' which is postmodernist in character. It assumes that: there is no firm foundation for establishing indubitable truth; bodies of knowledge consist of fragments of understanding, 'little narratives', rather than large logically integrated systems; these fragments are constructed in cultures; and, knowledge is tested pragmatically, by its usefulness. Polkinghorne links this postmodernist epistemology of practice to a range of studies of the ways in which professional practitioners in a variety of disciplines actually develop and apply knowledge in practice.

Donald Schon (1987), writing on professional practice, has, for instance, described the 'technical rationality model' as painting a picture of 'a high, hard ground overlooking a swamp'. In the swampy low-lands which are the 'indeterminate zones of practice' characterized by uncertainty, uniqueness and value conflict, the canons of technical rationality do not apply. Indeed technical rationality is not only an inadequate model for practice, it contributes to professional incompetence by focusing on problem-solving at the expense of the crucial task of problem-setting.

Schon finds that, rather than applying formal theory and research, successful practitioners learn from experience and that reflection-on-action, often with other practitioners, and reflection-in-action, the monitoring of practice in process, are the crucial factors in this learning and keep practitioners alive to the uniqueness and uncertainty of practice situations. The stress on a continuing supervision relationship, in counselling psychology, recognizes this reflective activity as central to the development of knowledge and good practice within the discipline.

We have, however, seen that the emphasis on 'little narratives', the context-bound nature of knowledge and on pragmatism or usefulness rather than truth carries the danger of relativism and the association of truth with power. Hence Lyotard's concern to rescue the concept of justice. John Shotter (1993) has taken up Schon's stress on the value dimension of practice. The limited applicability of formal knowledge brings into focus value conflicts and the unavoidable responsibility that we have to others. In the indeterminate zones of practice we are at least required to give good reasons and be accountable to others for our actions. This requires knowledge of quite a different order. It is 'rhetorical' rather than logical in nature. In taking science as the model of rational thought it can be argued that the Enlightenment project has led to the neglect of rhetoric or ethical and political thought and action. The main function of language has been identified with its capacity to represent the world and, in the pursuit of an objective representation, its role in argument, in persuasion and in justifying action has been

626

neglected. In practice many situations are vague and uncertain, decisions must be made, actions taken and accounted for. Social life is, in a real sense, radically open and 'essentially contestable' (Gallie, 1956). What is more, our actions have consequences which make a difference in people's lives. Under these conditions values, not truth, must provide the guiding principles.

In this context, then, we can perhaps see counselling psychology as a postmodern psychology which is practice-led, with its practice grounded in values which respect difference, feeling and subjective truths and emphasize choice and responsibility. As such, it has developed ways of being and knowing as well as methods of practice and research which offer real alternatives to psychology in the climate of questioning of our more traditional models.

We conclude then, on a positive note, emphasizing the potential of counselling psychology to contribute to the development of the profession. However, if counselling psychology is to realize the values embedded in its model, we must not neglect to challenge the more negative ideological functions addressed in the first half of the chapter.

References

Bleier, R. (ed.) (1986) *Feminist Approaches to Science*. Oxford: Pergamon.

Chapman, G. (1983) 'Ritual and rational action in hospitals', *Journal of Advanced Nursing*, 8: 13–20.

de Shazer, S. (1985) *Keys to Solution in Brief Therapy*. New York: W.W. Norton.

Egan, G. (1994) *The Skilled Helper*, 5th edn. Pacific Grove, CA: Brooks/Cole.

Gallie, W.B. (1956) *Proceedings of the Aristotelian Society*, 56.

Gramsci, A. (1971) *Selections from the Prison Notebooks* (trans Q. Hoare and G. Nowell-Smith). London: Lawrence and Wishart.

Harding, S. (1986) *The Science Question in Feminism*. Milton Keynes: Open University.

Howe, D. (1993) *On Being a Client: Understanding the Process of Counselling and Psychotherapy*. London: Sage.

Knorr-Cetina, K.D. and Mulkay, M.J. (eds) (1983) *Science Observed: Perspectives on the Social Study of Science*. London: Sage.

Kuhn, T.S. (1962) *The Structure of Scientific Revolutions*. Chicago: Chicago University Press.

Lakatos, I. and Musgrave, A. (1970) *Criticism and the Growth of Knowledge*. London: Cambridge University Press.

Lather, P. (1990) 'Postmodernism and the human sciences', in S. Kvale (ed.), *Psychology and Postmodernism*. London: Sage.

Lyotard, J.F. (1984 [1979]) *The Postmodern Condition: a Report on Knowledge*. Manchester: Manchester University Press.

Lyotard, J.F. and Thebaud, J.L. (1985 [1979]) *Just Gaming*. Manchester: Manchester University Press.

Marshall, R. (1988) 'The role of ideology in the individualisation of distress', *The Psychologist: Bulletin of the British Psychological Society*, 2: 67–9.

McLeod, J. (1994) 'Issues in the organisation of counselling: learning from NMGC', *British Journal of Guidance and Counselling*, 22(2): 163–74.

Menzies, I. (1970) *The Functioning of Social Systems as a Defence against Anxiety*. Tavistock Pamphlet no. 5. London: Tavistock.

Merton, R.K. (1957) *Social Theory and Social Structure*. London: Free Press of Glencoe.

Oliver, M. (1978) 'Disability, adjustment and family life', in A. Brechin et al. *Handicap in the Social World*. Sevenoaks: Hodder and Stoughton.

Pilgrim, D. (1990) 'Researching psychotherapy in Britain: the limits of a psychological approach', in I. Parker and J. Shotter (eds), *Deconstructing Social Psychology*. London: Routledge.

Pilgrim, D. (1991) 'Psychotherapy and social blinkers', *The Psychologist*, 2: 52–5.

Pilgrim, D. and Rogers, A. (1993) *A Sociology of Mental Health and Illness*. Buckingham: Open University Press.

Polkinghorne D.E. (1992) 'Postmodern epistemology of practice' in S. Kvale (ed.), *Psychology and Postmodernism*. London: Sage.

Popper, K. (1959 [1934]) *The Logic of Scientific Discovery*. London: Hutchinson.

Rogers, C. (1964) 'Towards a science of the person', in T.W. Wann (ed.), *Behaviorism and Phenomenology: Contrasting Bases for Modern Psychology*. Chicago: Chicago University Press.

Rose, N. (1989) *Governing the Soul: the Shaping of the Private Self*. London: Sage.

Ryle, A. (1990) *Cognitive-Analytic Therapy: Active Participation in Change*. Chichester: Wiley.

Schon, D.A. (1987) *Educating the Reflective Practitioner*. London: Jossey Bass.

Shotter, J. (1993) 'Rhetoric and the roots of the homeless mind', *Theory, Culture and Society*, 10(4): 41–62.

Smail, D.J. (1987) *Taking Care: an Alternative to Therapy*. London: Dent.

Spinelli, E. (1989) *The Interpreted World*. London: Sage.

Strawbridge, S. (1992) 'Counselling psychology and the model of science', *Counselling Psychology Review*, 7(1): 5–11.

Strawbridge, S. (1994) 'Towards anti-oppressive practice in counselling psychology', *Counselling Psychology Review*, 9(1): 5–12.

Thompson, E.P. (1967) 'Time, work-discipline and industrial capitalism', *Past and Present*, 38.

Walker, M. (1990) *Women in Therapy and Counselling*. Buckingham: Open University Press.

Watson, G. and Williams, J. (1992) 'Feminist therapy in practice', in J.M. Ussher and P. Nicholson (eds), *Gender Issues in Clinical Psychology*. London: Routledge.

Williams, J. and Watson, G. (1988) 'Sexual inequality, family life and family therapy', in E. Street and W. Dryden (eds), *Family Therapy in Britain*. Milton Keynes: Open University Press.

Woolfe, R. (1983) 'Counselling in a world of crisis: towards a sociology of counselling', *International Journal for the Advancement of Counselling*, 6: 167–76.

Woolley, M. (1993) 'Acquired hearing loss; acquired oppression', in J. Walmsley, J. Reynolds, P. Shakespeare and R. Woolfe (eds), *Health, Welfare and Practice: Reflecting on Roles and Relationships*. London: Sage.

28

Counselling Psychology: Into the New Millennium

Douglas Hooper

Never prophesy, especially about the future.   SAM GOLDWYN

The counselling psychologist is sitting in her counselling room on a bright sunny afternoon in May 1996. She works in a well-equipped primary health care centre on a sessional basis and has three clients 'booked' to see her.

She is to see Mrs Seagrove first, a 55-year-old married woman who has been chronically depressed for ten years. She has had a variety of interventions, none of which has been very successful, but she has not previously been offered counselling outside her medical consultations. The counselling psychologist has offered her a contract of eight sessions (of which this is the sixth) to focus on her self-image in relation to her depressive experience.

Next she is to see John Saddler. He is 35, unmarried and lives with his parents. He is an accountant but has developed acute anxiety about his work which has considerably disabled him although he struggles to continue. The counselling psychologist started a six-session contract with anxiety-control measures but quickly discovered life issues centring on his unexposed homosexuality.

Finally, she has an appointment with Tracey (19) and her mother and father. Tracey, away at university, came home after two terms because she could not cope with life away from home. Since returning, it has been quite difficult to get her motivated to 'do' anything. The counselling psychologist perceived an identity crisis and, after some single sessions with Tracey, has set up some conjoint sessions with her parents.

All run of the mill work which will be repeated hundreds of times on this particular afternoon throughout the country. But what might it all look like in 10 or 20 years time? Would the psychologist be in this setting, seeing these clients? Would she handle them differently – or at all? Would she use technology not in use at present? And so on.

It is of course virtually impossible to answer such questions with reliable accuracy, but it is possible to consider the broader issues of which this series of vignettes forms a part. This then may outline a possible framework for the future into which counselling psychology (and practices of like ilk) may fit. At least it enables us to lift our sights above the perplexing minutiae of daily professional life, even if we decide – having looked – that today might just possibly be preferable to tomorrow.

Let us begin with a brief discussion of futurology. It is, like economics, a rather dismal science with few successes to its credit except for some of the science fiction writers. It is as if the truly imaginative mind can sometimes see the shape of certain things in the future which requires one to leave behind the assumptions which currently form the basis for daily experience.

The writer of this chapter is not a science fiction writer and is therefore likely to be as wrong as everyone else would be who is dogged by a set of working professional assumptions. Nevertheless, he can draw to the reader's attention some intriguing possibilities in areas which will certainly change and which will certainly impinge on the counselling psychologist.

The over-riding issue is that of attitudinal stance about the future. Should we be optimistic or pessimistic about the next stage of human experience? In 1993, the weekly journal *The Economist* completed 150 years of publication. To mark the event, the editors commissioned a distinguished group of commentators to write about the next 150 years as best they could. The detail need not concern us further, but in the short editorial to the series, the editor wrote:

> The dominant sentiment (not at all prompted by us) is optimism: about . . . mankind's ability to solve as many problems as it causes, and about worries that the planet itself might give up the ghost. (*Economist*, 1993: 3)

This writer, too, is prepared to accept this stance.

Past and future

But first we need to look at the past decades which have shaped psychology in general and counselling psychology in particular, and look at ideas which have been critical. Of the bewildering variety available, we will select three, of which the first is *The Interpretation of Dreams*, published by Freud in 1900.

This book was seminal because it drew attention to psychological processes in the irrational world of individuals, and related these to distress and disturbance. The ideas were then elaborated and refined by innumerable writers into the psychodynamic view which informed much early counselling. Yet empirical psychologists found this approach hard to swallow, and as a result looked elsewhere for explanations of behaviour.

The classic text was that of J.B. Watson, the 'father' of behaviourism, writing *Psychology from the Stand-point of a Behaviorist* (1919). Unlike Freud's ideas, these were not immediately taken up by therapeutic workers but were influential in creating a second view of human problems.

Freud and his followers dominated the psychological care scene both theoretically and professionally for a number of decades, until Rogers broke with those views by proposing a much more optimistic and interactive approach which he set out in *Counselling and Psychotherapy* in 1942. The rest is history, but one important problem which this twentieth century poses is the nature of these developments. Each of these individuals – Freud, Watson, Rogers – were seminal people around and from whom significant change was created. Since that time, derivative counselling practice theories have grown rapidly, now numbering at least 400 recognizable 'brands' (Kanasu, 1986), each of which may have adherents.

This is an unsatisfactory state of affairs to which we shall return later in this chapter, but we may speculate as to whether the next major shift in ideas will be from a seminal person or alternatively from a seminal process. Most advances in thought do stem from a few individuals who challenge the current received wisdom and eventually change it. But it could be argued that there are no more moves to be had in grand theories about human behaviour. Lazarus (1989) proposed that to understand human experience we need to take account of seven modalities:

Behaviours
Affective processes
Sensations
Images
Cognitions
Interpersonal relationships
Biological functions

each of which may need appraisal and analysis for effective therapeutic work. The problem has been that each modality has considerable complexity, so that theories of therapy have been presented in a skewed and partial fashion, not necessarily able to handle both the modalities and dynamic interactions between them. In addition, the theory builder has also been the master practitioner, so that the apprentice practitioners have had to accept the master's view on many of the issues that puzzled them – and if not the master, then his later exponents. This has often served to intensify the problem of partial understanding rather than resolve it.

This will surely change as eclectic and integrative counselling practice education takes hold. We can expect that the 'schools' will vigorously defend their positions but that these will give way to reappraisal and synthesis in counselling psychology.

If we break up the future into areas of interest, then we can use the counselling psychologist–client–context as a convenient triad for getting purchase on each problem. However, we shall also have to take account of the triad as a system itself, and examine system change as well. Some help is at hand here in a special series of articles edited by Whiteley (1980) and entitled 'Counseling psychology in the year 2000 AD'. Although the cultural and professional context in the USA is in many respects different from that of the UK or Europe, some of the identified trends are very thought-provoking.

Allen (1980) catalogues what he calls the deadly delusions in the social and economic framework in which counselling psychology exists, all of which (he believes) will inevitably change. These are:

1 The growth myth: bigger is better.
2 The imperative of possibility: if it can be done it should be.
3 Linear history: the future must be better than the past.
4 Nature must be subjugated/domesticated for human happiness and meaning.

He believes that people will be living in a world in which all of these assumptions will be challenged or will no longer hold. In those circumstances, counselling psychology 'clients' will want help in facilitating the inward quest, moving from *having* to *being*; and maximizing their development, particularly in the social/moral and creative aspects, all of which sounds remarkably like the widely accepted philosophy of counselling already. Perhaps the important issue to which he draws attention is that if the broader systems fail or break down, then this will enhance personal and social turbulence.

In the same series, Ivey (1980) offers a shorter analysis but a fuller list of suggested change in counselling psychology. He believes that:

1 The person/environment focus will require much more attention, with the emphasis on the transactional processes.
2 Decision-making will be a dominant theme of the counselling process as compared with a internal search for psychological truth.
3 The use of a 'psychoeducational' model of practice rather than a 'remedial' model will become dominant.
4 Cultural and social factors will be increasingly important – the psychological world of the black/white person or the affluent/poor *are* different.
5 Psycho/socio-linguistics will be an important theoretical base for counselling psychology theories.

6   A new meta-theoretical framework for counselling and psychotherapy will evolve.

Both of these writers, as well as other writers in this series, regard the development of information technology as vital tools in the new millennium tool kit, but tools which will serve the counselling psychologists and their clients in supplementing the development of more effective practice.

The obvious place to start a more detailed analysis of future trends is with the first part of the triad.

The clients

Who will they be? The most important information for future patterns is yielded by the demographic data, and the most marked development is almost certainly the balance of the age structure. By 2020, the proportion of those aged 65 and over compared with those of 50 or under will be 20 per cent, as compared with 1990 figures of 15 per cent. This older age group is also likely to be uncharacteristically younger, both in physical and psychological terms than previous generations.

What are the consequences of this? One likely development is that the making and breaking of 'affectional bonds', as Bowlby (1979) called them, will be extended by one and possibly two decades. At present, there is very little evidence here except for the trend in divorce statistics. Even now these suggest that people are not satisfied with an intimate relationship for as long as in the past, and that bond-breaking is extending well into the later decades of life.

These young oldies will be more demanding of service than their forebears, who often appeared happy to struggle through crises of later life with little help outside of the family. There are few available figures, but at present, for example, the mean age of couples consulting counsellors in Relate centres is 38. If – as is very likely – relationships continue to become more vibrant and labile in later years, then this and other relationship counselling will both increase in scope and also be extended.

Family complexity is thus also likely to increase and not simply in two-generation families as at present, but in three-generation families as well. What is not possible to predict is whether relationship breakdown in couples will increase, plateau or diminish. Some writers have extrapolated from the remarkable growth in cohabiting and the linked growth of extra-marital birth to a situation where legal marriage becomes a minority interest. That presents important social and legal problems but there is little or no evidence that more corporate living styles will emerge. Intimate relationships are still both desired and emphasized as crucial personal values. And the crises and breakdown problems of intimate relationships take a great deal of counselling time and facility.

Next, the effects of discontinuity in parent–child relationships which are already apparent will increase through the decades. The current projection is that about 20 per cent of all children will experience the breakdown of their parental care because of divorce, and this figure is likely to be increased by breakdown of cohabitation into which an increasing percentage of children are now born.

The effects of these events on the children-as-adults is at present not easy to know, but the tentative information suggests that for some children there are marked effects and particularly for adolescent girls. In general, too, the crisis of divorce has a sharp effect on children, and we can expect that requests to help more children both by crisis counselling and more extended counselling help will increase.

There are demographic changes in the workplace which we can expect to continue. Recent employment patterns have changed markedly, as has the further education pattern of young people. The large bulk of 'structural' unemployment in much of Europe has been a significant problem for the last five years or more. The concept of structural unemployment implies that many jobs available to a previous generation are no longer going to be there for the foreseeable future, and that working life will be marked by job and career change, bringing (for some) early 'retirement', and for others an enhanced working life length. Overall, the percentage of men over 60 in employment is expected to diminish from 83 per cent in 1971 to 54 per cent by 2000, whereas the figures for women are hardly changing – indeed, if anything, increasing.

Within the working framework, service industries seem certain to continue their inexorable rise. These industries employ substantial numbers of women, often in increasingly complex and senior roles. We might anticipate that it would be the unemployed who would be in the greatest need of skilled counselling, but it seems unlikely that this will happen without significant political change. Unemployment has clear links now to increased physical and mental ill-health, and that is a possible route for counselling activity as a secondary service. On the assumption that unemployment remains a significant experience for the next decade at least, then this may absorb increasing counselling time in the future.

One area already showing significant growth is the so-called 'careers counselling'. This is dealt with earlier in this volume, but it seems likely that more people will be prepared to take advantage of this counselling approach if they are sensitized early on to the use of counsellors and counselling as effective supporters during personal change.

But will people wish to avail themselves of counselling psychology in increasing numbers? Certainly in recent years there has been a sharp rise in the publication of angry/aggrieved accounts, by both clients and journalists, of the failure of counselling and psychotherapy. This could suggest that people are becoming less happy to look for counselling for their difficulties. This, though, is in the context of a substantial increase in demand over the last decade which is very likely to continue. The reasons for this increase were outlined by Sherard (1993), and summarized as follows:

1 Dissatisfaction with orthodox treatment.
2 'New age' aspirations, and the desire to enhance human potential.
3 Not enough traditional professional help such as clinical psychology, psychiatry, psychiatric nursing.
4 Increasing income to finance fee-based counselling.

One further reason which is not covered by the author should also be added, namely:

5 Perception of personal distress as ameliorable rather than just sufferable.

Of these, points 3, 4 and 5 seem most likely to maintain the present trend towards the use of counselling. Undoubtedly the highly publicized allegations of incompetent counselling have some effect, but seem unlikely to weigh heavily with most people – despite some powerful critiques over the past 40 years by Eysenck, Halmos, Szasz and Masson. These critics and others have often argued that counselling (and psychotherapy of course) trades on the universal sufferings of people and is part of a much larger social process of control. Despite this trenchant critique, people will certainly continue to search for solutions to their life problems as they have done through the centuries. There is no doubt that the approach of counselling meets many needs like this – and that these needs are most unlikely to diminish because of societal change. We shall return to this theme later in the chapter. But now we will turn to the next element of the triad.

The counselling psychologist

We cannot take for granted that counselling psychologists will exist in 2010. But the discussion above of the social role of counselling leads directly into a discussion of the relationship between politics, policy and service provision. This is a necessary first step since the role will exist in these contexts.

In the formal sense it is impossible to predict the political framework in which counselling will be set in the next decades, but we can perceive

636

some of the issues which are likely to arise within the realm of applied psychology. First, let us try to see through the glass darkly as far as the broad political perspective is concerned.

Within certain limits, policy and politics travel together, and we have witnessed over the past decade a particularly active political period, in which policy has flowed from ideology. The ideology has favoured free enterprise, individualism, competition and 'freedom from interference'. This latter is in inverted commas because there is a substantial debate as to whether some freedom has been exchanged for a centralizing control.

The ideology, however, has clearly favoured multidimensional rather than monolithic responses to social problems, in particular, the shift of emphasis in service delivery from the centrally or regionally defined plan to a more local, client-orientated plan. The patient may not yet rule the professional, but at least he has a charter!

Purveyors of care will probably continue to be free to purchase and provide services such as counselling psychology – provided that it seems effective to do so. But the likelihood is that such services will vary greatly from area to area because of the differing perception of need.

During the next period, we shall probably see a shift towards a socially orientated policy again, but one in which the consumer has considerable power and rights and in which the professionals will be answerable both to the consumers and to the financial providers of services. Moreover, these two groups may be asking for services which are at opposite ends of a continuum. The providers are likely to demand shorter, cost- and change-effective intervention, whilst the clients may ask for sustained and extended contracts which they perceive as more supportive. Severe time-limited practice will drive up demand for a private fee-based service.

If counselling psychology can demonstrate its effectiveness, then it is likely to be in considerable demand as an alternative to other, more expensive modes of help such as biological and residential care. But this raises the politics of the professional position both within the caring professional groups and also within the range of psychological professions.

Counselling psychologists – a rival grouping?

The philosophy of practice within counselling psychology both in the UK and the USA emphasizes the importance of enhancing psychological function and well-being, and has sought to focus on those not labelled as 'ill'. But the problem of professional identity for those helping the normal is confusing. On balance, people do not seek help if they believe they are normal unless *either* their capacity starts to break down, *or* they experience bodily symptoms which concern them. They then become help-seekers – and turn to the 'helping professions'. These are ancient as well as modern patterns and will certainly be with us 100 years from now. This focus on the non-coping competent person has been widely recognized in the other professional groups, and some counselling or counselling skills have been added to personnel managers, many kinds of nurse, and a number of paramedical professions. In addition, there has been rapid growth *and* deployment of non-psychologist counsellors.

What may happen? The argument for counselling psychologists is that they have a distinctive academic learning background in psychology which enables them to draw directly on appropriate theory for application. This distinguishes the counselling psychologist from other professional groups who do not have this available to them. But this is changing. Increasingly, all 'people professions' are moving to a graduate intake which could include substantial learning in psychological matters.

At first, then, counselling psychologists will be (indeed, already are) seen as a rival group to others already active in this context. In particular, if they cost more money, then there will be economic rivalry and competition. There is no field of human activity in which counselling psychologists would like to practice which has not already been substantially colonized by others with a counselling orientation, perhaps with the exception of the workplace in which, given the very large number of workplace units, counselling development has so far been modest.

Counselling psychologists will therefore have to accommodate to those existing groups, either by becoming niche operators, or more specialist superordinate professionals directing the work of others less skilled and educated. One further possibility is that *all* counsellors will become counselling psychologists because employers will require this kind of grounding for every counselling service, which will push acolytes into this route for qualification. Given the size and strength of the non-psychologist groups at present, this seems unlikely.

By the year 2005 there will be, say, 4,000 counselling psychologists at most. They will therefore be a relatively small (but influential) cadre and very probably widely spread through organizational structure, both public and private, and client group. This will be rather like clinical psychology has become, unless they are organized on a totally different basis, perhaps within a College of Applied Psychology.

Counselling psychology and other applied psychologies

On the assumption that counselling psychologists stay firmly with the British Psychological Society, they will have to negotiate a clear position. What will it be? Certainly a real possibility is that they will be members of a College of Applied Psychology separate from the Society, but associated with it. It would have separate sub-groups for, perhaps, health/ illness, work, crime, childhood and adolescence, third age and others. But the interesting thing about counselling is that it already straddles all of these domains, which are a mixture of practice locus and client group. The much more likely event is that counselling psychology will sooner or later merge with others to form a broad grouping of, say, practitioner psychologists with specialisms in both area and client.

The politics here would be difficult. The British Psychological Society has given a fair wind to counselling psychology, but this will not be sustained forever. Other new groupings will need parental support, and the Counselling Division will become a peer with all the other Divisions. Since it has a wide remit, it will spread across other professional groups and probably meet opposition. It could be argued – and has been - that counselling psychology has separated out because clinical psychologists were too preoccupied with internal Health Service matters, and a narrower view of the field. The emerging sub-discipline of health psychology is also likely to achieve professional status. And what then? A superordinate body seems inevitable, certainly in the first decade of the millennium. Let's shift the hologram. How will counselling psychology *contribute* to psychology in general?

Counselling and psychological theory

Psychological scholarship linked to theory development has had a modest record in the UK. The strength has been in empiricism and also pragmatism, but the driving psychological theories have arisen from either the USA or other European countries. In academic psychology, little attention has been paid to the grand theories of human behaviour, whereas in counselling and psychotherapy such theories abound, often rivalrously. This is exemplified in this volume by seven chapters devoted to 'paradigms' of counselling, and a further one curiously included in this section called 'integrative' – perhaps a misnomer since integrative theory must be a new superordinate paradigm. All too frequently these theoretical bases of practice become articles of faith, to which the practitioners adhere closely without regard for efficacy.

If, however, counselling psychology sticks with the credo of being research-based, and if it follows both quantitative and qualitative traditions, then what should accumulate after 10–15 years should be a large volume of information about the actual experiences of counselling. This could have a major impact on laboratory-based approaches and influence academic psychology considerably, because the materials of counselling sessions (in whatever format) are the stuff of psychological life itself, and in particular developmental life. In a famous text, Gilmore (1973) refers to the core tasks of counselling as 'choice, change and confusion reduction', and even although these do not exhaust the issues that are involved, they do encapsulate much of the approach of the counselling world to life problems, which is sharply different from much academic psychological study. What may well emerge is not exquisite analysis of the minutiae of the counselling encounter, but broader, life-theme research in which the counselling intervention fits as part of an extended life process.

It is also likely that psychopharmacology and psychogenetics will become more sophisticated and increasingly able to modify or enhance particular parts of experience and behaviour. Counselling psychology will engage with these issues both at the level of simultaneous direct modification, but also at the secondary level of the consequences of pharmacology and genetics. This is already done to a limited extent, but will probably spread more widely as these biological interventions become both more effective and more available.

We have already discussed broadly the possible development of human behaviour theories in the first section of this chapter. But if we look more closely, then the counselling psychologist of 2010 ought not to be learning a set of axioms couched in a specific jargon, but using other methods to guide the counselling process wherever it is applied.

It could be argued, in line with postmodernist intellectual development (Harvey, 1989), that all theory is idiosyncratic to the contemporary problem tackled by the psychologist. There is then very little generalizability (required by most formal theories) because the interaction is unique. This forms the basis for a number of attempts to identify the substrata in any therapeutic encounter. It is likely that these attempts will make headway against the other theories of the first decades of the century – not because the assumptions from these theories are untrue, but because they have been worked out completely.

The business of developing new concepts and theories should, then, be bound into the experience of the clients. Howe (1993) has recently summarized much of the research which we already have about what clients distill from their counselling and therapeutic experiences. Viewed altogether, these research results are startling. He emphasizes that we must be much clearer about the difference between theories that *explain* people and those that seek to *understand* people. He further writes:

> What all clients bring to the counselling encounter is a socially formed self which arises ... between ... biology and social experience. It is the method of self-formation and the relationship between inheritance and social experience which explain why different people undergoing different types

of counselling report the *same* kind of experience. (1993: 190, original emphasis)

Distilling from these accounts, Howe says that the helpful process for the successful client is as follows:

Therapeutic alliance
Talk and dialogue
Making sense
Controlling the meaning of experience
Coping better with life.

It is in the period of 'making sense' that the counselling psychologists' theories come to the fore, and Howe insists that 'making sense' is a very critical element in client improvement, no matter what the 'sense' (i.e. the theory offered) might be. This broader discussion must be set in the counselling context, which brings us, then, to the third part of the triad.

Counselling psychology and context

Counselling is not a mature activity like that of a number of other professional work groups, but it has one important advantage. This is that the enterprise has developed a vigour and thrust that is autonomous. Because it clearly delivers a wide range of services in ways which the service providers want, it has not become an activity which is secondary to another, often senior, professional practice.

Indeed, the counselling product is generally so useful that it has spawned a series of programmes in counselling skills for other workers, so that some of the counselling universe has been 'given away' – a very different position from that adopted by much psychotherapy in which the appropriate guild protects the sacred text and its practitioners!

Counselling has developed as a practice most strongly by locating within an organizational structure, but one which is not, itself, devoted to counselling. Thus, schools, health centres, colleges, workplaces, have all increasingly taken on counsellors to handle the human downside of that particular activity. But as the patterns of these organizations change, will this change? The answer, of course, is yes – but in what ways is difficult to determine. Human interaction is fundamental to psychological health, and therefore the need for organizations will continue, despite the ability of information technology to disperse people away from a gathering place.

What will almost certainly happen will be an increase in counselling clusters, perhaps offering both a contracted service to organizations and also a private client payment service. Such clusters offer both strength and protection. Counselling centres of various kinds exist at present, but they have not often developed the strength in, say, research or practice differentiation which makes them as effective as they could be. This will undoubtedly require an accommodation between counselling psychologists and counsellors with other backgrounds, most of whom are now also graduates (British Association for Counselling, 1993). One hopes that pluralism and diversity will survive, and the issues of differentiation will certainly have to be resolved around the turn of the century. It is possible that clients will seek out a counselling psychologist, or a non-psychologist counsellor, in which case they will demonstrate a wish for a more widely based approach than the counselling psychologist provides. What is certainly clear is that non-psychologist counsellors will strongly resist becoming something like 'assistant' counselling psychologists.

One very probable development will be the provision of counselling/therapy insurance, in which individuals and families can ensure that such services are available to them as required. This will remove the many restrictions imposed by current medical insurance.

It is widely accepted that workplace counselling will become more available (Reddy, 1993) because that trend has already begun. But what other contexts might arise? One possibility is that government agencies in, for example, crime and deviance, will look to counselling psychology for a resource in dealing with deviant sexual, violent, or addictive behaviour. It is quite possible that if programmes of theory and practice develop in these areas, then psychological counselling could become prescriptive and mandatory. This may appear to offend one of the tenets of counselling about the freely given commitment of the client, but it could well be a serious alternative to other forms of intervention.

Changes in development in health care are very difficult to foresee, but each development, such as gene transplant or brain tissue replacement, will lead to the need for decision-making by the patient about participating in the process. It is highly likely that some biological advance will enable the ageing process to be more controlled, so that extended or enhanced life becomes available. Together with the inevitable development of genetic theory and practice, these will introduce complex choices for which a counselling intervention can prove helpful or even essential. The use to which counselling psychology will be put in this context will depend very much upon developing appropriate techniques alongside the physical and biological.

In general, what can be predicted is that the context for counselling psychology will broaden and spread – provided that the practitioners do not over-reach themselves in their claims for efficacy.

Counselling psychology, work and leisure

In our advanced urban industrial society, the issues of what is 'work' and 'not-work' have become important areas of discussion. Throughout the Western world, the pressure to train and educate has increased because the skilled workforce is seen as a prerequisite of economic development.

Alongside this, the phenomenon of mass and long-lasting unemployment had emerged as a major social issue. In this decade, and assuming that socio-economic factors do not change, the unemployment ratio is predicted to remain at around 8–10 per cent, of which the majority will be men.

But let's turn back, first, to working experience. The impact of the European Union, and the ability to conduct cross-border business with ease, suggests that the spread of advanced, integrated, international service and manufacturing will continue to grow. Much of this will be heavily dependent upon information technology. It is the demands of this kind which appear to lead to pools of non-employed, either because technology (and jobs) change fast or people are not equipped for the required work.

For those who have an employed life, the pattern is rapidly emerging as follows: assume a longevity of 80 years, then 25 per cent will be spent in development and education, 44 per cent in core work experience, and 30 per cent in post-work leisure and finally ageing. But the second two-thirds could quite easily be patterned very differently, so that as health and fitness improve, periods of work and non-work could alternate until well on into the life cycle with true retirement occupying only, say, the last 5–7 years of the life span.

Assuming that economic factors continue to improve, even moderately, then the time/money to pursue leisure pursuits in a work-disciplined way looks really likely. Leisure then becomes a very important area of human experience, which will produce its own human problems. It is assumed that leisure is always pleasurable and does not have the stresses and conflicts of working. But this is (and has been) unrealistic. Shall we then see counselling psychologists and others as leisure counsellors? Such people already exist in the ranks of trainers, coaches, couriers, etc. who recognize that much leisure pursuit is a search by individuals and groups for another road to fulfilment, and not just an opportunity for relaxation. As such, it could well become an avenue for counselling psychologists.

Counselling psychology, technology and human value

Some have argued that the growth of counselling and therapy has partly been an antidote to technology – that as natural science and technology have taken over some human functions, so the inner and interpersonal human world has become more important (van Deurzen-Smith, 1993). But counselling and particularly counselling psychology are also part of this technological advance, since the research base will not cease to have importance. This uneasy dilemma is likely to continue into the future because the human and the non-human will often be in apparent conflict, but also, perhaps, in some harmony or even synergy.

The core of counselling method is human interaction, but much help is sought by people using an intermediary technique. The obvious (and age-old one) is writing, and a newer and widely used one is the telephone. Both allow a troubled person to put some distance between themselves and their counselling psychologist — and thus establish control over the communication. It is, after all, much easier to put the telephone down peremptorily, than it is to walk out of the consulting room.

Multi-media communication will change and challenge that. The change could come in at least two ways. First, televisual communication does not require counselling psychologist and client to be in the same physical space. Counselling will take place via the network, and because of the convenience, can be scheduled at times and places suitable to both. So boundaries of time and place become much more flexible, but also more challenging, and will call into play technological methods to ensure confidentiality.

Into this picture, we can insert the technology of virtual reality in which the participant can immerse him/herself in a situation by means of controlled audiovisual imagery. What might this mean for counselling techniques? One possibility is that the process of imaginal participation in some sexual situation, for example, could be available directly to a client, the most important part being that the client could control the process — just as in imaginal work — but of course with greater reality. This would require sophisticated programmes, but these would be well within the present technical possibilities.

The other aspect of information technology is that of monitoring and analysing counselling sessions, and maintaining records. To deal with the last one first, it has taken a surprising length of time for records to be computer-based and -stored. A major problem, again, is that of confidentiality, and although there are evident ways of handling this problem, counsellors of all kinds remain (rightly) cautious. With the increasing miniaturization of systems, control over electronic records becomes easier, so that by, say, 2010, such records are likely to become commonplace.

Equally, with the use of this technology it will be possible not only to record counselling sessions, audiovisually, but also to carry out a continuous analysis against set criteria. Thus it may well be common practice to feed back to clients during or immediately after a session the problems and issues which have been identified or worked on during that session.

These techniques challenge the concept of the relationship between counselling psychologist and client which, some may feel, will be diminished and therefore produce less effective work. The final spectre, of course, is the computer-based 'interactor' using the undoubted development of voice simulation which, suitably programmed, could carry through a simple (or even complex) 'interview' for the client's benefit. The quotation marks are used because it is obvious that the many non-verbal factors which come into play would be entirely missing from such an encounter.

It seems that all these developments are adjunctive to the core interpersonal processes which counselling depends upon and which can usefully amplify or enhance what already exists. But this may limit the interactive properties of emerging technology too much, so that the penetration of these characteristics into counselling may be far more radical than we are proposing here.

Finally in this section, we should discuss the possibility that, for some, counselling and counselling psychology are seen as an anti-technology response. Many of the procedures of counselling have been developed as intense, personal encounters precisely because in other areas of life encounters were either superficial or faceless. The counselling space then becomes the place in someone's life where they can realize themselves as themselves and without any barrier, other than the internal psychological barriers. These human values are deeply embedded in the ethos of counselling psychology, and some practitioners may then offer what we may call an ecological counselling service, free from all technological aids and devices, perhaps using natural phenomena as a way of enhancing the relationship between the distressed person and the natural world.

This edge of counselling psychology will be more troublesome for psychologists than for non-psychologist counsellors, many of whom will continue to be drawn from backgrounds of the arts and humanities. The counselling psychologist will share the scientific value system of other psychologists which will challenge counselling theory builders to find conceptual tools for resolving these dilemmas.

Concluding thoughts

> What we call the beginning is often the end
> and to make an end is to make a beginning.
> The end is where we start from.   T.S. ELIOT, 'LITTLE GIDDING'

We are now in a position to return to the counselling psychologist whom we left at the beginning of the chapter in her sunny spring consulting room. We posed a series of questions, the first of which was about her clients in the new millennium. Hopefully, she would not be seeing Mrs Seagrove, the depressed woman, at this stage of her disorder. Either the depressive response would have been more swiftly improved, or the referrer, recognizing a counselling need, would have enabled the counselling psychologist to be involved at an early stage. This would obviously depend on several changes we have discussed, like availability of counselling, research-based practice to identify the need for counselling and its efficacy, and so on. But would we expect to find a depressed woman needing help? The answer, here, is surely yes. Would the intervention be different, however? If only some of the changes we anticipate are enacted or developed then the answer, too, is yes. Perhaps not in contract length, although we could and should expect that knowledge and technology may be able to focus the counselling task more rapidly. Finally, the client herself would be much more aware of, first, her difficulty, and secondly, how to understand it and find help.

What about the accountant, John? He might not even have come if societal values towards gay men continue to change towards a more libertarian view. Perhaps he would then have no cause to respond anxiously to his living situation. But if those changes do not come about, would he perhaps have received some help at his workplace, if the anxiety symptoms were interfering with his performance? Or – as a separate practitioner – he might have insurance cover to give him client access to a counselling psychologist.

Lastly, there is Tracey. Her problem of separating from her parents would not necessarily be different – except that her excessive dependence on her family might have been recognized earlier because of the family's familiarity with mental health and the availability of a counselling educational psychologist to work on it. Technology could certainly play a part in work with Tracey, in the sense that she could have the university environs displayed to her at home so that she could begin a process of re-entry into the student life at a sensory and emotional level.

But would the counselling psychologist be in the health centre in the first place? Indeed, would there be a health centre? The chances are that in health care the health centre would be a larger operation with possibly a psychological health facility alongside the physical health facility. This might well be staffed by psychologists and others who would not have the ascription 'counselling' in front of their title. We have not explored the growth and development of other professional groups in the health care facility – in particular the doctors and nurses, but here, too, there are likely to be substantial rearrangements of professional boundaries and responsibilities, especially the wider use of counselling psychology in the issues of chronic physical ill-health and psychosomatic problems.

The health setting is only one of the context scenarios we have discussed, and the imagination can be applied to the other contexts in the same manner. The fundamental human problems of a post-industrial, postmodern, post-divided world will be substantially the same as in today's world. Confusing, anxious, depressed or frightened responses to tomorrow's world will still be the stuff of the core experience upon which the counselling psychologist will work. These experiences may vary with a different life-span pattern and the help-seeking will take a different form, but the responses to the slings and arrows of outrageous fortune will be remarkably similar.

Our speculations in this chapter suggest that what *will* be different is the pattern of the counselling psychology services which should be available, as well as the ability of practitioners and collective services to deliver counselling much more efficiently and effectively than in the present. But only time will tell!

References

Allen, T.W. (1980) 'A counseling psychology for the new age?' *Counseling Psychologist*, 8: 38–43.

Bowlby, J. (1979) *The Making and Breaking of Affectional Bonds*. London: Tavistock.

British Association for Counselling (1993) 'Membership survey 1993', *Counselling*, 4: 243–4.

Deurzen-Smith, E. van (1993) 'Changing the world: possibilities and limitations', *Counselling*, 4: 120–3.

Economist (1993) 'The future surveyed', Supplement, 11 September.

Freud, S. (1900) *The Interpretation of Dreams*. London: Hogarth Press.

Gilmore, S.K. (1973) *The Counselor-in-Training*, Englewood Cliffs NJ: Prentice Hall.

Harvey, D. (1989) *The Condition of Post-Modernity: an Enquiry into the Origins of Cultural Change*. Oxford: Basil Blackwell.

Howe, D. (1993) *On Being a Client*. London: Sage.

Ivey, A.E. (1980) 'Counseling 2000: time to take charge!', *Counseling Psychology*, 8: 12–16.

Kanasu, T.B. (1986) 'The specificity against the non-specificity dilemma: towards identifying therapeutic change agents', *American Journal of Psychiatry*, 143: 687–95.

Lazarus, A.A. (1989) *The Practice of Multimodal Therapy*, 2nd edn. Baltimore, MA: Johns Hopkins University Press.

Reddy, M. (1993) 'The counselling firmament: a short trip around the galaxy', *Counselling*, 4: 47–50.

Rogers, C. (1942) *Counselling and Psychotherapy*. Boston, MA: Houghton Mifflin.

Sherard, C. (1993) 'The rise in the demand for counselling', in *Counselling Psychology Quarterly*, 6: 53–7.

Watson, J.B. (1919) *Psychology from the Stand-point of a Behaviorist.* Philadelphia: Lippincott.

Whiteley, J.M. (ed.) (1980) 'Counseling psychology in the year 2000 AD', *Counseling Psychologist*, 8: 4.

Notes on the Editors and Contributors

Editors

Ray Woolfe is Director of the MA/Diploma in Counselling at Keele University and is a Chartered Counselling Psychologist. He is Registrar for the Diploma in Counselling Psychology Examination Board of the British Psychological Society and is a former Chair of the Executive Committee of the Special Group (now Division) in Counselling Psychology. His publications include *Coping With Crisis* (1982), *Helping Families in Distress* (1985), *Guidance and Counselling in Adult and Continuing Education* (1987), *Handbook of Counselling in Britain* (1989) and *Health, Welfare and Practice* (1992).

Windy Dryden is Professor of Counselling at Goldsmiths' College, University of London. He has authored or edited over 90 books including *Facilitating Client Change in Rational Emotive Behaviour Therapy* (Whurr Publishers, 1995) and *Daring to be Myself: A Case of Rational-Emotive Therapy*, written with Joseph Yankura (Open University Press, 1992). In addition, he edits twelve book series in the area of counselling and psychotherapy including the *Brief Therapy and Counselling* series (Wiley) and *Developing Counselling* (Sage). His major interests are in rational emotive behaviour therapy, eclecticism and integration in psychotherapy and, increasingly, writing short, accessible self-help books for the general public.

Contributors

Anne Abel Smith is an independent research psychologist and an Associate Research Fellow at the Centre for Research in Social Policy at Loughborough University. Her special interests lie in identifying the needs of specific client groups – single parents, substance misusers, people with disabilities and older people – and evaluating new initiatives to address these needs. She has co-authored several journal articles on counselling, and has a continuing interest in how evaluation techniques can be applied to the counselling relationship.

Chris Barker is a Senior Lecturer in Psychology at University College London, and an Honorary Clinical Psychologist in Camden and Islington Community Health Services Trust. His main research interests are in interpersonal communication and the helping process, for example client/counsellor interaction, informal helping and clients' views of counselling and therapy. He is a co-author of *Research Methods in Clinical and Counselling Psychology* (Wiley, 1994).

Michael Barkham trained as a clinical psychologist and then spent ten years working at the MRC/ESRC Social and Applied Psychology Unit, University of Sheffield. He was involved in comparative studies of contrasting brief therapies focusing on both outcomes and processes. In 1995 he took up post as Senior Lecturer in Clinical Psychology and Deputy Director of the Psychological Therapies Research Centre at the University of Leeds. He is currently UK Vice-President of the international body of the Society for Psychotherapy Research.

649

Robert Bor is a Chartered Clinical and Counselling Psychologist, who specialized as a family therapist at the Tavistock Clinic, London. He has worked as a psychologist in the NHS and is now Reader in Psychology at City University, London. He is an Honorary Lecturer in Medicine at the Royal Free Hospital School of Medicine, a Clinical Member of the Institute of Family Therapy, a member of the Tavistock Society of Psychotherapists, UKCP Registered and a Churchill Fellow.

Paul Brown is a chartered and consulting clinical and occupational psychologist; the principal of the consultancy Jackson Brown & Co., specializing in the individual development and mentoring of senior individuals within organizations; and an honorary lecturer at Goldsmiths' College, University of London. He has co-authored the Penguin bestseller *Treat Yourself to Sex*; co-authored *Managing Meetings* for Longmans; has contributed to *The Oxford Companion to the Mind*; and was at one time Honorary Secretary of the Clinical Division of the British Psychological Society, Registrar of the Board of Examiners, and a member of the BPS Council.

Michael J. Burton is Director of Counselling and Psychotherapy at the University of Sussex with accreditation or registration with BPS, BAC and UKCP. He sees several hundred students per year as part of the service and teaches on a range of psychodynamically oriented programmes. He is interested in the provision of affordable therapy in which he can dare to say no to patients' narrative demands and subscribes to a view of therapy as the 'science of interruptions'.

Petrūska Clarkson is a Consultant Counselling and Clinical Psychologist, UKCP registered psychotherapist, accredited supervisor and accredited organizational consultant. She is Board of Examiners Chair for the British Psychological Society Diploma in Counselling Psychology and Honorary Reader in the Psychology of Supervision at Surrey University. She is the principal founder of several organizations (including BIIP), original author of eight books, several University validated Diploma courses and 80 articles. She has been internationally active for some 25 years and supervises and leads advanced programmes for supervisors, psychologists and individual and group psychotherapists using the principles of qualitative research including the five relationship model at PHYSIS, London.

Cassie Cooper is a Kleinian psychotherapist/psychologist formerly Head of Services for students at the Harrow Campus of the University of Westminster and Course Leader for its Diploma in Counselling Skills and ancillary counselling courses. She has authored many papers on psychotherapy and counselling published in learned journals and has contributed chapters in textbooks on these subjects. Current publications include chapters in M. Jacobs (ed.), *Charlie, an Unwanted Child* (Open University Press); W. Dryden (ed.), *Handbook of Individual Therapy* (Sage); Ved P. Varma (ed.), *Stresses in Psychotherapists* (Routledge). She is currently Editor of the *Newsletter* of the British Psychological Society (Psychotherapy Section) and Counselling Consultant to Age Concern UK. In addition, she has a large clinical practice.

Roslyn Corney is Professor of Psychology at the University of Greenwich. Previously she was a Senior Lecturer at the Institute of Psychiatry and the Department of Psychological Medicine, St Bartholomew's Hospital. Her research has mainly focused around mental health issues in general practice, in particular the evaluation of treatment offered by counsellors, social workers and community psychiatric nurses. She has co-edited a book on counselling in general practice, published by Routledge.

Tom Davey is a counsellor and psychotherapist in the Counselling and Psychotherapy Unit at the University of Sussex and is a registered psychotherapist with the UKCP. He is a graduate of the Regent's College MA in the psychology of therapy and counselling and teaches on a variety of university-based counselling programmes. His main research interest is in the issue of power in the supervisory relationship.

Jim Downey is a Chartered Clinical Psychologist working in South Wales. He works with children and families in the local Child Psychology Service as well as being Child Specialty Tutor of the South Wales Doctoral Training Course in Clinical Psychology.

Bill Farrell is a Chartered Counselling Psychologist, a UKCP registered psychoanalytic psychotherapist, and an organizational consultant. He was Honorary Secretary of the BPS Special Group in Counselling Psychology from 1990 to 1992. He now works as a psychologist and psychotherapist for Auckland Family Counselling and Psychotherapy Centre and in private practice in Auckland, New Zealand. He has worked as a psychological therapist with individuals, couples and groups in a wide range of settings, and has extensive experience as a trainer, supervisor and consultant.

Maria Gilbert has extensive experience in adult education, organizational consultancy, and psychotherapy, as well as in the supervision and training of psychotherapists and psychotherapists' supervisors in transactional analysis, Gestalt psychotherapy and integrative psychotherapy. She has been in private practice for 18 years and worked with a wide variety of clients, organizationally, individually and in groups. She is currently Head of the Integrative Psychotherapy Training at Metanoia in West London.

Douglas Hooper has been concerned with education, training and practice in the psychological caring field during his working life. He is presently Emeritus Professor University of Hull and Visiting Research Professor University of Bristol. He has had a particular interest in therapy and counselling with couples and has contributed to this literature particularly as the editor of *Couple Therapy* (Open University Press). He is immediate Past President of the British Association of Counselling. He is also a Fellow of the BPS and a Chartered Clinical Psychologist.

Jennifer M. Kidd is a Senior Lecturer in the Department of Organizational Psychology, Birkbeck College, University of London. Prior to this she worked as a Career Counsellor in further education and as a Research Fellow at the National Institute for Careers Education and Counselling. She is a Chartered Occupational Psychologist and her main areas of research and publication are career guidance and career development.

Charles Legg specializes in the biological bases of behaviour which he approaches from a systems viewpoint. His current research is on appetites and food cravings. He has recently trained as a counsellor and is currently involved in synthesizing biological concepts within a systemic counselling framework, working with clients who are on weight-loss programmes.

John McLeod is Professor in Counselling Studies and Director of the Centre for Counselling Studies at Keele University. He is a person-centred counsellor with interests in counselling research, the cultural context of therapy, and the role of narrative in therapeutic process. He is the author of *An Introduction to Counselling* (Open University Press, 1993) and *Doing Counselling Research* (Sage, 1994).

Vanja Orlans is a Chartered Counselling and Occupational Psychologist and Associate Fellow of the British Psychological Society. She has a private practice in organizational consulting, counselling and Gestalt psychotherapy, and she runs a variety of training workshops on themes such as the development of workplace counselling schemes and time-limited counselling and therapy. She has some 15 years' experience working with organizations and individuals on the problems and challenges of stress and change.

Stephen Palmer is the Director of the Centre for Stress Management and the Centre for Multimodal Therapy, London. He is an Honorary Visiting Lecturer in Psychology at Goldsmiths College, University of London. He is a Chartered Counselling Psychologist, a UKCP registered psychotherapist, and an Associate Fellow of the Institute of Rational-Emotive Therapy, New York and an accredited supervisor for training in Rational Emotive Behaviour Therapy. He edits *Counselling Psychology Review* published by the British Psychological Society Division of Counselling Psychology, and has authored eight books and manuals. His main interest is in the application of multimodal cognitive-behavioural techniques and therapies to the field of stress management in counselling, organizational and time-limited settings.

Peter Ross is Director of the University of Reading Counselling Service. He is an occupational psychologist and counselling psychologist. His clinical interests are in the psychology of belief systems; and his management interests are in quality issues in counselling. He is currently concerned with developing benchmarks for quality standards, evaluation, and audit of counselling services. He has published widely in these fields. He runs a private practice as a psychotherapist and is a regular consultant to many blue chip companies.

Isobel Scher is a clinical psychologist and family therapist who has worked at the Centre for Family Therapy at Groote Schuur Hospital, Cape Town. She has a special interest in the Narrative Approach in therapy and works at the Mental Research Institute at Palo Alto, California.

Michael Scott is a Chartered Counselling Psychologist and Honorary Research Fellow Department of Psychology, University of Manchester. His two most recent books are *Developing Cognitive-Behavioural Counselling* (Sage, 1995) and *Counselling for Post-Traumatic Stress Disorder* (Sage, 1992). He is a consultant psychologist to major organizations including ICI, Merseyside Police, Girobank and Glaxo, and also works as a psychologist in primary care.

Carol Shillito-Clarke was one of the first people to be Chartered as a Counselling Psychologist by the British Psychological Society. Integrating counselling and psychology, over the past ten years, has given her an important professional identity and focus for her work as a therapist, supervisor, trainer, lecturer and consultant. The promotion of high standards in training and practice has always been a particular interest.

Diana Shmukler was an Associate Professor and Head of Applied Psychology at the University of Witwatersrand, South Africa. Currently she is the Head of training in Integrative Psychotherapy at Sherwood Psychotherapy Training Institute in Nottingham. In addition to wide-ranging research and reading interests in developmental psychology, post-traumatic stress and cultural disadvantage, she is currently training and supervising psychotherapists in the UK, Europe and South Africa.

Ernesto Spinelli is a BPS Chartered Counselling Psychologist, a UKCP Existential Psychotherapist, and a BAC accredited counsellor. He is Principal Lecturer at the School of Psychotherapy and Counselling, Regent's College, London and the current Chair of the Society for Existential Analysis. He is the author of two books, *The Interpreted World: an Introduction to Phenomenological Psychology* (Sage, 1989) and *Demystifying Therapy* (Constable, 1994), and numerous papers.

Sheelagh Strawbridge is a Chartered Counselling Psychologist now practising independently. She has a background in university teaching on degree courses in Social Science and professional courses in Counselling and Social Work. Her particular interests in ethical and socio-political issues in counselling/psychotherapy are reflected in her publications and her committee work for the British Psychological Society's Division of Counselling Psychology.

Eddy Street is Consultant Clinical Psychologist at Llandough Hospital and Community NHS Trust. He is also Honorary Senior Research Fellow at the Department of Child Health, University of Wales, College of Medicine. His clinical work involves providing a whole range of services to children and families and he specializes particularly in chronic childhood illness and child abuse and neglect. He has contributed numerous chapters and articles on themes relating to family counselling and child psychology. He is the author of *Counselling for Family Problems* (Sage, 1994)

Léonie Sugarman is a Chartered Occupational Psychologist. She is Senior Lecturer in Psychology in the Department of Applied Social Sciences, University College of St Martin, Lancaster, and is Associate Editor of the *British Journal of Guidance and Counselling*. Her book *Life-Span Development: Theories, Concepts and Interventions* was published in 1986 by Routledge.

Maye Taylor, a life-long feminist, is a Chartered Counselling Psychologist and UKCP Registered Psychoanalytical Psychotherapist and she teaches, trains, researches, writes, broadcasts, supervises and practices in the general area of women's mental health with a specialist interest in trauma. She is based in the Centre for Counselling Psychology in the Department of Psychology at the Manchester Metropolitan University.

Charles Twining is Consultant Clinical Psychologist and Head of Psychology Services with Cardiff Community Health Care NHS Trust. He holds degrees in Natural Sciences from the University of Cambridge, Abnormal Psychology from the University of Oxford and a PhD from the University of Wales. He specializes in work with older people, their families and other carers.

David Winter is Head of Clinical Psychology Services for Barnet Healthcare NHS Trust and Visiting Professor in the Division of Psychology of the University of Hertfordshire. He is a UKCP Registered Personal Construct Psychotherapist, and has employed personal construct theory in his clinical practice and research for many years. His extensive publications in this area include *Personal Construct Psychology in Clinical Practice: Theory, Research and Applications* (Routledge, 1992; paperback edition 1994).

Index

Index

Index

Index

Index

Index

Index

Compiled by Meg Davies (Society of Indexers)